AF180595

Communications in Computer and Information Science 1022

Commenced Publication in 2007

More information about this series at http://www.springer.com/series/7899

Bruce M. McLaren · Rob Reilly ·
Susan Zvacek · James Uhomoibhi (Eds.)

Computer Supported Education

10th International Conference, CSEDU 2018 Funchal, Madeira, Portugal, March 15–17, 2018 Revised Selected Papers

Springer

Editors
Bruce M. McLaren
Carnegie Mellon University
Pittsburgh, PA, USA

Rob Reilly
MIT
Cambridge, MA, USA

Susan Zvacek
University of Denver
Denver, CO, USA

James Uhomoibhi
University of Ulster
Newtownabbey, UK

ISSN 1865-0929 ISSN 1865-0937 (electronic)
Communications in Computer and Information Science
ISBN 978-3-030-21150-9 ISBN 978-3-030-21151-6 (eBook)
https://doi.org/10.1007/978-3-030-21151-6

This Springer imprint is published by the registered company Springer Nature Switzerland AG
The registered company address is: Gewerbestrasse 11, 6330 Cham, Switzerland

Preface

The present book includes extended and revised versions of selected papers from the 10th International Conference on Computer Supported Education (CSEDU 2018), held in Funchal, Madeira, Portugal, from 15 to 17 March 2018.

CSEDU 2018 received 193 paper submissions from 43 countries, of which 14% are included in this book. The papers were selected by the event chairs and their selection was based on a number of criteria, including the classifications and comments provided by the program committee members, the session chairs' assessment, and the program chairs' global view of all papers included in the technical program. The authors of the selected papers were then invited to submit a revised and extended version of their papers with at least 30% new material.

CSEDU, the International Conference on Computer Supported Education, is an annual meeting place for presenting and discussing the role of computers and computing in new educational environments, best practices, and case studies on innovative technology-based learning strategies, institutional policies on computer supported education, and open and distance education. CSEDU 2018 provided an overview of the state of the art as well as upcoming trends, and promoted discussion about the pedagogical potential of new learning and educational technologies in the academic and corporate world.

The papers selected to be included in this book contribute to the understanding of relevant trends of current research on computer-supported education, including teaching methods, tools to support educational communication, and environments for learning. More specifically, these papers encompass topics such as e-learning, intelligent tutors, learning analytics, adaptive educational systems, game-based learning, and universal design. These papers reflect advances in and perspectives on the application of technologies designed to improve teaching and learning practices.

We would like to thank all the authors for their contributions and the reviewers who helped ensure the quality of this publication.

March 2018

Bruce M. McLaren
Rob Reilly
Susan Zvacek
James Uhomoibhi

Organization

Conference Chair

James Uhomoibhi	Ulster University, UK

Program Co-chairs

Bruce McLaren	Carnegie Mellon University, USA
Rob Reilly	MIT, USA
Susan Zvacek	SMZTeaching.com, USA

Program Committee

Dor Abrahamson	University of California, Berkeley, USA
Mehdi Adda	Université du Québec à Rimouski, Canada
Nelma Albuquerque	Concepts and Insights, Brazil
Efthimios Alepis	University of Piraeus, Greece
Eleftheria Alexandri	University of Patras, Greece
Abdulwahab Alharbi	University of Glasgow, UK
António Andrade	Universidade Católica Portuguesa, Portugal
Francisco Arcega	Universidad de Zaragoza, Spain
Anders Avdic	Dalarna University, Sweden
Breno Azevedo	Instituto Federal de Educação, Ciência e Tecnologia Fluminense, Brazil
Adriano Baratè	Università degli Studi di Milano, Italy
João Barros	Polytechnic Institute of Beja, Portugal
Marcelo Barros	Federal University of Campina Grande, Brazil
Antonio Bartolomé Pina	Universitat de Barcelona, Spain
Patrícia Bassani	Universidade Feevale, Brazil
Emad Bataineh	Zayed University, UAE
Patricia Behar	Universidade Federal do Rio Grande do Sul, Brazil
Kay Berkling	Cooperative State University Baden Württemberg, Karlsruhe, Germany
Gilda Bernardino de Campos	Pontifícia Universidade Católica do Rio de Janeiro, Brazil
Pavol Bistak	Slovak University of Technology, Slovak Republic
Andreas Bollin	Klagenfurt University, Austria
Katrin Borcea-Pfitzmann	Technische Universität Dresden, Germany
Elmar-Laurent Borgmann	Hochschule Koblenz, University of Applied Sciences, Germany
Ivana Bosnic	University of Zagreb, Croatia
Federico Botella	Miguel Hernandez University of Elche, Spain

François Bouchet	Laboratoire d'Informatique de Paris 6, France
Patrice Bouvier	XIWEN Studio, France
Tharrenos Bratitsis	University of Western Macedonia, Greece
Krysia Broda	Imperial College London, UK
Martin Bush	London South Bank University, UK
Egle Butkeviciene	Kaunas University of Technology, Lithuania
Santi Caballé	Open University of Catalonia, Spain
Manuel Caeiro Rodríguez	University of Vigo, Spain
Renza Campagni	Università di Firenze, Italy
Pasquina Campanella	University of Bari Aldo Moro, Italy
Chris Campbell	Griffith University, Australia
André Campos	UFRN, Brazil
Thibault Carron	Pierre-and-Marie-Curie University, France
Ana Carvalho	Universidade de Coimbra, Portugal
Manuel Castro Gil	National University for Distance Education, Spain
Cristian Cechinel	Universidad Federal de Pelotas, Brazil
Chia-Hu Chang	National Taiwan University, Taiwan
Amitava Chatterjee	Jadavpur University, India
Mohamed Chatti	University of Duisburg-Essen, Germany
Gwo-Dong Chen	National Central University, Taiwan
Maria Cinque	LUMSA Università, Italy
António Coelho	Universidade do Porto, Portugal
Robert Collier	Carleton University, Canada
Marc Conrad	University of Bedfordshire, UK
Fernando Costa	Universidade de Lisboa, Portugal
Gennaro Costagliola	Università di Salerno, Italy
Manuel Perez Cota	Universidade de Vigo, Spain
Braulio Couto	Centro Universitário de Belo Horizonte - UniBH, Brazil
Caroline Crawford	University of Houston-Clear Lake, USA
John Cuthell	Virtual Learning, UK
Rogério da Silva	University of Houston-Victoria, USA
Ines Dabbebi	LIUM, France
Ingo Dahn	Virtual Campus Rhineland-Palatinate, Germany
Thanasis Daradoumis	University of the Aegean / Open University of Catalonia, Greece
Sergiu Dascalu	University of Nevada, Reno, USA
Luis de-la-Fuente-Valentín	Universidad Internacional de la Rioja, Spain
Giuliana Dettori	Istituto per le Tecnologie Didattiche (ITD-CNR), Italy
Tania Di Mascio	University of L'Aquila, Italy
Yannis Dimitriadis	School of Telecommunications Engineering, University of Valladolid, Spain
Danail Dochev	Institute of Information and Communication Technologies, Bulgarian Academy of Sciences, Bulgaria
Toby Dragon	Ithaca College, USA

Jon Dron	Athabasca University, Canada
Benedict du Boulay	University of Sussex, UK
Amalia Duch	UPC - Politechnical University of Catalonia, Spain
Mihai Dupac	Bournemouth University, UK
Nour El Mawas	Université de Lille, France
Larbi Esmahi	Athabasca University, Canada
João Esteves	University of Minho, Portugal
Vladimir Estivill-Castro	Griffith University, Australia
Ramon Fabregat Gesa	Universitat de Girona, Spain
Si Fan	University of Tasmania, Australia
Michalis Feidakis	University of West Attica (UWA), Greece
Mingyu Feng	SRI International, USA
Richard Ferdig	Kent State University, USA
Gustavo Figueroa	Instituto Nacional de Electricidad y Energías Limpias, Mexico
Davide Fossati	Emory University, USA
Rita Francese	Università degli Studi di Salerno, Italy
Vittorio Fuccella	Università di Salerno, Italy
Rubén Fuentes-Fernández	Universidad Complutense de Madrid, Spain
Judith Gal-Ezer	The Open University of Israel, Israel
Francisco García Peñalvo	Salamanca University, Spain
Iván García-Magariño	Universidad de Zaragoza, Spain
Serge Garlatti	IMT ATlantique, France
Isabela Gasparini	UDESC, Brazil
Sébastien George	Le Mans University, France
David Gibson	Curtin University, Australia
Henrique Gil	Escola Superior de Educação do Instituto Politécnico de Castelo Branco, Portugal
Apostolos Gkamas	University Ecclesiastical Academy of Vella, Ioannina, Greece
Anabela Gomes	Instituto Superior de Engenharia de Coimbra (Coimbra Polytechnic - ISEC), Portugal
Maria Gomes	Universidade do Minho, Portugal
Nuno Gonçalves	Superior School of Technology, Politechnical Institute of Setúbal, Portugal
Carina Gonzalez	Universidad de la Laguna, Spain
Ana González Marcos	Universidad de la Rioja, Spain
Judith Good	The University of Sussex, UK
Anandha Gopalan	Imperial College London, UK
Christos Goumopoulos	Computer Technology Institute and Press, Diophantus, Patras, Greece
Angela Guercio	Kent State University, USA
Christian Guetl	Graz University of Technology, Austria
Raffaella Guida	University of Surrey, UK
Nathalie Guin	Université Claude Bernard - Lyon 1, France

Celina Leão	University of Minho, Portugal
Dominique Leclet	UPJV, France
Mark Lee	Charles Sturt University, Australia
Newton Lee	Newton Lee Laboratories LLC and Institute for Education Research and Scholarships, USA
Marie Lefevre	University Claude Bernard Lyon 1, France
José Alberto Lencastre	University of Minho, Portugal
Andrew Lian	Suranaree University of Technology, Thailand
Cheng-Min Lin	Nan Kai University of Technology, Taiwan
Chiu Lin	National Tsing Hua University, Taiwan
Andreas Lingnau	Ruhr West University of Applied Sciences, Germany
Martin Llamas-Nistal	University of Vigo, Spain
Sharon Locke	Southern Illinois University Edwardsville, USA
Luca Andrea Ludovico	Università degli Studi di Milano, Italy
Krystina Madej	Georgia Tech, USA
Maria Marcelino	UC, Portugal
Massimo Marchiori	University of Padua, Italy
Jacek Marciniak	Adam Mickiewicz University, Poland
Ivana Marenzi	Leibniz University Hannover, Germany
José Marques	FEUP, Portugal
Lindsay Marshall	Newcastle University, UK
Alke Martens	Universität of Rostock, Germany
Scheila Martins	Pontificia Universidade Católica de Minas Gerais - PUC Minas, Brazil
Bruce Maxim	University of Michigan-Dearborn, USA
Madeth May	Le Mans Université, France
Godfrey Mayende	University of Agder, Norway
Elvis Mazzoni	University of Bologna, Italy
Robert Meolic	University of Maribor, Slovenia
José Carlos Metrôlho	Instituto Politécnico de Castelo Branco, Portugal
Bakhtiar Mikhak	Harvard University, USA
Michihiko Minoh	Kyoto University, Japan
Andreea Molnar	Swinburne University of Technology, Australia
António Moreira	Universidade de Aveiro, Portugal
Leonel Morgado	Universidade Aberta, Portugal
Jerzy Moscinski	Silesian University of Technology, Poland
Maria Moundridou	School of Pedagogical and Technological Education (ASPETE), Greece
Antao Moura	Federal University of Campina Grande (UFCG), Brazil
Wolfgang Mueller	Weingarten University of Education, Germany
Michal Munk	Constantine the Philosopher University in Nitra, Slovak Republic
Yuko Murakami	Tohoku University, Japan
Antoanela Naaji	Vasile Goldis Western University, Romania
Hiroyuki Nagataki	Osaka Electro-Communication University, Japan
Minoru Nakayama	Tokyo Institute of Technology, Japan

Gali Naveh	Shamoon College of Engineering, Israel
Sotiris Nikolopoulos	Technological Educational Institute of Larissa, Greece
Kazunori Nozawa	Ritsumeikan University, Japan
Fátima Nunes	Universidade de São Paulo, Brazil
Dade Nurjanah	School of Computing, Telkom University, Indonesia
Emma O'Brien	Mary Immaculate College, Ireland
Ebba Ossiannilsson	The Swedish Association for Distance Education (SADE), Sweden
Kuo-liang Ou	National TsingHua University, Taiwan
Alessandro Pagano	University of Bari, Italy
José Palma	Escola Superior de Tecnologia de Setúbal, Portugal
Manuel Palomo Duarte	Universidad de Cádiz, Spain
Stamatis Papadakis	University of Crete, Greece
Kyparisia Papanikolaou	School of Pedagogical & Technological Education, Greece
Iraklis Paraskakis	South East European Research Centre, Greece
Emanuel Peres	University of Trás-os-Montes e Alto Douro/Inesc-Tec, Portugal
Paula Peres	ISCAP, Portugal
Arnulfo Perez	The Ohio State University, USA
Isidoros Perikos	University of Patras, Greece
Donatella Persico	Consiglio Nazionale Ricerche (CNR) - Italian National Research Council, Italy
Alfredo Pina	Public University of Navarra, Spain
Niels Pinkwart	Humboldt University, Germany
Elvira Popescu	University of Craiova, Romania
Petra Poulová	University of Hradec Králové, Czech Republic
Alexandra Poulovassilis	Birkbeck College, University of London, UK
Tamara Powell	Kennesaw State University, USA
Francesca Pozzi	CNR - National Research Council of Italy, Italy
Augustin Prodan	Iuliu Hatieganu University, Romania
Yannis Psaromiligkos	University of West Attica, Greece
Franz Puehretmair	Competence Network Information Technology to Support the Integration of People with Disabilities (KI-I), Austria
Clark Quinn	Quinnovation, USA
Muthu Ramachandran	Leeds Beckett University, UK
Altina Ramos	Universidade do Minho, Portugal
Fernando Ramos	University of Aveiro, Portugal
Eliseo Reategui	Universidade Federal do Rio Grande do Sul, Brazil
Petrea Redmond	University of Southern Queensland, Australia
Manuel Reis	University of Trás-os-montes e Alto Douro, Portugal
Fernando Ribeiro	Instituto Politécnico de Castelo Branco, Portugal
Razvan Rughinis	University Politehnica of Bucharest, Romania
Rebecca Rutherfoord	Kennesaw State University, USA
Demetrios Sampson	University of Piraeus, Greece

Juan M. Santos	University of Vigo, Spain
Georg Schneider	Trier University of Applied Sciences, Germany
Ulf Schreier	Furtwangen University, Germany
Wolfgang Schreiner	Johannes Kepler University, Austria
Ulrik Schroeder	RWTH Aachen University, Germany
Maria Serna	UPC - Technical University of Catalonia - Barcelona Tech, Spain
Haya Shamir	Waterford Research Institute, USA
Pei Siew	Universiti Tunku Abdul Rahman, Malaysia
Juarez Bento da Silva	Universidade Federal de Santa Catarina, Brazil
Natalya Snytnikova	Novosibirsk State University, Russian Federation
Filomena Soares	Algoritmi Research Centre, UM, Portugal
Michael Sonntag	Johannes Kepler University Linz, Austria
J. Michael Spector	University of North Texas, USA
Eliza Stefanova	Sofia University, Bulgaria
Claudia Steinberger	University of Klagenfurt, Austria
Craig Stewart	Indiana University, USA
Jun-Ming Su	National University of Tainan, Taiwan
Jarkko Suhonen	University of Eastern Finland, Finland
Katsuaki Suzuki	Kumamoto University, Japan
Karen Swan	University of Illinois at Springfield, USA
Nestori Syynimaa	University of Jyväskylä, Finland
Brendan Tangney	Trinity College Dublin, The University of Dublin, Ireland
Steven Tanimoto	University of Washington, USA
Luca Tateo	Aalborg University, Denmark
Dirk Tempelaar	Maastricht University School of Business and Economics, The Netherlands
Marco Temperini	Sapienza University of Rome, Italy
Uwe Terton	University of the Sunshine Coast, Australia
Neena Thota	University of Massachusetts Amherst, USA
Tomas Trescak	Western Sydney University, Australia
Abdallah Tubaishat	UAE
James Uhomoibhi	Ulster University, UK
Maria Uther	University of Wolverhampton, UK
Mario Vacca	Italian Ministry of Education, Italy
Leo van Moergestel	HU Utrecht University of Applied Sciences, The Netherlands
Ioannis Vardiambasis	Technological Educational Institute (TEI) of Crete, Greece
Norman Vaughan	Mount Royal University, Canada
Carlos Vaz de Carvalho	ISEP, Portugal
Andreas Veglis	Aristotle University of Thessaloniki, Greece
Ioanna Vekiri	Independent Researcher, Greece
Giuliano Vivanet	University of Cagliari, Italy
Harald Vranken	Open Universiteit, The Netherlands

Alf Wang	Norwegian University of Science and Technology, Norway
Fangju Wang	University of Guelph, Canada
Xinli Wang	Michigan Technological University, USA
Yuan-Kai Wang	Fu Jen Catholic University, Taiwan
Edgar Weippl	SBA & FHSTP, Austria
Christopher Wells	McGraw-Hill Education, USA
Martin Wessner	Darmstadt University of Applied Sciences, Germany
Leandro Wives	Universidade Federal do Rio Grande do Sul, Brazil
Jie Yang	National Central University, Taiwan
Katarina Zakova	Slovak University of Technology in Bratislava, Slovak Republic
Diego Zapata-Rivera	Educational Testing Service, USA
Thomas Zarouchas	Computer Technology Institute and Press Diophantus, Greece
Iveta Zolotova	Technical University in Kosice, Slovak Republic
Susan Zvacek	SMZTeaching.com, USA

Additional Reviewers

Susanne Haake	PH Weingarten, Germany
Benjamin Jones	University of Washington, USA

Invited Speakers

Liz Bacon	University of Greenwich, UK
Hamadou Saliah-Hassane	TÉLUQ University, Canada
H. Chad Lane	University of Illinois, Urbana-Champaign, USA

Contents

Effectiveness of Multisensory Methods in Learning Onomatopoeia for the Hearing-Impaired

Miki Namatame[1], Junichi Kanebako[2(✉)], Fusako Kusunoki[3(✉)], and Shigenori Inagaki[4(✉)]

[1] The National University Corporation of Tsukuba University of Technology, Amakubo, Tsukuba, Ibaraki 3058520, Japan
miki@a.tsukuba-tech.ac.jp
[2] Advanced Institute of Industrial Technology, Higashiooi, Shinagawa, Tokyo 1400011, Japan
kanebako-j@aiit.ac.jp
[3] Tama Art University, Yarimizu, Hachioji, Tokyo 1920394, Japan
kusunoki@tamabi.ac.jp
[4] Kobe University, Tsurukabuto, Nada-ku, Kobe 6578501, Japan
inagakis@kobe-u.ac.jp

Abstract. We examined the effectiveness of multisensory methods in learning animal sounds and the onomatopoeia that describe them. Hearing-impaired individuals find it difficult to learn onomatopoeia because they have limited or no access to auditory information. To address this problem, we developed a device that converts audio information into vibrations, and attempted to broaden the experience of sound by using multisensory methods to stimulate the senses of sight, hearing, and touch. In the rhythm discrimination test using the device, the hearing-impaired group showed better performance with vibration added to the audio information than without vibration. In addition, we designed a science lesson to help hearing-impaired individuals learn cicada songs. This lesson used multiple media including text, images, sounds, sound waveforms, onomatopoeia, and vibrations. The evaluation results showed a significant difference between the students who were able to distinguish the vibrations and those who could not. The former reported that they found the lesson enjoyable and that it was a useful way to learn science.

Keywords: Hearing-impaired · Science lesson · Cicada · Vibration · Onomatopoeia

1 Introduction

An onomatopoeia is a word that phonetically imitates the sound of a thing or action; it resembles or suggests the sound that it describes. Several examples of noises and sound effects in writing can be found in poems, comics, literature, and

B. M. McLaren et al. (Eds.): CSEDU 2018, CCIS 1022, pp. 1–13, 2019.
https://doi.org/10.1007/978-3-030-21151-6_1

slang. An onomatopoeia includes sound symbolism and exhibits cross-cultural differences. In a famous psychological experiment by Wolfgang Köhler in 1929 [1,2], the participants were asked to choose which of these shapes is named "Kiki" and which is named "Bouba". Most people agreed that Kiki represents the shape on the left and Bouba represents the one on the right in Fig. 1. This experiment suggests that sound symbolism may have a principle beyond cross-cultural differences.

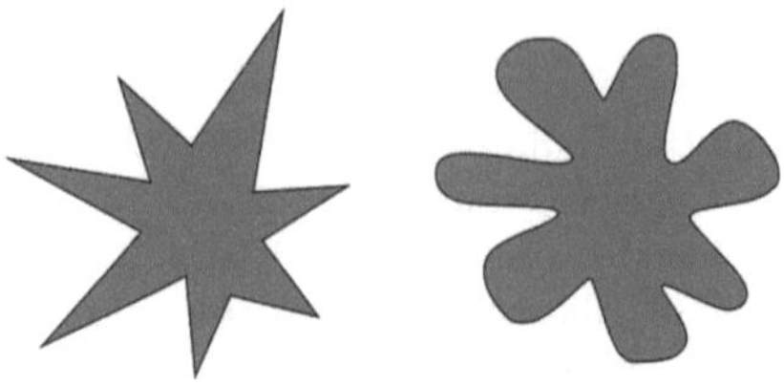

Fig. 1. The Kiki-Bouba shapes (From media Commons, the free media repository).

2 Background

2.1 Difficulties in Learning Onomatopoeia

An onomatopoeia plays an important role in word acquisition, child development, and education. It has also been found that, when using the auditory modality in the education of hearing-impaired children, onomatopoeia teaches vocalization patterns and how to associate meanings with words, thereby facilitating verbalization [3]. This suggests that onomatopoeic words are important for the hearing-impaired to learn. Other studies have found that when deaf individuals understood spoken sentences, not only the brain's left hemisphere (as in native speakers with normal hearing) but also the right hemisphere was extensively activated [4]. Moreover, it was shown that deaf individuals used phonological representations in visually presented verbal memory tasks similar to people with normal hearing [5]. However, when deaf subjects were asked to judge the appropriateness of the use of sound symbolic words depicting states, actions, or emotions to describe scenes in a video, the visual and auditory association areas in the brain were not activated [6]. These findings support the idea that it is difficult for hearing-impaired individuals, who have limited access to auditory information, to construct linguistic symbols using the sound symbolism of onomatopoeic words, in spite of their synaesthetic and sound-symbolic characteristics [7].

2.2 Importance of Learning Onomatopoeia in Japan

The Japanese language is said to use from three to five times as many onomatopoeic words as western languages or Chinese [8]. The dictionary of Japanese mimetics lists 4500 entries [9]. Educational research has suggested that onomatopoeia, that is, words which mimic animated sounds (giseigo) or inanimate sounds (giongo), or symbolize states (gitaigo), emotions (gijougo), or actions (giyougo), are easy to understand for students and enhance their comprehension and imagination [10]. It has also been said that high iconicity between the sound and the referent enables listeners to accurately generalize the meaning of the word and to make an immediate connection with the object being symbolized Furthermore, sound symbolic words referring to states, emotions, or actions facilitate the learning of verbs as children acquire vocabulary [11]. Therefore, learners of the Japanese language must master onomatopoeia to be able to communicate in a more descriptive and expressive manner [12]. Thus, onomatopoeias (also referred to as sound-symbolic words) are important for these individuals to learn.

2.3 Information Accessibility for the Hearing-Impaired

The elements of onomatopoeias are often described as pitch (low-high), tonality (pure tone-noisy), loudness (quiet-very loud), beginning (sudden-gradual), duration (short-long), constancy (smooth-intermittent). The difficulty faced by hearing-impaired individuals is understandable for the reason that these are the elements that constitute a sound. This highlights the importance of providing alternative information to sound to hearing-impaired individuals. Previous research on information accessibility and sensory substitution for the disabled has shown that haptic information is effective in speech training [13]. Practical applications using vibrations to provide alerts are already available, such as vibrating alarm clocks, vibrating devices worn in the hair [14], and applications that alert the user to sounds indicating danger [15]. In addition, information provided through vibrations enables hearing-impaired individuals to recognize rhythms and enjoy music [16]. In particular, hearing impairment has been linked to a heightened sense of touch [17]. Moreover, deaf children seem to be sensitive to their articulatory gestures in the context of sound symbolism [18,19]. It can be postulated that even without the ability to hold sound symbols in memory in the absence of auditory information, they may be able to construct other linguistic symbols if a multisensory environment is created to provide alternative sensory information, such as vibrations or visual information.

3 Research Questions

The purpose of this study was to determine whether vibration as a form of haptic information can broaden the learner experience of sound. Therefore, we constructed two research questions as follows.

1. How do hearing-impaired learners appreciate the component elements in an onomatopoeia lesson for animal sounds designed using multisensory methods?
2. Can vibration information play a complementary role to auditory information in learning onomatopoeia?

4 Research Features

Extensive research has been conducted on sound and vibration, ranging from characteristics extraction to virtual reality and science education. However, very little research exists that targets those with hearing disabilities. To address this problem, we developed learning materials targeting people with hearing difficulties that allow users to discover the differences in sounds made by insects through vibrations. In this report, we attempt to promote an understanding of synesthesia by considering a type of experience such as an insect (cicada) sound, which the hearing-impaired are unable to learn owing to their difficulty in acquiring auditory information.

We measure the learning effect by comparing the cases where vibration information is added or not. An evaluation of the methods and the teaching materials for providing the sense of touch (vibration) is presented. By further developing this research, we can expect to see an improvement in the rhythm perception of those who are hearing-impaired, while also seeing its benefits in science education.

5 Overview of Experiment

5.1 Prototype of Experimental Device

As the first step of the experiment, we developed a new hearing device that provides an experience of synesthesia. This device has piezoelectric elements mounted on its small housing and it converts audio information into vibrations that can be felt with the use of the five fingers (Fig. 2). By using five actuators, it is possible to feel different vibration frequencies on each finger. The device is connected to a PC to output a mono audio signal (5 ch) via an audio interface using an amplifier. The piezoelectric elements used in this device can generate frequencies between 100 Hz to 40 kHz. As it is suitable for producing low frequencies, it is possible to feel the audio information as vibrations. The frequency band allocation of the device is shown in Fig. 2(right); the horizontal axis represents the frequency band (Hz) and the vertical axis represents the volume (db). This system allows hearing-impaired individuals to extend their physical experience of sounds. We used this device in a preliminary experiment for discriminating the rhythm of the cicada's songs. The frequencies of the songs ranged between 2 kHz to approximately 10 kHz. It was difficult to represent the cicada's songs using this device, because of their small frequency range.

5.2 Design of Teaching Material

Therefore, we designed multimedia teaching materials that appeal to the senses of hearing, touch, and sight to aid the learning of the sound of the cicada.

The teaching material content includes a description of the habits of the cicada, the onomatopoeia of the cicada's song, images of the cicada, the sound information of the cicada's song, the waveform of the cicada's song, and vibrations. The presentation begins automatically when the learner clicks

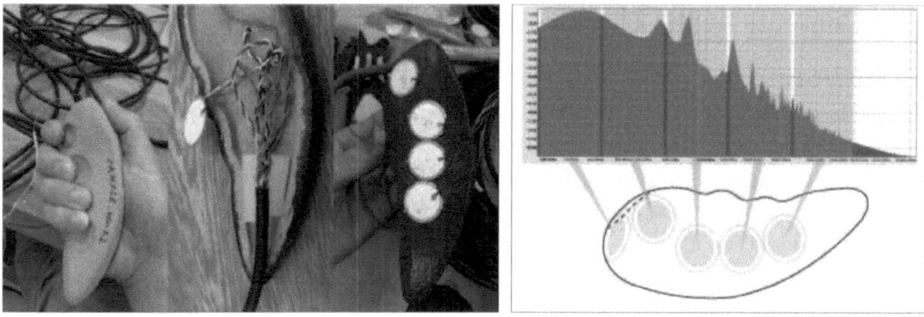

Fig. 2. Prototype of experimental device and allocation of frequency band.

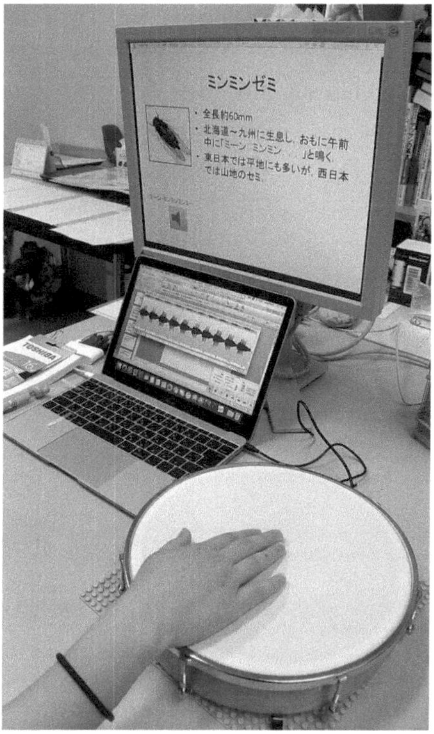

Fig. 3. Configuration of the learning materials [23].

the start button. On the main display, the description of the cicada, the onomatopoeia, image, and a button to play the cicada's song are shown. The learner can read the description of the cicada and the onomatopoeia, and then click the button to play the cicada's song. The sound waveform of the cicada's song emerges on a voice-display while the cicada's song is played. The vibration is linked to the cicada's song using a vibration speaker. The learner acquires the cicada's song and the sound waveform with the vibration. The configuration of the teaching material is shown in Fig. 3.

5.3 Contents of the Cicada's Song

We chose seven types of cicadas that are well-known in Japan. The sound specifications of each cicada are listed in Table 1, and the waveforms are depicted in Fig. 4. The cicada's song is edited such that it plays at a volume of 93 db (+−2 db) for approximately 40 s. In addition, the different types of cicadas are presented randomly each time the teaching material is used. Thus, the teaching material allows users to feel the rhythm and phrase of the cicada's song via vibrations and to experience the presence of the different types of cicadas.

Table 1. Specifications of the cicadas' song [23].

Cicada	Onomatopoeia	Time ms	Volume db	Vibration m/s^2
1: Graptopsaltria nigrofuscata	Jiri-jiri	45	95	2.8
2: Terpnosia nigricosta	Achi-achi	40	95	27.0
3: Tanna japonensis	Kana-kana	46	93	9.2
4: Kosemia radiator	chi. chi. chi	41	91	3.7
5: Meimuna opalifera	Tsuku-tusku	42	95	3.3
6: Hyalessa maculaticollis	min-min	46	95	3.0
7: Platypleura kaempferi	Chiiii...	45	100	0.6

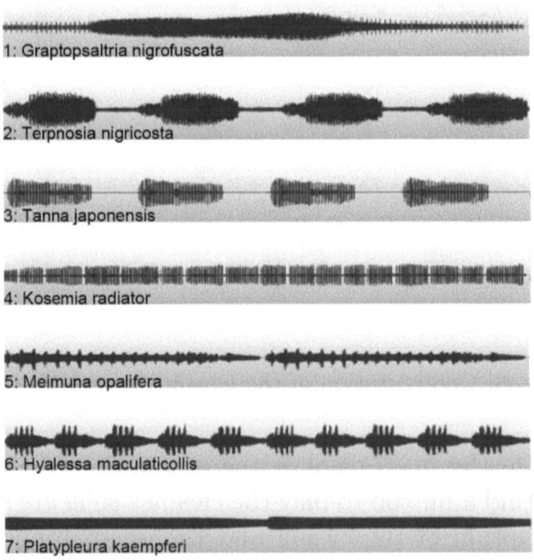

Fig. 4. Various sound waveform of the cicadas' song

6 Experiment

6.1 Preliminary Experiment

The preliminary experiment aimed to clarify the rhythm discrimination results when hearing-impaired participants listen to music using a device to supplement the sounds with vibrations. Using the developed device, a rhythm discrimination experiment was conducted for hearing-impaired people. The stimulus was presented under three different conditions: only auditory stimulation, adding vibration stimulus to auditory stimulus, and only vibration stimulation. The stimulus intensity was set to 74.0 dBSPL for auditory sound pressure and $2.3\,\mathrm{m/s^2}$ for tactile vibration acceleration. The results indicated that the rhythm discrimination performance improves by presenting the vibration stimulus at the same time as the sound, compared to only the sound stimulation.

6.2 Experimental Procedure

The experiment was conducted from 27th June to 6th July, 2017 A total of 26 individuals with hearing-impairments (average age: 21.1 years) participated in the experiment. The participants were divided into two groups. Group A comprised 17 participants using the vibration device, and Group B comprised 9 participants not using the vibration device. The experiment was conducted for 30 min in total per person. The experimental procedure was as follows:

1. Informed consent and experiment explanation
2. 2-back task (working memory task)
3. Pre-test
4. Learning
5. Post-test
6. Questionnaire evaluation

6.3 Evaluation Method of the Lesson

The lesson used multiple media including text, images, sounds, sound waveforms, onomatopoeia, and vibrations to stimulate the senses of sight, hearing, and touch. The following eight questions were prepared to evaluate the lesson:

Q1: Good material text, images, sounds, sound waveforms, onomatopoeia, (vibrations)
Q2: Did you hear anything?
Q3: Did you distinguish those vibrations?
Q3: (or Did you need vibration?)
Q4: The degree of easy intelligibility
Q5: The degree of usefulness
Q6: The degree of interest
Q7: The degree of enjoyability
Q8: The degree of being educative

7 Result

7.1 Learning Ability of Participants

As the baseline information, participants were assigned the 2-back task, in which they need to decide if the current number is the same as the one presented two trials ago, in order to assess their working memory. After a trial round, the formal experiment was conducted twice. The mean score of the experimental group was 53.2% and that of the control group was 57.9%. In order to assess the knowledge of the cicada's song, the participants had to connect the seven cicada's names to their respective songs (onomatopoeia), before and after the learning. The results showed that in the pre-test, the percentages of correct answers were 3.9 and 3.8 for the experimental group and control group, respectively; in the post-test, they were 6.8 and 6.6 for the experimental group and control group, respectively. That is, almost all the participants were able to match the cicada's name and song (onomatopoeia) after the learning. Therefore, we regarded the working-memory and learning effect of the participants as equal, and compared the subjective evaluation of the lesson between the experimental group and control group.

7.2 Evaluation of the Lesson

Figures 5 and 6 show the evaluation of good points of the lesson. The vertical axis shows the percentage and the horizontal axis shows the various elements. The elements are caption, photo, onomatopoeia, sound, waveform, and vibration. A multiple-choice question was answered by participants in each group: group A (with vibration) and group B (without vibration).

It can be seen from the figure that with or without vibration, the onomatopoeia was evaluated as an effective element of the lesson. In the absence of vibration, the sound was evaluated at the same level as the onomatopoeia, whereas the sound was not highly evaluated when vibration was provided.

7.3 Subjective Evaluation About the Lesson

The following Likert-scale was used for the subjective evaluation and the average was calculated.

+2point: strong-agree
+1point: agree
0point: neither
−1point: disagree
−2point: strong-disagree

To examine the differences between group A (with vibration) and group B (without vibration), a t-test was conducted; however, no significant differences were found.

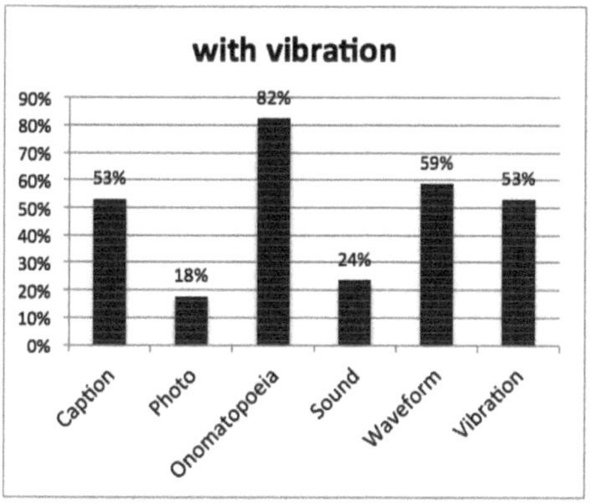

Fig. 5. Good element (Vib.) [23].

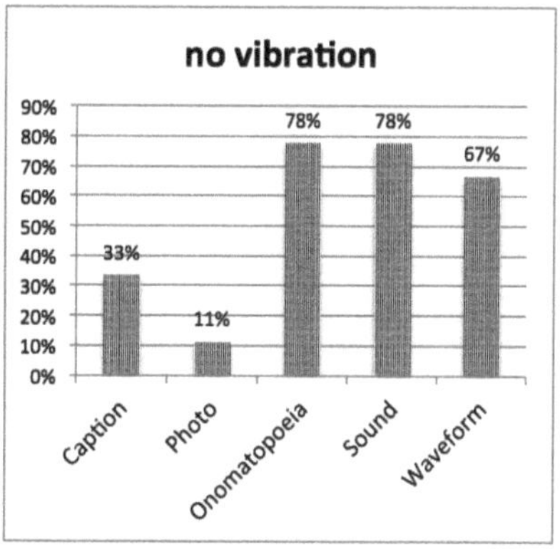

Fig. 6. Good element (no Vib.) [23].

7.4 Relation of the Senses

We asked two questions regarding the senses of hearing and touch. Q2: Did you hear anything?, Q3: Did you distinguish those vibrations? The t-test results were analyzed to find the differences in their feeling and subjective evaluation. The population was the 17 participants in group A (with vibration). They were separated into a positive group and a negative group. The positive group comprised "agree" and "strong-agree", and the negative group comprised "disagree", "strong-disagree", and "neither".

Q2: Did you hear anything? The result was that 11 participants responded "can hear something" and 6 participants responded "can't hear anything". There was no significant difference between the subjective evaluation (Intelligibility, Useful, Interesting, Enjoyable, Educative) and hearing-feeling. The result shows that there was no difference in the evaluation of the lesson by the degree of hearing.

Q3: Did you distinguish those vibrations? The result was that 11 participants responded "can distinguish" and 6 participants responded "can't distinguish". The Table 2 shows that the evaluation is higher for a person who was able to distinguish the vibration. There were significant differences between the subjective evaluation about "Interesting" ($t(15) = 3.05$, $p < .05$), and "Educative" ($t(15) = 2.49$, $p < .05$) (Fig. 7).

8 Discussion

The purpose of this study was to determine whether vibration as a form of haptic information can broaden the learner experience of sound. The haptic information provided by a vibration device allowed hearing-impaired individuals to extend their physical experience of sounds. A multisensory lesson to teach sound-symbolic onomatopoeias for animal sounds by broadening the learner experience of sound beyond auditory information could facilitate learner comprehension.

Table 2. Distinction of the vibration and evaluation of the lesson [23].

	Distinguish average (S.D.)	No distinguish average (S.D.)
Intelligibility	1.09 (0.70)	0.50 (0.84)
Usefulness	1.27 (0.47)	0.33 (1.21)
Interest	0.45 (0.82)	0.17 (0.75)
Enjoyability	1.27 (0.65)	0.33 (0.52)
Being educative	1.00 (0.77)	−0.17 (1.17)

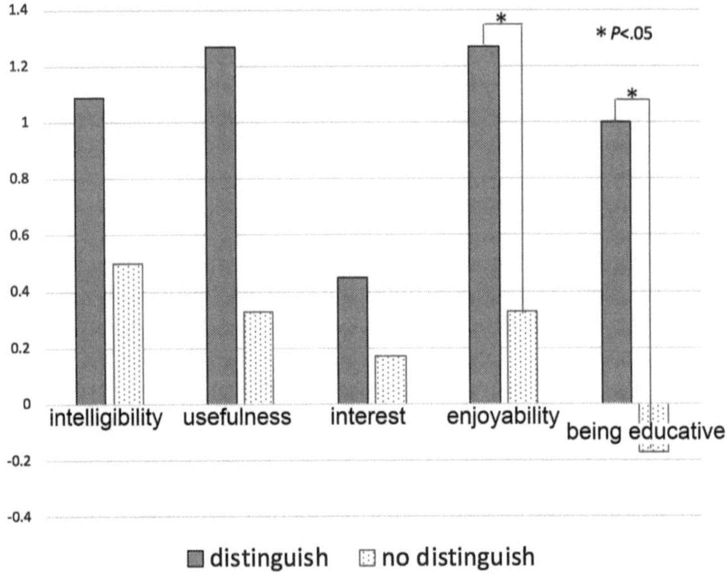

Fig. 7. Comparison of the subjective evaluation [23].

The subject of the lesson was cicada songs. The lesson content consisted of an explanation of cicada ecology, the onomatopoeia for the cicada's song, a picture of the cicada, the cicada's song (auditory information), its sound waveform, and, for one of the groups, a vibration. Analyses were based on participants' evaluations of the lesson and on tests to determine if the lesson had an effect on participants' learning.

The results showed no significant difference in learning between the two groups of participants (26 in total): one that was provided with vibrations as part of the lesson and the other that was not. Post-lesson test results showed improvement over the pre-lesson results with almost all participants ultimately answering all the questions correctly (the score was 6.8/7.0 and 6.6/7.0 points for the two groups, respectively). However, to accurately assess the lesson's effectiveness, knowledge retention needs to be measured by conducting another test at some fixed period of time after the lesson.

There were inconsistencies in how participants were able to feel the vibrations in the lesson, which suggested that the vibrations were not provided in a way that everyone could understand them. Regardless of whether vibrations were included, most participants rated the onomatopoeias for the songs as a good element of the lesson. A total of 82% of the participants provided vibration and 78% of participants not provided vibration answered that onomatopoeias were good teaching material for the lesson. This result, although a slight difference, indicates the possibility that vibration helps the understanding of sound-symbolic words.

For the group for which vibrations were included as an element of the lesson, fewer participants selected the song's auditory information rather than the vibration as a good element of the lesson. They evaluated the vibration, waveform, and caption at the same level. The result suggests that the participants may have tried to make more use of vibrations and other elements than auditory information when they were available. In contrast, when vibrations were not included, more participants appreciated the inclusion of the song's auditory information. This indicates that these hearing-impaired individuals concentrated on the auditory information by using their residual hearing.

No statistically significant difference was found in the subjective evaluations of the lesson between the groups given and not given the vibrations. Nor was there any significant difference in evaluation results due to the degree to which participants reported they were able to hear sounds.

However, a significant difference was shown due to differences in how participants were able to feel the vibrations. Those who were able to distinguish the vibrations reported they found the lesson "fun" and that "it could be used for teaching science". Considering that including vibrations in a lesson can make learning sound-symbolic words enjoyable, it may be promising to apply them in science lessons for hearing-impaired individuals.

9 Conclusion and Future Work

This study aimed to determine how hearing-impaired learners evaluate the component elements of a multisensory lesson on onomatopoeia. The experimental results demonstrated that the elements of the multisensory lesson that broadened the learner experience of sound and that were most appreciated by the participants in this study were the onomatopoeia, the sound waveforms of the cicada songs, and either the song itself or its vibration, depending on the group they were assigned to.

Secondly, the study investigated whether vibration information could complement auditory information in learning onomatopoeia. The results demonstrated that haptic information like vibrations was a useful alternative to sound that complements auditory information for people with difficulty in hearing. While the results did not show that the inclusion of vibrations in the lesson facilitated learner comprehension of sound-symbolic onomatopoeia, they did show vibration to be a promising element for inclusion in educational materials for the hearing-impaired.

In the future, it may be possible to develop more effective lessons by using better vibration devices that can vibrate in more distinctive ways. Better devices are needed that can convey more nuances and higher registers of sound, and not vibrate the way an alarm clock does. By further developing this work, we can expect to see an improvement in the rhythm perception of those who are hearing-impaired, while also seeing its benefits in science education. In addition, we need to consider that there may be biased correspondences between the sound symbolism of onomatopoeia and haptics in the same way as "a correspondence between vowel sound and shape".

WHO has declared that over 5% of the world population (or 466 million people) has disabling hearing loss [22]. Therefore, we believe that we need to construct an inclusive and sustainable society with hearing-impaired individuals. We may also overcome cross-cultural differences by utilizing sound-symbolic onomatopoeia.

Acknowledgements. This paper is an extension of our presentation [23] at the CSEDU2018 conference. We sincerely thank the CSEDU2018 committee.

We thank the students of the Tsukuba University of Technology who cooperated on the experiment and Kitamura M. who supported the experiment[1].

This work was supported by JSPS KAKENHI Grant Numbers 18H01046 and 15K12122.

References

1. Kohler, W.: Gestalt Psychology. Liveright Google Scholar, New York (1929)
2. Köhler, W.: Gestalt psychology. Psychologische Forschung **31**(1), 28–30 (1967)
3. Nakamura, K.: Use of the auditory modality and language acquisitiony. J. Logopedics Phoniatrics **48**, 254–262 (2007)
4. Neville, H.J., et al.: Cerebral organization for language in deaf and hearing subjects. Proc. Natl. Acad. Sci. USA **95**(3), 922–929 (1998). https://doi.org/10.1073/pnas.95.3.922. National Center for Biotechnology Information
5. Okada, R., et al.: The deaf utilize phonological representations in visually presented verbal memory tasks. Neurosci. Res. National Center Biotechnol. Inf. **90**, 83–89 (2015). https://doi.org/10.1016/j.neures.2014.11.004
6. Arata, M., Imai, M., Namatame, M., Okuda, J., Okada, H., Matsuda, T.: Semantic processing of mimetic words in deaf individuals. An fMRI study. In: 26th O2-3, Japanese Cognitive Science Society (2009). (in Japanese)
7. Hinton, L., Nichols, J., Ohala, J.J.: Sound Symbolism. Cambridge University Press, Cambridge (2006). Digitally printed first paperback version
8. Yamaguchi, N.: Giongo gitaigo jiten (Onomatopoeia Mimetic words Dictionary). Kodansha, Tokyo (2003). (in Japanese)
9. Ono, M.: Nihongo onomatope jiten (Japanese Mimetics Dictionary). Shogakkan, Tokyo (2007). (in Japanese)
10. Miyazaki, A., Tomimatsu, K.: Onomato planets: physical computing of Japanese onomatopoeia. In: Proceedings of the 3rd International Conference on Tangible and Embedded Interaction. ACM, Cambridge (2009)

[1] This study was accepted by the ethics committee of the Tsukuba University of Technology.

11. Imai, M., Kita, S., Nagumo, M., Okada, H.: Sound symbolism facilitates early verb learning. Cognition **109**, 54–65 (2008). https://doi.org/10.1016/j.cognition.2008.07.015
12. Yusuf, M., Asaga, C., Watanabe, C.: Onomatopeta!: developing a Japanese onomatopoeia learning-support system utilizing native speakers cooperation. In: Proceedings of the 2008 IEEE/WIC/ACM International Conference on Web Intelligence and Intelligent Agent Technology, pp. 173–177. IEEE Computer Society Washington, DC (2008). https://doi.org/10.1109/WIIAT.2008.300
13. Alves, R.L., Lima, C.S., Freire, R.: Correction of the fundamental voice frequency using tactile and visual feedback. In: Proceedings of the 17th International ACM SIGACCESS Conference on Computers & Accessibility. ACM (2015). https://doi.org/10.1145/2700648.2811378
14. Honda, T., Okamoto, M.: User interface design of sound tactile. In: Miesenberger, K., Fels, D., Archambault, D., Peňáz, P., Zagler, W. (eds.) ICCHP 2014. LNCS, vol. 8548, pp. 382–385. Springer, Cham (2014). https://doi.org/10.1007/978-3-319-08599-9_57
15. Henriquez, P., Travieso, C.M.: Review of automatic fault diagnosis systems using audio and vibration signals. Trans. Syst. Man Cybern.: Syst. **44**(5), 642–652 (2013). https://doi.org/10.1109/TSMCC.2013.2257752
16. Kanebako, J., Yamanaka, T., Namatame, M.: Effect of vibration on listening sound for a person with hearing loss. In: Miesenberger, K., Bühler, C., Penaz, P. (eds.) ICCHP 2016. LNCS, vol. 9759, pp. 419–423. Springer, Cham (2016). https://doi.org/10.1007/978-3-319-41267-2_59
17. Heidenreich, M., et al.: KCNQ4 K+ channels tune mechanoreceptors for normal touch sensation in mouse and man. Nat. Neurosci. **15**, 138–145 (2012). https://doi.org/10.1038/nn.2985
18. Shinohara, K., Kawahara, S.: A cross-linguistic study of sound symbolism: the images of size. In: Berkeley Linguistics Society, the Linguistic Society of America, pp. 396–410 (2010) https://doi.org/10.3765/bls.v36i1.3926
19. Eberhardt, M.: A study of phonetic symbolism of deaf children. Psychol. Monogr. **52**, 23–42 (1940)
20. Kanebako, J., kusunoki, F., Inagaki, S., Namatame, M.: Proposal for science learning materials using a "VibGrip". In: Proceedings of the 12th International Conference on Advances in Computer Entertainment Technology, no. 36, pp. 1–3 (2015). https://doi.org/10.1145/2832932.2832935
21. Spector, F., Maurer, D.: Early sound symbolism for vowel sounds. i-Perception **4**(4), 239–241 (2013). https://doi.org/10.1068/i0535
22. WHO news deafness and hearing loss, 15 March 2018. http://www.who.int/news-room/fact-sheets/detail/deafness-and-hearing-loss
23. Namatame, M., Kusunoki, F., Inagaki, S.: Basic research on multisensory methods for teaching onomatopoeia to the hearing-impaired - broadening the experience of sound. In: Proceedings of the 10th International Conference on Computer Supported Education, vol. 1, pp. 22–27. SciTePress, INSTICC (2018). https://doi.org/10.5220/0006665800220027

Using Spinoza Log Data to Enhance CS1 Pedagogy

Fatima Abu Deeb, Antonella DiLillo, and Timothy Hickey(✉)

Computer Science Department, Brandeis University,
415 South Street, Waltham, MA 02453, USA
{abudeebf,dilant,tjhickey}@brandeis.edu

Abstract. Active learning in Computer Science classrooms often involves having students solve programming problems in class using a web-based interpreter. Spinoza is one such system which captures all of the student attempts and uses it to provide actionable learning analytics for the instructor. In this paper we present several new pedagogical applications of the log data from Spinoza, including two approaches to team formation and an in depth analysis of the Solve-Then-Debug debugging pedagogy in Spinoza. We provide some initial evidence that the Team Formation strategies may be effective methods for forming either diverse or homogeneous teams. The second application we examine in depth is the Solve-Then-Debug pedagogy in which students who correctly solve a Spinoza programming problem are then asked to analyze and debug the most common errors that the class has made so far on that problem. This is a social debugging process and in this paper we provide a detailed explanation of the learning goals for each step of this pedagogy. We also give an example of how students engaged with one particular Solve-Then-Debug problem. This provides initial evidence that the Solve-Then-Debug pedagogy engages students in effective program bug analysis activity.

Keywords: Solve-Then-Debug · Near-peer mentoring · Peer led team learning · Study group formation · Online IDEs · Educational data mining · Hierarchical clustering · Classroom orchestration · Markov Models · Machine learning · Learning analytics

1 Introduction

In this paper we describe our experience in using log files from an online Integrated Development Environment (IDE) to enhance the pedagogy in two large courses introductory programming courses (CS1) – one taught in Java and the other in Python. There are many on-line IDEs available today (e.g. codingbat.com, repl.it, pythontutor.com). We developed the online IDE Spinoza [1–3] which differs from the others in that it has a much greater focus on orchestration support for the instructor. Spinoza provides real-time views of the performance of the entire class as well as individual students and off-line access to

B. M. McLaren et al. (Eds.): CSEDU 2018, CCIS 1022, pp. 14–36, 2019.
https://doi.org/10.1007/978-3-030-21151-6_2

the detailed log files. The most recent version of Spinoza [3] is publicly available and provides an IDE for Python with a rich set of tools for classroom orchestration and learning analytics. An earlier version of this paper appeared in CSEDU2018 [5].

One of the main benefits of using an on-line IDE in Introductory Programming Classes (usually referred to as CS1 classes) is that it provides immediate access to the students' attempts at solving a problem, and this data can be used in a variety of ways, such as forming study groups using knowledge of the kinds of errors the students make, as well as providing in-class activities that use the students' own mistakes to provide a basis for discussion and debugging practice.

Spinoza provides a wealth of real-time learning analytics collected while the students are attempting to solve programming problems. This learning analytics data can be used in real-time to improve the effectiveness of classroom orchestration. For our purposes, orchestration refers to the instructor's ability to respond effectively to a diverse class of learners in real-time. Prieto [17] provides a comprehensive overview of the theory and practice of classroom orchestration. Ihantola et. al. [12] provide an extensive overview of educational data mining and learning analytics for programming classes and its use in improving the instruction and guiding at-risk students. This kind of data can also be used to study particular styles of student learning, for example, Berland [8] collected log data for novice programmers and used it to study their learning pathways. Spinoza has been designed to support collaborative learning.

The rest of this paper is organized as follows. In Sect. 2, we give an overview of Spinoza and its primary features. In Sect. 3, we present our results on two different approaches to using Spinoza log data to form study groups for collaborative learning. In Sect. 4, we provide a careful description of the Solve-Then-Debug pedagogy and the design decisions made to create this six step learning cycle. In Sect. 5 we look closely at how student interact with one particular Solve-Then-Debug problem and summarize the results of a large qualitative analysis of that data. Finally, we discuss our connections to related research in Sect. 6 and we discuss future work in Sect. 7.

2 Spinoza

Spinoza is an on-line problem solving learning environment for coding (PSLEC) designed to allow the instructor to create and share small programming problems. Each problem asks the student to write the body of a method that would automatically be checked for correctness by running a suite of instructor-supplied unit tests. Each time a student clicks the "run" button, Spinoza runs the unit tests and displays the results to the user. It also stores a copy of the submitted code, a time stamp, the userId, the percentage of correct unit test results, the type of error (e.g. syntax error, run-time error) and the hash of the vector resulting from the instructor supplied unit tests.

Figure 1 shows the Spinoza user interface with the problem description before the user presses the "run" button and Fig. 2 shows interface after "run" is pushed, where the problem description is replaced by the unit test results tab. There are some correct (green) and some incorrect (red) results in the unit tests in this example.

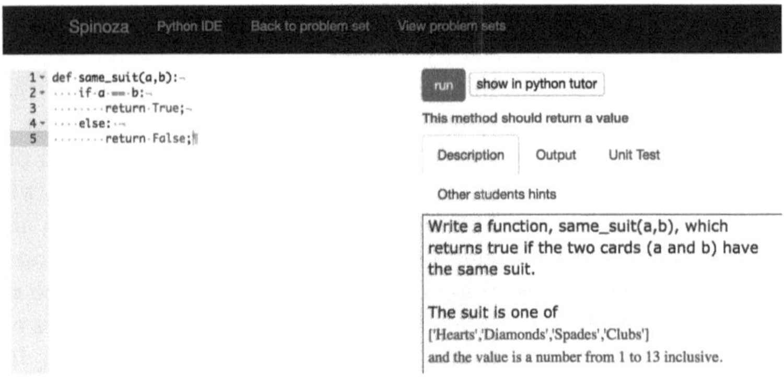

Fig. 1. An example of Spinoza problem with description tab before they push the "run" button.

Fig. 2. An example of Spinoza problem with unit tests tab after they push the "run" button. (Color figure online)

2.1 Spinoza Markov Models

Spinoza is coupled with features that facilitate teacher orchestration. It provides a dashboard for the instructor to see the progress of the entire class working on the current problem in real time using multiple views. One of these sophisticated views is the Spinoza Markov Model (SMM) [4]. An example is shown in Fig. 3. The SMM is a graph whose nodes are the equivalence classes of student programs submitted for the current problem. Two programs are equivalent if they produce the same values on the instructor-supplied unit tests. The size of each node is the number of programs in that equivalence class. The color corresponds to the percentage of unit tests that the programs satisfied. An edge between nodes A and B is labeled by the number of times students first submitted a program in equivalence class A and then submitted their next attempt in equivalence class B. In this way it gives an overview of the common programming errors and the common order in which they appear.

Each SMM has a start node, representing the starting state of the programming exercise, the correct solution node if at least one student solved the problem correctly, and a 'give up' node. All the other nodes represent students' incorrect attempts at solving the problem. The SMM is drawn in real-time and the instructor can click on each node and use the arrow keys to page through each of the programs in that equivalence class and discuss it with the class. The color and the size are chosen to represent the correctness of the attempts and how often this error are made by the students respectively.

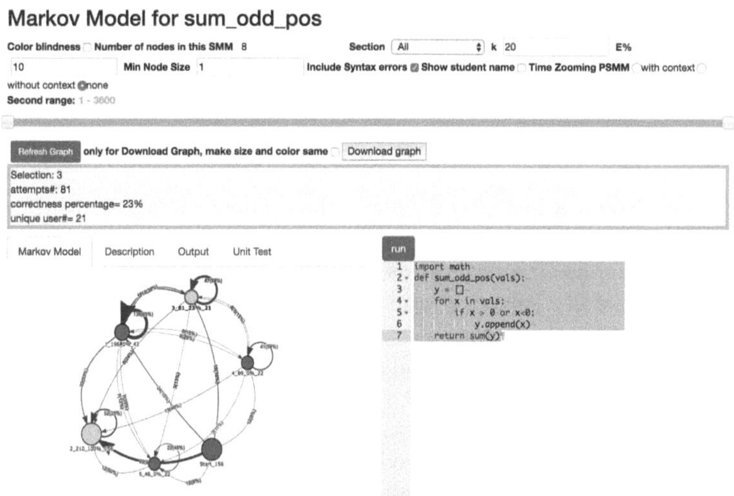

Fig. 3. Spinoza Markov Model. (Color figure online)

During class, it can be effective to look at the most common errors (as classified by their behavior on unit tests) and then look at each of the different ways students were able to make that error, i.e. using the Spinoza feature that lets the instructor browse each of the programs in that equivalence class. It is also helpful to scan all of the successful programs to comment on programming style.

2.2 Solve-Then-Debug

One issue with having students work on programming problems in class or in a recitation is that students work at different rates. The fast students will complete the problem in a few minutes and typically have nothing to do while everyone else completes the problem. Initially, we would wait until a threshold number of students had completed the problem (typically 75–80%) before discussing the solutions and errors, but this meant that over half of the students would be non-engaged during at least part of the exercise.

Spinoza provides a solution to this challenge by requiring students who solved a programming problem to get experience in debugging by analyzing the most common errors that the class has made (and is making) on that problem. This is called the "Solve-Then-Debug" activity, which was introduced in [3]. This activity becomes visible when the students have solved the problem correctly and it allows them to debug the most common errors that their classmates have made in the process up to that point in time. They classify the kind of error (syntax, run-time, incomplete program, "I don't know") and give a comment describing the error and how it could be fixed. If the instructor so chooses, these comments can then become accessible to students who are still trying to solve the problem and are generating similar errors (i.e. in the same equivalence class). The comments are meant to be hints that may or may not be helpful. In Sect. 4, we provide a detailed pedagogical analysis of the Solve-Then-Debug activity and in Sect. 5 we look closely at how students interacted with this tool in a Python programming class with about 150 students.

2.3 Spinoza Problem Solving Engagement Graphs

Another useful Spinoza instructor view is the student engagement graph Fig. 4 that gives the instructor an idea, in real time, of how many students have started working on the exercise (i.e have pressed the run button at least one time), how many have successfully solved it and how many have submitted at least one Solve-Then-Debug comment.

The graph in Fig. 4 represents the students' interaction with one of Spinoza problems, where the x axis represent the minutes and the y axis represents the number of students in each category. The top section are students who have started the problem but not yet solved it correctly (red). The middle group are those who have solved it, but haven't begun to classify other students' errors (green). The lower group are those who have started to classify other students' errors (gray).

This engagement graph is generated in real-time and can be used by the instructor to guide the class. Students are asked to solve the problem and then were required to make at least 10 solve-then-debug comments.

3 Team Formation in Spinoza

3.1 Team Formation Using Spinoza Activity Measures

In this section we describe the use of Spinoza log data to form groups in a large Java programming class (CS11a in Fall 2016). For this class we only used gross

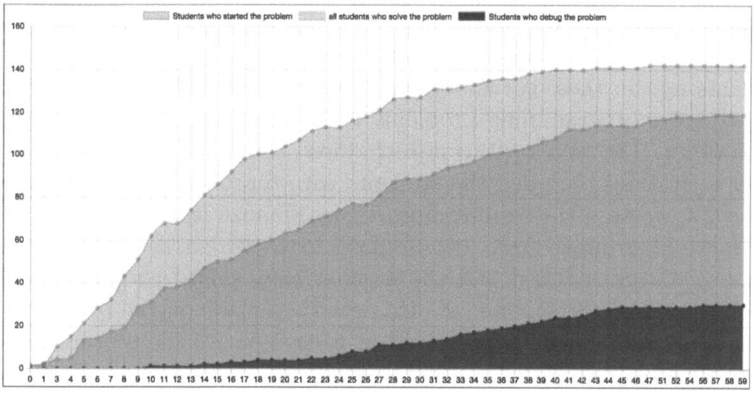

Fig. 4. Spinoza engagement graph. The horizontal axis is number of minutes since the first run time attempt. The vertical axis represents the number of students who are in a particular stage of the process of working on a problem. (Color figure online)

activity measures such as how many problems a student attempted and how many times they pressed the run button. The class had almost 280 students in two sections of 140 each with a wide variety of different backgrounds and exposures to programming and mathematics. Teaching a large class with such disparities between students is a challenging task. To improve student retention, we introduced a peer-led team learning approach (PLTL) for the recitations in which the teams would change every week, based on the student's performance the previous week.

The mandatory PLTL recitation was based on a variation of the near-peer mentoring technique, in which a group of students (ranging from 5–20) worked on a set of programming problems with an undergraduate mentor to help them whenever they were stuck. In these recitations, students worked on the same problems and were encouraged to talk with other students about the programming problems but every student needed to write their solution alone using the Spinoza web application. The mentors were selected based on their performance when they took the class in a previous semester as well as their ability to work with students. They had an initial mentor training session at the beginning of the semester and they met weekly with the instructor to debrief the previous week's recitation and plan for the next week's recitation.

Our hypothesis, based on our experience with unbalanced groups in previous years, was that in order for the groups to be effective, students with roughly the same level should be placed together.

To form effective groups initially, we sent a survey to all CS11a students. This survey contained questions about their goals in taking the class, their previous Math experience, and their programming experience. It also challenged them to solve a few programming problems (in the language of their choice). The women in the class were also asked if they preferred to work in a women-only group. We grouped the 230 (out of 280) students who answered the survey into 13 groups based on interests and experience. The remaining 50 students who didn't answer the survey were randomly assigned to three new groups.

Students met in these survey-based groups for the first two weeks and used Spinoza to solve programming problems with help from the near-peer mentors and each other. The first recitation introduced the students to Spinoza. All of the other recitations provided the students with 6 problems to work on.

In week 3, we used the results captured by Spinoza from their week 2 recitation to form 17 groups. From the Spinoza logs, we extracted the number of problems each student tried and the number they solved correctly during the recitation as well as the number of attempts they made on the problems.

We moved any students who solved at least 4 out of the 6 problems during recitation time to group 17 there were 93 students in this group and we assigned 3 mentors to them. This was the group of students who generally understood the material and had mastered the skills for that week.

We grouped the rest based on how many problems they solved correctly. The group size ranged from 20 to 5, where students who seemed to be struggling more were put into smaller groups. The larger groups (that contained 20 or so) are the ones whose students solved 3 programming problems. The smaller groups (with 5 or so students) were formed from students that tried some problems but were not able to correctly solve any problems. For the students that solved the same number of problems, we ranked them according to the average number of attempts for each problem and used this to form groups.

Assessing Effectiveness. Students were asked to complete a survey after each recitation which would allow us to estimate the effectiveness of the recitation groups. We collected 1298 survey responses after 8 recitations (about 160 responses per recitation). The results indicate that the recitation groups were generally successful, from the students' point of view.

Students felt that their mentor was helpful (7.8/10) and that the recitation itself was helpful (6.9/10) and they enjoyed the recitation (6.7/10). About 78% felt the groups were the right size. About 20% felt their recitation group was too large, these were mostly students in the one large recitation group.

We asked how confident they were of their coding skills before and after the recitation on a 0 to 10 scale. Looking at change in individual students we found that 45% of the time students had no change in confidence of their programming ability, while 45% felt that they had increased confidence. A small percentage of the times (10%), they felt less confident. The average change in confidence was 0.59 on a ten point scale (which is a 5.9% change).

We performed a paired T-test on the confidence levels of students before and after the recitations. The mean level of confidence increased from 6.74/10 (sd = 2.23) before the recitations to 7.33/10 (sd = 2.18) after the recitations. The difference is 5.8% (0.58/10–95% CI [0.5, 0.68]) which is statistically significant ($t = 13.53$, $p < 0.0001$). This result indicates that the recitations increased the confidence of the students, as we would expect from previous research on the effectiveness of collaborative learning.

We repeated the paired T-test looking only at novices (as self reported by the students), or only at non-novices who had some previous programming experience before taking this introductory class. We found the same statistically significant increase in confidence for both groups. The novices increase in confidence went from 6.41/10 (sd = 2.1) to 7.07/10 (sd = 2.4) which was an increase of 6.6% which was statistically significant at the $p < 0.0001$ level. The non-novices went from 7.45/10 (sd = 2.0) to 7.99/10 (sd = 1.8) which was an increase of 5.4% which was statistically significant at the $p < 0.0001$ level. The non-novices were 10.4% more confident than the novices before the recitations and about 9.2% more confident than the novices after the recitations, but there was no statistically significant difference in the amounts that they increased in confidence. The recitations were effective for both novices and experts.

3.2 Clustering Students Using Error Logs

In this section we present another approach to clustering students using Spinoza data that can be used to form recitation or other groups based on the kinds of errors students make. We also give an example of how it could be used. In our previous approach we grouped students using the number of problems they solved correctly, in this approach we use their actual errors to cluster them. We have not used this approach to form teams, but our results suggest that this form of clustering can identify groups of students with similar programming styles.

There are two basic approaches to using data about student's programming errors to form groups:

- form groups of students who make similar mistakes which could make it easier for their mentor to help them,
- form groups of students with different issues, so that each group has a diversity of strengths and weaknesses and they can help each other understand the concepts.

The second approach can be realized by first forming groups of similar students, and then picking one or two students from each of the "similarity" groups to form a "diversity" group, so we focus here on the "similarity" group formation.

The key idea is to create a boolean-valued table where the rows correspond to the students and the columns correspond to all equivalence classes of attempted solutions to problems for which at least 10% of the class made that attempt. Each row specifies which of the attempts were made by that particular student. We can then apply hierarchical clustering on the rows to automatically create a cluster dendrogram whose subtrees corresponds to groups of students with similar sets of programming errors. By cutting this dendrogram at a particular depth, the subtrees at that depth provide a classification of students into groups with roughly the same level of similarity.

Figure 5 shows such a clustering of all of the novice students (as self-reported on an initial survey) using the data from about halfway through the semester, immediately before the second quiz. This graph was previously presented in [5].

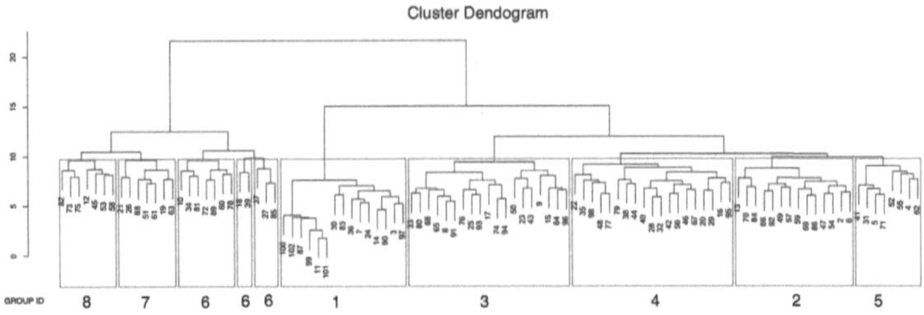

Fig. 5. Hierarchical clustering of novice programmers based on their programming errors. The leaves of the tree are labeled with the anonymized student id number. The groups are formed from subtrees of the cluster dendrogram which correspond to groups of students whose collection of incorrect attempts are somewhat similar. The vertical axis is a measure of the number of differences between the problems sets in a subtree. This graph was previously shown in [5].

This dendrogram was generated using using the `hclust` command in the statistical programming system R. There were 158 students in the class, but we only classified the 101 students who self-identified as novices.

Each leaf of the tree in Fig. 5 corresponds to a single novice student and the interior nodes of the tree correspond to groups of students appearing as descendants of that node. The students are represented by a binary vector encoding which of 198 possible attempts were actually made by that student over the semester. The 198 attempts correspond to all incorrect attempts made by at least 10% of the students over the course of the semester; we call these the common attempts. For each particular student, their vector has a 1 for each common attempt they made and a 0 for each common attempt they didn't make.

The y axis of an interior node is a measure of the variance of the students in that cluster. Larger numbers correspond to clusters with a greater amount of variance. The clustering algorithm initially puts all students in their own cluster and then iteratively selects a pair of clusters whose union has the smallest variance, and joins those two to form a new cluster.

We grouped the three smallest clusters into a single cluster, labeled group 6, this corresponds to cutting the dendronic tree one level higher for those clusters.

We would hope that students in the same group as formed by this hierarchical clustering method would also share other behavioral similarities in addition to making similar errors. Figure 7 validates this hypothesis by showing a box and whisker plots of the number of attempted solutions to all problems. The students in group 1 generally made fewer than 1000 attempts to solve Spinoza problems, while those in group 8 clustered around 2000 attempts each. The groups were numbered for this paper so that the average number of attempted solutions for the groups would be linearly ordered.

Figure 6 shows another clustering using the same approach, but for this dendrogram we included the novice programmers as before, but also those students who self-reported some previous programming experience; we call them the non-novices. The non-novices are highlighted in the figure with thick green bars at

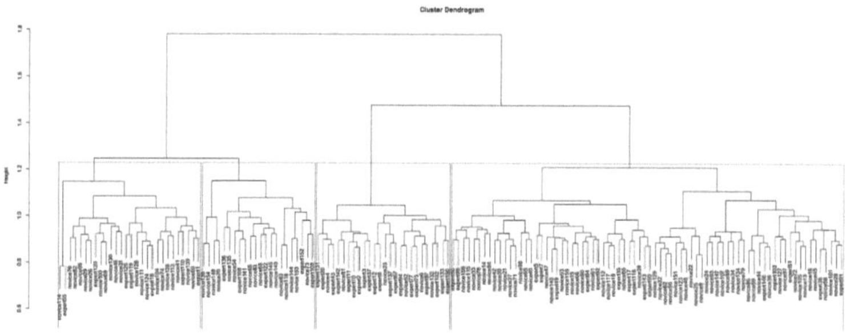

Fig. 6. Hierarchical clustering of novice and non-novice programmers based on their programming errors. Those students with some self-reported prior experience are highlighted. (Color figure online)

the connecting the dendrogram to the non-novice leaf containing their ID number. We can see that this dendrogram clusters many of the the non-novices into one group. Each of the four groups indicated in the figure by the vertical red dividing lines has a 25/75% split between novice and non-novices. With one group having more non-novices and the other three having more novices. Since this was self-reported data the actual difference in ability between novices and self-reported non-novices is unclear.

In the future, we plan to use hierarchical clustering based groupings to form Peer Led Team Learning groups for Introductory Programming courses. This particular class was fully flipped with almost no lecturing, and we didn't require recitations; but the current study suggests that this approach would be useful in team formation and in future versions of the class we may attempt to form recitations in this manner.

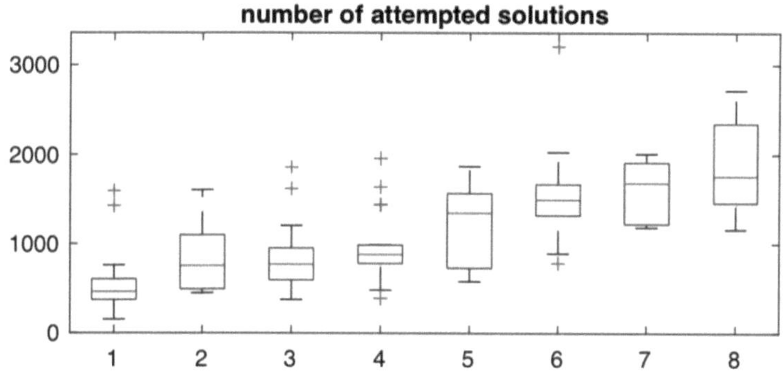

Fig. 7. Difference in the number of attempted solutions between the 8 groups.

In this section, we demonstrated how Spinoza log data might be used to characterize student programming behavior up to the current point of the semester and to use that to form homogeneous or diverse teams. In the next section, we describe how that data can be used in real-time to help students develop their skills in debugging and analyzing code that others have written.

4 Solve-Then-Debug

In Sect. 2 we presented a brief overview of the Solve-Then-Debug pedagogy. This pedagogy was developed to keep all students in a class engaged in developing their coding skills by having students who quickly complete their programming problem move on to practicing their debugging skills on the most common errors that they and their classmates have made and are currently making.

In this section, we give a detailed description of the pedagogical considerations arising in the design of this activity. In the next section we look at some data from actual student engagement in a Solve-Then-Debug activity to see whether these pedagogical goals are being achieved.

A Solve-Then-Debug activity from the student perspective consist of 6 cognitive steps. Each step in the process has been designed with the goal of maximize student engagement and learning during the activity during a class.

The 6 steps in the student view of the Solve-Then-Debug activity are as follows:

1. Try to solve a programming problem
2. Start the "Debug Others" phase after solving the problem
3. View another student's buggy code and the results of unit tests
4. Try to classify the bug(s) and submit a comment explaining the bug(s)
5. Look at other students' comments and try to debug the code
6. Go to the next debugging challenge for this same problem

If the instructor allows hint generation, then there is one more step in the process which happens while the student is trying to solve the problem. If the student's current attempt belongs to a Spinoza Markov Model node which other students have commented on in the Debug Other Code phase, then that student can click the "Show Other Hints" tab and

(1a) View others' debug comments as hints.

Each one of these items will be discussed in more detail in its own section below.

4.1 Step 1: Try to Solve a Programming Problem

During a lesson after the instructor explains a concept, they can test their students' understanding of the concept by assigning a Spinoza problem. Each student works individually on their computer to solve the problem, they can run the code many times and each time they press "run" the results of running their code on a special set of unit tests is compared to the results from the instructor's solution to test for correctness. The results of the unit tests and the student's code are then stored on the server along with the student's id and a time stamp.

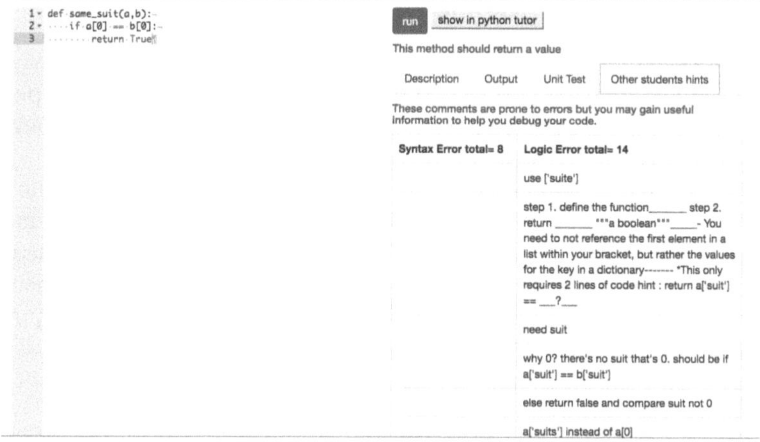

Fig. 8. The student's problem view with hint.

This approach of having students solving programming problems with an online unit testing IDE is a common way to add active learning to a programming class. Figures 1 and 2 show a student's view of the "same_suit" Spinoza problem before and after they press the run button, respectively.

Optional Step 1a: View Other Students' Debug Comments as Hints. While the students who solved the problem are engaged in the debug phase, the slower, struggling students are still in the Solve phase. The Solve and Debug phases were designed to engage all students in the problem solving activity. If the instructor permitted Hint Generation for this problem, the students who are still in the Solve phase, can view the debug comments that their peers have made on a similar problem (in the same SMM equivalence class) as a kind of hint.

Figure 8 shows the Hint view for a particular problem.

Students know their comments might be visible as hints and this encourages them to try to create helpful comments, but the comments might not be appropriate since they are commenting on a different attempt which happens to be in the same SMM equivalence class. In a way this is a good feature, as the students are not able to fully trust the hint and so have to think critically about whether the hints make sense. Also there are typically dozens of these debug comments for each of the common errors so they need to read them and see which, if any, are appropriate. This exercises higher thinking skills. They can also look to see if any idea appears multiple times in the comments, and perhaps try that one first!

4.2 Step 2: Start the "Debug Others" Phase

The Debug Others phase starts after a student solves a problem by having their code pass all the unit tests. If the student returns to the problem set page that contains the solved problems, the problem will be green and the Debug Other button will appear next to the problem as shown in Fig. 9.

In the Solve-Then-Debug activity, students are asked to click the Debug Other Code button as soon as they have successfully solved the problem. When they click on the button, Spinoza finds the most common class of mistakes that the students have made and ranks them by the number of the students who made that mistake. This phases uses the Spinoza Markov Model equivalence relation defined in Sect. 2 which groups two attempts in the same class if they take exactly the same (possibly incorrect) values on all of the unit tests.

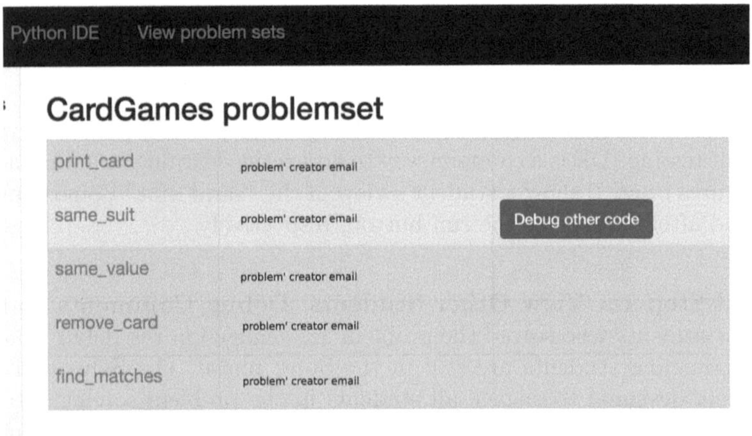

Fig. 9. Spinoza Card Game problemset view with debug other button. (Color figure online)

The mistake class with the highest number of students will be chosen first and the first version of code in that class will be displayed to this student. These common mistake classes are represented by SMM nodes. The size of the nodes are changing from time to time in this activity. Each time a student clicks the debug other code button, the Spinoza algorithm picks the largest SMM node that the student has not yet analyzed. Only SMM nodes with more sufficiently many common attempts will be chosen. For the current version of Spinoza we require only 2 or more attempts.

All students debug the same problem for each SMM node chosen. If a student has debugged one problem instance from all of the mistake classes, then they start again with a second member of each of the equivalence classes. If the students finish analyzing all the versions of codes in the common SMM nodes, which is unlikely in large classes, the students will continue to loop through these problems and see the debug comments but cannot make any changes until a new problem attempt arises.

The way in which students are given debug problems was designed to expose students to the most common mistakes that they are their peers have been making in the problem solving activity and also to expose them to the variety of ways that lead to the same mistake. The reason that we decide to have every student debug the same problem in each equivalence class was because we wanted students to see other students' comments, and if we showed them different problems they would not benefit from seeing each others' comments.

4.3 Step 3: View the Buggy Code and the Results of the Unit Tests

An example of the initial student view of the buggy code is shown in Fig. 10. At this stage, students are able to run the code to see the output or the unit test results for this buggy code, but are not be allowed to edit the code. They are also not yet allowed to see the debug comments that other students have made.

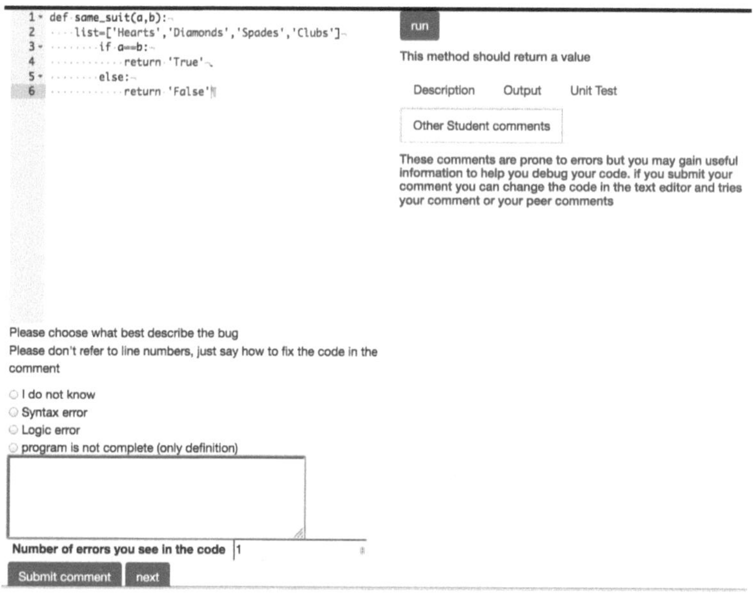

Fig. 10. The student's debug problem view.

Not allowing the student to change the code is a way to make them focus on analyzing the error through logical thinking rather than just making changes to the code to see if they can fix it. If we were to allow the student to edit the code, they could easily forget the initial bug even if they got it to work. They could also just cut/paste in their own correct code, which defeats the purpose of this exercise.

By not allowing students to see other students' debugging comments we also force them to rely on their own judgment, with the expectation that this could help them develop their own debugging skills.

4.4 Step 4: Classify and Comment on Bugs

When the students are shown the debug other problem they need to choose the type of error. Their choices are

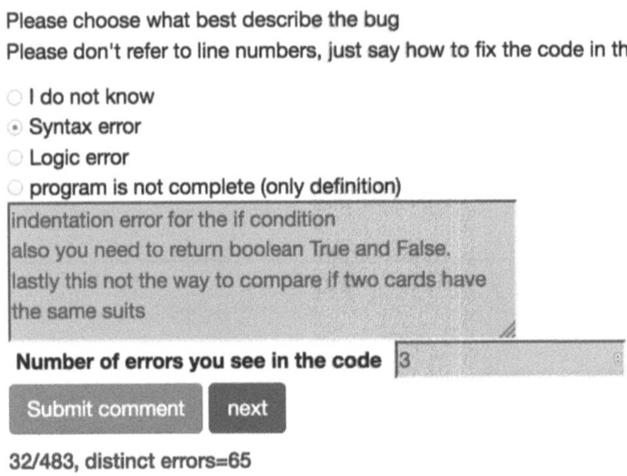

Fig. 11. The student's debug problem view classification part.

- "I do not know"
- syntax error
- logic error
- incomplete code

Then they have to describe how to fix the error in a few words and specify how many errors this code has. Finally, they press the Submit button to finalize their choices. Figure 11 shows an example of that part of the screen.

We ask the students to classify the bug using one of the four choices so that they understand that there are different classes of bugs. One issue is that a program could easily have multiple bugs: syntax errors, logic errors, and also be incomplete. They simply need to choose one bug to focus one for this activity.

Asking the students to write a comment about the bug they discovered encourages them to think about the bug and write a clear description of how to fix the code to be free of this bug. If the students select "I don't know" then they are not required to submit a comment. The students know that their comments could appear in the "Other Student Hints" tab for students who are still working on the problem and whose current error is in the same equivalence class. This potentially motivates them to provide helpful comments.

The "number of errors" question was added recently and is intended to be used to have the student look in depth at the code to find all of the bugs, rather than just stopping after finding the simplest error.

4.5 Step 5: Look at Other Students' Comments and Try to Debug the Code

When the student clicks submit, Spinoza provides a view that allows them to check on the correctness of their debug comments and classification.

Although they can no longer change their classification or their comments on the debug problem, they can now edit the code and run it to see if their debugging analysis was correct or not.

They can also see the comments of other students for that same debugging problem in the Other Students Comments tab (Fig. 12). The debug comments are arranged in vertical columns based on the classifications. So the Syntax error comments are in one column, the logic error comments in another, etc. This allows the student to see if other students agreed with them or not.

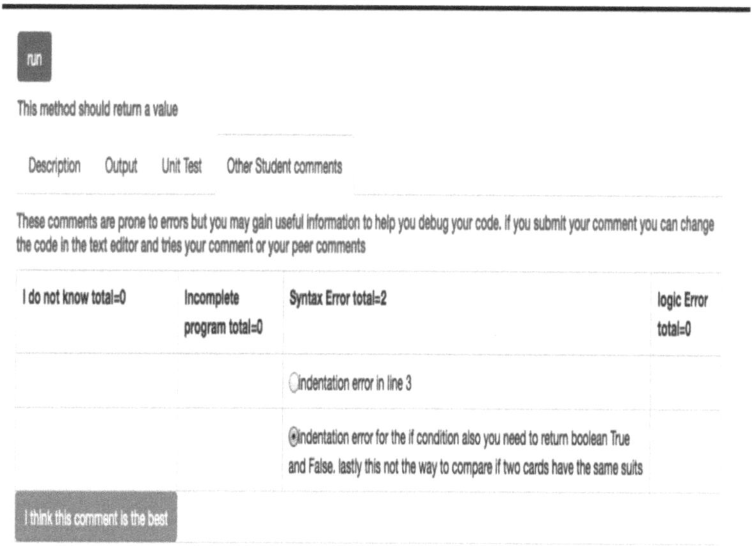

Fig. 12. The student's debug problem view other students' comments part.

If the student's debug analysis was incorrect and their attempted fix didn't remove the error, then the student can try the suggestions that other students have made to see if they work.

To encourage students to read the debug comments of other students, we require them to select the best comment describing the bug before they can move on to the next debug problem. We want to encourage the students to read other students' comments because we think they could learn more deeply by reviewing the correctness of other students analyses. We have not, however, gathered any evidence to support this hypothesis.

Our approach requires the students to engage in higher level thinking. They not only have to critique other students attempts, they need to review other students critiques. It would be infeasible to have the instructor give individual feedback on all of the debug problem comments, but we have found that the current process is similar to peer review and the "wisdom of the crowd" almost always generates the correct debugging analysis from at least a few of the other student comments. This is especially true for students who come to the problem later in the process when there are many student comments already there. These are the students who are most likely to be struggling so it is beneficial for them to see many comments on each program. In Sect. 5, we report on our analysis of the debug comments submitted on the most common error for one particular problem. Our experience was that approximately 75% of our students debugging comments were accurate.

Students are not allowed to edit their classification and comments, because they may feel tempted to make an initial "I don't know" choice, and then later choose one of other students comments and classification without actually thinking or trying to critique the problems by themselves.

4.6 Step 6: Go to the Next Debugging Challenge Problem

When the student clicks the "Next": button, Spinoza will find the next biggest SMM node that this student has not yet analyzed and will show the (chronologically) first attempt in that node. If the student had already analyzed all the common SMM nodes, the subsequent versions of code in each SMM node will be presented until the student has finished debugging all the versions in each SMM, but this is unlikely to happen in a medium to large size class.

When the student is shown the next debug problem the cycle repeats.

5 Analysis of Student Interaction with Solve-Then-Debug

The Solve-then-Debug model requires the students to solve the problem first before debugging other students' code. Typically, the Solve-Then-Debug activity is ended before all students have completed the Solve phase. Waiting for 60–80% to finish is usually a good goal. With this in mind, the 60% that have finished can be thought of as writing hints for the 40% who are still struggling. Also, the students who finish the Solve phase first, do so with very few hints (as there has been little Debugging) and hence they are more likely to have a solid understanding of the problem. Hence, they will have a better chance of correctly diagnosing bugs if they have solved the problem themselves first with few hints. Fitzgerald et al. [10], provides some evidence that good debuggers are generally also good programmers, while the converse is not necessarily true – good programmers are not always good at debugging. So this phase of the Solve-Then-Debug activity was designed to both help provide struggling students with decent hints and to help students who are good at programming to also develop strong debugging skills. We have some anecdotal data that supports these hypotheses but their verification will require further study.

The Solve-Then-Debug activity was created to keep all students engaged while working on a Spinoza problem, especially when some are much faster coders than others. In this section, we discuss some of the data we collected during the Spring 2017 semester. The students were required to make at least 100 Solve-Then-Debug comments by the end of the semester, but this was entirely a participation score and their grade would not depend on the correctness of their comments. They did know that their comments might appear as hints for other students still working on the problem however, and we felt that this might encourage them to put more effort into their comment writing.

5.1 Most Students Are Able to Make a Comment

Since the students' grades were not dependent on the quality of their comments, we suspected that many busy students might just choose the "I do not know" option which doesn't require any written comment. We found, however, that only 5 students out of 148 (3.3%) used the "I don't know option" more than 50% of the time, and only 34 out of 148 (23%) students used it more than 10%. So 114/148 (77%) of the students gave a substantial comment at least 90% of the time.

By comparing the grades in quiz 2 for students who chose "I do not know" more than 10% of the time versus those who chose it ≤10% of the time, we found that those who selected "I don't know" more than 10% of the time had a average score on the 6 point quiz that was 0.61 (or 10%) lower than the score of the rest. This difference was not statistically significant at the 0.05 level (but it was almost at the 0.10 level).

One interesting observation is that of the 34 students who selected "I don't know" as a debug comment 10% or more of the time, 20 of them scored a perfect 6/6 on final in-class programming exam for the course, which provides more evidence for Fitzerald's claim [10] that good programmers are not necessarily good debuggers.

5.2 Analyzing Student Debug Comments

In this section we explore the accuracy of the students' debugging comments in the debug phase of the Solve-Then-Debug activity. Our goal is to demonstrate some of the pedagogical benefits that students obtain by engaging in this activity both by writing comments and by receiving hints if they are still working on the problem.

The fact that there are so many comments and that not all of them are correct, or clear, in a way makes this Hint Generation more valuable, as the students need to decide which hints they want to explore. It can be difficult to give hints that are both useful and don't give away the answer. By having the student see so many comments, we will see that most problems have several good comments and most of the issues get covered by some students' comments, but some comments are just completely wrong, so students can not just blindly follow the commented suggestions.

A correct comment, for our purposes, is one that correctly describes some issue with the code, perhaps not the most important or obvious bug, but an issue none the less. We also count comments where the student seems to have the correct idea, but has not expressed themselves very clearly. So we are looking for evidence of debugging understanding, not of clear communication about bugs. We suspect that asking students to verbalize their understanding of bugs and seeing other students explanations would have a positive effect on their ability to explain bugs themselves over time, but we have not collected data to support this hypothesis.

In this section we look in depth at the debug comments for one particular debugging question from the `isLeapYear` problem where students were asked to write a function with one parameter `year` which returns true if that year is a leap year and false otherwise. The five most common incorrect attempts were in the following SMM equivalence classes:

- The first corresponds to functions which return "False" on all inputs.
- The second is in the class of functions that returns True if the year is divisible by 4.
- The third returns True for all years.
- The fourth returns True for all multiples of four that are not centuries (but misses the case of years divisible by 400).
- The fifth was a syntax error with a missing colon after an if statement.

We found that the students supplied 44 correct debug comments out of 59 total comments, which means that the students' comments were accurate 75% of time. We did not consider their classification when determining correctness, so if a comment correctly described a logic error but was in the syntax error category or vise versa, we counted that as a correct comment.

5.3 Detailed Analysis of a Debugging Problem

We look at one example here (debug problem number 1) to illustrate a number of points. Here is the buggy code they were asked to analyze:

```
def is_leap_year(y):
    if y%4==0 and y%100==1 and y%400==0:
        return "True"
    else:
        return "False"
```

This attempted solution has four main issues:

(a) the return type should be `boolean` not `String`
(b) the middle test should be `y%100!=0` not `y%100==1`
(c) the last `and` operator should be an `or` operator
(d) a simple return of the boolean expression would be better than using an if expression.

In this debug problem, 16 students submitted debugging comments and 11/16 correctly classified the error as a logic error. Of the rest, 4 of them classified the error as syntax, and one classified it as an incomplete program. All but one, however, gave a correct comment, in our sense.

In this analysis we ignore the correctness of the classification. We are mostly interested in if the students are able to give a good comment to describe some issue with the code.

Figure 13 shows an annotated version of the "Show Other Student Comments" view where we have indicated with a checkmark those comments which we deemed to be correct, and we have indicated with one or more letters (a, b, c, d) which of the errors we think they are referring to. For this problem, all four errors were mentioned by at least one commenter. Error (c) was the most frequently mentioned error and in fact is the most obvious error if you know the right answer.

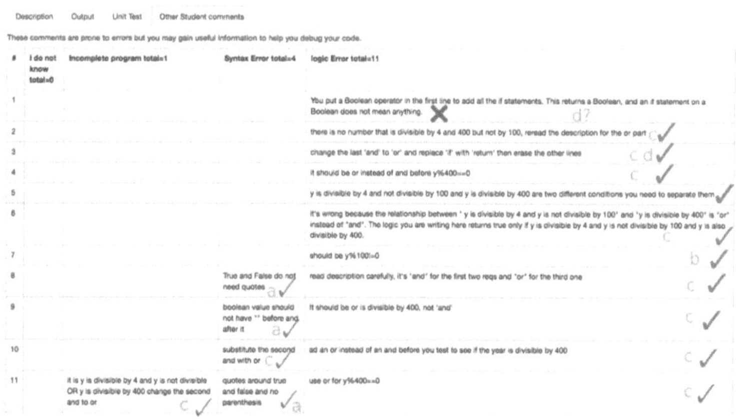

Fig. 13. Student comments to a debug problem, #1

Even though we put a lot of thought into the design of the debug phase, as described in the previous sections of this chapter, the way students interacted with the debug phase was somewhat different that we had expected.

The classification of the bug into one of 4 categories was not as clear as we thought it would be. The students' comments show that there was some confusion among the syntax error, logic error and problem not complete choices.

For example, when a student returns a string "True" instead of the boolean True, we would classify that as a logic error, but students quite reasonably felt that it was a syntax error.

The "program not complete" option was added to cover the cases where a student's attempt was either completely empty or just contained a stub program (returning 0 or some fixed value). This was a common strategy of students who used a step-wise refinement strategy so as to avoid having to debug an entire program. Some students in the debug phase, however, used this category to indicate that code is missing some important logic and so is incomplete.

6 Related Work

In response to the pressing need to increase the retention rates in Introductory Computer Science classes while simultaneously dealing with rapidly increasing enrollments in those courses and a relatively slow growth in teaching faculty, many researchers have attempted to use technology and new pedagogical practices to provide additional academic support. Our work can be seen in this context as we have tried to form supportive recitation groups and to use Spinoza log data to more effectively orchestrate large class lessons.

There is a growing body of research focused on creating applications that support collaboration [11]. In computer science, the most common collaboration style is in the form of pair programming which shows various benefits including improving the quality of submitted programs by the pair, increased engagement and more positive attitudes toward the field [14,16]. These benefits depend on choosing the right pair, since an ineffective pairing could hinder learning.

Many researchers have indicated that the most effective pairs are the ones matched by similar skill levels, but it is difficult to measure skill level. Some researchers have used grades on the exam as a factor to form the group, others have used a combination of exam scores and SAT scores, but exam and SAT scores do not necessarily correlate to programming skill [9,13,19]. Our approach of using fine-grained log data from online IDEs potentially provides a much more accurate model of programming skill.

The research that is most similar to ours is that of Berland et al. In their paper [7], they describe a teacher orchestration tool that gives instructors real-time information about possible pairs in a visual programming environment. The idea is to have students initially work on a problem individually and then to ask students who are generating similar approaches to work together. Their system converts the students' visual block code to normalized parse trees and identifies pairs of students with similar parse trees. Students continue working on their own code and if a pair diverges, then the instructor may choose to put them in different pairs during the same problem solving activity.

Sadeghi [18] reviews previous work on group formation. These groups could be homogeneous or heterogeneous and the groups formation can be based on many criteria such as previous knowledge level, learning style, thinking style, personal traits, degree of interest in the subject and the degree of the motivation. Bekele's [6] work indicates that homogeneous groups are suited more for achieving particular educational goals, while heterogeneous groups tend to be more innovative and creative and hence better for open-ended projects.

Our work on hierarchical clustering has some similarities to [15] in which they report on their work on clustering students based on their mistakes in an on-line educational tool, called Logic-ITA, for teaching Formal Proof techniques. The target of their clustering was the students who tried, but were not able to solve, a collection of problems. Using a two step clustering technique which combined k-means and hierarchical clustering, they were able to form two groups of students based on this error data. The students in one cluster made more mistakes than the other and by looking closely at the sequence of errors they discovered that one group used a guessing strategy to approach the problem while the other group got confused and gave up rapidly. The goal of this clustering was to give the instructors an evaluation of the students so based on the cluster they could explain the problem again or appropriately readjust the difficulty of the exercises for the students in each cluster.

7 Final Remarks and Future Work

In this paper we have presented two approaches for forming teams using Spinoza log data and provides some preliminary evidence that these might be helpful in identifying groups of students with similar learning patterns. We also provided an in depth pedagogical analysis of the Solve-Then-Debug pedagogy that was first introduced in [3] and we also explored how students interacted with a particular Solve-Then-Debug problem.

In the future we continue to explore pedagogically effective applications of programming error data. In particular, we will be looking for variations of the Solve-Then-Debug pedagogy which use the attempts made by the class to form new problems.

References

1. Deeb, F.A., Hickey, T.: The Spinoza code tutor: faculty poster abstract. J. Comput. Sci. Coll. **30**(6), 154–155 (2015a)
2. Deeb, F.A., Hickey, T.: Spinoza: the code tutor (2015b)
3. Deeb, F.A., Hickey, T.: Flipping introductory programming classes using Spinoza and agile pedagogy. In: 2017 IEEE on Frontiers in Education Conference (FIE), pp. 1–9. IEEE (2017)
4. Deeb, F.A., Kime, K., Torrey, R., Hickey, T.: Measuring and visualizing learning with Markov models. In: 2016 IEEE on Frontiers in Education Conference (FIE), pp. 1–9. IEEE (2016)
5. Deeb, F.A., Hickey, T.J., DiLillo, A.: Using fine grained programming error data to enhance CS1 pedagogy. In: CSEDU (2018)
6. Bekele, R.: Computer-assisted learner group formation based on personality traits (2006)
7. Berland, M., Davis, D., Smith, C.P.: AMOEBA: designing for collaboration in computer science classrooms through live learning analytics. Int. J. Comput.-Supp. Collab. Learn. **10**(4), 425–447 (2015)

8. Berland, M., Martin, T., Benton, T., Petrick Smith, C., Davis, D.: Using learning analytics to understand the learning pathways of novice programmers. J. Learn.Sci. **22**(4), 564–599 (2013)
9. Byckling, P., Sajaniemi, J.: A role-based analysis model for the evaluation of novices' programming knowledge development. In: Proceedings of the Second International Workshop on Computing Education Research, pp. 85–96. ACM (2006)
10. Fitzgerald, S., et al.: Debugging: finding, fixing and flailing, a multi-institutional study of novice debuggers. Comput. Sci. Educ. **18**(2), 93–116 (2008)
11. Flieger, J., Palmer, J.D.: Supporting pair programming with JavaGrinder. J. Comput. Sci. Coll. **26**(2), 63–70 (2010)
12. Ihantola, P., et al.: Educational data mining and learning analytics in programming: literature review and case studies. In: Proceedings of the 2015 ITiCSE on Working Group Reports, pp. 41–63. ACM (2015)
13. Katira, N., Williams, L., Wiebe, E., Miller, C., Balik, S., Gehringer, E.: On understanding compatibility of student pair programmers. In: ACM SIGCSE Bulletin, vol. 36, pp. 7–11. ACM (2004)
14. MarTin, T., Berland, M., BenTon, T., SMiTh, C.P.: Learning programming with Ipro: The effects of a mobile, social programming environment. J. Interact. Learn. Res. **24**(3), 301–328 (2013)
15. Merceron, A., Yacef, K.: Clustering students to help evaluate learning. In: Courtiat, J.-P., Davarakis, C., Villemur, T. (eds.) Technology Enhanced Learning. IIFIP, vol. 171, pp. 31–42. Springer, Boston, MA (2005). https://doi.org/10.1007/0-387-24047-0_3
16. Nagappan, N., et al.: Improving the CS1 experience with pair programming. ACM SIGCSE Bull. **35**(1), 359–362 (2003)
17. Prieto, L.P., Holenko Dlab, M., Gutiérrez, I., Abdulwahed, M., Balid, W.: Orchestrating technology enhanced learning: a literature review and a conceptual framework. Int. J. Technol. Enhanc. Learn. **3**(6), 583–598 (2011)
18. Sadeghi, H., Kardan, A.A.: A novel justice-based linear model for optimal learner group formation in computer-supported collaborative learning environments. Comput. Hum. Behav. **48**, 436–447 (2015)
19. Watkins, K.Z., Watkins, M.J.: Towards minimizing pair incompatibilities to help retain under-represented groups in beginning programming courses using pair programming. J. Comput. Sci. Coll. **25**(2), 221–227 (2009)

Improving Student Learning Experience by the Full Integration of Classroom Response Systems into Lectures

Jalal Kawash[1(✉)] and Robert Collier[2]

[1] Department of Computer Science, University of Calgary, 2500 University Dr. NW, Calgary, AB, Canada
jalal.kawash@ucalgary.ca

[2] Department of Computer Science, Carleton University, 1125 Colonel By Dr., Ottawa, ON, Canada
robert.collier@scs.carleton.ca

Abstract. Classroom response systems are widely recognized as an effective way to engage and motivate students, improve knowledge retention, and provide formative feedback opportunities for both students and educators, and as such present an excellent opportunity to improve the student classroom experience. Unfortunately, there remain concerns in the pedagogical research community that the use of classroom response systems can distract, confuse, or intimidate students. The authors believe that these concerns can be mitigated by fully integrating classroom response system technologies into the classroom, such that the systems become an integral part of the lecture experience and not simply a intermittent supplementary activity. To fully integrate classroom response systems into a course, it is necessary for educators to unlock the full potential of classroom response systems. Over the past several years, the authors were able to achieve this full integration and gather data from almost 500 computer science students. The findings, presented in this paper, clearly indicate that students appreciate the activity and fully recognize its value as an enhancement to their learning experience, and do not, for the most part, consider these systems to be a source of distraction or confusion.

1 Introduction

Classroom response systems (CRS) present an excellent opportunity for instructors to integrate technology into the classroom and with increasing class sizes it has become more important than ever to devise creative methods for improving student engagement and motivation. Thankfully, many of the new CRS solutions available to instructors have replaced the hardware "clickers" (which often represented an additional cost to students) with an application for the ubiquitous smartphone. These systems have also been expanded to include a better interface for students to review their CRS activities, while still providing exceptional opportunities to improve participation and provide for formative feedback.

B. M. McLaren et al. (Eds.): CSEDU 2018, CCIS 1022, pp. 37–55, 2019.
https://doi.org/10.1007/978-3-030-21151-6_3

Typically, CRS activities are included during a lecture period by presenting the entire class with a question and then using the CRS to gather and analyze the responses provided by participants.

Although the most predominant opinion supports the use of CRS in the classroom for improving engagement and feedback, their remain some studies claiming that such activities can be detrimental because they can distract or confusion students. It is the position of the authors that this risk can be minimized through the careful integration of CRS throughout the course, so that the CRS activities themselves are not viewed by the students as a supplemental (and disrupting) "accessory". The authors also believe that this integration is not prohibitively difficult to achieve, and that traditional lectures present several opportunities. In addition to an obvious application for the reinforcement of lecture content, CRS can be used for preparative or introductory exercises, for a review of a previous lecture, for an opportunity for in-class discussion, etc. CRS need not be used at every opportunity, but by using the system frequently and for a variety of purposes, its use in the classroom is less likely to be considered a disruption by the students.

The authors both deliver undergraduate-level courses in computer science at their respective institutions, and have each successfully integrated CRS into several of their courses. These courses, on topics ranging from operating system design and computer architecture to discrete mathematics and introductory programming, would each use several different types of CRS questions on a regular basis for several different express purposes. From reviewing their own course content, the authors have identified ten different (but not mutually exclusive) categories of CRS questions, and that these questions can be used effectively to meet the needs of the classroom. With this chapter the authors will explore how this deep integration of CRS into the classroom addresses many of the concerns that might prevent other educators from doing the same. This chapter revisits and expands on the conference paper originally presented by Jalal Kawash at Computer Supported Education (CSEDU) 2018 [1].

The remainder of this chapter is organized as follows. Section 2 discusses related work in the context of the use of CRS. The categories of CRS questions that the authors have identified are discussed in Sect. 3 and an example CRS is discussed in Sect. 4. Section 5 examines two of the authors' courses (into which a CRS was integrated) and critically reflects on the student feedback that was received. Section 6 reviews and concludes the chapter.

2 Related Work

Many educators first consider the inclusion of CRS activities in their courses as opportunities to improve student engagement, particularly in courses with very large class sizes. This significant application notwithstanding, CRS systems offer another, unique opportunity for formative feedback that can be generated immediately, even in large populations. The feedback provided by CRS can be used by students to discretely self-assess themselves on a specific facet of a larger topic by comparing their own performance against that of the rest of the class. Simultaneously, the instructor can review the performance of all participants and assess how well the corresponding material has been understood by the class, adjusting the pace of the lecture to match the immediate learning needs of the participants.

Many extensive studies [2–6] support the effectiveness of CRS in delivering these invaluable opportunities, and nearly all of the surveyed literature supports the claim that participants are satisfied with the CRS activities themselves. That said, on more than one occasion [7,8], it has been suggested that benefits attributed to CRS by these research studies might simply be the result of improving interactivity in the classroom. Nevertheless, since CRS represent an interactive activity that can be used with a class of virtually any size, it is not unreasonable to state that this application of CRS is almost universally accepted. Furthermore, it has been demonstrated that CRS activity performance is a good predictor of overall performance [9], and that, with no additional effort, CRS can be used to identify participants that might be struggling [10]. Others [11,12] also indicated that they used CRS as one of their best practices for student retention.

The effective use of CRS has been shown to benefit student performance as well. Simon et al. [13] contrasted the performance of students instructed traditionally against a peer-instructed offering, finding that the peer-instructed subjects (that made extensive use of CRS) outperformed those who were instructed in a more traditional manner. Similarly, Huss-Lederman [14] reported on a 2-year experiment in which first-year students showed better learning gains as a result of using a CRS. More recently, Collier and Kawash [15] presented quantitative evidence that CRS questions can be structured and presented in such a way as to improve a participants ability to retain content, by allowing students to revisit content that has already passed from short-term memory.

In contrast with these results, some studies have suggested that the inclusion of CRS activities may not yield any benefits and could in fact actually create a barrier for some students. Vinaja presented [16] the results of an experiment where the use of a CRS (alongside recorded lectures, videos, and other electronic materials) did not result in a performance improvement. In a broader criticism of in-class discussion in general, Kay and Lesage [4] discussed how exposure to differing perspectives (that could potentially arise during the discussion following a CRS question) might cause confusion. Similarly, Draper and Brown [17] suggested that CRS activities might distract students from their actual learning outcomes.

Although those findings are not consistent with the authors' own experiences, CRS do require an investment (with respect to both lecture time and preparation time) and the concern that the activity might be confusing or distracting cannot be summarily dismissed. Nevertheless, the authors believe that the concerns about CRS activities being disruptive or confusing can be addressed by an integrated approach. The authors conjecture that, when a CRS is carefully integrated into the classroom flow (as opposed to being treated as a novel but disjoint activity) these potential barriers will no longer exist.

3 Categorization of CRS Questions

The exposure to a different perspective a student might receive notwithstanding, for a CRS itself to be considered confusing it would have to represent an activity that was unfamiliar to the class. This concern can be easily addressed by increasing the frequency with which CRS activities appear in the classroom, and since the investment associated with the use of CRS can be weighed against the potential benefits previous noted, the greatest barrier to an education choosing to employ a CRS may be the perception that the system itself might be a distraction. The authors believe this concern can be addressed as well, but in order to properly integrate CRS activities in such a way as they are neither distracting nor disruptive, it must first be recognized that a single CRS activity can take many different forms and address many different needs. By recognizing the role of a question (and answering the question "what do I expect to gain from this activity?") an educator is able to integrate that question into the lecture such that it will not present a distraction. To this end the authors have established a collection of categories for the different classes of questions that can be asked using a CRS. It should be noted that these categories are not necessarily mutually exclusive – an individual question could belong to more than one category.

Ice Breakers: Ice breaker questions are intended to change or influence the classroom social atmosphere in a positive way. These are especially important in the first lecture of a course but can be useful at other times as well. Icebreaker questions can be used to address any stereotypes and misconceptions about the course, the instructor, and the students themselves. In the authors' respective courses, for instance, the authors have used icebreaker questions to address misconceptions about the difficulty of a subject or the importance and relevance of a particular topic.

Being aware and addressing social dynamics in the classroom is crucial. The use of power by educators in learning environments necessitates continued attention because it strongly influences educator-student relationships, students' motivation to learn, and the extent to which learning goals are met. Icebreaker questions can be used to reinforce positive powers (such as reward and expert powers) and avoid the use of negative powers (such as coercive power).

Material Reinforcement/Content Retention: Questions in this category typically include variations of the material being discussed and directly apply the content most recently presented to the students. The interval between the delivery of the CRS question and the presentation of the corresponding material can determine how useful a question can be in improving content retention. The most common practice is to pose CRS questions during or immediately after the presentation of the corresponding material and, in so doing, the CRS question becomes a reinforcing activity (e.g., an additional example), albeit one where student engagement is improved by transitioning students from a passive recipient role into an active participant role. Alternatively, this type of question can be posed after a significant period of time (typically at the beginning of the following lecture). This interval entails that the relevant knowledge has passed out of the short-term memory of the students, and, as a result, the question becomes an opportunity to revisit and review the corresponding content, improving the likelihood that it will be retained.

Feedback: Questions in this category are designed to provide immediate and formative feedback to the students and/or the instructors. Students can use their performance (relative to the other participants in the class) to self-assess their knowledge in the topics being presented, identify gaps that may exist in their current understanding, and even respond immediately to fill those gaps. With CRS systems that allow students to revisit past questions outside of the lectures, student can also review their performance over a particular set of questions, seeking out further resources or assistance as warranted.

The feedback from a CRS activity can also be important to the instructor, since it allows for the immediate assessment of the understanding of the class, providing information on whether and where a specific subject needs reinforcement. If the class (as a whole) under-performs on a particular question, the instructor can respond immediately by providing more examples or by approaching the subject from different angles. Instructor feedback questions can also help in identifying student pitfalls in certain subjects, which can be invaluable in future course development.

Bridging: Often the best way to transition between one subject to another in the classroom is through a problem or discussion and these transitions can be accomplished using CRS questions. While students may not score well on these questions (as they do not reference specific material that has already been presented), they provide an opportunity for students to be challenged by thinking "outside the box" and/or trying to relate different concepts together. These bridging questions can be designed to motivate the inclusion of the next topic in the course, while, at the same time, relating it to the material most recently presented.

Reflection: After a lecture, The authors often challenge their students to apply their knowledge using higher-level thinking problems. CRS questions can be readily used at the end of a lecture, where the questions are discussed and left with students as homework to answer until the following lecture.

Review: The use of CRS questions in review sessions can make these sessions more engaging and beneficial to students. The authors were able to organize review sessions that required little or no lecturing, and these sessions were highly welcomed by the students. The authors would typically provide students with a practice set of problems in advance and then, during the review session, the students were given a series of quizzes (to be completed in small groups). Each of these quizzes ended in at least one CRS question, testing certain critical aspects of that particular quiz.

Fun Injection: Fun injection is a common technique used to keep a relaxed atmosphere in the classroom, balance the serious tone of the lectures, and give the students the opportunity to stay engaged. CRS questions can be used to occasionally inject fun and these questions need not be orthogonal to the lecture (i.e., there need not be an abrupt transition from a serious topic into a fun injection question). As a clarifying example, a multiple-choice question for which all of the answers are correct can spark an engaging and entertaining discussion, while still focusing on the corresponding material! It should be noted that a question from virtually any other category can be restructured such that it belongs to the fun injection category as well.

Polling: Since most CRS questions can be configured such that the collection of responses can be reviewed anonymously, students can participate in polls to assess their learning, preferred delivery styles, etc. without discomfort. Polling students on the pacing of the lectures or the difficulty of the exams, for instance, can grant students a safe way to voice their concerns without sacrificing the feedback for the instructors.

Attendance: It is worth noting that, in institutions or settings where attendance is a requirement, attendance questions can be easily incorporated into CRS, avoiding the overhead associated with keeping an attendance tally at the beginning of every lecture.

Series: While some may argue that the nature of CRS does not allow working on complex problems and thorough problem-solving techniques, the authors have used CRS to solve complex problems by presenting them as a series of interrelated questions. The step-by-step solution to a complex problem can be converted to a relevant series of CRS questions that will ultimately form a complete solution to the problem. This is, in fact, a very practical and effective approach for teaching students the "divide-and-conquer" problem solving technique.

4 Example CRS: "Tophat"

As noted previously, CRS have developed considerably beyond the initial hardware "clicker"-based systems, and instructors now have a wide variety of solutions to consider that require only that students have access to a smartphone or laptop computer. Many of these solutions can be easily integrated with whatever learning management systems is in use a given institution, and many more have data collection and analysis capabilities that can be used by instructors for statistical analysis and by students for summative feedback. For this chapter, the authors have decided to present results from a course into which the *Tophat* classroom response system was integrated. Unsurprisingly, the authors observed that the vast majority of students use their smartphones for this purpose.

The initial interaction point with Tophat is a website www.tophat.com at which students register a new account. This web interface can be used by students for registering their responses to CRS questions or, upon creation, accounts can be associated with a mobile phone number, allowing students to interact with the system using text messaging. For instructors, a Tophat CRS account can be organized into separate courses, with each course being associated with a set of "invitations", broadcasted to the populations of students enrolled in the course. Figure 1 shows the main course screen for an example course in Tophat.

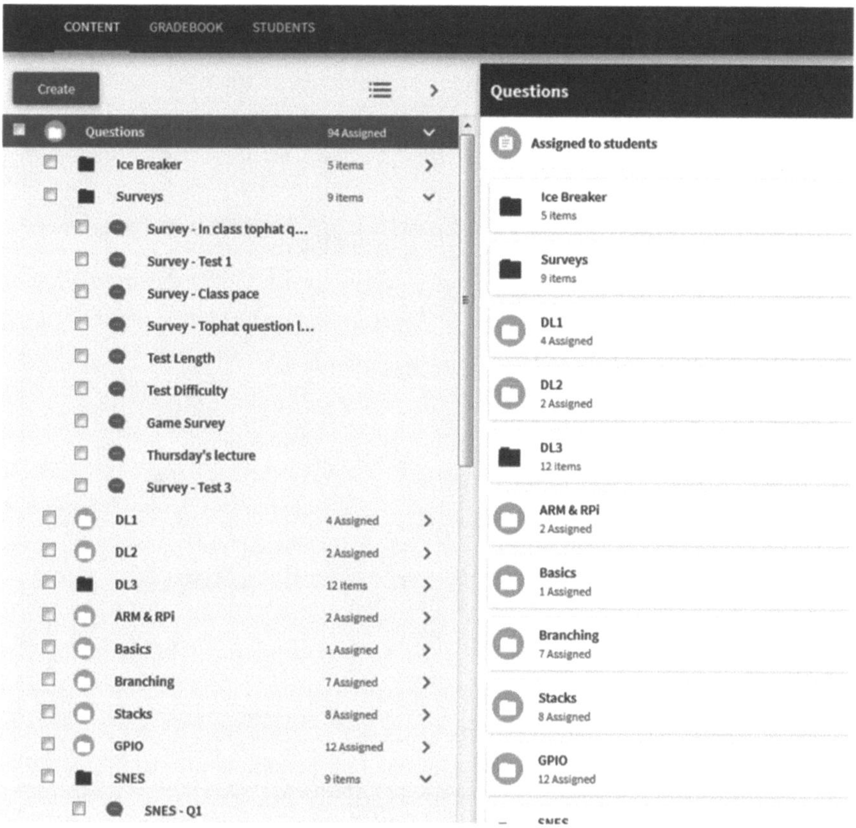

Fig. 1. Main course screen in Tophat [1].

Figure 2(a) shows an example CRS question as it appears to students; Fig. 2(b) also shows the question the class response statistics screen with the highlighted correct answer.

Each course has three main areas:

- Content: where questions and other content are created.
- Gradebook: a database of student activity regarding answering questions. This activity can be downloaded as a spreadsheet or synchronized with student records on a LMS.
- Students: A list of enrolled students and a mechanism to invite more students.

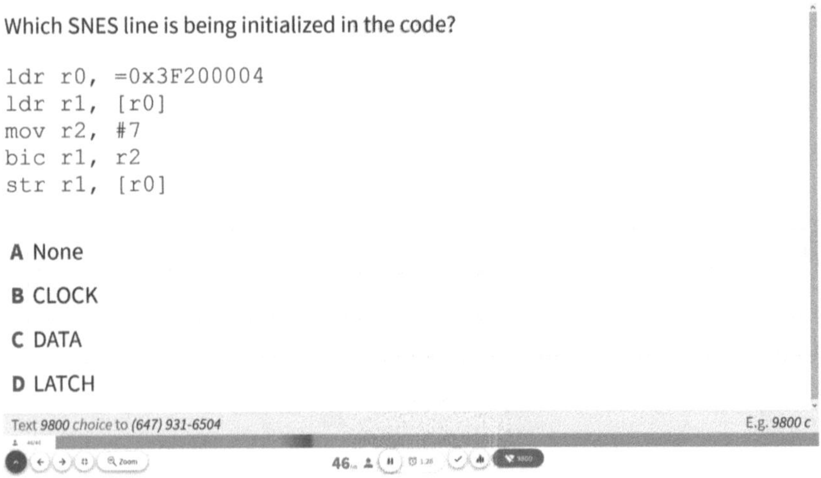

(a)

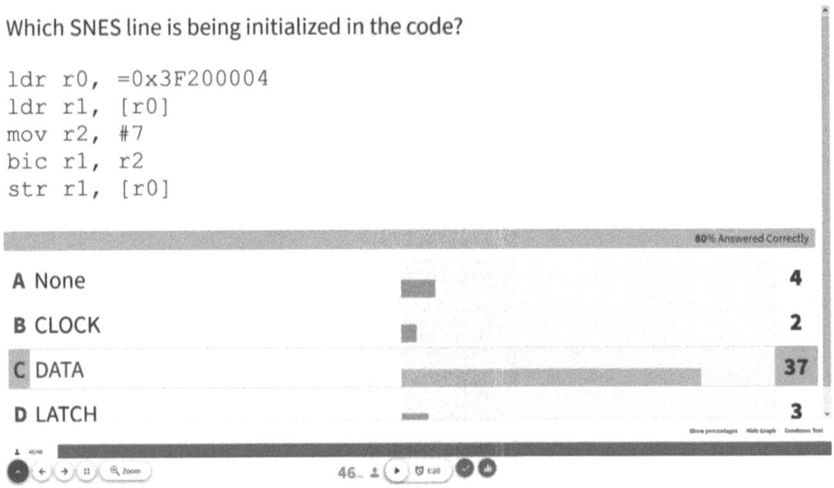

(b)

Fig. 2. Asking a question in Tophat (a) Question screen (b) Class responses and correct answer [1].

Student responses need not be evaluated by correctness alone, and it is possible for instructors to reward participation to whatever degree is desired by specifying the relative weight of each question and the relative weights of the participation and correctness components. Instructors are also able to specify the duration of the question (if they wish the question to be restricted to a set period of time) with students being allowed to resubmit their answers as often as they wish during that period.

Many modern CRS offer a variety of question types, taking full advantage of the different ways a participant can interact with their smartphone or laptop computer. For the Tophat CRS, there are six question formats that can be created:

Multiple-choice: Although the best practices associated with multiple-choice item creation is a completely separate (albeit worthwhile) topic for research, multiple-choice questions are easily created with Tophat and certainly represent one of the most widely used formats. These questions can be supported by charts, tables, or images as required and can be constructed with any number of possible answers and no restrictions on how many answers should be considered correct. Since many students are already familiar with multiple-choice questions, this format is probably the least likely to make students feel uncomfortable (Fig. 3).

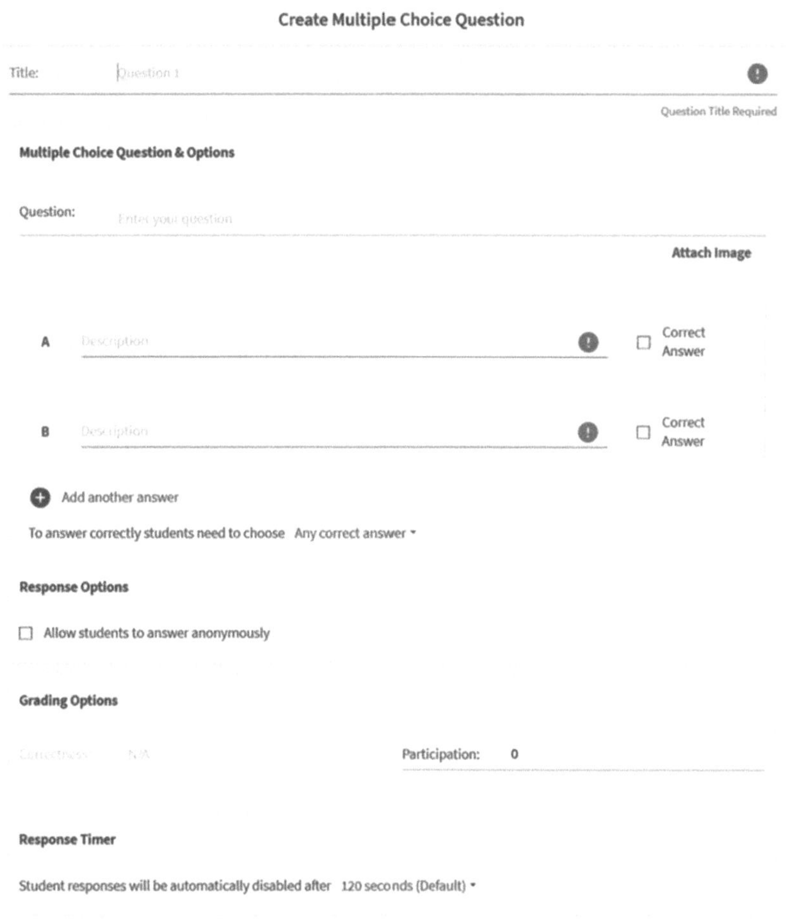

Fig. 3. Creating a multiple-choice question in Tophat [1].

Word Answer: This format is typically used for questions requiring that students respond with only a single word or a short phrase. It is the belief of some instructors that this format is superior to the multiple choice format because it requires students to generate a response rather than simply apply a process of elimination. That said, instructors designing such a question must be careful to consider all the different variations of the correct response that may be supplied by the student population.

Numeric Answer: A numeric answer question requires students to enter a single number as a response, and while this is obviously very useful for evaluating a student on his or hers ability to perform a calculation correctly and accurately, this format shares the same weakness as the previously mentioned word answer format, in that there may be different variations that should still be considered correct. In addressing this, the designer of a number answer question with Tophat can specify a tolerance range for the incoming responses. As a clarifying example, a tolerance of 1 and a correct answer of 50 would mean that any of the the values 49, 50, and 51 would be accepted as correct.

Matching: For this format the instructor specifies a list of ordered pairs (e.g., corresponding elements, numerical values, etc.) and Tophat shuffles the elements before presenting. It is then the task of the students to select the corresponding elements from each ordered pair and reconstruct the underlying relation. Figure 4 shows an example matching question with more responses than premises.

Sorting: Similar to the matching format above, for this format the instructor provides a sorted list of items that is shuffled before presentation. Students are then expected to resort the elements of the list before proceeding. Figure 5 shows an example sorting question.

Click-on-Target: For these questions an image is uploaded and, upon releasing the question to the students, students are able to click on certain areas of the image, with the CRS recording the position or region selected by each student.

It is worth noting that the wide variety of question types discussed in this section can support instructors pursuing a learner-centered approach, because students of different learning styles may find some types of questions easier to process (and thus more useful) that others. Verbal learners, for instance, may find themselves more comfortable with multiple-choice questions, while visual learners might be better served by questions with the matching or click-on-target styles. This diversity in the collection of formats available to designers facilitates attempts to include activities for students of each learning style.

It is worth noting that Tophat (and many other CRS) also feature discussion forums and subsystems for storing and delivering lectures notes and supporting files. Although these solutions are certainly useful, they are not necessary for the integration of CRS activities in the classroom and as such are beyond the scope of this chapter.

5 Student Feedback

Both authors of this chapter have used CRS as an integral part of most of their courses, and in the authors' experiences, it was only rarely encountered that CRS were distracting, confusing, or unhelpful. Although it is not unusual for a student to become confused by a particular question (which is obviously something that can occur regardless of how the question was presented) it is virtually always confusion surrounding the material, and not the interface to the CRS. Furthermore, since the authors integrate CRS into their courses very early

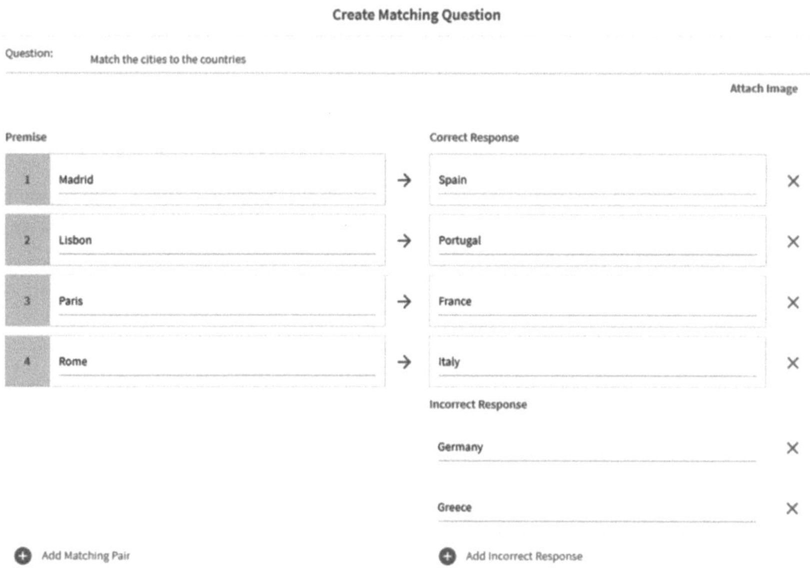

(a)

(b)

Fig. 4. A matching question in Tophat (a) Creating the question (b) Students' view [1].

in the semester, the activity becomes a familiar component of the classroom and is not typically considered a distraction.

In supporting our claims that an integrated approach addresses concerns about confusion and distraction, this section presents data collected from two courses into which CRS was fully integrated. Both are required courses for the Bachelor's of Science and the Bachelor's of Science with Honours programs in Computer Science. The first is a second-year course dealing with computer architecture and low-level programming, and the second is a third-year course dealing with the principles of operating systems.

For the second-year computer architecture course, the data was collected over a period of two years from 2015 to 2016 and involved 292 surveyed students - a survey participation rate of 63.6%. During this 2-year period, the course was offered six times: four offerings during regular terms (one offering per term) and two accelerated offerings in during summer terms. Consequently, the total number of students registered in this course during that period was 459, with class sizes ranging between 43 and 131 students. For the third-year operating systems course, the data was collected over three regular term offerings from the period from 2015 to 2017 and involved 327 students, with class sizes ranging between 90 and 115 students.

Fig. 5. A sorting question in Tophat [1].

Each of the nine offerings described above (in both the former and the latter course) was developed and delivered by the same instructor, and the Tophat classroom response system was thoroughly integrated into both sets of lectures. The university requires instructors to provide anonymous, voluntary surveys towards the end of each course each semester, so for these surveys, students were asked to include statements about what the instructor did to help their learning and were given the chance to name one aspect that was especially effective in supporting their learning. It should be noted that, for this question, no options were presented to the students and the question itself was entirely free-form.

In the computer architecture course, 292 valid surveys were received and an overwhelming 76.7% of the surveyed students mentioned CRS (specifically, Tophat) as the most effective aspect in the course that helped their learning. The remaining 23.3% mentioned visual aids used by the instructor, group work activities, open-book exams, and the lab assignments. Figure 6 clearly shows that the CRS dominated the survey participant responses concerning especially effective supports for each of the six semesters (which have been arranging according to class size, from lowest to highest).

The authors should note that in Canadian universities, the Fall semester spans September to December, the Winter Semester covers January to April, and the Spring semester consists of May and June (there is also a second short Summer semester in July-August.)

A full table of the values used to create the previous chart is presented in Table 1. In this table, the rows correspond to the semesters (listed in chronological order) and each row shows the class size, number of students participating in the survey, and the number of survey participants mentioning the CRS as an effective learning support. The fact that the number of students that mentioned CRS specifically never dropped below 73% of the total number of survey participants is a testament to how well the CRS was integrated into this course.

In the operating systems course, 191 valid surveys were received. Once again a substantial majority – 73.8% – of the surveyed students mentioned CRS as the course element that they believed to be most helpful to their learning. The responses received for this course mirror the data collected for the former course, and are depicted in Fig. 7 (with offerings again arranged according to class size, from lowest to highest) and Table 2 (wherein the rows are listed in chronological order).

The surveys also included questions where participants could specify what they believe should be changed in order to improve future offerings. Only 2 out of the 292 survey participants in the computer architecture course complained about the CRS – one student considered it to be a distraction, and the other, while openly recognizing the value of CRS, believed the number of CRS questions presented could be reduced. This means that less than 0.35% of the participants considered the use of a CRS as a distraction, in stark contrast with some of the earlier studies mentioned in Sect. 2. Furthermore, less than 0.70% of the subjects had anything negative to say about the use of CRS. Similarly, in the operating systems course there were 2 participants (of the 191 surveyed) that expressed concerns that the CRS questions were distracting and intimidating (respectively), and an additional 2 participants that echoed the suggestion that the number of questions be reduced (while still citing the CRS system itself as a particularly effective learning support.) We attribute this overwhelming positive response to the fact that our integrated approach has made the activity familiar and non-disruptive, without sacrificing its effectiveness as an engagement and feedback tool.

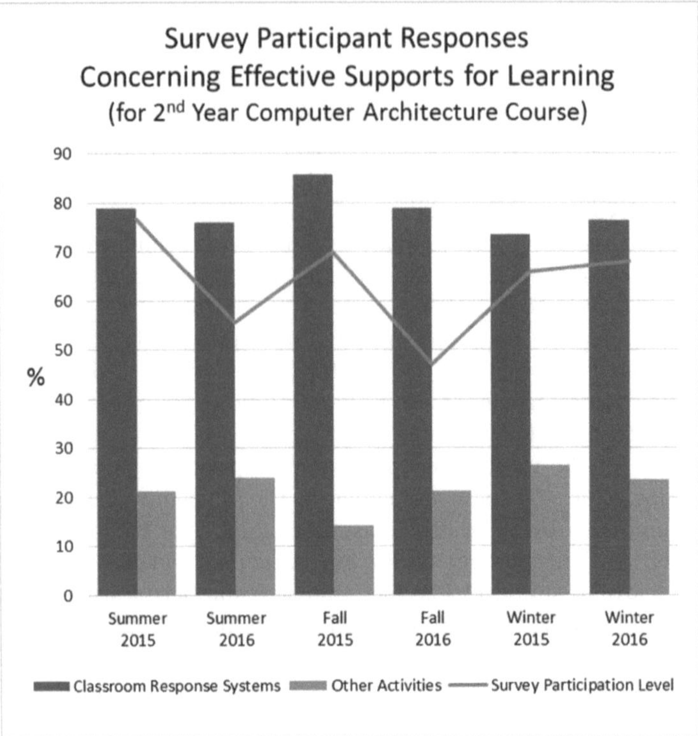

Fig. 6. Summary of student feedback for the computer architecture course [1].

Table 1. Student feedback details for the computer architecture course [1].

Semester	Course enrollment	Survey participants	Participants citing CRS specifically
Winter 2015	120	79	58 (73.4%)
Spring 2015	43	33	26 (78.8%)
Fall 2015	50	35	30 (86%)
Winter 2016	131	89	68 (76%)
Spring 2016	45	25	19 (76%)
Fall 2016	70	33	26 (79%)
Total	459	292	224 (77%)

Digging deeper into the student free-form written comments, many students thought the use of Tophat CRS was engaging. As one student put it:

"Tophat kept me motivated to come to class and made the class fun."

The students also praised the usage of the CRS for its ability to reinforce the material. Some of the student comments included:

"Tophat clarified confusing concepts."
"Tophat cements the knowledge in your head."
"The Tophat questions worked great and help ensure you actually understood what you though you understood."

It is obvious from these comments that well-crafted questions, when properly integrated into the lectures, can help alleviate the illusion of understanding and deal with learning uncertainties by providing an opportunity to practice material and receive immediate, formative feedback. Other participants added:

Table 2. Student feedback details for the operating systems course.

Semester	Course enrollment	Survey participants	Participants citing CRS specifically
Winter 2015	90	54	44 (81.5%)
Fall 2016	122	85	53 (62.4%)
Winter 2017	115	52	44 (84.6%)
Total	327	191	141 (73.8%)

"Tophat ironed out pretty much all mid-lecture uncertainties." "The feedback from the Tophat questions allowed you to adjust your focus to areas of need."

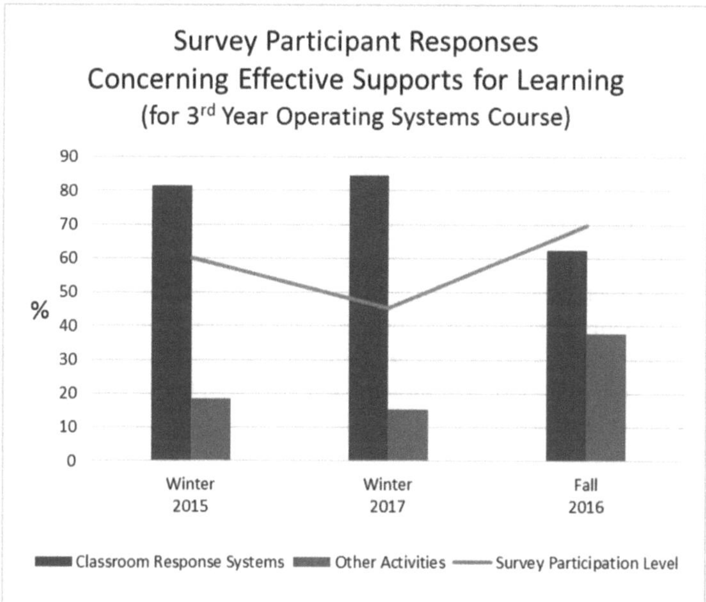

Fig. 7. Summary of student feedback for the operating systems course.

Properly integrated questions can help the instructor better explain difficult concepts, by deconstructing the problem into smaller pieces and giving the students the chance to actively work on these problems, rather than turning the students to passive recipients of information. In support of this claim, we received the following participant comments:

> *"Tophat was particularly helpful in understanding tricky concepts."*
> *"Tophat questions were very effective in providing a chance for students to try out new concepts."*
> *"The Tophat questions basically forced you to focus and apply the knowledge."*
> *"Tophat are some of the most effective tools and more effective than how other profs use them."*

It is clear that many of these comments echo the well-established benefits associated with the use of CRS. We also believe that the results of our two-year investigation provide strong support our claim that a full integration of CRS into the classroom addresses virtually every concern an instructor might have about adding CRS to their own courses. Although effective CRS integration represents the same kind of investment of time and effort that would be expected of any best practice, we believe our investigation has clearly demonstrated that the barriers can be addressed without sacrificing any of the benefits.

The authors have both witnessed this firsthand in their respective courses. The following case (exemplifying this feedback process) occurred in an introductory computer science course during a module on database management. By this point in the course (typically week 9 of 14), students have been exposed to both propositional logic and set theory and have explored (and been assessed on) both topics in detail, and the lessons in question are part of an introduction to structured query language (SQL). Since elementary query design is a problem that requires both propositional logic and set theory, it is a logical "next step" in the course. After a discussion of query design with SQL, the following "feedback-type" classroom response system question was presented to one of the classes (alongside specifications for a Children table and a Mother table):

"Which of the following SQL statements will get back all the Children that have a biological Mother from Calgary? (You may assume that, because Children and biological Mothers have a one-to-many relationship, the primary key (SIN) of Mother was added as the column MOTHERSIN to the Child table.)" The format of this question was multiple-choice, which the following responses available to the students:

(a) SELECT * FROM CHILD, MOTHER
WHERE MOTHER.CITY = "Calgary"
(b) SELECT * FROM CHILD UNION SELECT * FROM MOTHER
WHERE CITY = "Calgary"
(c) SELECT * FROM CHILD IN SELECT * FROM MOTHER
WHERE CITY = "Calgary"

(d) SELECT * FROM CHILD INNER JOIN MOTHER ON
MOTHER.SIN = CHILD.MOTHERSIN and MOTHER.CITY = "Calgary"

The correct answer to this question is response "d" but when reviewing the responses received (with the class, very shortly after query design with SQL had been discussed) it was found that only 22.9% of respondents submitted the correct answer. The response distribution for this question is shown in Fig. 8.

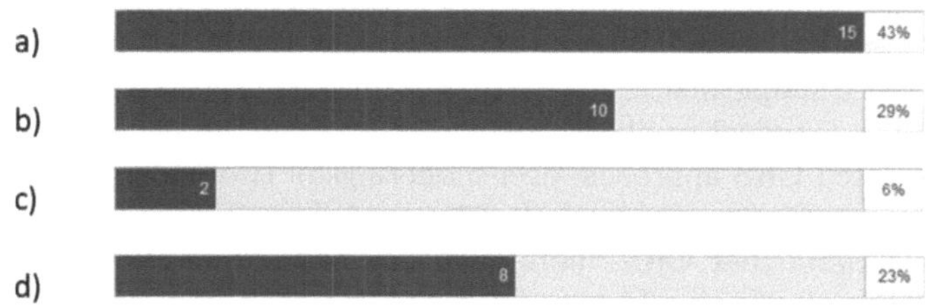

Fig. 8. Response distribution for the SQL question.

Although this result, in and of itself, is invaluable for instructors (and indicates that the majority of students are not yet comfortable with this topic and the lecture should not yet proceed to subsequent material), a quick, "on the fly" examination of the response distribution is very informative.

Response "c" was syntactically incorrect and invalid, but the fact that this response was chosen by only 5.7% of respondents indicates that SQL syntax was not an issue at the moment. Incorrect response "b", on the other hand, was selected by 28.6% of respondents and so any possible explanations should not be summarily dismissed. This option was included to ensure the participants understood the role of the set theory operations discussed earlier in the semester, and the incorrect respondents (although somewhat understandable since union was a set theory concept that had been practiced mostly on numbers and not database table records) could be easily corrected by revisiting the concept. Similarly, response "a" (the most frequently selected incorrect response at 42.9%), differs from the correct response by only the absence of a join condition, and it was thus decided by the instructor to revisit the concept of joining tables before proceeding further.

6 Conclusion

The body of research supporting the claim that classroom response systems improve the learning experience (and are thus valuable to students) is extensive. Numerous studies have discussed the benefits associated with CRS - for providing feedback opportunities, improving student engagement, motivation, knowledge retention, etc. - but contrary to this large body of research there remain concerns that CRS can present a barrier to learners that perceive its usage as diverting or confusing. With this examination, the authors (each of whom have delivered courses that used CRS extensively) have demonstrated that CRS can be fully integrated into courses such that the system becomes comfortable and familiar to students, while still delivering the benefits noted previously. In these courses, the use of the CRS was not a gratuitous activity, and as a result the overwhelming majority of students did not consider the CRS to be an unnecessary disruption. In this chapter, the authors have provided a classification of categories for the different CRS questions that the authors believe clarifies how these activities can be fully integrated during lecture design. The authors have also discussed a well-known CRS system, called Tophat, exploring how it can be effectively used as more than just a supplementary activity. The authors have also presented a large body of data and student feedback, collected from hundreds of students subjected to this integrated CRS approach, over 9 offerings of two undergraduate courses in computer science over the period of 2 years. This feedback overwhelmingly supports the claim that CRS, more than any of the many other activities in use, was the most effective feature for enhancing student learning. Only three students from a population of 483 expressed concerns that CRS was a distraction from their learning, and as this is a mere 0.62% of the surveyed population, the authors believe that the full integration of CRS into the classroom will obliterate any perceived dangers of impeding student learning.

References

1. Reading, A.: Kawash, J., Collier, R.D.: On the use of classroom response systems as an integral part of the classroom. In: Proceedings of the 10th International Conference on Computer Supported Education, CSEDU 2018, 15–17 March 2018, Funchal, Madeira, Portugal, vol. 1, pp. 38–46 (2018)
2. Boscardin, C., Penuel, W.: Exploring benefits of audience-response systems on learning: a review of the literature. Acad. Psychiatry **36**, 401–407 (2012)
3. Moss, K., Crowley, M.: Effective learning in science: the use of personal response systems with a wide range of audiences. Comput. Educ. **56**, 36–43 (2011)
4. Kay, R.H., LeSage, A.: Examining the benefits and challenges of using audience response systems: a review of the literature. Comput. Educ. **53**, 819–827 (2009)
5. Bruff, D.: Teaching with Classroom Response Systems: Creating Active Learning Environments. Jossey-Bass, San Francisco (2009)
6. Moredich, C., Moore, E.: Engaging students through the use of classroom response systems. Nurse Educ. **32**, 113–116 (2007)
7. Blasco-Arcas, L., Buil, I., Hernandez-Ortega, B., Sese, F.J.: Using clickers in class. The role of interactivity, active collaborative learning and engagement in learning performance. Comput. Educ. **62**, 102–110 (2013)
8. Webb, A., Carnaghan, C.: Investigating the effects of group response systems on student satisfaction, learning and engagement in accounting education. Issues Acc. Educ. **22**, 391–409 (2006)
9. Porter, L., Zingaro, D., Lister, R.: Predicting student success using fine grain clicker data. In: Proceedings of the Tenth Annual Conference on International Computing Education Research, ICER 2014, pp. 51–58. ACM, New York (2014)

10. Liao, S.N., Zingaro, D., Laurenzano, M.A., Griswold, W.G., Porter, L.: Lightweight, early identification of at-risk CS1 students. In: Proceedings of the 2016 ACM Conference on International Computing Education Research, ICER 2016, pp. 123–131. ACM, New York (2016)
11. Porter, L., Simon, B.: Retaining nearly one-third more majors with a trio of instructional best practices in CS1. In: Proceeding of the 44th ACM Technical Symposium on Computer Science Education, SIGCSE 2013, 165–170. ACM, New York (2013)
12. Simon, B., Kinnunen, P., Porter, L., Zazkis, D.: Experience report: Cs1 for majors with media computation. In: Proceedings of the Fifteenth Annual Conference on Innovation and Technology in Computer Science Education, ITiCSE 2010, pp. 214–218. ACM, New York (2010)
13. Simon, B., Parris, J., Spacco, J.: How we teach impacts student learning: Peer instruction vs. lecture in CS0. In: Proceeding of the 44th ACM Technical Symposium on Computer Science Education, SIGCSE 2013, pp. 41–46. ACM, New York (2013)
14. Huss-Lederman, S.: The impact on student learning and satisfaction when a CS2 course became interactive (abstract only). In: Proceedings of the 47th ACM Technical Symposium on Computing Science Education, SIGCSE 2016, p. 687. ACM, New York (2016)
15. Collier, R.D., Kawash, J.: Improving student content retention using a classroom response system. In: CSEDU 2017 - Proceedings of the 9th International Conference on Computer Supported Education, Volume 1, 21–23 April 2017, Porto, Portugal, pp. 17–24 (2017)
16. Vinaja, R.: The use of lecture videos, ebooks, and clickers in computer courses. J. Comput. Sci. Coll. **30**, 23–32 (2014)
17. Draper, S.W., Brown, I.M.: Increasing interactivity in lectures using an electronic voting system. J. Comput. Assist. Learn. **20**, 81–94 (2004)

A Virtual Learning Environment to Acquire Orientation Skills in the LUSI Class Context

Lahcen Oubahssi(✉) and Claudine Piau-Toffolon

LIUM Laboratory, EA 4023, UBL, Le Mans University, 72085 Le Mans, France
{lahcen.oubahssi,
claudine.piau-toffolon}@univ-lemans.fr

Abstract. Virtual Reality (VR) technologies become a promising tool in the context of learning especially for learners with learning disabilities, because of their technological specificities that differentiate them from the traditional learning environments. The development of educational virtual environment is a complex task due to the interdisciplinarity intrinsic to VR and its cognitive aspects. This paper describes a research work whose objective is to propose a solution based on virtual reality to enhance the traditional learning to acquire orientation skills in the LUSI class. This research work identifies some limitations with existing solutions and studies the design and operationalization of learning situations in the form of scenario models. Our aim is providing trainers with an educational toolkit, thus allowing them to recreate virtual reality scenarios and assess the learners' progress for learning orientation skills.

Keywords: Virtual learning environments · Educational virtual environment · Pedagogical scenario · Orientation skills

1 Introduction

Virtual Reality (VR) technologies become a promising tool in the context of learning especially for learners with learning disabilities, because of their technological specificities that differentiate them from the traditional learning environments. VR can be described as a set of technological tools that support the creation of synthetic, highly interactive three dimensional (3D) spatial environments that represent real or non-real situations. This description shows that VR can be pedagogically exploited through its unique technological characteristics that can be compiled as follows [31–33]: creation of 3D spatial representations, namely virtual environments (VE); multisensory channels for user interaction; immersion of the user in the VE and intuitive interaction through natural manipulations in real time.

Mikropoulos and Natsis [33] define a Virtual Learning Environment (VLE) or Educational Virtual Environment (EVE) as a virtual environment that is based on a certain pedagogical model, incorporates or implies one or more didactic objectives, provides users with experiences they would otherwise not be able to experience in the physical world and redounds specific learning outcomes. Huang et al. [23] refer to Virtual Reality Learning Environments (VLRE) when they speak about environments based on VR used in educational applications.

B. M. McLaren et al. (Eds.): CSEDU 2018, CCIS 1022, pp. 56–76, 2019.
https://doi.org/10.1007/978-3-030-21151-6_4

There are numerous research studies on VR technologies for teaching and learning [13, 22, 30] establishing the advantages of using VR in education. We also note that with the appearance of the virtual reality, the computing allows to offer new experiences to the users thanks to possibilities of interaction and immersion which are even more performing. These possibilities are of great interest in the learning domain because they allow the creation of original and dynamic learning situations detached from the constraints that can exist during real training (danger, cost, uncertainty) and bringing specific advantages (enrichment of situations, replay, etc.) [3, 4, 10, 26, 35]. But Martin-Gutierrez et al. [29] note also some limitations due to the missing of studies on educational designs for a better integration of VR. Existing design-oriented studies are limited [5] but educational design is an integral part of the work all teachers perform [21] and there is a shortage of relevant practical and conceptual tools to support teacher design [5, 36]. Design is a complex task, in particular in the domain of virtual learning environments, due to the interdisciplinarity intrinsic to VR and its cognitive aspects.

We present in this paper a research work whose objective is to propose a solution based on virtual reality to enhance the traditional learning to acquire orientation skills in the LUSI[1] class. This research work took part of the ARVAD project [1, 39]. As part of this research project, we worked with a LUSI class of twelve learners aged 16–18. The major difficulty of this public is managing their stress, which can be caused by several factors, including their own delay or the forgetting of the transport card, the delay of the bus, the noise, and the crowd. Our aim is to provide solutions to this problem of autonomy by using the techniques of virtual reality.

We shall propose in this project solutions to structure the learning situations in formalism understandable for teachings and interpretable by the machine, adaptive and reusable according to the context. The research questions of this study are relative to the activity of design and operationalization of the pedagogical scenarios by the teachers-designers [30] in the target VRLEs. As part of this research, we study the design and operationalization of several learning situations in a virtual reality environment. The initial proposal of this research effort has been discussed in [11, 38, 39, 45].

This paper is structured as follows: the next section will present context and objectives of our project and the main stages of the design of the orientation skills process. We present in Sect. 3 the related research works on virtual reality and instructional design. Our proposal is presented in Sect. 3. A discussion is made in Sect. 4 on results of the pilot study we carried out to verify the usability of the developed environment [37]. We draw a conclusion and present our research perspectives in the last section.

[1] Local Units for School Inclusion.

2 Context of This Research Work

2.1 The ARVAD Project

The ARVAD project was conducted in collaboration with the Technology Enhanced Learning (TEL) Engineering research team of the LIUM[2] laboratory, the INSH[3] laboratory and the Robert Buron High School[4] in Laval (France). This project is financed by Laval-Agglomeration. The aim of this research project is to propose a solution implemented in virtual reality environment to enhance the traditional learning to acquire orientation skills in the LUSI class. Our goal is to facilitate this learning through digital, and to provide trainers of the LUSI class with an educational toolkit, allowing them to recreate virtual reality scenarios and to assess the learner's progress. We followed a constructivist teaching approach based on problem situations, and a virtual reality environment to develop automation that can be latter exploited in a context of orientation skill acquisition. The challenge of this research project relies on the interest of digital technologies in the learning for young people with cognitive disabilities.

2.2 The Local Units for School Inclusion

The Local Units for School Inclusion (LUSI) welcome pupils with cognitive or mental learning disabilities. The main goal of education in LUSI class is the development of autonomy and long-term professional integration in the labor market. LUSI class provides to pupils classroom accommodations and a specific educational program consolidating and developing adapted apprenticeships (general and professional education) with the alternation of collective and individual workshops. Teaching program includes general and specific learning facilitating social integration and autonomy (orientation skills, hygiene, etc.). As lack of skills for independent mobility can be a real barrier in everyday life, orientation activity becomes a daily practice. Different pedagogical learning approaches are taken: from the study of reading a map to real orientation activities in the city.

In LUSI class we distinguish two types of disorders, cognitive [25] and psychosocial [2, 15]. Some characteristic behavior of pupils is to adapt themselves to places; to the people they meet by having the proper attitude. They have no introspection activity and they have major difficulty explaining why they are doing some action. Major cognitive problems are located in four domains: memory, sense of time, reasoning and the space notion. The identified psychosocial problems are located on three domains: attention, motivation and self-esteem.

Several research studies have studied the issues related to the assessment and rehabilitation of these disorders. Sehaba and Hussaan [43] cited some examples based on clinical tests dealing with different cognitive functions, such as working memory [16], attention [27], auditory perception [35], oral and written language [8].

[2] https://lium.univ-lemans.fr/.

[3] https://www.esiea.fr/equipe-insh/.

[4] http://reaumur-buron.paysdelaloire.e-lyco.fr/.

The evolution of computer science has led to the development of several digital solutions for cognitive and linguistic remediation.[7, 9, 14, 40, 42, 43] noted that these kinds of solutions have the advantage of being more flexible and easily accessible. However, most of them do not adapt to the specificities and needs of each user. Research works establish a close relationship between digital environments and teachers' practices and responsibilities in defining new pedagogical strategies within this type of training units. In our work, we address the issues of designing and operationalizing pedagogical situations enhanced by VR environments in an engineering approach based on scenario models.

3 Learning Scenarios Oriented Virtual Reality

3.1 Related Work

Design of Virtual Reality learning environments (VRLEs) or Educational Learning Environments (EVEs) is a task that poses new technical difficulties, induced by the interdisciplinary intrinsic to the VR (graphic computer, haptic devices, distribution, etc.) and cognitive aspects (respect of the learned task characteristics, transfer of learning to the real world, etc.) [6, 28, 44]. Research has often focus on technical issues and discussions on how VR can be integrated into curriculum and relate to the learning process. Huang et al [23] propose a theoretical framework supporting instructional principles to facilitate building novel VRLEs. But they discussed only the pedagogical aspects influencing the learning process when designers apply a new VR technology to educational settings. According to the model of technology integration [34], VRLE's design should combine three sources of knowledge: technology, pedagogy and content. A VRLE includes an educational simulation, which is built around a set of learning objectives. The description of the educational simulations has to take into account the technological environment specificities (structure and dynamics). To fully describe the learning experience, designers of VLREs also need to specify the pedagogical requirements, in order to describe precisely the operationalization and the control of the activities in the environment. Tools by themselves do not teach; appropriate theories and/or models to guide the design and development of this technology are needed [12]. We might consider both didactic situations and scenario model. We analyzed the various research works that studying the question of scenario model design in VR domain.

[10, 4] propose a model based on a centralized and indirect control of an emergent simulation from learning scenario content model. In this model, the environment is populated with autonomous virtual characters and the user is free from his/her actions. Learning scenario design is realized in two steps: dynamic objectives are determined from the user activity, and then a learning scenario is generated by these objectives and implemented through simulation adjustments.

Trinh et al. [46] provide models for the knowledge explanation for virtual agents populating virtual environments. This knowledge focuses on the structure and dynamics of the environment as well as procedures that teams can perform in this environment. This makes it possible to ensure the different semantic constraints in VR: (1) internal properties of the spatial object, (2) spatial relationships between a set of spatial objects, and (3) semantic of spatial interactions (for example, before and after the state of the spatial tasks).

Sehaba and Hussaan [43] propose a serious adaptive game for the evaluation and rehabilitation of cognitive disorders; their system makes it possible to personalize the course of games to each patient according to their capacities and competences. The architecture of the system organizes the knowledge in three layers: domain concepts, pedagogical resources and game resources. The main objective of this work is to reuse this architecture in different fields of applications and different serious games.

Fahim et al. [18] ensured that the generic side of the POSVET pedagogical scenario model through the use of the MASCARET meta-model, allows to reuse pedagogical scenarios on different platforms. The main advantage of POSVET is to allow the adaptation of educational activities and to offer to learners a control on their learning. This work aims at adapting the educational scenario to the learners' needs but doesn't offer solutions for assisting the teachers in their design process.

Marion et al. [28] propose a learning scenario model that describes machine-readable educational activities in a virtual environment, in a generic way in terms of learning domain, type of task to carry out and learning strategy. The author uses a virtual environment meta-model that provides an abstract representation of virtual environments to allow its model to be both generic and machine-readable.

Chen et al. [13] propose an analysis that focuses on the improvement of a pedagogical design model of virtual environments using formative research. They propose a theoretical framework which identify four principles of pedagogical scenarios' realizations: (1) the conceptual principle that guides the learner towards the information he must consider; (2) the principle of metacognition that explains to the learner how to think during learning; (3) the procedural principle that indicates how to use the information available in the VRLEs; (4) the "strategic" principle that allows the learner to analyze the learning task or problem to be solved.

3.2 Lessons Learned and Issues from Existing Works

These research works overcome some limits identified in [10] that are related to the limited reactivity of the system or pedagogical control of the adaptation approaches. The models proposed improve the way to explicit knowledge [5, 46] or the pedagogical design of virtual environment [13] or permit the personalization of the course [43]. To overcome the lack of dynamic of the pedagogical scenario design, some works [10, 46] embed virtual agents in the virtual environment. But these works still limit the use of the virtual environment to predefined knowledge and learning activities. In [10], experts can enter their own model in a graphical editor that relies on a formal representation directly interpretable by computer systems. The meta-model approach developed by [28] also permits to experts to generate their virtual environment. But, despite these interesting approaches, they do not address in particular, the problem of the definition and adaptation of scenario models directly by the trainers according to the pedagogical situations they might encounter and the technical VR environment. Trainers/Teachers can still not adapt by themselves the pedagogical scenario according to the learner profiles and enable a gradual learning process. Our main concern is to propose solutions to trainers to help representing scenario according to their own pedagogical needs in new environments such as those dedicated to virtual reality. As part of this research, we study the design and operationalization of several learning situations in a virtual reality environment. We are particularly interested in learning design activities by means of scenarios models, by the teachers themselves, to enable them to design learning situations in virtual reality environments to ensure the achievement of their educational objectives. Last but not least, it is important to take note that the implementation of these scenarios always requires an extra effort in order to meet different technical, pedagogical and content constraints required by this type of environment [34].

4 Our Contributions

As stated by [29] younger students have always lived surrounded with technologies and are digital natives [41] but relationships between technology and learning are not evident and virtual technologies are not an exception to this. But an investigation by [32] found that students had a favorable attitude towards these technologies in the educational process. Studies in the scientific literature linking virtual technologies with improvements in particular in students' social and collaborative skills [24] and students' psychomotor and cognitive skills [19] allowed us to suppose that the use of tablets, smartphones or video games in their daily life, and the attraction they show for all these devices suggest that virtual technologies can be beneficial for both learning and autonomy development.

In order to achieve our objectives, we adopt an iterative and participative approach involving a representative teacher [44]. Design occurred before, during and after prototype's implementation. Participants (teacher and researchers) to the design process developed their design using a broad-to-specific pattern in iterations [5]. In a first time we analyze and model existing learning situations, develop a functional demonstrator and test the usability and relevance of the demonstrator in real situations. During the analysis phase, we tested the technical acceptance of virtual reality environments through the manipulation by the LUSI class learners of two well-known 3D video games based on displacement situations using a joystick. This test proved that learners were very comfortable with these environments and associated peripherals. In order to define the practices and put them into perspective with the theories and methods of learning adapted to the target audience, we observed for a period of three months in the LUSI class the different pedagogical situations. Based on this study, we proposed pedagogical models to be implemented in the future virtual environment. These models may offer the possibility to trainers to define their own scenarios according to the learner's profile and the pedagogical situation.

4.1 Example of a Learning Scenario Oriented LUSI Class

The LUSI class learners were asked to carry out various educational activities related to orientation skills so that they could develop more autonomy in their personal and professional lives. We observed these activities, depending of two categories of pedagogical situations (High School category and City category) and synthesized them in

Table 1. The activities being carried out can be characterized with different variables and parameters in accordance with the needs of the teaching staff of the LUSI class. For instance, an activity "*work stress management*" can be adjusted with the variation of the level of stress by adding "noise" as parameter (Table 1).

Table 1. Example of variables for an orientation skill activity [39].

Activity name	Stress Parameters							
	Noise		Timer				Obstacle	
	With	Without	Display		Duration		Present	Absent
			Yes	No	Limited	Unlimited		

Thanks to the observation process, we are able to propose a version of a model of scenarios (as illustrated in Fig. 1), which leads us to propose a conceptual model of different pedagogical scenarios based on the needs of the referring teacher. Figure 1 illustrates the course of the learning situation related to *Activity 1,* beginning with Activity 0 (Table 2). The objective of this activity is to locate different places on a map. The pedagogical strategy being used in this example is to work individually, and afterwards collectively for the correction.

Thus far, we note that the given scenarios are adaptable to the learners' progress (suggesting an itinerary to be followed first with visual and/or audible indications or without indication, adding noises from environments, etc.). In the suggested scenarios, the general objective of having learners move independently while managing stress with a map and benchmarks in the environment is fulfilled. In the meantime, we have identified several intermediate objectives that allow for a gradual learning towards this general objective (Fig. 2). Each intermediate objective is composed of a pedagogical sequence, which is divided into activities. The sequences are independent of one another because they do not respond to the same intermediate objectives.

Table 2. Example of orientation skills activities achieved in LUSI class [39].

Activities	Objectives	Variables
High School category		
Activity 0	Preparation for activity 1 & activity 2	No variable
Activity 1	Locate places in high school (with numbers)	Type of maps (1a: map with many words and images indices, 1b: map with many word indices, 1c: map with few words and image indices)
Activity 2	Identify places in high school (with colours)	No variable, only the map with many indices is used
City category		
Activity 0	Preparation for activity 1 & activity 2	No variable
Activity 1	Locate on a city map	No variable
Activity 2	Locate important places with a grid	Search strategy with imposed grid

The set of these sequences constitutes a group of activities. The teacher assigns a specific sequence to one or more learners depending on their competency levels on orientation skills. In our study, we distinguish two groupings of learners according to two competence levels:

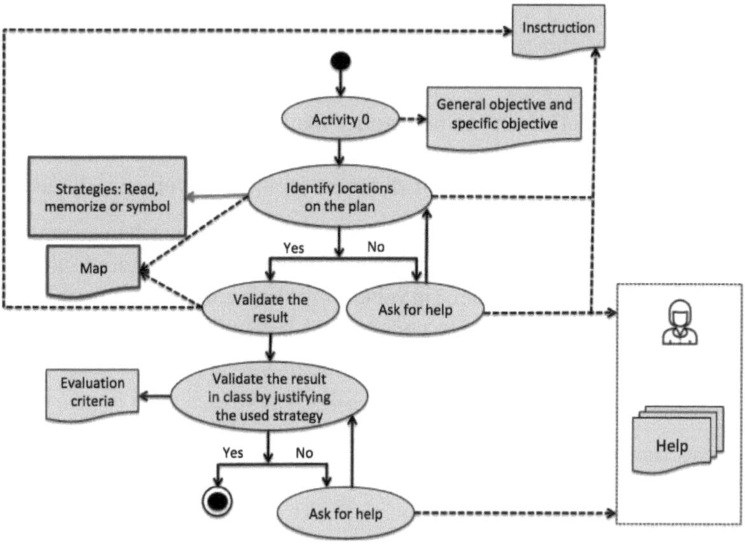

Fig. 1. High School category – Progress of activity 1 (Table 1) [39].

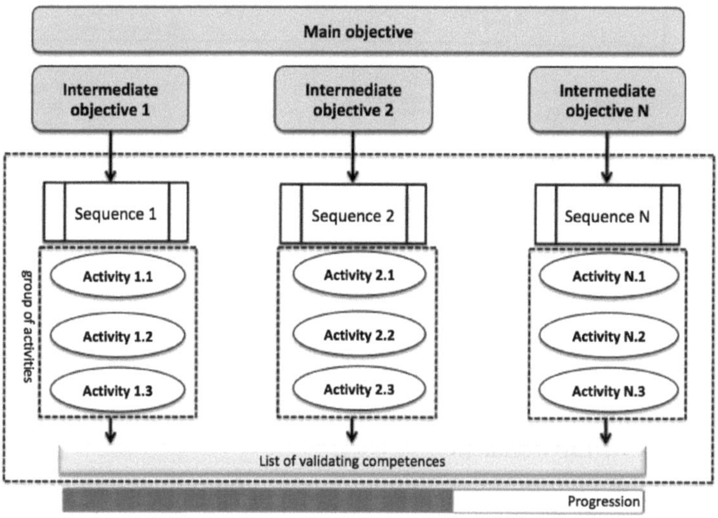

Fig. 2. Progress of activity 1 (Table 1) [39].

- Group 1: is the grouping of learners with a low level of competence on orientation skills. For example, group 1 always starts activities with a simplified map because they have difficulty moving on a complex map (with a lot of path choices).
- Group 2: is the grouping of learners with an average level of competence on orientation skills. For example, group 2 always begins activities with a complex map because we consider that they are able to move with a simple map.

We found that for the same objective, the teacher does not evaluate the same competency:

- For the same objective, the same activity may be used, but with lower or higher level of requirements according to the handicap and education level.
- For the same objective, activities of different (gradual) levels may be used.

To evaluate the learner progress, a scale is used by the teacher according to the academic evaluation system (acquired, being acquired, almost acquired, not acquired). This makes it possible to locate them in relation to their competence booklet. Figure 3 illustrates an example of a learner's pedagogical path with the different adaptations (change of activities, adaptation of objectives, etc.).

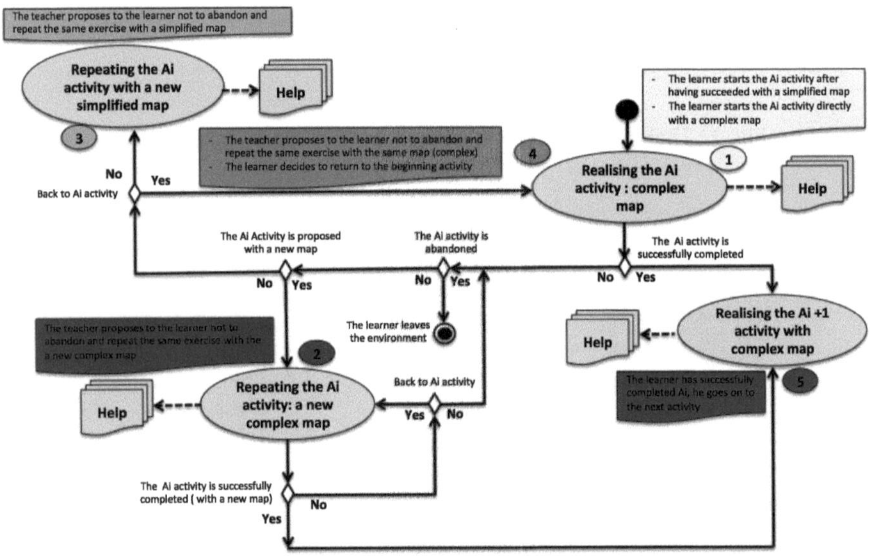

Fig. 3. The progression of a learning path with a complex map [39].

4.2 The ARVAD Environment

We proposed a set of specifications characterizing a virtual reality environment and adapted to specific needs and scenarios according to the analysis and modeling of existing pedagogical situations. This allowed the development of a virtual environment enabling the pedagogical team to define orientation skills scenario sand learners to carry out the activities related to the objectives set. For carrying out these activities, the learner has a joystick, a synchronized tablet displaying a 2D map, and visual indices (images or texts) (Fig. 4). We developed a non-immersive virtual reality environment in the form of a window into a virtual world displayed on a computer monitor and the interaction made via a mouse or a joystick.

To set up the orientation skills activities, the teacher uses a configuration interface communicating with the ARVAD execution environment. This interface permits:

- Management and configuration of the travel plans;
- Management of learners or group of learners, set up of activities according to learning profile and pedagogical progression;
- Analysis of the results of the activities achieved;
- Management of the learner's accounts.

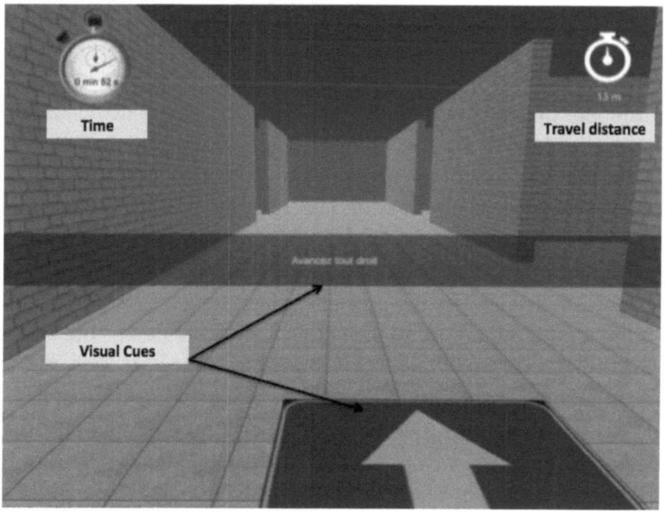

Fig. 4. ARVAD environment screenshot [39].

As shown in Fig. 5, the ARVAD execution environment integrates a model of orientation skills scenario and the 3D environment (a labyrinth). A server is dedicated to the management of data and resources. An instance of the 3D orientation skills scenario model is defined through the setting up of the activities generating a scenario for a learner or a group of learners.

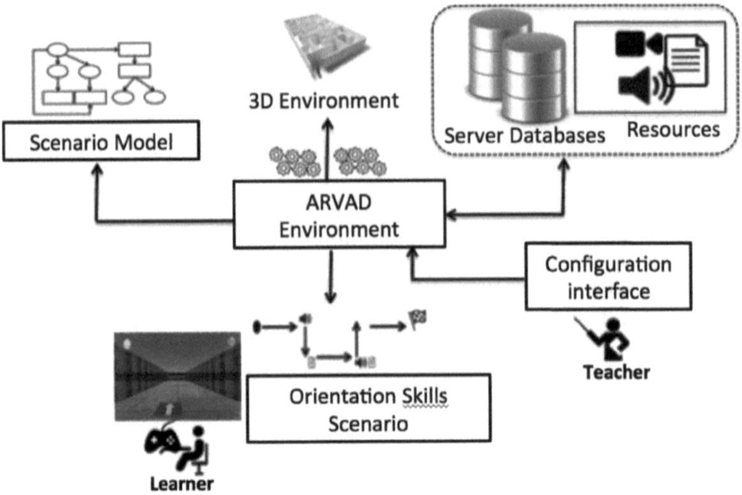

Fig. 5. The ARVAD execution environment [39].

The environment includes two main parts. The first one is dedicated to the learner, playing the scenario defined by the trainers. The second part (not developed at this time) will allow the teacher to set pedagogical scenarios according to the learner's profiles and their pedagogical progression and save the results to track the progress of these learners.

The virtual environment has been developed with the cross-platform game engine Unity as a desktop version, where the user navigates using a joystick, related to a tablet. The design of the scenes did not try to provide authentic situations but only one close to the reality. Data of the various games play by each learner are recorded in databases.

The software architecture of the ARVAD environment is illustrated in Fig. 6. It is composed of two functionalities modules, a teacher's module and a learner's module. The teacher may *manage a learner sessions* to create, modify or remove a learner profile, and define activities for learners or group of learners. During a session, he can *manage tracks/indicators* to visualize the different activities achieved by learners or group of learners for a period of time selected. Some indicators may be: date, learner code, number of activities achieved by a learner, distance travelled (by activity), and success or not of an activity. The teacher can export the results. When defining a scenario, the teacher can *manage orientation skills activities* and set up or associate a map (*mapping map*). When learners play a session they can *read the instructions* at any moment to achieve their activities (hear or read the indication) according to the teachers' settings before *moving into the environment* with the joystick. They can *visualize their orientation plan* and gets their position in the environment and *ask for help* at any moment in the game by clicking. Different types of aid are given according to the teachers' settings. At any moment it is possible to *restart the activity* from the beginning. The last attempt is recorded. *Pause/Exit* permits to the learners to take a break at any moment. This pause is not taken into account when the activity is timed.

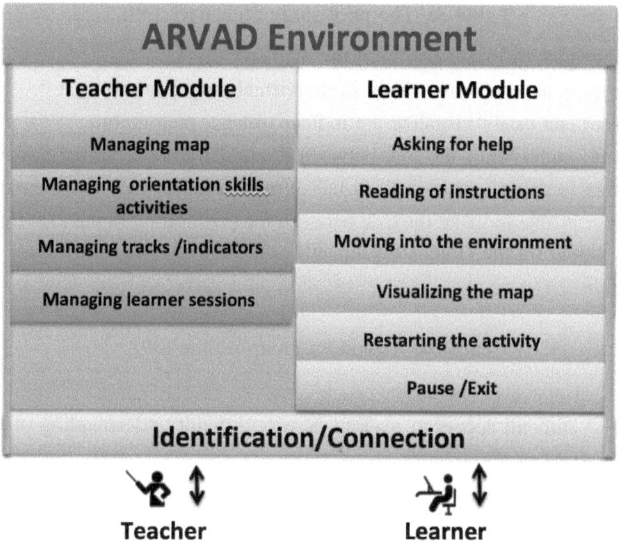

Fig. 6. ARVAD software architecture [39].

5 Pilot Study and Results

This section provides first a description of the pilot study and then describes the methodology for the evaluation of the VR based environment and gives and discusses results.

5.1 User Story

In order to assess the feasibility and the usability of the ARVAD environment, we conducted a pilot study. We defined with the teacher referent a set of objectives to evaluate if the functionalities and modalities of interactions (Table 3):

- Are well adapted to the LUSI class learners;
- Allow one or more skills to be easily worked;
- Allow one or more skills to be easily evaluated.

The experiment scope does not still permit to evaluate the pedagogical approach effectiveness. This pilot study was realized with nine learners (aged between 15 and 18) from the LUSI class at the Laval Robert Buron high school, in France. With the pedagogical team, we organized the learners into two groups according to the abilities and skills of each one. Table 4 shows an overview of the profiles of each group.

Table 3. The pilot study objectives [39].

O1	The learner gets to locate easily on the map (tablet)
O2	The learner is able to move easily in the virtual environment
O3	The learner can easily visualize the indices (image, pictogram)
O4	The learner understands the link between the tablet and the virtual environment
O5	The learner is able to move with visual or textual aid in the virtual environment
O6	The learner is able to make the link between the positioning in the 3D environment and the positioning on the tablet (use the aid)

Table 4. Learner's group profile [39].

Group	Size	Capacities and skills
1	4	Difficult access to reading or very difficult understanding of instructions. Use of pictograms
2	5	Easy access to write and understand a simple instruction

5.2 Research Methodology

The pilot study was used for this research along with quantitative and qualitative data. The aim was to evaluate qualitatively the feasibility of the pedagogical approach and some aspects of the usability of the virtual environment. We empirically verify usability criteria of the environment such as learnability, efficiency, memorability, errors or satisfaction [37]. According to the model of [17], we evaluate the concept of attitude, mainly the concept of perception of the user. To do so, we define a list of objectives (Table 3) to observe how the perception of content on the screen (visibility, display, texture) was perceptible, the perception of the contents on the shelf and the link between the tablet and the main screen. We define a protocol based on two learning groups (Group 1 and 2) and four steps: pre-test, test, post-test and results analysis. Figure 7 proposes an activity diagram of the pilot study process.

During the first step, the pedagogical team organized learners in two groups (Table 4), prepared an orientation map (on paper), the activities to be realized (duration, objective) and defined evaluation criteria (according to the skills to be tested for each group). The teacher then worked the orientation activity with the learners of the two groups (paper based map). For the post-test phase, an evaluation grid has been developed by researchers and a questionnaire for learners according to the objectives of the pilot experiment to evaluate the virtual environment during the learner's activities (Table 3). The map and the learning game scenario model were operationalized on the tablet and in the prototype of the virtual environment. In the second step (test), each group of learners plays their learning game scenario in the virtual environment. During each game session, the research team observes the learners' activities and notes their observations on the evaluation grid. For each objective (Table 3) we evaluate if the learner was able to achieve it. In the third step, the researchers submit a questionnaire to the two groups of learners. The objective of this questionnaire is to have a learner's feedback on the realized activities. The questionnaire was submitted by oral and the

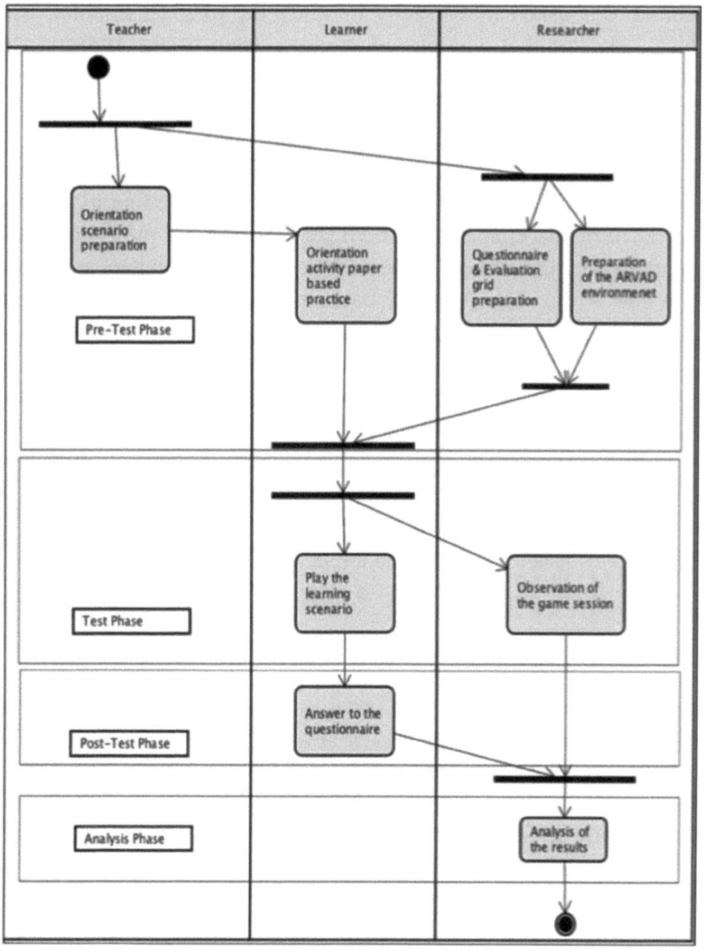

Fig. 7. Activity diagram of the pilot study process [39].

research team recorded answers. Finally, in a last step, the researchers conducted an analysis of the results and defined the improvements elements to the virtual environment.

During the test step, each group realized 3 sets of scenarios of the same activity (*moving from point A to point B*) but with a different variant depending on the group (with visual aid for Group 1 and with textual indications in Group 2). The skills to be evaluated were not the same for the two groups.

For example, among the skills to be assessed for Group 1, we can cite:

- I know how to go from a point A to a point B on the tablet map without indices.
- I know how to go from a point A to a point B using the visual aid in the virtual environment.

Each learner was asked individually to study the map on a tablet, which is the reproduction of the one that was played in class. Then he/she explains what he/she should do, before realizing his/her activities in the virtual environment. At any moment they could get help (by asking directly to the project team members conducting the experiment) or by clicking with the joystick to spot on the map of the tablet where they were located in the environment. The time (in seconds) and distance covered (in meters) were recorded in order to evaluate the efficiency according to the mode of use.

Three series of displacement (scenarios) per learner were proposed (Table 5). The project team monitored the process, observed the learner's activities and questioned the learner at the end of the session on the basis of the planned questionnaire and noted observations on the evaluation grid.

Table 5. Displacement series for the two groups of learners [39].

Series	Description
1	Same departure and arrival point of the paper map
2	A new departure and arrival point with indications
3	A new departure and arrival point without indications

5.3 Results and Discussions

The analysis of the results from the post-test questionnaire submitted to the learners and the evaluation grid completed during the test (results presented for Group 1 in Tables 6, 7 and Figs. 8, 9), made it possible to verify some of the usability criteria. The feasibility of the approach was validated as learners of the two groups were able to move in the virtual environment, locate themselves on the map in the tablet (tracing the requested itinerary) and achieved a series of activities (no abandonment). Only one learner (learner 4) unfamiliar with the joystick had some difficulties during the series (can be observed through the travel time recorded). Objectives O1 to O3 in Table 3 were satisfied. Some learners had more difficulties to understand and use the link between the tablet and the virtual environment (O4, O6 in Tables 3 and 7). Those who did not use the link with the tablet and the help proposed (by clicking with the joystick), randomly explored the environment for the first attempt in search of the arrival point. Then they used their memory to locate objects to achieve the series of displacement, thus the time taken to complete the activity or the covered distance in the two first series was greater, in a ratio of 1 to 3 for the time in the case of learner 4 compared to the best results of learners of the Group 1.

The time taken to complete the activity and the covered distance was variable according to the learners without being directly linked to the different types of help proposed. Objective O6 seems more difficult to achieve. We still noted in series 3 (changed start and arrival points - no indices provided in the virtual environment) that time and covered distance was greater for the two groups (see results Table 6, Figs. 8 and 9 for Group 1- except for learner 2 and 4). We observed that Learner 2 used systematically the aid provided in the environment but the results (in terms of distance and time) were not better than the others (except for the last series).

Table 6. Results of Group 1 [39].

Learner	Series	Distance	Time	Help
1	1	31.2	51	0
	2	25.9	47	0
	3	51.5	133	2
2	1	30.8	66	5
	2	25.8	58	5
	3	21.3	34	6
3	1	36.1	82	0
	2	21.7	51	0
	3	53.9	122	1
4	1	32.1	143	0
	2	24.9	103	0
	3	28.4	127	0

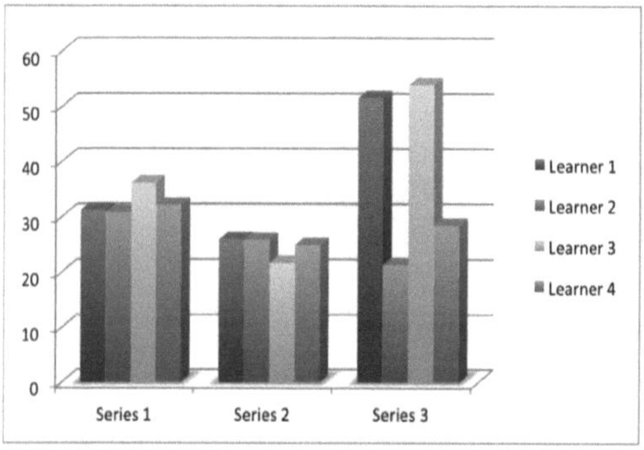

Fig. 8. Results of Group 1: distance travelled (in meters) [39].

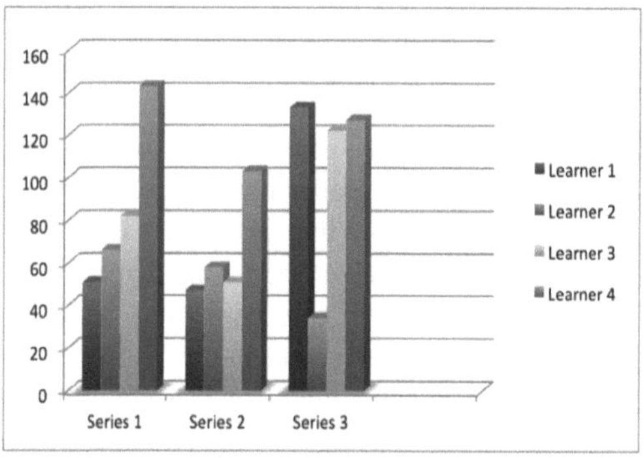

Fig. 9. Results of Group 1: time of travel (in seconds) [39].

The first two series permit to verify the usability of the prototype and the skill (I know how to go from a point A to a point B using the visual aid in the virtual environment). In the last serie, learners enable to locate themselves in the environment with the use of indices despite change with the points of departure and arrival. Learners used more internal skills instead of exploiting the link between the map on the tablet and the environment. Group 2 presented results rather similar as Group 1.

Table 7. Results of Group 1 by objectives for each series of activities [39].

Learner	Series	O1	O2	O3/O5	O4	O6
1	1	Ok	Ok	Ok	Ok	No
	2	Ok	Ok	Ok	Ok	No
	3	Ok	Ok	-	Ok	Ok
2	1	Ok	Ok	Ok	Ok	Ok
	2	Ok	Ok	Ok	Ok	Ok
	3	Ok	Ok	-	Ok	Ok
3	1	Ok	Ok	Ok	Not clear	No
	2	Ok	Ok	Ok	Ok	No
	3	Ok	Ok	-	Ok	Ok
4	1	Ok	Ok	Ok	Ok	No
	2	Ok	Ok	Ok	Ok	No
	3	Ok	Ok	-	Ok	Ok

6 Conclusion and Perspectives

The use of virtual reality techniques has shown their effectiveness in the field of learning, but some limitations have been identified notably for the design of learning environment by teachers themselves. We based our research study on the framework proposed in [36] and results of previous works [11, 38, 45]. Design of VRLE should combine three sources of knowledge: technology, pedagogy and content beginning with pedagogical affordances to maximize learning outcomes [20]. Existing research works exploiting pedagogical scenario model do not always allow teachers to adapt the learning situation to the learner's course. Our findings from these works show that the learning scenario design is tackled with virtual agents embedded in the environment. Most models proposed are specific to a particular domain and technical environment. The scenario model must be planned from the early times of design of the environment where all the possible situations must have been considered.

The aim of the research presented in this paper has been to propose a learning environment exploiting virtual reality and scenario-based models that could be adapted by teachers to learning situations in the context of learners with cognitive disabilities. This research work identifies some limitations with existing solutions and studies the design and operationalization of learning situations in the form of scenario models. It takes place in the context of LUSI class and involves a specific learning situation of acquisition of orientation skills. We propose a solution based on virtual reality technology to enhance traditional learning and provide trainers with an educational toolkit, thus allowing them to recreate virtual reality scenarios and assess the learners' progress for learning orientation skills.

We have developed our own environment rather than reusing existing solutions because they do not allow us to deploy our learning scenario oriented LUSI class. The solution produced is authentic but in a simplified reality that can be complicated according to the learner's learning profile and promotes repetition which is an important learning spring for this learner audience. The pilot study based on qualitative evaluation validated the feasibility and usability of the pedagogical approach implemented in the virtual environment. The main improvements relate to the teacher part, to permit the adaptation of learning scenario to the learners and enable their monitoring. We aim to develop an editor that will facilitate the simple conception or parameterization of scenarios in different environments (simple labyrinths or 3D cities) and the monitoring of different paths by teachers and in a reflexive way by the learners (applicable to several environments, regardless of the field or type of simulation to play).

Future experiments should evaluate interfaces and usability on the part of the teacher and the effectiveness of pedagogical approach. We will also need to address the follow-up of learners and the adaptation of scenarios by teachers according to profiles and learning situations.

Acknowledgements. This work was funded by Agglomeration-Laval (France). We want to thank all partners of this project. We would also like to thank especially the learners and teachers for their full support and key contributions: the Laval Robert Buron high school, France.

References

1. ARVAD: Project Web site (2017). http://perso.univ-lemans.fr/~loubah/ARVAD/
2. ASH02: Troubles des fonctions cognitives – pistes pédagogiques. Enseigner - Aux élèves en situation de handicap - En unité d'enseignement (2011). http://ash.ia02.ac-amiens.fr/IMG/article_PDF/Troubles-des-fonctions-cognitives-pistes-pdagogiques_a220.pdf
3. Barot, C., Lourdeaux, D., Burkhardt, J.-M., Amokrane, K., Lenne, D.: V3S: a virtual environment for risk-management training based on human-activity models. Presence Teleoper. Virtual Environ. **22**(1), 1–19 (2013)
4. Barot, C., Lourdeaux, D., Lenne, D.: Using planning to predict and influence autonomous agents behaviour in a virtual environment for training. In: 2013 12th IEEE International Conference on Cognitive Informatics & Cognitive Computing (ICCI*CC), pp. 274–281 (2013)
5. Bennett, S., Agostinho, S., Lockyer, L.: The process of designing for learning: understanding university teachers design work. Educ. Res. Dev. **65**(1), 125–145 (2017)
6. Bossard, C., Kermarrec, G., Buche, C., Tisseau, J.: Transfer of learning in virtual environments: a new challenge? Virtual Real. **12**(3), 151–161 (2008)
7. Botella, C., Banos, R., Villa, H., Perpina, C., Garciapalacios, A.: Virtual reality in the treatment of claustrophobic fear: a controlled, multiple-baseline design. Behav. Ther. **31**, 583–595 (2000)
8. Broomfield, J., Dodd, B.: Children with speech and language disability: caseload characteristics. Int. J. Lang. Commun. Disord. **39**, 303–324 (2004)

9. Campos, E., Granados, A., Jiménez, S., Garrido, J.: Tutor Informatico: increasing the selfteaching in down syndrome people. In: Miesenberger, K., Klaus, J., Zagler, Wolfgang L., Burger, D. (eds.) ICCHP 2004. LNCS, vol. 3118, pp. 202–205. Springer, Heidelberg (2004). https://doi.org/10.1007/978-3-540-27817-7_30
10. Carpentier, K., Lourdeaux, D.: Generation of learning situations according to the learner's profile within a virtual environment. In: Filipe, J., Fred, A. (eds.) ICAART 2013. CCIS, vol. 449, pp. 245–260. Springer, Heidelberg (2014). https://doi.org/10.1007/978-3-662-44440-5_15
11. Chaabouni, M., Piau-Toffolon, C., Laroussi, M., Choquet, C.: Indexing learning scenarios by the most adapted contexts: an approach based on the observation of scenario progress in session. In: The 15th IEEE International Conference on Advanced Learning Technologies – ICALT 2015, 6–9 July 2015, Hualien (Taiwan), pp. 39–43 (2015)
12. Chen, C.J.: The design, development and evaluation of a virtual reality based learning environment. Australas. J. Educ. Technol. **22**(1), 39–63 (2006)
13. Chen, C.J., Teh, C.S.: Enhancing an instructional design model for virtual reality based learning. Australas. J. Educ. Technol. **29**, 699–716 (2013)
14. Conde, A., et al.: LAGUNTXO: a rule-based intelligent tutoring system oriented to people with intellectual disabilities. In: Lytras, M.D., et al. (eds.) WSKS 2009. LNCS (LNAI), vol. 5736, pp. 186–195. Springer, Heidelberg (2009). https://doi.org/10.1007/978-3-642-04754-1_20
15. De Gasparo, S., Van Belleghel, L.: L'ergonomie face aux nouveaux troubles du travail: le retour du sujet dans l'intervention, in Hubault (coord.). Actes du séminaire de Paris 1 du 11, 12 et 13 juin 2012. Persistances et évolutions: les nouveaux contours de l'ergonomie. Toulouse, Octarès (2012)
16. Diamond, A., Goldman-Rakic, P.S.: Comparison of human infants and rhesus monkeys on Piagets AB task: evidence for dependence on dorsolateral prefrontal cortex. Exp. Brain Res. **74**(1989), 24–40 (1989)
17. Dillon, A., Morris, M.: User acceptance of information technology: theories and models. Ann. Rev. Inf. Sci. Technol. **1996**, 3–32 (1996)
18. Fahim, M., Jakimi, A., El Bermi, L.: Pedagogical scenarization for virtual environments for training: towards genericity, coherence and adaptivity. IJAERS **3**(12), 96–103 (2016)
19. Feng, Z., Duh, H.B.L., Billinghurst, M.: Trends in augmented reality tracking, interaction and display: a review of ten years of ISMAR. In: the 7th IEEE/ACM International symposium on mixed and augmented reality (ISMAR), Cambridge, UK (2008). https://doi.org/10.1109/ismar.2008.4637362
20. Fowler, C.: Virtual reality and learning: where is the pedagogy? Br. J. Edu. Technol. **46**(2), 2015 (2015)
21. Goodyear, P.: Teaching as design. HERDSA Rev. High. Educ. **2**, 27–50 (2015)
22. Gutiérrez, J.M., Domínguez, M.G., González, C.R.: Using 3D virtual technologies to train spatial skills in engineering. Int. J. Eng. Educ. **31**(1), 323–334 (2015)
23. Huang, H.M., Rauch, U., Liaw, S.S.: Investigating learners 'attitudes toward virtual reality learning environments: based on a constructivist approach. Comput. Educ. **55**(2010), 1171–1182 (2010)
24. Kaufmann, H., Steinbugl, K., Dunser, A., Gluck, J.: General training of spatial abilities by geometry education in augmented reality. Cyberpsychol. Behav. **8**(4), 330 (2005)
25. Lahav, O., Mioduser, D.: Multisensory virtual environment for supporting blind persons' acquisition of spatial cognitive mapping, orientation, and mobility skills. In: Proceedings of the 4th Conference on Disability, Virtual Reality and Associated Technologies, Veszprém, Hungary, pp. 213–220 (2002)

26. Lourdeaux, D., Fuchs, P., Burkhardt, J.-M., Bernard, F.: Relevance of an intelligent tutorial agent for virtual reality training systems. Int. J. Contin. Eng. Life-Long Learn. **12**, 214–230 (2002)
27. Manly, T., Anderson, V., Nimmo-Smith, I.: The differential assessment of children attention: The Test of Everyday Attention for Children (TEA-Ch), normative sample and ADHD performance. J. Child Psychol. Psychiatry **42**, 1065–1081 (2001)
28. Marion, N., Querrec, R., Chevaillier, P.: Integrating knowledge from virtual reality environments to learning scenario models-a meta-modeling approach. In: INSTICC International Conference of Computer Supported Education, pp. 254–259 (2009)
29. Martín-Gutiérrez, J., Mora, C.E., Añorbe-Díaz, B., González-Marrero, A.: Virtual technologies trends in education. Eurasia J. Math. Sci. Technol. Educ. **13**(2), 469–486 (2017). https://doi.org/10.12973/eurasia.2017.00626a
30. Martinez-Ortiz, I., Moreno-Ger, P., Sierra-Rodríguez, J.-L., Fernández-Manjón, B.: Supporting the authoring and operationalization of educational modelling languages. J. Univ. Comput. Sci. **13**(7), 938–947 (2007)
31. Mikropoulos, T.A., Bellou, J.: The unique features of educational virtual environments. In: Isaias, P., McPherson, M., Banister, F. (eds.) Proceedings E-Society 2006, International Association for Development of the Information Society, vol. 1, pp. 122–128. IADIS (2006)
32. Mikropoulos, T., Chalkidis, A., Katskikis, A., Emvalotis, A.: Students' attitudes towards educational virtual environments. Educ. Inf. Technol. **3**(2), 137–148 (1998)
33. Mikropoulos, T.A., Natsis, A.: Educational virtual environments: a ten-year review of empirical research (1999–2009). Comput. Educ. **56**(3), 769–780 (2011)
34. Mishra, P., Koehler, M.J.: Technological pedagogical content knowledge: a framework for teacher knowledge. Teach. Coll. Rec. **108**(6), 1017–1054 (2006)
35. Mody, M., Studdert-Kennedy, M., Brady, S.: Speech perception deficits in poor readers: auditory processing or phonological coding? J. Exp. Child Psychol. **64**, 199–231 (1997)
36. Mor, Y.: Embedding design patterns in a methodology for a design science of e-learning. In: Kohls, C., Wedekind, J. (eds.) Problems Investigations of E-Learning Patterns: Context Factors Solutions (2010)
37. Nielsen, J.: Usability Engineering. The Book. Academic Press, Boston (1993)
38. Oubahssi, L., Piau-Toffolon, C., Clayer, J.P., Kammoun, F.: Design and operationalization of patterns: case of a training situation of personal assistance for public in professional integration. In: International Conference on Software Technologies, ICSOFT 2013, 29–31 July 2013, Reykjavik (iceland), pp. 488–495, July 2013
39. Oubahssi L., Piau-Toffolon C.: Virtual learning environment design in the context of orientation skills acquisition for LUSI class. In: The 10th International Conference on Computer Supported Education, Madeira, Portugal, pp. 47–58, March 2018
40. Parfitt, L., Jo, J., Nguyen, A.: Multimedia in distance learning for tertiary students with special needs. ASCILITE, Australas. Soc. Comput. Learn. Tary Educ. **1998**, 561–569 (1998)
41. Prensky, M.: Digital natives, digital immigrants. Horizon **9**(5), 1–6 (2001). https://doi.org/10.1108/10748120110424816
42. Sehaba, K., Estraillier, P., Lambert, D.: Interactive educational games for autistic children with agent-based System. In: Kishino, F., Kitamura, Y., Kato, H., Nagata, N. (eds.) ICEC 2005. LNCS, vol. 3711, pp. 422–432. Springer, Heidelberg (2005). https://doi.org/10.1007/11558651_41
43. Sehaba, K., Hussaan, A.M.: Adaptive serious game for the re-education of cognitive disorders. AMSE J. Adv. Model. Ser. Model. C (Spec. Issue Handicap) **73**(3), 148–159 (2013)

44. Shrader, G., Williams, K., Lachance-Whitcomb, J., Finn, L.E., Gomez, L.: Participatory design of science curricula: the case for research for practice. Paper Presented at the Annual Meeting of the American Educational Research Association, Seattle, WA (2001). http://www.letus.org/PDF/ShradervaeraSpencer.pdf. Accessed 11 May 2018
45. Tadjine, Z., Oubahssi, L., Piau-Toffolon, C., Iksal, S.: A process using ontology to automate the operationalization of pattern-based learning scenarios. In: Zvacek, S., Restivo, M.T., Uhomoibhi, J., Helfert, M. (eds.) CSEDU 2015. CCIS, vol. 583, pp. 444–461. Springer, Cham (2016). https://doi.org/10.1007/978-3-319-29585-5_26
46. Trinh, T.-H., Querrec, R., Loor, P.-D., Chevaillier, P.: Ensuring semantic spatial constraints in virtual environments using UML/OCL. In: VRST 2010 Proceedings of the ACM symposium on Virtual reality software and Technology, United States, pp. 219–226 (2010)

A Layered Approach to Automatic Essay Evaluation Using Word-Embedding

Tsegaye Misikir Tashu(✉) and Tomáš Horváth

Faculty of Informatics, Department of Data Science and Engineering (Telekom Innovation Laboratories), ELTE – Eötvös Loránd University, Pázmány Péter Sétány 1/C, Budapest 1117, Hungary
{misikir,tomas.horvath}@inf.elte.hu
http://t-labs.elte.hu/

Abstract. Automated Essay Evaluation (AEE) use a set of features to evaluate and score students essay solutions. Most of the features like lexical similarity, syntax, vocabulary and shallow content were addressed but evaluating students essays using the semantics and context of the essay are not addressed well. To address the issue which are related to the semantics and context, we propose a layered approach to AEE which uses neural word embedding in order to evaluate student answers semantically and the similarity will be computed by using Word Mover's Distance. We also implemented a plagiarism detection algorithms to protect the students from submitting someone else solution as their own using k-shingles and local sensitive hashing. We also implemented an algorithm that penalize students who are trying to fool the system by submitting only content bearing works. The performance of the proposed AEE was evaluated and compared to other state-of-the-art methods qualitatively and quantitatively. The experimental results show that the proposed AEE approach using neural word embedding achieve higher level of accuracy as compared to others baselines and are promising in evaluating students essay solutions semantically.

Keywords: Automatic essay scoring · Automatic essay evaluation · Word mover's distance · Semantic analysis · Neural word embedding

1 Introduction

Automatic essay evaluation, also called Automated Essay Scoring, plays an important role in the educational process and scoring subjective type of questions is one of the most expensive and time-consuming activity for educational assessments. As a consequence, the interest and the development of automated assessment systems are growing.

Tomáš Horváth is also associated with the Institute of Computer Science of the Faculty of Science at the Pavol Jozef Šafárik University in Košice, Slovakia.

B. M. McLaren et al. (Eds.): CSEDU 2018, CCIS 1022, pp. 77–94, 2019.
https://doi.org/10.1007/978-3-030-21151-6_5

Automated Essay Evaluation (AEE) can be seen as a prediction problem, which automatically evaluates and scores essay solutions provided by students by comparing them with the reference solution via computer programs [1]. For academic institutions, AEE represents not only a tool to assess learning outcomes, but also helps to save time, effort and money without lowering the quality of teacher's feedback on student solutions.

The area has been developing since the 1960s when Page and his colleagues [2] introduced the first AEE system. Various kinds of algorithms, methods, and techniques have been proposed to implement AEE solutions, however, most of the existing AEE approaches consider text semantics very vaguely and focus mostly on its syntax.

We can assume that most of the existing AEE approaches give much more focus on syntax, vocabulary and shallow content measurements and only limited concerns for the semantics. This assumption follows from the fact that the details of most of the known systems have not been released publicly. To semantically analyze and evaluate documents in these systems, Latent Semantic Analysis (LSA) [3], Latent Dirichlet Allocation (LDA) [4], Content Vector Analysis (CVA) [5] and Neural Word Embedding (NWE) [6,7] are mostly used.

NWE [6,8] is similar to other text semantic similarity analysis methods such that LSA or LDA. The main difference is that LSA and LDA utilize co-occurrences of words while NWE learns to predict context. Moreover, training of semantic vectors is resulted from neural networks. NWE models have increased acceptance in recent years because of their high performance in natural language processing (NLP) tasks [9].

In this work, the Relaxed Word Mover's Distance (WMD) is used which uses NWE, vector representations of terms, their embedding is computed from unlabeled data that represent terms in a semantic space in which proximity of vectors can be interpreted as semantic similarity [6,7]. The proposed layered pair-wise method computes the semantic similarity between individual word vector values of the reference solution and a student answer. To the best of authors' knowledge, this work is the first effort in utilizing WMD for AEE.

The main objective behind our proposed layered pair-wise AEE using the NWE approach is not to exactly reproduce the human grader's scores, which are varying in their evaluation but to provide acceptable and reliable scores and also to provide immediate and helpful feedback to the students and also to show that essay can be evaluated using semantic features as well. The proposed AEE approach is compared with approaches using LSA, Wordnet and cosine similarity.

The performance of the algorithm was evaluated both qualitatively and quantitatively. A qualitative evaluation measure based on pairwise ranking, called *prank*, for assessing the performance of various models w.r.t. the human scoring is also used in this paper [10] and for quantitative evaluation the normalized root mean squared error ($nRMSE$) between human's and machine's scores was used.

The experiments was conducted on real-world datasets, provided by the Hewlett Foundation for a Kaggle challenge, showed the proposed layered pair-wise AEE using NWE approach is promising such that, in general, it achieved higher performance than the used baseline for AEE approaches according to both quantitative ($nRMSE$) and the qualitative ($prank$) performance evaluation metrics.

The rest of this paper is organized as follows: Sect. 2 reviews existing AEE approaches. In Sect. 3, the proposed Layered Pair-Wise AEE approach is introduced. Experiments and results are described in Sect. 4. Section 5 concludes the paper and discusses prospective plans for future work.

2 Related Work

The research on automatically evaluating and scoring essay question answers is ongoing for more than a decade where Machine Learning (ML), NLP and artificial neural network (NN) techniques were used for evaluating essay question answers.

Project Essay Grade (PEG) was the first AEE system developed by Page and his colleagues [2]. Earlier versions of this system used 30 computer quantifiable predictive features to approximate the intrinsic features valued by human markers. Most of these features were surface variables such as the number of paragraphs, average sentence length, length of the essay in words, and counts of other textual units. PEG has been reported as being able to provide scores for separate dimensions of writing such as content, organization, style, mechanics (i.e., mechanical accuracy, such as spelling, punctuation and capitalization) and creativity, as well as providing an overall score [11–13]. However, the exact set of textual features underlying each dimension and the details concerning the derivation of the overall score were not disclosed [11,14].

E-Rater [15], the basic technique of which is identical to PEG, uses statistical and NLP techniques. E- Rater utilizes a vector-space model to measure semantic content. It examines the structure of the essay by using transitional phrases, paragraph changes, etc., and examines it's content by comparing it's score to other essays. However, if there is an essay with an unfamiliar argument style, E-rater will not notice it.

[16] used natural language processing techniques to develop a system capable of automatically assessing short-answers based on the linguistic features of student response. The system reduces the supplied answer as well as the student response to their canonical form through a comprehensive text pre-processing phase. All words in the canonical form are tagged based on their part of speech. The student response and the supplied answer are then compared. In this comparison, features encapsulated within Word Net are utilized to ensure that exact word matches are not necessary for determining the level of equivalence between the student response and the supplied answer.

Intelligent Essay Assessor (IEA), based on LSA, is an essay grading technique developed in the late 1990s that evaluates essays by measuring semantic features

[17]. IEA is trained on a domain-specific set of essays that have been previously scored by expert human raters. IEA evaluates each ungraded essay by comparing through LSA, i.e. how similar the new essay is to those it has been trained on. By using LSA, IEA is able to consider semantic features by representing essays as multidimensional vectors.

As the existing AES techniques which are using LSA do not consider the word sequence of sentences in the documents and the creation of word by document matrix is somewhat arbitrary, [18] proposed an automated essay scoring system using generalized latent semantic analysis (GLSA) which address word sequence of sentences in a sentence problem of latent semantic analysis. The proposed AES system grades essays with more accuracy than the previous LSA based AES. In order to reduce memory and time consumption without lowering the performance of automated scoring in comparison with human scoring, [13] proposed incremental singular value decomposition as a part of incremental LSA to score essays when the dataset is massive.

IntelliMetric [19], uses a blend of Artificial Intelligence (AI), NLP and statistical techniques. IntelliMetric needs to be trained with a set of essays that have been scored before by human expert raters. To analyze essays, the system first internalizes the known scores in a set of training essays. Then, it tests the scoring model against a smaller set of essays with known scores for validation purposes. Finally, once the model scores the essays as desired, it is applied to new essays with unknown scores.

Three deep semantic features based on the continuous bag-of-words (CBOW) and recursive auto-encoder models were proposed in [20]. They used support vector machine for ranking to learn a rating model and test the performance of the three new features. The experiment carried out on publicly available English essay data showed that their proposed features are beneficial to automated essay scoring using semantic features.

A deep NN capable of representing both local contextual and usage information as encapsulated by essay scoring was introduced in [21]. This model yields score specific word embedding used by a recurrent NN in order to form essay representations. They have shown that this kind of architecture is able to surpass similar state-of-the-art systems, as well as systems based on manual feature engineering which have achieved results close to the upper bound in past works. They introduced a novel way of exploring the basis of the network's internal scoring criteria and showed that such models are interpretable and can be further exploited to provide useful feedback to the author.

Authors of [22] have also proposed AES that accepts an essay text as input directly and learns the features automatically from the data. For this purpose, they developed a method based on recurrent NN to score the essays in an end-to-end manner based on long short-term memory NN which is trained as a regression method.

An investigation on the effectiveness of using semantic vector representations for the task of automated essay scoring (AES) was performed in [23]. According to the evaluation results on the standard English dataset, the effectiveness brought by the proposed semantic representations of essays depends on the learning algorithms and the evaluation metrics used. On the other hand, the effectiveness of individual semantic features is stable with respect to different numbers of dimensions.

In [24], an ontology-based tool for automatic evaluation for free-text short responses submitted by users in learning management systems (LMS) based discussion forums or community-based question answer forums was proposed. Their architecture is based on simple NLP techniques, WordNet and hand-coded logic to make sense of user questions and submitted responses using the semantic web ontology language (OWL). The experimental results show that their approach, which is tested on computer science subject operating systems, can be effectively used to evaluate the response by providing a score that a learner uses to satisfy the learner's objective.

In [25], an automatic essay scoring system based on n-gram and cosine similarity was described. N-gram was used for feature extraction and modified to split by word instead of by letter so that the word order would be considered. Based on evaluation results, this system got the best correlation of 0.66 by using unigram on questions that do not consider the order of words in the answer. For questions that consider the order of the words in the answer, bi-gram has the best correlation value by 0.67.

An extension of existing AEE systems was introduced in [26] by incorporating additional semantic coherence and consistency attributes. They design coherence attributes by transforming sequential parts of an essay into the semantic space and measuring changes between them to estimate coherence of the text and consistency attributes that detect semantic errors using information extraction and logic reasoning. The resulting system (named "sage-semantic automated grader for essays") provides semantic feedback for the writer and achieves significantly higher grading accuracy compared with nine other state-of-the-art AEE systems.

An architecture of automated essay scoring system based on a rubric, which combines automated scoring with human scoring, was proposed in [27]. The proposed rubric has five evaluation viewpoints contents, structure, evidence, style, and skill and 25 evaluation items which are subdivided viewpoint. At first, the system automatically scores 11 items included in the style and skill such as sentence style, syntax, usage, readability, lexical richness, and so on. Then it predicts scores of style and skill from these items' scores by multiple regression models. It also predicts contents' score by the cosine similarity between topics and descriptions

AEE systems that use LSA ignore the order of words or arrangement of sentences in its analysis of the meaning of a text because LSA does not have such a feature. A text document in LSA is simply treated as a "bag of words" – an unordered collection of words. As such, the meaning of a text as derived by LSA is not the same as that which could be understood by human beings from grammatical, syntactic relations, logic, or morphological analysis. The second problem is that LSA does not deal with polysemy. This is because each word is represented in the semantic space as a single point and its meaning is the average of all its different meanings in the corpus [28]. In this paper, we used the "skip-gram" model of word2vec [6] to obtain word embedding that learns to predict the context and to train the semantic vectors that is resulted from neural networks to address the issue of word polysemy [6,7].

3 The Layered Pair-Wise AEE Approach

The most common way of computing a similarity between two textual documents is to have the centroids of their word embedding and evaluate an inner product between these two centroids [6,7]. However, taking simple centroids of two documents is not a good approximation for calculating a distance between these two documents [7]. In this paper, the similarity between individual words in a pair of documents, i.e. the student's answer and the reference (a good) solution, is measured as opposed to the average similarity between the student's answer and the reference solution. Therefore, the Word Mover's Distance (WMD), calculating the minimum cumulative distance that words from a reference solution need to travel to match words from a student answer, is used in this paper.

3.1 Word Mover's Distance

First, it is assumed that text documents are represented by normalized bag-of-words (nBOW) vectors, i.e. if a word w_i appears f_i times in a document, its weight is calculated and defined as in [10]

$$d_i = \frac{f_i}{\sum_{j=1}^{n} f_j} \tag{1}$$

where n is the number of unique words in the document. The higher it's weight, the more important the word is. Combined with a measure of word importance, the goal is to incorporate semantic similarity between pairs of individual words into the document distance metric. For this purpose, their Euclidean distance over the word2vec embedding space was used [6,7]. The dissimilarity between word w_i and word w_j can be computed and defined as in [10]

$$c(w_i, w_j) = \|x_i - x_j\|^2 \tag{2}$$

where x_i and x_j are the embedding's of the words w_i and w_j, respectively.

Let $\mathbf{D}$ and $\mathbf{D'}$ be nBOW representations of two documents D and D', respectively. Let $T \in \mathbb{R}^{n \times n}$ be a flow matrix, where $T_{ij} \geq 0$ denotes how much the word w_i in D has to "travel" to reach the word w_j in D', and n is the number of unique words appearing in D and D'. To transform $\mathbf{D}$ to $\mathbf{D'}$ entirely, we ensure that the complete flow from the word w_i equals d_i and the incoming flow to the word w_j equals d'_j. The WMD is defined as the minimum cumulative cost needed to move all words from D to D' as [10], i.e.

$$\min_{T \geq 0} \sum_{i,j=1}^{n} T_{ij}\, c(w_i, w_j) \tag{3}$$

subject to

$$\sum_{j=1}^{n} T_{ij} = d_i, \forall i \in \{1, \ldots, n\}, \sum_{i=1}^{n} T_{ij} = d'_j, \forall j \in \{1, \ldots, n\}$$

The solution is achieved by finding T_{ij} that minimizes the expression in Eq. 1. In [7], this was applied to obtain nearest neighbors for document classification, i.e. k-NN classification which produced outstanding performance among other state-of-the-art approaches. Therefore, WMD is a good choice for semantically evaluating a similarity between documents. The features of WMD can be used to semantically score a pair of texts such that, for example, student's answers and reference solutions.

In this regard, in order to compute the semantic similarity between the student's answer, denoted here by Sa, and the reference solution, denoted here by Rs, Sa is mapped to Rs using a word embedding model. Let **Sa** and **Rs** be nBOW representations of Sa and Rs, respectively. The word embedding model is trained on a set of documents. Since the goal is to measure a similarity between **Sa** and **Rs**, $c(w_i, w_j)$ is redefined as a cosine similarity as in [10], i.e.

$$c(w_i, w_j) = \frac{x_i\, x_j}{\|x_i\| \|x_j\|} \tag{4}$$

A much tighter bound results can be obtained by relaxing the WMD optimization problem and removing one of the two constraints and, since similarity is used in the Eq. 4 instead of distance (Eq. 2), Eq. 3 is also modified to

$$\max_{T \geq 0} \sum_{i,j=1}^{n} T_{ij}\, c(w_i, w_j) \tag{5}$$

subject to

$$\sum_{j=1}^{n} T_{ij} = d_i, \forall i \in \{1, \ldots, n\}$$

according to the previous case.

3.2 A Layer Based Pair-Wise AEE Architecture

On Layer One, the candidate answer and the student answer are provided to the algorithm as an essay input. These inputs will be sent to Layer Two for text preprocessing and the following activities will be carried out: Tokenization; Removing punctuation marks, determiners, and prepositions; Transformation to lower-case; Stopword removal [29] and word stemming [30]. In Layer Three, shingle based plagiarism (see Sect. 3.3) and foolish detection tasks (see Sect. 3.4) are carried out. Those essays which passed certain threshold of Layer Three are sent to Layer Four for scoring and those who failed to pass are discarded. Layer Four is where the actually Semantic similarity between the candidate answer and student solution is computed using NWE (see Sect. 3.1) and the result is forwarded to Layer Five for storage (Fig. 1).

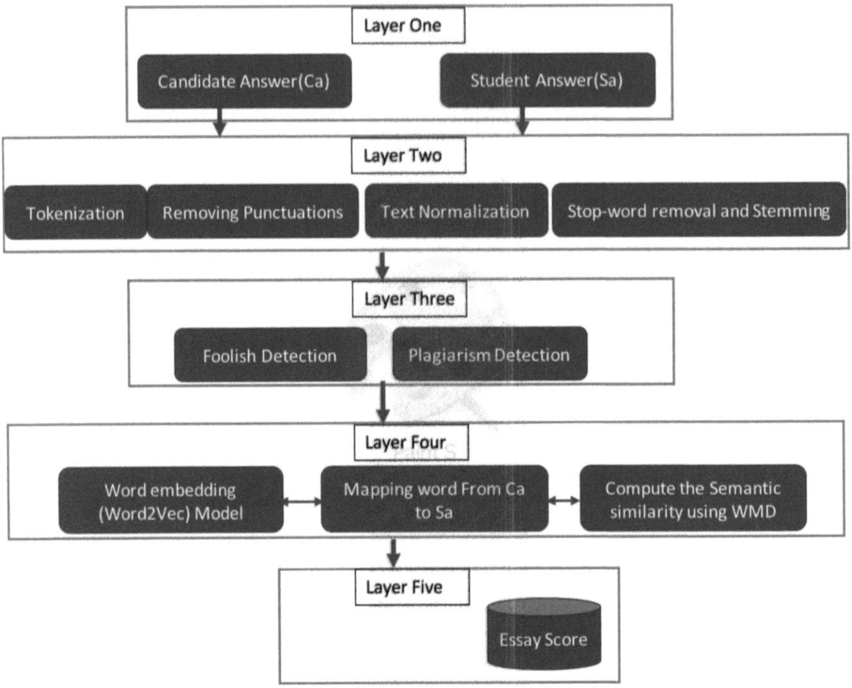

Fig. 1. The architecture of the proposed layered based Pair-Wise AEE approach.

For word embedding model, the freely available word2vec word embedding which has an embedding for 3 million words/phrases from Google News, trained using the approach in [6], was used in the implementation of the Layer based Pair-Wise AEE approach.

3.3 Plagiarism Detection Using Shingles

Plagiarism is one of the growing issues in academic and research field, raising more concerns in university systems. During submitting solutions to essay exams using on-line systems, students may commit plagiarism by copying and pasting solutions from other students. It has become a very common issue when evaluating the students work and their creativeness.

In order to address this issue, we propose a plagiarism detection approach that identifies duplicates within the submitted solutions by comparing each student's solution with others student's solution for the specific essays based on the k-shingles [31] approach. The most effective way to represent a document, for the purpose of identifying lexically similar documents, is to construct from the document a set of short strings that appear within it using shingles [31]. If we do so, then documents that share pieces as short as sentences or even phrases will have many common elements in their sets, even if those sentences appear in different orders in the two documents. By defining a k-shingle for a document to be any substring of length k found within the document, we can associate with each document the set of k-shingles that appear one or more times within that document.

As the objective is to identify lexical similarity, we keep punctuation and whitespace in the process. This way of document representation keeps word order and allows comparing documents based on the sets of character shingles. The similarity of two documents can be defined as the Jaccard similarity of the two sets of shingles: the number of elements (shingles) they have in common as a proportion of the combined size of the two sets, or the size of the intersection divided by the size of the union. The Jaccard similarity between two sets X and Y is defined as

$$S_j(X,Y) = \frac{|X \cap Y|}{|X \cup Y|} \tag{6}$$

3.4 Foolish Detection

Another issue in AEE is that it might be easily tricked or fooled by the students. One of the fooling methods that students could use for getting higher scores is just to list high profile words related to the topic and submit those words as a solution to the essay. In order to penalize such attempts of the students we implemented a simple foolish detection algorithm in two ways.

The first method is done by computing similarity between the student's solution with text preprocessing and without text preprocessing. If the student answer contains only high profiled words then the similarity between the two pairs will be almost the same. Therefore, the student is trying to fool the system and the system automatically discards the student's solutions.

The second method works as follows: The algorithm first generates content bearing words or high-profile words from the candidate answer using inverse document frequency (IDF). Then similarity is computed between the submitted students answer without any text preprocessing and content bearing words. If the similarity between the two is greater than or equal to some threshold level then the student is trying to fool the system and the system also automatically discards the student's solutions.

4 Experiment

The experiment was carried out on datasets provided by the Hewlett Foundation at a Kaggle[1] competition for an AEE. There are ten datasets containing student essays from grade ten students. All the datasets were rated by two human raters. The features of the datasets are shown in Table 1.

[1] https://www.kaggle.com/c/asap-sas.

Five datasets, numbered 1, 2, 5, 9 and 10 in this paper, are provided with the correct, reference solution to which student answers are compared to. In case of the other five datasets (no. 3, 4, 6, 7 and 8) the reference solution was created according to the score given by human raters, i.e. ten students' answers which got full score were randomly selected as reference solutions.

Python was used to implement the algorithms discussed. As the Pair-Wise approach is dependent on a word embedding, we used the freely-available Google News word2vec[2] model. Additionally, Scikit-learn[3] and Numpy[4] Python libraries were also used.

The performance of the proposed Pair-Wise approach is compared to that of other three approaches utilizing LSA [3,32], Wordnet [33–35] and cosine similarity [36,37].

Table 1. Essay sets used in the experiment and their main characteristics [10].

Essay set	Grade level	Domain	Score range	Average length in words	Training set size	Test set size	Total size
1	10	Science	0–3	50	1672	558	2230
2	10	Science	0–3	50	1278	426	1704
3	10	English, arts	0–2	50	1891	631	2522
4	10	English, arts	0–2	50	1738	580	2318
5	10	Biology	0–3	60	1795	599	2394
6	10	Biology	0–3	50	1797	599	2396
7	10	English	0–2	60	1799	601	2400
8	10	English	0–2	60	1799	601	2400
9	10	Science	0–2	60	1798	600	2398
10	8	Science	0–2	60	1799	599	2398

4.1 Quantitative Evaluation

The machine score of each essay was compared with the human score to test the reliability of the proposed Layer based Pair-Wise approach. Normalized root mean squared error ($nRMSE$) was used to evaluate the agreement between the score given by the Pair-Wise approach as well as baseline AEE algorithms and

[2] https://code.google.com/archive/p/word2vec/.
[3] http://scikit-learn.org/.
[4] http://www.numpy.org/.

the actual human scores. The essay scores provided by human raters were normalized to be within [0, 1]. $nRMSE$ is widely accepted as a reasonable evaluation measure for AEE systems [38] and is defined as in [10]

$$nRMSE(ES) = \left(\frac{\sum_{Sa \in ES} (r(Sa) - h(Sa))^2}{|ES|} \right)^{\frac{1}{2}} \tag{7}$$

where ES is the Essay Set used, $r(Sa)$ and $h(Sa)$ are the predicted rating for Sa by the used AEE approach and the human rating of Sa, respectively. Rating here means how the student answer is similar to the reference solution. The lower the $nRMSE$ the better the performance of the measured approach is.

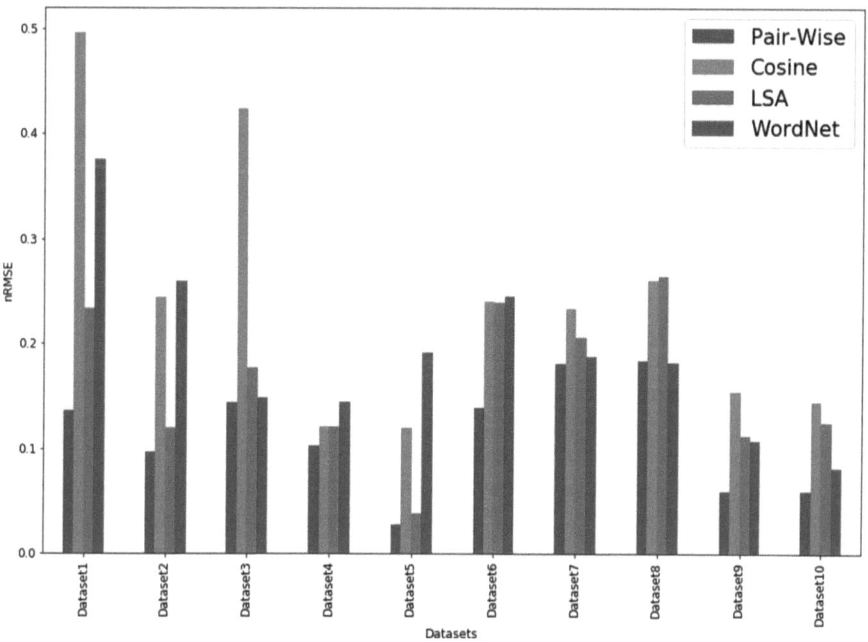

Fig. 2. A quantitative comparison using $nRMSE$ (Eq. 7) of the proposed Pair-Wise AEE and the baselines using LSA, WordNet and cosine similarity. In case of the datasets no. 3, 4, 6, 7 and 8, the average performance from 10 runs (corresponding to the 10 randomly chosen reference solutions) is reported while in case of the other five datasets (where only the one reference solution indicated in the data is used), the result from one run is reported [10].

Figure 2 shows the $nRMSE$ between the human score and the tested AEE systems for the datasets used in the experiment. Except the Dataset8, where Pair-Wise was performing slightly worse than the winner Wordnet baseline, Pair-Wise was outperforming the baseline approaches.

Table 2. The p-values resulting from the Wilcoxon signed-rank test between the *nRMSE* results of the proposed AEE and the baselines using LSA, WordNet and cosine similarity [10].

Datasets	Pair-Wise vs.			LSA vs.		Cosine vs. WordNet
	LSA	WordNet	Cosine	WordNet	Cosine	
Dataset3	0.005	0.005	0.005	0.005	0.005	0.007
Dataset4	0.005	0.005	0.005	0.005	0.005	0.005
Dataset6	0.005	0.005	0.005	0.005	0.005	0.005
Dataset7	0.005	0.005	0.005	0.005	0.005	0.005
Dataset8	0.005	0.005	0.005	0.005	0.005	0.074

In case of the datasets 3, 4, 6, 7 and 8, the average values of $nRMSE$ from the ten runs corresponding to ten randomly chosen reference solutions are indicated in the Fig. 2. To test if the differences between the tested AEE approaches indicated in the Fig. 2, in case of these 5 datasets, are statistically significant, the non-parametric Wilcoxon signed-rank test was used. The resulting p-values from these tests are reported in the Table 2 showing that the differences between Pair-Wise and the baselines as well as between the baselines are statistically significant.

4.2 Qualitative Evaluation

$nRMSE$ measures the performance of the tested AEE approaches quantitatively, i.e. by how much the predicted score of an approach differs from the human ratings. Since the proposed and baseline approaches are based on different models, their results might be biased. Thus, a qualitative evaluation measure, named *prank*, referring to "pairwise ranking" is defined as in [10]

$$prank(ES) = \frac{1}{Z} \sum_{Sa_i \neq Sa_j \in ES} \delta(Sa_i, Sa_j) \tag{8}$$

where $Z = |ES|(|ES| - 1)/2$ is a normalization constant and $\delta(Sa_i, Sa_j) = 1$ if $\big(h(Sa_i) < h(Sa_j) \,\&\, r(Sa_i) < r(Sa_j)\big)$ or $\big(h(Sa_i) > h(Sa_j) \,\&\, r(Sa_i) > r(Sa_j)\big)$ while in cases where $h(Sa_i) = h(Sa_j)$, $\delta(Sa_i, Sa_j) = 1 - |r(Sa_i) - r(Sa_j)|$.

In other words, $\delta(Sa_i, Sa_j)$ results in it's maximal value 1 when the predicted ratings for two student answers Sa_i and Sa_j do not change the human "ranking" of Sa_i and Sa_j w.r.t. their similarities to the reference solution. If the human ranking can not be determined, i.e. the human rated the similarities of Sa_i and Sa_j to the reference solution equally, then the lower the difference between the predicted ratings the better.

As far as the knowledge of the authors goes, none of the state-of-the-art approaches have been evaluated in a qualitative way, only $nRMSE$ (or it's variants) was used in all the recent works found.

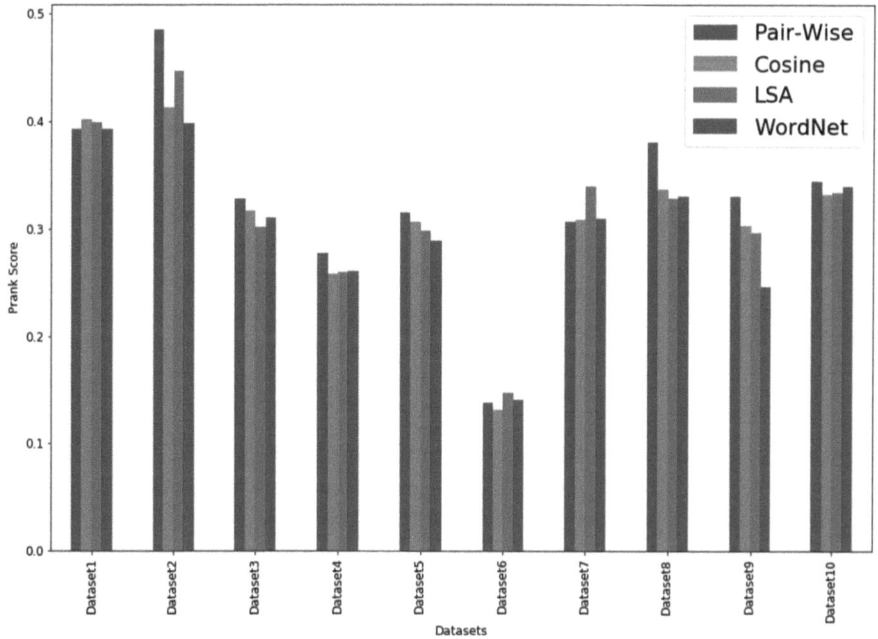

Fig. 3. A qualitative comparison using *prank* (Eq. 8) of the proposed Pair-Wise AEE and the baselines using LSA, WordNet and cosine similarity. In case of the datasets no. 3, 4, 6, 7 and 8, the average performance from 10 runs (corresponding to the 10 randomly chosen reference solutions) is reported while in case of the other five datasets (where only the one reference solution indicated in the data is used), the result from one run is reported [10].

Figure 3 shows the results when measuring the (average) performance of the discussed approaches qualitatively using the proposed *prank* measure. Pair-Wise outperforms the baselines in 7 from the 10 essay sets used for evaluation. In 2 cases, the *prank* score was very close to the winner approaches while only in one case the proposed approach was substantially outperformed by the LSA baseline.

In case of the datasets 3, 4, 6, 7 and 8, the average values of *prank* from the ten runs corresponding to ten randomly chosen reference solutions are indicated in the Fig. 3. To test if the differences between the tested AEE approaches indicated in the Fig. 3, in case of these 5 datasets, are statistically significant, the non-parametric Wilcoxon signed-rank test was used, as in the case of quantitative evaluation, above. The resulting p-values from these tests are reported in the Table 3 showing that the differences between Pair-Wise and the baselines are statistically significant.

4.3 Plagiarism Detection Evaluation

The dataset used for this task was provided by Clough [39] that was collected from students in Sheffield University studying for a degree in Computer

Table 3. The p-values resulting from the Wilcoxon signed-rank test between the *prank* results of the proposed AEE and the baselines using LSA, WordNet and cosine similarity [10].

Datasets	Pair-Wise vs.			LSA vs.		Cosine vs. WordNet
	LSA	WordNet	Cosine	WordNet	Cosine	
Dataset3	0.005	0.005	0.005	0.878	0.878	0.241
Dataset4	0.012	0.005	0.053	0.012	0.078	0.170
Dataset6	0.006	0.005	0.028	0.005	0.005	0.005
Dataset7	0.016	0.005	0.005	0.053	0.721	0.006
Dataset8	0.005	0.005	0.005	0.332	0.044	0.006

Science at either undergraduate or postgraduate level and the dataset is publicly available. The dataset contains 100 students answers from which 95 answers provided by the 19 participants and the five Wikipedia source articles for five learning tasks. For each learning task, there are 19 examples of each of the heavy revision, light revision and near copy levels and 38 non-plagiarized examples written independently from the Wikipedia source. The answer texts contain 19,559 words in total while the Wikipedia pages contain 14,242 words in total. The average length of files in the corpus is 208 words and 113 unique tokens. The metrics used to check the performance of shingle based plagiarism detection are Precision, Recall and Accuracy [40] defined in Eqs. 9, 10 and 11, respectively

$$Precision = \frac{TP}{TP + FP} \tag{9}$$

$$Recall = \frac{TP}{TP + FN} \tag{10}$$

$$Accuracy = \frac{TP + TN}{TP + TN + FP + FN} \tag{11}$$

where True Positives (TP) is the number of documents actually plagiarized and predicted as plagiarized, False Positives (FP) is the number of documents predicted as plagiarized but actually are non-plagiarized, True negatives (TN) is the number of documents actually non-plagiarized and predicted as non-plagiarized and False Negatives (FN) are the number of documents actually plagiarized but predicted as non-plagiarized.

The challenge faced in evaluation of "as plagiarized" or not is to set a minimum threshold level. We were unable to find any baseline used so far for this purpose and it's not actually easy to say that students' solution are plagiarized or not because sometimes students might use and read the same reference materials. With the assumption that the students might use the same reference material and as they are asked the same type of questions, there might be some level of similarity in their solutions. Therefore, we set the threshold value to 5%,

10%,15% and 20 % to get a clear separating line between actually plagiarized and predicted plagiarized documents.

Table 4. Shingle based Plagiarism detection results.

Metrics	5%	10%	15%	20%
Precision	0.62	0.78	1	1
Recall	1	0.96	0.94	0.77
Accuracy	0.62	0.82	0.96	0.86

The results of shingle based plagiarism detection is reported in Table 4 using four different threshold values (5%, 10%, 15% and 20%). The experiment showed that as the threshold value increases from 5% to 10% and from 10% to 15%, the overall accuracy is increasing. But when the threshold value increases from 15% to 20%, the overall accuracy starts to decrease. Therefore, we can deduce that the minimum threshold level that can be used to detect plagiarized student solutions can be 15% for this specific case. In other words, 15% of similarity between students solution can be tolerable and will not be considered as plagiarized.

5 Discussion and Conclusion

In this paper, a layer based automated essay evaluation (AEE) using neural word embedding has been proposed to address the issues related with semantics of essays. The layered pair-wise AEE not only evaluates students answers semantically, it also has a feature to automatically detect plagiarized solution and also have the capability to detect and penalize attempt of the students to fool the system. During evaluating essays, the system accepts two values, i.e. student answer and reference solution. Before computing the semantic similarity, the students answer should pass both the plagiarism and foolish detections. If the student answer fails to pass one of them, then the algorithm will discard that student's specific answer. The performance of the semantic scoring was evaluated both by a qualitative accuracy measure and a qualitative accuracy measures. The performance of plagiarism detection method was also evaluated using precision and recall measures.

From the experimental results we can deduce that the proposed layer based pair-wise AEE using neural word embedding approach can be used as a state-of-the-art in evaluating and scoring essay questions using semantic features and opens the opportunity in scoring essay exams using unsupervised machine learning algorithms. AEE systems with such features can be integrated with massive open on-line course (MOOC) systems to give automatic feedbacks to the students and as the level of awareness increases, the number of participants in using MOOC will also increase.

The plagiarism detection algorithm implemented here uses k-shingles and are only capable in identifying lexically similar documents. K-shingles by their nature require large memory space as the size of the documents grow and high execution time. In the future we will work on designing an efficient and effective plagiarism detection for lexical similarity and also a possible way of paraphrased texts. Thus, decreasing the time and space complexity of the proposed approach is also an important phase of future development.

Acknowledgements. The research has been supported by the European Union, co-financed by the European Social Fund (EFOP-3.6.2-16-2017-00013).

Supported by Telekom Innovation Laboratories (T-Labs), the Research and Development unit of Deutsche Telekom.

References

1. Miller, M.D., Linn, R.L., Gronlund, N.E.: Measurement and Assessment in Teaching, 11th edn. Pearson, London (2013)
2. Page, E.B.: Grading essays by computer: progress report. In: Invitational Conference on Testing Problems (1966)
3. Deerwester, S., Dumais, S.T., Furnas, G.W., Landauer, T.K., Harshman, R.: Indexing by latent semantic analysis. J. Am. Soc. Inf. Sci. **41**, 391–407 (1999)
4. Blei, D.M., Ng, A.Y., Jordan, M.I.: Latent dirichlet allocation. J. Mach. Learn. Res. **3**, 993–1022 (2003)
5. Attali, Y.: A differential word use measure for content analysis in automated essay scoring. ETS Res. Rep. Ser. **36**, i–19 (2011)
6. Mikolov, T., Sutskever, I., Chen, K., Corrado, G.S., Dean, J.: Distributed representations of words and phrases and their compositionality. In: Advances in Neural Information Processing Systems, vol. 26, pp. 3111–3119 (2013)
7. Kusner, M.J., Sun, Y., Kolkin, N.I., Weinberger, K.Q.: From word embeddings to document distances. In: International Conference on Machine Learning, vol. 37, pp. 957–966 (2015)
8. Bengio, Y., Ducharme, R., Vincent, P., Janvin, C.: A neural probabilistic language model. J. Mach. Learn. Res. **3**, 1137–1155 (2003)
9. Li, Y., Xu, L., Tian, F., Jiang, L., Zhong, X., Chen, E.: Word embedding revisited: a new representation learning and explicit matrix factorization perspective. In: IJCAI International Joint Conference on Artificial Intelligence, pp. 3650–3656 (2015)
10. Tashu, T.M., Horváth, T.: Pair-wise: automatic essay evaluation using word mover's distance. In: Proceedings of the 10th International Conference on Computer Supported Education, CSEDU, INSTICC, vol. 2, pp. 59–66. SciTePress (2018)
11. Shermis, M.D., Koch, C.M., Page, E.B., Keith, T.Z., Harrington, S.: Trait ratings for automated essay grading. Educ. Psychol. Measur. **62**, 5–18 (2002)
12. Wang, X.B.: J. Educ. Behav. Stat. **30** (2005)
13. Zhang, L.: Review of handbook of automated essay evaluation: Current applications and new directions. Lang. Learn. Technol. **18**, 65–69 (2014)
14. Ben-Simon, A., Bennett, R.E.: Toward more substantively meaningful automated essay scoring. J. Technol. Learn. Assess. **6**(1) (2007)
15. Attali, Y., Burstein, J.: Automated essay scoring with e-rater® V.2. J. Technol. Learn. Assess. **4** (2006)

16. Cutrone, L., Chang, M.: Kinshuk: auto-assessor: computerized assessment system for marking student's short-answers automatically. In: Proceedings of the IEEE International Conference on Technology for Education, pp. 81–88 (2011). https://doi.org/10.1109/T4E.2011.21
17. Foltz, P.W., Laham, D., Landauer, T.K.: Automated essay scoring: applications to educational technology. In: World Conference on Educational Multimedia, Hypermedia and Telecommunications (ED-MEDIA) (1999)
18. Islam, M., Hoque, A.S.M.L.: Automated essay scoring using generalized latent semantic analysis. In: IEEE 13th International Conference on Computer and Information Technology, vol. 7, pp. 616–626 (2012)
19. Shermis, M.D., Burstein, J.: Automated essay scoring a cross-disciplinary perspective. Br. J. Math. Stat. Psychol. (2003)
20. Jin, C., He, B.: Utilizing latent semantic word representations for automated essay scoring. In: 12th International Conference on Ubiquitous Intelligence and Computing and IEEE 12th International Conference on Autonomic and Trusted Computing and IEEE 15th International Conference on Scalable Computing and Communications and Its Associated Workshops (UIC-ATC-ScalCom) (2015)
21. Alikaniotis, D., Yannakoudakis, H., Rei, M.: Automatic text scoring using neural networks. In: Proceedings of the 54th Annual Meeting of the Association for Computational Linguistics, pp. 715–725 (2016)
22. Taghipour, K., Ng, H.T.: A neural approach to automated essay scoring. In: Proceedings of the 2016 Conference on Empirical Methods in Natural Language Processing, pp. 1882–1891. Association for Computational Linguistics (2016)
23. Jin, C., He, B., Xu, J.: A study of distributed semantic representations for automated essay scoring. In: Li, G., Ge, Y., Zhang, Z., Jin, Z., Blumenstein, M. (eds.) KSEM 2017. LNCS (LNAI), vol. 10412, pp. 16–28. Springer, Cham (2017). https://doi.org/10.1007/978-3-319-63558-3_2
24. Thanawala, P., Pareek, J., Shah, M.: OntoBAeval: ontology-based automatic evaluation of free-text response. In: 2014 IEEE Sixth International Conference on Technology for Education (2014)
25. Fauzi, M.A., Utomo, D.C., Setiawan, B.D., Pramukantoro, E.S.: Automatic essay scoring system using N-gram and cosine similarity for gamification based E-learning. In: Proceedings of the International Conference on Advances in Image Processing, ICAIP 2017, pp. 151–155. ACM, New York (2017)
26. Zupanc, K., Bosnifć, Z.: Automated essay evaluation with semantic analysis. Knowl.-Based Syst. **120**, 118–132 (2017)
27. Yamamoto, M., Umemura, N., Kawano, H.: Automated essay scoring system based on rubric. In: Lee, R. (ed.) ACIT 2017. SCI, vol. 727, pp. 177–190. Springer, Cham (2018). https://doi.org/10.1007/978-3-319-64051-8_11
28. Dumais, T.K., Landauer, S.: Latent semantic analysis. Scholarpedia **3**(11), 4356 (2008)
29. Salton, G.: Automatic Text Processing: The Transformation, Analysis, and Retrieval of Information by Computer. Addison-Wesley Longman Publishing Co., Inc., Boston (1989)
30. Porter, M.: The Porter Stemming Algorithm (1980)
31. Rajaraman, A., Ullman, J.D.: Mining of Massive Datasets. Cambridge University Press, New York (2011)
32. Islam, M., Latiful Hoque, A.S.M.: Automated essay scoring using generalized latent semantic analysis. In: International Conference on Computer and Information Technology (2010)

33. Atoum, I., Otoom, A.: Efficient hybrid semantic text similarity using wordnet and a corpus. Int. J. Adv. Comput. Sci. Appl. (IJACSA) **7**, 124–130 (2016)
34. Wan, S., Angryk, R.A.: Measuring semantic similarity using WordNet-based context vectors. In: IEEE International Conference on Systems, Man and Cybernetics (2007)
35. Zhuge, W., Hua, J.: WordNet-based way to identify Chinglish in automated essay scoring systems. In: International Symposium on Knowledge Acquisition and Modeling (2009)
36. Ewees, A.A., Eisa, M., Refaat, M.M.: Comparison of cosine similarity and k-NN automated essays scoring. Int. J. Adv. Res. Comput. Commun. Eng. **3** (2014)
37. Xia, P., Zhang, L., Li, F.: Learning similarity with cosine similarity ensemble. Inf. Sci. **307**, 39–52 (2015)
38. Williamson, D.: A framework for implementing automated scoring. In: The Annual Meeting of the American Educational Research Association (AERA) and the National Council on Measurement in Education (NCME) (2009)
39. Clough, P., Stevenson, M.: Developing a corpus of plagiarised short answers. Lang. Resour. Eval. **45**, 5–24 (2011)
40. Powers, D.M.W.: Evaluation: from precision, recall and F-measure to ROC, informedness, markedness & correlation. J. Mach. Learn. Technol. **2**, 37–63 (2011)

Generation of Adapted Learning Game Scenarios: A Model-Driven Engineering Approach

Pierre Laforcade(✉) and Youness Laghouaouta

Computer Science Laboratory of Le Mans University, Le Mans, France
{pierre.laforcade,youness.laghouaouta}@univ-lemans.fr

Abstract. Adaptativity is a key-concern when developing serious games for learning purposes. It makes it possible to customize the game according to each learner individuality. To deal with adaptativity, this chapter proposes a Model-Driven Engineering approach that supports dynamic scenarization instead of implementing fixed configurations of learning scenarios. The base principle is to consider the generation of scenarios as a model transformation of a learner profile and a game description models toward adapted scenarios. This proposal has been applied to the context of the *Escape-it!* research project that aims to propose an "escape-room" game for helping children with Autistic Syndrome Disorder (ASD) to learn visual performance skills.

Keywords: Serious game · Autism · Learning scenarios · Adaptation · Model Driven Engineering

1 Introduction

The use of serious games [3] in Autistic Syndrome Disorder (ASD) interventions has become increasingly popular during the last decade [4]. They are considered as effective new methods in the treatment of ASD. Computerized interventions for individuals with autism may be much more successful if motivation can be improved and learning can be personalized by leveraging principles from the emerging field of serious game design in educational research [19].

This chapter tackles the challenge of adapting learning sessions to the needs of individual learners. Our research is conducted in the context of the *Escape it!* project. The objective is to develop a serious game to train visual skills of children with ASD. This serious game uses mechanics from "escape-room" games: the player's goal is to open a locked door to escape the room. To this end, the user has to solve numerous puzzles often requiring observation and deduction. We adapted it for our targeted audience, requiring to solve only one puzzle per scene.

In the context of this project, we are focusing on the generation of learning scenarios adapted to the current learning progress of children with ASD. Indeed,

B. M. McLaren et al. (Eds.): CSEDU 2018, CCIS 1022, pp. 95–116, 2019.
https://doi.org/10.1007/978-3-030-21151-6_6

this generation is difficult because there are a lot of elements and rules involved in the set up of an adapted game session. Our proposal to deal with this issue is based on Model-Driven-Engineering (MDE) principles and tools. MDE [14] is a research domain promoting an active use of models throughout the software development process, leading to an automated generation of the final application. We already tackled instructional design challenges with MDE techniques in the past [11] however the learning scenarios were specified by teachers and not generated by machine.

The remainder of this chapter is organized as follows. The next section presents the *Escape it!* project contextualizing our research. Section 3 discuses related work. Our model-driven based approach for the adaptive generation of learning scenarios is presented in Sect. 4. Section 5 illustrates the application of our proposal and discusses the obtained results. Finally, Sect. 6 concludes this chapter and presents the next directions for further research.

2 Context and Motivation

This section presents the *Escape it!* project that contextualizes our research. Before presenting the main gameplay we draw the project rationale.

2.1 Objectives of the Project

The project aims at designing and developing a mobile *learning game* (a serious game with learning purposes) dedicated to children with ASD (Autistic Syndrome Disorder). The game intends to support the learning of visual skills (based on the ones described in the ABLLS-R® curriculum guide [15]): matching an object to another identical object, sorting objects into different categories, making seriation of objects, etc. The mobility feature will allow the learning to take place wherever the parents, therapeutics, as well as the child himself want it. The game will be used both to reinforce and generalize the learning skills that will be initiated by "classic" working sessions with tangible objects.

The project involves autism experts, parents and Computer Science researchers and experts in the engineering of Technology-Enhanced Learning systems.

2.2 General Overview and Principles for the Serious Game

The serious game is based on the *escape-the-room* structure: players have to find hidden cues and objects, sometimes combine objects or interact with the playing scenes, in order to unlock a door. The door symbolizes the end of the level and gives access to the next level. We made a cross analysis between mechanisms from various escape-the-room-*like* games and best practices for designing serious games for children with ASD [4,20].

We then sketched with experts, during participatory design sessions, the major directions and requirements to take into account. Some of them are related to the game aesthetics and sound environment (to be adapted to the child sensory profile), other about the regulation of the child activity (prompts, guidance, feedback, reinforcements have to be adapted to every children profile), or about the tracking system that will be used to update the children profiles after a game session. We only focus here on the scenario involving the resolution activities, and list, below, the most appropriate information for our concern:

- targeted skills: a subset from the 27 visual performance skills depicted in the ABLLS-R, the relevant ones for a mobile game-play adaptation.
- variable game sessions: a session will propose from 3 to 6 levels according to a start menu choice (to the convenience of the pairing adult with the child or the child him-self).
- levels as meaningful living places: the whole screen will display a fixed (no scrolling or change of point of view) and enclosed (with a door to open) easily identifiable living places. These scenes are related to themes. For example, the *bedroom, kitchen and living room* are related to the *home* theme, whereas *classroom* and *gymnasium* are related to the *school* theme.
- adapted difficulty: according to the current child progress in the targeted skills; difficulty raises after three succeeded activities for a same skill (along one or several game sessions).
- generalizing the acquired skills: to this end, the scenes have to change, in accordance with the previous difficulty level, in order to propose non-identical challenges for the same skill; i.e.:
  - changing the scene (background and elements).
  - adding background elements to disrupt visual reading.
  - changing the objects to find and handle.
  - adding other objects not useful to the resolution.
  - hiding objects behind or into others.

Figure 1 depicts an example of a scene which targets the B8 skill (i.e. sort non-identical items) in the '*Expert*' difficulty level. Various trucks and balls have to be found and moved into the appropriate storage boxes before the door opens. Interactive hiding places, like the closet and its drawer, can be opened showing hidden objects.

Figure 2 illustrates an example of another scene which targets the B13 skill (i.e. matching a sequence of objects) in the '*Intermediate*' difficulty level. Mustard and ketchup dispensers, and coke bottles have to be found and moved into their appropriate locations in the middle fridge door shelf with the aim of matching the sequence on the top shelf. Some of the objects to found are already visible, others can be hidden in the shopping bags. Note that experts validated objects and gameplay in order to avoid inappropriate interactions or explicit actions that children do not normally realize in everyday life.

Figure 3 shows a bedroom scene variant which targets the B3 skill (i.e. matching identical objects) in the '*Elementary*' difficulty level. Dinosaurs toys have to be found and moved in the top shelf of the drawer wherein an exemplar is already visible. The desk is an example of randomized additional decor that can provide new locations for placing objects. In Fig. 3 two dinosaurs toys are placed in potential locations provided by the desk.

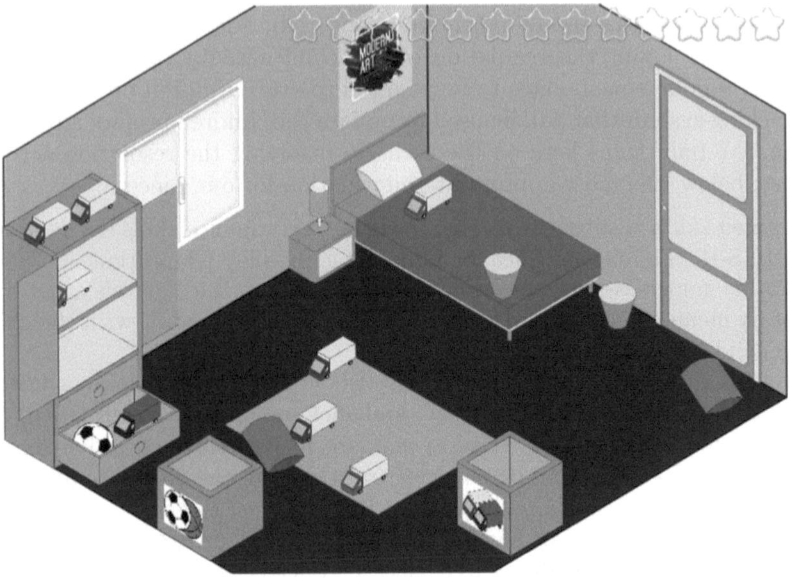

Fig. 1. An example of the *bedroom* scene.

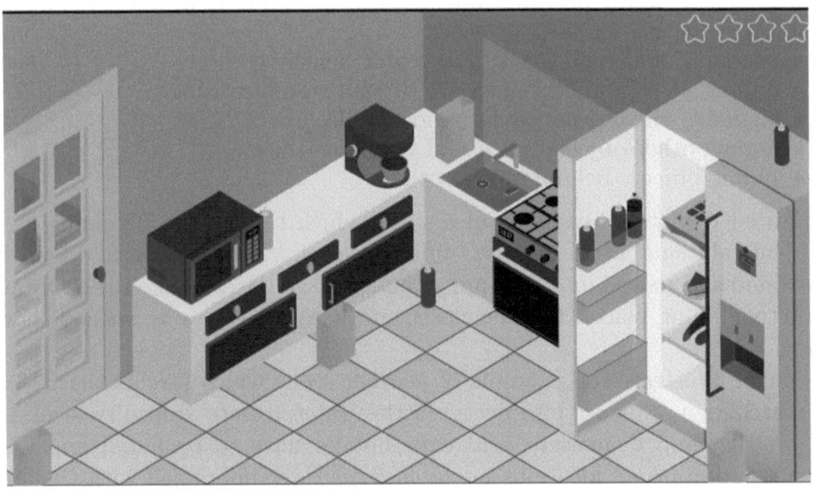

Fig. 2. An example of the *kitchen* scene.

2.3 Anatomy of a Scene

Whichever scenes are selected for the learning scenario, they share common features:

- a background image that depicts a familiar scene for children, with a few recognizable objects;

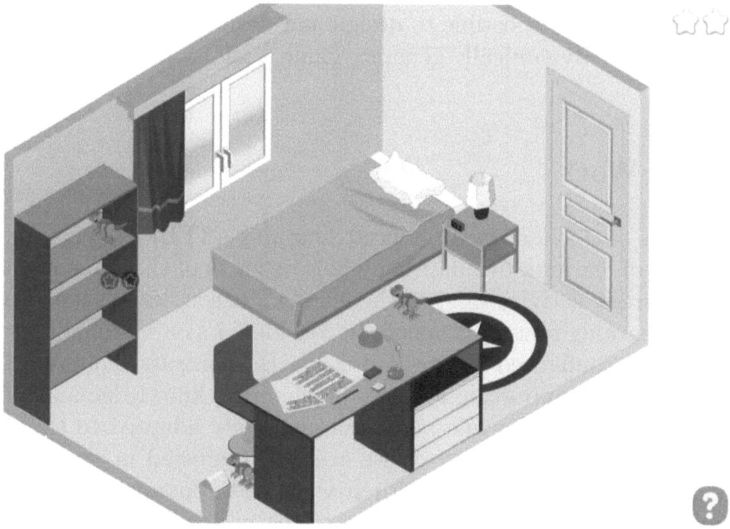

Fig. 3. An example of the *bedroom-2* scene.

- several empty slots where objects to find can be later positioned.
- additional decorations to impair visual reading (in relation to the difficulty rules); each one can:
  - appear in different locations.
  - create new slots for other game objects.
- interactive *hiding objects*: provide new hidden objects slots and reveal them when touched.
- solution objects where game objects have to be dropped in/on.
  - one or several places can be proposed to place a solution object or the different instances required to solve the level (e.g. for sorting objects two or more storage boxes can be used).
  - zero or several places can be proposed if dropped objects have to appear specifically.

2.4 Motivation

As stated above, a game scenario is composed of an ordered sequence of scenes including precise descriptions of each scene components and locations. All this information has to be adapted to the child's profile when starting a new game session. There are various profile variables (current progress during learning skills, preferences/dislikes, level difficulties for every skill...) and a lot of combinations of elements to set-up a scene. In addition, generalization is very important in autism. It can be defined as the process of taking a skill learned in one setting and applying it in other settings or different ways [1]. To support the learning of generalization, we have to propose a large variety of scenes settings.

Nevertheless, it is not possible to design and develop all the combinations of settings. We need to dynamically generate game sessions adapted to each child's profile.

3 Related Work

The adaptation of Technology-Enhanced Learning (TEL) systems allows the personalization of learning by adapting whole or parts of the presented systems (contents, resources, activities...) to the learner's needs, interests and abilities. An adaptable learning system is generally considered as a learning system that can be manually configured by its end-users. By contrast, adaptive learning environments aim at supporting learners in acquiring knowledge and skills in a particular learning domain while being automatically adapted to the changing needs of the learner. In our context, we are not interested in the adaptability of the mobile learning game for children with ASD but on the adaptivity of the game (i.e. to provide adapted game sessions in accordance to the children profiles).

3.1 Generation of Adaptive Scenarios

The motivation for steering adaptivity in serious games is to improve the effectiveness of the knowledge transfer between the game and its players. Several studies tackled the adaptation issue in order to find a balance between the player's skills and the game challenge level. The learning goals to achieve are usually strongly coupled with the gradual personal improvement of a skill set. Generally, adaptive serious games have specialized *ad hoc* approaches where game components are adjusted in order to encourage training of a specific skill.

Research work dealing with adaptivity have different targets: game worlds and its objects, gameplay mechanics, nonplaying characters and AI, game narratives, game scenarios/quests... They also rely on various methods: bayesian networks, ontologies, neuronal networks, rules-based systems, procedural algorithms... [2,7,17]. Game scenarios are generally defined as *the global progression within a game level, its initial settings and the logical flow of events and actions that follow* [5], whereas game worlds are *the virtual environments within which gameplay occurs*. In our context, our interest is about learning game scenarios, because each scene to achieve targets a specific skill, while disregarding the flow of events or actions. The resolution of a scene only requires that the learners find and move objects to their appropriate target locations. Our context partially maps the game world and its object definition in the way that the available objects of scenes can have zero or more instances according to the generation process.

Reaching beyond skill-driven adaptivity and integrating scenario with world adaptation/generation while the game is running remains a research challenge [12]. There are two approaches to tackle it: (1) during the loading stage of a game session by considering player-dependent informations, and (2) in real-time during game playing. Our concern relies on the first approach: scenarios are generated before starting every new game sessions (the 3-to-5 levels).

In [13], the authors have proposed a system for generating content highlights the involvement of domain experts (i.e. teachers) to control the content generation. Teachers can select pre-created game objects, add new learning content to them and create relationships between objects. Knowledge about objects and their relationships seems a basis for solving and generating all the appropriate content. It could be a valuable contribution to control the generation of our learning game scenarios by using knowledge on the objects of each scene and their relationships. Such game knowledge should be specified at a high semantic level in order to involve domain experts. That approach is very interesting in our context. We could specify every game scenes (bedroom, kitchen...) in a descriptive way of all available slots, additional decors, selectable objects... (cf. elements listed in Sect. 2.3), as well as their restrictive relations (i.e. solution objects).

3.2 An Architecture and Approach for Generating Scenarios

Closer to our concerns, the work presented in [16] proposes a generic architecture for personalizing a serious game scenario according to learners' competencies and interaction traces [6]. The architecture has been evaluated with the objective to develop a serious game for evaluating and rehabilitating cognitive disorders. It is organized in three layers: domain concepts (i.e. the domain-specific concepts and their relations), pedagogical resources (i.e. "*any entity used in the process of teaching, forming or understanding, enabling learning or conveying the pedagogical concepts*" [16]) and game resources (i.e. "*either static objects or those endowed with an interactive or proactive behavior according to the game*"). Machine learning is used to update the learner profile based on interaction traces.

In addition, this proposal allows the generation of three successive scenarios (conceptual, pedagogical and serious game scenarios) according to the three presented layers. As for the validation of the generated scenarios, the authors used an evaluation protocol. For that, experts were involved at first to validate the domain rules, *a priori* of the generator implementation, and then to produce scenarios for specific contexts. These scenarios are compared to the generated ones. Hence, experts guide the requirements specification and validation activities, but they are not directly involved in the generation process.

4 A Model-Driven Approach to Support Adaptive Generation of Scenarios

4.1 Overview of the Approach

Our proposal is based on the idea to combine the general architecture of a scenario generator from the CLES project [16] with the Model-Driven Engineering approach and process used in the EmoTED project [10] to support the specification of the elements (concepts, properties and rules) required to drive the adaptive generation of scenarios. From the first architecture, we follow the generator principle where the final learning game scenario is built after 3 steps. Similarly we propose to split the final scenario generation into three scenarios:

- the **objective scenario** refers to the selection of the targeted learning objectives according to the user's profile including his current progress. In the *Escape it!* context, this is related to the elicitation of the visual performance skills in accordance to the number of levels to generate.
- the **structural scenario** refers to the selection of learning game exercises or large game components. In the *Escape it!* context, this concerns the various scenes where game levels will take place. This scenario extends the previous one (i.e. the objective scenario elements are included in this one). It is generated from user profile elements and knowledge domain rules stating the relations between these pedagogical large-grained resources and the targeted skills they can deal with.
- the **features scenario** refers to the additional selection of the inner-resources/fine-grained elements. In the *Escape it!* project, this concerns all objects appearing in a scene. The game scenario includes both previous scenarios components. It specifies the overall information required by a game engine to drive the set-up of a learning game session.

It is worth noting that the final scenario is only composed of required descriptive information to adapt the game sessions to a user's profile. Information about how these descriptions elements are functioning (static and dynamical dimensions) might be addressed by the generator and the serious game engine: they are out the scope of the scenarization process.

From the EmoTED project [10], we follow the metamodeling/modeling approach using the EMF framework (*Eclipe Modeling Framework*) [18]. We propose to capture the global domain elements, required for the generation, into three inter-related parts of a general metamodel: profile-related elements, game description elements, scenario elements. Contrary to the EmoTED project, the scenarios elements have to be generated, not specified (see Fig. 4). Nevertheless we still have to specify the metamodel in order to detail the components of the three scenarios in terms of elements/properties and relations to be generated. From this metamodel, different models have to be considered:

- The Game Description Model: it describes all the game elements (skills, resources or exercisers, in-game objects...). It is an input model for the generator.
- The Profile Model: it describes the user's profile for one child. It is also an input model for the generator.
- The Scenario Model: it embeds the 3-dimensions global scenario (objective, structural and features scenarios). It is an output model of the generator.

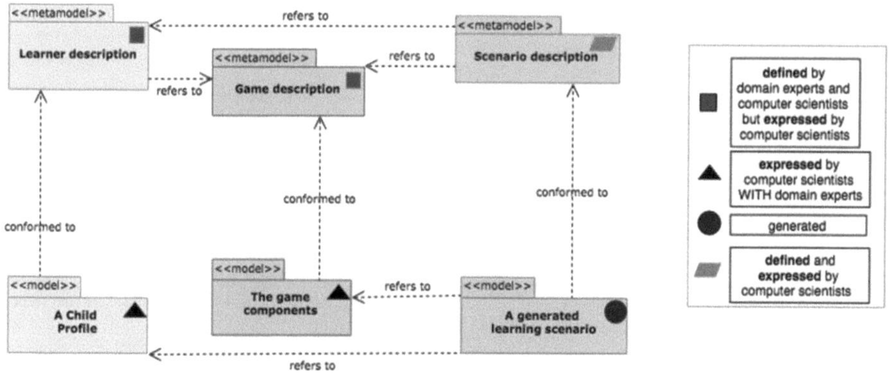

Fig. 4. The proposed 3 × 3 metamodel-based architecture.

The structuring of the elements related to the game as well as generation rules of learning scenario rely on the ASD experts recommendations/requirements. The following section details this aspect.

4.2 Game Analysis

Several collaborative sessions with autism experts led us to progressively explicit:

- the global 'escape-the-room' game-play adaptation.
- the visual performance skills in conformance with this game-play.
- a more detailed description of the scene resolution in terms of objects, hiding elements, solution objects...
- the domain rules to apply when generating a scenario.

Some of these generation rules as well as the elements from the profile and game components models in relation to them, are sketched in Table 1. The generator we developed do not yet tackle the child's profile elements for the *resource* and *game* levels of the generator (gray cells from Table 1). This choice allowed us to focus on the high-priorities elements and rules.

As mentioned in Table 1, some mapping rules have been made explicit in order to guide the generator in deciding how a scene is composed according to a specific difficulty level. For example, here are the mappings for the 'intermediary' level:

- some background elements can appear.
- some hiding objects can appear with 0 or several hidden objects inside according to their available slots.
- all selectable objects are in relation to the problem resolution (no objects for disturbing purposes).

Some mapping rules have also been established to guide scenes construction according to a specific difficulty level (cf. Table 2). Additional information like the different ranges according to the difficulty level have been specified.

Table 1. The different domain rules and relevant elements according to our metamodeling architecture (from [9]).

	Game description	**User profile**	**Generation rules for scenarios**
Objective scenario	-visual skills to acquire. -*dependency* relations between skills.	-acquired or in progress skills. -their difficulty level. -number of levels to generate.	-only skills with *parents* at *'Intermediate'* level or higher are eligible. -80% of targeted skills with a difficulty level less than *'Intermediate'*.
Structural scenario	-themes and associated scenes. -skills targeted by each scene.	-themes/scenes to exclude/favour according to child's preferences/dislikes. -history of proposed scenes.	-generate different scenes from the same theme.
Feature scenario	-background elements, hiding objects, available object places of each scene.	-scene objects to exclude/favour according to child's preferences/dislikes. - objects involved in previous sessions.	-mappings between each difficulty level and the objects to select and place into the scene.

Table 2. Difficulty levels and their impacts on the generation process.

	Additional decors	Hidding objects	Number-of-objects-to-place indicator on solution objects	All movable objects are parts of the solution	Range of objects to find
Beginner	No	No	Yes	Yes	Low
Elementary	Yes	No	Yes	Yes	Low
Intermediate	Yes	Yes	Yes	Yes	Medium
Advanced	Yes	Yes	No	Yes	Medium
Expert	Yes	Yes	No	No	Large

4.3 Metamodeling Architecture

The domain elements and relations required for the adaptive generation of scenarios are structured according to three metamodels (i.e. the *Profile*, *Game Description*, and *Scenario* metamodels). We have used the EMF platform[1] to express the relevant metamodels (see Fig. 5). We have to notice that Fig. 5 depicts all related constructs as one metamodel for better comprehending the inter-metamodels references.

We have to notice that each scenario's perspective (i.e. objective, structural and features) has been considered when defining the implied metamodels (see Fig. 6). For example, the generation of an objective scenario considers a relevant subsets of the profile elements (e.g. skills and their levels for a specific child) and the game description elements (the ones representing the skills that are tackled by the game).

A *Scenario* instance contains three inter-related elements: objective, structural and feature scenarios. By following the same decomposition approach, the *Game Description* constructs are decomposed into three subsets that match the scenario's perspectives: the skills elements (visual skills), the exercises elements (scenes and themes) and the game components associated with a concrete exercise (background, objects, locations...). Some elements from *Exercises* and

[1] http://www.eclipse.org/modeling/emf/.

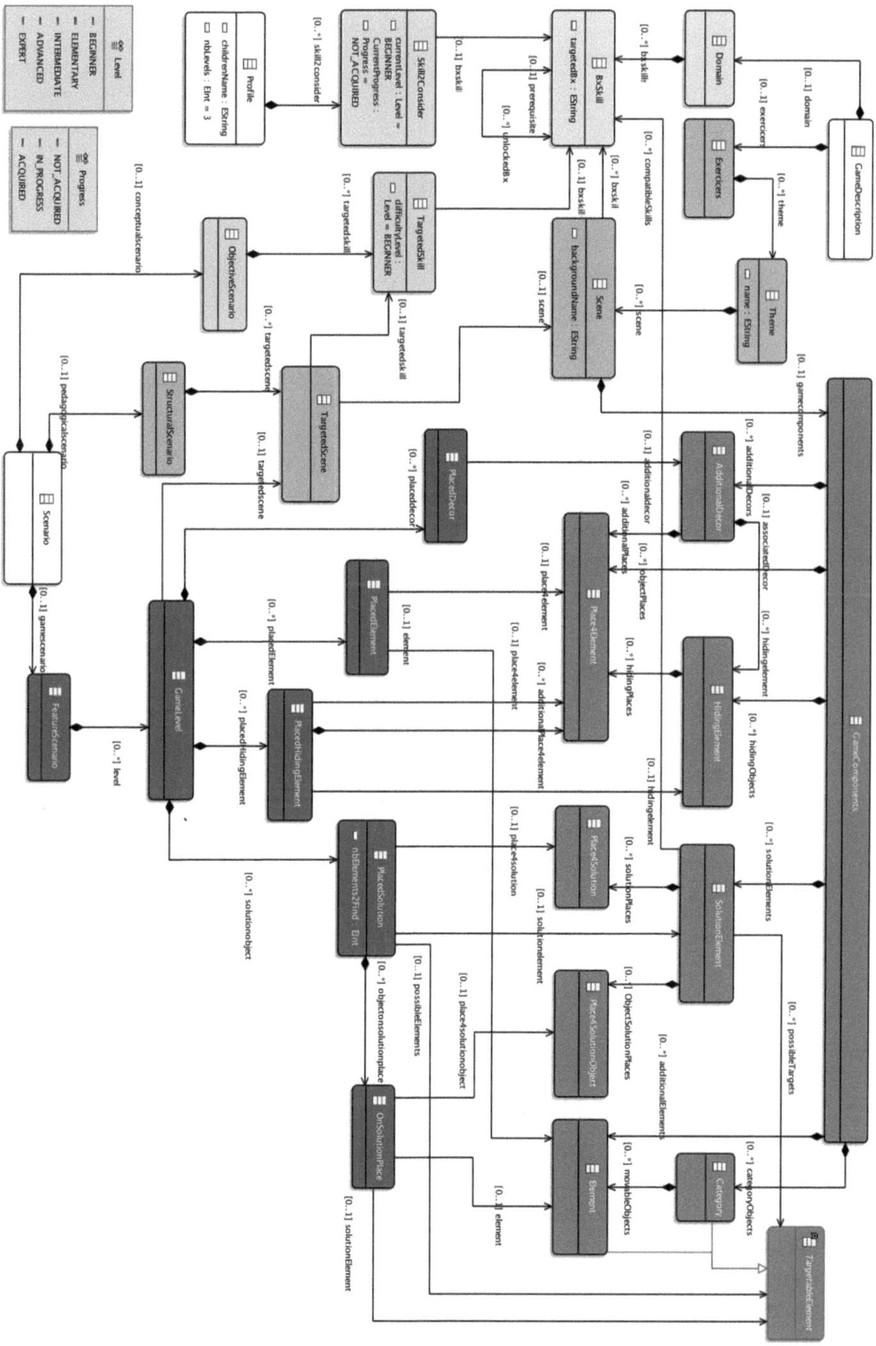

Fig. 5. Complete view of the metamodels with variations of colors to discern the different dimensions/perspectives.

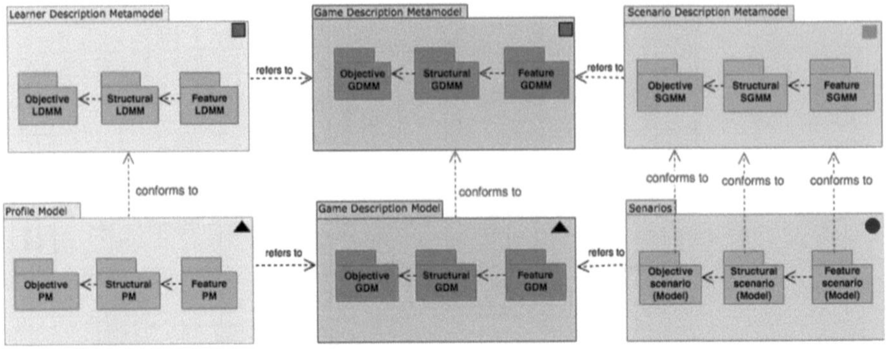

Fig. 6. The detailed proposed 3 × 3 metamodel-based architecture.

Game Components parts will refer to specific skills elements (e.g. scenes must specify which targeted skills they can deal with). As for the *Profile* constructs, they are limited to elements required for generating the objective scenario. The remaining perspectives are not yet handled by our proposal (they are highlighted with grey color in Table 1).

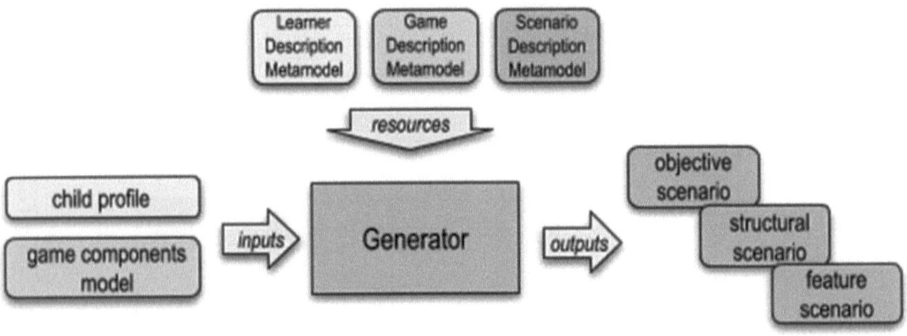

Fig. 7. Conceptual view of the transformation.

4.4 Generation of Learning Scenarios

The generation of scenarios adapted to child profiles is implemented as a model transformation written in Java/EMF. It uses the profile and game description models as inputs to allow the successive generation of the three perspectives of an adapted scenario (cf. Fig. 7). The generation rules are then hard-coded with randomness when several choices are met. It is worth noting that the experts requirements related to dynamic domain rules are not easy to implement. In fact, the implemented model transformation uses sometimes an external constraints solving library to tackle some very specific generation steps.

Employing the transformation presented above performs the generation of adapted scenarios. However, interpreting the generated models using basic EMF editors is not appropriate to perform domain rules validation. As a solution, we have implemented a support for integrating the generated scenarios in the learning game prototype (developed using Unity[2]). This concerns the low level scenario (i.e feature scenario) and makes it possible to visual and play the corresponding scenes in order to carry out effective tests of the game. It allow us to propose more accurate validations with respect to the prototype independence to changes on the generator. The scene depicted in Figs. 1, 2 and 3 were generated using the proposed integration support.

The main technical key points of this integration are illustrated in Fig. 8:

1. The learning game serializes the profile of the current log in user as an XML-based file.
2. The learning game makes a Web service call using an HTTP POST request in order to upload the profile file.
3. The Web service executes at first an *unflatten* service for getting the profile file as a model conformed to our profile metamodel. Indeed, the generator requires the profile input model in a very specific format. Skills do not have to be declared in the profile: the profile have to reference skills defined in the *Game Description* input model. This mapping is concretely realized by the mean of an MDE model transformation using the *Epsilon Transformation Language* (ETL) [8].
4. The target profile is now in an XMI format in conformance to the profile metamodel.
5. The Web service calls the generator that makes use of the new conformed profile file (with all other model and metamodels as mentioned in Fig. 7 that are already located on the Web service side).
6. The generation produces the output scenario model.
7. The Web service executes a *flatten* service. It has the opposite objective of the unflatten service: current scenario makes a lot of references of game elements (objects, decors...) from the *Game Description* model. The scenario must be self-sufficient for being handled by the game prototype. A dedicated ETL model transformation performs this task.
8. The resulting XML scenario is returned by the Web service to the prototype. This scenario will be parsed and used in the learning game.

5 Validation

This section is dedicated to the description of one use-case among those we experimented with domain experts in order to verify the generator (whether the system is well-engineered and error-free) and validate the generation rules (whether the generator and generator rules meet the experts expectations and requirements). All those use cases were fictive but realistic according to experts suggestions.

[2] https://unity3d.com/.

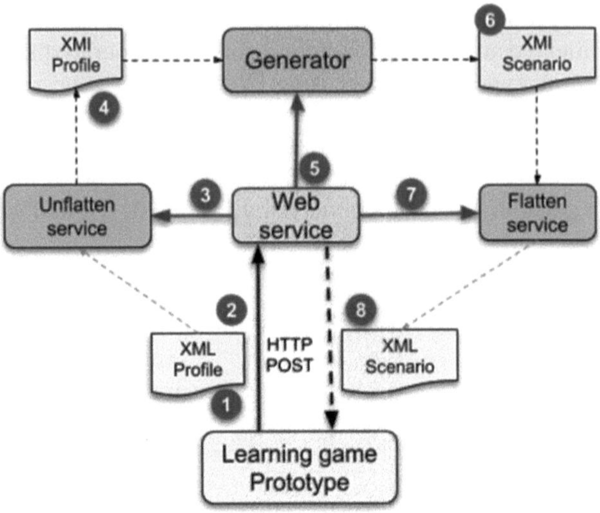

Fig. 8. Integration of the generator service into the learning game.

5.1 Input Models

The generator requires two input models. The first one specifies the game components involved with the various scenario levels whereas the second one simulates a child's profile.

In our experiments with autism experts, the first model has been specified based on the experts' requirements. We modeled the B3-B4-B8-B9-B13-B19-B25 visual performance skills (respectively matching object to object, matching object to image, sorting non-identical items into categories, placing objects on their marks, sequencing pattern to match visual model, sorting by feature, making a seriation - ordering by size, shapes...) and added their dependency relations (e.g. Fig. 9 shows that the B3 skill unlocks the B4 and B8 skills, i.e. completing B3 at least at a sufficient difficulty allows to progress independently with the learning of the B4 and B8 skills). We then specified the description of the game *scenes* according to their relative *theme* (Fig. 10). Finally, we specified the elements involved in the different scenes. As an example, Fig. 11 depicts the detailed description of the *gymnasium* scene.

This game description has been modeled using the tree-based editor generated from our metamodel. Figures 9, 10 and 11 show different extracts of this unique model. The model root is a *Game Description* instance. The *composition* relations are naturally represented within this tree-based representation whereas properties and other relations are detailed in the *Properties view* according to the element currently selected.

In opposition to the *game description* model that is unique, several children profile models have been specified in order to test the correct application of the generation rules related to the difficulty progress. Figure 12 shows one of these

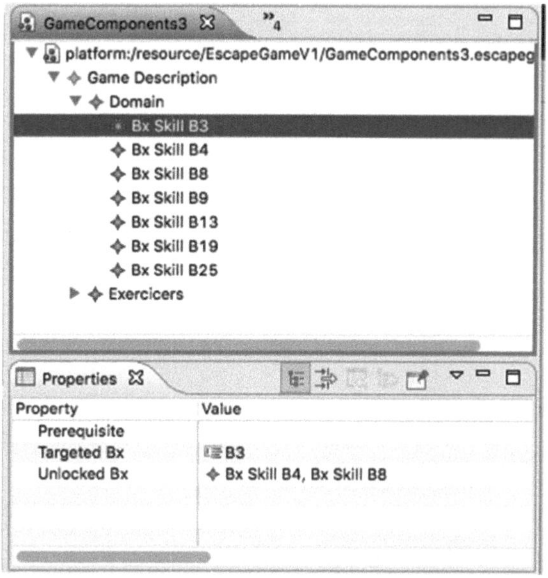

Fig. 9. Partial view of the game description input model for level 1 (objective perspective).

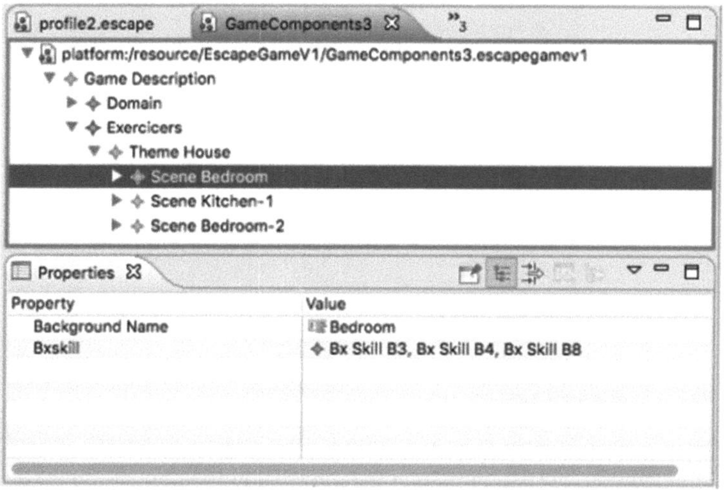

Fig. 10. Partial view of the game description input model for level 2 (structural perspective).

profile models. It describes a child's profile wherein the B3 skill is acquired at its highest (*expert*) level. The B4 skill is at the *elementary* level, B8 is at the *intermediate* level, and all other skills are at the *beginner* level.

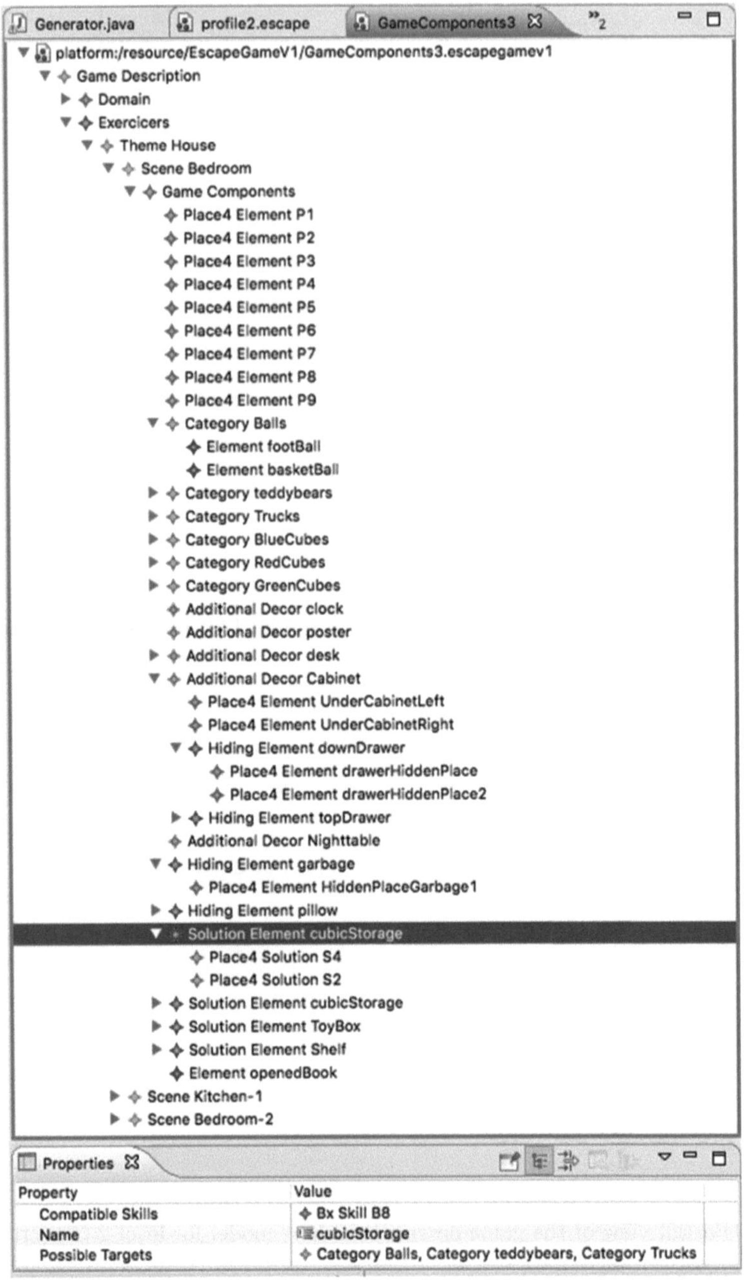

Fig. 11. Partial view of the game description input model for level 3 (feature perspective).

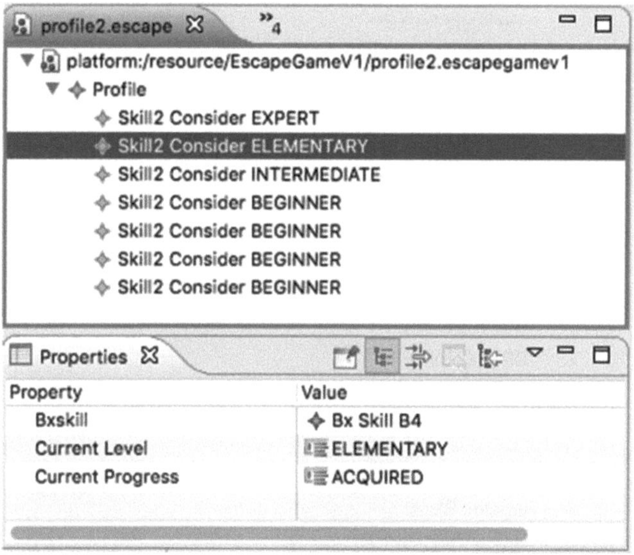

Fig. 12. Partial view of a child's profile input model.

5.2 Analysis of the Generated Scenario

We only depict the output scenario generated from the child's profile described in the previous section.

The generator displays in the console user-friendly prints of the resulting scenario. First prints remind the input child's profile and the number of levels to generate. Then the objective scenario is displayed, followed by the additional information generated with the resource scenario (see Fig. 13). For example, experts can verify that, for this very generation execution, 4 levels are proposed for the respective targeted and ordered skills: B25/B4/B8 and B25 again (with their difficulty level corresponding to the one specified in the child's profile). In this execution, the generator succeeded in proposing different scenes from the same theme (*home*).

As for the examination of the third level scenario (i.e. feature scenario), we used the integration support based on Unity (c.f. Sect. 4.4) which provides a playable prototype of the corresponding related game level. The integration architecture presented in Fig. 8 is used: Fig. 14 shows the resulting XML scenario of the 8-point. This scenario is then parsed and used by the Unity game in order to set-up the successive 4 levels. Finally, Fig. 15 illustrates the matching in-game scene for the second B4 level.

5.3 Validation of Generating Rules

We have conducted several collective validation sessions with two ASD experts. The proposed MDE based approach allowed us to varying situations proposed

```
******* INIT *********
Profile and game description models loading...
DONE

******* Child Profile *******
This is the profile for: Tom
Skills:
- B3 (EXPERT)
- B4 (ELEMENTARY)
- B9 (INTERMEDIATE)
- B13 (BEGINNER)
- B8 (BEGINNER)
- B19 (BEGINNER)
- B25 (BEGINNER)

******* Objective Scenario *******
Targeted Skills:
- B25 (BEGINNER)
- B4 (ELEMENTARY)
- B8 (BEGINNER)
- B25 (BEGINNER)

******* Structural Scenario *******
Targeted Scenes:
- Bedroom-2 - B25
- Bedroom - B4
- Kitchen-1 - B8
- Bedroom-2 - B25
```

Fig. 13. Console prints after the generation of an adapted scenario: readable view of the *objective* and *structural* parts of the output model.

to domain experts without significant effort. Indeed, we have expressed several profiles and apply the same transformation to automatically generate the consequent scenarios.

As a first feedback, the experts decided to disregard the 80/20 generation rule. This rule stipulates that 80% of the skills referenced by the generated *objective* scenario must be at a difficulty level less than '*Intermediate*' against 20% at higher level. Indeed, the experts realized that this rule cannot be satisfied in all possible cases (basically for children not familiar with the game and those at an advanced stage). On the other hand, the experts have proposed new rules concerning the selection of candidate scenes about the *structural* scenarios. The base principle is to diversify the scenes offered to the child while trying to use the same theme.

Another collaborative session focused on validating the good matching between the difficulty levels and the different game rules. Some of these rules are

```xml
<?xml version="1.0" encoding="ASCII"?>
<flatModel4Unity:Game xmi:version="2.0" xmlns:xmi="http://www.omg.org/XMI" xmlns:
flatModel4Unity="flatModel4Unity">
  <level scene="Bedroom-2" nbElementsToPlace="1" difficulty="BEGINNER">
    <element pos="P2" name="CubeBlue2"/>
    <solutionobject pos="Pos4ShelfB25" name="ShelfB25" acceptedElements="
    CubeBlueB25" targetedSkill="B25" nbSol2Find="1">
      <element pos="Shelf1" name="CubeBlue5"/>
      <element pos="Shelf2" name="CubeBlue4"/>
      <element pos="Shelf5" name="CubeBlue1"/>
      <element pos="Shelf3" name="CubeBlue3"/>
      <solutionarea pos="Shelf4" acceptedElement="CubeBlue2"/>
    </solutionobject>
  </level>
  <level scene="Bedroom" nbElementsToPlace="2" difficulty="ELEMENTARY">
    <placeddecor name="desk">
      <element pos="D2" name="basketBall"/>
    </placeddecor>
    <element pos="P8" name="basketBall"/>
    <solutionobject pos="S2" name="cubicStorage" acceptedElements="basketBall"
    targetedSkill="B4" nbSol2Find="2"/>
  </level>
  <level scene="Kitchen-1" nbElementsToPlace="1" difficulty="BEGINNER">
    <element pos="B5" name="RedPlate"/>
    <solutionobject pos="SolTopPlates" name="WallCupboardOpenedPlatesSol"
    acceptedElements="Plates" targetedSkill="B8" nbSol2Find="1"/>
  </level>
  <level scene="Bedroom-2" nbElementsToPlace="1" difficulty="BEGINNER">
    <element pos="P6" name="CubeBlue3"/>
    <solutionobject pos="Pos4ShelfB25" name="ShelfB25" acceptedElements="
    CubeBlueB25" targetedSkill="B25" nbSol2Find="1">
      <element pos="Shelf5" name="CubeBlue1"/>
      <element pos="Shelf1" name="CubeBlue5"/>
      <element pos="Shelf4" name="CubeBlue2"/>
      <element pos="Shelf2" name="CubeBlue4"/>
      <solutionarea pos="Shelf3" acceptedElement="CubeBlue3"/>
    </solutionobject>
  </level>
</flatModel4Unity:Game>
```


Fig. 14. XML-based version of the generated scenario.

depicted in Table 2. Other rules detail for each skill and each difficulty level, how many solution objects and movable objects can be instantiated. For example the *B8* - sorting - skill at the *beginning* level requires one solution object and one object to find, whereas the same skill at *expert* level requires 2 solution objects with a different random number of corresponding movable objects for each solution object (from 0 to the number of available spots specified for the scene). A fictive child's profile was used to drive the focus on a targeted skill and therefore experimenting all difficulty levels mappings, one-by-one. These experiments with experts highlighted some misconceptions about some min/max ranges for randomized instantiations. Some generated scenes were too complex to solve because the randomize algorithm chose the max number of possible objects for a scenes declaring a large number of objects locations. Ranges have been then reviewed to fixed values and that are not dependent of other elements.

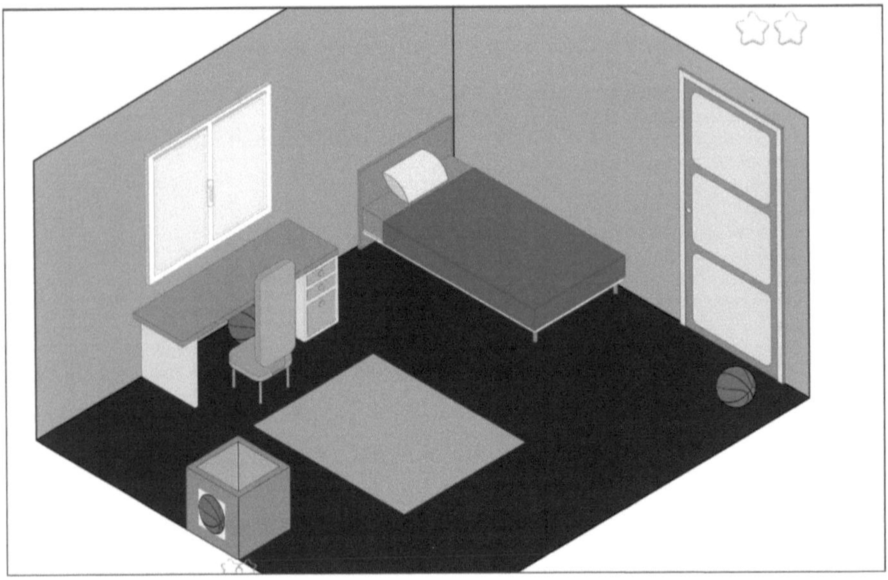

Fig. 15. The B4/bedroom scene set-up according to the data from the generated XML-based scenario.

6 Conclusion

This chapter focuses on the development of a learning game for helping young children with Autistic Syndrome Disorder to learn and generalize visual performance skills. It tackles the issue of generating adapted learning game scenarios by proposing a Model-Driven Engineering approach. The proposal is based on a metamodel specifying at first the domain elements according to both a 3-incremental-perspective on the resulting scenario, and a 3-dimensions specification of domain elements. The approach proposes to model the game description and the child's profile as input models for the generator that will produce the adapted scenario as an output model.

The generation rules and the mapping rules between the difficulty levels and the game objects involved within a scene resolution, are not explicit: they are hard-coded in the generator. These dynamical domain rules being doomed to evolve by the expert after validation sessions, we are working to make them explicit with a view to manipulating these rules as additional inputs of the leaning scenarios generator.

References

1. Burton, L.R., McEachin, J.: A Work in Progress: Behavior Management Strategies and a Curriculum for Intensive Behavioral Treatment of Autism. DRL Books, New York (1999)
2. Callies, S., Sola, N., Beaudry, E., Basque, J.: An empirical evaluation of a serious simulation game architecture for automatic adaptation. In: Munkvold, R., Kolas, L. (eds.) Proceedings of the 9th European Conference on Games Based Learning, ECGBL 2015, pp. 107–116 (2015)
3. Deterding, S., Dixon, D., Khaled, R., Nacke, L.: From game design elements to gamefulness: defining "gamification". In: Proceedings of the 15th International Academic MindTrek Conference: Envisioning Future Media Environments, MindTrek 2011, pp. 9–15. ACM, New York (2011). https://doi.org/10.1145/2181037.2181040
4. Ern, A.: The use of gamification and serious games within interventions for children with autism spectrum disorder, January 2014. http://essay.utwente.nl/64780/
5. van Est, C., Bidarra, R.: High-level scenario editing for simulation games. In: Proceedings of the 6th International Conference on Computer Graphics Theory and Applications (2011)
6. Hussaan, A.M., Sehaba, K.: Consistency verification of learner profiles in adaptive serious games. In: Verbert, K., Sharples, M., Klobučar, T. (eds.) EC-TEL 2016. LNCS, vol. 9891, pp. 384–389. Springer, Cham (2016). https://doi.org/10.1007/978-3-319-45153-4_31
7. Janssens, O., Samyn, K., Van de Walle, R., Van Hoecke, S.: Educational virtual game scenario generation for serious games. In: Proceedings of the IEEE 3rd International Conference on Serious Games and Applications for Health, SeGAH 2014, June 2014
8. Kolovos, D.S., Paige, R.F., Polack, F.A.C.: The epsilon transformation language. In: Vallecillo, A., Gray, J., Pierantonio, A. (eds.) ICMT 2008. LNCS, vol. 5063, pp. 46–60. Springer, Heidelberg (2008). https://doi.org/10.1007/978-3-540-69927-9_4
9. Laforcade, P., Loiseau, E., Kacem, R.: A model-driven engineering process to support the adaptive generation of learning game scenarios. In: CSEDU, vol. 1. INSTICC, Funchal, March 2018. https://hal.archives-ouvertes.fr/hal-01740062
10. Laforcade, P., Vakhrina, V.: A domain-specific modeling approach for a simulation-driven validation of gamified learning environments - case study about teaching the mimicry of emotions to children with autism (2015)
11. Loiseau, E., Laforcade, P., Mawas, N.E.: Turning recurrent uses of e-learning tools into reusable pedagogical activities - a meta-modeling approach applied to a moodle case-study. In: Proceedings of the 7th International Conference on Computer Supported Education, pp. 64–76 (2015). https://doi.org/10.5220/0005434000640076
12. Lopes, R., Bidarra, R.: Adaptivity challenges in games and simulations: a survey. IEEE Trans. Comput. Intell. AI Games **3**(2), 85–99 (2011). https://doi.org/10.1109/TCIAIG.2011.2152841
13. Bieliková, M., Divéky, M., Jurnečka, P., Kajan, R., Omelina, L.: Automatic generation of adaptive, educational and multimedia computer games. Sig. Image Video Process. **2**, 371–384 (2008)
14. Mussbacher, G., et al.: The relevance of model-driven engineering thirty years from now. In: Dingel, J., Schulte, W., Ramos, I., Abrahão, S., Insfran, E. (eds.) MODELS 2014. LNCS, vol. 8767, pp. 183–200. Springer, Cham (2014). https://doi.org/10.1007/978-3-319-11653-2_12. https://hal.inria.fr/hal-01081848

15. Partington, J., Analysts, P.B.: The assessment of basic language and learning skills-revised (the ABLLS-R) (2010)
16. Sehaba, K., Hussaan, A.: GOALS: generator of adaptive learning scenarios. Int. J. Learn. Technol. **8**, 224–245 (2013)
17. Sina, S., Rosenfeld, A., Kraus, S.: Generating content for scenario-based serious-games using crowdsourcing. In: Proceedings of the Twenty-Eighth AAAI Conference on Artificial Intelligence, pp. 522–529. AAAI Press (2014)
18. Steinberg, D., Budinsky, F., Paternostro, M., Merks, E.: EMF: Eclipse Modeling Framework 2.0, 2nd edn. Addison-Wesley Professional, Boston (2009)
19. Whyte, E.M., Smyth, J.M., Scherf, K.S.: Designing serious game interventions for individuals with autism. J. Autism Dev. Disord. **45**(12), 3820–3831 (2015). https://doi.org/10.1007/s10803-014-2333-1
20. Zakari, H.M., Ma, M., Simmons, D.: A review of serious games for children with autism spectrum disorders (ASD). In: Ma, M., Oliveira, M.F., Baalsrud Hauge, J. (eds.) SGDA 2014. LNCS, vol. 8778, pp. 93–106. Springer, Cham (2014). https://doi.org/10.1007/978-3-319-11623-5_9

An Approach to Advance STEM Education Practices Based on IoT Technologies and the CoPs Paradigm

Christos Goumopoulos[1,2(✉)], Athanasios Iossifides[1,3], Olga Fragou[1], Ioannis D. Zaharakis[1,4], and Achilles Kameas[1,5]

[1] Computer Technology Institute and Press, Diophantus, Research Unit 3 "DAISSy", Patras, Greece
{goumop, aiosifidis, jzaharak, kameas}@cti.gr, fragou0@gmail.com
[2] Information and Communication Systems Engineering Department, University of the Aegean, Samos, Greece
[3] Department of Electronics Engineering, Alexander Technological Educational Institute of Thessaloniki, Thessaloniki, Greece
[4] Computer and Informatics Engineering Department, Technological Educational Institute of Western Greece, Patras, Greece
[5] School of Science and Technology, Hellenic Open University, Patras, Greece

Abstract. Internet of Things and other state-of-the-art technologies like mobile and ubiquitous computing present ample opportunities for developing novel solutions almost in every domain of modern life. The research work presented here aims to leverage on the potential of such technologies in the direction of enhancing learning practices in secondary level education and promoting positive attitudes towards the corresponding scientific and engineering disciplines. The originality of the proposed approach lies on the provision of an educational platform, framed by contemporary pedagogical principles, and with an aim to stimulate collaboration between the relevant stakeholders in the form of operational communities of practice. Such communities are brought together on the basis of participating in on line activities, problem solving, exchanging reflections and experiences in the context of educational scenarios that incorporate modern technologies. The platform development is discussed in terms of the underlined conceptual models, the defined stakeholders' requirements, the online services developed, the software tools integrated and the data management supported. An example educational scenario, the corresponding IoT application developed and preliminary evaluation results of this approach are also reported.

Keywords: Internet of Things · Ubiquitous computing · Communities of practice · UMI technologies · STEM education

1 Introduction

Currently, there is a growing body of research about emerging technologies, such as, ubiquitous computing, mobile computing and the Internet of Things (IoT), collectively mentioned in the literature as UMI technologies [1]. Despite the many challenges that

B. M. McLaren et al. (Eds.): CSEDU 2018, CCIS 1022, pp. 117–141, 2019.
https://doi.org/10.1007/978-3-030-21151-6_7

must be overcome in terms of lack of standards, service adaptation, privacy and trust concerns [2], it is considered that the proliferation of these niche technologies may offer a wide range of learning opportunities, especially in the context of Science Education [3]. Undoubtedly, such technologies can be used either as educational subjects or as facilitators of the educational practice [4].

In parallel, there is a growing market need for jobs that fall within this professional domain. An analysis of Eurostat data on STEM employment indicates that in the next ten years, there will be 8 million new STEM jobs in the EU [5]. However, an argument is where the designers and developers of these technologies and related products will be educated and with what skills and training programs.

The UMI-Sci-Ed (Exploiting Ubiquitous Computing, Mobile Computing and the Internet of Things to promote Science Education) is a Horizon 2020 project (http://umi-sci-ed.eu/) related to the EU work program "Innovative ways to make science education and scientific careers attractive to young people" aiming to provide efficient practices into this technology training issue. UMI-Sci-Ed approach is to introduce several model educational scenarios that incorporate UMI technologies, in order to cultivate relevant competences to high school students. The core objectives of the project are stated in terms of delivering:

- Novel educational services – the aim is to develop and evaluate a training mechanism for UMI to help students acquiring relevant competences.
- Career consultancy services - the aim is to develop and sustain Communities of Practice for UMI and materials to motivate students pursuing a career in related domains.
- Supporting software tools, through the development of an online platform.
- Supporting hardware tools, through the delivery of a dedicated hardware kit.

In the context of UMI-Sci-Ed, UMI technologies are introduced in the learning process of secondary schools' students (i.e. 9th and 10th grade). In particular, the students attend to specially designed learning activities concerning UMI technologies under the guidance of the *Communities of Practice* (*CoPs*) paradigm [6]. The proposed methodology adheres to a number of robust educational principles. Firstly, in order to bond theory with practice, students are encouraged to develop technology-based applications acquiring thus an "attitude of creation". Secondly, by exploiting the UMI-Sci-Ed platform on-line services, students exchange material, results and good practices with other members of the community disseminating and reflecting upon important information. Thirdly, by following contemporary pedagogical approaches that promote active learning practices in a structured way promoted by proper educational scenario models.

The students are invited to explore IoT technologies through hands-on activities. The principal tools that are used are advanced System on Chip boards like the UDOO Neo board (https://www.udoo.org/udoo-neo/) and the Raspberry Pi board (https://www.raspberrypi.org/) (Fig. 1). Both offer a versatile sensor kit and wireless communication allowing high performance at a low price and enabling the creation of various IoT applications.

Given the pivotal role of CoPs, emerging learning and consequently the knowledge is constructed by interactions and communications between the relevant stakeholders.

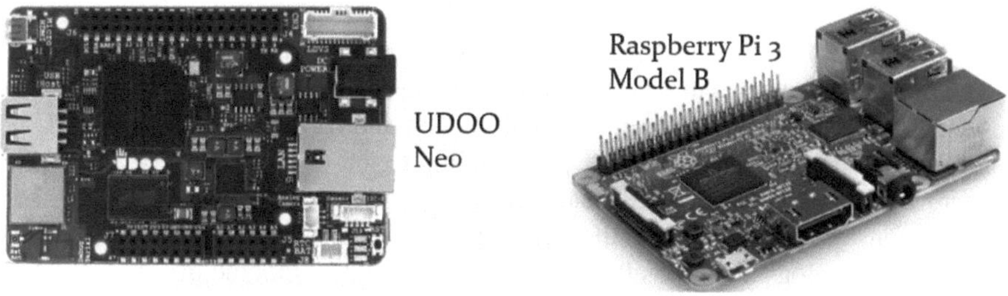

Fig. 1. IoT technologies for hands-on activities in UMI-Sci-Ed.

Under this scope, the UMI-Sci-Ed platform aims to bring together practitioners, students, school teachers, instructional designers, academics and IT specialists, who actually are going to act as members of the UMI-Sci-Ed CoPs. Such communities are brought together on the basis of participating in on line activities, problem solving, exchanging reflections and experiences in the context of educational scenarios that incorporate UMI technologies, in order to cultivate relevant competences.

An example of educational scenario and application using IoT technologies is discussed in this chapter whereas the members of the assembled CoP included students, teachers, and technology/domain experts with a mentoring role. UMI experts who involved originated from the postgraduate program on engineering of pervasive computing systems of the Hellenic Open University [7].

The remainder of the chapter is organized as follows. In the next section a discussion on related work is provided and the distinction of our approach is argued. The background conceptual models that underpin the development of the UMI-Sci-Ed platform is discussed in Sect. 3. The role of CoPs theory and the devised UMI-Sci-Ed Educational Scenario Template in shaping the UMI-Sci-Ed platform operational characteristics are explained. The UMI-Sci-Ed platform development is discussed in Sect. 4 in terms of user requirements, on-line services developed, software tools integrated and data management. We discuss also the platform architecture and the main modules that support the involvement of the stakeholders. Next, we present an example educational scenario, the corresponding UMI application developed, and report on preliminary evaluation results of this approach. Finally, we provide our conclusion and future work.

2 Related Work

The multifaceted nature of UMI-Sci-Ed platform to promote science education creates an intersection between different tool areas such as online CoPs management, computer-supported collaborative learning (CSCL), learning management systems (LMS) and IoT platforms. Although there is no complete match of each of the above tool areas with the aims of the UMI-Sci-Ed platform there are certain aspects of the respective field that have been encapsulated in the developed platform.

Although it is quite frequent phenomenon that social networking tools (i.e. Facebook, Twitter etc.) are used to build online CoPs, on the other hand, it is not common to identify general purpose platforms that address the needs of any CoP [8]. In this context the tendency is that CoPs platforms are built on demand for specific domains, or CoPs members use one or more different tools according to the task at hand (e.g. DISCUSS, Twitter, YouTube, Moodle, wikis, and forums).

In response to the popularity of Web 2.0 technologies, LMSs evolved to include features such as blogs and wikis [9]; it has been recognized, that the majority of LMSs introduced friction for instructors, trying to reuse and share course materials. To adhere to these market needs, tools for establishing collaboration between software community members so as to process code or software development material, have been recently introduced and developed, such as GitHub [10]. Environments as such provide social and collaborative features in conjunction with distributed version control. GitHub is a popular Web based social code sharing service that utilizes the Git distributed version and control system. The rationale of circulating educational material and collaborating on this basis for further developing software applications is quite important in an effort to develop a culture of collaboration, transparent and active, for teachers, practitioners, and educational policy makers involved in this creative and dynamic process.

Lamer et al. suggest the use of robotics as an enabling ICT platform for promoting STEM education [11]. The multidisciplinary nature of the robotics field offers the opportunity for young children to enhance their creativity and problem-solving abilities. An open framework is proposed to bring together the main stakeholders of educational robotics, i.e. teachers, educational researchers and providers of educational robotics, in terms of a common ground based on an activity centered repository. The framework offers different perspectives and approaches such as learning through making to trigger the curiosity and interest of students about science and technology.

Lehman et al. discuss the use of HUBzero, an open software platform operated by Purdue University in US to support scientific collaboration, for the development of STEMEdhub which is a tool for collaboration, research and education in STEM domain [12]. STEMEdhub users can find resources such as lessons plans, simulations and publications in the content repository. Moreover, using search engines they can find the most appropriate content in terms of topic, field domain, grade level or rating scores. The hub supports the concept of groups as the main organizational unit to elaborate on the capabilities of the platform. A group can define a custom template design for unique view of the interface and associate key terms with STEM resources. The use of collaboration tools such as wikis, blogs, forums, calendars, and project management allow groups to build various communities among their members.

The STEM4youth project builds a repository of educational content and teaching scenarios with a goal to make science education and scientific career more attractive to youngsters [5]. Various methodologies and tools such as learning by experiment, demonstrations, social media and games are employed to present the scientific challenges in several disciplines and their impact in everyday life. The STEM4youth approach emphasizes the social dimension and the career prospects associated with the science education by indicating the specific skills that are developed.

IoT platforms like Arduino and Raspberry PI provide tools through their web portals for creating and maintaining their communities. Such tools include forums with topics spanning from hardware and software to education and tutorials, wikis, blogs, newsletter, etc. Project repositories created and documented by the users are also maintained. Furthermore, Arduino Creative Technologies in the Classroom, or CTC [13], is a program focusing on STEM teaching for students of secondary education in collaboration with their teachers. The program provides IoT resources, learning materials and educational services to enable participants to create a more hands-on learning experience in the topics of programming, mechanics and electronics.

The UMI-Sci-Ed platform shares common characteristics and goals with the above approaches and other online portals that collect and present STEM educational material and provide collaboration support to active groups (e.g., Scientix, eTwinning, Micro:bit and Make World). However, it is diversified by integrating under a common technological environment CoPs management and the UMI/IoT technical tools to assist students both acquiring relevant competences and being motivated in pursuing a career in related domains. On the operational level, the integration of the UDOO Neo IoT platform allows to perform remote management of the device, visualize the data, and trigger actions as a result of rules on the received data.

Another differentiation of UMI-Sci-Ed platform is its orientation in instructional design: the educational scenario as a flexible structure has been the basis for designing the platform mechanism for leveraging UMI-Sci-Ed communities. CoPs' members create groups on the basis of designed educational scenarios and further negotiate and experiment on their implementation and splitting in smaller projects in a variety of educational contexts.

3 Background Conceptual Models

3.1 The Role of Communities of Practice in UMI-Sci-Ed Platform Modeling

Students as future practitioners, need to be able to perform analytic reasoning, interpret information and demonstrate personal and social responsibility. Designing and establishing thus Knowledge Management schemata such as *Communities of Practice* (*CoPs*) in the context of corporate or academic organizations is strongly related to enhancing professional development in the following axes: (a) personal commitment, (b) building trusting relationships with collaboration, (c) opportunities and ongoing support for continuous learning, (d) inquiry based, practice based learning within school settings, (e) respect for differences in practitioners' theoretical backgrounds, prior knowledge, experiences, and expertise, (f) risk taking, and (g) evaluation and feedback [14].

Reflective practice, on the other hand, has significant potential to create educational improvement because it is situation specific and places the professional in the very centre of the attempt to create improvement: this, supported by the use of social networking systems for knowledge management, seems to result in evident advantages such as documenting tacit knowledge and building a sense of community in the context of corporate or academic organizations.

Furthermore, the practice based approach to continuing education aims to create a common ground for individuals and teams to work, jointly reflect, explore alternatives and support each other. A strong assumption in a practice based approach is that CoPs cultivate professional learning and instructional improvement. The framework provided by Wenger et al. on CoPs, defines these as *"groups of people that cohere to through sustained mutual engagement on an indigenous enterprise, and creating a common repertoire"* [15]. The message conveyed by the CoPs theory is that even in apparently routine or unskilled work, there is a large amount of interaction and sense making in completing the task(s) involved.

A knowledge schema as CoPs, needs an identity defined by a *shared domain of interest* and membership implies a commitment to the domain and therefore a shared competence that distinguishes this group from other people. These community members, as they pursue their interest in their domain, engage in joint activities and discussions, build relationships, help each other and share information. The community members as active practitioners deploy practices and use the same tools, working together. Through such interaction they come to hold similar beliefs and value systems: its members are colleagues committed to jointly develop best practices.

In the case of implementing CoPs in the field of education, their perspective affects educational practices along three dimensions: (a) internally, in the sense of organizing educational experiences that ground school learning in practice through participation in communities around subject matters, (b) externally, in the sense of connecting students' experience with actual practice through peripheral forms of participation in broader communities, (c) over the lifetime of students, in the sense of tracing students' learning needs and organizing communities on topics around these.

The model by Wenger et al. [15] in this context is based on social learning; participation is voluntary, membership can be self-selected or assigned, based on the expertise or a passion of the topics. Leadership comes from both formal and informal leaders while organization values innovation and knowledge sharing; knowledge sharing occurs mainly within the community as an emerging and tie bonding process. Under this model the designed and developed learning environment has to incorporate the basic array of CoPs framework tools to achieve, knowledge presentation, communication and collaboration.

In UMI-Sci-Ed approach, the strategic decision has been to design a simple but robust structure supporting CoPs avoiding to a priori structure the educational environment before taking into consideration members' interaction and launching of pilot educational activities. For that reason, knowledge management and collaboration tools are incorporated in the UMI-Sci-Ed platform as will be discussed in the following sections of the chapter. In UMI-Sci-Ed CoPs, a major part is to explore existing processes and then refine those processes through collaboration among UMI-Sci-Ed stakeholders. The collaborative practices that practitioners, as CoPs members, learn to use will enable them to share knowledge and disseminate best practices within their organization and other agencies.

UMI-Sci-Ed CoPs are expected to create, develop and disseminate new tools, systems, and resources based on applications developed via UMI technologies. For creating and supporting the UMI-Sci-Ed CoPs we have selected the model by Snyder & Brigg, as composed by the following phases [16]: (a) discovering the potential,

(b) coalescing, (c) maturity/growth, (d) advocacy/stewadership, and (e) transformation. Each stage has a number of associated goals and activities or tasks. Identifying issues that the CoPs will address, identifying the target population, defining the roles and processes of involving key stakeholders, recruiting participants and identifying key content for CoPs are important actions on following the aforementioned stages.

3.2 Instructional Design Considerations and the Role of UMI-Sci-Ed Educational Scenario Template (UMI EST)

The hypothesis examined and explored in this work is that students studying science topics can be empowered by using UMI applications which are developed in the context of model educational scenarios whereas students are provided with meaningful opportunities to participate in the learning process such as in terms of building applications that are relevant to the subject they like. On the described basis vivid interactions take place within student groups accustomed to a practice oriented experience model targeted to provide them with a rich context to grasp scientific knowledge.

Therefore, the pillar of the UMI-Sci-Ed educational learning platform had to be a pedagogical framework, adequately structured, however "open" so as to encourage users' actual engagement with authentic learning activities regarding STEM and involving state of the art IoT technologies such as UDOO Neo. *Problem oriented project pedagogy (POPP)* is a pedagogical framework that incorporates a series of integrated didactical principles as the basis for the design of this learning environment: problem formulation, enquiry of exemplary problems, participant control, joint projects, interdisciplinary approaches, and action learning [17].

Important issues on applying the POPP are the following: who is formulating the problem to work with, as well as the balance between problem formulation and problem solving. This framework integrates pedagogical principles such as problem-orientation, interdisciplinarity, participant control, exemplary projects, team work and action learning. An important pillar of the educational process is users' *enquiry on scientific problems* and is the focal center of users' engagement. In order to understand the problem and find a solution to the problem, users have to go through different stages of systematic investigations: preliminary enquiry, problem formulation, theoretical and methodological considerations, investigations, experimentation and reflection. When users themselves define and formulate the enquiry, they have conscious relation of ownership to it, and they experience the problem fact which encourages involvement and motivation. This enquiry and negotiation between users and experts/mentors sets the learning process in a CoP.

The preliminary phase of problem setting is quite important and has to be supported by materials, lectures, preliminary investigations and review of former work so as users to focus on exemplary and principal problems. *Collaboration in projects* is another design principle embraced by the UMI-Sci-Ed platform's architecture. In such collaborative learning projects participants have a joint project and a shared enterprise, participants are interdependent, participants own and share the problem, participants have mutual responsibility of learning and collaboration among participants is a long term process.

What consists a design pillar of the UMI-Sci-Ed platform architecture is its focus on the structure and use of educational scenarios. Their formats and use are quite broad, targeted at all levels of typical and vocational education and training. There are limited examples of extending STEM curriculum by employing scenario based e-learning opportunities using state of the art technologies. Educational theories support learning approaches that make learning engaging and meaningful, however the experientalism approach is linked to improving student performance [18].

In this context, to launch orchestrating the learning process the UMI-Sci-Ed Educational Scenario Template (UMI EST) has been designed [19]; the template as the core instructional tool, has been aims to encapsulate all important components of the learning process. In UMI education we need to design "user experiences". Figure 2 shows part of the UMI EST components.

For successful integration of STEM education, there are several characteristics that have to be implemented. The four major features of STEM education include STEM being collaborative, hands–on, problem solving and project-based [20]. Educational scenarios have been used in educational and training practices so as to discuss which futures are preferred or disliked, or pin down the direction of observable trends, or revealing patterns of viewpoints than of a general consensus regarding the future. Different stakeholders develop different - perhaps conflicting-interpretations filtered through their experiences and their own professional and personal values. Since the use of CoPs implies also supporting innovation mechanism through revelation of tacit knowledge, a critical decision has been to incorporate educational scenario structure in shaping the use of the UMI-Sci-Ed platform. Thus, using tools to start constructing a common understanding and springboard for interaction and engagement among different stakeholder groups has been a critical decision and factor of differentiation of UMI-Sci-Ed platform regarding other CoPs' platforms.

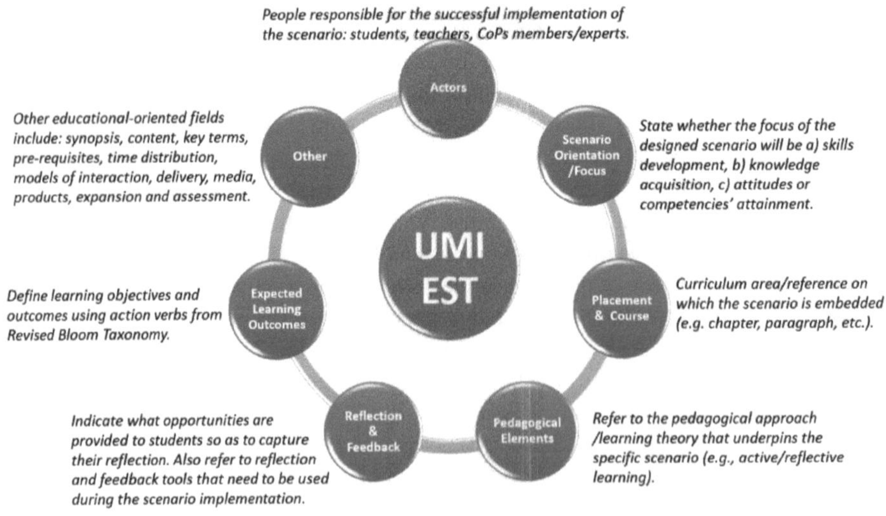

Fig. 2. UMI EST representative components.

4 Platform Development

4.1 Requirements

Social media and Web 2.0 tools have been quite important in forming communities on which users, communicate, collaborate or interact based on digital resources. Given that, systematic attempts in designing and developing web based platforms for supporting CoPs, have emerged in various domains. Typical characteristic of these platforms is the fact that they aim to function as a full-service, digital learning environment, supporting important processes for information sharing, communicating, collaborating on the basis of topics and predefined tasks. These platforms cater for content management services, project coordination services, providing to members feedback mechanisms and the ability to research on already provided content, as well as the ability for members to construct artefacts or digital products on line. These services actually take place in both individual and group level; the working group is the mediator between the individual knowledge as it transforms to community knowledge.

Web supported technological environments for CoPs, by default have to be oriented to uncover the principles embedded in existing learning practices (i.e. a problem of engineering), develop technologies to help students participate in these practices (i.e. a problem of engineering and technology development), and create experimental learning environments designed to develop life skills through participation in a community of practice (i.e. a problem of program design and action research). For these purposes tools for content research and management are important, synchronous and asynchronous communication tools, on line collaboration tools as well as space for presenting co-creation of artefacts or digital products.

Important aspects on the design of UMI-Sci-Ed platform have been the following: (a) relating sensitively to learners and working through agreed processes to build trust and confidence, (b) modeling expertise in practice or through conversation, (c) observing, analyzing and reflecting, (d) providing information, (e) relating guidance to evidence, (f) broker access to a range of opportunities (i.e. discussions with a specialist), (g) providing feedback, (h) target setting and action planning, (i) tailor activities in partnership with the professional learner. It is unlikely however that a self-selected, immediate needs-related form of self-development will produce transformational learning. The provision of online resources, need to be balanced with opportunities for interaction with others who can provide some sort of impetus to inspire a paradigm shift: this could be achieved by supervisors or link tutors working in tandem with mentors and coaches to draw their attention to specific resources which are particularly pertinent to issues arising from practice.

The aforementioned features inform the UMI-Sci-Ed platform development as outlined in the following sections.

4.2 Users

The UMI-Sci-Ed platform provides services to support the goals of many different user roles according to the requirements and the background concepts discussed previously. Consolidating all the requirements regarding the users and their roles in the platform, we concluded in the hierarchy depicted in Fig. 3.

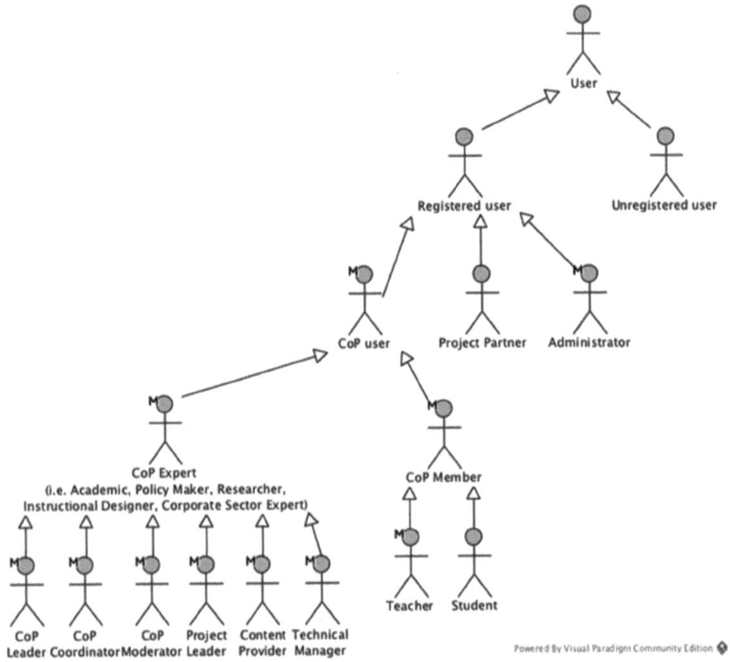

Fig. 3. UMI-Sci-Ed platform users' hierarchy.

Table 1 summarizes the goals of the primary users of UMI-Sci-Ed platform.

Table 1. User roles and their goals.

User role	Goals
CoP leader	- Identify important issues in the domain - Manage the boundary between community and formal organization - Provide leadership in resolving the problems with and in the practice - Arrange for communication support - Overlook the potential needs of CoPs changes
CoP coordinator	- Coordinate information from CoP members to avoid side effects - Inform CoP members about relevant activities elsewhere - Inform others about CoP's activities
CoP moderator	- Clarify communications - Ensure that dissenting points of view are heard and understood - Keep discussions on topic and reconcile opposites of view
Project leader	- Plan and supervise projects running in CoPs - Monitor members' progress on project completion
Content provider	- Design and develop educational material for CoPs - Upload/make public educational material through platform tools
CoP member	- Share knowledge and experience - Participate in discussions and other sessions - Raise issues and concerns regarding common needs and requirements - Devise solutions to shortcomings in formally documented methods and procedures
Technical manager	- Provide technical support/guidance to CoP members

The purpose of this analysis is to define the platforms' services that match the requirements of the various CoPs. It should be noted that in practice for CoPs targeting very busy professionals which are overloaded with tasks and information, what is needed is simplicity and flexibility regarding the accessing of the information that will be helpful in their job. For example, finding quickly the current pending tasks for the group someone belongs to or finding the artefacts someone needs to study to be prepared for the next meeting. Such requirements affect the platform presentation layout.

4.3 Services

The UMI-Sci-Ed platform offers services that are aligned with the POPP framework and support the goals of the user roles specified in the previous section. The main service categories are outlined in the following.

Content Management Services. Content and media sharing are central to the operation of CoPs. Therefore UMI-Sci-Ed platform supports various forms of content management from typical file organization in folders to metadata annotated resource filtering. Given the large amount of data the UMI-Sci-Ed platform needs to handle it is required to provide the proper functionality to organize and navigate such kind of content. In UMI-Sci-Ed the following content management services are supported:

- Management of educational content
- Management of student project specification and results
- Management of UMI app store
- Management of career opportunities/advertising.

For all the above categories of content management metadata editing is a provided feature especially for large document repositories.

Besides content management other collaboration services are evolved around content. Several such services are included in UMI-Sci-Ed platform:

- Collaborative document authoring
- Collaborative UMI app authoring
- Management of discussion forum content
- Management of blogs/microblogs content
- Management of wikis content
- Support social bookmarking
- Import on-line content libraries.

Project Coordination Services. Here we have services that implement the project management module that support the creation of a project, allocation of tasks including documents (e.g. the informed consent of the participants) and organizing activities with relevant information. Managing a calendar of events is mandatory so that all CoPs members can be informed of scheduled tasks and find information on previous tasks and meetings. Each user can add a new event to the platform and can visit the calendar section where all events are presented. Access rights can be also defined, i.e. for a new event a user could set the group audience and visibility properties so that the calendar's view can be only seen by members that have access rights.

Evaluation of tasks and project milestones assessment are also provided. Since the participants in a project may create artefacts to solve problems of practice various decision making tools can be used to assist this process (e.g. rank ideas, establish consensus, and systematically analyze information through series of steps).

Member Feedback and Research Services. CoPs workings are facilitated by allowing their members to provide feedback in the form of rating a type of content, providing comments, and finding information according to the ratings and access frequency of their colleagues. For a large content repository, like the UMI-Sci-Ed repository, such feedback can be a powerful service to quickly discover the most appropriate content (e.g. a UMI project with specific characteristics and rating) and assist the comprehension on the details of development and usage of such a content.

Poll and survey services are provided to facilitate participation to the workings of a community task from a broader group of users. Different types of questions are supported such as select options, likert-scale, and date and text fields. Analysis of the results is also provided (number of submissions per component value, calculations, and averages).

Social Media Sites Services. Although content management systems such as Drupal Commons provide basic services to build social networking capabilities within the UMI-Sci-Ed platform, mainstream social media such as Facebook and Linkedin could also be exploited by CoPs for their collaboration and interaction. As a design decision, a mix of both worlds can bring more benefits where the basic activities are supported by the platform and in addition some discussions and activities are extended into external social networking systems. Some of the mainstream platforms (e.g. Facebook) support programming linkages to their systems through Application Programming Interfaces (APIs) to allow custom integration.

Supporting Utility Services. A number of supporting utility services are provided in the UMI-Sci-Ed platform:

Login: Allowing user authentication either in the traditional way or login via Web-wide authentication services (e.g. authentication from social networking sites such as Facebook, Twitter, and Linkedin). Existing open standards are used such as OpenID or OAuth.

Access Rights Setting: Different roles may have different access rights on the stored content.

Characterize Content Visibility: A key feature of this service is a versatile set of access controls that facilitates imposing a variety of privacy policies. The dynamicity of the environment allows for setting access permissions on a fine-grain level allowing a post to be shared to a specific group of users and the next one to be shared with all the participants of a network.

Notification RECEive: Notifications are important for the operation of an active CoP. Various forms of notifications are supported such as e-mails, SMSs and social network notifications.

Web Metric Reports: Metrics reports provide information about the ways visitors (members and non-members) access, use, and benefit from CoPs content. At the initial stage of evaluating UMI-Sci-Ed platform, it is important to use metrics reports to provide statistics on the number of new members, total number of page views, average number of page views per visit, average number of messages posted per week, total number of messages posted, etc.).

Submit UMI App to Execution: Instead of the user downloading a UMI project, this is an advanced feature that is supported by the platform's middleware where the user can submit remotely the application to the h/w platform.

4.4 Data

The UMI-Sci-Ed approach generates, uses, circulates and disseminates a big amount of diverse data. These include data that support the educational and training activities, the artefacts and derivatives of the piloting and implementation phases, data that drive the research process that justifies the UMI-Sci-Ed methodology, etc. Both qualitative and quantitative in nature, may either be automatically or manually generated. The origin differs substantially, e.g., data are generated by the participants to the educational activities (e.g., students, tutors, researchers, project members or professionals), researchers that process and analyze the activities and data created in the context of the educational scenarios implementation, sensors or other artefacts producing data in the context of the pilot and implementation phases as well as the UMI-Sci-Ed platform itself. Furthermore, it is clear that the generated data follow different formats and standards due to their diverse nature and post-processing requirements. Almost all types of data are managed through the UMI-Sci-Ed platform in order to support the activities that are realized in the context of various educational scenarios.

Aiming to provide easy access and processing capabilities, all generated data by UMI-Sci-Ed platform have been classified into six dataset categories. This categorisation achieves the provision of a simple structure while keeping the major relevant data collections compact, in terms of the origin of creation and the post-processing that will be applied to the data collections. In specific, the six datasets are:

- DS1: Educational scenarios derivatives. This is the family of datasets that contains all the raw or processed data that are generated during the execution of the pilots as learning artefacts, mainly by the students and the tutors.
- DS2: Research data. This dataset includes all the quantitative and qualitative data (pre- and post-processed questionnaires, reflections, evaluations, etc.) that support educational research.
- DS3: Educational material. This dataset includes all the educational material that is developed by tutors, professionals, domain experts etc.

- DS4: Platform and market analysis data. This dataset includes information about the usage of the platform in the form of log files and evaluation forms as well as overall evaluation data that are used for market analysis and exploitation.
- DS5: Project working data. This dataset includes working documents in the context of the project, such as presentations, draft deliverable documents, deliverable review documents, etc.
- DS6: Other data. This dataset includes other types of information that are gathered in the UMI-Sci-Ed platform that cannot be categorized in one of the above datasets.

Major importance for ethical aspects is data collected as part of DS2 and DS4 datasets. For example in DS2, all data are stored without any reference to the student interacting with the platform and are password protected. In the case of the tutors collecting or generating information (interviews, assessments, reflections, etc.), the information is directly stored to the platform via proper forms with no reference to student personal data. In such cases, only demographic student data are stored (e.g., gender, age) and are password protected. Along the same lines, DS4 data including platform log files are encrypted, statistically processed and aggregated to ensure anonymity.

The UMI-Sci-Ed platform that hosts the above mentioned data has been organized in specific content types that support the educational/training/mentoring etc. activities, the most important being the *UMI Scenario*, *UMI Project*, *Group Article*, *Repository Entry*[1], *Blog*, *Survey*, *Wiki*, *Forum Topic*, *Poll*, and *Event*. In addition, a *Filedepot* is included in the platform that supports information exchange among UMI-Sci-Ed stakeholders. Table 2 provides the platform content types that are used for collecting or exchanging data of the defined datasets.

Table 2. Datasets and UMI-Sci-Ed platform content types relation.

Content Type	DS1	DS2	DS3	DS4	DS5	DS6
UMI scenario		×	×	×		
UMI project	×		×	×		
Group article		×		×		×
Repository entry		×	×	×		
Forum topic	×		×	×		×
Blog				×		×
Survey	×	×		×		
Poll	×	×		×		
Wiki			×	×		

The UMI-Sci-Ed platform is the major place of data collection and presentation either raw or processed data generated by the involved communities of practice. Additionally, publications and related research data are uploaded to Zenodo open

[1] *Repository entry* refers to entries in the Open Repository of the UMI-Sci-Ed platform.

platform (https://zenodo.org/), after proper anonymization, in order to expand visibility. All data of the content types described above that are uploaded in the project platform, including attachments, have a unique and persistent identifier of URI type that is automatically generated by the platform. Research data uploaded to Zenodo also have a unique DOI provided by Zenodo platform.

A first set of metadata has been declared for each of the content types of the platform focusing in educational research while general metadata are also going to be generated. The specific set for each content type has been decided as a compromise between a full descriptive set of metadata for educational research and low requirements of user input, so that to avoid end user dissatisfaction that will prevent users from using the platform. Therefore, *UMI Scenario* and *UMI Project* content types that are basically developed and supported by the project partners and the tutors require a significant set of metadata (provided by user input) during the setup of a scenario or a project. In all other cases user input related to metadata has been minimised.

Following the same principle, attachments in the platform are classified in two major categories: attachments including educational material that supports educational scenarios and activities under the *UMI Scenario* content type and attachments for all other content types. In the former case, educational material is classified in 5 categories, that is, Source Code, URL, Digital Document, Media Object and Rich Text, each one accompanied by a detailed set of metadata that is generated either by user input or automatically by the platform. In the latter case, attachments are categorized as file attachments, image/photos and YouTube videos and are accompanied by a minimum set of metadata that will be generated by user input in order to ease file and media exchange.

The metadata schema for educational research in the framework of the project follows the Learning Resource Metadata Initiative (LRMI) version 1.1 of Dublin Core Metadata Initiative (DCMI)[2], properly adapted and expanded to fulfil the needs of UMI-Sci-Ed. Table 3 provides the properties of *Schema.org/CreativeWork* that were adopted from LRMI specification, new properties introduced, the metadata collection method in the platform and some clarifying comments.

Table 3. LRMI properties adopted in UMI-Sci-Ed.

Property	LRMI	New	Generation method
educationalAlignment	×		User input
educationalUse	×		Automatically by the platform
timeRequired	×		User input
typicalAgeRange	×		Automatically by the platform
interactivityType	×		User input or automatically by the platform
learningResourceType	×		User input or automatically by the platform
artefactType		×	User input
licence	×		User input
educationalRole	×		User input

[2] http://dublincore.org/dcx/lrmi-terms/1.1/.

A new set of values has been defined in addition to the recommended by LRMI 1.1 values for the *alignmentType* property. These are used primarily with *UMI Scenario* and secondarily with *UMI Project* content types and are expected to enhance discoverability and reusability of UMI-Sci-Ed data. Table 4 summarizes the use of *AlignmentObject* type and its properties that are used as a basis for detailed metadata in the context of educational research. All metadata are saved in the platform for further use and presentation and they will follow the Schema.org structure.

UMI Scenario, *UMI Project*, *Group Article*, *Repository Entry*, *Blog*, *Wiki* and *Forum Topic* content types include a mandatory field for Key Terms or Tags. All of them are mapped to *schema.org/CreativeWork:keywords* property for metadata generation. Therefore, all datasets are accompanied by keywords. Keywords are available as a list (autocomplete feature) while typing new key terms or tags in the above-mentioned content types in order to enhance reusability. Keywords are searchable through the main search function of the platform.

Table 4. Properties of Schema.org/Intangible/AlignmentObject used in UMI-Sci-Ed.

AlignmentType value	LRMI	New
"learningOutcomes"		×
"educationalLevel"	×	
"educationalSubject"	×	
"umiDomain"		×
"educationalScenarioOrienation"		×
"pedagogicalTheory"		×
"requires"	×	
"activityType"		×
"learningObjectives"		×
"difficulty"		×

Versioning of *UMI Scenario*, *UMI Project* and *Wiki* content types is preserved automatically by the platform. Additionally, versioning is available for *UMI Scenario*, *UMI Project* and *Wiki* content types by user input.

4.5 Architecture

The goal of the UMI-Sci-Ed platform is to support CoPs through socialization, delivery specific of educational material, entrepreneurship training, showcases, self-evaluation, mentoring, and conceptualization of content and information management. Figure 4 shows the main components of the UMI-Sci-Ed system architecture.

The platform mainly combines a content management system with collaboration tools under a common digital environment and provides a special-purpose middleware for integrating applications with the hardware educational kit for retrieving and visualizing data.

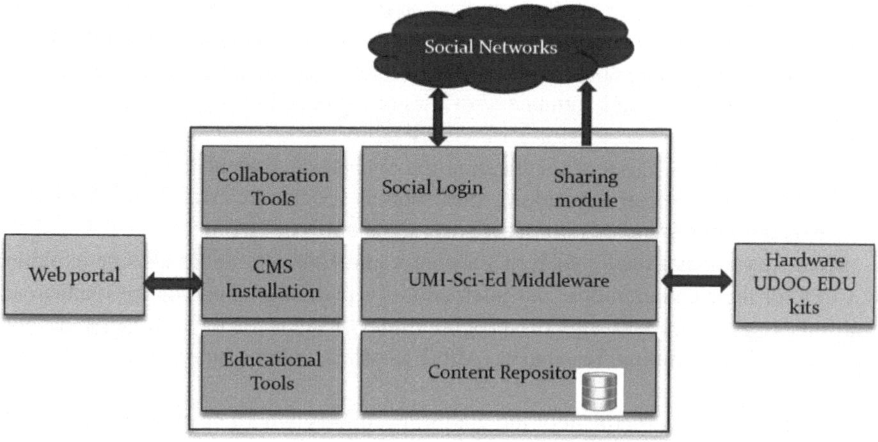

Fig. 4. UMI-Sci-Ed platform architecture

The web portal[3] is the front end of the platform and allows stakeholders to access the tools and services of the platform. The portal provides a single-entry point to the digital environment offering a unified user experience to the participants as soon as they familiarize with the environment. Instead of using multiple systems and layouts and keeping track of different streams of information the users are focusing on a single environment. The web portal gives access to services such as content repository access, forum/blog/wiki management, announcements and notifications, user profile area management, commenting and project planning and development.

The educational tools for reinforcing peer learning and mentoring include:

- An open repository of educational material on UMI.
- Self-education, training and evaluation questionnaires and tests.
- A set of training activities that allow the educational community to implement UMI scenarios in real world settings.
- A set of educational scenarios that convey both technological and pedagogical approach to future users.
- A set of UMI projects implementing the educational scenarios.

The content repository includes various forms of content such as educational material, UMI projects and results developed by the students, research results on educational approaches and methodologies, and links to tools for information extraction, management and diffusion of the produced knowledge. A key goal is to provide an "application store" of the UMI projects offering all the necessary information such as: hardware resources for program execution, a library of training materials and other information to support application use.

The collaboration tools enable CoP members to: (a) upload content and publish it to a wide audience, (b) work together in private spaces where they can share documents

[3] https://umi-sci-ed.cti.gr.

and send messages to one another, and (c) ask questions and post responses about project concepts. Other services enable students to work collaboratively on the source code of their projects and share with other CoP members and allow registered users to post ratings (e.g. 5-star) and comments/reviews on uploaded resources so as to produce rankings.

Social login allows user authentication via Web-wide authentication services (e.g. authentication from social networking sites such as Facebook, Twitter, and Linkedin). Here, existing open standards are used such as OpenID or OAuth.

Mainstream social media such as Facebook and Linkedin could also be exploited by CoPs for their collaboration and interaction. In particular, some of the mainstream platforms (e.g. Facebook) support programming linkages to their systems through Application Programming Interfaces (APIs) to allow custom integration within our platform.

The middleware component of the platform supports two kinds of communications: user-to-device and M2M communication. In the first case the middleware supports through a user interface operations such as controlling an IoT device over the web, collecting data from the devices (e.g. temperature), visualizing the collected data and exporting the collected data to various formats. In the second case instead of downloading a UMI project from the repository and installing it on the hardware kit, the user can submit remotely the application to the h/w platform. The communication between the hardware kits and the middleware is based on the HTTP protocol using JSON streams.

4.6 Implementation

The core of the platform is based on Drupal 7, an open source CMS with a variety of contributed modules from the community. The current version of the platform has over 90 Drupal modules enabled and properly configured to provide the wanted functionalities. The platform is installed on a web server running Ubuntu Server, Apache 2 as a web server with PHP 7 and MySQL 5 as a database server.

On the user interface, the approach of a user's dashboard is followed where user's information is clearly provided and is associated with relevant content (created by the user, recent used content, etc.). The current version of the platform supports 11 content types (Fig. 5). A user can create a new group, upload a UMI scenario, upload a UMI project, post a new group article, add a new entry to platform's repository, write a new post to a blog, create a survey, write a new wiki page, create a forum topic, create a new poll or create a new event. Users can also create relations between certain content types. For example, a blog post may belong to a specific group, a UMI project may be related to a specific forum topic, calendar event etc.

In particular, the "UMI project" content type allows users to upload to the platform their UMI projects or download projects created by other groups. Each UMI project has a number of specification fields to assist searching and comprehension of the corresponding applications. Fields are emanated from the UMI-Sci-Ed Educational Scenario Template discussed in Sect. 3.2. Figure 6 shows an example UMI scenario definition where a subset of the available fields have been captured.

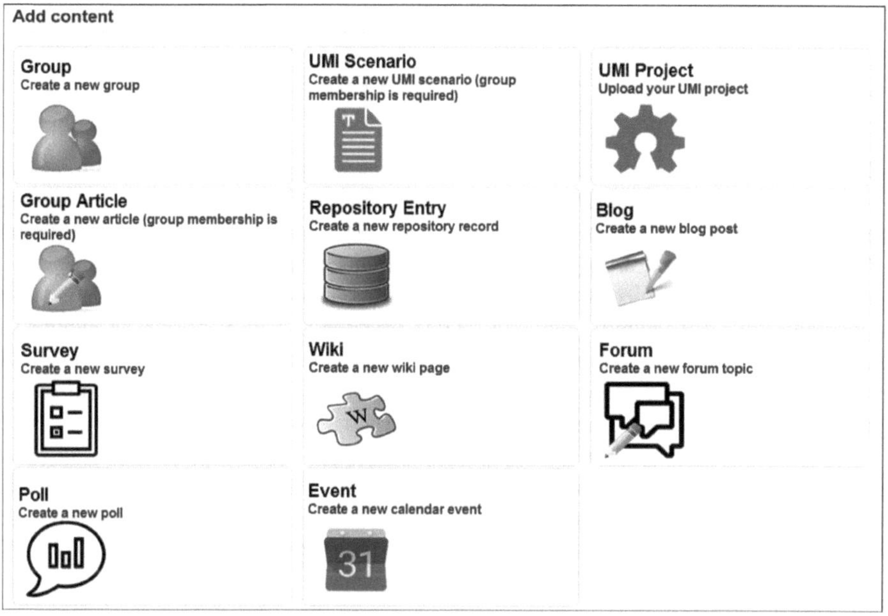

Fig. 5. UMI-Sci-Ed portal UI for content management.

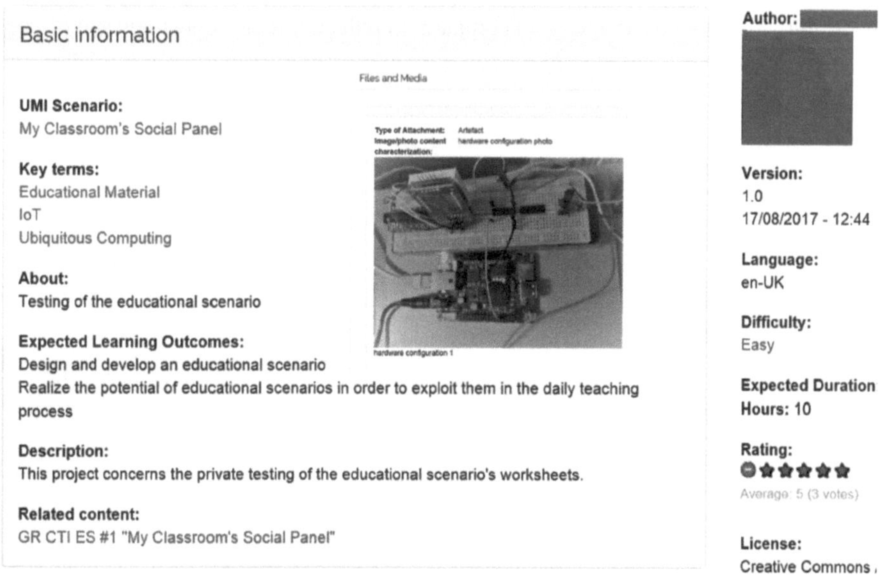

Fig. 6. UMI project definition example.

5 Evaluation

5.1 Example Educational Scenario and UMI Project

The aim of this specific scenario is to explore the Physics laws and the related theory behind the absorption of thermal radiation on surfaces of different colour and material. The students by first configuring and then using the appropriate hardware and software components are able to measure, observe and explain the details of the different behavior of materials regarding thermal radiation absorption.

Its major learning objectives are: (a) to bring about problem solving skills that are connected with UMI technologies and STEM practice, (b) to elaborate on synthesis, analysis, critical thinking and decision making, (c) to provide an insight on how UMI technologies could be used as a means for updating educational practice, and (d) to support students in developing UMI projects through experts' feedback.

One of the experiments designed included the use of a desktop incandescent lamp as a heat source and paperboards placed underneath the lamp (Fig. 7). The distance, position and angle of the material have to be specific according to the instructions and experiment scenario. Under the material a thermistor sensor is placed to monitor its temperature.

From the platform UI students can configure the experiment variables and parameters and give the command to start the measurements. When the lamp is turned on a timer is set typically to 1 min or more depending on the scenario. During the experiment the students are able to observe the temperature graphs displayed depending on the behavior of the material they test each time. So they have the opportunity to make observations, to compare, to reflect or to ask questions and discuss with their teacher.

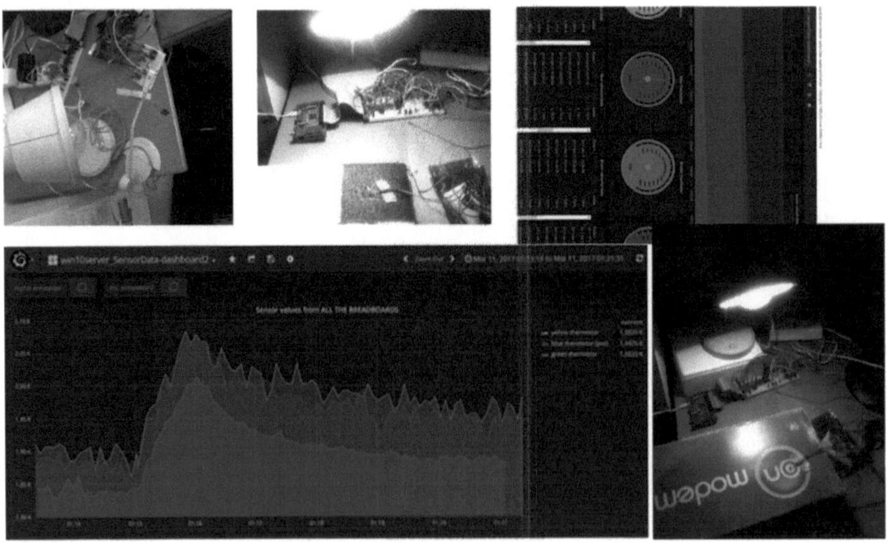

Fig. 7. Experimental setup for the educational scenario "thermal radiation absorption" [3].

The open source s/w platforms used to develop the application include:

- Node-red which is an IoT s/w platform that is used to integrate devices, APIs and on-line services with applications. We used this platform to build the user interaction environment of the application, to control devices like the lamp, and to gather values from the sensors in order to store them in the DB.
- The influxDB which implements our database to store the sensor measurements.
- The Grafana, which is the s/w tool used to create diagrams and graphs in order to visualize the sensor measurements.

5.2 Preliminary Results

A two days pre-pilot evaluation of the proposed methodology took place in a Greek high school. Fourteen (n = 14) students participated (64% female, 36% male). During the first day students were involved in introductory activities including experimental setup in terms of the required hardware and software components, presentation of material on the course subject, acquaintance with the IoT platform features, testing of the UMI-Sci-Ed platform on-line services and configuration of the UMI applications to be used in the experiments. To collect research data an initial questionnaire has been delivered to participating students, aiming to assess their knowledge on the course topic, their familiarity to technology, as well as to assess attitudes and openness regarding UMI technologies exploitation in education. The students replies showed that: (a) all of them had adequate familiarity with technology; (b) they did not know much about the microprocessor boards and had little knowledge about IoT; and (c) they had a positive attitude and expectation regarding the UMI enhanced educational activity.

During the second day the designed experiments were conducted and the UMI application was used to measure, display and record temperature changes under different conditions and various materials in order to have a hands-on experience regarding thermal radiation absorption mechanisms and make associations with the relevant physics laws.

On the educational part active exploration techniques was possible to apply in line with the principles of reflective and peer learning. For example, the students were asked through worksheets to explore the factors that affect thermal absorption, i.e. distance of material from the heat source, material colour/thickness, position angle, heating duration and amplitude, heat type (radiation, current, conduction, combination), ambient temperature, surface/material temperature etc. They repeated the experiment by changing one factor each time, measured the temperature and compared the results to identify causality or correlations. A playful and participatory approach to increase engagement through gamification was also possible. Given certain task characteristics each team picked the materials that they believed can satisfy the requested properties and behaviour, and validated their hypothesis by using the UMI application. The teams that reached closer to the specifications won.

A second questionnaire was handed to the students with an aim to evaluate both the robustness of the application components and the learning benefits as a result of using IoT technology and applications. The graph at the lower left in Fig. 8 depicts the

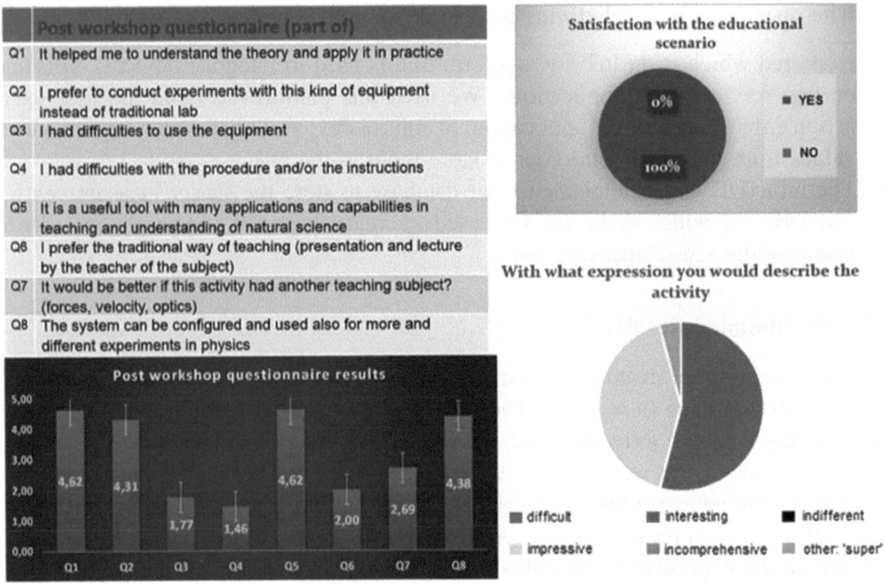

Fig. 8. UMI application evaluation results [3].

questionnaire results using a cumulative scoring scale method (Likert scale 1–5). Almost all students conveyed a clear benefit in understanding the theory and its connection to practical use through UMI applications. They also expressed a preference for using the IoT toolkit in combination with configurable software programs compared to traditional analogue instruments and manual recordings. We also surveyed whether the students realized that the approach presented was not representing a monolithic system serving a single purpose but a platform that can be adapted, configured and used in many other Physics experiments. The majority of the students embraced that view which justifies the point that such systems can be accepted as learning tools in school communities.

The overall impression obtained from this first assessment was positive based on the comments expressed by the students. In addition they found the educational scenario to be helpful, the tasks performed useful and rated positively the overall learning experience. The message delivered is that the UMI approach is promising and can be developed to a valuable educational tool empowering students learning experiences. Even with this form of limited evaluation it was possible to test several aspects of the UMI-Sci-Ed platform including the versatility of the IoT toolkit towards supporting the circuit design and implementation of educational scenarios as well as the supporting services of the software platform including delivering of educational material on UMI technologies, sharing of UMI applications, gathering and storing experimental data, supporting polls and surveys and disseminating results and experiences via social media.

6 Conclusions

Using scenarios in education enables the orchestration of the learning process as well as the gradual employment of technological tools that further support the learning process as a whole. In our work the structure of the UMI EST has been the pillar and semiotic artefact based on which secondary school teachers, researchers, practitioners, design their own educational scenarios and collaborate on the basis of designing also small projects that actually interrelate with their educational scenarios. The added value of such an inclusion, providing an instructional tool for CoPs' members, so as users to collaborate has been: (a) to create an integrated learning environment with multiple of stimuli for engaging in the design process, (b) to organize design products, emerging out of the design process, and (c) to provide a common basis to all CoPs' stakeholders so as to start building common understanding on communities' purposes, goals and final products. The strength of the scenario approach lies in separating between an intellectual fiction and complex realities as a means to acquire a better understanding of commonalities between "real" organizations (i.e. firms, schools etc.) and an intellectual design.

Although the UMI platform shares common characteristics with other online portals that collect and present STEM educational material and provide collaboration support to active groups it is diversified from them because it integrates under a common technological environment CoPs management and the UMI technical tools to assist students both acquiring relevant competences and being motivated in pursuing a career in related domains. On a technical level, the middleware layer of the platform allows to perform remote management of the IoT device, visualize the data, and trigger actions as a result of rules on the received data. Another differential aspect is the use of the designed Educational Scenario Template as the core instructional tool, to encapsulate all important components of the learning process.

The evaluation presented represents a set of preparatory activities required for the official UMI-Sci-Ed pilot studies setup. Field research will follow in educational conditions involving five European countries (Finland, Greece, Ireland, Italy and Norway) in order to test in a broad educational context the UMI-Sci-Ed methodology. The research sample includes five schools from each country and about 25 students per class.

The participation of the students, the teachers and the school community members is expected to produce several outputs. Variables to be analyzed include usability, motivation interest, knowledge and engagement. Media include surveys, interviews, observations and cognitive tests. The collected quantitative and qualitative feedback elements are going to be analyzed to construct knowledge about the whole process. The results of using an evaluation framework that will assess the impact of such activities in terms of learning gains are also expected.

Acknowledgements. The UMI-Sci-Ed project has received funding from the European Union's Horizon 2020 research and innovation programme under grant agreement No 710583. The authors would like to thank the fellow researchers who participated in this project.

References

1. Goumopoulos, C., Xanos, N., Kameas, A.: Leveraging STEM education via UMI technologies. In: 16th World Conference on Mobile and Contextual Learning, p. 11. ACM, Larnaca (2017)
2. Goumopoulos, C., et al.: ATRACO: adaptive and trusted ambient ecologies. In: 2nd IEEE International Conference on Self-Adaptive and Self-Organizing Systems Workshops (SASOW 2008), pp. 96–101. IEEE, Venice (2008)
3. Goumopoulos, C., et al.: The UMI-Sci-Ed platform: integrating UMI technologies to promote science education. In: 10th International Conference on Computer Supported Education (CSEDU 2018), vol. 1, pp. 78–90. SCITEPRESS, Funchal (2018)
4. Delistavrou, K.T., Kameas, A.D.: Exploring ways to exploit UMI technologies in STEM education: comparison of secondary computer science curricula of Greece, Cyprus and England. In: Proceedings of the 2017 Global Engineering Education Conference (EDUCON), pp. 1824–1830. IEEE, Athens (2017)
5. Brzozowy, M., et al.: Making STEM education attractive for young people by presenting key scientific challenges and their impact on our life and career perspectives. In: 11th International Technology, Education and Development Conference (INTED 2017), pp. 9948–9957. IATED, Valencia (2017)
6. Wenger, E.: Communities of practice: a brief introduction. University of Oregon (2011)
7. Goumopoulos, C., Nicopolitidis, P., Gavalas, D., Kameas, A.: A distance learning curriculum on pervasive computing. Int. J. Contin. Eng. Educ. Life Learn. **27**(1–2), 122–146 (2017)
8. Gunawardena, C.N., Hermans, M.B., Sanchez, D., Richmond, C., Bohley, M., Tuttle, R.: A theoretical framework for building online communities of practice with social networking tools. Educ. Media Int. **46**(1), 3–16 (2009)
9. Dalsgaard, C.: Social software: E-learning beyond learning management systems. Eur. J. Open, Distance E-Learn. **9**(2), 1–7 (2006)
10. Wu, Y., Kropczynski, J., Shih, P.C., Carroll, J.M.: Exploring the ecosystem of software developers on GitHub and other platforms. In: 17th ACM Conference on Computer Supported Cooperative Work, pp. 265–268, ACM, Baltimore (2014)
11. Lammer, L., Lepuschitz, W., Kynigos, C., Giuliano, A., Girvan, C.: ER4STEM educational robotics for science, technology, engineering and mathematics. In: Merdan, M., Lepuschitz, W., Koppensteiner, G., Balogh, R. (eds.) Robotics in Education. AISC, vol. 457, pp. 95–101. Springer, Cham (2017). https://doi.org/10.1007/978-3-319-42975-5_9
12. Lehman, J.D., Ertmer, P.A., Bessenbacher, A.M.: STEMEdhub: supporting STEM education initiatives via the HUBzero platform. Educ. Technol. **55**(2), 31–34 (2015)
13. CTC by Arduino: Creative Technologies in the Classroom (2017). http://www.electronics-lab.com/ctc-arduino-creative-technologies-classroom/
14. Penuel, W.R., Frank, K.A., Krause, A.: The distribution of resources and expertise and the implementation of schoolwide reform initiatives. In: 7th International Conference of the Learning Sciences, pp. 522–528, International Society of the Learning Sciences, Bloomington (2006)
15. Wenger, E., McDermott, R.A., Snyder, W.: Cultivating Communities of Practice: A Guide to Managing Knowledge. Harvard Business Press, Boston (2002)
16. Snyder, W.M., De Souza Briggs, X.: Communities of practice: a new tool for government managers. November 2003 Series Collaboration. IBM Center for the Business of Government (2003)

17. Dirckinck-Holmfeld, L.: Designing virtual learning environments based on problem oriented project pedagogy. In: Dirckinck-Holmfeld, L., Fibiger, B. (eds.) Learning in Virtual Environments, pp. 31–54. Samfundslitteratur Press, Frederiksberg (2002)
18. Elmore, B., Mariappan, J., Hays, G.: Improving performance through simulation - a scenario based learning approach. White Paper, Experia Solutions (2003)
19. Fragou, O., Kameas, A., Zaharakis, I.: An instructional design process for creating a U-Learning Ecology. In: Proceedings of the 2017 Global Engineering Education Conference (EDUCON), pp. 1817–1823. IEEE, Athens (2017)
20. Carnegie Science Center: The role of STEM education in improving the tri-state region's workforce (2014). http://www.carnegiesciencecenter.org/stemcenter/stemcenter-work-to-do-the-role-of-stem-education/

Developing an Online Authoring Tool to Support Teachers in Designing 21st Century Design Based Education in Primary School

Tilde Bekker[1], Ruurd Taconis[2(✉)], Saskia Bakker[1], and Bernice d'Anjou[1]

[1] Department of Industrial Design, Eindhoven University of Technology, Den Dolech 2, Eindhoven, The Netherlands
{m.m.bekker,s.bakker}@tue.nl, b.e.m.d.anjou@student.tue.nl
[2] Eindhoven School of Education, Eindhoven University of Technology, Den Dolech 2, Eindhoven, The Netherlands
r.taconis@tue.nl

Abstract. Design Based learning (DBL) as an educational approach which is emerging in primary education. Because of the limited availability of prescribed teaching materials for DR, learning activities are often developed by instructors themselves. However, it is often difficult for teachers to develop DBL activities. The paper investigates how primary school teachers can be supported in developing successful DR learning activities, in which pupils can develop both core curriculum objectives and 21st century skills. The research questions are: How can teachers be supported in the design of DBL activities aimed at concrete learning objectives? Are teachers able to apply the DBL creation tool as intended; to follow the design strategy offered, to reflect on the DBL activities using the tool and to improve the design iteratively? Are teachers able to successfully develop DBL learning activities using the tool?

The paper describes the development of a tool that supports primary school teachers in creating DBL teaching materials. A web-based tool has been realized iteratively by means of design research. The resulting supports the teachers in developing 21st century education and encourages the teacher to reflect, even if it does not yet produce complete teaching materials for the classroom. However, in order to be effective in promoting DBL, there is a need to integrate the underlying concepts of DBL (such as incorporating design generations into the course material) even more extensively into the tool and to supplement it with an explicit pedagogical strategy and concrete assessment procedures.

Keywords: Design Based Learning · Authoring tool · Primary education

1 Introduction

In order to be carefully prepared for the future, children today are increasingly encouraged to learn 21st century skills such as working together and solving problems. Teachers are faced with the challenge of integrating these skills into their lessons, in

B. M. McLaren et al. (Eds.): CSEDU 2018, CCIS 1022, pp. 142–165, 2019.
https://doi.org/10.1007/978-3-030-21151-6_8

addition to achieving the regular core curriculum objectives such as arithmetic, writing and subject knowledge. Interest in Design Based Learning (DBL) [1, 2] is growing among primary school teachers. They see it as helpful in teaching children 21st century skills. DBL (Design Based Learning) is an educational approach in which pupils learn by developing ('designing') solutions for (open) social challenges in cooperation with each other through design-methodology. During DBL the pupils work on authentic challenges, which often lead to intrinsic motivation, and provide insight into how the learned knowledge and skills can be applied in practice.

Despite the fact that DBL is seen as an appropriate approach to learning 21st century skills [3], there are practical obstacles, which often prevent primary school teachers from (successfully) implementing DBL in class. There are no fully developed textbooks, the teacher has to take on a coaching role as opposed to the traditional role of teacher [4] and the teaching materials often have to be developed by the teachers themselves [5]. The development of suitable DBL teaching materials is also challenging and time-consuming; teachers are often unfamiliar with the concept of DBL, unable to determine the appropriate level of openness in the assignment for the pupils, and experience difficulties in linking DBL activities to the development of crucial basic skills (such as numeracy and language skills).

The project was carried out in very close cooperation with three schools of PlatOOlab [24]. PlatOOlab is an organisation of schools in the south of the Netherlands that is interested in educational innovation and seeks to implement the teaching of 21st century skills.

This chapter presents the development of an online tool that supports primary school teachers in creating DBL learning activities. This DBL creation tool seeks to help teachers to integrate 21st century learning goals into DBL activities. In this, it also seeks to encouraging teachers to reflect on the DBL activities they have developed, thus strengthening the teachers' professional agency. The DBL creation tool has been developed in three iterative cycles, in collaboration with teachers and the directors of the three participating schools. The design of the tool is based on the design in the master thesis of van der Sanden [30].

2 Related Work

2.1 Design Based Learning and 21st Century Skills

Europe is facing an "innovation crisis": research needs to be better translated into new and better products and services in order to improve quality of life in Europe and to remain competitive in the global marketplace. To counter this crisis, Europe needs people with an entrepreneurial and creative way of thinking. However, current education largely concentrates on knowledge acquisition, automated skills, and little emphasis is put on understanding, critical thinking, the ability to apply knowledge in new situations, creativity and collaborative skills. As a result, teachers, entrepreneurs, academics and public authorities are increasingly calling for the implementation of the so-called 21st century skills [3], that particularly focus on the less traditional academic skills needed for the future.

Trilling and Fadel [6] have divided 21st century skills into three categories (see Fig. 1):

- Learning and innovation skills, including critical thinking, Problem-solving thinking, Communication, Collaboration, Creativity, Innovation and entrepreneurial skills;
- Digital literacy skills, including information literacy, media literacy and information and communication technology (ICT) literacy;
- Career and life skills, including flexibility and adaptability, initiative and self-management, social and multicultural interaction, productivity and responsibility.

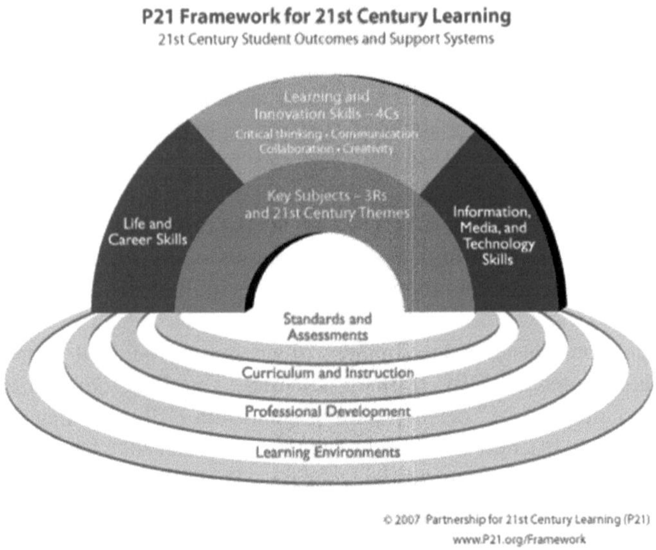

Fig. 1. A model of learning 21st century skills [6].

As a teaching/learning strategy, Design Based Learning facilitates various of these 21st century skills. Since DBL focusses on solving complex and poorly defined design problems, this would challenge pupils critical thinking, creativity and self-directed learning ability [7].

The Design Based Learning process follow consists of a series of steps, such as: exploring the problem, developing ideas, building and testing prototypes and evaluating the outcome. In projects, some of these steps may be performed more than once, since during the process new temporary designs become available to be tested, new perspectives may be discovered instigating re-testing of re-design, and new aspects to the problem may become visible pointing for solutions in new directions that are to be explored. However, a DBL project will typically start with a divergent, chaotic phase and then gradually move forward towards a solution; a process in which the emphasis gradually shifts towards convergent thinking (Fig. 2).

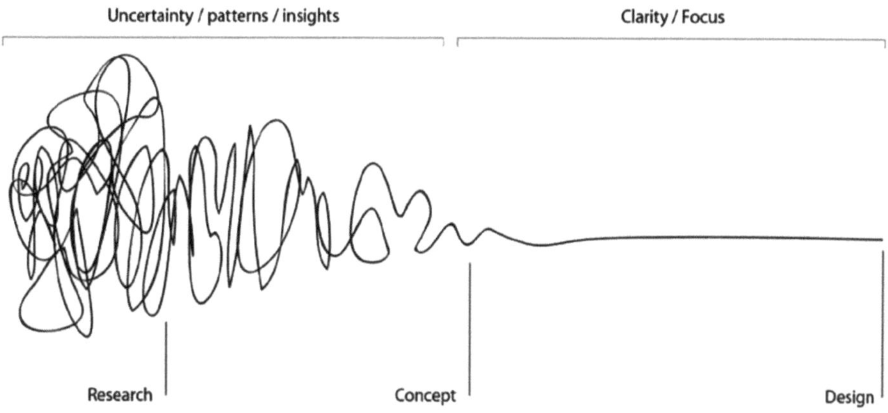

Fig. 2. How the process of divergence and convergence proceeds to a clear final design [34].

Teaching using DBL is attracting increasing interest [7]. However, it has been little applied in schools, mainly due to practical problems such as a lack of Design Based teaching materials and un acquaintance of the teachers with DBL. Moreover, examination syllabi may get in the way, putting pressure on classroom practice preventing teacher to explore with new forms of education, even those aiming for the learning of the desired 21st century skills.

Nevertheless, DBL has been identified as an innovation with the potential to bring about a major change in learning and can contribute to a new pedagogy, which may transform education [7].

Teachers are the key to the successful educational change and the implementation of DBL. In order to bring a change, teachers must understand the principles of DBL, integrate these into their professional conception of teaching, and need an overview of means and techniques to practically implement DBL in their classrooms. To do this, teachers need resources, examples and professional development opportunities [8].

Such implementation will very much involve the teacher in the role of 'learning activity/material designer'. For this, a variety of educational frameworks is available, such as Van den Akker's spider web (Fig. 3) [9]. Such frameworks can help to structure educational processes and their design. In this study, the 'spider web framework' was used to develop a practical tool for primary school teachers to design their own DBL learning activities.

The various learning elements in the spider web al interact in establishing effective education. The spider web gives an overview of the learning elements that are to be orchestrated in order to arrive at a coherent lesson or lesson series. We used it as a basis for the lay-out of our educational design support tool. In this, we downplayed the learning elements 'forms of collaboration' and 'sources and materials' but put extra emphasis on the element 'role of the pupil'. The results form a solid foundation for our design support tool that will assure that the teachers will pay adequate attention to all elements.

Fig. 3. The curricular 'spider web' by Van den Akker [9].

2.2 Tools for Teachers

No 'plug and plan' teacher design support tools are available. Existing educational materials that focus on promoting Design Based learning in education, such as Stanford 'd.school' [10], focus on the Design Based learning materials, rather than on supporting the instructor to design the learning materials himself. A toolkit that helps teachers to integrate Design Based learning into their lessons, an approach that has much in common with DBL, has been developed by the IDEO [11]. This toolkit uses Design Based learning to support teachers in developing new teaching materials. But this not necessary is Design Based Learning Material. Unlike these toolkits, our approach is specifically focused on supporting teachers in creating DBL in which students learn 21st century skills.

To support designing teachers, it is crucial to reduce the 'design space'. A first component is structuring the design process. This takes away much of the interrelatedness of the various design choices which is difficult to understand for the novice teacher/designer. Structuring can be less strict for more proficient teachers/designers that already can understand the 'when and why' of various choices [35]. A second component is to make design options transparent, and to reduce their number through pre-selection.

To make websites that present complex processes or situations in an intuitive and predictable way, these should be structured according to users' mental model(s) of these processes or situations. An example is the lay-out of the railway station manager's dashboard. Hence the online design tool should be organized according to the teachers' perception of the process of 'planning education'. This model can be found by examining how a representative group of teachers views this [36, 37].

Structuring the design process and pre-selecting design options alone would 'robotize' the teachers' design process, frustrate teachers as autonomous professionals and hinder their development as reflective practitioners [27]. Hence the online support system should give room for teachers' professional autonomy and professional decisions. Moreover, it should stimulate reflection while designing education. Even more so for designing DBL since reflection is in the heart of the design process itself [2].

Hence, structuring and pre-selection of design choices should be minimized, but must also be rigorous enough to prevent cognitive overload. Scaffolding and guidance to support teacher in taking the remaining design-decisions is key. An adaptive strategy was developed [38]: Guided Learner Adaptable Scaffolding (GLAS). They distinguish 3 types of scaffolds: supportive (e.g. advise, highlighting options), reflective (e.g. clarifying alternatives and criteria, asking for deliberations), intrinsic (e.g. relating to the design process as a whole).

2.3 Properties of DBL Activities

In developing a tool that supports teacher in the creation of DBL learning activities, we need to start from a clear description of DBL and its characteristics. Here only a short description can be given - a more detailed description based on various resources [12–14] can be found in [2]. Design Based learning activities consist of the following six components:

1. *Design Elements and a Design Process*

The design process should move through various steps and the focus should gradually shift from divergence (e.g. generating directions and ideas) and to convergence (e.g. deciding on the size of the challenge and selecting ideas). In DBL, the design problem that students work on should be valuable for real life. The project should aim for adding value for the user, subject and possibly for other stakeholders.

2. *Collaborative Learning and Reflection Process*

Reflection plays a crucial role in the design processes [39]. Through reflection, questions are articulated concerning the aim, design or current prototype. Seeking answers can involve theoretical exploration, a shift in view-point, information search of testing. At the same time, reflection plays an important role in the learning process since it contributes to understanding and personal internalization of results. Hence, it directly contributes to 21st century learning. In DBL, the pupils learn by iteratively switching between doing and reflecting. Group work and collaborating promotes this process.

3. *Assessment and Learning Objectives*

Learning objectives of DBL activities should comprise both skills (e.g. design skills, 21st century skills) and the 'classical' learning goals such as knowledge (e.g. mother tongue) or domain-specific skills (e.g. arithmetic).

4. *Project Properties and Design Assignment*

The design assignment, i.e. the (social) challenge for which the pupils are asked to come up with a solution, should be open and should provide the pupils with the opportunity to work on relevant learning objectives. The design project must be recognizable and motivating for the pupils. In addition, it should match the level of the students. Based on the similarities between learning from inquiry and learning from DBL, the level scheme of Ireland, Watters, Lunn Brownlee and Lupton [22] and with the addition of the degree of self-determination by the pupils, can be elaborated into a level scheme that indicates at which levels in DBL can be worked. Levels are: experienced, getting acquainted, challenging, guided design, targeted design, coached design.

5. *Teacher and Pupil Role*

In DBL, it is important that the instructor properly fulfils his/her coaching role. Pupils should increasingly take responsibility for the design process, products and learning outcomes. They themselves are the driving force behind their design and learning process. Teachers must give room for this but should offer just as much support that the tasks for the individual students are manageable, challenging and motivating [6].

6. *Teaching Materials and Learning Environment*

Just like the design assignments, the learning environment is open to be decided on by the teachers. This means that the local school environment and/or parents are principally involved in the project. This gives external confirmation and value to the entire effort. It creates meaning, relevance and motivation in the pupils.

These six components serve as a beacon in developing the DBL support tool.

3 Methodology

3.1 Research Questions

The central research question is: *Can an online tool be developed that supports primary school teachers creating 21st century lessons that include 'classical learning goals' using DBL?*

This question is structured on the basis of the following sub-research questions:

(1) Are primary school teachers able to apply the DBL creation tool as intended; in particular, to follow the design strategy offered, to reflect on the DBL learning activities using the tool and to improve the design from there iteratively?
(2) Are primary school teachers able to successfully develop DBL learning activities by means of the DBL creation tool?;
  (a) Are the DBL learning activities, which the instructors develop by means of the tool, generally practical and educationally sound (can be implemented)?
  (b) Do the DR learning activities, which teachers develop by means of the tool, have the intended characteristics (authentic, open, limited problem space, core objectives, etc.)?
  (c) Do the DR learning activities, which teachers develop by means of the tool, enable pupils to achieve the desired learning objectives of both types?

3.2 Research Setup

The development of the DBL creation tool was done using the methodology of Design Research [15–17]. Design research has many similarities with e.g. a design approach used for developing computer-based products [18]. In this educational methodology research and design move forward simultaneously. After an initial design, 'experimental phases and evaluation' and 'redesign' alternate. The entire process can consist of several rounds.

The first evaluation round usually deals with basic issues occurring in the designed material such as missing communications, smaller structural inconsistencies, technical flaws of textural errors that hamper classroom process. Hence open data-collection methods are preferred, while additional information is usually collected, for example by expert reviews. The first round usually only produces indicative answers to the research questions. In the second and following round, the full focus is on answering the research questions.

Evaluation is often carried out using a multi method approach in which the results of e.g. material-analysis, classroom observations and interview or questionnaires are combined [19]. Data from these different sources are combined by triangulation providing internal confirmation [e.g. 19].

The various data sources principally address the education to be evaluated at different curriculum levels [20]. Interviews with teachers – for example - address the 'perceived curriculum', whereas classroom observations address the 'observed curriculum'. Hence, the data from the various sources supplement each other. Alignment and discrepancies point out the level to which the 'intended curriculum' was actually transformed in 'classroom reality'.

Data collection and analysis was organized according to the evaluation scheme shown in Table 1). Five 'main variables' are evaluated on 4 of the Goodlad - curriculum levels: Theoretical, Perceived, Material and Experienced curriculum. For each level particular data-sources are available (bottom row in Table 1). When used, the cell of the scheme fill, and comparison of the findings in one row over various columns reveals how the intentions underpinning the tool worked through in e.g. teacher perceptions, teaching materials created and/or classroom reality.

Table 1. General evaluation scheme [24].

	Curriculum level			
	T	P	M	E
General **A**spects of education: goals, methods, evaluation, … [26]				
Adoption and **I**mplementation: understandability, usefulness, easy to use, congruence [21]				
DBL characteristics: structure, steps, reflection (Rotherham and Willingham [40]), [1]				
Teacher **G**uidance: structure/fit to teachers mental model, option reduction/cognitive load, guidance, reflectiveness, [28]				
Learning **G**oals within DBL created: classical learning goals, 21st century goals				

Goodlad [20] levels of curriculum:
T = Theoretical curriculum: analysis of the tool, expert panel, user interviews
P = Perceived curriculum: teacher interviews, classroom observations
M = Material curriculum: analysis of classroom materials
E = Experienced curriculum: classroom observations, student interviews

The categories reflect the studies research questions. The first category is fundamental to evaluate the general effects off the tool on the created education and concern general aspects of learning environments according to [26]. The second employs the work of [21] on adoption of educational innovations and implementability. Key factors considered here are: understandability, usefulness, ‘easy to use’, and congruence with the teachers’ convictions.

The third category ensures the evaluation of the way the tool addresses the various DBL components (Table 1). The fourth category focusses on teacher support and the stimulation of reflection. The fifth category concerns the educational goals.

3.3 Participants and Data Collection

The project was performed in a team of 6 researchers including an ICT specialist, and one researcher who was not part of the designing team. An expert panel was formed that comprised 7 experts in the field of education and/or the use of ICT in education. The various versions of the tool were tested by 7 teachers. Three school directors were involved, making up stakeholder-board and feedback group.

Instruments. Our multi-method [19] approach comprises: formative analysis of the tool by stakeholders and experts, interviews with teachers, observation of teachers who design lessons with the DBL tool, observations in the class that apply the course material made, and an analysis of the course material designed with the tool.

Workshops. During the development of the tool, three co-creation sessions with stakeholders were organized, at which school leaders and teachers of the PlatOO schools were present. In addition, a number of educational researchers/teachers from and around the Eindhoven School of Education were asked to assess the tool formatively as an expert. In the first research round no format was not imposed beforehand [8] and the results of this were immediately incorporated into the first design. Questions that were raised in the co-creation sessions of the first round:

- How can a DBL activity be organized in practice?
- What are the characteristics of a DBL activity to be a good learning activity?
- How can a tool support the creation of DBL activities?

Expert Panel. In sessions of 30–60 min, five educational experts were interviewed individually about the DBL properties that the tool weighs up and how reflection can best be stimulated among teachers during the design process. Furthermore, the tool was evaluated in terms of ‘practical ease of use for teachers’. The questions put central in this expert panel were:

- Background; (Experience, expertise)
- What is your prior knowledge of Design Based Learning?
- To what extent is DBL being stimulated by this tool?
- Does the DBL become clear in this tool for teachers who have no previous experience in this field?
- To what extent is this tool supportive for teachers?
- To what extent does the tool encourage the teacher to reflect on the composition of the lesson?
- And how could this best be facilitated?

Background Interview. Prior to the experimental use of the tool by teachers, a 'background interview' was held with these teachers to get a clear picture of their background, previous knowledge, perspective on teaching, etc. The topics discussed were:

- Background; (experience, age, training, classes taught, ...)
- How do you design your lessons?
- Proficiency concerning design and DBL: (knowledge, experience, tool seen previously, expectation, motivation, ...)
- Perceived issues in current education that DBL could help to solve
- 21st century skills:
  - Knowledge
  - How do you already do this in your education?
  - Reflection by pupils in your education; importance? how? How many?
  - Planning by pupils in your education; importance? how? How many?
  - Practical: What is going to happen? Planning; (when in lesson, number of lessons, group, time, subject, ...)

Observation of Designing Teachers. In a 60-min session, the teachers were observed while using the tool to design a Design Based learning activity. During the design process, the actions carried out by the teachers and the discussions were recorded: by observation, audio-taping as well as 'digitally'. A researcher was present to help the teachers in case they got stuck. After the design session there will be a short interview. Topics of the interview/observations are derived from the general analysis schedule, in particular: the ease of use of the tool; the workflow (are the design steps in the tool understandable and logically organized/sequenced in the experience of the teacher); the considerations/reflection that the tool provokes; comments from the designing teacher.

Observation in the Classroom. Lessons were observed in which the teachers used their self-designed DBL-material in classroom. Special attention was paid to the points indicated in the last column of Table 1. In classroom the DBL-characteristics of the education in practice can be evaluated. Also, it can be seen to what extent the use of the tool has contributed to a lesson design that may or may not function properly. In the first round this usually is a 'rough picture' due to the practical and functional issues concerning the tool and its use (see above).

4 Developing the DBL Creation Tool – Round One

The development of the DBL creation tool presented in this paper happened in two iterative development rounds. This section reports on round one.

4.1 Starting Point and Paper Version of the DBL Creation Tool

The development of the DBL creation tool is based on the experiences gathered in earlier work by the authors [2] in which several design explorations investigates how digital means can support children and teachers in the Design Based Learning process.

The focus was mainly on supporting the children. As part of this earlier work, a literature study was carried out to determine the important characteristics of Design Based learning activities, as described in the related work section. These activities have also led to a paper version of an 'initial' DBL creation tool (see Figs. 4 and 5) [30].

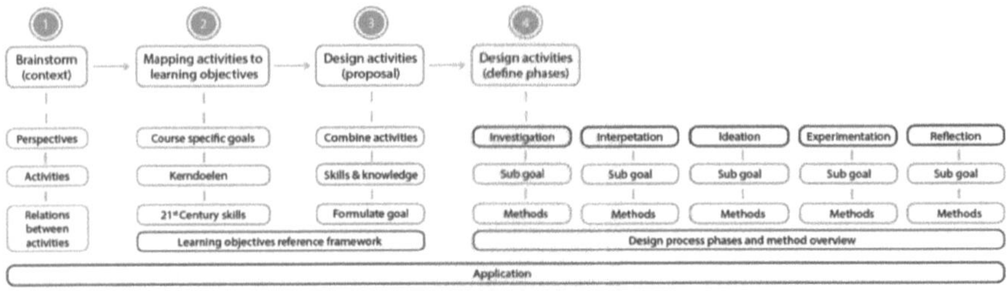

Fig. 4. The paper based first iteration of the DBL creation tool.

In the first phase of the development of this paper-based tool, we looked at how the structure of a design process can be linked to topics and practice of today's primary school class. Co-creation sessions were held with three teachers from two primary schools. During these sessions, DBL activities were created using the initial DBL-framework as shown in Fig. 4. The main insights of these activities were that teachers can develop learning activities on the basis of this framework and that a mind map activity can be used by teachers to brainstorm about how to link the learning objectives to a design assignment that is meaningful to their pupils [30]. The created learning activities also showed that dividing the design process into design phases, learning objectives and (suggested) design methods, was a useful structure for the teachers [30].

To give an example, one teacher made a DBL activity for 3 sessions in which the pupils had to develop a menu for the school restaurant that would appeal to the user group and that would be healthy. A mind map allowed the teacher to brainstorm on the topics that come up in the design assignment, such as user requirements, cooking and healthy eating considerations, the knowledge that should be provided to the students during the different phases of the process and the learning goals that could be assessed. Using this first paper prototype of the tool resulted in a paper-based lesson planning made by the teachers (see Fig. 5) [30].

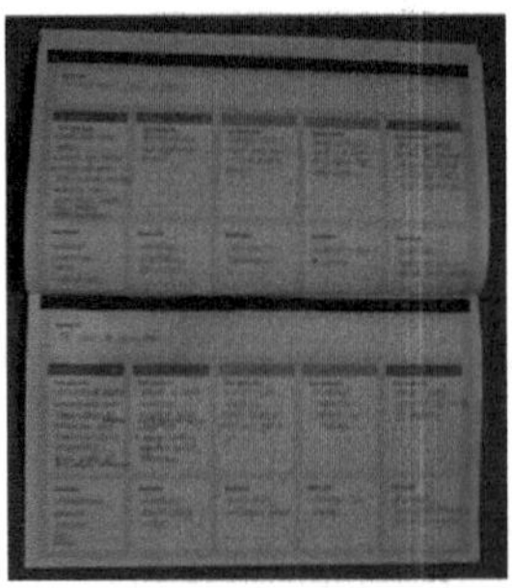

Fig. 5. The paper-based lesson planning made by the teachers.

4.2 Developing the First Digital Version of the DBL Creation Tool

To make the tool more dynamic and accessible, we aimed to further develop it into a digital DBL creation tool. To do so, two co-creation workshops were organized with teachers, school principals and design-researchers. The first workshop aimed to gather further requirements for a DBL creation tool and the second workshop aimed to elicit and verify the 'building blocks' that are needed to create successful DBL learning-activities.

The discussion during the first workshop confirmed that the workshop-participants considered the concept of DBL to be very well suited for the learning of 21st century skills. The participants experienced that teachers are often uncertain about which regular core curriculum objectives can be addressed in DBL learning activities. A tool to create DBL activities should therefore help teachers, during the process of designing the activities, to get a clear picture of the possible core objectives that can be addressed. Additionally, the participants noted that not all teachers have the same level of experience in creating DBL activities, therefore the tool might support different experience levels of users (e.g. a more step-by-step approach for novices, and more freedom for experienced teachers). Practical requirements that surfaced during the workshop included the suggestion that the tool must deliver a very concrete product that can be stored and shared; the suggestion to make the tool suitable for different grades of primary school; and the suggestion that the tool should match with infrastructures already available in schools.

Based on the insights from the first workshop, a 'workflow' or step-by-step process was identified that teachers could go through when developing DBL learning activities. This workflow was further discussed in a second workshop. Participants in this workshop concluded that most teachers will use this workflow in a step-by-step fashion, starting with the decision on the general design assignment context and theme, and ending by deciding on the specific methods used. However, to accommodate more experienced teachers, the tool should also support a flexible workflow, in which teachers can choose the order in which they develop the DBL activities.

By discussing the workflow, the workshop participants also formulated a number of new requirements for the DBL creation tool. Firstly, the tool should provide help in selecting different learning goals (e.g. 21st century goals and subject-specific goals). Secondly, it should support the practical planning of the design process. Thirdly, it should support an iterative and reflective approach to designing teaching materials, by stimulating teachers to regularly reflect on the materials they developed.

As a result of the two workshops, the workflow what translated into 7 concrete building-blocks that are required to design a DBL activity. These building-blocks, visualized in Fig. 6 form the basis of the DBL creation tool. The tool guides teachers through these building blocks and thus helps them to set up a Design Based learning activity.

As visualized in Fig. 6, teachers are recommended to start with the bottom three building blocks, 'Authentic learning environment', 'Theme' and 'Class', which together form the context in which the Design Based learning activity takes place. Following, in the 'Assignment frame' building block, the teacher records certain choices that together form a direction (assignment frame) for the assignment. The teacher can use this frame when writing the draft project brief. This brief describes the assignment frame for the students. The building block 'Design process' then helps to translate the project brief into concrete Design Based learning activities for the pupils.

While working on a Design Based learning activity, pupils go through a Design Based design process (learning process). This process consists of different phases that are determined by the teacher and/or pupils. Each phase consists of a design activity and one or more design methods. In each phase, the teacher can define what the pupils should do (design activity) and in what way (design methods).

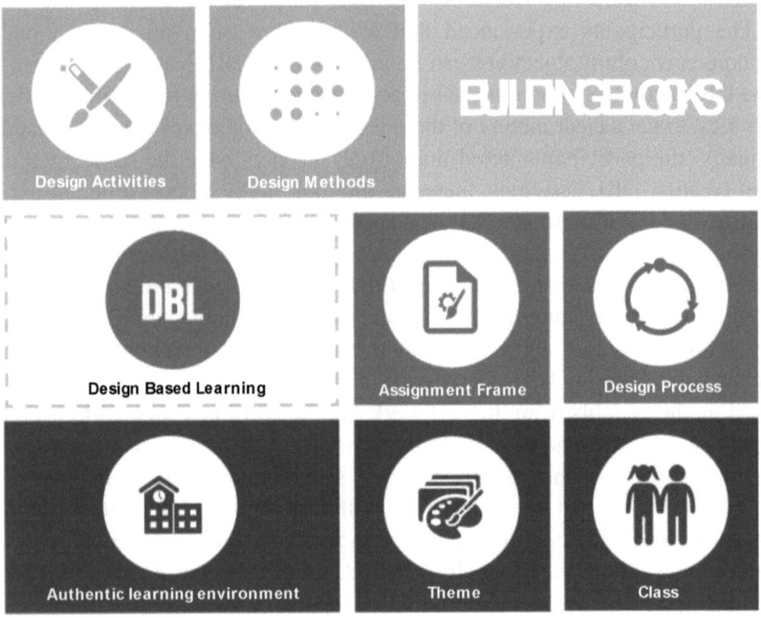

Fig. 6. The building blocks of the DBL creation tool.

4.3 Evaluation of the First Digital DBL Creation Tool

Evaluation Approach

To gain insights into the potential of the DBL creation tool, and to pinpoint points for improvement, it was evaluated with educational experts and teachers. Firstly, the tool was demonstrated to, and discussed with a panel of experts.

Secondly, 4 teachers used the tool individually or in pairs to create a Design Based learning activity of their choice during sessions of 60 min. During these sessions, a researcher was present to observe and offer explanations when needed, and the teachers were interviewed to gather their experiences. All participants were experiences teachers, but none of them were experienced with developing or teaching Design Based learning activities. See Fig. 7 for an impression.

Thirdly, one of the designed learning activities was tried out in class by the teacher who designed it, a researcher observed the lesson. See Fig. 8 for an impression.

Fig. 7. Evaluation sessions with teachers.

Fig. 8. Impression of evaluation in class.

Findings

Educational Design. The evaluation of the first round identified a number of practical problems regarding the design of educational activities using the tool. It appeared that there was a need for a specification of the Design Based learning properties in the tool.

Furthermore, the tool lacked elements that are relevant for designing lessons, such as homework and testing. The experts argued that the tool was more structured along the design-process, rather than along the educational process. Interestingly, all elements of the educational design were considered by the teachers in the learning activities they developed, also those that were not included in the tool itself. This was also observed in the lessons. The tool led to more awareness on the complete package of educational design elements among the teachers.

Adoption and Implementation. The workflow of the tool was not always clear for the teachers. Additionally, observing a lesson in which a designed activity was conducted with pupils revealed that the tool lacked concrete output materials that teachers can use while teaching. Teachers also felt that it yielded a lot of extra work in addition to the regular work when designing lessons, which meant that it was not experienced as time effective. All participants recognized that 21st century skills are important but insufficiently supported in current materials, and that DBL offers an opportunity to solve this. However, since it was not yet possible with the first version of our DBL creation tool to link the activities to specific (21st century) learning goals it was difficult for the teachers to experience it as a useful product for education.

Experts recognized that the tool forces teachers to make concrete decisions as part of the process of designing a lesson, which can stimulate reflection. This was confirmed by teachers who mentioned there were more reflective in their educational design when using the tool.

Characteristics of DBL. The sessions in which teachers used the tool showed that the concrete specifications of what makes a good DBL activity were not yet clear, both for the teacher and the designers of the tool. The design process which pupils that conduct DBL go through in their projects was linearly incorporated in the tool, as a result of which it was not experienced by the teachers as intended by the designers. As a result, the teaching materials that were designed did contain the necessary DR specifications, but in the lesson the focus on these disappeared. It also appeared that the teachers needed to redesign the lessons during the lesson, because at that moment the needs and strengths of the pupils in relation to the teaching material became clear.

Educational Concerns. The evaluation revealed that the cognitive workload of the teachers was not balanced, because the tool was not perceived as clear and comprehensible. Furthermore, the link between the didactic learning process of the pupils and the activities in the tool was lacking, as a result of which the role of knowledge in the designed lessons was missing for the teachers. It also turned out that the tool could steer more towards reflective design of lessons.

4.4 Improvements to the DBL Creation Tool

Based on interpretation of the results of the evaluation we have concluded the following improvements, which steered the development of the second digital version of the tool. The characteristics have been developed on the basis of the needs and feedback of the participating teachers and the observations of the researchers.

- The tool - and in particular the workflow – needs to be made more recognizable from the point of view of teachers: it must be more closely aligned with the workflow of educational design with which teachers are familiar. For example, by relying on 'Van den Akker's spider's web' [17].
- The desired workflow should be presented more clearly in the tool.
- It must be made clear which practical educational product the tool delivers.
- All the elements of lesson design [17] need a clear place in the tool - including homework and testing. For example, homework can be another 'design phase' or 'design step'.
- The specific characteristics of DBL need to be made clearer and these must be included explicitly in the tool.

5 Developing the DBL Creation Tool – Round Two

5.1 Redesign of the DBL Creation Tool

In order to improve the DBL creation tool, a new tool was developed based on the results of the first evaluation round (see Fig. 9).

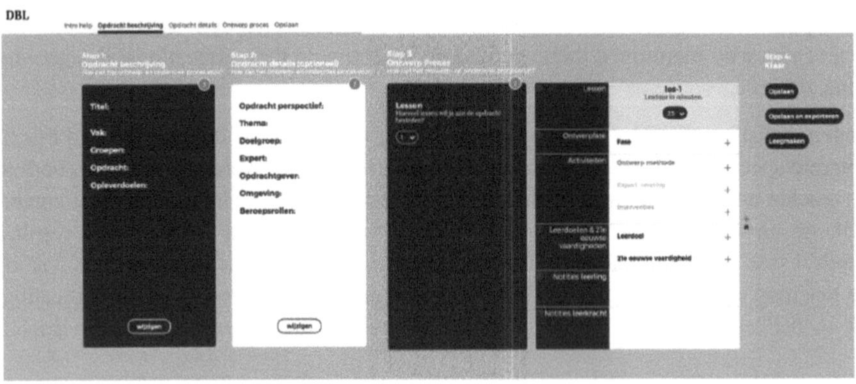

Fig. 9. Screenshot of the second iteration of the DBL creation tool.

One aspect related to educational design has been added in the second DBL creation tool: an option for defining homework. This option supports teachers in linking different lessons of the DBL project. Furthermore, a conscious decision was made not to add the option for defining the assessment to this version of the tool yet, because it requires its own specification. This would be a next step for the further development of the tool.

The workflow of the tool has been clarified, to make the adoption and practical use easier for to teachers. The theory of Van den Akker [17], which is closer to educational design, was used to make the design process of the lessons more explicit for instructors.

The iterative process of designing lessons by instructors will also be better facilitated in the new tool, in which there is a clear distinction between making fundamental choices for the basis of the DR project and the elaboration of each of the activities. The space for redesigning the elaboration is built into the tool.

Furthermore, the lesson description that that can be saved, after all aspects have been completed, is tailored more to be practically applicable by teachers and students.

5.2 Evaluation of the DBL Creation Tool

For the second iteration, the evaluation of the DBL creation tool, consisted of different methods. First, observations were conducted of teachers using the tool, in which the teachers designed a series of lessons. The tool was used by the teachers to create a Design Based learning activity in 60 min (see Fig. 10). These observations were followed by a short interview of the teacher about the experiences of using the tool.

The second method was an evaluation of the tool using expert interviews. Five educational experts were interviewed, while conducting a walk-through of the tool. The experts gave feedback on the interface of the tool and on the educational and Design Based learning aspects of the tool. The results of the methods were incorporated into the Evaluation matrix (Table 2).

Fig. 10. An impression of the observation session with the teachers.

Table 2. Evaluation matrix of design round 2 [24].

	T	P
General Aspects of Education	All lesson components are in the tool	Teachers consider all lesson components
Adoptation and Implementation	Workflow is clear, output of use to teachers	Fits very well to teachers' convictions of modern education; output is usable
Characteristics of **DBL**	The concept of DBL is clear	Teachers value the tool for the structured way of designing modern education (rather that DBL per se)
Teacher Guidance	The tool follows the mental model of 'lesson planning' and guides teacher choices on learning activities	Teachers report being more reflective; and are inspired by the suggested learning activities

Goodlad [20] *levels of curriculum:*
T = Theoretical curriculum: analysis of the tool, expert panel, user interviews
P = Perceived curriculum: teacher interviews, classroom observations

5.3 Results

Educational Design General. One aspect that was missing from the tool was more details with regard to the lesson preparation. This includes lesson planning with "start", "core" and "finish", which for the teachers was an essential part of the lesson planning. The terminology used for the (design) activity lists needed further explanation. Also a link was lacking in the tool between the learning objectives and the activities, which can be explained by the lack of explanation for each activity. A positive aspect of the activities was that the teachers gained a lot of inspiration from the many possibilities in choosing activities and thus started to think more clearly about the design of their lessons. There was also a lack support for the assessment of lessons. However, this was deliberately chosen by the designers of the tool since the support of testing for teachers did not fit in the scope of this project.

Adoption and Implementation. The teachers experienced the tool as clear and logical. The tool led to depth and awareness of the lessons of teachers. The teachers also felt that the tool could lead to modern education due to the clear link with 21st century skills in the designed lessons. However, the terminology from the design domain that was used in the tool still needs to be explained better and tailored to terminology of teachers.

Characteristics of DBL. The sequential structure of the tool fits well with the teachers, however, it does not yet support the complex structure of iterative thinking of Design Based Learning. This can limit the iterative thinking of instructors to a certain level. Teachers also indicated that you can develop other learning activities with the tool, not specifically DBL learning activities. This indicated that the management of the

DR characteristics was lacking in the tool to a certain extent or was unclear to the teachers.

Educational Perspective. The cognitive load of the new tool on the teachers is well balanced, the teachers understand what is expected. The missing aspect of the tool, which was defined in the goals of this project, was the reflection of the designing teachers during the development of lessons. The teachers also experienced this as lacking, some teachers indicated that they would like to have an inbuilt reflection moment per lesson and overall. There was also a lack of freedom of movement for some teachers in the tool, although this is built into the tool, so we need to look at how this can be made clearer in the tool.

5.4 Recommendations

Based on the results of the user tests, we have drawn up certain recommendations for the development of the latest digital version of the tool. The most important adjustments for the latest version of the online tool are listed below.

- Reflection triggers should be embedded in the tool for interim reflection by the teacher. These reflections could best take place after the conclusion of a "phase". The reflection triggers can best be presented in the form of questions, which are not too guiding and stimulate reflection; not focusing on the teachers accountability.
- The evaluation showed that the teachers do not see the tool as specific to DR learning activities. In order to clarify this and to give teachers more guidance to develop real DR learning activities, certain DR triggers need to be added to the tool. One of these is a feedforward system comprising a tick-box where teachers can choose whether the lessons should follow an open (diversifying) or more converging strategy, that would filter the learning activities suggested by the tool during the rest of the design process. An option must also be added for each lesson in which the teacher can indicate which iteration the pupils should work on per lesson. Furthermore, in the first "phase" of the tool, more questions need to be asked of the teacher who focuses on Design Based learning, such as "how many iterations do you want the students to go through in this lesson package? and "Do you want the students to evaluate their ideas themselves and reflect on them?".
- The list of teaching activities should be described more clearly and clustered. First of all, the teaching activities need to be worked out in detail, with regard to the role of the pupils and of the teacher, and which learning objectives these activities fulfil. Second, the list of teaching activities should be clustered by design phase, in order to provide more guidance to the teachers in developing a design process.
- An improvement must be made in the terminology of the tool, in order to attune this more to the target group primary school teachers.
- The core objectives and 21st century skills should already be chosen by the teachers in the first phase of the tool. When selecting specific activities, it must be possible to select the sub-learning objectives.

5.5 Final Version of the DBL Creation Tool

In the latest version of the DBL creation tool, several improvements have been made compared to the previous tool. First of all, in order to improve the workflow, the phases are visually more clearly indicated by means of color gradation, an adapter bar and numbering. This leads to clearer navigation and a better overview. Furthermore, some functionalities have been moved in order to improve the workflow: for example, it can be indicated earlier in the process which core objectives are to be worked on.

In order to better support inexperienced teachers in the design of DBL learning activities, the DBL characteristics have been added in the form of tips. E.g. an option to indicate if this lesson is about converging or diverging and in which iteration the students are. It is now possible to add or remove lessons and move them back and forth.

Screenshots are presented of the project overview screen (Fig. 11), the fields to define the project, fields to fill in the lesson and the final reflection suggestions (Fig. 12).

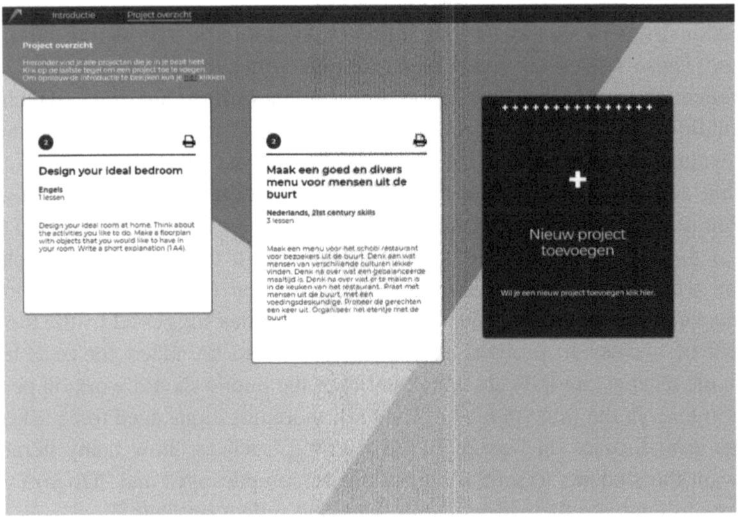

Fig. 11. Screenshot of the project overview screen.

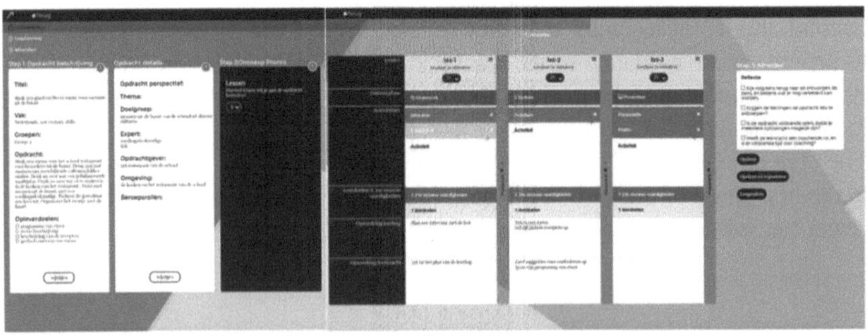

Fig. 12. Screenshot of the field to define the project with the reflection suggestions.

6 Discussion and Conclusion

This report describes the development of a tool that supports primary school teachers in creating teaching materials for teaching 21st century skills, mainly by DBL. After defining initial conditions, the study progressed as "design research" consisting of several iterative design rounds. From this study, a detailed DBL creation tool has been developed as an end product and conclusions have been drawn for improvements that require further research.

6.1 Progress of the Project

The first design round showed that an in-depth redesign was still needed for the DBL creation tool, which led to 2 evaluation rounds. This was demonstrated by the fact that the second evaluation was more focused on the practical aspects of the tool. Because of this need for evaluation and time problems due to the duration of the second redesign, an extensive test of the tool in the classroom was not done. This time shortfall is also due to the planning in schools, time for building the second tool, and that turned out during the construction of the second tool that a sharper definition of DBL properties was needed. Because of this, evaluation could hardly involve the fourth level of Goodlad.

Throughout the project, it became apparent that there was a need to shift and sharpen the concept of Design Based Learning. This is a result of this research, but also a factor that has influenced the course of the project. The didactics of Design Based Learning have also been better defined through this project. This was done by elaborating on the basis of the theory of Ireland [22] about how DBL is offered to the teacher, which has consequences for the design space in the tool. This scheme supports teachers in understanding and selecting classroom learning activities based on the didactic level and direction of the activity.

The DBL creation tool wants to support teachers in applying didactics when creating DBL activities. Because it is a relatively unknown approach in education, it is important to ensure that the didactics of the learning activities fit in well with the level of the pupils. Students should not be over-questioned but challenged at the right level. In order to support the instructor in these choices, the tool provides guidance and regulation for the preparation of a project with various learning activities.

6.2 Conclusion

The central research question was:

How can PO instructors be supported in the design of DBL learning activities aimed at concrete learning objectives?

This question was examined on the basis of the following sub-research questions:

(1) *Are PO teachers able to apply the DBL creation tool as intended; in particular, to follow the design strategy offered, to reflect on the DBL learning activities using the tool and to improve the design from there iteratively?*

Both research rounds have shown that the teachers very clearly apply the DBL creation tool as intended. The evaluation shows that the DBL creation tool fits in well with their mental model of their vision on education. It has not been demonstrated in the evaluation moments that the teachers improve the designs step by step over a longer period of time. Instead they are continuously improving there lessons. The tool therefore stimulates designing the lessons as an iterative process. Furthermore, during the first round, it appeared that many iterations on the elaborations of the design were devised by the teacher in (not during lesson preparations) the classroom, while the pupils carried out the learning activities.

(2) *Are PO teachers able to successfully develop DBL learning activities through the DBL creation tool?*

2(a) *Are the DBL learning activities, which the instructors develop by means of the tool, generally practical and educationally sound (can be implemented)?*

The learning activities developed are practical and contribute to modern education. The learning activities do not necessarily meet the characteristics of Design Based learning. So, a clarification of the concept of Design Based Learning is required, in order to build it into the tool more clearly, so that the message also gets across better to the teachers. To this end, a first step has been taken, based on the results of the last evaluation round. The learning activities that have been developed have been recognized by the experts as being appropriate from an educational perspective. There are several aspects built into the tool that create this educational accountability.

2(b) *Do the DR learning activities developed by the instructors using the tool have the intended characteristics (authentic, open, limited problem space, core objectives, etc.)?*

After the first evaluation in this project, there appeared to be a need for a new definition of the characteristics of Design Based Learning. As a result, the properties mentioned in this research question have also shifted, as the property of "limited problem space" is no longer considered essential. The DBL learning activities do, however, comply with the rest of the intended Design Based characteristics, as also mentioned in the Related Work section. This can be seen in the built-in aspects of the tool and in the teaching material that has been developed.

2(c) *Do the DR learning activities, which the teachers develop by means of the tool, enable pupils to achieve the desired learning objectives of both types?*

Whether the DBL learning activities developed enable pupils to achieve the desired learning objectives of both types cannot be substantiated on the basis of the results of the evaluations carried out. However, we have positive expectations about this, because the learning objectives are linked to the DBL activities in the tool and by the designing teachers. This was also reflected in the course material developed, so the expectations are that this goal will be met during the implementation. These expectations were also confirmed by the educational experts interviewed.

6.3 Adaptation and Implementation of the Tool

The final version of the DBL tool, called TEACH21, was delivered as a standalone web tool, which can be used free of charge via the website (http://platoolab.id.tue.nl). A paper version of the tool and a manual can also be downloaded from the website.

The contribution of this tool to modern education is clear. Although teachers are able to develop their own teaching materials, they often do not know enough about the characteristics of DBL to develop their own well-designed DBL-type learning materials. TEACH21 takes the instructor step-by-step through the course material development process. TEACH21 then helps the teacher to describe a project, define the context of the design problem, and then fill it in by working out the details of a flexible number of lessons. TEACH21 provides suggestions for design activities, learning objectives and reflection questions so that instructors think about the characteristics of DBL and the quality of the teaching material.

References

1. Scheltenaar, K.J., van der Poel, J.E.C., Bekker, M.M.: Design-based learning in classrooms using playful digital toolkits. In: Chorianopoulos, K., Divitini, M., Baalsrud Hauge, J., Jaccheri, L., Malaka, R. (eds.) Entertainment Computing. LNCS, vol. 9353, pp. 126–139. Springer, Cham (2015). https://doi.org/10.1007/978-3-319-24589-8_10
2. Bekker, T., Bakker, S., Douma, I., Van Der Poel, J., Scheltenaar, K.: Teaching children digital literacy through design-based learning with digital toolkits in schools. Int. J. Child-Comput. Interact. **5**, 29–38 (2015)
3. Thijs, A., Fisser, P., Van Der Hoeven, M.: Digitale Geletterdheid En 21e Eeuwse Vaardigheden in Het Funderend Onderwijs: Een Conceptueel Kader. SLO (Digital Literacy and 21st century skills in primary education: a conceptual framework), Enschede (2014). http://www.slo.nl/nieuws/dig-gelett/
4. Den Ouden, E., Valkenburg, R., Den Brok, P.: Leren in Eindhoven 2030. (Learning in Eindhoven 2030, Vision and Roadmap) (2014). http://www.ililighthouse.nl/Images/VisieRoadmapLerenEindhoven2030LR.pdf
5. van Cuijk, L., van Keulen, H., Jochems, W.: Are primary school teachers ready for inquiry and design based technology education? In: Proceedings of the PATT-22 Conference, pp. 108–121 (2009)
6. Trilling, B., Fadel, C.: 21st Century Skills: Learning for Life in Our Times. Wiley, Hoboken (2009)
7. Sharples, M., et al.: Innovating pedagogy 2016: open university innovation report 5 (2016)
8. Bocconi, S., Kampylis, P.G., Punie, Y.: Innovating learning: key elements for developing creative classrooms in Europe. JRC-Scientific and Policy Reports, Luxembourg (2012)
9. Van den Akker, J.: Curriculum perspectives: an introduction. In: Van den Akker, J. (ed.) Curriculum Landscapes and Trends, pp. 1–10. Springer, Dordrecht (2004). https://doi.org/10.1007/978-94-017-1205-7_1
10. Kim, C., Tranquillo, J.: K-WIDE: Synthesizing the Entrepreneurial Mindset and Engineering Design, p. 24 (2014)
11. IDEO: Design thinking for educators v2 (2013). https://designthinkingforeducators.com/toolkit/

12. Gómez Puente, S.M., Van Eijck, M., Jochems, W.: Towards characterising design-based learning in engineering education: a review of the literature. Eur. J. Eng. Educ. **36**(2), 137–149 (2011)
13. Puente, S.M.G., van Eijck, M., Jochems, W.: A sampled literature review of design-based learning approaches: a search for key characteristics. Int. J. Technol. Des. Educ. **23**(3), 717–732 (2013)
14. Puente, S.G., Van Eijck, M., Jochems, W.: Empirical validation of characteristics of design-based learning in higher education. Int. J. Eng. Educ. **29**(2), 491 (2013)
15. Plomp, T.: Education design research: an introduction. In: Plomp, T., Nieveen, N. (eds.) An Introduction to Educational Design Research, pp. 9–35. SLO: Netherlands Institute for Curriculum Development, Enschede (2009)
16. Plomp, T., Nieveen, N.: An introduction to educational design research. Paper presented at the Proceedings of the Seminar Conducted at the East China Normal University. SLO: Netherlands Institute for Curriculum Development, Shanghai (2007)
17. Van den Akker, J., Gravemeijer, K., McKenney, S., Nieveen, N. (eds.): Educational Design Research. Routledge, Abingdon (2006)
18. Zimmerman, J., Forlizzi, J., Evenson, S.: Research through design as a method for interaction design research in HCI. In: Proceedings of the SIGCHI Conference on Human Factors in Computing Systems, pp. 493–502. ACM, April 2007
19. Meijer, P.C., Verloop, N., Beijaard, D.: Multi-method triangulation in a qualitative study on teachers' practical knowledge: an attempt to increase internal validity. Qual. Quant. **36**(2), 145–167 (2002)
20. Goodlad, J.I.: Curriculum inquiry: the study of curriculum practice (1979)
21. Doyle, W., Ponder, G.A.: The practicality ethic in teacher decision-making. Interchange **8** (3), 1–12 (1977)
22. Ireland, J., Watters, J.J., Lunn Brownlee, J., Lupton, M.: Approaches to inquiry teaching: elementary teacher's perspectives. Int. J. Sci. Educ. **36**(10), 1733–1750 (2014)
23. Bekker, T., Bakker, S., Taconis, R., van der Sanden, A.: A tool for developing design-based learning activities for primary school teachers. In: Lavoué, É., Drachsler, H., Verbert, K., Broisin, J., Pérez-Sanagustín, M. (eds.) EC-TEL 2017. LNCS, vol. 10474, pp. 532–536. Springer, Cham (2017). https://doi.org/10.1007/978-3-319-66610-5_56
24. Taconis, R., Bekker, T., Bakker, S., van der Sanden, A.: Developing the TEACH21 online authoring tool supporting primary school teachers in designing 21st century design based education. In: 10th International Conference on Computer Supported Education, CSEDU 2018, 15–17 March 2018, Funchal, Madeira, Portugal (2018)
25. Verpoorten, D., Westera, W., Specht, M.: Using reflection triggers while learning in an online course. Br. J. Educ. Technol. **43**(6), 1030–1040 (2012)
26. van Gelder, L., et al.: Didactische Analyse Werk-en Studieboek, 2nd edn. Wolters-Noordhoff, Groningen (1973)
27. Schon, D.A., DeSanctis, V.: The Reflective Practitioner: How Professionals Think in Action. Routledge, London (1986)
28. Kirschner, P.A., Sweller, J., Clark, R.E.: Why minimal guidance during instruction does not work: an analysis of the failure of constructivist, discovery, problem-based, experiential, and inquiry-based teaching. Educ. Psychol. **41**(2), 75–86 (2006)
29. Griffin, P., Care, E., McGaw, B.: The changing role of education and schools. In: Griffin, P., McGaw, B., Care, E. (eds.) Assessment and Teaching of 21st Century Skills, pp. 1–15. Springer, Dordrecht (2012). https://doi.org/10.1007/978-94-007-2324-5_1
30. Van der Sanden, A.: Eduvation: a toolkit that empowers teachers to create DBL activities, Eindhoven (2016)

31. Fang, X., Holsapple, C.W.: An empirical study of web site navigation structures' impacts on web site usability. Decis. Supp. Syst. **43**(2), 476–491 (2007)
32. Razzouk, R., Shute, V.: What is design thinking and why is it important? Rev. Educ. Res. **82** (3), 330–348 (2012)
33. Zhang, F., Markopoulos, P., Bekker, T.: Children's emotions in design-based learning activity: a systematic review. Submitted to journal: Review of Educational Research
34. Damien Newman (2006). http://designsojourn.com/design-processed-explained/
35. Silver, M.S.: Decisional guidance for computer based decision support. MIS Q. **15**(1), 105–122 (1991)
36. Bernard, M.: Constructing user-centered websites: design implications for content organization. Usability News **2**(2) (2000)
37. Roth, S.P., Schmutz, P., Pauwels, S.L., Bargas-Avila, J.A., Opwis, K.: Mental models for web objects: where do users expect to find the most frequent objects in online shops, news portals, and company web pages? Interact. Comput. **22**(2), 140–152 (2009)
38. Jackson, S.L., Krajcik, J., Soloway, E.: The design of guided learner-adaptable scaffolding in interactive learning environments. Paper presented at the Proceedings of the SIGCHI Conference on Human Factors in Computing Systems (1998)
39. Hummels, C., Frens, J.: The reflective transformative design process. In: CHI 2009 Extended Abstracts on Human Factors in Computing Systems, pp. 2655–2658. ACM, April 2009
40. Rotherham, A.J., Willingham, D.T.: 21st-Century skills. Am. Educ. **17**(1), 17–20 (2010)

Personalized Recommendation of Open Educational Resources in MOOCs

Hiba Hajri(✉), Yolaine Bourda, and Fabrice Popineau

LRI, CentraleSupelec, Bat 650 (PCRI), Rue Noetzlin, Gif-sur-Yvette 91405, France
{hiba.hajri,yolaine.bourda,fabrice.popineau}@centralesupelec.fr

Abstract. Today Online Learning Environments (OLE) like MOOCs and LMS are very commonly used and a huge number of students with very different profiles and backgrounds follow the same online courses. Still, personalized experience for attendees is not widely spread on the platforms hosting these courses. At the same time, there is a growing number of open educational resources (OER) that can helpfully enrich the content of online courses and even be chosen to match one-by-one the student tastes. Recommender systems may support personalization in OLE by providing each learner with learning objects carefully selected to help reaching their learning objectives. This kind of recommendation is more specific to compute than usual recommendations like consumer products: the recommendation depends not only on the learner profile, but also on the content of the course, because the recommendation needs to fit precisely with the course format at any point. In this article, we introduce MOORS, a MOOC-based OER recommender system that can be plugged in an OLE to dynamically provide recommendations of OER to learners on the basis of their profiles and the profile of the MOOC. We also describe the process for calculating recommendations from OER metadata, assuming these metadata follow the Linked Opend Data (LOD) principles. Our implementation has been done in Open edX, an open source MOOC platform widely used, however the same approach could be implemented in any OLE as long as the learners profiles and the course profile can be extracted. Finally, we discuss a life-size evaluation of our recommender system.

1 Introduction

For many years now, personalization in technology enhanced learning (TEL) is a major subject of intensive research. But, with the spreading of Massive Open Online Courses (MOOCs) and their open and massive nature, the personalization issue is becoming ever more important. Indeed, a learner who follows a MOOC, freely shared on the web and without any commitment related to a registration fees he paid or a diploma he must obtain, may decide not to finish it at any time, when the MOOC no longer meets his needs. To support personalization in MOOCs, recommender systems are increasingly introduced to enable learners to finish MOOCs and take the better advantage from its content. Recommendations

B. M. McLaren et al. (Eds.): CSEDU 2018, CCIS 1022, pp. 166–190, 2019.
https://doi.org/10.1007/978-3-030-21151-6_9

offered to each learner are adapted to his needs and his learning objectives. They can take the form of pedagogical resources, other learners, discussions, etc.

At the same time, the amount of Open Educational Resources (OER) available on the web is permanently growing. These OERs have to be reused in contexts different from the initial ones for which they were created. Indeed, producing quality OER is costly and requires a lot of time. Reusing OERs can provide an efficient way to enrich online courses content and particularly MOOCs content. But the reuse of OERs depends on the ease with which we can identify them on the web and on the quality and the availability of their descriptions (metadata). In this context, linked Open Data principles are sometimes used for describing OERs in order to facilitate their discovery automatically by machines and then their reuse.

In this paper, we introduce a MOOC-based OER recommender system (MORS). MORS assists learners, who are attending a MOOC, by offering to them complementary OERs, in addition to the internal resources of the MOOC, when these resources are not sufficient for them. MORS recommendations aim to remedy some of learners deficiencies during the MOOC, in order to help them to assimilate the MOOC's knowledge. Recommendations provided by MORS are computed dynamically based on learner profile and on the MOOC profile. MORS is implemented in MOOCs but it can be integrated in other OLE as the course and the learner profiles can be extracted. We choose MOOCs because (1) their large number of learners with varied profiles make them good candidates for personalization, and (2) because targetting an open platform like Open edX will allow us to widely disseminate our system and to make it reusable.

This paper is an extended version of our previous work [8]. We extend our previous work by presenting the experiments conducted to evaluate our solution and discussing the results. This paper begins with related work. In Sect. 3 we introduce the recommendation scenarios proposed by our solution. Section 4 draws the architecture of the proposed system. Section 5 presents how we implemented our solution. The evaluation protocol and results are proposed in Sect. 6. Section 7 concludes the paper and presents future directions.

2 Related Works

Even though Personalization in TEL is a research topic with a long history, studies on MOOCs personalization have started since 2012 [17]. In order to address issues related to the open and the massive nature of MOOCs, different personalization approaches have been introduced. One of the most popular techniques relies on recommender systems. We have studied some of the proposed approaches to personalize MOOCs and adapt their content to the needs and objectives of each learner, based on different criteria.

The studied approaches offer different types of recommendations as pedagogical resources and other learners who can help the learner during the MOOC. Regarding the recommendation of pedagogical resources, we noticed that most approaches compute their recommendations based on internal resources of the

MOOC. For example, [1] targets learners who post a question in a MOOC discussion which reflects a confusion and recommends educational videos related to the confusion subject. [3] recommends additional learning activities to learners who show a lack of knowledge in a particular subject. However, it is interesting to offer to the learner external resources from the web, when the resources of the MOOC fail to meet his needs or do not allow him to assimilate the lacking knowledge.

For approaches that recommend external resources to the learner, we found that they rely on a static set of resources selected from the web. For example, [2] recommends to the learner a set of MOOCs which mostly match his learning objectives. Another approach [14] offers a scenario of activities to each group of learners according to the gap between their actual competencies and the target ones. This scenario can perform a number of recommendations of either internal or external educational resources, captured from the web. It is therefore interesting to be able to select external resources dynamically to take into account the changes on the web.

On the other hand, the approaches offering recommendations of external pedagogical resources to a learner who is following a MOOC are based on some of his characteristics: his knowledge, his preferences, his learning objectives, etc. They are therefore centered on the learner. But, these new resources will complement a MOOC, which represents an initial and main learning path and will enrich its content, for example to remedy the learner gaps or to present a set of alternative resources to those proposed in the MOOC. It is therefore important to propose resources that are both adapted to the characteristics of the learner and to the specificities of the MOOC that they will complete. It is also necessary to take into account the stage of the MOOC in which the recommendations are proposed. The interest of the dynamic calculation of the recommendations compared to the static calculation is that it allows taking into account, on the one hand the evolution of the profile of the learner throughout the MOOC and, on the other hand, the updates and the changes made on external pedagogical resources and repositories storing these resources descriptions.

We have also noticed that most of the approaches have been implemented in specific platforms, such as a specific university or laboratory, and are dedicated to a specific area. For example, the approach proposed by [13] is specific to health MOOCs in the area of Motivational Interviewing. It recommends to the learner the MOOC resources related to concepts they only need to know, by analyzing learners contexts. That is why it is important to introduce a generic solution, independent of the MOOC domain and implemented in one of the MOOC platforms which are accessible to everyone, such as Open edX.

In our work, we propose a generic solution providing recommendations of OERs in a MOOC platform when a lack of knowledge is detected for a learner. These recommendations are computed dynamically based on different learner characteristics and also on MOOC specificities.

3 Recommendation Scenarios

In this section, we describe how our system personalizes a MOOC for a learner. More precisely, we introduce some realistic scenarios of recommendation offered by MORS: where and when exactly the recommendation process is triggered for a learner during the MOOC.

Let's consider the MOOC as a set of sections. Each section offers pedagogical resources as video, text, quiz, etc. We consider also that studying the MOOC requires some prerequisites with a certain performance level defined by the MOOC creator who is the teacher. Each MOOC section provides some learning objectives with a certain performance level defined by the teacher. In our solution, we decide to recommend OERs to the learner at two different kind of stages of the MOOC: before starting the MOOC and after each MOOC's section.

Before Starting the MOOC. Once a learner is enrolled in a MOOC and decides to start its first section, MORS verifies if the learner has the prerequisites of the MOOC with the appropriate performance degrees. If a lack of knowledge is detected in at least one of the MOOC prerequisites, the recommendation process is triggered and a set of OERs dealing with the appropriate prerequisites are recommended to the learner.

At the End of Each MOOC Section. As stated earlier, each MOOC section has at least one learning objective. This learning objective can also be a prerequisite for the following section. So it is important to ensure that the learner has assimilated the section content. That is why at the end of each section, a quiz is presented to the learner where each question aims to assess his assimilation level of at least one of the section learning objective. Now if the learner gets bad results in the quiz, MORS triggers the recommendation process in order to recommend to him a set of OERs dealing with the learning objectives where he failed.

4 System Architecture

In this section we describe the architecture of our system for recommending OERs in a MOOC (MORS). MORS is composed of four major process (Fig. 1): process of generating the MOOC profile, process of generating the learner profile, PreSelection process and refinement process.

Once MORS is integrated in the MOOC to be personalized, the process of generating the MOOC profile generates the profile of the MOOC based on the MOOC model defined in our solution. Then the process of generating the learner profile generates the learner profile based on the learner model defined in our solution. When the system identifies gaps in student mastery of a certain topic, before starting the MOOC or at the end of one of its sections, the PreSelection process requests the external OERs descriptions repositories to collect an initial set of OERs dealing with this topic. This initial set is transmitted to the refinement process that performs selection and ranking operations based on the learner and the MOOC profiles content at the time of the calculation of the recommendations.

4.1 Process of Generating the MOOC Profile

The role of this process is to generate the profile of a specific MOOC from the MOOC model defined in our approach.

MOOC Model. In the MOOC Model, we represent some of its characteristics: the knowledge elements of the MOOC and the corresponding performance degrees, the domain of the MOOC and the effort needed in terms of time. We consider two types of knowledge elements: learning objectives of each MOOC section and prerequisites of the MOOC.

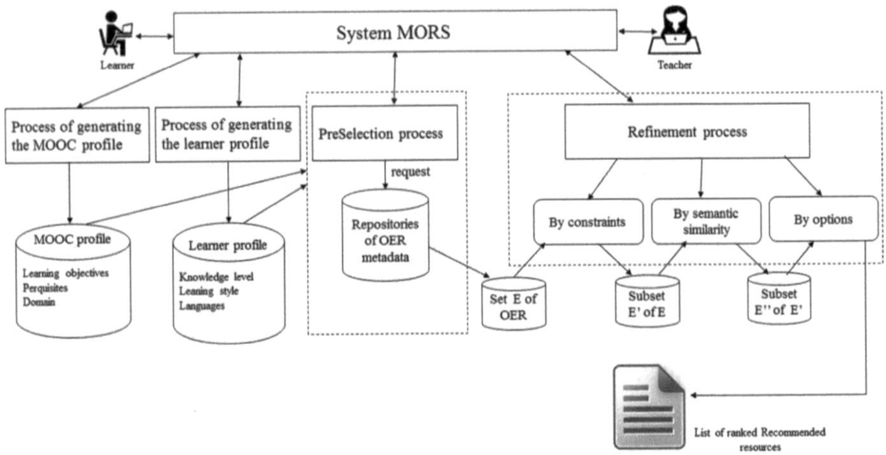

Fig. 1. The architecture of MORS.

Notations. In this paper, we denote the number of MOOC sections by $n_{section}$, the set of MOOC knowledge elements as KE, the set of MOOC prerequisites as P, the set of the learning objectives provided by the kth section as LO_k, where $1 \leq k \leq n_{section}$ and the set of the learning objectives provided by the entire MOOC as LO. Then $LO = \cup_{k=1}^{n_{section}} LO_k$ and $KE = LO \cup P$.

The teacher defines the MOOC knowledge elements together with their performance degrees. In this work, we use the performance degrees as introduced in [9] (1: beginner, 2: intermediate and 3: expert) to which we add (0: no performance).

Definition 1 (Performance Degree by Teacher): *Given a knowledge element ke from KE, the performance degree of ke, set by the teacher, is defined by the function LP_T.*

$$LP_T : \begin{cases} KE \longrightarrow \{0,1,2,3\} \\ ke \longmapsto lp \in \{0,1,2,3\} \end{cases}$$

The prerequisites and the learning objectives of the MOOC associated to their performance degrees are modeled respectively by the vectors $V_{P,MOOC}$ and $V_{LO,MOOC}$. We represent in (Fig. 2) the evolution of knowledge elements during the MOOC. As input, we represent in $V_{P,MOOC}$ the required performance degrees for each prerequisite. Then we represent the evolution of $V_{LO,MOOC}$ during the MOOC. At first, $V_{LO,MOOC}$ is initialized to zero. Thus, at the end of each section, $V_{LO,MOOC}$ is updated with new values. These values correspond to performance degrees expected to be acquired in learning objectives provided by the section.

The MOOC domain and the MOOC effort are represented respectively by the variables D_{MOOC} and Eff_{MOOC}.

Generation of the MOOC Profile. The data required to generate the profile of a specific MOOC based on our MOOC model are collected from the information entered by the teacher when creating this MOOC. The teacher defines the prerequisites of the MOOC, the learning objectives of each of its sections and the corresponding performance degrees. He defines also the domain and the effort of the MOOC.

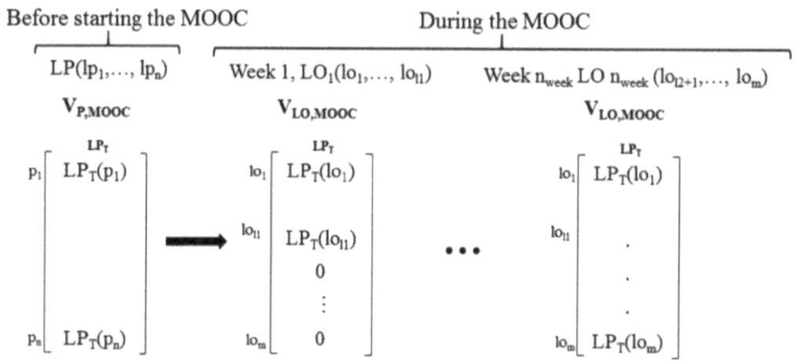

Fig. 2. The evolution of the knowledge elements during the course (from [8]).

4.2 Process of Generating the Learner Profile

The role of this process is to generate and update the profile of a specific learner from the learner model defined in our approach.

Learner Model. In the learner Model, we represent some of his characteristics: his knowledge level, his learning style and the languages he knows. Concerning the learner knowledge level, we consider only his level in the knowledge elements of the MOOC. More precisely, the learner model contains the performances degrees of the learner in the prerequisites and the learning objectives of the MOOC.

Definition 2 (Performance Degree of Learner): *Given a knowledge element ke from KE, the learner performance degree in ke is defined by the function LP_L.*

$$LP_L : \begin{cases} KE \longrightarrow \{0, 1, 2, 3\} \\ ke \longmapsto lp \in \{0, 1, 2, 3\} \end{cases}$$

The prerequisites and the learning objectives of the MOOC associated to the learner performance degrees are modeled respectively by the vectors $V_{P,Learner}$ and $V_{LO,Learner}$. A quite similar modeling process is proposed in [15]. In (Fig. 3) we represent the evolution of the knowledge elements in the learner profile during the MOOC. Before starting the MOOC, the learner performance degrees in MOOC prerequisites are stored in $V_{P,Learner}$. During the MOOC and after each section, $V_{LO,Learner}$ is updated with the new learner performance degrees acquired with the learning objectives provided in this section.

The learning style refers to the way a learner receives and processes information [6]. In the literature, many profiles are defined to analyze learners learning styles like Kolb [10] and Felder and Silverman [6]. In our work, we use the frequently used, Index of Learning Style (ILS) questionnaire [16]. It was developed by Felder and Soloman to identify learning styles based on Felder and Silverman Learning style Model (FSLSM) [6]. The FSLSM classifies learning styles along to four dimensions which are active/reflective, sensorial/intuitive, visual/verbal and sequential/global. In our work we also use the patterns introduced by [5] to identify the type of learning resources to be provided to the learner based on his answers to the ILS questionnaire. For example, sensing learners prefer to get more examples and exercises [5]. We model the learning style by using the term $S_{learner}$.

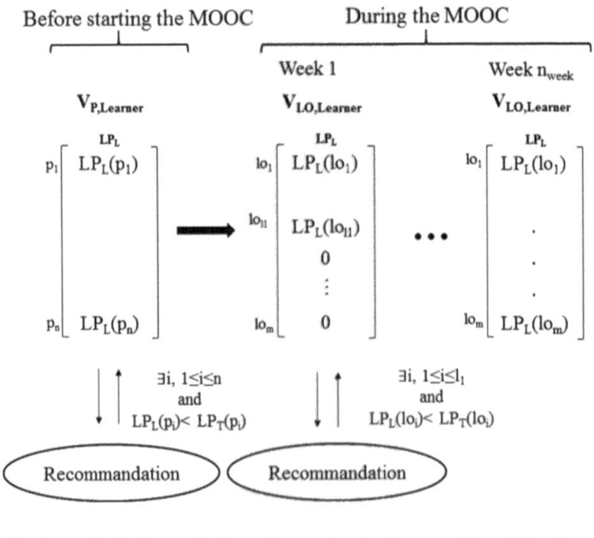

Fig. 3. The evolution of the knowledge elements in the profile of the learner during the course (from [8]).

The languages known by the learner are modeled by using a list $L_{learner}$.

Generation of the Learner Profile. The data required to generate the profile of a specific learner are collected with different methods. The learner performance degrees on MOOC prerequisites are determined by browsing his knowledge base storing the knowledge elements acquired by the learner previously on the same MOOC platform. If no significant evidence is collected this way, because the learner is a new user of the platform for example, then we ask the learner a few questions about the prerequisites in order to evaluate his performance degrees.

Each MOOC section ends with a quiz. The learner results on those quiz are used to compute the learner performance degrees on MOOC learning objectives. For the learning style of the learner, we use his answers to the questionnaire ILS [16] to deduce his learning style. We ask him also about the languages he knows.

4.3 PreSelection PROCESS

As indicated in (Fig. 3), the recommendation process is triggered for a learner L at two different kind of steps of the MOOC.

Before Starting the MOOC. Let $LP_L(p)$ the performance degree of a learner L in $p \in P$, the recommendation process is triggered if:

$$LP_L(p) = V_{p,L}(p) < LP_T(p) = V_{p,MOOC}(p)$$

During the MOOC. At the end of the kth section of the MOOC, let a learner L who acquires $LP_L(lo)$ in $lo \in LO_k$, the recommendation process is triggered when:

$$LP_L(lo) = V_{LO,L}(lo) < LP_T(lo) = V_{LO,MOOC}(lo)$$

Where $V_{LO,MOOC}$ and $V_{LO,L}$ considered are those updated after the kth section.

The aim of this module is to select a set of candidate OERs dealing with the knowledge element for which the recommendation process has been triggered. In order to find these resources, the system performs a keyword search in metadata stored in external accessible repositories of OERs metadata [7]. The metadata used in this search is "the description of the resource" introducing the subject and the global idea of the resource.

For keywords, the first keyword is the knowledge element which is the subject of the recommendation. The objective of the search is, therefore, to select resources with descriptions containing this knowledge element. However, we must also solve the problems of synonymy and polysemy that may arise in our search.

Polysemy. The same knowledge element can be expressed differently. For example "conditional statements" in computer science are also "if-then-else".

Synonymy. The same expression can be used to represent different knowledge elements that belong to different domains. For example the notion of "graph" is used in a variety of disciplines as "computer science", "mathematics", etc.

To solve synonymy problems, we used a second keyword, in addition to the knowledge element, which is the domain of the MOOC. We introduced also a module of synonyms detection[1] to address synonymy problems. This module is based on DBpedia[2] structured data that has been extracted from Wikipedia. Some possible synonyms of the knowledge element and the MOOC domain are inferred using this module that will increase the number of selected resources.

Overall, we select descriptions including the knowledge element and the MOOC domain or at least one of their synonyms.

In a formal way, let *OER* be the set of Open educational resources, $R \in OER$, $ke \in KE$, $Meta_R$ is the set of the metadata of R where $\text{Meta}_R = \{\text{Descript}_R, \text{Lang}_R, \text{Prereq}_R, \ldots\}$, $Syn_{D_{mooc}}$ the set of the synonyms of the domain of the MOOC, D_{mooc} and Syn_{ke} is the set of the synonyms of the ke generated by our module of synonyms detection.

$$(R \text{ is dealing with } ke) \equiv ((ke \in \text{Descript}_R) \text{ OR } (\exists i : Syn_{ke}[i] \in \text{Descript}_R)) \text{ AND } ((D_{mooc} \in \text{Descript}_R) \text{ OR } (\exists j : Syn_{D_{mooc}}[j] \in \text{Descript}_R)).$$

To select the candidate resources, our PreSelection process requests external repositories providing SPARQL endpoints with an initial query. In order to manage the diversity of metadata schemas employed by these repositories, we use classes and properties as defined in the Learning Object Ontology of Mapping (LOOM) introduced in [7].

4.4 Refinement Process

The PreSelection process returns as result an initial set E of OER and as we explained in the previous part the PreSelection is based on keywords. This initial set E is transmitted to this refinement process which applies selection and sorting operations according to several criteria. These operations are performed in three stages.

- Selection by constraints.
- Selection by semantic similarity.
- Sorting by options.

Selection by Constraints. In this first step, we select a subset E' of E which contains only the resources that respect certain constraints. The constraints are firm criteria that must be respected by the resources recommended to the learner. In other words, these are criteria without which it will be difficult for the learner to understand the content of the resource or it will impact the MOOC follow up. The three constraints we consider are the following. The first one is: "Resources must not require prerequisites not assimilated by the learner" **(C1)**. The second constraint is: "Resources must be presented in a language known by the learner" **(C2)**. The third constraint is: "The resource has to bring a performance level which is greater than or equal to the level defined in the MOOC" **(C3)**.

[1] https://davidallenfox.wordpress.com/2013/09/05/generating-synonyms/.
[2] http://wiki.dbpedia.org/.

Constraint C1 Violation. Let $R \in E$, R doesn't respect the constraint C1 if:

$$\exists ke \in \text{Prereq}_R : (LP_L(ke) = 0) \vee (\exists i, LP_L(\text{Syn}_{ke}[i]) = 0)$$

In order to identify the performance degree $LP_L(ke)$ of the learner in the prerequisite ke of the resource R, we start with browsing his knowledge base looking for the information. Otherwise, we ask the learner some questions to deduce his $LP_L(ke)$.

Constraint C2 Violation. Let $R \in E$, R doesn't respect the constraint C2 if:

$$(\text{Lang}_R \notin \text{L}_{learner})$$

Where $\text{L}_{learner}$ is the set of the languages known by the learner and Lang_R the metadata presenting the language of the resource.

Constraint C3 Violation. As we did previously for the learner and the MOOC, each resource $R \in E$ is modeled by a vector $V_{KE,R}$ that represents the performance degrees acquired in each ke of the MOOC after following this resource.

Definition 3 (Resource Performance Degree): *The performance degree acquired by the learner with regard to a specific knowledge element ke, from KE, after following the resource R is defined by the function LP_R.*

$$LP_R : \begin{cases} KE \longrightarrow \{0,1,2,3\} \\ ke \longmapsto lp \in \{0,1,2,3\} \end{cases}$$

As shown in (Fig. 3), the recommendation process is triggered when $LP_T(ke) > LP_L(ke)$. Indeed, the goal of the recommendation of the resource R to the learner is the improvement of his level of performance in the knowledge element ke.

So, Let $R \in E$, R doesn't respect the constraint C3:

$$LP_R(ke) < LP_T(ke).$$

As the OERs metadata do not specify the performance degrees of OREs, we need to estimate them from learners who have already used the resources. For a new OER we use two performance degrees 0: a resource doesn't deal with the knowledge element and 1: the resource deals with the knowledge element. Then once the resources are studied by the learners, we plan to collect the results from them according to their responses to the knowledge test once they have followed a recommended resource.

Definition 4 (A Knowledge Element derived from a Resource):

$$(ke \textit{ is provided by } R) \equiv (\text{V}_{KE,R}(ke) \neq 0) \equiv$$
$$\{ke \in \text{Descript}(R) \vee \exists i : \text{Syn}_{ke}[i] \in \text{Descript}(R)\}.$$

Selection by Semantic Similarity. Once resources respecting the defined constraints have been identified, we select resources which are close to the initial query (the query defined in the PreSearch module). For that purpose, we calculate the similarity between selected resources and the initial query terms (IQT). The IQT are the terms used in the initial query: the knowledge element, the domain of the MOOC and their synonyms generated by our module of synonyms detection. We denote IQT as a set.

$$IQT = \{\mathrm{T}_1, ..., \mathrm{T}_{nt}\}$$

Where T_{nt} is one of the initial query terms and nt is the total number of terms used in the initial query.

We start with using Term Frequency Inverse Document Frequency (TF-IDF) [4] to identify the importance of IQT inside the selected resources descriptions. Each selected resource R is represented by a vector V_R.

$$\mathrm{V}_R = (\mathrm{V}_{R_{T_1}}, ..., \mathrm{V}_{R_{T_{nt}}})$$

Where $\mathrm{V}_{R_{T_1}}$ is the TF-IDF value of the term $operatorname T_1$ in the description of the resource R.

The IQT is also represented by a vector V_{IQT}.

$$\mathrm{V}_{IQT} = (\mathrm{V}_{IQT_{T_1}}, ..., \mathrm{V}_{IQT_{T_{nt}}})$$

Where $\mathrm{V}_{IQT_{T_1}}$ is the TF-IDF value of the term $\mathrm{V}_{R_{T_1}}$ in the descriptions of all selected resources.

Then a cosine measure is employed to compute the similarity between each resource vector V_R and the initial query vector V_{IQT}. As result each selected resource R is characterized by one measure which is his cosine measure, CosSim(R). The resource R with higher value of CosSim(R), is the closest to the initial query.

At the end of this step, the result is the set E' of resources ordered by their semantic similarity with the IQT. We select the subset E'' of the first n ones to be the input of the next step. We take a limited number of resources because the objective of our recommendations is to help the learner to improve his knowledge level in a certain knowledge element by following at least one resource rather than recommending a large number of resources. The number n is defined arbitrarily and in our case study, n has been fixed to 4 but the teacher can change its value. We define the relation of preference ($\geq$).

Definition 5 (Preference Relation $\geq$): *Given two resources $R_1 \in OER$ and $R_2 \in OER$:*

$$R_1 \geq R_2 \text{ means } R_1 \text{ is at least as good as } R_2.$$

In this first step $R_1 \geq R_2 \Leftrightarrow \mathrm{CosSim}(R_2) \geq \mathrm{CosSim}(R_1)$.

Sorting by Options. The last step is to classify resources based on options. The options are other criteria defined to reflect the adaptation to some characteristics of the MOOC and the learner. However, these options are not mandatory criteria as the constraints used in the first step. In other words, recommended resources may not be consistent with all options, but they are presented to the learner in an order depending on how much they satisfy the options. Let *Op* the set of options and n_{op} the total number of options.

Definition 6 (Score Function): *For each* $op_i \in OP$*, where* $1 \leq i \leq n_{op}$*, we define the score function* U_i*:*

$$U_i \colon \begin{cases} E'' \longrightarrow [0,1] \\ R_j \longmapsto a_i^j \end{cases} \tag{1}$$

U_i assigns a score a_i^j, between 0 and 1, to each candidate resource R_j depending on how much it satisfies the op_i. The scores a_i^j are calculated differently depending on the options op_i type.

For each option, the resource score represents its option satisfaction percent. Then we consider each option as a fuzzy set and the score of each resource as its membership degree to this set. We represent each resource R_j by a vector S_{R_j} whose components are the values of its score for each option.

$$S_{R_j} = (a_1^j, a_2^j, ..., a_2^{n_{op}})$$

The ideal resource *id* has a vector S_{id} whose components are equal to 1. This means that the resource meets all the options at 100%.

A weight value $p_i \in 1, 2, 3$ is assigned to each option in order to characterize its importance (1: less important, 2: important and 3: very important).

Initially all options have the same importance ($p_i = 3$) but we give the teacher the possibility to change weights values of options defined to reflect coherence with the MOOC. In MORS, we defined these options: "Recommended resources should respect the learning style of the learner." (Op_1) and "Recommended resources should have a 'typical Learning Time' similar or bellow the mean effort needed to assimilate a MOOC resource, as defined by the teacher." (Op_2).

For Op_1, we define the corresponding score function U_1 as below:

$$U_1(R) = \begin{cases} 1 \text{ if } \mathrm{Typ}_R \in RT_L \\ 0 \text{ else.} \end{cases}$$

where Typ_R is the type of the resource $R \in E''$ and RT_L is the set of resources types corresponding to the learner L learning style.

Concerning op_2, we define the corresponding score function U_2 as below:

$$U_2(R) = \begin{cases} 1 & \text{if } LT_R \leq ME_{W/R} \\ (\varepsilon + ME_{W/R} - LT_R)/\varepsilon & \text{elseif } LT_R \\ & \in [ME_{W/R}, ME_{W/R} + \varepsilon] \\ 0 & \text{else } LT_R \geq ME_{W/R} + \varepsilon \end{cases}$$

where $R \in E''$, $ME_{W/R}$ (Mean Effort section) corresponds to the quotient of the section effort defined by the teacher and the number of the section resources and LT_R corresponds to the value of the metadata 'typical Learning Time' for R. The value ε is defined arbitrarily and has been fixed to ME_W in our case study.

To rank candidate resources, we use the Chebyshev distance to compute the distance between the ideal resource and each resource to recommend. The smaller the distance is the better the resource is. This distance is defined as below:

$$\mathrm{DCH}_{R_j,id} = max_{i \in n_{op}} \lambda_i |V_{R_j}[i] - V_{id}[i]|$$

where λ_i is defined as below:

$$\lambda_i = p_i / (\mathrm{Sup}_{R_j \in E''}(V_{R_j}[i]) - \mathrm{Inf}_{R_j \in E^*}(V_{R_j}[i]))$$

where E^* is a subset from E'' of candidate resources that not have a maximal satisfaction degree for any option.

In conclusion,

$$R_1 \geq R_2 \Leftrightarrow \mathrm{DCH}_{R_2,id} \geq \mathrm{DCH}_{R_1,id}$$

5 Implementation

In order to implement our solution, we choose edX as the MOOC platform. First, it is an open platform which is widely used. Then, this choice allows us to offer our solution to the vast community of OpenEdX users and hope to replicate experiments about personalization, then gather more data about its efficiency. Furthermore, the documentation of Open edX is well detailed and the community is very active. Finally, the platform is characterized by a modular architecture thanks to XBlocks [11] that we will detail later.

The XBlock is a component architecture developed in 2013 by edX, which allows developers to create independent course components (xBlocks). These components can be combined together to make an online course [11]. The advantage of XBlocks is that they are deployable. The code that you write can be deployed in any instance of the edX Platform or other XBlock runtime application[3]. We found also that there is a recent focus on using these XBlocks to add personalization in MOOCs, for example the work [12] where a recommender XBblock was created in order to recommend resources for remediation in a MOOC. Once developed, each XBlock can be installed and added by the MOOC creator, in the appropriate unit of the appropriate section of his MOOC[4]. In fact, Open edX organized the courses in a hierarchy of sections, sub-sections and units, where the unit is the smallest component in the MOOC.

[3] https://open.edx.org/about-open-edx.

[4] http://edx.readthedocs.org/projects/open-edx-building-and-running-a-course/en/latest/.

For these reasons, we use XBlocks to implement our solution in edX. Three XBlocks have been implemented.

An XBlock to Generate the MOOC Profile and the Static Part of the Learner Profile. This XBlock is developed to be added at the first unit of the MOOC first section. It is responsible for collecting information about the learner and the MOOC: learner languages, learner learning style, MOOC knowledge elements and corresponding performance degrees (see Fig. 4).

An XBlock to Compute Recommendation at the Beginning of the MOOC. This XBlock checks the performance degree of the learner in the prerequisites of the MOOC. In order to ensure this, it starts with determining whether this prerequisite is stored in the knowledge base of the learner. In case the prerequisite is not found in the knowledge base, the XBlock asses the knowledge level of the learner in the MOOC prerequisites by asking him some questions (an example for the prerequisite "structure data" (Fig. 5)). Then if he doesn't answer the questions correctly, a set of OERs links are recommended to him. These links are ranked by descending order by satisfaction of the criteria defined at the previous section (Fig. 6).

An XBlock to Compute Recommendation after Each MOOC Section. A third XBlock is developed to be added at the end of each section. This XBlock computes recommendations of OERs to the learner based on his answers to the quiz presented at the end of the section. These OERs links are presented to the learner sorted based on the criteria we defined in the previous section.

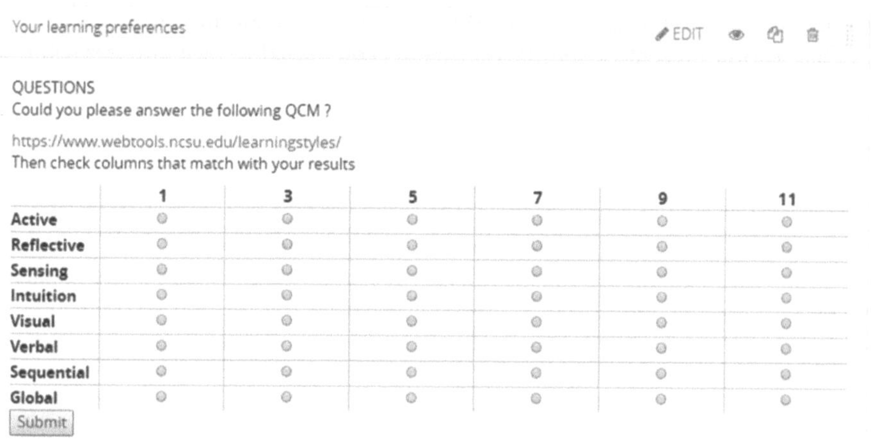

Fig. 4. Interface to collect information about the learning preferences of the learner (from [8]).

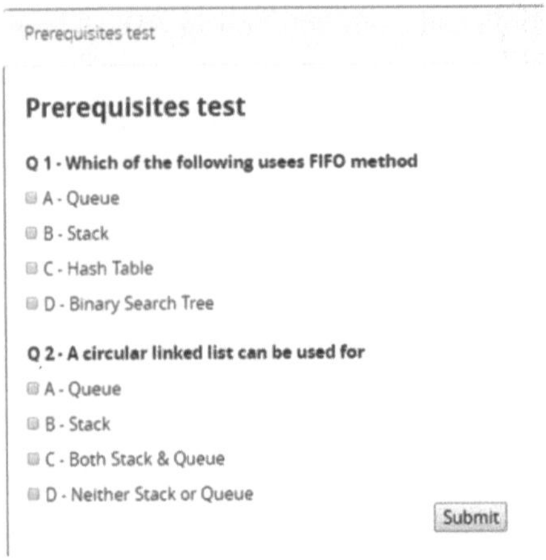

Fig. 5. Interface for testing the assimilation of the prerequisites (example "Data structure") (from [8]).

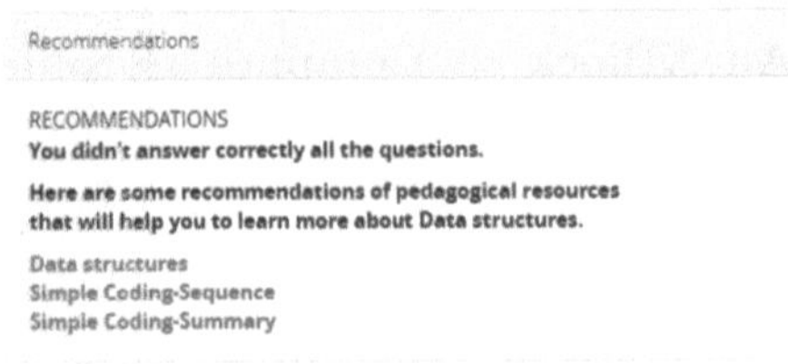

Fig. 6. Interface for recommended resources (from [8]).

6 Evaluation

Our recommender system MORS presents some specific characteristics that come firstly from the open and the massive nature of MOOCs and secondly from OERs referenced in external and dynamic repositories. For this reason, it is difficult to reuse evaluation protocols mentioned in the literature for classic recommender systems and it is important to introduce a new evaluation protocol.

This section presents a set of experiments conducted to evaluate our solution and discuss the results. The purpose of the evaluation is to assess our algorithm of recommendation and the relevance of the recommended resources. The recommended resources have to be adequate with the criteria defined previously, to exhibit some characteristics consistent with both the learner and the MOOC. The scalability and the versatility of OERs repositories means that OERs and their descriptions change dynamically, so there is no "best OERs", only best OERs at some time point. Given OERs vary over time, during the evaluation process, we are not interested in assessing whether our system recommends all the "good" resources, but rather in assessing whether the retrieved resources are "good" resources.

6.1 Evaluation Process

In order to evaluate our system, we chose the MOOC[5] "Design a Database with UML" in the domain of computer science, from the platform OpenClassrooms. This MOOC is composed of three sections. Each section represents a set of pedagogical resources. An assessment quiz is presented at the end of the section to

[5] https://openclassrooms.com/courses/faites-une-base-de-donnees-avec-uml.

evaluate the assimilation of its learning objectives by the learner. In our evaluation, we were interested in a learning objective of each section: "Relationnel model" presented in the first section, "Database management system (DMS)" presented in the second section and "SQL" presented in the third section.

Our evaluation process is based on two questionnaires. The first one is dedicated to experts and the second one is intended to learners. The questionnaire for experts has been sent by e-mail to four teachers which are experts in the domain of database. We had several constraints to respect for learners. The MOOC can be followed by a large number of learners with various profiles. To collect a large number of various users profiles without having to wait until they subscribe and follow the MOOC from the beginning to the end, we used the website Foule Factory. It is a micro-service platform which offers the possibility to ask the crowd to do some tasks as answering questions or finding data. It also allows recovery of rapid results. 117 Foule Factory respondants answered our questionnaire.

In the questionnaire dedicated to teachers, we present the REL selected by the initial query which are expected to provide the three learning objectives of the MOOC as well as some questions to assess these resources. Concerning the questionnaire for learners, we start with assessing the knowledge level of each learner in each learning objective. Therefore, we invite the learner to answer a set of questions about the learning objective, selected from the assessment quiz of the corresponding section. In this context, we chose three questions to evaluate his knowledge in the notion of "relational model", three questions to evaluate his knowledge in the notion of SMD and two questions to evaluate his knowledge in the notion of "SQL". For each set of questions, if the learner answers correctly, he is redirected to the questions about the learning objective of the next section. Otherwise, we consider that the learner has not sufficiently assimilated the corresponding notion and we present to him the resources selected by the initial query as well as some questions to evaluate these resources.

Adequacy of Recommendations with the MOOC and the Learner Profiles

A set of questions asked to Foule Factory respondents and to the teachers had the objective to assess the adequacy of selected OER with the criteria fixed, with regard to our approach, to express the recommendations adaptation with the learner and the MOOC profiles.

Application of Semantic Similarity Measure. The first criterion to evaluate is the selection of the closest resources to the initial query by applying the semantic similarity measure. In this context, for each learning objective: "relational model", "DMS" and "SQL", we present the initial set selected using the initial query to the teacher. For each resource, a closed question is presented to the teacher asking whether this resource is relevant or not. Relevance in this context refers to the fact that studying the resource allows the learner to acquire knowledge on the notion.

The synthesis of teachers replies will help us to assess the interest applying the semantic similarity measure on REL descriptions is interesting and whether it allows eliminating non relevant resources selected by the initial query and keeping the most relevant resources.

Adequacy of Recommended Resources with the MOOC Profile. In order to assess the adequacy of the OER recommended by our solution with some specificities of the MOOC, the teachers are invited to rate the relevance of the recommended OER in accordance with the criteria fixed in our approach: the granularity, the learning time and the provided performance degree.

For each resource that provides the learning objective, according to the teacher, he is invited to answer three questions:

1. A closed question asking the teacher to rate the resource on a scale of 1 to 5 according to how much its granularity is more or less adequate with the MOOC content.
2. A closed question asking the teacher to rate the resource on a scale of 1 to 5 according to how much its learning time is more or less adequate with MOOC specificities.
3. A closed question asking the teacher to rate the resource on a scale of 1 to 5 according to how much the knowledge level provided by the resource in the notion in question is more or less adequate with the level supposed to be provided in the MOOC.

Adequacy of Recommended Resources with the Learner Profile. The assessment of the adequacy of the resources recommended by our solution with some characteristics of the learner is conducted according to this protocol. As a first step, we ask Foule Factory respondents to rate the pertinence of the OER in accordance with the criteria fixed in our approach: the learning style and the knowledge of the learner. For each resource, they are invited to answer two questions:

1. A closed question asking the respondent to rate the resource on a scale of 1 to 5 according to how much the resource is more or less pleasant to follow and matches with his learning habits.
2. A closed question asking the respondent to rate the resource on a scale of 1 to 5 according to how much the resource is more or less easy to follow.

In a second step, we ask the respondents to choose one resource to follow from the list of OER presented to them for each notion. Our aim is to examine the learner's choice to compare it with his characteristics and then to detect what makes him choose one resource over than other. Learners are invited to answer two questions.

1. A closed question asking them to tick the resource they choose to study.
2. An open question asking them to justify choosing this resource and abandoning the others.

Evolution of learners Knowledge after Recommendations

Another set of questions proposed to Foule Factory respondents aims to evaluate the effect of the recommended resources on the evolution of learner knowledge in general and on the evolution of his knowledge in the learning objective of the MOOC.

For this purpose, learners are invited, firstly to answer a closed question asking him whether the recommended resources allowed him to acquire new knowledge. Secondly, the same questions selected from the evaluation quiz and asked to evaluate his knowledge level in each notion, are addressed to the learner for a second time after he studied at least one recommended resources for each notion. The purpose is to study and compare his answers before and after recommendations.

Overall evaluation of the Approach

A last set of questions asked to learners and teachers concerns assessing globally our solution. As experts, after consulting the recommended resource for each notion, the teachers are invited to express their views on the interest of recommendations, the method we use to propose recommendations and more precisely the importance of the criteria used to adapt the resources to the specificities of the MOOC and to propose other criteria they find interesting.

The teachers questionnaire contains 4 questions dedicated for that purpose.

1. An open question asking the teacher's view on the idea of recommending external resources for a learner who is attending a MOOC.
2. A closed question presenting the different criteria used in our solution to the teacher and asking him to rate them according to their importance on a scale from 1 to 3 (not very important, important, very important).
3. An open question inviting the teachers to propose other criteria to take into account when choosing resources to recommend, in order to respect the specificities of the initial course and to facilitate the integration of the resources in its content.
4. An open question asking teachers to propose other suggestions.

As playing learner role, Foule Factory respondents are also invited to express their views on recommending external resources, after consulting the recommended resources and studying some of them.

The learners questionnaire contains 3 questions dedicated for this purpose.

1. An open question asking the respondents to suppose they are attending an online course and express their views about recommending to them other resources when they don't answer correctly to the evaluation test of a certain course's section. The respondents are invited to choose between: (1) It is a good idea but I will study some of them; (2) It is a good idea but I don't have the time to study them; (3) It is not a good idea, because I don't want to disperse myself with studying external resources; (4) other point of view.

2. A closed question asking respondents to suppose they are attending an online course and to precise their behavior when they don't understand some of its notions. Do they repeat the course or look for other online courses ?
3. For the learners who prefer looking for other courses, another closed question asks them to precise whether the recommended resources allow them to save time compared to the time they spend to look for external resources by themselves.

6.2 Evaluation Results

In this chapter we summarize the responses of teachers and learners to the questions presented in the evaluation questionnaires.

Overall evaluation of the Approach

Experts Opinions. After consulting the resources selected by our system, all experts agreed that recommending external resources, during a MOOC, is a good idea. Regarding the criteria defined in our solution to take into account the specificities of the MOOC in the recommended resources, we obtain these results. All experts assigned the maximum score of 3 to the criterion relating to the level of knowledge provided by the resource. All experts agreed on the importance to recommend resources allowing the learner to acquire the knowledge level supposed to be acquired by attending the MOOC. Three of the experts assigned the maximum score of 3 to the criterion relating to the learning time. According to them, it is very important to take into account the learning time of the recommended resources. The fourth expert assigned the score of 2 to this criterion. He considers that it is an important criterion but still less important than the one relating to the knowledge level.

Two experts assigned the maximum score to criterion relating to the granularity of the resource. The other two experts assigned the score 2 to this criterion. For them, the fact that the granularity of the recommended resources is adequate with the internal resources of the MOOC is important, but it is less important than the adequacy of the knowledge level and the learning time.

Learners Opinions. After consulting the resources selected by our solution, 60% of Foule Factory respondents endorse the recommendation of external pedagogical resources, when they didn't correctly answer the evaluation test presented in a course they are attending. Another 25.7% of the respondents consider that it is a good idea but they have a problem with the time they will spend to learn additional resources. The lack of additional time available to study the recommended resources, confirms the importance of the learning time criterion taken into account in our solution. The last 14.3% of respondents don't consider the recommendation of external resources as a good idea and they do not want to disperse themselves by studying external resources in addition to the course they are attending.

On the other hand, 55.2% of the respondents prefer to search for other online courses when they are taking a course and they don't understand some of its notions. The remaining respondents prefer to repeat the same course. Among those who prefer to search for other online courses, 72.4% find that the recommended resources allow them to save time, compared to the time they would have spent looking for resources on the web.

Evolution of Learners Knowledge after Recommendations

After consulting the recommended resources, 81.6% of Foule Factory respondents find that those recommended for the notion "relational model" allowed them to acquire new knowledge. 69.5% find that those recommended for the notion "DBMS" allowed them to acquire new knowledge about this notion and 60.5% find that those recommended for the notion "SQL" helped them to learn new knowledge.

Based on the respondents answers to the same quiz presented before and after recommendations, the Table 1 resumes the percentages of correct answers. By examining the results, we note an improvement in all the answers after the recommendations except for one question dealing with the notion of "Relational Model" Q_2 for which the percentage of correct answers decreased. To understand the causes of this decrease, we started with studying the resources we recommend to the respondents to help them to acquire the notion of "Relational Model". Among the four recommended resources, there is R_1 that does not contain the information which is the subject of the question Q_2. There are also two resources R_2 and R_3 that include the information and the resource R_4 that includes the information but that is very voluminous with 37 modules and that require at least 3 hours to learn its content.

Table 1. Answers to the evaluation quiz before and after recommendations.

Recommandations	Relationnal model			DBMS			SQL	
	Q_1	Q_2	Q_3	Q_4	Q_5	Q_6	Q_7	Q_8
Before	48%	42%	41%	31%	51%	24%	42%	16%
After	76%	34%	52%	41%	68%	28%	43%	20%

Then we selected the 15 respondents who answered correctly the question Q_2 before the recommendations and incorrectly after the recommendations. By looking the resources attended by these respondents, we found that 10 of them have opted to attend the resource R_1 not dealing with the information processed by the question Q_2 and 3 of them choose the voluminous resource R_4. So, a possible explanation for these results is that the respondents didn't find the answer in the chosen resource or they didn't follow it until the end and they replied randomly to the question.

It is also important to note that two of the three respondents who opted to attend R_4 left some comments about its length: *"many pdf documents to open"* and *"too long"*. Hence the importance of the criteria relating to the granularity and the learning time of the recommend resources, defined in our solution and the importance of describing these information in the metadata of the OER to improve the recommendation's results.

Adequacy of recommendations with both the MOOC and the Learner Profiles

Application of Semantic Similarity Measure. For each MOOC's notion, the fourth experts ticked the resources allowing to acquire knowledge about this notion, from the set of all the resources selected by the initial query of our MORS system (the query defined in the PreSearch module). To assess the benefit of using the semantic similarity measure, we define two measures of precision. The first one is carried out on the resources selected by the initial query to assess whether the keyword search adopted in this query allows selection of relevant resources dealing with of knowledge element (subject of the recommendation). The second measure of precision aims to assess whether the refinement of the initial set of resources by using the semantic similarity measure increases the precision rate. Our objective is to have a precision rate closer to 100% after applying the semantic similarity on the descriptions of the resources selected by the initial query.

As explained previously, our goal is not to select all the relevant resources that exist in the external repositories but to be assured that the limited resources recommended to learners are relevant. In this context, the relevance is that the resource allow the acquisition of the notion which was not well mastered by the leaner and whose lack of knowledge triggered the recommendation process. For this reason, we define to measures of precision adapted to our goals:

- A first precision rate Precision_{ad1}. Precision_{ad1} represents the percentage of relevant resources among all the resources selected by the initial query.

$$\text{Precision}_{ad1} = \frac{|R_{RT}|}{|R_{IQ}|}$$

  Where R_{RT} represents the resources ticked by experts as relevant resources and R_{IQ} represents the set of the resources selected by the initial query of our system MORS.
- A second precision rate Precision_{ad1}. Precision_{ad2} represents the percentage of relevant resources among all the resources selected after the refinement using semantic similarity.

$$\text{Precision}_{ad1} = \frac{|R_{RT}|}{|R_{SS}|}$$

  Where R_{RT} represents the resources ticked by experts as relevant resources and R_{IQ} represents the set of the resources selected after applying semantic similarity.

By reviewing the results, we notice a significant increase in precision rates for resources related to the notion "Relational Model" and "DMS". For the notion "SQL", an increase is detected depending on the answers of two experts (expert 1 and expert 3) whereas a decrease is detected depending on the answers of the two others (expert 2 and expert 4). To understand this decrease, we studied the answers of the fourth experts on the relevance of the resources selected after applying the semantic similarity. Among the four selected resources, there is a resource which is considered as relevant by the expert 1 and 3 and no relevant by the expert 2 and 4. This is a course on database with a section introducing the notion "SQL", without giving details. A possible explanation of the difference between experts' opinions is that presenting not detailed information about the notion is considered, by some experts, sufficient to acquire some basic knowledge about the notion and not sufficient by the others.

In our case, the objective of recommendations is to help the learner to acquire a knowledge level allowing him to attend the MOOC until the end. From that comes the importance of the constraint defined in our solution to just retain resources which provide a knowledge level in a specific knowledge element (prerequisite or learning objective) upper or equal to the knowledge level defined in the MOOC. Unfortunately this information doesn't exist in the metadata of OER but recovering it later from learners who consult the recommendations may improve the results.

Adequacy of Recommendations with the MOOC Profile. In this step, we calculated the averages of scores given by the experts to each resource according to its satisfaction to the criteria related to the granularity and the learning time and the knowledge level.

It is important to note that in this step we are interested in the resources of the final set which is recommended to the learner (after applying the selection by constraints and the selection by semantic similarity).

Concerning the criterion related to the learning time of the resource, we obtain these results. For the notion "Relational Model", the resource with the worst note, represents a voluminous course with 37 modules and 3 hours at least to learn its content. The resource which receives the best note is a pdf of 84 pages in the form of slides where each page some lines. Therefore, we can deduce that the resource's volume (the number of its pages in this case) cannot give the exact information about the duration needed to assimilate its content.

Having the exact information about the learning time of the resource could support its recommendation by our approach. Unfortunately, information about learning times, in the majority of cases, is not included in the OER descriptions.

Concerning the notion "DBMS", the two best notes were assigned to resources presented as HTML pages. Although these courses are long, the notes can be explained by the fact that each of them offers a well presented summary that allows learners to go directly to a section dealing with a specific notion. The worst rating was assigned to a resource in the form of a quiz. A quiz presents questions and answers to learners and in most cases, it is used for the assessment of knowledge. Therefore, to answer a quiz, the learner is, in many cases, obliged to consult other courses which will increase the duration necessary to master the knowledge.

For the notion "SQL", the best note was assigned to a resource presented as a set of short videos of 2 to 4 min. A quiz resource is considered as the resource that requires the longer learning time.

Based on the experts responses on the relevance of OERs according to the criterion of the learning time, we can notice that two learning durations are to be taken into consideration.

The first duration concerns that necessary to assimilate the total content of the resource, and the second duration concerns that necessary to acquire knowledge about a specific notion, by consulting the resource. We can also notice that the way in which the resource is presented influences the duration to be spent by the learner to master its content.

In some cases, we noticed that experts have difficulty to rate resources criterion-by-criterion and their scores are influenced by several criteria at once. Such is the case of the criterion of granularity and knowledge level. For example, for the notion "DBMS", the same resource received the worst notes about its satisfaction to the criterion of granularity and knowledge level. The same resource received also the best note for its satisfaction to the criterion about granularity and knowledge level.

Adequacy of Recommendations with the Learner Profile. A large proportion of respondents, between 40% and 90%, considered the recommended resources as difficult resources in relation to their knowledge. Some of them left comments to express this difficulty: *"quite complex"*, *"very technical"* and *"I do not have the necessary bases"*.

This highlights the constraint defined in our approach that the prerequisites of recommended resources must be mastered by the learner.

As regards the criterion about learner's learning style, we calculated the average values of the scores assigned by respondents. After reviewing the results, we noticed that the resources presented in the form of videos and HTML pages with a properly presented menu to access resources' sections, are the most appreciated. Long resources are less appreciated. The worst notes were assigned to quizzes. This can be explained by the fact that a quiz does not explain the notion especially for beginner learners.

By studying respondents' learning styles based on their answers to the (ILS) questionnaire [16], we found that 29% of respondents are visual rather than verbal and 16% are 100% visual. This can explain the fact that the resources properly presented and including videos and images received better notes. We also found that 36% of respondents are sensorial rather than intuitive and 18% are 100% sensorial. This can explain the fact that resources containing exercises and applications were more appreciated than those based solely on theory.

7 Conclusions

In this article, we have presented our recommender system MORS. It dynamically recommends external OERs during a MOOC when a lack of knowledge of the learner is detected. To this end, we use performance degrees to qualify the difficulty of the MOOC knowledge elements and also to measure the acquisition of these elements by the learner. MORS adapts the results according to the progress of the MOOC and the knowledge acquired by the learner.

The resources to be recommended by MORS, at the beginning of the MOOC or at the end of each section, are calculated so that they are adapted to some characteristics of the learner and of the MOOC he is attending, at the moment of the recommendation. Therefore, our system consists of two processes responsible for generating and updating the learner profile and the MOOC profile throughout the MOOC, by extracting the necessary information. Based on these two profiles, if a lack of knowledge is detected for a certain knowledge element, the calculation of the recommendation is triggered. It starts with the PreSelection process that requests the repositories of OERs descriptions to select an initial set of OERs dealing with the knowledge element. Then, the refinement process generates the final set of OERs to be recommended to the learner. To his end, the refinement process performs selection and ranking operations based on mandatory and optional criteria. These criteria are defined to take into account both some characteristics of the learner and some specificities of the MOOC.

The first assessment of our system showed the importance of the criteria used in our recommendation algorithm to satisfy some learner and MOOC characteristics. This also allowed us to have an idea about the criteria priority according to the experts and to retrieve other proposals of criteria like the difficulty and the creation's date of the resource to enhance our solution. The evaluation also showed that in most cases, the resources recommended to the learners allowed them to acquire better knowledge in the notions of the MOOC. It is also necessary to perform another qualitative assessment to understand some of the experts answers that were not clear and easy to interpret. It is important to note that our solution uses the OERs metadata stored in accessible repositories, hence depends on the availability and the quality of these metadata. Therefore, in some cases, we have not been able to verify the fulfillment of certain criteria by the recommended OER because of the lack of metadata information, which affects the quality of recommendations.

Our short-term objective in the intermediate future is to improve our solution in the light of the results obtained from the evaluation, for example by adding other criteria in the recommended resources and assigning weights values to the optional criteria based on the experts answers. We also seek to integrate our recommender system in an existing MOOC in order to assess how it will be working under real conditions. This integration will allow us to get better feedback on the quality of recommended OERs and how much they support learners during the MOOC. We will be able also to deduce the performance degrees provided by the OERs based on learners responses to the MOOC quiz, after attending the recommended OERs.

References

1. Agrawal, A., Venkatraman, J., Leonard, S., Paepcke, A.: YouEDU: addressing confusion in MOOC discussion forums by recommending instructional video clips (2015)
2. Alario-Hoyos, C., Leony, D., Estévez-Ayres, I., Pérez-Sanagustín, M., Gutiérrez-Rojas, I., Kloos, C.D.: Adaptive planner for facilitating the management of tasks in MOOCs. In: V Congreso Internacional sobre Calidad y Accesibilidad de la Formación Virtual, CAFVIR, pp. 517–522 (2014)
3. Bansal, N.: Adaptive recommendation system for MOOC. Indian Institute of Technology, pp. 1–40 (2013)
4. Chowdhury, G.G.: Introduction to Modern Information Retrieval. Facet Publishing, London (2010)
5. Fasihuddin, H.A., Skinner, G.D., Athauda, R.I.: Personalizing open learning environments through the adaptation to learning styles. In: ICITA (2014)
6. Felder, R.M., Silverman, L.K., et al.: Learning and teaching styles in engineering education. Eng. Educ. **78**(7), 674–681 (1988)
7. Hajri, H., Bourda, Y., Popineau, F.: Querying repositories of OER descriptions: the challenge of educational metadata schemas diversity. In: Conole, G., Klobučar, T., Rensing, C., Konert, J., Lavoué, É. (eds.) EC-TEL 2015. LNCS, vol. 9307, pp. 582–586. Springer, Cham (2015). https://doi.org/10.1007/978-3-319-24258-3_64
8. Hajri, H., Bourda, Y., Popineau, P.: A system to recommend open educational resources during an online course. In: 10th International Conference on Computer Supported Education, pp. 99–109 (2018)
9. Imran, H., Belghis-Zadeh, M., Chang, T.-W., Graf, S., et al.: PLORS: a personalized learning object recommender system. Vietnam J. Comput. Sci. **3**(1), 3–13 (2016)
10. Kolb, A.Y.: The Kolb learning style inventory-version 3.1 2005 technical specifications, vol. 200, p. 72. Hay Resource Direct, Boston (2005)
11. Kolukuluri, S.: XBlock-courseware component architecture. Ph.D. thesis, Indian Institute of Technology, Bombay, Mumbai (2014)
12. Li, S.-W.D., Mitros, P.: Learnersourced recommendations for remediation. In: 2015 IEEE 15th International Conference on Advanced Learning Technologies (ICALT), pp. 411–412. IEEE (2015)
13. Maran, V., de Oliveira, J.P.M., Pietrobon, R., Augustin, I.: Ontology network definition for motivational interviewing learning driven by semantic context-awareness. In: 2015 IEEE 28th International Symposium on Computer-Based Medical Systems (CBMS), pp. 264–269. IEEE (2015)
14. Paquette, G., Mariño, O., Rogozan, D., Léonard, M.: Competency-based personalization for massive online learning. Smart Learn. Environ. **2**(1), 4 (2015)
15. Sahebi, S., Lin, Y.-R., Brusilovsky, P.: Tensor factorization for student modeling and performance prediction in unstructured domain. In: Proceedings of the 9th International Conference on Educational Data Mining, pp. 502–506. IEDMS (2016)
16. Soloman, B.A., Felder, R.M.: Index of learning styles questionnaire (1999). Accessed 26 Mar 2003
17. Sunar, A.S., Abdullah, N.A., White, S., Davis, H.C.: Personalisation of MOOCs: the state of the art (2015)

TECMap: Technology-Enhanced Concept Mapping for Curriculum Organization and Intelligent Support

Toby Dragon(✉) and Elisabeth Kimmich Mitchell

Department of Computer Science,
Ithaca College, 953 Danby Road, Ithaca, NY, USA
{tdragon, ekimmichmitchell}@ithaca.edu

Abstract. This paper extends a previous publication describing a system that utilizes a wide variety of available assessment information to automatically analyze students' understanding at a conceptual level and offer relevant automated support to teachers and students. This organization and support can be at the course level or at the level of curriculum for an entire program of study. Intelligent support includes interactive visualization of the conceptual knowledge assessment, individualized suggestions for resources, and suggestions for student groups based on conceptual knowledge assessment. This system differs from prior related work in that it can operate on entire program curricula, and that the basis for analysis and feedback is entirely customized to the individual instructors' course content. We discuss how the system is configured for courses and the curriculum levels, and describe our experience that indicates the benefits of the approach. We then provide detailed descriptions of how the system performs analysis and offers support in both course and curriculum scenarios.

Keywords: Concept maps · Automated assessment · Intelligent Tutoring Systems (ITS) · Expert Knowledge Bases (EKB) · Curriculum mapping · Curriculum assessment · Program assessment

1 Introduction

Instructors currently face an ever-wider variety of resources to support their courses. These options range from traditional textbooks to fully interactive online learning environments. Instructors can take a traditional approach, relying on a single source for their material. However, instructors have a different option as well: to use several different types of resources at once, pulling from traditional text, online articles, online practice environments, video tutorials, etc. While these materials may rapidly change for a variety of reasons, most instructors also have an understanding of the core concepts and organization of a course that remains consistent across iterations of the course and changes in materials. Our system supports instructors that want to apply their own organization to a variety of content in this way.

Similarly, instructors overseeing the organization of entire programs of study (for example a degree program at a university) are responsible for organizing all courses in a cohesive fashion in order to ensure that certain high-level learning goals are met. This

B. M. McLaren et al. (Eds.): CSEDU 2018, CCIS 1022, pp. 191–213, 2019.
https://doi.org/10.1007/978-3-030-21151-6_10

requires not only defining these learning goals, but also aggregating assessment information from a variety of sources to evaluate the effectiveness of the current approach.

These challenges can be seen as the same problem at different levels of abstraction, namely the challenge of organizing a set of concepts and their related resources in such a way as to clarify the intent of instruction. Our system, TECMap, allows instructors to encode their conceptual organization for a course or the curriculum of an entire program. They can then attach the varied types of educational materials and assessments. Once this structure is defined, the artifacts created through this process can be used to provide a variety of intelligent feedback, including an open-learner-model visualization of conceptual understanding, direct feedback for teachers and students, and intelligent grouping suggestions. We discuss the general manner in which the framework can be used for such feedback, and the specific implementation we currently employ.

This paper is an extension of prior work presented in CSEDU 2018 [7], and is organized as follows. First, we present relevant related work (Sect. 2), our goals in context of that prior work (Sect. 3), and the underlying structure on which our system is based (Sect. 4). We then present the manner in which the system is configured by instructors for course work, our experience configuring the system (Sect. 5), and the manner in which the same system can be applied at the curriculum level (Sect. 6). Finally, we present the various types of feedback the system provides in either of these scenarios (Sect. 7) and discuss plans for future work (Sect. 8).

2 Related Work

Current education technology systems may provide either instruction, practice environments, or both. These systems may also provide automated feedback to students, tools to support teachers in the grading process (including automation) or both. Finally, there are several full-fledged Intelligent Tutoring Systems (ITS) that perform automated analysis and use it to offer individualized feedback and educational information.

We consider our system to offer something different from these other tools in several aspects. We offer full customization of content and concept structure. We also offer estimated knowledge at the conceptual level, rather than having assessment tied to assignments. Finally, we offer a higher level of abstraction where assessment and feedback can apply to an entire program, which is not offered by other current systems to our knowledge. We see our work as complimentary, in that any of these other systems can actually be used to collect information at the assignment level and considered input to our system to provide more precise knowledge estimates, as discussed in Sect. 4.3.

Online textbooks and practice systems are available for many subjects and offer advantages over standard textbooks. They are more easily edited, customized, updated and can also offer interactive practice interleaved with content. Examples in the domain of computer science (our chosen domain) include Runestone Interactive[1], Zybooks[2],

[1] http://interactivepython.org/runestone/default/user/login.

[2] http://www.zybooks.com.

and Codio[3]. The information that these systems provide to instructors and students is rooted in specific individual assignments or questions, rather than any type of summary of what concepts the students understand. Our system uses that type of assignment-specific information as a basis for assessment at a higher level of abstraction, namely the conceptual level.

In the ITS field, there are many systems that organize analysis at a higher level of abstraction in order to base feedback on a conceptual level, rather than remaining assignment–specific. For example, Butz et al. present a system employing Bayesian networks to estimate higher-level assessment [3]. Sosnovsky and Brusilovsky present a system that organizes both content and assessment by topic, and present compelling evidence of the system's success with extensive usage [20]. These systems demonstrate the potential for a system to offer high-level assessment and feedback, but they are tied to a certain knowledge base and a certain set of resources. Even when automating the process of creation [14], the product is a single set of content organized by the ITS developers. Many instructors desire this type of "out-of-the-box" functionality. However, our system is aimed at instructors that want automated support but also want to exert a high level of control of the content and organization of their course.

Our system provides the ability to assess students at the conceptual level using each specific instructor's understanding of their course, their materials, and their assessment metrics. Those metrics could include any of the assignment-specific assessment offered by the aforementioned computer science education technology, as we discuss further in Sect. 4.3. We offer a solution that includes the benefits of ITS techniques combined with the variety of content and assessment available through the plethora of online tools and offline resources and catered to the individual instructors' needs and understanding of the course.

Our approach to offering this customization is based on concept mapping. Concept mapping has been shown to be a useful tool for science education, helping students organize their knowledge and to demonstrate their understanding of interconnections between concepts [19]. Likewise, instructors who are planning courses or curricula can use the same technique to explicate the concepts and the interconnections to be taught. This application of concept mapping during curriculum development has demonstrated benefits in biology and medicine, including improved cohesion and clarification of concepts and their interconnections [9, 21].

A potential concern we consider about this prior work is that these concept maps were not connected to the actual assignments given in class, were not used in the practice of the class, and therefore were most likely left behind at some point. Khan academy offered a similar vision of a concept map to organize course content and offer assessment, but it was only used in their math domain [17], and is no longer in active development[4]. The closest effort to our own technique was presented by Kumar, who demonstrated the use of concept maps as a basis for intelligent tutoring [12]. We apply this technique in a way that uses the instructor's concept map in the classroom process and ties it directly to the specific course content, rather than using it only as authoring for an ITS.

[3] https://codio.com/.

[4] http://khanacademy.wikia.com/wiki/Knowledge_Map.

3 Goals

Our approach leverages the ideas and technology from the fields of education, ITS, and concept mapping to accomplish one major overarching goal: to support students and instructors in situations where instructors want fine-tuned control over the content and organization of their courses and curricula. We provide a holistic system that helps instructors improve their organization and content while simultaneously creating a data structure enabling intelligent, automated assessment and feedback. This goal can be broken down into 3 component parts:

1. Creating a generic underlying structure that can be customized for individual courses or programs and then used by an ITS (Sect. 4).
2. Creating a customization process that helps instructors improve their course organization and content (Sect. 5) or their curriculum organization and assessment (Sect. 6).
3. Using that customized structure to provide automated assessment and feedback (Sect. 7).

Considering these goals, our approach will only be successful if:

- The effort expended customizing the system for a given class or program actually helps the instructors.
- If this customization process can be accomplished in a reasonable amount of time, such that it is feasible for instructors.
- If the system using the structure can provide useful assessment and feedback.

4 The System Foundation

All analysis performed by our system is based upon a data structure we term the concept graph. For an instructor to use our system with their course, they must define a concept graph and connect the resources they intend to use. This process explicates what concepts need to be taught and the manner in which the resources used for the course are related to those concepts. We have seen indication that the instructor's role in creating these graphs has direct benefits for the instructor's course (see Sect. 5).

4.1 The Concept Graph

The concept graph is a Directed Acyclic Graph (DAG) explicating the specific concepts to be taught in the course and their inter-relations, see Fig. 1. We draw these graphs with high-level concept nodes appearing at the top of the graph, and low-level nodes appearing underneath. Low-level nodes have edges that point to higher-level nodes. Each edge represents roughly the relationship "is-a-part-of". Node B pointing to node A would indicate that the knowledge of topic B is part of the necessary knowledge for topic A. In ITS terms, this model serves as the domain model, an Expert Knowledge

Base (EKB) [22]. It also serves as the basis for a student model. Namely, our student model is an overlay model because we hold an estimate of the student's knowledge for each node (concept) in the EKB.

This concept graph structure serves as the core representation that the system uses to provide automated analysis and support to students. The structure is encoded in JSON text format as a list of nodes and links, making it easily customizable and configurable.

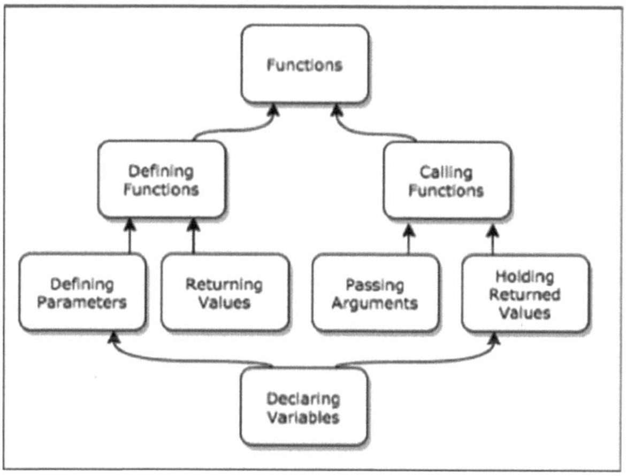

Fig. 1. An example concept graph explicating the concepts related to functions that are taught in an introductory computer science course. Image from [7].

4.2 Connecting Resources

Beyond the basic concept graph that encodes the important concepts and their interconnection, the system also requires a record of the resources and how these resources relate to the concepts in the graph. We use the term resource to refer to any artifact that imparts information to a student or offers information about a student related to the content (subject matter). We consider two main categories of resources: assessments and materials.

Assessments are any resources about which a student receives a grade, or number-based evaluation. Instructors generally have this information stored in some master list where student grades are organized and calculated (e.g., spreadsheet or student information system). However, the system can include information that is not used in course grade calculation. For example, teachers could include evaluation from more formative feedback, such as practice exercises, group evaluation, or rubrics. These evaluations might be indicative of mastery of concepts, even if the teacher prefers not to use them for grading. For each assessment, the system currently tracks: the ID, the display name, the maximum possible score for that assessment, and each student's score on that assessment.

We use the term materials to refer to any resource that provides information or opportunity for practice to the student, such as handouts, textbook chapters, and websites. The system currently only maintains an ID, a display name, and optionally a URL for materials, it does not attempt to track their content. The distinction between assessments and materials is important because the system uses assessments to calculate the knowledge estimate for each concept (see Sect. 6.1) and then uses materials when making suggestions (see Sect. 6.2). It is important to note that a certain resource could be both assessment and material. For example, many online learning environments provide both instruction and assessment information.

The resources and their connections for an entire course can be large and complex, with each resource potentially linked to several concepts. This creates certain challenges and requirements on the authoring process (see Sect. 5).

4.3 Providing Assessment Data

The system now needs data for individual students. These data can be imported from any source containing the assessment ID and the scores for each student on that assessment. Our initial efforts indicate that the most common format available for grade information is a spreadsheet in the form of a CSV file. Therefore, the system's current default behavior to directly import any number of CSV files related to a course. Many common computer systems offer this format including basic spreadsheets (e.g., Microsoft Excel, Google Sheets) learning management software (e.g., sakai[5]), and many online learning tools (e.g., Runestone, Zybooks and Codioas mentioned in Sect. 2).

5 Improving Course Content Through Authoring

The prior section describes the process by which the system is customized for a given course, namely creating a concept graph, connecting resources, and finally providing grade files. This work can be considered an authoring task for an ITS. Authoring related to ITS is traditionally considered challenging due to the effort required [18]. Therefore, we need to consider carefully the time, effort, and payoff involved to understand the likelihood of instructors successfully adopting the system. We now offer some detail of the authoring process we employ for creating graphs for course work, and describe our experience using the system with real instructors. We argue that the effort necessary for our authoring process is not overwhelming, can be completed incrementally, and most importantly has direct benefit for the author. Section 6 describes the similar authoring process as applied to an entire curriculum at the program level.

[5] https://sakaiproject.org/.

5.1 The Authoring Process

The first step in creating a concept graph for a given course is to define a set of concepts that students should learn in that course. There are many sources from which to derive this set, including the syllabus, student learning objectives associated with the course, the schedule, and the table of contents of any associated texts. Creating a single set from all these varied sources may seem daunting due to the sheer size and varied levels of abstraction. To relieve some of this stress, we must understand that this is merely a brain-storming step with no single right or wrong outcome. We have also found that, when given examples, instructors are intuitively aware of such a set of concepts for classes they have already taught (see Sect. 5.2). Once a general set of concepts is established, the next step is to draw a graph structure representing the connections between these concepts. This will likely cause revision of the concept list: addition, subtraction, merging for simplification, dividing for clarification, etc.

This mapping moves the author beyond isolated concepts such as those addressed by concept inventories [1], and also beyond organizations like course schedules (ordered list) and tables of contents (tree). Each of these data structures have their own inherent limitations beyond that of a graph. In a list, concepts can only be associated as before or after another concept. In a tree, each concept can only have one parent concept (i.e., the concept can only appear under one heading in the table of contents). You can note the redundant and sometimes awkward representation in the table of contents of texts where multiple chapters contain the same concept revisited. By allowing a many-to-many mapping when considering topics, we loosen the constraints to allow important distinctions, such as clarifying that a single concept learned early on in the course will be used and reinforced when learning higher-level concepts covered later in the course. While we consider this freedom crucial to accurately representing certain scenarios, it should be noted that a tree or list organization is perfectly acceptable as a DAG, and therefore can be used when an instructor considers it the ideal representation. In the extreme, a course can be represented by a set of distinct, unrelated concepts, although the utility of the automated analysis is limited in that case.

The process of mapping the interrelations of concepts can aid instructors in improving the overall organization of their course content (see Sect. 5.3). Instructors find relations that were not made clear to students, identify redundant presentation of concepts, and recognize better ordering in which to present concepts.

Once a first draft version of the concept graph has been drawn, the next task is to associate the resources used in the course with this concept graph. The concept graph itself can become large and complex, and in practice we have found it generally too complicated to visualize resources as separate items in the same diagram as the concept graph (as mentioned previously). Instead, we engage in the resource relation process by considering each individual resource and identifying the connection to concepts, rather than attempting to draw a diagram of the relations. We use a tabular format to allow instructors to list resources and to select the specific concepts to which the resource is related (see Fig. 2).

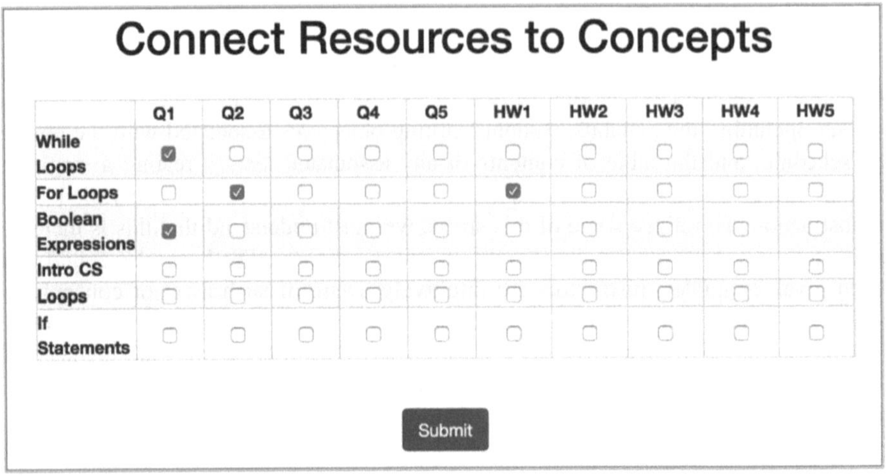

Fig. 2. Teachers use this tabular interface to denote the relations between resources and concepts. In the example shown above, Q1 is related to while loops and Boolean Expressions, while Q2 and HW1 are related to For Loops.

The process of identifying relations between resources and concepts is productive because it informs the instructor as to how the actual assessment and materials provided are related to their intention of teaching specific concepts. Through this process, instructors can recognize areas for improvement in their course content. Examples of problems recognized include: few or no assessments on key concepts; too little material directly related to a concept or assessments that should be divided in order to help their students and themselves pinpoint areas of misconception (see Sect. 5.3).

5.2 Authoring in Action

To test the practicality and potential benefit of this authoring process, we engaged seven different instructors (including one author of this paper) to create seven concept graphs for six different courses in our departmental curriculum. In most of the cases, individual instructors created the graph for their course. Alternatively, for certain courses with multiple sections, pairs of instructors who co-teach created the graphs together. Each graph creation started with a 30–45 min introduction and discussion with our team to communicate the task and the purpose as described in Sect. 5.1. Instructors then created graphs on their own time by drawing on white boards (tracking their time investment). They delivered their initial attempts to our team, who analyzed the results and conducted another 30–45 min of clarification and discussion with the participants for each graph.

A graph was created for each course, although some graphs represented only a subsection of a course and others did not have resources associated with them. We do not consider these partial creations an incomplete attempt, but rather a step in an iterative process from which we can learn (for further discussion see Sect. 5.3). Table 1 summarizes the courses and the respective effort to create a concept graph for each.

Table 1. Individual courses and their respective authoring efforts. Different instructors created two different graphs for different implementations of Comp. Sci. I. The * indicates instructor is an author of this paper. Table from [7].

Course title	# of instructors	Hours authoring	# of concepts	Complete course?	Resources connected?
Comp. Sci. I	1*	4	42	Yes	Yes
Comp. Sci. I	2	1	21	Yes	No
Comp. Sci. II	2*	1	17	Yes	No
Data Structures	1*	4	36	Yes	Yes
Discrete Structures	1	1	10	No	Yes
Website Dev.	1	3	39	Yes	Yes
Comp. Info. Tech.	1	3	19	Yes	No

Overall, the average creation time for a complete graph (rows 1, 4, and 6) is 3.7 h and average authoring time spent over all graphs including partial solutions is 2.4 h. We recognize the weakness of small sample size, and the specific bias that an author created several of the most complete graphs. Even with this considered, we see indication that productive graphs can be created on the order of hours, which we consider to be a time expense that most instructors could afford as long as there is recognizable benefit to their class.

We see that increased time also indicates increased complexity in the graph structure, and that connecting resources seems to also be correlated with more complex graphs. Figures 3 and 4 show two different concepts graphs, one simpler example created in a short period of time without connecting resources, and another created by the author demonstrating more complexity. We consider both of these efforts to have been successful in their own right, as both instructors found significant value in the process.

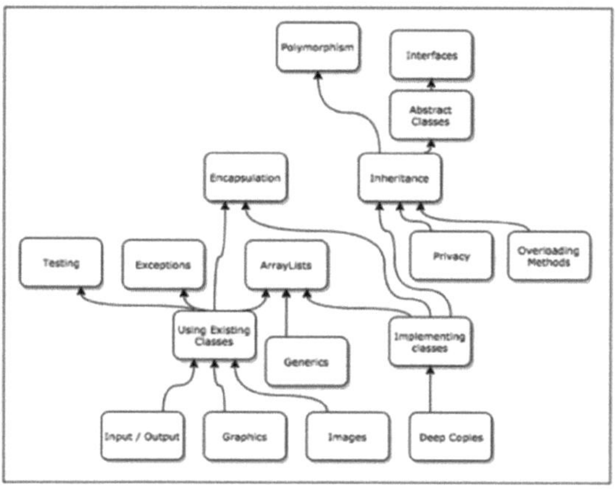

Fig. 3. The concept graph created for Comp Sci. II demonstrates the results of a shorter effort without connecting resources. The course is focused on Object Oriented Programming. Image from [7].

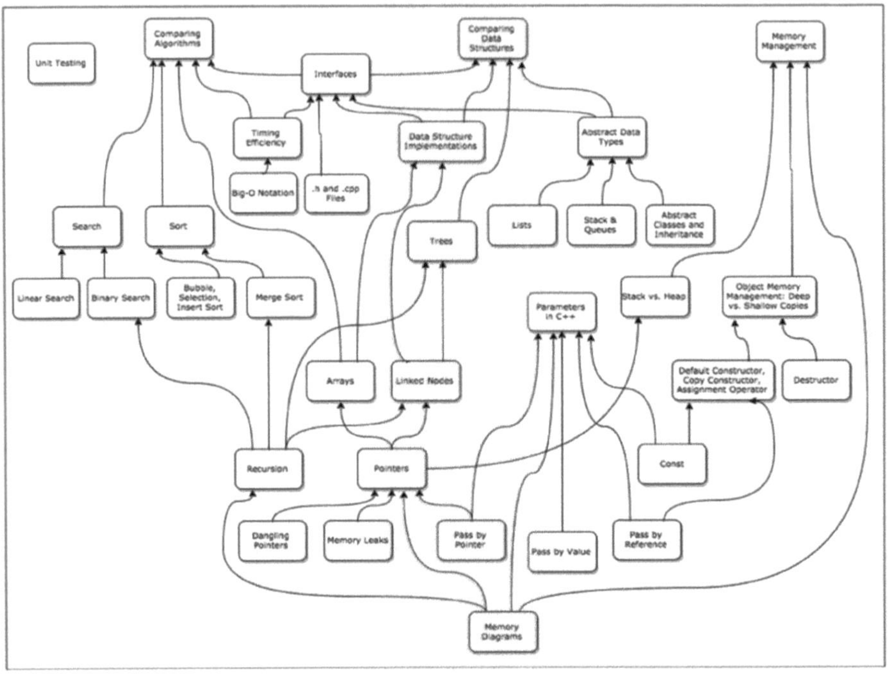

Fig. 4. The concept graph created for data structures demonstrates a more complex graph resulting from a longer effort that included the process of connecting related resource. The course covers memory management and data structures in C++. Image from [7].

5.3 Benefits and Challenges of Authoring

There was general consensus that the authoring process urged instructors to improve both organization and content within their courses. The process required instructors to carefully consider the order in which concepts are introduced and clarified. For example, two instructors noticed overarching concepts that were not being addressed as such. The issue was mitigated by reordering the topics to group around the actual concept in one case, and, in another case where this wasn't possible, by introducing the general concept more clearly in the beginning and noting the various applications as they occur.

In terms of content, the most common realization was that assessments were broad; covering many different concepts e.g., "Lab 8 covers these six concepts." When a student scores poorly on such an assessment, neither the instructor nor the student receive clear information about which specific concepts are the root of the issue. Several professors are currently re-working their assessments to include smaller, more targeted assessment. Other realizations included excessive assessment of one topic, missing direct assessment of others, and assessments on topics where very few materials are available for individual study (an indication more materials might be helpful).

The overall process was reportedly helpful for both revisiting familiar material and developing a new course. Most instructors were applying this technique to a course that they had already taught. These instructors reported that the process helped them formalize and clarify a structure for information with which they were already somewhat familiar. One pair of instructors was applying the process to a new course and reported that the process helped them realize that the course might be covering too much information and therefore provide too little practice when considering assessments and materials for each of the given concepts.

The main concern expressed by instructors about the process was managing the complexity of the task at hand. While the process is not overly time consuming (as shown in Table 1), the scope and ambiguity can be challenging. To complete a detailed concept graph for an entire course in addition to connecting relevant resources offers a daunting challenge. We discuss approaches to mitigate this issue in Sect. 5.4.

Another specific concern worthy of note was raised in regard to the level of abstraction (e.g., "How detailed should the graph be?"). We established a rule of thumb that if you have, or should have, distinct assessment that relates to a proposed concept, that concept should be its own node in the graph. If the proposed concept is simple enough or too entwined with other concepts to be assessed individually, then it is not abstract enough to include as a node in the graph. This is pragmatic but is also directly tied to the ITS which uses these graphs to offer support (Sect. 7).

A final recurring concern during the graph creation process was ambiguity. Participants found it challenging to create a "correct" graph. This was often due to the general debate about the manner in which a course should be taught. Our suggestion is to enjoy the discussion and remember that the graph is a living artifact. The main utility of this process is to generate formalized thought on the best content and organization of the course. This type of discussion will clearly lead to debate and discussion. We observed this debate particularly with pairs of instructors working together to make a graph, which we consider positive. There should be discussion when teaching a course together, and participants noted that the discussion was more clear and structured due to the graph. In the end of the discussion, a decision must be made, and this is the time to remember that changes can and will happen in the classroom and those changes can easily be reflected in later iterations of the graph.

5.4 Incremental Development to Address Complexity

Both the complexity concern and the ambiguity concern can be mitigated by working incrementally on the authoring process. One manner of incremental development is already built into our process; the idea of splitting this task into two distinct portions, creating the concept graph and then linking the resources. These steps can operate fairly independently. As we described in Sect. 4, performing the linking process for each resource in isolation simplifies and clarifies the task, rather than mapping each resource as a node in the graph, which can become overwhelming.

In practice, some instructors used the graph/resource split to limit their upfront effort. As seen in the table, some instructors did not link their resources during this exercise. Rather, they intend to link resources as they use them in class during the semester. This is a particularly practical approach for those that are either starting a new course or drastically altering the resources provided.

A different approach to iteration is to build the graph and link the resources for only a subsection of the course. In this way, the instructor has a full description of conceptual basis and the link to the resources for that part of the course.

Both of these approaches yield an incomplete concept graph artifact. We still consider the effort to be meaningful in two distinct ways. First, given the amount of time invested, we consider it to be reasonable that full graphs can be completed by instructors during any given semester. Second, even in situations where the graph creation was limited to a portion of the course, the product is still useful. The instructor still noted the benefits of improved course organization and content, and as long as relevant resources were connected the to graph, the incomplete work can still be used by the ITS.

6 Curriculum-Level Application

This project was conceived as a system to organize, assess and provide feedback related to course content [7]. However, we find that the system has an equally interesting and potentially important function in organizing, assessing, and providing feedback for entire program curricula. We now describe the application of the system at the curricular level, and then describe the types of support offered for both course and curricular level (Sect. 7).

6.1 Approach

The system applied to the curricular, or program level requires no functional changes. The main difference is the level of abstraction in the graph. When considering the entire curriculum, the concepts should be, by definition, higher-level. These high-level learning goals are often related to Student Learning Objectives (SLOs) in programs of study. Student Learning Objectives are goals for student achievement and growth, which are generally created by first deciding a set of target skills and concepts for students to learn, and then designing a set of assessment metrics by which to judge this acquisition [13]. These concepts and target skills can translate directly into concepts to be used in the concept graph. The assessment metrics can then be considered assessment resources in the system.

However, the graph structure and the system's ability to process a wealth of complex data allows us to consider both the conceptual and the assessment-related parts of program evaluation in a different and perhaps more meaningful manner than standard SLO evaluation. We applied our mapping process to our Computer Science curriculum to consider the utility of this process. Figure 5 shows the concept graph that was created from the five original SLOs. We consider several important weaknesses of SLOs that are potentially mitigated by the mapping process, indicating that using our system at the curriculum level might be a fruitful addition to curriculum mapping and assessment practices.

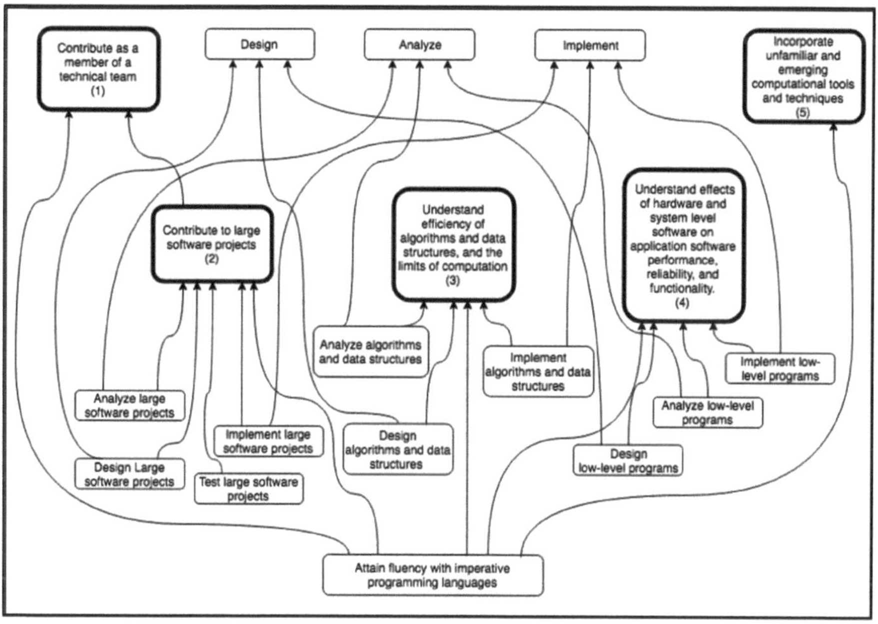

Fig. 5. The concept graph of a computer science curriculum as derived from iterative process considering the original SLOs of the program. The nodes representing the original SLOs are numbered and highlighted with bold outline.

6.2 Benefits

The first consideration is the assumption of independence built into the SLO process. SLOs are typically written as independent, measurable variables. However, in reality, SLOs may rely directly on one another. For example, we recognize that one important aspect of contributing successfully on a technical team in our department (SLO 1) is that you can contribute to large software projects (SLO 2). Beside direct relations, there may also be lower-level factors that have an impact on multiple SLOs (hidden factors). For example, we recognized that our SLOs did not include any reference to basic programming skills, which are necessary to meet any of our SLOs. The graph structure allows us to make these types of relationships explicit. By adding the node to represent fluency with imperative programming languages, we can now assess that aspect by collecting data independently and begin to understand if students not meeting SLOs are lacking high-level skills such as understanding efficiency of algorithms, or if they are missing basic skills that would allow them to succeed in more lofty goals. This is also now under consideration to become an SLO, but again, if it does become an SLO, it will be important to recognize the dependence of all other SLOs on it.

The second consideration is the data processing aspect as related to assessment of SLOs. Generally, the list of SLOs for a program will be fairly short. We believe this is at least partly due to the burden of data collection and analysis to evaluate the SLOs. Rather than make many fine-grained SLOs, in practice SLOs tend to evaluate broad ideas with a limited amount of assessment information. Our assessment structure allows for the creation of lower-level breakdown of an SLO. For example, each of the SLOs 2, 3, and 4 are broken down into respective abilities of students to design, analyze, and implement. The wording to represent this breakdown by ability was present in the original SLOs (although inconsistent), but these aspects were not evaluated independently, meaning single data points represented students' abilities in all three aspects combined. Considering aspects as separate entities in our system allows us to collect data from multiple sources to assess the different parts of an SLO, and the overall SLO evaluation can be related to the higher-nodes in the graph. In our example, we can collect data from points in the curriculum where students implement algorithms and data structures but do not analyze or design them yet (for example an introductory course). This information allows for evaluation of progress on SLOs as students move through the curriculum, see Sect. 7.1.

The final aspect that we consider beneficial to curriculum assessment is the ability to slice and unify assessment data in different ways. The system allows for lower-level information to be used by multiple high-level concepts. For example, several of our original SLOs are broken down by topic (e.g., large software projects, algorithms, etc.). Alternatively, these same SLOs could have addressed important abilities (e.g., design, analyze, implement). The breakdown in our graph allows the same low-level nodes and all their respective assessment to provide us understanding across all data from both the topic and the abilities perspectives.

6.3 Combining Course-Level and Curriculum-Level Graphs

When mapping both curriculum and courses, an obvious consideration is the manner in which these can be combined. From a naïve perspective, one could just make a graph that includes the entire curriculum from program SLOs down to each assignment given in all classes. This is theoretically possible but not practical in the current system. The graph would be complex to the point of being confusing rather than illuminating, and the amount of effort needed to create the graph would be enough to negate the claims in Sect. 5 that this can be achieved in a matter of hours. Currently, we suggest creating the graphs for curriculum and courses separately, while potentially using the information from course graphs to inform curriculum graphs. For example, knowledge estimates for students on specific nodes from course graphs could be output and used as input to the curriculum graph. We discuss further integration ideas in Sect. 8.

7 Support Offered

Now that there is an understanding of the underlying data structure (the concept graph), and we see that the creation process can be productive, we can discuss the manner in which this structure is used to provide automated support for students and teachers. The system provides a direct view of the conceptual-level assessment for students and teachers to better understand their situation, suggests resources on which students should focus; and identifies groups of students that are potentially helpful to each other.

7.1 Knowledge Estimation

The system provides estimates of students' knowledge for each concept in the concept graph. These concept knowledge estimates can be calculated for any student, or for any group of students. To perform this analysis, the system must have a concept graph definition and connected assessments (as described in Sect. 4). These definitions provide student data connected to the resources in the graph, those resources connected to concepts, and those concepts inter-connected in a DAG. Our algorithm for making knowledge estimates is a recursive bottom-up traversal of the graph. In an effort to maintain simplicity until there is solid rationale for complexity, each node's estimate is currently a weighted average of all the resources connected directly to that node, along with recursive estimates of all other concepts below that node. We plan for a system in which the formula for aggregation can be altered at runtime, to allow experimentation with more sophisticated calculation techniques.

Weights of specific assessments are set by the author. Weights of any given node are currently calculated as a sum of the weights of all assessments and nodes connected to that node. This weighting system is naïve in several ways (e.g., direct assessment of a concept is weighted equally to indirect assessment), but again we choose to maintain simplicity until we have clear justification for added complexity.

To visualize the concept graph and the knowledge estimates for each concept, we present an html page using google charts[6], see Fig. 6. Each node displays the knowledge estimate as a number between zero and one, and is color coded to indicate areas of concern. The color coding is adjustable by the instructor's choice.

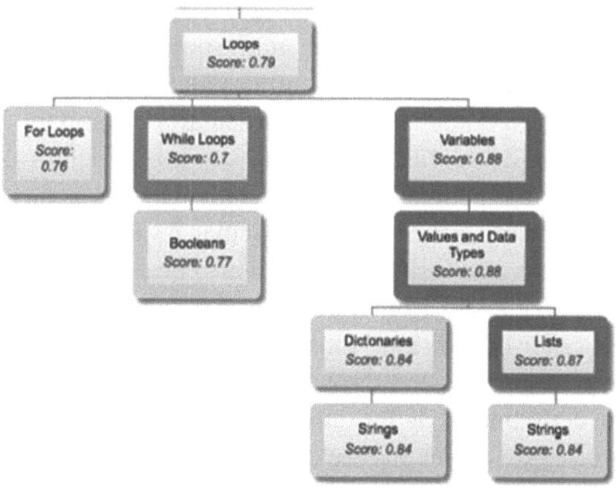

Fig. 6. An example portion of the visualization of a students' knowledge estimates as displayed by our system for the introductory computer science course. Image from [7].

Clicking on a concept will display the resources related to that concept, and if the resource is an assessment, the score received on the assessment. Concept nodes in this

[6] https://developers.google.com/chart/.

display can be collapsed to hide the lower-level nodes. It should be noted that the google charts tool can only display tree structures and so our graph is converted to a tree by making duplicate nodes with the same titles and information. This is not ideal, and a direct visualization of the graph is an area of active research.

Use at the Course Level
Considering concept graphs that represent a course, this visualization provides a quick artifact that students or teachers can review in order to see strengths and weaknesses at a conceptual level rather than an assignment level. The ability to open and close nodes and see associated resources also allows students to explore the reason behind the knowledge estimates. This type of display can be considered an Open Learner Model (OLM), as it displays the automated analysis to the student in order to allow them to consider and reflect on their current state of knowledge. OLMs have been demonstrated to have positive effects on learning, even without offering further feedback [2] and have shown promise in closing the achievement gap [16]. The use of color-coded visualization has been demonstrated to allow users to gain useful assessment information in a brief interaction [15]. Visualizing the average of all students in a single graph is useful to instructors to understand full class dynamics (e.g., that concept was not covered well), and potentially also useful to students for comparing themselves to an average of their peers.

Use at the Curriculum Level
Considering concept graphs for an entire program curriculum, this visualization provides aggregate assessment information about SLOs. Each node in the graph that represents an SLO informs the assessment team about how students have performed across all assessments in the department that are related to that SLO. Instructors can then navigate to the lower connected nodes and resources for a more in-depth view of precisely where problems might be occurring.

This visualization has potential to be particularly important when considering monitoring progress on SLOs. Instructors can monitor progress of specific cohorts (e.g., freshman, juniors, first-generation college students, etc.) as they move through the degree program, giving early notice about curricular issues for certain cohorts.

On an individual scale, this visualization can also be used in advising. Students can use what they should be gaining from a program, i.e., what the department intends for them to learn. This color-coded, individualized graph can be used to help a student understand how they are progressing through the program and could be compared with the average in the department, at the advisor's discretion, to discuss the student's relative success or struggle at this higher conceptual level.

7.2 Resource Suggestion

In addition to visualizing knowledge estimates, the system uses these estimates to suggest resources that should be useful to a student. We encode certain pedagogical principles in order to automatically suggest on which concepts students should focus, and which resources are best to study the selected concepts. In this way, the following suggestion algorithm represents a pedagogical model [22] because it controls the manner in which the ITS uses the assessment to offer pedagogically-meaningful recommendations. Figure 7 represents the algorithm used to make suggestions based on the concept graph. We now explain each step in the process, and the pedagogical rationale for each. Italics indicate steps that are directly represented in the diagram.

Starting from the concept graph, the first step is to choose concepts on which the student should focus. A common pedagogical theory based in Vitgostky's theory of Zone of Proximal Development [4] is that we must choose topics that are not already known, but also not too far beyond student's current knowledge. To identify these concepts, we choose the concepts in range from yellow to orange, leaving out known concepts (green), and potentially unreachable concepts (red). The next step does an ancestry check in the graph to ensure that if many related concepts might be suggested, only the lowest level concepts are included. This decision is based on the theory that we should work on simpler concepts before the concepts that build on them. These steps result in a specific set of suggested concepts for which we now need to find appropriate related resources to suggest. The system also has a mode that allows users to directly specify the concepts to study rather than employing the algorithm for this step.

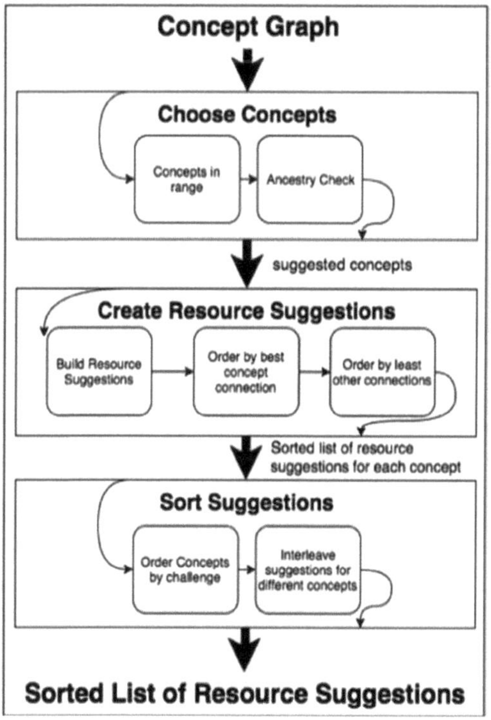

Fig. 7. The algorithm for producing suggested resources based on the concept graph structure and knowledge estimates. Image from [7].

For each concept that has been identified as in need, the system now identifies related resources. The system *creates resource suggestions* for each concept to link the suggested resource with the given concept. This ensures the student receives information not only about which resource they should study, but also why they should study it (the important associated concept that is a weakness for them specifically). For each concept, all related resources are then sorted by multiple criteria. The most important criterion is the strength of the relationship between the resource and the concept at hand. Resources directly connected within the concept graph (strongest connections), or they could be found by recursively exploring the concept graph for indirect connections. We judge indirect connections by counting the number of paths from an indirect resource to the relevant concept. Each path found represents one set of sub-concepts that connect the resource to the concept. Many of these paths indicate that a resource contains many relevant sub-concepts of the desired concept. Using this count of paths, r*esources are then ordered by best concept connection*, being direct and then strongest indirect connections. In practice with sample data from our work with real concept graphs (see Sect. 5.2), we observed that many resources are equal by this standard, and so to further sort the list, we *find resources with least other connections*. This indicates that a resource directly addresses the concept at hand and is not muddied by other concepts. This entire process creates a *sorted list of resource suggestions related to each concept*.

Considering this list of resource suggestions for each concept, the system now chooses the ordering of resources to be presented to the user. First, the system chooses an ordering of concepts by challenge. The system identifies knowledge estimates that are closest to the center of the range of concepts to study. This approach attempts to balance the need for concepts that are the most likely to be necessary to study with the need for concepts most likely for a student to be ready to study. Finally, the system *interleaves suggestions for different concepts* in the order of concept priority, offering the best suggestion about the top concept, followed by the best suggestion for the second concept, etc. This decision is driven by the theory that variety in educational materials is beneficial, and also by pragmatism, in that the best suggestions will appear first, rather than some sub-par suggestions for the most important concept appearing before the best suggestion for another important topic.

Overall, this algorithm considers the individualized knowledge estimates and utilizes the concept graph structure to automatically create intelligent suggestions for reflection and study. These suggestions not only provide the user with the resources, but also with the related concept that should be the focus of their use of each suggested resource. These suggestions are intuitively useful to students, but instructors can use them as well. This same algorithm can be applied to a graph containing estimates for an entire class, and suggestions would be relevant to the average student in the class, representing good potential classroom exercises. We envision this current system as more useful for course-level feedback, but the same tools can be applied to curriculum-level graphs.

We note that the pedagogy encoded is debatable and changeable. Further research in educational theory could warrant changes and classroom use will define our understanding of the success/failure of this specific pedagogy. However, the system source code is developed in a modular fashion with clean software interfaces that allow for alteration or multiple interchangeable pedagogical models for experimentation.

7.3 Dynamic Group Suggestion

Similar to resource suggestions, we have defined an algorithm for dynamic group selection based on the concept graph and certain pedagogical principles [8]. Automated group selection is a challenging problem [5] that is addressed by a large body of research, including the fields of Computer Supported Collaborative Learning (CSCL) and Computer Supported Cooperative Work (CSCW). We are not seeking to replicate the large body of work based on grouping students by traits or roles. Rather, we seek to understand the effect of basing groups on concept knowledge, similar to techniques pioneered some time ago [10, 11], but less explored in recent literature.

The system employs a generic grouping mechanism by which different grouping methods can be applied in any order. Figure 8 offers a visualization of the technique. Any type of grouping method can be applied in any order to allow for experimentation.

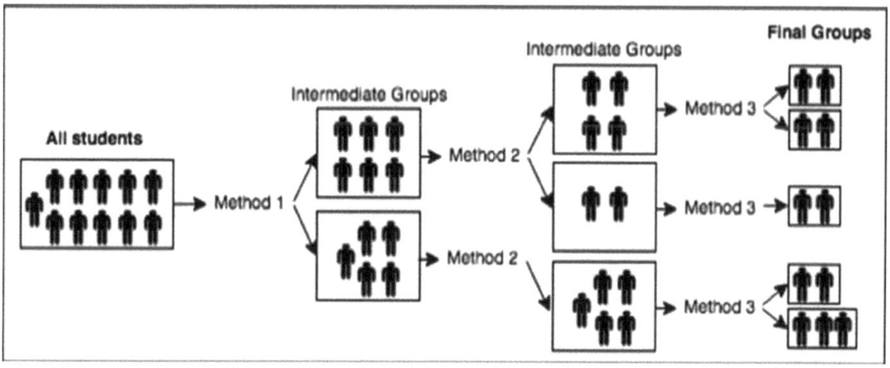

Fig. 8. The result of applying 3 different grouping methods in our generic grouping system. Each consecutive method will produce more groups with less students in each group. Image from [7].

Considering specific grouping methods, the system has can use the individual concept graphs for each student to make choices. Figure 9 shows the specific grouping methods currently implemented by our system, and their ordering.

The algorithm takes the set of knowledge graphs and computes an overall knowledge estimate for each one by finding the sum of all knowledge estimates in the given graph. The system then uses this score to divide the set of students into buckets. The number of buckets is relative to the size of the class. For our current class sizes of 20–30 students, we are using three buckets, representing advanced, average, and struggling students respectively. The theory behind this step is to group students with similar abilities. Our experience tells us that small groups with large gaps in ability tend to devolve into advanced students completing the work while struggling students disengage.

Within these large subsets of students with similar abilities, the system identifies common concepts that are in need of improvement. The system builds a list of the students most in need of work on each concept. If a student is in need of multiple concepts, they are grouped with the concept closest to the center of the range of need, for the same reasons described in Sect. 7.2.

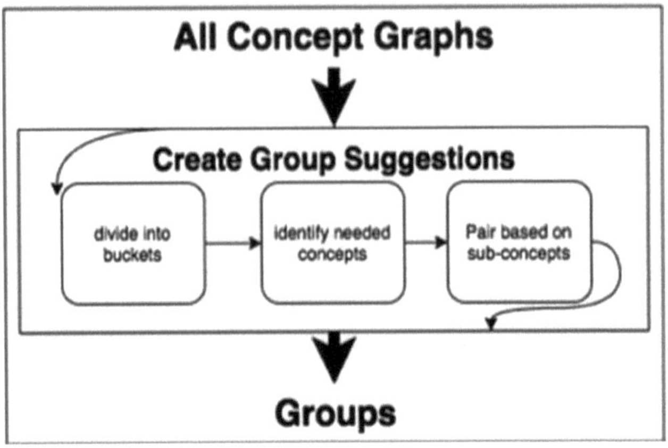

Fig. 9. The algorithm for producing suggested groups based on the concept graph structure knowledge estimates of each student. Image from [7].

Finally, within these sub-sets of students with similar abilities that need work on the same concepts, we make the actual group suggestions (of 2–4 students). The system makes this final determination of the best groups by examining the concept graphs of the involved students. The system searches for sets of students that have differences in knowledge estimates of sub-concepts directly related to the chosen concept. This identifies sets of students that have a similar level of understanding of the concept to study but have differing levels of understanding of the sub-concepts. Theoretically, this will bring together sets of students that have complimentary parts of the overall necessary knowledge for the concept at hand.

Once the group and concept has been identified, the system uses the suggestion algorithm from Sect. 7.2 to also identify a list of potential resources with which the group could be tasked.

By the third level of selection, the system is looking for something very specific, which will likely not be found for every group. However, the system then defaults to simply grouping only by concept, or finally grouping by ability. The worst-case scenario is that groups need to be made across buckets.

Use at the Course Level

The methodology above was developed to address a specific classroom grouping need. Instructors in our department often create dynamic groups for single class periods or even part of a class period. Students are grouped differently each class period. Currently, students are grouped randomly or self-selected. These approaches both have strengths and weaknesses, but neither approach addresses the need to have students work in groups that are beneficial based on their knowledge of the material in class.

Similar to the suggestion algorithm, the algorithm described above is an initial attempt at a pedagogically–driven group selection process for this small, short-term group scenario. Considering that one current benchmark for comparison is random, we hypothesize that even with potential flaws, the system might offer added benefit. We will test this theory with experimentation. We have currently also developed a random group selection mechanism to provide a control group for experimentation with this grouping policy.

Use at the Curriculum Level
While originally developed for short-term in-class interaction, the generic framework and even the specific grouping mechanisms can also be used for a curriculum-level concept graph. One example use is identifying peer tutoring and mentoring opportunities. As described in Sects. 7.1 and 7.2, the system can allow instructors to identify and even suggest specific students who are struggling. The grouping mechanisms described above can help to identify subsets of students with similar problems. This cohort of students (if they are interested in support) can then be paired with a peer tutor/mentor. The same mechanism that can identify the group of students and the concepts (or SLOs) with which they are struggling can be used to identify students who excel in this aspect. In this way, the system can suggest groups of students that need support, and students that could provide that support. It should be noted that, due to the many potential pitfalls inherent to creating such groups, this entire process requires monitoring and administration by instructors that use the system only for guidance at first. After experimentation and refinement, we can evaluate the potential for direct use by the students.

8 Conclusions and Future Work

We see potential in this systemto support students and instructors at both the course level and program level. As a tool at the course level, instructors can map the conceptual basis for their courses, organize, and relate their materials and assessments. At the curriculum level, instructors planning entire programs can map their SLOs in a more in-depth manner, and clearly relate any number of assessment metrics. In either case, the system then provides students and instructors a more detailed vision of the goals of the course or program, individual progress, and intelligent suggestions of resources and student groups.

We also recognize the ability for the system to provide a more stable and yet dynamic basis for the organization of both courses and curricula. In general, curriculum mapping and reflection on course organization occurs less often than it is ideal. These types of documents often become stale. Meanwhile, when such documents aren't regularly referenced and content or assessment shifts within a class, the conceptual basis of the course or program can shift inadvertently or arbitrarily. A correctly-used concept graph could prevent some of these problems by providing a stable base that changes less often than the transient resources but is updated more often than curriculum maps that may only be referenced during program reviews.

Aside from general experimentation to demonstrate the efficacy of the system in real classroom use, we have several avenues for future work. The first is prediction. As described in Sect. 7.1, the system currently uses a bottom up traversal in order to calculate knowledge estimates from related assessment. This means we have no estimates for any node without assessment complete at that node or below it, leaving us in the dark about how a student will theoretically perform on future tasks related to those nodes. We are currently testing different machine learning techniques to offer prediction of both incomplete assessments and nodes that do not have sufficient data for estimation. The most interesting aspect of this work is testing whether additional information from the concept graph can improve accuracy of prediction.

We are also focused on improving methods of providing feedback to the authors to help them improve their concept graphs, using both theoretical and statistical approaches [6]. This work is particularly important when considering curriculum-level concept graph because this type of feedback could offer suggestions for improvement to both assessment techniques for academic programs and curriculum design.

Finally, in the long-term, we envision the system as a cloud-based web service, where concept graphs and resource links can be saved, shared, and edited by the community. In this way, any instructor could review many other concept graphs related to a given course, adapt any of them to their own purposes by changing concepts and resources, and share their own version back to the community.

References

1. Almstrum, V.L., et al.: Concept inventories in computer science for the topic discrete mathematics. In: ITiCSE-WGR 2006, pp. 132–145. ACM, New York, June 2006. https://doi.org/10.1145/1189215.1189182
2. Bull, S., Kay, J.: Open learner models. In: Nkambou, R., Bourdeau, J., Mizoguchi, R. (eds.) Advances in Intelligent Tutoring Systems. SCI, vol. 308, pp. 301–322. Springer, Heidelberg (2010). https://doi.org/10.1007/978-3-642-14363-2_15
3. Butz, C.J., Hua, S., Maguire, R.B.: A web-based Bayesian intelligent tutoring system for computer programming. Web Intell. Agent Syst. **4**(1), 77–97 (2006)
4. Chaiklin, S.: The zone of proximal development in Vygotsky's analysis of learning and instruction. Vygotsky's Educ. Theory Cult. Context **1**, 39–64 (2003)
5. Dillenbourg, P.: Over-scripting CSCL: the risks of blending collaborative learning with instructional design. In: Three Worlds of CSCL. Can We Support CSCL? pp. 61–91 (2002)
6. Dragon, T.: Turning the tables: authoring as an asset rather than a burden. In: Proceedings of the 10th International Conference on Computer Supported Education, CSEDU 2018, pp. 308–315. SciTePress (2018)
7. Dragon, T., Kimmich Mitchell, E.: Improving course content while creating customized assessment and support at the conceptual level. In: Proceedings of the 10th International Conference on Computer Supported Education, CSEDU 2018, pp. 110–121. SciTePress (2018)
8. Dragon, T., Lindeman, C., Wormsley, C., Lesnefsky, D.: Better than random: can we use automated assessment to form productive groups on the fly? In: The Workshop on Intelligent Support for Learning in Groups, 13th International Conference on Intelligent Tutoring Systems, ITS-2016 (2016)
9. Edmondson, K.M.: Concept mapping for the development of medical curricula. J. Res. Sci. Teach. **32**(7), 777–793 (1995)
10. Greer, J.E., Mccalla, G., Collins, J.A., Kumar, V.S., Meagher, P., Vassileva, J.: Supporting peer help and collaboration in distributed workplace environments. Int. J. Artif. Intell. Educ. (IJAIED) **9**, 159–177 (1998)
11. Hoppe, H.U.: The use of multiple student modeling to parameterize group learning. In: Proceedings of AI-ED 1995, 7th World Conference on Artificial Intelligence in Education (1995)

12. Kumar, A.N.: Using enhanced concept map for student modeling in programming tutors. In: FLAIRS Conference, pp. 527–532 (2006)
13. Lachlan-Haché, L., Cushing, E., Bivona, L.: Student Learning Objectives as Measures of Educator Effectiveness: The Basics. American Institutes for Research, Washington, DC (2012)
14. Lin, Y.L., Brusilovsky, P., He, D.: Improving self-organising information maps as navigational tools: a semantic approach. Online Inf. Rev. **35**(3), 401–424 (2011)
15. Mavrikis, M., Gutierrez-Santos, S., Poulovassilis, A.: Design and evaluation of teacher assistance tools for exploratory learning environments. In: Proceedings of the Sixth International Conference on Learning Analytics & Knowledge (LAK 2016), pp. 168–172. ACM (2016). ISBN 9781450341905
16. Mitrovic, A., Martin, B.: Evaluating the effects of open student models on learning. In: De Bra, P., Brusilovsky, P., Conejo, R. (eds.) AH 2002. LNCS, vol. 2347, pp. 297–305. Springer, Cham (2018). https://doi.org/10.1007/3-540-47952-X_31
17. Morrison, B.B., DiSalvo, B.: Khan academy gamifies computer science. In: Proceedings of the 45th ACM Technical Symposium on Computer Science Education, pp. 39–44. ACM, March 2014
18. Murray, T.: An overview of intelligent tutoring system authoring tools: updated analysis of the state of the art. In: Murray, T., Blessing, S.B., Ainsworth, S. (eds.) Authoring Tools for Advanced Technology Learning Environments, pp. 491–544. Springer, Dordrecht (2003). https://doi.org/10.1007/978-94-017-0819-7_17
19. Novak, J.D.: Concept mapping: a useful tool for science education. J. Res. Sci. Teach. **27** (10), 937–949 (1990)
20. Sosnovsky, S., Brusilovsky, P.: Evaluation of topic-based adaptation and student modeling in QuizGuide. User Model. User-Adap. Inter. **25**(4), 371–424 (2015)
21. Starr, M.L., Krajcik, J.S.: Concept maps as a heuristic for science curriculum development: toward improvement in process and product. J. Res. Sc. Teach. **27**(10), 987–1000 (1990)
22. Woolf, B.P.: Building Intelligent Interactive Tutors: Student-Centered Strategies for Revolutionizing E-Learning. Morgan Kaufmann, Burlington (2010)

Improving STEM Learning Experience in Primary School by Using NEWTON Project Innovative Technologies

Nour El Mawas[1(✉)], Irina Tal[2], Arghir Nicolae Moldovan[2], Diana Bogusevschi[3], Josephine Andrews[2], Gabriel-Miro Muntean[3], and Cristina Hava Muntean[2]

[1] CIREL(EA 4354), University of Lille, Lille, France
nour.el-mawas@univ-lille.fr

[2] School of Computing, National College of Ireland, Dublin, Ireland
{Irina.Tal,ArghirNicolae.Moldovan,Josephine.Andrews, Cristina.Muntean}@ncirl.ie

[3] School of Electronic Engineering, Dublin City University, Dublin, Ireland
{diana.bogusevschi,Gabriel.Muntean}@dcu.ie

Abstract. Nowadays school curriculum is changing and more and more teachers are incorporating STEM content and themes into their classrooms. Students need to be proficient in STEM fields in order to be ready for the new technology driven society. Game-based learning and the latest visual technologies such as Augmented Reality, Virtual Reality and Virtual Labs can motive students to study STEM topics through an immersive and engaging environment. This research introduces NEWTON project that integrates into a learning platform (NEWTELP) different innovative technologies and deploys them in various European learning environments. In particular, Final Frontier, a novel interactive educational video game about solar system designed for primary school children is presented. A research study that involved the use of the game in a primary Irish school from Dublin, has investigated the learner experience. An analysis of the results show that over 90% of students confirmed that the game helped them to learn about the characteristics of the planets from the Solar system and they enjoyed the game and the game features in particular the fun aspect, the exploration tasks, stars and meteorites collection, avatar, use of jetpack, and the interactive puzzles.

Keywords: Technology enhanced learning · STEM · Educational video game · Primary education · Solar system

1 Introduction

STEM stands for science, technology, engineering, and math and it has become more than a popular buzzword. Nowadays school curriculum is changing and more and more teachers are incorporating STEM content and themes into their classrooms. Students need to be proficient in STEM fields in order to be ready for the new technology driven society. The new 21st century STEM oriented teaching and learning paradigm replaces the old approach in which the teacher is the only source of all the knowledge, everyone

B. M. McLaren et al. (Eds.): CSEDU 2018, CCIS 1022, pp. 214–230, 2019.
https://doi.org/10.1007/978-3-030-21151-6_11

learns the same way, and the class is the only place in which knowledge is transmitted. The 21st century teaching and learning paradigm is dynamic, technology-enabled, student-centric and develops 21st century competencies and skills such as digital literacy, communication, collaboration, critical thinking, problem solving, decision making and creativity.

The latest technological innovations such as virtual reality (VR), augmented reality (AR), educational 3D games integrated into the teaching and learning process increase student motivation and engagement. in STEM subjects, demystify the pre-conceived idea among students that science and technologies subjects are difficult and not at last improve learning outcome and increases student motivation and engagement.

Many VR applications are currently designed for entertainment, but VR's potential for education is huge. VR devices are expected to increase 85% by 2020, with gaming and educational applications driving most of that growth [49]. A few companies (e.g. ZSpace), have already created specialized VR systems for education purpose that help children complete STEM tasks in a hands-on environment.

AR technology integrates digital information with real environments in which people live. AR offers a new form of interactivity between the physical and virtual world and has become one of the key emerging technologies in education. A systematic review on the use of AR technology to support STEM learning found that most augmented reality applications for STEM learning offered exploration or simulation activities However, few studies provided students with assistance in carrying out learning activities [17].

Game-based learning involves the use of gaming technology for educative purposes where students explore concepts in a learning context designed by teachers. Game-based learning helps the students learn in an immersive and engaging environment.

Educational games are now applied at all levels of education, from primary school to the third level education. In 2015, 47% of K-12 teachers reported that they use game-based learning in their classrooms, and almost 66% of K-5 teachers mentioned the use of digital games in their curriculum [8]. Currently increasing number of students are exposed to game-based learning in their formal, non-formal and in-formal education and this trend is expected to continue. For instance, the TechNavio's report published in August 2017 [40] forecasts that K-12 game-based learning market is expected to grow at a compound annual growth rate of nearly 28% during the period 2017–2021.

The growing importance of Science, Technology, Engineering, Mathematics (STEM) education is also driving the growth of game-based learning market. This is due to the fact that educational games encourage students to get involved in live projects or real-time activities so that they can learn by experimenting [34]. The game-based learning pedagogy also boosts students' confidence in STEM-related subjects, increase their interest in complex topics and helps teachers to deal with disengagement of young people from STEM.

The research work reported in this paper focuses on the use of the latest technological innovations to help students learn about STEM. A review on the use of games, Virtual Reality, Augmented Reality, Virtual Labs, Multimedia and mulsemedia in education is presented. In this context, the European Union-funded Horizon 2020 NEWTON project [30] is introduced. NEWTON Project proposes and integrates diverse novel technologies in STEM education including adaptive multimedia and multi-sensorial content delivery mechanisms [1, 25, 48] personalisation and gamification solutions [21, 32], introduces virtual labs and fabrication labs [22, 43] and employs problem-based, game-oriented, and flipped-classroom-based learning [28]. As part of the NEWTON project, a number of small and large scale pilots were run. In particular, the large scale Earth Science pilot includes a set of educational applications for primary school education, that cover a set of topics in the areas of Atmosphere, Geosphere, Biosphere and Astronomy. The Astronomy topic is taught through an immersive educational game called Final Frontier. The paper also presents a research study on learner experience when the game was used in the class.

The paper is organized as follows. Section 2 introduces some research projects that investigated the use of various technologies in the teaching and learning process. Sections 3 and 4 details our scientific positioning, gives an overview of the NEWTON project focusing on the *Final Frontier* game description and game design methodology. Section 5 presents research methodology of the case study and its results. Section 6 summarizes the paper, draws conclusions regarding the research study performed and presents future perspectives.

2 Related Work

2.1 Gamification and Game-Based Learning

Gamification and game-based learning (GBL), have drawn the attention of many researchers and educators over the past years. While there are various definitions and interpretations of gamification, one common definition is that gamification represents the integration of game elements into gameness objects in order to have gameful characteristics [45]. Such game elements or mechanics include: points, badges, levels, progress bars, leader boards, virtual currency, and avatars [7]. Some criticism of gamification is that often the implementations lack thorough theoretical foundation and are too focused on extrinsic motivation by being too reliant on points, badges and leader boards [35]. A number of research studies have showed that gamification can have positive effects on the learning performance as well as on motivational aspects such as engagement, participation and enjoyment [15, 35]. However, the results were not always consistent, with some arguing that the results may be the result of the novelty aspect and not have long-term impact [15].

GBL represents an educational approach that integrates video games with defined learning outcomes. The appeal of using video games in education can be partially explained by the need to reach today's digital learners that have continuous access to entertainment content through the Internet. At the same time, games provide highly engaging activities that are stimulating, generate strong emotions, require complex information processing, provide challenges and can support learning and skill acquisition [3]. The learning experiences and outcomes of educational games can be classified into several classes which include: knowledge acquisition, practising and processing (content understanding), knowledge application (skill acquisition), reflection (behaviour change) and knowledge anticipation (motivation outcomes) [18].

Previous research works have shown that game-based learning can have positive effects on important educational factors such as student motivation and engagement [13], learning effectiveness [10], as well as learning attitude, achievement and self-efficacy [39]. Moreover, game-based learning has the potential to facilitate the acquisition of 21st century skills such as critical thinking, collaboration, creativity and communication [33]. While there is much research evidence of GBL benefits, some studies failed to reproduce them or obtained contradictory findings. Tobias et al., argue that this may be due to lack of design processes that effectively integrate the motivational aspects of games with good instructional design to ensure learners acquire the expected knowledge and skills [42]. The authors also made recommendations for educational game design, such as to provide guidance, use first person in dialogues, use animated agents in the interaction with players, use human rather than synthetic voices, maximise user involvement and motivation, reduce cognitive load, integrate games with instructional objectives and other instruction, use teams to develop instructional games [42].

One common criticism of game-based learning studies is that they lack foundation in established learning theories. A meta-analysis of 658 game-based learning research studies published over 4 decades, showed that the wide majority of studies failed to use a learning theory foundation [44]. Among the studies that had a pedagogical foundation, constructivism appears to be the most commonly used as indicated by multiple review papers [20, 33, 44]. Other learning theories that were also implemented by different research studies include: cognitivism, humanism and behaviourism. Common learning principles employed by game-based learning studies include among others: experiential learning, situated learning, problem-based learning, direct instruction, activity theory, and discovery learning [44].

Few studies have proposed and/or evaluated educational games related to planets or the solar system [28]. *HelloPlanet* is a game where the player can observe and interact with a planet that has a dynamic ecosystem, where the player can simulate organisms, non-organisms, terrains, and more [37]. The game evaluation results from 41 primary and secondary school children, showed a statistically significant learning gain for both girls and boys, and an effect on interest in STEM for girls, but not for boys. The *Space Rift* game enables students to explore the Solar system in a virtual reality environment [31]. However, the game evaluation involved only 5 students and was mostly focused on usability rather than educational aspects. The *Ice Flows* game aims to educate the users about the environmental factors such as temperature and snowfall on the behaviour of the Antarctic ice sheet [19]. However, the game was either not evaluated or the results were not published yet.

A recent systematic review of game-based learning in primary education has indicated that games were used to teach a variety of subjects, among which the most popular being Mathematics, Science, Languages and Social Studies [14]. However, the review authors also concluded that more research studies are needed to evaluate the pedagogical benefits of GBL at primary level.

2.2 Multimedia, Mulsemedia and Virtual Reality in Learning

In the last years, the technological landscape allowed for the usage of multimedia in education to become quite common. There is a lot of research that demonstrated the benefits of multimedia in education, benefits that can be augmented with the adaptation and personalization of the content to the learner context and needs [26, 46]. Learner context can encompass for instance characteristics of the device used during learning (e.g. CPU, screen resolution, battery life, etc.) or network conditions (e.g. throughput, loss, latency, etc.). Finding the right balance between content adaptation and learner quality of experience is difficult, but highly important. However, there is a natural desire to increase learner quality of experience, especially in learning context [27].

Multimedia is popular in education as it was demonstrated that when both text and supporting pictures are used in the learning process, a higher level of understanding and recall is achieved by learners than when text only is used in the learning process [11]. Moreover, neuroscience states that human brain is multisensorial and the more senses are involved in the learning process the deeper the learning is [36]. Mulsemedia represents a step further to the classic multimedia; it is a type of media that involves more than the two senses (i.e. sight and hearing) stimulated by multimedia. There are very recent studies that are focused on analysing the impact of mulsemedia on the learning process and the degree of acceptability of mulsemedia by the students as a technology used in learning [6]. In [47], a study carried out with 42 master students employed a mulsemedia-enhanced teaching approach in order to assess the impact of mulsemedia content on learner experience. The results of the study demonstrated that mulsemedia had a very positive impact on students' experience. All the students that participated in the study stated that they enjoyed the multisensorial experience during the class. Additionally, a vast majority of students agreed that the multi-sensorial effects associated with mulsemedia have not distracted them from learning and that they would like to have more such classes. More recent studies have assessed the influence of mulsemedia content on learning process, showing how it helps increase not only learner satisfaction, but also learning outcome [1, 41].

Virtual Reality is able to provide immersive experiences using a computer-generated environment. In general, it is focused on the two senses that multimedia is focused on, but the trend is to combine multi-sensorial effects (e.g. haptic effects, tactile effects, etc.) for a truly immersive experience, just like mulsemedia. Virtual reality in education provides students with authentic learning experiences and facilitates students in visualizing different complex and difficult models [16]. There are a considerable amount of studies and surveys that are analysing the impact of virtual reality in education [12, 16, 24]. The general conclusion is that virtual reality has a very positive impact on learning, it increases learner engagement, allows for constructivist learning and stimulates learner creativity.

It is envisioned that mulsemedia and virtual reality will become very popular in education, similar to how popular multimedia is today, as the devices that allow for such experience are becoming increasingly popular and more affordable and as more and more technical solutions to support such technologies are proposed [5, 6, 16].

2.3 Virtual Labs

Virtual labs refer to a set of electronic resources which provide a virtual working environment that allows to perform experiments without the need of any actual physical presence. They offer rich environments for learners to interact and use virtual objects and apparatus, through a software interface. Virtual labs offer a solution to the limitations of traditional practical classes which are resource intensive both in terms of personnel and maintenance.

Diverse virtual labs are in use world-wide, including some which target science, technology, engineering and mathematics (STEM) education.*ChemCollective*[1] is a Carnegie Mellon University virtual lab used to teach chemistry to college and high school students. Apart from the virtual labs, there are also available scenario-based learning activities, tutorials, and concept tests. *SpongeLab*[2] is a virtual lab based on a platform that provides students and educators with online free or premium resources for teaching and learning basic sciences and biology. The platform offers digital content for course development, online tools to create and share lessons and educational material and assessment tools.

Many US digital libraries and educational projects have joined the *National Science Digital Library* (NSDL)[3], which supports development of a digital online library of teaching and learning resources oriented to STEM disciplines. *TeachEngineering*[4], *Howtosmile*[5] and *Open Learning Initiative (OLI)*[6] areamong important NSDL projects. For instance, *TeachEngineering* is a National Science Foundation (NSF)-funded project which provides "*a searchable, web-based digital library collection populated with standards-based engineering curricula for use by K-12 teachers and engineering faculty to make applied science and math come alive through engineering design in K-12 settings. The TeachEngineering collection provides educators with free access to a growing curricular resource of activities, lessons, units and living labs*". OLI is a NSF-funded Carnegie Mellon project which offers an open platform to provide online content such as simulation environments, virtual labs, etc. and personalized learning to its users. The system analyzes the user experience and provides a personalized feedback to improve student-teacher interaction and maximize the success rate in the learning path.

In EU context, employing technology-enhanced teaching practices and methodologies is fundamental and several educational projects are funded, including *inGenious*[7], *iTec*[8], *Go-Lab*[9] *and NEWTON*[10]. The first three EU projects indicated are mainly focused on the development of digital repositories, and virtual labs or on experimenting new technology-enhanced teaching practices. NEWTON addresses all these aspects under a common umbrella and builds a platform NEWTELP[11] which deploys them. More details about the NEWTON project are presented next.

---

1 ChemCollective, Website http://www.chemcollective.org, Accessed: July 8th 2018.

2 Spongelab, Website http://www.spongelab.com, Accessed: July 8th 2018.

3 National Science Digital Library, Website https://nsdl.oercommons.org, Accessed: July 8th 2018.

4 TeachEngineering, Website http://www.teachengineering.org/, Accessed: July 8th 2018.

5 Howtosmile, Website http://howtosmile.org/, Accessed: July 8th 2018.

6 Open Learning Initiative (OLI), website http://oli.cmu.edu/, Accessed: July 8th 2018.

7 InGenious, Website http://www.ingenious-science.eu/web/guest, Accessed: July 8th 2018.

8 iTec Website, http://itec.eun.org/, Accessed: July 8th 2018.

9 Go-lab Website, http://go-lab-project.eu/, Accessed: July 8th 2018.

10 NEWTON Website, http://newtonproject.eu/, Accessed: July 8th 2018.

11 NEWTELP Website, http://newtelp.eu/, Accessed: July 8th 2018.

3 The NEWTON Project

NEWTON is a large European innovation action project that looks at how to use latest technological innovations to help students learn about science, technology, engineering and mathematics (STEM). It is funded by the EU Horizon 2020 programme and involves 14 academic and industry project partners from around Europe. The NEWTON project partners have designed different innovative technologies and are deploying and testing them out in various learning environments.

NEWTON technologies include solutions for adaptation and personalisation of content creation, distribution and presentation in order to increase learner quality of experience, improve learning process, and potentially increase learning outcome. Games and gamification are used to stimulate and motivate students, augmented reality allows learners to access computer generated models of scientific content, while interactive avatars guide students with special learning needs in a manner which suits them the best. Virtual and fabrication learning labs allow students to experiment in simulated environments and eventually transform their solutions into real life products. Finally and not the least important, multi-sensorial media (or “mulsemedia”) helps engage three or more human senses in the learning process, including smell and touch. Innovative pedagogies such as 3D interactive educational games [9], flipped classroom [4], virtual labs-based teaching and learning, enhanced learning experiences through augmented and virtual reality, gamification, and personalised learning path through educational content are used by NEWTON learners.

Fundamentally, in the NEWTON project, these new technologies are deployed under the same umbrella: there is a newly built common platform called NEWTELP (http://newtelp.eu). NEWTELP allows educational content to be stored and delivered to learners using these NEWTON technologies as part of real life pilots to see whether and how they help students to engage more with STEM subjects. NEWTON pilots target primary and secondary schools, university and vocational institutions. There are over thirty NEWTON pilots on various technologies, among which three are large scale deployments on Programming, Gamification and Earth science. The latter is labelled “Earth Course” and focuses on primary school education across Europe.

Earth Course consists of eight separate sessions in each school and includes a set of educational applications, developed as part of the NEWTON project in an effort to attract students to STEM subjects, which cover a set of topics in the areas of Atmosphere, Geosphere, Biosphere and Astronomy. The main applications employed in this pilot are:

- Water Cycle in Nature, focusing on precipitation formation and related topics, such as vaporisation, evaporation and condensation [2];
- Wildlife, focusing on a set of terrestrial animals, such as deer, brown bear, lynx, wolf, wild boar, fox, hare and moose;
- Sea-Life, focusing on the aquatic world and presenting educational material on sea creatures such as sharks, stingrays, dolphins, puffer fish, jellyfish, octopus, orc, turtle, clownfish, seahorse;
- Final Frontier, which presents the Solar system in two parts: a game focusing on a set of astronomical bodies situated closest to the Sun: Mercury, Venus, Moon and Mars, and a virtual lab concentrating on the large gaseous planets: Jupiter, Saturn, Uranus and Neptune; and

- Geography application, which is focused on educational content about Ire-land and United Kingdom, including its monuments and archaeological sites.

This chapter focuses on the Final Frontier Game and describes the results obtained following its deployment as part of a real life pilot in an Irish primary school. Next the game, testing methodology, practical deployment and results are presented in separate sections.

4 The Final Frontier Game

4.1 Game Description

Final Frontier [9] is an interactive 3D educational video game about space for children up to 12 years old. The game supports knowledge acquisition on Solar system planets (i.e. Mercury and Venus were targeted in this study) through direct experience, challenges and fun. The topics coved by the game are part of the Geography curriculum, section "Planet Earth and Space", defined for the primary school in Ireland. The game has different levels, each level containing different models and landscapes. In each level, the game requires meeting a game objective (i.e. mission), collection of stars and meteorites and has con-strains e.g. coolant time. Information regarding the number of stars and meteorites col-lected, coolant time and game level mission is displayed on the screen.

Once a level is completed, the player must answer correctly a multi-choice question in order to be able to progress to the next level. The player is allowed to try to answer the question multiple times if a wrong answer is provided.

The game starts by bringing the player on a spaceship where he game mission is explained. There are two activities that the player has to complete during the first activity, the player is instructed to visit the first planet, Mercury. The game goal related to this planet is to explore the environment and to collect five meteorites hidden in the craters that exist on Mercury (see Fig. 1). The player may use the jetpack to get in and out of the craters. An avatar provides extra information (facts) about the planet during the play time.

Figure 2 illustrates how the level mission as well as the number of meteorites and stars a player has collected are displayed on the screen for the entire duration of playing a level.

Once the mission on Mercury was completed, the player returns to the spaceship, in the puzzle room where he/she must answer a question (e.g. What is the closest planet to the Sun?).

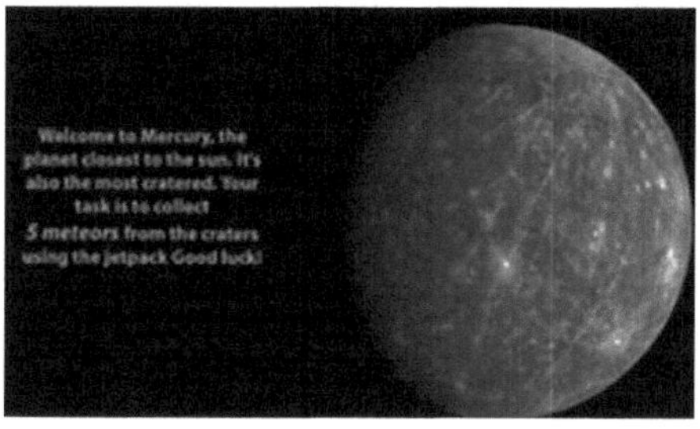

Fig. 1. The goal of the mission to Mercury [40].

Fig. 2. The player using jetpack on Mercury [40].

Fig. 3. Puzzle room and the question about Mercury [40].

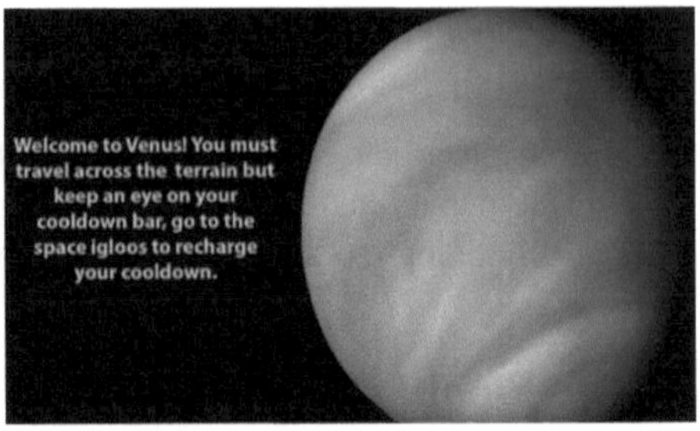

Fig. 4. The objective of the mission to Venus [40].

Fig. 5. The player on Venus planet [40].

Fig. 6. Puzzle room and the question about Venus [40].

A screenshot of this game activity is presented in Fig. 3. The aim of this mini-quiz is to check player's knowledge about Mercury. The player interacts with the game environment when answering the question by picking up the correct object (e.g. planet Mercury) and placing it beside the Sun.

Once this question is answered correctly, the player is awarded a key that is used to open a door on the spaceship and progress to the next level.

The second level is associated with another activity which requires the player to explore the planet Venus and complete a given task. The mission is to traverse the Venus environment without letting their cooldown bar get to zero. Buildings called igloos may be used to recharge their coolant supply (see Fig. 4).

Next, the player is teleported to the Venus planet surface. There are four buildings (igloos) that the player may enter while crossing the terrain. The cooldown bar depletes when traversing the planet surface, which is very hot (Fig. 5), but regenerates when the player enters any of the buildings. While traversing the terrain, the player may collect stars that are added up to the overall stars' score. Facts about Venus are displayed during the play time.

Once the player reaches the fourth igloo, he/she is returned to the spaceship, into the puzzle room and asked to complete the second puzzle. A multi-choice question about Venus (see Fig. 6) must be answered correctly in order to complete this level.

The puzzle asks the player to identify which planet is the hottest in the Solar system. Three planets are displayed. The player must walk towards the planet that represents the correct answer. Once this is done the game is complete. The overall number of collected starts is also displayed.

4.2 Game Design Methodology

The methodology for designing the Final Frontier game [9] is based on that described in [23]. However, two steps related to the learning puzzle such as the general description of the learning puzzle and detailed description of the learning puzzle were added.

The authors believe that recall is a very important step in the learning process. Moreover, the recommendations on efficient game design proposed by [42] were taken into account.

The game design methodology proposed in this research is composed of the following steps:

- specification of the pedagogical objectives,
- choice of the game model,
- general description of the scenario and virtual environment,
- general description of the learning puzzle,
- choice of a software development engine,
- detailed description of the scenario,
- detailed description of the learning puzzle,
- pedagogical quality control, and
- game distribution.

Specification of the Pedagogical Objectives: The proposed 3D interactive educational game shall be used to teach concepts on the solar system in primary schools. The first step of the conception phase consists of defining the concepts that must be learned by the students. For this reason, the authors worked with teachers from European primary schools that teach the Geography subject to make sure that the designed game covers the required topics specified in the curriculum. The pedagogical objectives of the game were defined and presented in Table 1.

Table 1. LOs of the final frontier game [9].

Planet	LOs
Mercury	- Closest planet to the sun (LO1) - Planet with the most craters (LO2) - Smallest planet (LO3)
Venus	- Hottest planet due to the greenhouse effect (LO1) - Spins opposite direction to Earth (LO2) - High Gravity cannot jump very high (LO3)

Choice of the Game Model: Once the pedagogical objectives were defined, *Adventure* was selected as the game model for the *Final Frontier*. The *Adventure* game model involves the player assuming the role of the protagonist in the game, exploring the environment and completion of puzzles in order to progress. Collectable objects such as stars and meteorites are also included. The jetpack allows the player to go higher than the jump. The puzzle embedded in the game requires the player to complete various tasks in order to progress through the game. The collectable stars are used to guide the player and encourage him/her to explore the environment. The meteorites are used on the Mercury planet as a collectable to gauge the players' progress. The cooldown feature is used on Venus and gives the player a challenge, as they go through the level.

The game design has considered three areas: the spaceship where the game starts and finishes and where the player goes back to after visiting a planet; planet Mercury which the player visits during the first activity; and planet Venus that hosts the second activity to be completed.

The *Adventure* game model is one of the most popular among children. The children get more immersed and motivated when they play adventure games over other types. Moreover, the *Adventure* game model involves a linear story that can be easily defined in the game. Various gameplay features such as jetpack, puzzle solving, collectable stars and meteorites, cooldown bar were also defined in this game mode.

General Description of the Scenario and Virtual Environment: The aim of this part is to structure the pedagogical scenario and match it up with a fun based scenario. The main focus was to make the game familiar to the learners. The characters are simple human characters so the player can easily interact with. The story of the game is that the player is on a field trip, and he/she visits some planets. The player is assigned a task to do on each planet and learns implicitly facts about the planet while playing.

General Description of the Learning Puzzle: When the player completes a given task, he/she is brought back to the spaceship to solve a puzzle and when successful, to progress to the next level. The puzzle learning was added because it was believed that active recall is a principle of efficient learning. Many studies demonstrate the role of active recall in consolidating long-term memory e.g. [38].

Choice of a Software Development Engine: Concerning the game development engine, Unreal Engine 4 or Unity, two of the most popular game development engines, can be used. Unreal Engine 4 was used in this game development due to its graphic potential, especially as it was aimed to give to the player the most realistic environment of the planets.

Detailed Description of the Scenario: This step involves the illustration of each scene with all the details and interactions to be integrated into the game.

Detailed Description of the Learning Puzzle: The game has two puzzles that correspond to the two planets. Once the puzzle is answered correctly the player is allowed to go to the next planet. The player is allowed to try to answer the puzzle multiple times if a wrong answer was given.

Pedagogical Quality Control: The developed game was shown to the teacher to validate it and to approve the pedagogical quality of the game. Feedback was considered and the game was improved.

Game Distribution: Once the teacher was satisfied and the game was approved, the game was ready to be distributed to the students in the class.

5 Case Study

The goal of the research study [9] was to investigate learner experience when the Final Frontier game was used in the class to teach scientific knowledge of the planets from the Solar system to primary school children.

This section presents the evaluation methodology applied, case study set-up and results analysis for of the collected data.

5.1 Research Methodology

The evaluation included a group of children who were taught by using the Final Frontier game. The learning activity took place in class, during the normal hours of study. A total of 53 children of age 9–10 years from Saint Patrick Boys National School located in Dublin, Ireland took part in the case study. Team members from the National College of Ireland and Dublin City University (DCU) have prepared and helped perform the tests.

The evaluation meets all Ethics requirements (Table 2). Prior to running the case study, the Ethics approval was obtained from the DCU Ethics Committee and all required forms were provided to the children and their parents, including informed consent form, informed assent form, plain language statement and data management plan. These documents include a detailed description of the testing scenario, as well as information on study purpose, data processing and analysis, participant identity protection, etc.

The flow of the evaluation is illustrated in Fig. 7 that presents in details the steps followed by the researchers. It can be seen that prior to beginning the evaluation, the consent forms signed by parents were collected. Then the children were introduced to the research case study and asked to review and sign the assent form. The children had roughly 20 min to play the game or till they finished the game before doing a survey.

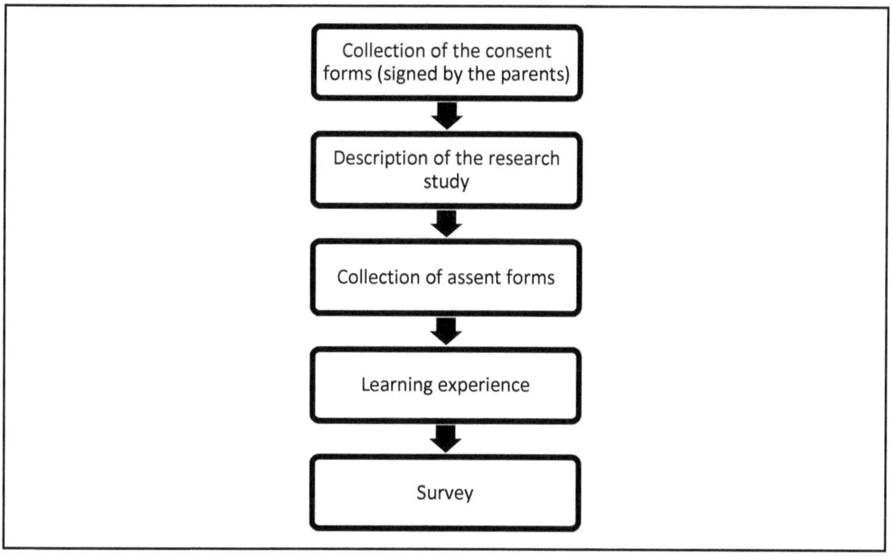

Fig. 7. Evaluation process [40].

Table 2. Survey questions [9].

Question	Answer/Scale
Q1. The video game helped me to better understand the characteristics of different planets	- Strongly Disagree, - Disagree, - Neutral, - Agree, - Strongly Agree
Q2. The video game helped me to learn easier about planets	- Strongly Disagree, - Disagree, - Neutral, - Agree, - Strongly Agree
Q3. I enjoyed this lesson that included the video game on planets	- Strongly Disagree, - Disagree, - Neutral, - Agree, - Strongly Agree
Q4. The quizzes that I did in the game helped me better remember what I learned	- Strongly Disagree, - Disagree, - Neutral, - Agree, - Strongly Agree
Q5. The video game distracted me from learning	- Strongly Disagree, - Disagree, - Neutral, - Agree, - Strongly Agree
Q6. I would like to have more lessons that include video games	- Strongly Disagree, - Disagree, - Neutral, - Agree, - Strongly Agree
Q7. What did you like most about the game?	Students to provide their feelings toward the experience
Q8. Comments/Suggestions (optional)	Students to provide their comment if they wished
Q9. What way of learning you would like (tick one answer)?	- Teacher based learning - Computer game based learning

The case study investigated the learner experience with the game and the game usability. A learner satisfaction questionnaire assessing student level of experience and game usability was collected. Standard emojis were associated with each answer to the questionnaire's questions.

5.2 Results Analysis

5.2.1 Micro-IHM Analysis

Learner experience in using the *Final Frontier* game was investigated and evaluated by questions Q1 to Q6 in the survey. The experience was analysed in terms of number of *Strongly Agree/Agree* answers for Q1, Q2, Q3, Q4, and Q6 and *Strongly Disagree/Disagree* for Q5.

The overall learner experience of children was excellent (see Table 3). 92.5% of children confirmed that the video game helped them to better understand the characteristics of the two planets. 88.8% of children thought that the video game helped them to learn easier about planets. 98.1% of students enjoyed the lesson that included the video game. 84.9% of children agreed on the fact that quizzes embedded in the game helped them better remember what they have learned. 70.1% of children disagreed that the video game distracted them from learning. 96.2% of children expressed that they would like to have more lessons that include video games.

Table 3. Children answers on the user experience survey [9].

	SD	D	N	A	SA
Q1	0	0	7.5%	60.5%	32%
Q2	0	0	11.2%	45.4%	43.4%
Q3	0	0	1.9%	19.1%	79%
Q4	0	1.9%	13.2%	52.9%	32%
Q5	45.4%	24.7%	15%	3.7%	11.2%
Q6	1.9%	0	1.9%	7.5%	88.7%

Note that for clarity reasons, in Table 3, SD refers to *Strongly Disagree*, D refers to *Disagree*, N refers to *Neutral*, A refers to *Agree*, and SA refers to *Strongly Agree.*

5.2.2 Game Usability

The game usability of the *Final Frontier* was also analysed through Q7, Q8 and Q9 from the survey.

An analysis of the answers provided for Q7 and Q8 shows that 92.6% of children mentioned that they have enjoyed the game, in particular the fun aspect, learning aspects, stars and meteorites collection, avatar, use of jetpack, and interactive puzzle room.

Regarding Q9, 94% of children mentioned that they prefer computer game-based learning during the normal teaching class, which is an outstanding result for the deployment of this game.

6 Conclusion

The growing importance of Science, Technology, Engineering, Mathematics (STEM) education requires innovative teaching and learning approaches in order to increase the number of students that follow STEM career. This paper addresses the problem of motivating, engaging, and improving learning experience of students in the STEM field. NEWTON is an ambitious EU Horizon 2020 funded innovation action project that seeks to integrate innovative technologies in STEM education. A novel interactive and immersive video game (Final Frontier) was designed as part of this project. A case study that involved 53 children of age 9–10 years from Saint Patrick Boys National School located in Dublin, Ireland was run in order to assess how the game supports knowledge acquisition about the Solar system through direct experience, active recall, challenges and fun.

A survey that gathered information about learner experience with the game, and game usability was distributed to the children after they played the game. An analysis of the survey answers shows that over 90% of the children were satisfied with the game usability and they enjoyed the game. The children have also appreciated various game features including the fun aspect, learning aspects, stars and meteorites collection, avatar, use of jetpacks, and the interactive puzzles. The game will be extended to include adaptive features such as personalised learning paths and extra learning support when a wrong answer is given to a puzzle. Future tests will include the deployment of the Final Frontier game through the NEWTELP platform developed as part of the NEWTON project [29] in different European primary schools. Usability, learner satisfaction and knowledge achievements analyses will be performed across the countries.

Acknowledgements. This research is supported by the NEWTON project (http://www.newtonproject.eu/) funded under the European Union's Horizon 2020 Research and Innovation programme, Grant Agreement no. 688503.

References

1. Bi, T., Pichon, A., Zou, L., Chen, S., Ghinea, G., Muntean, G.-M.: A DASH-based mulsemedia adaptive delivery solution, pp. 1–6. ACM Press, Amesterdam (2018)
2. Bogusevschi, D., et al.: Water cycle in nature: small-scale STEM education pilot. In: World Conference on Educational Media and Technology (EdMedia), Amsterdam, Netherlands (2018)
3. Boyle, E., Connolly, T.M., Hainey, T.: The role of psychology in understanding the impact of computer games. Entertain. Comput. **2**, 69–74 (2011). https://doi.org/10.1016/j.entcom.2010.12.002
4. Bradford, M., Muntean, C., Pathak, P.: An analysis of flip-classroom pedagogy in first year undergraduate mathematics for computing. In: 2014 IEEE Frontiers in Education Conference (FIE), pp. 1–5. IEEE (2014)
5. Comsa, I.-S., Trestian, R., Ghinea, G.: 360 mulsemedia experience over next generation wireless networks-a reinforcement learning approach (2018)
6. Covaci, A., Zou, L., Tal, I., Muntean, G.-M., Ghinea, G.: Is multimedia multisensorial? - a review of mulsemedia systems. ACM Comput. Surv. **51**, 1–35 (2018)
7. Dicheva, D., Dichev, C., Agre, G., Angelova, G.: Gamification in education: a systematic mapping study. J. Educ. Technol. Soc. **18**, 75–88 (2015)
8. Doran, L.: Games, videos continue to make big gains in classrooms, survey finds. In: Education Week - Digital Education. http://blogs.edweek.org/edweek/DigitalEducation/2016/05/games_videos_continue_to_make_.html?cmp=SOC-SHR-FB. Accessed 7 Jun 2018
9. El Mawas, N., Tal, I., Bogusevschi, D., Andrews, J., Muntean, G.-M., Muntean, C.: Final frontier game: a case study on learner experience. In: Proceedings of the 10th International Conference on Computer Supported Education (CSEDU), Madeira, Portugal (2018, accepted)
10. Erhel, S., Jamet, E.: Digital game-based learning: impact of instructions and feedback on motivation and learning effectiveness. Comput. Educ. **67**, 156–167 (2013). https://doi.org/10.1016/j.compedu.2013.02.019
11. Fletcher, J., Tobias, S.: The multimedia principle. In: The Cambridge Handbook of Multimedia Learning, pp. 117–133 (2005)
12. Freina, L., Ott, M.: A literature review on immersive virtual reality in education: state of the art and perspectives. In: eLearning and Software for Education (2015)
13. Ghergulescu, I., Muntean, C.H.: Measurement and analysis of learner's motivation in game-based e-learning. In: Ifenthaler, D., Eseryel, D., Ge, X. (eds.) Assessment in Game-Based Learning, pp. 355–378. Springer, New York (2012). https://doi.org/10.1007/978-1-4614-3546-4_18
14. Hainey, T., Connolly, T.M., Boyle, E.A., Wilson, A., Razak, A.: A systematic literature review of games-based learning empirical evidence in primary education. Comput. Educ. **102**, 202–223 (2016). https://doi.org/10.1016/j.compedu.2016.09.001

15. Hamari, J., Koivisto, J., Sarsa, H.: Does gamification work? – a literature review of empirical studies on gamification. In: 2014 47th Hawaii International Conference on System Sciences, pp. 3025–3034 (2014)
16. Hu-Au, E., Lee, J.J.: Virtual reality in education: a tool for learning in the experience age. Int. J. Innov. Educ. **4**, 215–226 (2017)
17. Ibáñez, M.-B., Delgado-Kloos, C.: Augmented reality for STEM learning: a systematic review. Comput. Educ. **123**, 109–123 (2018)
18. Jabbar, A.I.A., Felicia, P.: Gameplay engagement and learning in game-based learning a systematic review. Rev. Educ. Res. **85**, 740–779 (2015). https://doi.org/10.3102/0034654315577210
19. Le Brocq, A.: Ice flows: a game-based learning approach to science communication, p. 19075 (2017)
20. Li, M.-C., Tsai, C.-C.: Game-based learning in science education: a review of relevant research. J. Sci. Educ. Technol. **22**, 877–898 (2013). https://doi.org/10.1007/s10956-013-9436-x
21. Lynch, T., Ghergulescu, I.: Large scale evaluation of learning flow. In: 2017 IEEE 17th International Conference on Advanced Learning Technologies (ICALT), pp. 62–64. IEEE (2017)
22. Lynch, T., Ghergulescu, I.: NEWTON virtual labs: introduction and teacher perspective. In: 2017 IEEE 17th International Conference on Advanced Learning Technologies (ICALT), pp. 343–345. IEEE (2017)
23. Marfisi-Schottman, I., George, S., Tarpin-Bernard, F.: Tools and methods for efficiently designing serious games. In: Proceedings of 4th European Conference on Games Based Learning, Copenhagen, Denmark, pp. 226–234 (2010)
24. Merchant, Z., Goetz, E.T., Cifuentes, L., Keeney-Kennicutt, W., Davis, T.J.: Effectiveness of virtual reality-based instruction on students' learning outcomes in K-12 and higher education: a meta-analysis. Comput. Educ. **70**, 29–40 (2014)
25. Moldovan, A.-N., Muntean, C.H.: QoE-aware video resolution thresholds computation for adaptive multimedia. In: 2017 IEEE International Symposium on Broadband Multimedia Systems and Broadcasting (BMSB), pp. 1–6. IEEE (2017)
26. Moldovan, A.-N., Weibelzahl, S., Muntean, C.H.: Energy-aware mobile learning: opportunities and challenges. IEEE Commun. Surv. Tutor. **16**, 234–265 (2014)
27. Molnar, A.: Content type and perceived multimedia quality in mobile learning. Multimed. Tools Appl. **76**, 21613–21627 (2017)
28. Muntean, C.H., Andrews, J., Muntean, G.M.: Final frontier: an educational game on solar system concepts acquisition for primary schools. In: 2017 IEEE 17th International Conference on Advanced Learning Technologies (ICALT), pp. 335–337 (2017)
29. NEWTON: H2020: networked labs for training in sciences and technologies for information and communication. Newton (2016). http://www.newtonproject.eu/. Accessed 10 Nov 2017
30. Peña, J.G.V., Tobias, G.P.A.R.: Space Rift: an oculus rift solar system exploration game. Philipp. Inf. Technol. J. **7**, 55–60 (2014)
31. Playfoot, J., De Nicola, C., Di Salvadore, F.: A new experiential model to innovate the stem learning processes
32. Qian, M., Clark, K.R.: Game-based learning and 21st century skills: a review of recent research. Comput. Hum. Behav. **63**, 50–58 (2016). https://doi.org/10.1016/j.chb.2016.05.023
33. Ravipati, S.: Trends: STEM game-based learning to see surge in immersive tech. Transform. Educ. Technol. (2017)
34. Seaborn, K., Fels, D.I.: Gamification in theory and action: a survey. Int. J. Hum Comput Stud. **74**, 14–31 (2015). https://doi.org/10.1016/j.ijhcs.2014.09.006

35. Shams, L., Seitz, A.R.: Benefits of multisensory learning. Trends Cogn. Sci. **12**, 411–417 (2008)
36. Sin, Z.P.T., Ng, P.H.F., Shiu, S.C.K., Chung, F.L.: Planetary marching cubes for STEM sandbox game-based learning: enhancing student interest and performance with simulation realism planet simulating sandbox. In: 2017 IEEE Global Engineering Education Conference (EDUCON), pp. 1644–1653 (2017)
37. Spitz, H.H.: Consolidating facts into the schematized learning and memory system of educable retardates. Int. Rev. Res. Ment. Retard. **6**, 149–168 (1973)
38. Sung, H.-Y., Hwang, G.-J.: A collaborative game-based learning approach to improving students' learning performance in science courses. Comput. Educ. **63**, 43–51 (2013). https://doi.org/10.1016/j.compedu.2012.11.019
39. TechNavio: Global K-12 Game-based Learning Market 2017–2021 (2017)
40. Ting, B., Silva, F., Ghinea, G., Muntean, G.M.: Improving learning experience by employing DASH-based mulsemedia delivery, Galway, Ireland (2018)
41. Tobias, S., Fletcher, J.D., Wind, A.P.: Game-based learning. In: Spector, J., Merrill, M., Elen, J., Bishop, M. (eds.) Handbook of Research on Educational Communications and Technology, pp. 485–503. Springer, New York (2014). https://doi.org/10.1007/978-1-4614-3185-5_38
42. Togou, M.A., Lorenzo, C., Lorenzo, E., Cornetta, G., Muntean, G.M.: Raising students' interest in STEM education via remote digital fabrication: an Irish primary school case study, Palma de Mallorca, Spain (2018)
43. Wu, W.-H., Hsiao, H.-C., Wu, P.-L., Lin, C.-H., Huang, S.-H.: Investigating the learning-theory foundations of game-based learning: a meta-analysis. J. Comput. Assist. Learn. **28**, 265–279 (2012). https://doi.org/10.1111/j.1365-2729.2011.00437.x
44. Yohannis, A.R., Prabowo, Y.D., Waworuntu, A.: Defining gamification: from lexical meaning and process viewpoint towards a gameful reality. In: 2014 International Conference on Information Technology Systems and Innovation (ICITSI), pp. 284–289 (2014)
45. Yousafzai, A., Chang, V., Gani, A., Noor, R.M.: Multimedia augmented m-learning: issues, trends and open challenges. Int. J. Inf. Manag. **36**, 784–792 (2016)
46. Zou, L., Tal, I., Covaci, A., Ibarrola, E., Ghinea, G., Muntean, G.M.: Can multisensorial media improve learner experience. In: Proceedings of the 8th ACM on Multimedia Systems Conference, pp. 315–320. ACM (2017)
47. Zou, L., Trestian, R., Muntean, G.-M.: E^3DOAS: balancing QoE and energy-saving for multi-device adaptation in future mobile wireless video delivery. IEEE Trans. Broadcast. **64**, 26–40 (2018)
48. VR Trends to Watch in Education – Campus Technology. https://campustechnology.com/articles/2017/05/16/5-vr-trends-to-watch-in-education.aspx. Accessed 9 Jul 2018

Pathways to Successful Online Testing: eExams with the "Secure Exam Environment" (SEE)

Gabriele Frankl(✉), Sebastian Napetschnig, and Peter Schartner

Alpen-Adria-Universität, Klagenfurt, Austria
{gabriele.frankl, sebastian.napetschnig, peter.schartner}@aau.at

Abstract. eExams can potentially improve didactics, efficiency, objectivity, flexibility, accessibility, and even sustainability compared to written exams. However, they also present great challenges such as security, reliability, integrity, as well as the availability of computer rooms of sufficient size. To conduct large-scale online exams, we implemented the "Secure Exam Environment" (SEE) in 2011. The SEE enables online testing in any lecture hall using students' own devices – and loan devices if needed – while blocking access to unauthorized files or internet pages. After booting the SEE, assessment is conducted via Moodle and additional software (e.g. GeoGebra, Excel or Eclipse) can be used as well. To maintain quality of service, we developed a monitoring solution to control the technical infrastructure of the SEE. As of July 2018, we have conducted 1,605 such online exams with 57,607 students. Moreover, the SEE offers the possibility for slotted exams where students can choose freely the time of their exam within a week. Since technical solutions cannot solve all problems, the organization of eExams is vital to guarantee smooth operations as well as integrity. This paper offers a technical solution for the implementation of a secure and highly available exam environment with the various benefits of eExams, and provides organizational recommendations for the successful roll out of online exams as well as for overcoming technical challenges.

Keywords: Secure online testing · Secure Exam Environment · Benefits of eExams · Organization of eExams · Security · High availability · Monitoring

1 Introduction

Assessment methods have a profound influence on how students learn [1, 2]. Assessment generates students' activities and engagement, heavily influences student behaviour, shapes students' experiences, and generates feedback and thus opportunities for improving students' knowledge as well as reflection and removing misunderstanding [3–5]. Unfortunately, current assessment approaches have proved to be unsuitable for measuring complex learning [6]. In spite of the considerable importance of assessment and the increasing availability of alternative methods for assessing students' knowledge and competencies like dynamic question types, training software, videos, or games,

B. M. McLaren et al. (Eds.): CSEDU 2018, CCIS 1022, pp. 231–250, 2019.
https://doi.org/10.1007/978-3-030-21151-6_12

paper-and-pencil exams and written summative assessments continue to be the dominant method of assessment. This leads, among other things, to learning processes being directed towards the acquisition of factual knowledge and towards rote learning at schools, at universities as well as in organizational training. Even though the didactical opportunities of paper-and-pencil exams are quite limited, their management costs various resources, visible mainly as increased workload for academic staff. While technology has proven its potential for enhancing learning processes [7–10], it offers opportunities for improving assessment methods as well. However, we found a lack of technical solutions for conducting secure online exams for larger audiences. The problems we encountered were twofold: first, classical computer rooms were simply too small for large-scale exams. Second, like in all other electronic "business scenarios", confidentiality, integrity, authenticity, accountability, privacy, and reliability (and thus availability) are also mandatory in the context of electronic exams. Especially, if they come with the property "secure". The first five aspects are commonly addressed by the use of cryptography (e.g. encryption of transmitted and stored data, network-based security mechanisms like firewalls, and authentication of messages and users) as well as organizational measures to compensate for the limits of technical solutions. The last one may be overcome with physical and logical redundancy and continuous monitoring of the IT system [11]. This includes the continuous monitoring of the infrastructure (hardware, software and network) as a preventive measure to help detect issues before they cause any major problems.

To overcome these shortcomings, we implemented the Secure Exam Environment (SEE). This paper demonstrates how the technical implementation of the SEE can make eExams "*secure*", and provides recommendations for extending Moodle as a learning platform for conducting "*exams*", as well as expertise for the organization and design of an "*environment*" for successful eExams.

2 Benefits Offered by eExams

Online testing has great potential as a tool for conducting exams. Next to didactical benefits, they improve the efficiency and objectivity of exams, offer increased flexibility for lecturers as well as students, are sustainable if the personal devices of the students are used and offer students with disabilities increased accessibility.

2.1 Didactical Benefits

From a didactic point of view, eExams improve the execution of traditional question types like free text answers or multiple choice questions, and expand the range and variety of assessment methods by offering a number of new question types. Thus, online exams provide didactical benefits and have the potential to assess higher order thinking skills and different kinds of knowledge, e.g. procedural knowledge.

Free text questions remain invaluable even in the digital era when it is crucial to let learners explain something in their own words and thus to check if they understand more complex concepts adequately. With online exams, students can structure their answers in a clear and concise manner while making as many revisions and corrections as necessary. This provides students and teachers with increased clarity about the basis of the evaluation.

Multiple-choice or -response questions are appropriate if the recognition of the correct information within a set of selection options, the analysis of situations or scenarios, or the evaluation of adequate options is of interest. For didactical reasons, multiple-response questions should be preferred as this reduces the likelihood of students simply guessing the right answers. Cloze is suitable if the context of the learning content is essential, and particularly for short answers and terms that should be used correctly. The electronic delivery of cloze allows various forms of gaps to be filled via selection options, as short answers or drag-and-drop operations.

In addition to optimizing traditional question types, online exams also expand the repertoire of questions. While paper-and-pencil question types remain static, online testing offers variety, e.g. calculations with ranges of validity, and even dynamic types of questions, like drag-and-drop questions, the integration of variables into the question text or into items of multiple-choice questions, or the integration of videos or games (if sound is necessary for these questions, headphones should be available to not disturb colleagues during exams). Drag-and-drop questions within online testing include dragging of texts and/or images, for example, dragging several texts into an image and thus marking special areas of this image. Consequently, this question type is well suited when learners need to assign related elements, prioritize or organize elements. Videos and games may include procedural and complex information in questions, offering a new dimension in the assessment of situations, procedures, and dynamic content. Thus, analysis and evaluations of social dynamics, e.g. the communication between doctors and patients, technical procedures or meteorological processes, to name a few, are quite easily assessable. To sum up, question types should be selected based on the content being assessed.

Another and outstanding advantage of online testing is the opportunity to push the boundaries of static question types by including additional software in exams, making software, which is available for teaching and learning, also available for testing. More complicated problems can be solved in this way. According to Biggs and Tang [1] and their concept of "constructive alignment", coherence between all phases and elements of the learning process is essential for high quality education. Intended learning outcomes, teaching/learning activities, assessment tasks as well as grading should support one another [1, 12]. Thus, the software tools used for teaching and learning - e.g. mathematical or statistical calculations and analysis, programming, literature essays - should be used during the examination process as well. Being able to use specific software and multimedia in electronic exam environments paves the way to promising (hands-on) performance assessments too.

Beyond this, eExams can extend general feedback to each question and thus to all students without additional work for lecturers, leading to more valuable feedback for students about their level of knowledge [13]. Moreover, individual feedback may be made available to every student. We have observed that while students do not necessarily come to personal feedback talks they always want to see online feedback for an eExam.

In addition, opportunities for statistical analysis of questions may be utilized to improve the quality of questions over time.

2.2 Efficiency

Online exams result in a noticeable reduction of academic workload and thus result in significant savings [14] due to the improved readability, structure and clarity of typed open-text answers, along with automatic delivery, storage and (semi-)automated correction of (semi-)standardized question types. Handwritings in paper-and-pencil exams are often difficult to decipher and answers are quite often supplemented and extended using any blank regions on the paper sheet. Thus, the correction of free text answers takes a lot of time without any benefit for teachers or students. With online exams, the answers to free text questions are effortlessly readable. Additionally, eExams bring further advantages such as improved correction possibilities. The sorting of all students' answers to one question is done by the machine, which means an ease of correction. For exams conducted by several lecturers, e.g. for qualifying subject examinations, the correction can be done by several colleagues simultaneously. In addition, correction work can be done more easily while traveling since all exams are available online, eExams do not get lost, and – compared to paper-and-pencil exams - they may be copied effortlessly. The question pool may be improved over time through the adaptation, modification or extension of questions, thus simplifying the creation of new exams. Finally, as technical support staff may take over the supervision of the exams, lecturer may concentrate on other activities.

The greater efficiency of eExams provides students with instant grading and - if supported by lecturers - feedback [15]. Moreover, since today's students are more used to typing than to extensive handwriting [16], online exams prevent hand pains and bad handwriting related to paper-and-pencil exams.

2.3 Objectivity

eExams restrict the halo-effect which occurs when different handwriting styles influence the lecturer when grading [4, 17–19]. Online exams enable each question to be evaluated on its merits without being influenced by other answers provided by the student and thus subjective construction processes. Furthermore, online exams facilitate blind grading in many learning management systems, e.g. in Moodle, increasing objectivity.

Importantly, cheating may be minimised through the shuffling of questions and test-items and thus the avoidance of simultaneously displayed questions and test-items, the automatic selection of random questions out of a sufficiently large question pool as well as the opportunity to create questions including variables which are assigned different values for each student. Additionally, technical security concepts go far beyond the security possibilities of paper-and-pencil exams.

2.4 Flexibility

Furthermore, online exams provide greater flexibility compared to traditional testing methods [14]. Next to the extended correction possibilities mentioned above (simultaneous correction, correction on mobile devices whilst traveling) candidates are able to use their own familiar devices for an exam which helps to reduce stress as well as costs. In addition, implementing our secure exam environment (SEE) enabled us to offer so-called "slot-exam-weeks" where students can freely choose their examination date within one week (see Sect. 3.8).

2.5 Sustainability

Students usually have their own computers. Using these existing devices of the students (bring your own device – BYOD) minimizes institutional asset requirements to a few loan devices for students without portable computer or in case of a computer failure during the exam. Thus, the acquisition of new computers, which are mainly used for auditing purposes, is minimized. Additionally, eExams save paper and consequently contribute to the environmental protection.

2.6 Accessibility

Display magnifiers (screen loupes), screen readers, Braille input and output devices, mouth sticks or other devices allow students with disabilities to take an exam in a way quite similar to their colleagues. Thus, easy access to exams for people with disabilities is much more convenient with online exams. eExams are therefore also in compliance with the Austrian law which grants students with disabilities unrestricted accessibility to exams. In particular this means that students have the right "to be examined according to an alternative method if they suffer from a permanent disability which makes it impossible for them to take an examination in the prescribed manner and the other method does not limit the content and standards of the examination" [20].

3 The Secure Exam Environment (SEE)

Our efforts to take advantage of the above mentioned benefits together with an unsuccessful search for a satisfactory technical solution for eExams led to the development of the Secure Exam Environment (SEE) for online testing at the Alpen-Adria-Universität Klagenfurt (AAU) in 2011 [21]. The aim to make use of modern teaching and testing strategies next to the need to support large class sizes while working within budgetary and organizational constraints required a flexible and thin development. By making use of the students' existing personal computers (laptops), the SEE increases efficiency since ordinary lecture halls can be used for large scale online testing as well as effectiveness since the students are presumably familiar with their own devices. The SEE disables access to students' own files, data, and external hardware as well as to unwanted internet sites. Loan devices are offered for those who do not own a laptop or whose laptop is not compatible with the SEE. As a result, institutional asset requirements as well as the associated maintenance costs are minimized. We are currently able to test up to 220 students simultaneously with a stock of 80 loan devices [22].

3.1 Integration with Moodle

The actual exams are presented as quizzes, a key component of the Moodle learning management system (LMS) utilized by the AAU. Moodle offers various types of questions:

1. Questions which require manual grading like free text answers (called "essays" in Moodle).
2. Questions which are graded semi-automatically such as short answers. For these, examiners define a set of answers which allow the question to be evaluated automatically. Since students' responses might be correct but not included in this set, markers should manually check answers where students did not receive the maximum points available.
3. Question types which are evaluated automatically, including true/false questions, multiple choice and - response questions, numerical as well as calculated questions and calculated multichoice, matching, embedded answers (cloze), select missing words as well as drag-and-drop into text, onto image or drag-and-drop markers.

In the context of testing, archiving exams is another important aspect. According to Austrian legislation [23], documents related to written exams have to be archived for at least six months. Moodle, however, offers a practical solution as it automatically archives exams, which dramatically reduces the physical storage requirements and, as a positive environmental side-effect, the amount of paper needed (especially in the case of no-shows).

Furthermore, Moodle settings allow additional security measures to be defined such as the IP-range within which eExams can be taken.

3.2 Additional Software and Resources

The SEE facilitates the integration of different software tools and programmes, which are increasingly used for teaching and learning into the exam environment, fostering pedagogical coherence [1]. At the moment we support GeoGebra, Eclipse, Office-products like Excel or Word, calculators, PSPP, as well as any combination of these tools.

Furthermore, PDF-documents or websites which are allowed and could be used during an exam can be provided.

3.3 Security and Bring Your Own Device – BYOD

In contrast to other electronic exam environments (e.g. [24]), we avoid the use of special equipment and encourage students to use their own device. However, accessing the Moodle server directly via a common web browser running on the student's operating system (OS) is an insecure approach. In this case, blocking connections to Wikipedia or other online resources may be simple, but cheating by using materials stored on the local hard drive is rather easy. Since we do not want to force students to install additional software (such as lockdown modules) on their personal laptops, we have to use our own OS in order to restrict the access to the local resources and programmes that are prohibited during the exam. We decided to boot this OS via the Preboot eXecution Environment (PXE) protocol over a local area network (LAN), since the handling of USB sticks or DVDs is very error-prone, time-consuming and inflexible, especially when additional software is needed [22]. Using wireless LANs (WLANs) would be an alternative solution, but with technical limitations to guarantee security since WLANs are very interference-prone. Each student with an easily obtainable jammer could interfere the WLAN. Nonetheless, we developed organizational security concepts for the SEE via WLAN, but are still focusing on LAN as it is sufficient for our current requirements and technically more secure.

Clearly, booting our own OS requires that the client is able to boot via the network. In order to support a very broad range of (private) laptops, our solution is designed as a minimal Linux system. At the moment, this OS is realized using Fedora and Knoppix, which enables us to boot Legacy and UEFI devices. To support Apple hardware we boot a minimal macOS image. In order to restrict the access to external resources, we implemented corresponding firewall rules. Since Moodle as an LMS not only provides exam features but also chatting capabilities and course related material, a solution was needed to prevent access to such resources and activities during exams. Running an ordinary web browser – even when restricted with firewall rules – would not have completely solved the cheating problem. Fortunately, the Safe Exam Browser (SEB – [25]) is fully supported by Moodle-core. The SEB is far more than an ordinary browser. Beside it's common browser functionality it offers a complete lockdown of all OS interface functions as opening, switching and closing applications other than the SEB itself. Furthermore, together with a SEB moodle plugin it also guarantees (when set up appropriately) that a moodle quiz can only be accessed by the SEB and all moodle graphical user interface (GUI) functions which would allow interaction outside the quiz are suppressed. However, the SEB is only available for Windows and macOS. Therefore, we boot a minimized Windows 7 as a virtual machine on the minimized Linux system via VirtualBox [26] (see Fig. 1). Despite the availability of online tools and platforms, proprietary software which only runs on Windows remains widespread in the educational sector. On the one hand, the reliance on a virtual machine and Windows 7 is a drawback in terms of performance, on the other hand, it adds flexibility regarding the management of the virtual machine image. Furthermore, hardware driver management is done completely in Linux, which is known for its broad, out of the box hardware support especially for older devices. The selection of the allowed programmes during the exam (in addition to the SEB) is set via a configuration file, which is retrieved from an intranet service. In the GUI of this service, administrators are able to configure different combinations of GeoGebra, Excel, Word, Calculator, Eclipse, and PDFs for the exam.

Starting an online exam using the SEE begins by booting a minimized Linux from the LAN, then the minimized Linux automatically starts the Windows 7 virtual machine (VM), Window 7 automatically starts the SEB, the SEB automatically connects to the homepage of the AAU's learning management system Moodle, and finally users have to log in to Moodle with their own account and enter the Moodle course in order to select the exam they want to take [22].

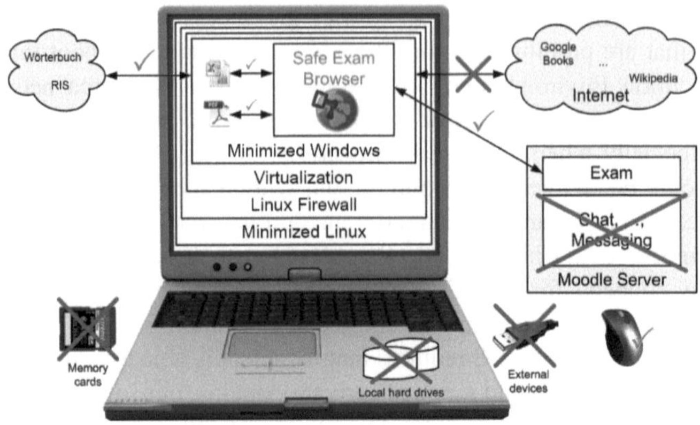

Fig. 1. The operating principle of the Secure Exam Environment (SEE).

3.4 Maximizing the Availability of the SEE

The availability of an exam environment is an issue of critical importance. Even a short downtime of the SEE could prevent hundreds of students from taking exams which might be urgently needed to get marks or certificates, take new courses, finish modules, classes or studies, get financial aid for higher education studies, or even get a new job. Furthermore, students tend to be quite nervous before an exam and a technical glitch would undoubtedly increase stress and erode trust in the exam environment. Thus, perception of the SEE's reliability (from both for examiner's and examinees' viewpoint) depends on the availability of the (information) technology during the exam [5].

During the SEE boot process, the SEE-servers (and the personal computers with which the exams are written) have to operate properly as well as the network including the switches in the lecture halls. At the time of writing an eExam, the SEE depends on the online connection between the SEB and the Moodle-server. Consequently, the availability of the SEE can be affected by hardware failure, network drop-outs or service outages. Analyzing and identifying failures when a breakdown occurs usually costs a lot of time, which is at a premium while conducting an eExam. Thus, a continuous monitoring solution of the various IT components involved - e.g. servers and computer networking technologies – to prevent failures and optimize the availability of the SEE is mandatory, particularly considering the SEE is based on various hardware components which are administered by different departments of the university.

Drop-outs of components or services or deviations from thresholds within defined time intervals result in alerts, allowing support staff to react to and resolve issues immediately, leading to crucial time-savings within the failure identification process. Monitored components and services include the availability of the SEE-servers (implemented with centOS) including CPU and storage, as well as DHCP, NFS, TFTP, and HTTP services; the availability of the administration backend of the SEE including the corresponding HTTP service; the availability of Moodle including HTTP-access as well as end-to-end-tests in the lecture halls with minimal computers (Raspberry Pi); the availability of the network (connection between SEE-server, clients and Moodle), and end-to-end performance tests within the network with low-cost probes (Raspberry Pi).

Monitoring the High-Availability SEE-Host and Including Services. The availability of the server, providing the SEE for network boot, as well as services like DHCP, NFS, HTTP and TFTP is one of the key requirements of online testing with the SEE.

We operate the SEE-server as a high-availability and stable system by running multiple redundant SEE-servers. Using DRBD/Heartbeat or Pacemaker/Corosync in a failover setup (to define one server as the master server and the other one as slave) enables us to switch from one server to the other automatically in case of a failure or manually in case of scheduled maintenance. Thus, a new update can be safely implemented within the system by installing it on one server and, after careful testing, on the other and thus the production system.

While monitoring the services mentioned above, we log CPU utilization, RAM and hard disc usage, and the status as well as the utilization of the network interface. Additionally, we periodically check for pending updates, especially security updates, to eliminate failures or prevent hack-attacks on the system and improve performance. Controlling upcoming updates enables us to schedule maintenance periods efficiently around exams.

Measuring Network Performance. Measuring the run-time of the network including the connection between the SEE-server, clients and Moodle during an eExam in real time generates significant data about the latency and utilization of the network. The open source software SmokePing is a suitable tool for measuring and visualising the round-trip-time (RTT) of Linux-based systems by defining the specific hosts as well as relevant external hosts which are reachable via ICMP. By default, every five minutes twenty ICMP-packages are transmitted to each specified host and used to calculate RTTs. Package loss is a signal for capacity overload of the main host or related hosts, or for a failure or an erroneous configuration of a network device. Black ‘smoke’ at an interval of measurement shows the range of fluctuation of the RTT. Increased smoke indicates a high variation of the RTT per ping and thus capacity overload of the network. The combination of SmokePing and probes (Raspberry Pi’s) placed in the SEE-network enables us to monitor all servers and network devices and thus to recognise network bottlenecks and failures at an early stage.

Maximizing Availability of the Network Connection. In order to maximise network availability, we only use wired LAN connections at this point of time. Despite recent developments, WLAN remains too error-prone and, additionally, a malicious user could easily perform a denial-of-service (DoS) attack on the WLAN access points and hence prevent all users from taking the exam. To achieve such an attack, a battery-powered pocket-sized WiFi jammer could be placed close to or in the room where the eExams take place.

To ensure the maximum stability of the network system, the network department of our university provides high redundancy within the network-core, distribution-switches, firewalls, and the border-router, as well as load sharing via the Border Gateway Protocol (BGP) in a multihomed environment and redundant cables. In addition, the equipment used in the core and distribution layer are high-end components.

Infrastructure. The availability of our Secure Exam Environment (SEE) is affected by the infrastructure in which the SEE components are embedded. One critical issue is an Uninterruptible Power Supply (UPS) for the SEE-server as well as for the network to protect the system from power failures. The UPS also guards against over - and under voltage and is backed by means of batteries (short-term power failures) and a diesel generator (long-term power failures).

Another important topic is the geographical distribution of the (redundant) hardware components. The two SEE-servers are located in different areas of the university and thus, in the case of an extended power failure, fire or flooding, it is unlikely that both servers will be affected.

Backups. One indirect approach to guarantee the availability of the SEE-servers, and thus the SEE, is frequent, well organized backups. In case of an outage like hardware failure, the SEE-server must be restored to the most recent valid state. An up-to-date, functioning backup reduces the mean time to repair (MTTR). A well-organized backup-strategy includes the evaluation of functionality of the frequently executed backups as well as the documentation and frequent testing of the backups and training of the responsible staff. Furthermore, it should be guaranteed that spare hardware (like hot-standby harddisks, power supplies and spare network components) is immediately available in case of serious hardware failure.

Monitoring the Availability of the Administration Backend of the SEE Including the Corresponding HTTP Service. The administration backend is another key component of the SEE, offered via web interface and used by the supporting staff to activate any additional software (e.g. a calculator or Eclipse) for an exam. The administration backend is accessible only via a URL https://backend.spu.aau.at. A periodical check of the HTTP server's reachability is performed monitoring the HTTP status code. If the wrong status code is returned from the backend, an alarm is sent to the service team. Additionally, it is possible to check the server's response times. Longer response times could be an indicator of network outages or a server problem.

Centralized Monitoring of all SEE-Components and Services. Deviations from threshold values of all components and services of the SEE are reported at regular intervals. Every outage triggers an alarm (via e-mail or SMS) which, together with centralized monitoring, helps the service team to rapidly identify the cause of a failure, saving additional time.

Optimizing the SEE Based on Monitoring Data. The constant monitoring of all components and services of the SEE offers the opportunity for (trend) analysis (also see Sect. 5.1 "Further developments") as a basis for the continuous optimization of the systems' performance.

3.5 Reliability

Reliability for examiner and examinee is a critical issue and depends on the availability of (information) technology - e.g. computers and computer networking technologies -

during the exam [5, 11]. At the time of writing, the SEE depends on the online connection between the SEB and the Moodle-server. As a result, users cannot save current results or proceed to the next question during a network failure. Thus, the temporary storage of the answers (during network failures) remains a problem. Fortunately, Moodle saves the last answer received and the progress of each examinee. Therefore, the examinee is allowed to continue the exam from the point where the error occurred after potential network problems are solved. In the worst case scenario, the last answer of the examinee is lost. Similarly, laptop failure is not a severe problem because all answers provided up to the failure would have been stored on the server and the student can simply continue his or her exam on one of our loan devices.

3.6 Loan Devices

Loan devices serve two purposes within the SEE: Firstly, it cannot be assumed that all students have a portable device, and secondly, they may substitute a student's personal device in the case of technical problems or breakdowns during the exam. The AAU currently has approximately 80 laptops serving as loan devices for students.

3.7 Secure Exams for Students with Disabilities

Impaired students have very different needs. Thus, one single standard solution for students with disabilities would not meet the requirements. Therefore, we provide for each student with specific needs a unique solution for eExams using different tools (see Sect. 2.6). Since the integration of these tools would pose severe security problems for the SEE, we conduct eExams for students with disabilities on their own, familiar device but with local restrictions or, if required, on loan devices.

3.8 Offering Flexibility with Slot-Exams

One service for students, which followed from the development of the SEE, are so-called slotted eExams. For the execution of eExams with the SEE, we developed an online-process to register for an eExam some time before the test takes place as well as an online-registration process right before the exam in the lecture hall. Thus, exams, registration data as well as access rights are available online. These processes enabled us to offer several time-slots for an eExam within a week, from which students can freely choose when they want or are able to take an exam. Especially for students who are employed next to their studies, who need to foster children or relatives or whose mobility is restricted, this service is very helpful.

The decision as to whether an eExam is conducted in a traditional way on a fixed examination date or as a slotted eExam is made by the lecturer: slotted eExams can only work if a suitably large question pool is available, such that on different days randomly generated questions and/or exams are sufficiently dissimilar from each other [11].

4 Organizational Issues of eExams

Careful planning and organization are crucial for the smooth, secure and reliable operation of eExams. Organization is vital not only for the preparation of eExams but also to close security gaps. As a result, many aspects have to be considered before, during and after exams.

4.1 Organizational Measures Beforehand

In addition to informing teachers and students about the basics of eExams before an exam, support staff must be trained and available, rooms must be booked and tests must be created correctly.

Provide Information. Some lecturers, particularly if they have only recently taken up their position at the university or are external teachers, are not aware of the possibilities of online testing and especially not of the SEE as a specific solution at the AAU. Hence, we offer videos introducing the SEE, clearly arranged checklists for the preparation of casual eExams or slotted eExams with the SEE, a Moodle-course with information and a ‘playground’ to try online-tests and get familiar with eExams as well as advanced training courses and personal trainings.

The eLearning-hotline is available 24/7 to support lecturers as well as students in case of open questions, e.g. if a personal device fails immediately before an exam and a loan device is needed.

Support Students with the Preparation of Their Devices. Since students have to change the boot-order of their devices to start the SEE, we offer special information days once or twice a week to support them with this task. Over a six hour period, students are offered the opportunity to change the boot order of their device and test if it is compatible with the SEE. In addition, first time students learn something about the eExam process. The type of device, the key combination to enter the boot-menu or the need for a loan device are stored in a database to improve preparations for future eExams.

Training of a Flexible Support-Team and Team-Building. Successful written exams require the cooperation of multiple staff members. As the Alpen-Adria Universität Klagenfurt conducts online exams from 8 a.m. to 10 p.m., five days a week, we supplement our core team of four employees which are responsible for the entire eLearning services of the university, with students trained as e-tutors. At the moment our team includes 12 e-tutors working between two and 12 h a week to successfully deliver a growing number of tests.

The team has received significant coaching and teambuilding to manage the technical, organizational as well as personal challenges related to online exams. For example, the support staff must remain calm in the event of failures, errors or problems, particularly as students are already under stress due to the examination situation and should not be subjected to further strain. Students who start as e-tutors initially perform simple tasks like the transport of loan and registration devices into the lecture hall, setting up loan devices for replacement in the lecture hall or supervision of the exam.

Once they have gained experience with the handling of eExams, they receive further training as 'lead-e-tutors', taking over contact with lecturers before the exam, the final check of the test-setting and questions in Moodle, and the activation of the correct exam-version (e.g. unlocking additional software).

To schedule availability of the support staff for each eExam, we use a shared spreadsheet (ev. Screenshot) where each team-member fills out his or her (non-) availability for each exam-slot. The core-team then decides who will be the lead of an eExam and who will be in the support team.

Organizing Lecture Halls for eExams. The room for an eExam is booked mainly by the lecturers in coordination with our eLearning-team and the room administration of the university. Obviously, it is important to ensure that not too many eExams take place simultaneously, overstraining support staff and loan device capacities. Furthermore, enough time must be allocated for test-settings (e.g. additional software or websites allowed) before and after an exam and for setting up registration and loan devices in the lecture hall as well as the registration process itself.

Organizing Tests and Questions. Many lecturers need support with didactical and technical issues surrounding the creation of test questions and tests when starting out with eExams. Moreover, the general conditions must be set for each exam: Will subject-specific supervision be available? Are written materials allowed during the exam? Should websites and/or additional software be available and, if yes, which ones?

As Moodle's test settings are crucial for successfully conducting secure eExams with the SEE, the settings for each eExam are checked along with the questions themselves by the support team.

Registration of Students Before an Exam. Students have to register for any exam. During the registration process for an eExams students must confirm that they attended an information day for eExams and that they have had their device checked for compatibility with the SEE and they will bring it to the eExam, or that they will use a loan device. In addition, students can indicate if they require a barrier-free exam environment, in which case communication with the support staff follows to clarify the conditions for the accessibility of the exam.

If the number of registered students exceeds the capacity of the lecture hall, a second exam slot is typically organized. Students who cannot prebook a loan device due to unforeseen demand are placed on a waiting list.

4.2 Organizational Measures at the Time of the eExam

eTutors ensure that the exam venue is open and that the required registration and loan devices are available. The support team receives instructions from the lead-e-tutor about the specific exam requirements then (e.g. permitted software, websites, - documents, notes or materials).

Additional loan-devices are set up as backups for any computers that fail during the exam. The number of the replacement devices depends on the number of registered students. Experience shows that one backup device for every 10 to 20 students is sufficient.

The identities of students are verified upon arrival in the lecture hall by scanning their student card using a card reader. Following processing via our university's examination administration system, eLearning staff are informed if the student registered for the specific eExam, if s/he needs a barrier-free examination environment and if s/he will use his or her personal device or a loan device.

After checking in, students receive a LAN-cable and a loan device if needed and are seated appropriately in the lecture hall. In the meantime, the specific exam is made visible in the Moodle-course, the proper version of the SEE is activated (with a correct selection of additional software, websites as well as documents) and the network switches are activated.

Powerpoint slides are presented in the lecture hall with detailed step-by-step instructions for the installation of the LAN-cable, the booting-process and as well as for navigating through and eventually submitting the test. Afterwards, the students boot the SEE. During the booting process, and a video is played to inform students about the examination modalities in a comprehensible and traceable way, e.g. about how to start the eExam, how to navigate between test questions, how to submit the eExam, which actions are considered cheating and the corresponding consequences.

Fig. 2. Instructions for students in the lecture hall before an eExam.

Finally, once the support staff has informed the students about any special features of the exam, the exam starts.

During the exam, the support staff verifies if each student has logged into Moodle with his or her proper account by matching their physical student identity card with the login data. Furthermore, the e-tutors supervise the exam and support in case of technical failures or problems.

After submitting the exam, the students return the LAN-cable, the loan devices (where applicable) and check out by replacing their student identity card on the card reader.

4.3 Organizational Measures After the eExam

After all, students have submitted the exam or the examination period has expired, the exam-slot is closed, the test is made invisible for students in the Moodle-course and a backup of the exam is created.

5 Experiences with eExams at the AAU and Further Developments

In June 2011 we began offering online exams with the SEE. Table 1 shows the growth of eExams conducted with the SEE at the AAU over the last six years.

Table 1. The Progression of eExams with the Secure Exam Environment (SEE), * in progress.

	2011	2012	2013	2014	2015	2016	2017	2018*	Total
eExams	10	59	159	208	234	286	373	276	1,605
Examinees	288	2,717	7,475	7,082	8,954	10,352	12,252	8,487	57,607

5.1 Experiences with Supporting Students' Own Devices

The aim of supporting all student laptops is quite challenging because the dedicated installation of drivers would be too time consuming and risky. Nonetheless, we try to support as many devices as possible. [27] Fig. 2 shows the proportion of supported devices over time.

As shown in the Fig. 3, in 2012 the SEE system supported 65% of the hardware provided by the students. As hardware evolved and, in particular with the introduction of UEFI in newer laptops, the percentage of supported devices decreased until 2016. In response to this, in 2016 we began to work on a second OS image (based on Fedora) and as a result, the number of supported laptops has begun to increase.

Most of the remaining compatibility problems stem from exotic hardware (Linux integrates the most common and widespread hardware components), which mainly appear in low budget and top end laptops as well as sub notebooks. For example, gaming laptops with GeForce graphic cards are often unsupported since NVIDIA only provides proprietary drivers and the open source drivers lack support for mobile gaming graphic cards.

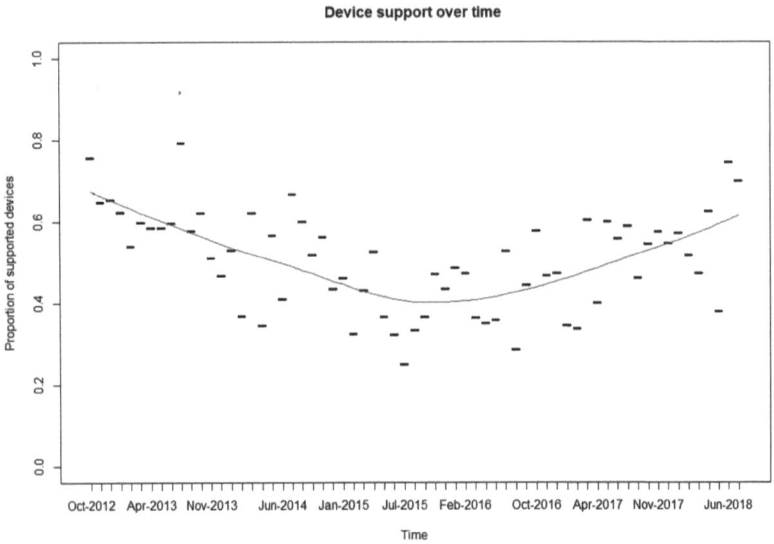

Fig. 3. Supported Student Laptops from 2012 to (ongoing) 2018.

Unfortunately, device support data from 2012 until the beginning 2016 is somewhat incomplete, as during the early stages of the implementation of the SEE we focused on the technical solution. Data was collected to find out which devices were bootable with the SEE and which devices not, thus, where effort should be invested, i.e. which devices were popular enough to require a technical solution. As testing procedures were not standardized the data does not distinguish between when the tester could not get a device to work and when it was not supported, and how this information was recorded was not standardized. Over time, we have standardized the procedure for testing students' devices as well as the documentation of device support.

Since every supported laptop currently needs to be fully functionable without the installation of additional drivers or custom configurations for specific hardware combinations, we consider a support rate of over 70% as a success. In combination with our 80 loan devices we have been able to offer eExams as required and conduct online assessment of up to 300 students.

5.2 Further Developments

Didactical Improvements. Although online testing has the potential to extend the variety of question types as well as software and multimedia available for an exam, the question types offered by LMS are nevertheless rather limited and the software available restricted to licensing agreements. Hence, examination has improved with eExams, but has not reached a new level yet. Consequently, we are continuing our work to improve the ways in which knowledge is tested and adapt it to current knowledge requirements.

Stable and Flexible Network Connection. One of the current challenges of online exams is the necessity of a stable and preferably flexible network connection. As WLAN is still prone to failure, LAN is the best option for stability, especially for larger groups of students. This results in another challenging aspect, namely that lecture halls require LAN and power sockets near at least every second seat. Unfortunately, not all lecture halls fulfill these requirements and retrofitting is extremely expensive, resulting in a lack of flexibility. The obstacle with the LAN sockets could be overcome with access points. Thus, we are evaluating solutions to provide eExams for devices without ethernet port via WLAN or a hybrid boot (usb/ethernet) solution. To compensate technical weaknesses, we defined organizational measurements to increase the availability of WLANs. However, running laptops purely on battery power is risky.

New Generations of Hardware. New generations of laptops, requiring continuous adaptation of the SEE, remain a persistent challenge. For example, we had to invest significant effort to support UEFI as a new interface between the hardware and the OS. As laptops become slimmer, more devices come without dedicated ethernet ports, forcing us to support adapters within the SEE. Unfortunately, some manufacturers do not support even PXE boot with USB ethernet adapters, leading to the need to find workarounds.

Improved Monitoring. Further developments in monitoring will include the integration of the students' devices and the loan devices into the monitoring concept and predictive maintenance (for details refer to [28–30]). In more detail, we will pursue the following ideas:

- By gathering and analyzing the devices' log-files, whenever they are connected to the SEE, *students' devices* and the *loan devices* may be directly integrated into the monitoring system. This will help to keep the loan devices up-to-date, because a problem detected on a single device (currently in use) can (automatically) be fixed on all other instances of the same model. A similar process can be applied for the students' devices: a problem detected with one device can either trigger an update of the SEE (e.g. with respect to drivers) or a warning for other students using the same model. In the long-term, the log-data may be included in a predictive model.
- The goal of *Predictive Maintenance* is to determine the condition of equipment (servers, laptops, and network-infrastructure such as switches and cabling) in order to predict when maintenance should be performed in order to avoid failures. This is contrary to the classical approach, where maintenance is either triggered by a concrete failure (aka the break-fix model [31]) or an interval-based approach, which often causes unnecessary costs. In short, predictive maintenance promises time and cost savings and a higher level of availability.

Different Versions of Simultaneous eExams. Currently, we are only able to execute one eExam with specific settings, e.g. additional software, at the same time. Therefore, we are developing a boot environment that supports multiple eExams with different additional software simultaneously by recognizing the identity of the lecture hall and subsequently by recognizing the identity of the student and transmitting the proper exam environment.

Identity Verification. Checking the identity of an examinee by verifying the picture on his/her (student) identity card is a quite common process at the beginning of exams. However, when it comes to large scale exams (say 200 or more examinees), this process in total gets quite time consuming. In order to enhance the efficiency of the identity verification process we plan to integrate authentication by use of biometric features. These features might include a picture of the face (available on the identity card and in the students' record) or even a fingerprint. If the (students) hardware provides the according sensor, the identity checking could take place at his/her seat. In case of a camera needed to verify an image of the face, this is quite likely with modern laptops. Since fingerprint readers are most commonly only available to the operating system (or special) applications, a fingerprint reader could be placed next to the RFID-reader that reads the students identity card.

General Data Protection Regulation (GDPR). Of course, the processing of personal data calls for compliance to the GDPR [32], especially when biometric data (Art. 9 GDPR: special categories of personal data) is processed. When conducting electronic exams, besides of identity verification, there are several processes that have to be concerned. Some of them are already compliant with the GDPR (e.g. notification of the outcome/grade, or right of access to the exam), but some are not or have to be implemented yet (e.g. right for a copy of the exam, or automatic compliance to deadlines for storage or deletion). So another open topic is to adapt the SEE concept and Moodle for GDPR-compliance.

6 Conclusion

eExams extend the possibilities for assessment in many ways, especially in terms of quality (e.g. didactics and objectivity) and efficiency. However, the transition from paper-based to electronic exams raises "new" security-related problems. Traditional paper-based exams handled requirements like confidentiality, privacy, integrity, authenticity, accountability and availability in a straight-forward manner: simply preventing access before and after the exam guarantees their confidentiality, the paper and well established organizational and personnel processes do the rest (privacy, integrity, authenticity, accountability, and availability). The security gaps in paper exams have not always been sufficiently taken into account, especially due to the lack of an alternative. For eExams, all the aforementioned aspects have to be addressed by complex, often technical mechanisms.

One solution to overcome these challenges is the Secure Exam Environment (SEE) used at the Alpen-Adria-Universität Klagenfurt (AAU) as presented in this paper. The SEE provides didactical benefits of online testing by extending the questions types offered by the LMS Moodle with additional software, multimedia and online resources, all within a secure environment. The system's BYOD-approach, utilizes students' familiarity with their devices to provide efficiency and sustainability while restricting access to local resources and to the Internet. Furthermore, this paper contains a description of our low-cost monitoring system that helps us achieve a high quality of service level with respect to the availability of the SEE. Finally, this paper considers the underlying organizational measurements supporting pathways to successful online testing.

References

1. Biggs, J., Tang, C.: Teaching for Quality Learning at University. McGraw Hill, Berkshire (2011)
2. UK Quality Code for Higher Education. Part B: Assuring and Enhancing Academic Quality. Quality Assurance Agency of Higher Education (2001). http://www.qaa.ac.uk//en/quality-code/the-existing-uk-quality-code/part-b-assuring-and-enhancing-academic-quality. Accessed 13 July 2018
3. Marriott, P.: Students' evaluation of the use of online summative assessment on an undergraduate financial accounting module. Br. J. Edu. Technol. **40**(2), 237–254 (2009)
4. Müller, F.H., Bayer, C.: Prüfungen: Vorbereitung - Durchführung - Bewertung. In: Hawelka, B., Hammerl, M., Gruber, H. (eds.) Förderung von Kompetenzen in der Hochschullehre, pp. 223–237. Asanger, Kröning (2007)
5. Sharpe, R., Oliver, M.: Designing courses for e-learning. In: Beetham, H., Sharpe, R. (eds.) Rethinking Pedagogy for a Digital Age. Designing and Delivering E-Learning. Routledge, London and New York (2007)
6. Clarke-Midura, J., Code, J., Mayrath, M.C., Dede, C., Zap, N.: Thinking outside the bubble: virtual performance assessments for measuring complex learning. In: Technology-Based Assessments for 21st Century Skills, pp. 125–146 (2012)
7. Benkada, C., Moccozet, L.: Enriched interactive videos for teaching and learning. In: Conference Paper: 8th International Workshop on Interactive Environments and Emerging Technologies for eLearning (IEETeL2017) and 21st International Conference on Information Visualisation, London (2017)
8. Põldoja, H., Väljataga, T., Laanpere, M., Tammets, K.: Web-based self- and peer assessment of teachers' digital competencies. World Wide Web **17**(2), 255–269 (2012)
9. Howell, D.D., Tseng, D.C.Y., Colorado-Resa, J.T.: Fast assessments with digital tools using multiple-choice questions. Coll. Teach. **65**(3), 145–147 (2017)
10. Ardito, C., et al.: Usability of e-learning tools. In: AVI 2004 Proceedings of the Working Conferences Interfaces, pp. 80–84 (2004)
11. Frankl, G., Schartner, P., Jost, D.: The "secure exam environment": e-testing with students' own devices. In: Tatnall, A., Webb, M. (eds.) WCCE 2017. IAICT, vol. 515, pp. 179–188. Springer, Cham (2017). https://doi.org/10.1007/978-3-319-74310-3_20
12. Müller, A., Schmidt, B.: Prüfungen als Lernchance: Sinn, Ziele und Formen von Hochschulprüfungen. Zeitschrift für Hochschulentwicklung **4**(1), 23–45 (2009)
13. Price, M., Handley, K., Millar, J., O'Donovan, B.: Feedback: all that effort, but what is the effect? Assess. Eval. High. Educ. **35**(3), 277–289 (2010)
14. Anakwe, B.: Comparison of student performance in paper-based versus computer-based testing. J. Educ. Bus. **84**, 13–18 (2008)
15. Hewson, C.: Can online course-based assessment methods be fair and equitable? Relationships between students' preferences and performance within online and offline assessments. J. Comput. Assist. Learn. **28**, 488–498 (2012)
16. Fluck, A.: eExaminations Strategic Project Final Report for Academic Senate, University of Tasmania (2011). Meeting 1/2011, cited in Fluck, A., Hillier, M.: Innovative assessment with eExams. Paper presented at the Australian Council for Computers in Education (ACCE) Conference, 29 September–2 October, Brisbane, Queensland (2016)
17. Fleming, N.D.: Biases in marking students' written work: quality? In: Brown, S., Glaser, A. (eds.) Assessment Matters in Higher Education: Choosing and Using Diverse Approaches, pp. 83–92. McGraw-Hill Education, London (1999)

18. Sweedler-Brown, C.O.: Computers and assessment: the effect of typing versus handwriting on the holistic scoring of essays. Res. Teach. Dev. Educ. **8**(1), 5–14 (1991)
19. Brown, S., Glaser, A.: Assessment Matters in Higher Education: Choosing and Using Diverse Approaches. McGraw-Hill Education, London (2003)
20. Bundeskanzleramt Österreich, Universitätsgesetz 2002, § 59 Abs. 1. Z 12. https://www.ris.bka.gv.at/Dokumente/Erv/ERV_2002_1_120/ERV_2002_1_120.pdf. Accessed 13 July 2018
21. Frankl, G., Schartner, P., Zebeding, G.: The "secure exam environment" for online testing at the Alpen-Adria-Universität Klagenfurt/Austria. In: World Conference on E-Learning in Corporate, Government, Healthcare, and Higher Education. Association for the Advancement of Computing in Education (AACE), Hawaii (2011)
22. Frankl, G., Schartner, P., Jost, D.: Guaranteeing high availability of the "secure exam environment" (SEE). In: Proceedings of the 10th International Conference on Computer Supported Education, no. 2, pp. 130–136 (2018)
23. Bundeskanzleramt Österreich, Universitätsgesetz 2002, §79 Abs. 3 and 4 and § 84 Abs. 1, https://www.ris.bka.gv.at/Dokumente/Erv/ERV_2002_1_120/ERV_2002_1_120.pdf. Accessed 13 July 2018
24. SoftwareSecure. http://www.softwaresecure.com/. Accessed 16 Aug 2017
25. Safe Exam Browser (SEB). http://www.safeexambrowser.org/news_en.html. Accessed 13 July 2018
26. Virtual Box. http://www.virtualbox.org. Accessed 13 July 2018
27. Frankl, G., Napetschnig, S.: Bring your own device to secure online exams. In: Technology Enhanced Assessment (in press)
28. Sasisekharan. R., Seshadri, V., Weiss, S.M.: Proactive network maintenance using machine learning. In: Workshop on Knowledge Discovery in Databases (KDD 1994), pp. 453–462 (1994)
29. Susto, G.A., Schirru, A., Pampuri, S., McLoone, S., Beghi, A.: Machine learning for predictive maintenance: a multiple classifier approach. IEEE Trans. Ind. Inform. **11**(3), 812–820 (2015)
30. Hashemian, H.M., Bean, W.C.: State-of-the-art predictive maintenance techniques. IEEE Trans. Instrum. Meas. **60**(10), 226–236 (2011)
31. General Electric Company: Beyond the break-fix model: predictive services to leverage GE's record $229 billion backlog. GE Reports, 18 October 2003. http://www.gereports.com/beyond-the-break-fix-model. Accessed 17 Aug 2017
32. Regulation (EU) 2016/679 of the European Parliament and of the Council of 27 April 2016 on the protection of natural persons with regard to the processing of personal data and on the free movement of such data, and repealing Directive 95/46/EC (General Data Protection Regulation - GDPR). https://publications.europa.eu/en/publication-detail/-/publication/3e485e15-11bd-11e6-ba9a-01aa75ed71a1/language-en. Accessed 13 July 2018

A Space-Efficient Technique of Policy Trees for an Intelligent Tutoring System on POMDP

Fangju Wang(✉)

University of Guelph, Guelph, ON N1G 2W1, Canada
fjwang@uoguelph.ca

Abstract. Adaptive tutoring is essentially a decision process, in each step of which an optimal tutoring action is chosen and taken. In recent years, researchers have been increasingly interested in applying the partially observable Markov decision process (POMDP) model to build intelligent tutoring systems (ITSs). The POMDP model may enable an ITS to optimize tutoring when uncertainties exist. Computing in a POMDP is characterized by exponential costs, in both time and space, which obstruct the POMDP model for practical applications. In our research, we develop techniques to improve computing efficiency in a POMDP based ITS. In this paper, we report a space-efficient technique of policy trees. The technique may help achieve high space efficiency by grouping policy trees and dynamically creating the policy trees to be evaluated in making a decision.

Keywords: Intelligent tutoring system · Computer supported education · Partially observable Markov decision process · Computational complexity

1 Introduction

An intelligent tutoring system (ITS) is an interactive computer program for adaptive teaching. Computational complexity is a key issue in building an ITS, which must reside on a computing platform, and respond to student questions or requests in a timely fashion. Many mathematical models underlying ITSs are computationally intractable. Huge space consumption and lengthy computing time have been major obstacles to applying the models to intelligent tutoring. The partially observable Markov decision process (POMDP) model is one of them.

A major goal for building an ITS is adaptive teaching. To be adaptive, in each tutoring step a system should be able to choose the action that is most beneficial to the student it teaches. Mathematically, adaptive tutoring can be modeled by a *Markov decision process* (*MDP*), in which the agent makes optimal decisions considering the current states. In an MDP, states can be observed completely,

B. M. McLaren et al. (Eds.): CSEDU 2018, CCIS 1022, pp. 251–267, 2019.
https://doi.org/10.1007/978-3-030-21151-6_13

and the agent knows exactly what the current states are. However, in a tutoring process, the teacher may be uncertain about student states and unsure about the most beneficial teaching actions [12].

The POMDP model is an extension of MDP for handling uncertainties. In a POMDP, the task of choosing an optimal action is referred to as *solving the POMDP*. This task is computationally expensive. A simplified, less expensive technique for POMDP-solving is to use *policy trees*, in which decision making involves evaluating a set of trees and choosing an optimal one. However, the technique of policy trees is still too expensive to be used in practical applications. In making a decision, the number of trees to evaluate is exponential, and the number of operations in evaluating a tree is also exponential. To apply the POMDP model to intelligent tutoring, we must address the problems of computational complexity.

In our research, we develop new techniques to improve computing efficiency in a POMDP based ITS. In this paper, we report a space-efficient technique of policy trees. The work is an extension of the research described in [8,9]. The technique helps achieve high space efficiency by grouping policy trees and dynamically creating the policy trees to be evaluated in making a decision.

In the following, we first introduce the technical background of the POMDP model that is needed for discussing our technique, followed by reviewing the existing work related to our research. Then we present our techniques for tree grouping and dynamic tree creation, and finally discuss some experimental results.

2 Partially Observable Markov Decision Process

2.1 POMDP as an Extension of MDP

A Markov decision process (MDP) can model a process in which different actions can be chosen in different states to maximize rewards. The core of an MDP includes S, A, T, and ρ, which are a set of states, a set of actions, a set of state transition probabilities, and a reward function. In a decision step, the agent is in $s \in S$, takes $a \in A$ that is available in s, enters $s' \in S$, and receives reward $\rho(s, a, s')$. The MDP model is stochastic. $P(s'|s, a) \in T$ is the probability that the agent enters s' after taking a in s. In addition, an MDP includes a core component of *policy*, denoted by $\pi(s)$:

$$a = \pi(s). \tag{1}$$

It guides the agent to choose the optimal action available in s to maximize rewards. The MDP model is suitable for decision processes in which states can be observed completely and exactly.

A POMDP, as an extension of an MDP, has two additional core components: O and Z, which are a set of observations and a set of observation probabilities. A POMDP can model a decision process in which the agent is not able to observe states completely, and does not know which state it is in exactly. In a POMDP, the agent infers information about states and represents the information by a *belief*, denoted by b. In a decision step, the agent is in $s \in S$ that it is not able to see, chooses $a \in A$ based on its current belief b, enters $s' \in S$ that it is not able to see either, observes $o \in O$, and infers information about s' by using $P(o|a,s') \in Z$ and $P(s'|s,a) \in T$.

Belief b is defined as

$$b = [b(s_1), b(s_2), ..., b(s_Q)] \tag{2}$$

where $s_i \in S$ $(1 \leq i \leq Q)$ is the ith state in S, Q is the number of states in S, $b(s_i)$ is the probability that the agent is in s_i, and $\sum_{i=1}^{Q} b(s_i) = 1$ [9].

In a POMDP, the policy is $\pi(b)$. In a decision step, it guides the agent to choose an action considering the current belief b to maximize the long term reward.

2.2 State Transition and Belief Update

After the agent takes a in s, the action causes a state transition, and the agent enters s'. The new state s' may or may not be s. Since s' is not completely observable either, the agent updates its belief each time after it takes an action. Figure 1 illustrates state transition and belief update in a decision step. It is assumed that at t, the agent is in $s1$ and has belief b, while at $t+1$, it is in $s2$ and has belief b'.

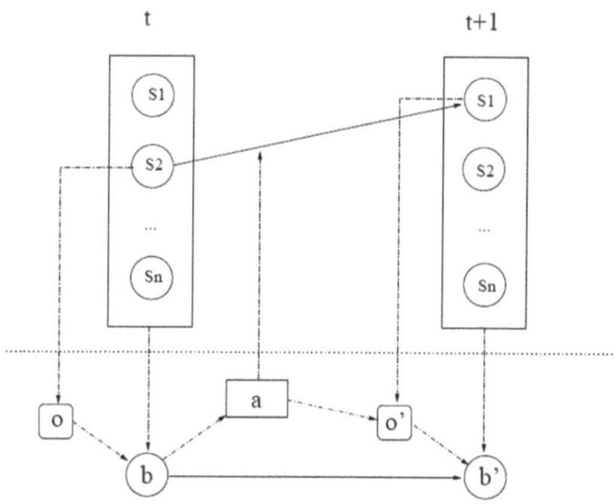

Fig. 1. State transition and belief update in a decision step.

A belief is a set of probabilities (see Eq. (2)). To update a belief, we update each of the probabilities. The following is the formula to calculate element $b'(s')$ in updated belief b':

$$b'(s') = \sum_{s \in S} b(s)P(s'|s,a)P(o|a,s')/P(o|a) \tag{3}$$

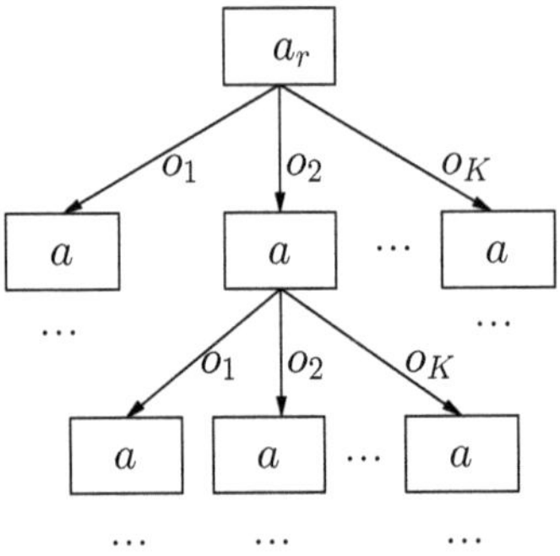

Fig. 2. The general structure of a policy tree (from [9]).

where $P(s'|s,a) \in T$ and $P(o|a,s') \in Z$ are transition probability and observation probability, $P(o|a)$ is the total probability for the agent to observe o after a is taken, calculated as

$$P(o|a) = \sum_{s \in S} b(s) \sum_{s' \in S} P(s'|s,a) P(o|a,s'). \tag{4}$$

$P(o|a)$ is used in Eq. (3) as a normalization.

2.3 POMDP-Solving by Policy Trees

For a given b, an optimal π returns an optimal action. In a POMDP, finding the optimal π is referred to as *solving the POMDP*. For most practical application problems, POMDP-solving is a task of great computational complexity [1,5]. A simplified, less expensive technique for POMDP-solving is to use *policy trees*.

When a technique of policy trees is used, finding the optimal policy is to evaluate a set of policy trees, and identify the optimal tree. In each decision step, the agent finds the optimal tree considering its current belief, and takes the root action of the tree.

In a policy tree, nodes are actions, and edges are observations. The action at the root is called *root action*. An action node has observation edges to actions at the next level. After an action is taken, the next action to take is one of the actions at the next level, depending on what the agent observes. Figure 2 illustrates the general structure of a policy tree, in which a_r is the root action, a is an action in A, and K is the number of all possible observations in O. That is, $K = |O|$, where $|\ |$ is the operator for measuring a magnitude. In the following, we discuss a method for finding the optimal tree.

Each policy tree is associated with a *value function*, which evaluates the long term reward of taking the tree (policy). Let τ be a policy tree. The value function of state s given τ is

$$V^{\tau}(s) = \mathcal{R}(s,a) + \gamma \sum_{s' \in S} P(s'|s,a) \sum_{o \in O} P(o|a,s') V^{\tau(o)}(s') \tag{5}$$

where a is the root action of τ, s' is the next state, i.e. the state that the agent enters into after taking a, γ is a discounting factor ($0 \leq \gamma \leq 1$), o is the observation after a is taken, $\tau(o)$ is the subtree in τ which is connected to the root by the edge of o, and $\mathcal{R}(s,a)$ is the expected immediate reward after a is taken in s [9]. $\mathcal{R}(s,a)$ is calculated as

$$\mathcal{R}(s,a) = \sum_{s' \in S} P(s'|s,a)\mathcal{R}(s,a,s') \tag{6}$$

where $\mathcal{R}(s,a,s')$ is the expected immediate reward after the agent takes a in s and enters s' [9]. The second term on the right hand side of Eq. (5) is the discounted expected value.

From Eqs. (2) and (5), we have the value function of belief b given τ:

$$V^{\tau}(b) = \sum_{s \in S} b(s)V^{\tau}(s). \tag{7}$$

Thus we have $\pi(b)$ returning the optimal policy tree $\hat{\tau}$ for b:

$$\pi(b) = \hat{\tau} = \arg\max_{\tau \in \mathcal{T}} V^{\tau}(b), \tag{8}$$

where $\mathcal{T}$ is the set of trees to evaluate in making the decision [9].

The costs of the method of policy trees depend on the number of trees in $\mathcal{T}$, and the number of nodes in individual trees. The size of a policy tree depends on the number of possible observations and the horizon. When the horizon is H, the number of nodes in a tree is

$$\sum_{t=0}^{H-1} |O|^t = \frac{|O|^H - 1}{|O| - 1}. \tag{9}$$

At each node, the number of possible actions is $|A|$. Therefore, the total number of all possible policy trees is

$$|A|^{\frac{|O|^H - 1}{|O| - 1}} \tag{10}$$

when the horizon is H [9]. Both numbers are exponential.

3 Related Work

Researchers in the fields of ITSs have seen the great potential of the POMDP model in building ITSs. Extensive research has been conducted in applying POMDPs to intelligent tutoring [2–6,10,11]. In the work related to applying the model to ITSs, POMDPs were used to model student states, and to customize and optimize teaching. In a commonly used structure, student states had a boolean attribute for each of the subject contents, actions available to a tutoring agent were various types of teaching techniques, and observations were results of tests given periodically. The goals were to teach as many of the contents in a finite amount of time, or to minimize the time required to learn the entire subject. In the following, we review some work in which policy trees were used for POMDP-solving in ITSs.

Rafferty and co-workers created a POMDP-based system for teaching concepts [5]. A core component of the system was a technique of fast teaching by POMDP planning. The technique was for computing approximate POMDP policies, which selected actions to minimize the expected time for the learner to understand concepts. The researchers framed the problem of optimally selecting teaching actions by using a decision-theoretic approach, and formulated teaching as a POMDP planning problem. In the POMDP, states represented the learners' knowledge, and transitions modeled how teaching actions stochastically changed the learners' knowledge.

For solving the POMDP, the researchers developed a method of forward trees, which are variations of policy trees. A forward tree is constructed by interleaving branching on actions and observations. For the current belief, a forward trees was constructed to estimate the value of each pedagogical action, and the best action was chosen. The learner's response, plus the action chosen, was used to update the belief, and then a new forward search tree was constructed for selecting a new action for the updated belief. The cost of searching the full tree is exponential in the task horizon, and requires an $O(|S|^2)$ set of operations at each node. To reduce the number of nodes to search through, the researchers restricted the tree by sampling only a few actions, and limited the horizon to control the depth of the tree.

In the work reported in [8], an experimental ITS was developed for teaching concepts in computer science. A POMDP was used in the system to model processes of intelligent tutoring. In the POMDP, states, actions, and observations modeled student knowledge states, system tutoring actions, and student actions, respectively. A method of policy trees was proposed for POMDP-solving. In the method, policy trees were created and stored in a tree database. To choose an optimal action to respond to a given student query, the agent searched the database and evaluated a set of trees. For reducing the costs in making a decision, techniques were developed to minimize the tree sizes and decrease the number of trees to evaluate. A major disadvantage of the proposed policy tree method was its space complexity.

The techniques of policy trees for improving POMDP-solving have made good progress towards building practical POMDP-based ITSs. However, they were still too costly to use. For example, as the authors of [5] concluded, computational challenges existed in their technique of forward trees, despite sampling only a fraction of possible actions and using short horizons. Also, how to sample actions and how to shorten a horizon were challenging problems. Computational complexity has been a bottleneck in applying the POMDP model to intelligent tutoring.

4 The New Technique and Testing Bed

We develop new techniques to address the problems of computational complexity in applying the method of policy trees in a POMDP-based ITS. In the following sections, we will discuss a space efficient technique. The discussion is in the context of an experimental ITS, which we developed for testing our techniques. The instructional subject is software basics. The ITS teaches concepts in the subject. It tutors a student at a time, interactively, on a turn-by-turn base. Typically, in a tutoring step, the student asks a question about a concept, and the system takes a teaching action that it believes to be the optimal according to the student's current knowledge state.

A POMDP helps the ITS choose optimal teaching actions. We cast the ITS on to the POMDP, by using POMDP states to represent student knowledge states, and actions to represent system tutoring actions. We treat student actions (asking questions, accepting answers, etc) as observations. For POMDP-solving, that is, for choosing optimal actions, we use a technique of policy trees.

In the technique, policy trees are grouped and dynamically created. With this technique, sizes of policy trees are minimized, and the agent evaluates a small set of trees when making a decision. Also, trees in the set are dynamically created. Evaluating a small set of trees helps improve time efficiency, and dynamically creating the tree set helps improve space efficiency. Minimizing tree sizes may improve both time and space efficiencies.

5 State Space Partitioning

To have small tree sets, we partition the state space into subspace, and then group trees in each subspace into tree sets. Before discussing the tree grouping algorithm, we introduce our method for state space partitioning.

We define states in terms of concepts in the instructional subject. In software basics, concepts include *program*, *instruction*, *algorithm*, and many others. We associate each state with a *state formula*, which is of the form:

$$(\mathcal{C}_1 \wedge \mathcal{C}_2 \wedge \mathcal{C}_3 \wedge ... \wedge \mathcal{C}_N), \tag{11}$$

where $\mathcal{C}_i$ is the variable for the ith concept C_i, taking a value $\surd C_i$ or $\neg C_i$ $(1 \leq i \leq N)$, and N is the number of concepts in the subject [9]. We use $\surd C_i$ to represent that the student understands C_i, and $\neg C_i$ to represent that the student does not. A state formula is a representation of a student knowledge state. For example, formula $(\surd C_1 \wedge \surd C_2 \wedge \neg C_3 \wedge ...)$ is a representation of the state in which the student understands C_1 and C_2, but not C_3, ... States thus defined have Markov property.

When there are N concepts in an instructional subject, the number of state formulas is 2^N. This implies that the number of possible states is 2^N. As can be seen in Eq. (5), the cost for evaluating a value function is proportional to the size of state space. To reduce the cost, we partition the state space into smaller subspaces. The partitioning technique is based on prerequisite relationships between concepts.

Prerequisite relationships are pedagogical orders of concepts. A concept may have zero or more prerequisites, and a concept may serve as a prerequisite of zero or more concepts. For example, in mathematics, *derivative* has prerequisites

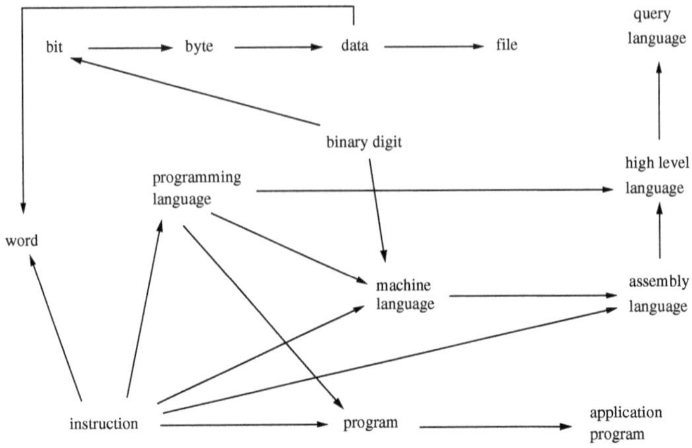

Fig. 3. A directed acyclic graph (DAG) of 14 concepts and their prerequisite relationships. An edge represents "is a direct prerequisite of".

function, *limit* and so on, and *function* is a prerequisite of *derivative*, *integral*, and so on. To understand a concept well, a student should understand all its prerequisites first. In this paper, when a concept is a prerequisite of another, we call the latter a *successor* of the former. For a set of concepts, the prerequisite relationships can be represented by a directed acyclic graph (DAG). Figure 3 illustrates a DAG of 14 concepts in software basics and their prerequisite relationships. In the DAG, an edge represents "is a direct prerequisite of". For example, the edge from *bit* to *byte* represents that *bit* is a prerequisite of *byte*.

Figure 4 shows our algorithm for space partitioning. In the first step of the algorithm, we subdivide concepts such that those having prerequisite relationships are in the same group. Some very "basic" concepts may be in two or more groups. In the second step, for each group, we create a state subspace by using concepts in the group to define states, in the way just discussed. In this step, we first eliminate invalid formulas. By a *invalid formula*, we mean a formula representing that the student understands a concept but does not understand one or more prerequisites of the concept. For details of the partitioning technique, please see [7]. After space partitioning, we create policy trees for each subspace. In a tree, the nodes and edges concern concepts in the subspace only, instead of all the concepts.

This partitioning method is based on our observation that in a window in a tutoring process, student questions likely concern concepts that have prerequisite relationships with each other. The observation suggests that we could localize the computing for choosing an optimal teaching action within a smaller state subspace defined by concepts having prerequisite relationships.

The total number of states in the subspaces are much smaller than the number of states in the space defined by using all the concepts. In addition, the number and sizes of policy trees in subspaces are much smaller because the sets

```
ALGORITHM PartitioningSpace (C)
    Input:  C is an array of concepts

    Create a DAG for the concepts in C
    Represent the DAG by an adjacency matrix
    Identify direct and indirect prerequisites for each concept
       by using the matrix
    Group concepts based on prerequisite relationships

    for each concept group
       Generate all the possible state formulas
       Eliminate invalid state formulas
       Define states by using the valid state formulas
```

Fig. 4. Algorithm for partitioning state space.

of actions and observations are smaller, which determine the numbers of nodes and edges in policy trees.

6 Policy Tree Grouping

As discussed, the cost for making a decision depends on the number of trees to evaluate, that is, the size of $\mathcal{T}$ in Eq. (8). For lower costs, we group the trees in each subspace into small tree sets. When choosing an optimal teaching action, the agent evaluates trees in a single set. For discussing the grouping algorithm, we first define *optimal action* and *tutoring session.*

In science and mathematics subjects, many concepts have prerequisites. When the student wants to learn a concept, the system should decide whether it would start with teaching a prerequisite for the student to make up some required knowledge, and, if so, which one to teach. The *optimal* action is to teach the concept that the student needs to make up in order to understand the originally asked concept, and that the student can learn it without making up other concepts.

A *tutoring session* is a sequence of interleaved student and system actions, that is, questions and answers, starting with a question about a concept, possibly followed by answers and questions concerning the concept and its prerequisites, and ending with a student action accepting the answer to the original question. If, before the acceptance action, the student asks a concept that has no prerequisite relationship with the concept originally asked, we consider that a new tutoring session starts.

We classify questions in a session into the *original question* and *current questions.* The original question starts the session, concerning the concept the student originally wants to learn. We denote the original question by $(?C^o)$, where C^o is the concept concerned in the original question and the superscript o stands for "original". A current question is the question to be answered by the agent at a point in the session, usually for the student to make up some knowledge. A current question may be asked by the student, or made by the agent. We denote a current question by $(?C^c)$, where C^c is the concept concerned in the current question, and the superscript c stands for "current". Concept C^c is in $(\wp_{C^o} \cup C^o)$, where $\wp_{C^o}$ is the set of all the direct and indirect prerequisites of C^o.

In the following, we discuss an example, which involves concepts *database* and *file*. We assume that *file* is a prerequisite of *database*. At a point in a tutoring process, the student asks question "What is a database?" If *database* has no prerequisite relationship with the concepts asked/taught right before the question, we consider the question starts a new tutoring session, and it is the original question of the session. If the agent believes that the student already understands all the prerequisites of *database*, and answers the question directly, the question is also the current question when the agent answers it. If the agent teaches *database* as "A database is a collection of interrelated files", and then the student asks question "But what is a file?", this system action of teaching *database* is not an optimal because the student needs to make up a prerequisite. At this point the question about *file* is the current question. If the agent answers the question about *file* and the student has no difficulty to understand *file*, the action of teaching *file* is optimal.

Now we consider the grouping of trees. When the agent has current question $(?C^c)$ to answer, it needs to choose an optimal action. The optimal action may be to teach C^c or teach one of the prerequisites of C^c, depending on the agent's belief about the student's knowledge state. Recall that in a tutoring step, the agent evaluates a set of trees and chooses the root action of the tree that has the highest value. The set of trees to evaluate to answer $(?C^c)$ should include trees in which root actions are to teach C^c or prerequisites of C^c. Since the ultimate goal to answer $(?C^c)$ is to answer the original question $(?C^o)$, actions to answer $(?C^o)$ should be included in the trees in the set.

Based on the above consideration, we have our grouping strategy: for each possible pair of $(?C^o)$ and $(?C^c)$, we create tree set $\mathcal{T}_{C^c}^{C^o}$. In a tutoring session with original question $(?C^o)$, to choose an optimal action to answer current question $(?C^c)$, the agent evaluates trees in $\mathcal{T}_{C^c}^{C^o}$. Since $\mathcal{T}_{C^c}^{C^o}$ is normally much smaller than the set of all the possible trees, the cost for choosing an optimal tree can be significantly reduced. The tree structure will be discussed in the next section.

7 Dynamic Creation of Policy Trees

7.1 Structure of the Policy Trees

In the following, we denote the system action for teaching concept C by $(!C)$, and denote a student acceptance action by (Θ). An acceptance action can be something like "I understand", and "I see".

As just discussed, in a state subspace, for each possible pair of original and current questions, denoted by $(?C^o)$ and $(?C^c)$, we create tree set $\mathcal{T}_{C^c}^{C^o}$. The optimal action to answer current question $(?C^c)$ may be to teach C^c, or to teach one of the prerequisites of C^c. Therefore, the trees in $\mathcal{T}_{C^c}^{C^o}$ have root actions $(!C)$

where $C \in (\wp_{C^c} \cup C^c)$. For each $C \in (\wp_{C^c} \cup C^c)$, we have a tree in $\mathcal{T}_{C^c}^{C^o}$, of which the root is $(!C)$. We denote a tree in $\mathcal{T}_{C^c}^{C^o}$ with root action $(!C)$ by $\mathcal{T}_{C^c}^{C^o}.\tau_C$.

Now we discuss leaf nodes and paths in a tree. In a tutoring session started by $(?C^o)$, the ultimate goal of the agent is to teach C^o. In a policy tree in $\mathcal{T}_{C^c}^{C^o}$, any leaf node must be a system action to terminate the session, after a student acceptance action that accepts $(!C^o)$. A path in the tree includes possible questions and answers concerning prerequisites of C^o. A policy tree with root $(!C)$ includes all the possible paths starting with $(!C)$ and ending with a terminating action. Since possible student questions in the session concern concepts in $(\wp_{C^o} \cup C^o)$, we limit the observation set O to questions concerning concepts in $(\wp_{C^o} \cup C^o)$ only. (Student actions are treated as observations.)

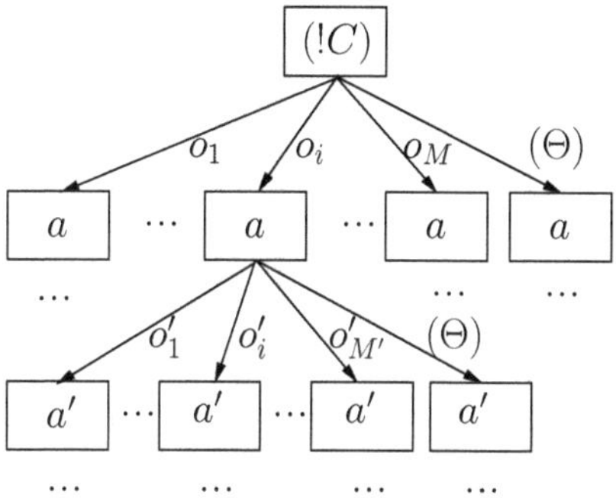

Fig. 5. The general structure of policy tree $\mathcal{T}_{C^c}^{C^o}.\tau_C$ (from [9]).

Figure 5 illustrates the general structure of policy tree $\mathcal{T}_{C^c}^{C^o}.\tau_C$. The root of $\mathcal{T}_{C^c}^{C^o}.\tau_C$ is $(!C)$, i.e. an action for teaching $C \in (\wp_{C^c} \cup C^c)$. When C has M prerequisites C_1, ... C_M, the root has $M+1$ children. The observations $o_1, ..., o_i, ..., o_M$ are student actions $(?C_1), ..., (?C_i), ..., (?C_M)$. The first M children are sub-trees connected by the observation edges. Actions at the sub-tree roots are in the set of $(!C_1), ..., (!C_M)$. Note that edge o_i $(1 \leq i \leq M)$ connects to one of them. The last edge is labeled with (Θ), and the last child is a sub-tree rooted by $(!C^u)$, where C^u is one of the direct *successors* of C. When C has more than one direct successor, C^u is the one on the path from C^o to C. The semantics of such root-children structure is that after $(!C)$, if the student accepts $(!C)$, teach the direct successor C^u, if the student asks about a prerequisite of C, teach a prerequisite. The prerequisite to teach is dynamically selected. The selection will be discussed in the next subsection.

In a policy tree, each sub-tree is structured in the same way, for example the sub-tree connected by the edge of o_i in Fig. 5. The root has edges for prerequisites of the concept in the root action and an acceptance edge, illustrated by o'_1, ..., o'_i, ..., $o'_{M'}$ and (Θ), where M' is the number of prerequisites of the concept in the root action. However, if a prerequisite has been taught in the path from the tree root, no edge is created for it. If a root action is $(!C^o)$ for answering the original question, its acceptance edge connects to an action for terminating the session.

7.2 Creation of the Policy Trees

When the student asks question $(?C^o)$ starting a new tutoring session, the agent goes to the subspace that contains C^o and all the prerequisites of C^o. To answer current question $(?C^c)$ in the session, it evaluates all the trees in tree set $\mathcal{T}_{C^c}^{C^o}$. We have developed a new technique to dynamically create the tree set right before it is evaluated. This technique has better space efficiency than the method of storing a tree database.

As discussed in the previous subsection, root actions in trees in $\mathcal{T}_{C^c}^{C^o}$ teach concepts in $(\wp_{C^c} \cup C^c)$. In the general structure of a policy tree (illustrated in Fig. 2), each edge (observation) connects to all the possible actions (in different trees). With this structure, for each $C \in (\wp_{C^c} \cup C^c)$ the number of trees with root action $(!C)$ is exponential in the number of possible observations (see Eq. (10)). That is, the number of trees having the same root action is exponential.

To reduce the cost for evaluating policy trees, in $\mathcal{T}_{C^c}^{C^o}$ we create only one tree for each $C \in (\wp_{C^c} \cup C^c)$, and use it to approximate an exponential number of trees. To have only one tree for each $C \in (\wp_{C^c} \cup C^c)$, we connect each edge to one action, instead of all the possible actions. For example, when creating the tree in Fig. 5, we select one action for edge o_1, one action for o_2, ... one action for o'_1, one action for o'_2, and so on.

In experiments, we discovered that in a state only a very small number of actions have large enough chances to be taken. Also, in computing Eq. (5) for evaluating trees, most actions contribute little to tree values. This suggests that we would not lose much information when ignoring the actions that have little chance to be taken and contribute little. In the following, using the tree in Fig. 6 we discuss the selection of one action for each edge.

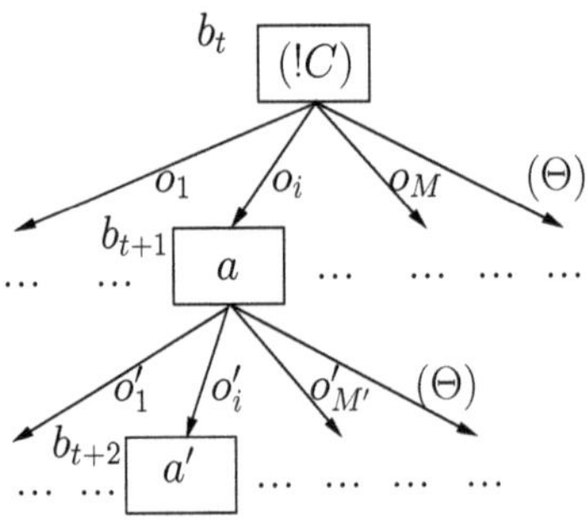

Fig. 6. Action selection in the general structure of policy tree $\mathcal{T}_{C^c}^{C^o}.\tau_C$ (from [9]).

Assume at time step t, the agent has belief b_t, and will evaluate tree set $\mathcal{T}_{C^c}^{C^o}$, and assume the tree in Fig. 6 is $\mathcal{T}_{C^c}^{C^o}.\tau_C$. In creating the tree, we select $(!C)$ as the root, which is a possible action to take at t, and then select an action for each edge based on an updated belief at the next level, and so on. For example, we need to select action a for edge o_i based the updated belief b_{t+1}, select a' for o'_i based on the updated b_{t+2}, and so on [9].

Let b_{t+1} be

$$b_{t+1} = [b_{t+1}(s_1), b_{t+1}(s_2), ..., b_{t+1}(s_Q)]. \tag{12}$$

In b_{t+1} we can find the j such that $b_{t+1}(s_j) \geq b_{t+1}(s_k)$ for all the $k \neq j$ $(1 \leq j, k \leq Q)$. Assume the state formula of s_j is

$$(\surd C_1 \surd C_2 ... \surd C_{l-1} \neg C_l ... \neg C_{N'}). \tag{13}$$

The belief and state formula indicate that most likely the student does not understand C_l, but understands all of its prerequisites. Considering a single step, we select $(!C_l)$ as an optimal action at b_{t+1}. Thus we select $(!C_l)$ as a, and connect the edge of o_i to it. Figure 7 summarizes the algorithm for creating a policy tree.

```
ALGORITHM CreateTree (a, b)
    Input: a is action teaching concept c
           b is the current belief
    Return: subtree t rooted at a

    Create subtree t
    Create root for a
    for each prerequisite p of c
        if p has not been taught
            Create an edge for o = (?p)
            Choose action a' for the edge
            Calculate updated belief b' from a, b, o
            Connect the edge with CreateTree(a', b')
    Create an edge for acceptance action
    if c is the concept in original question
        Connect the edge with an action to terminate the session
    else
        a' is to teach the successor of c
        Calculate updated belief b' from a, b, o
        Connect the edge with CreateTree(a', b')
    return t
```

Fig. 7. Algorithm for tree creation.

7.3 Choosing Optimal Action and New Current Question

As has been discussed, when the original question is $(?C^o)$ and the agent needs to answer the current question $(?C^c)$, it evaluates all the policy trees in $\mathcal{T}_{C^c}^{C^o}$ based on its current belief, and finds the tree that has the highest value (optimal tree). When choosing the optimal policy tree by using Eq. (8), we substitute $\mathcal{T}$ with $\mathcal{T}_{C^c}^{C^o}$.

A policy tree is not a tutoring plan that the agent will follow in the future. It is the strategy for the current step: After choosing the optimal tree, the agent takes the root action. Then it will terminate the session, or have a new current question, depending on the student action (observation):

1. If the student action is (Θ), and the (Θ) edge connects to a terminating action in the tree, the agent terminates the tutoring session;
2. If the student action is (Θ), and the (Θ) connects to $(!C)$ where C is a direct successor of the concept in the root action, the agent considers $(?C)$ as the new current question;
3. If the student action is $(?C)$, where $C \in (\wp_{C^c} \cup C^c)$, the agent considers $(?C)$ as the new current question.

In the second case above, the agent will teach C without further computing. In the third case, the agent chooses an optimal action in the same way, i.e. by evaluating a set of policy trees and finding the tree having the highest value.

8 Experimental Results and Discussion

8.1 Evaluating Adaptive Teaching

In this section, we present two sets of experimental results. The first set includes the results of evaluating adaptive teaching of the system, and the second set includes the results of testing the technique for dynamic creation of trees. The data set used in the experiments included 90 concepts in software basics. Each concept had zero to five prerequisites.

We used a two-sample t-test method to evaluate the system performance in adaptive teaching. The test method was the *independent-samples t-test.* 30 students participated in the experiment. They were adults who knew how to use word processors, Web browsers, etc., but had no formal training in computing. The students were randomly divided into two equal size groups. Group 1 studied with the ITS with the POMDP turned off, and Group 2 studied with the POMDP turned on. Each student studied with the ITS for about 45 min. The student asked questions about concepts in the subject, and ITS taught the concepts. The performance parameter was *rejection rate*, which was the ratio of the number of system actions rejected by a student to the total number of system actions for teaching the student.

For each student, we calculated a rejection rate. For the two groups, we calculated mean rejection rates $\bar{X}_1$ and $\bar{X}_2$. The two sample means were used to represent population means μ_1 and μ_2. The alternative and null hypotheses are:

$$H_a : \mu_1 - \mu_2 \neq 0, \qquad H_0 : \mu_1 - \mu_2 = 0$$

The means and variances calculated for the two groups are listed in Table 1. In the experiment, n_1=15 and n_2=15, thus the degree of freedom is $(15-1)+(15-1) = 28$. With alpha at 0.05, the two-tailed t_{crit} is 2.0484 and we calculated $t_{obt} = +8.6690$. Since the t_{obt} is far beyond the non-reject region defined by $t_{crit} = 2.0484$, we could reject H_0 and accept H_a. The analysis suggested that the POMDP could significantly reduce the rejection rate. This implies that the POMDP helped the system significantly improve adaptive teaching.

Table 1. Number of students, mean and estimated variance of each group (from [9]).

	Group 1	Group 2
Number of students	$n_1 = 15$	$n_2 = 15$
Sample mean	$\bar{X}_1 = 0.5966$	$\bar{X}_2 = 0.2284$
Estimated variance	$s_1^2 = 0.0158$	$s_2^2 = 0.0113$

8.2 Evaluating Space Efficiency

We tested the dynamic tree creation technique with the same data set of software basics, on a desktop computer with an Intel Core i5 3.2 GHz 64 bit processor and 16 GB RAM. For comparison, we also tested a static tree creation technique. Both the static and dynamic tree creation techniques shared the same algorithms for partitioning state space and grouping trees. The difference is that in the static technique all the tree sets were created and stored in a database before the ITS started teaching students, while in the dynamic technique a tree set was created right before it was evaluated. In both techniques, the state space was subdivided into six subspaces. The largest subspace included 27 concepts, 4,970 valid states, 170 tree sets, and 688 trees.

Table 2. Comparison between static and dynamic tree creation methods (from [9]).

	Static creation	Dynamic creation
Permanent pace usage	1.078 GB	0
Max space usage	1.078 GB	215.68 MB
Database creation time	36,888 ms	
Max tree creation time		158 ms
Belief update time	525 ms	518 ms
Max decision time	147 ms	152 ms
Max response time	669 ms	828 ms

In Table 2 we list results of the two techniques. The space usage includes that for the tree database or tree sets only. The maximum tree creation time was for creating the largest tree set, of which the size was 215.68MB. The maximum decision time was for evaluating trees in the largest tree set and choosing the optimal tree. Response time included the time for calculating a new belief, and evaluating a tree set to choose an optimal tree. The maximum response time was recorded when the largest tree set was evaluated.

The experimental results indicated that the dynamic tree creation technique was effective for building space-efficient ITSs. Its space usage was a small fraction of that of a static tree creation technique. In terms of time efficiency, the dynamic technique was comparable to a static technique. Since the time for dynamically creating a tree set is short, the total response time was only slightly longer. As can be seen in Table 2, the maximum response time with dynamic tree creation was less than a second. For a tutoring system, such response time could be considered acceptable. Time efficiency can be improved with a cache of tree sets.

9 Conclusion

POMDP-solving is a key operation for choosing optimal teaching actions in an ITS based on the POMDP model. Solving a POMDP in tutoring a practical subject is intractable in both computing time and space usage, even when the technique of policy trees is employed, which is considered the most efficient currently. The research reported in this paper is aimed at addressing the space complexity problem. It has obtained encouraging initial results: The space usage has been significantly reduced while response time remains acceptable. The techniques of dynamic tree creation and tree grouping contribute to the achievement. With dynamic tree creation, no space is required to store a tree database. The technique of tree grouping helps improve time efficiency. The techniques enable ITSs to teach "practical" subjects. They are especially useful for building ITSs on handheld devices, which usually have limited storage spaces and computing power.

Acknowledgements. This research is supported by the Natural Sciences and Engineering Research Council of Canada (NSERC).

References

1. Carlin, A., Zilberstein, S.: Observation compression in DEC-POMDP policy trees. In: Proceedings of the 7th International Joint Conference on Autonomous Agents and Multi-agent Systems, pp. 31–45 (2008)
2. Cassandra, A.: A survey of POMDP applications. In: Working Notes of AAAI 1998 Fall Symposium on Planning with Partially Observable Markov Decision Process, pp. 17–24 (1998)
3. Chinaei, H.R., Chaib-draa, B., Lamontagne, L.: Learning observation models for dialogue POMDPs. In: Kosseim, L., Inkpen, D. (eds.) AI 2012. LNCS (LNAI), vol. 7310, pp. 280–286. Springer, Heidelberg (2012). https://doi.org/10.1007/978-3-642-30353-1_24
4. Folsom-Kovarik, J.T., Sukthankar, G., Schatz, S.: Tractable POMDP representations for intelligent tutoring systems. ACM Trans. Intell. Syst. Technol. (TIST) **4**(2), 29 (2013). Special section on agent communication, trust in multiagent systems, intelligent tutoring and coaching systems archive

5. Rafferty, A.N., Brunskill, E., Griffiths, T.L., Shafto, P.: Faster teaching by POMDP planning. In: Biswas, G., Bull, S., Kay, J., Mitrovic, A. (eds.) AIED 2011. LNCS (LNAI), vol. 6738, pp. 280–287. Springer, Heidelberg (2011). https://doi.org/10.1007/978-3-642-21869-9_37
6. Theocharous, G., Beckwith, R., Butko, N., Philipose, M.: Tractable POMDP planning algorithms for optimal teaching in SPAIS. In: IJCAI PAIR Workshop (2009)
7. Wang, F.: Handling exponential state space in a POMDP-based intelligent tutoring system. In: Proceedings of 6th International Conference on E-Service and Knowledge Management (IIAI ESKM 2015), pp. 67–72 (2015)
8. Wang, F.: A new technique of policy trees for building a POMDP based intelligent tutoring system. In: Proceedings of The 8th International Conference on Computer Supported Education (CSEDU 2016), pp. 85–93 (2016)
9. Wang, F.: Dynamical creation of policy trees for a POMDP-based intelligent tutoring system. In: Proceedings of The 10th International Conference on Computer Supported Education (CSEDU 2018), pp. 137–144 (2018)
10. Williams, J.D., Poupart, P., Young, S.: Factored partially observable Markov decision processes for dialogue management. In: Proceedings of Knowledge and Reasoning in Practical Dialogue Systems (2005)
11. Williams, J.D., Young, S.: Partially observable Markov decision processes for spoken dialog systems. Comput. Speech Lang. **21**, 393–422 (2007)
12. Woolf, B.P.: Building Intelligent Interactive Tutors. Morgan Kaufmann Publishers, Burlington (2009)

A Learning Analytics Dashboard to Analyse Learning Activities in Interpreter Training Courses

Davide Taibi[1], Francesca Bianchi[2], Philipp Kemkes[3], and Ivana Marenzi[3](✉)

[1] Institute for Educational Technology, National Research Council of Italy, Palermo, Italy
davide.taibi@itd.cnr.it
[2] University of Salento, Lecce, Italy
francesca.bianchi@unisalento.it
[3] L3S Research Center, Hannover, Germany
{kemkes,marenzi}@L3S.de

Abstract. Learning analytics dashboards constitute an effective tool for monitoring learning activities that take place in online learning environments. Thanks to dashboards, teachers can promptly detect low levels of student engagement in given tasks, incorrect usage of a system, and other types of pedagogically relevant information, which helps them to better support students in achieving their learning objectives. This study describes the integration of a dashboard in an online learning system. The system includes a tool that guides students in the creation of highly informative bilingual glossaries, a service that traces student searches on the web for reference material, and a service that tracks student interactions with the glossary. The data thus collected are selectively displayed in the newly developed dashboard. The dashboard was specifically designed to allow teachers to monitor the students' approaches to glossary building and to provide individual remedial feedback, if necessary. It was also intended to spur students to keep on a par with the rest of the class, by seeing their status compared to the rest of the class. The system was tested with two groups of university students specializing in interpreting, and two different teachers. The results of the experiments suggest that this integrated system manages to achieve its goals and provides students and teachers of interpreting with an innovative online tool that concretely fosters and supports vocabulary building.

Keywords: Learning analytics dashboard · Interpreting · Tracking systems

1 Introduction

In interpreter training, the creation of personal glossaries constitutes a relevant learning activity to develop students' abilities related not only to terminology acquisition [1], but also to content acquisition in a specific knowledge domain [2]. Both abilities are fundamental requirements for interpreters (e.g. [3, 4]).

B. M. McLaren et al. (Eds.): CSEDU 2018, CCIS 1022, pp. 268–286, 2019.
https://doi.org/10.1007/978-3-030-21151-6_14

Moreover, the creation of personal glossaries is a learning activity that involves a wide range of cognitive, linguistic and practical skills (e.g. [5, 6]) and it is a primary and largely used method for acquiring technical vocabulary.

As a complex process, consisting of several steps, the creation of a glossary can benefit from the use of software programs. The most widely used applications for creating glossaries include programs specifically developed by or for interpreters and translators, such as Interplex[1], Lookup[2], and SDL Multiterm[3], as well as components of the MS Office suite, such MS Word or MS Excel (e.g. [7, 8]). However, these tools are not integrated within online learning environments and do not include learning analytics dashboards for teachers and/or students. In other words, they lack features that monitor the overall learning process and that could make the learning activity more effective.

In this paper, we present a learning analytics dashboard that allows teachers to analyse the way students populate a bilingual glossary and to monitor their progress in such a task. The dashboard has been integrated in the LearnWeb environment, an online learning platform that supports competence development through specifically designed (autonomous as well as collaborative) learning tasks. The LearnWeb environment keeps track of the students' activities in the glossary and of their searches on the Web for reference material. This integrated system aims to support students in the creation of glossaries, and teachers in monitoring the students' approaches to this particular task and in providing individual remedial feedback, if necessary.

The paper is organized as follows: Sect. 2 introduces the dashboard, which was specifically designed to analyse learning activities involved in the creation of personal glossaries, and illustrates the theoretical considerations that guided its creation; Sect. 3 describes the new functionalities that were developed in the LearnWeb environment to support the creation of the glossaries, including a description of the dashboard's interface; Sect. 4 reports on the testing of the glossary tool and dashboard with two groups of university students specializing in interpreting and focuses on advantages and limitations of the current version of the system; finally, Sect. 5 draws conclusions based on the current experimentations, and outlines perspectives for future research.

2 Designing a Learning Analytics Dashboard to Support Interpreter's Training

2.1 Dashboard Design

Dashboards are used in several fields to support decision-making processes and, with the development of Learning Analytics approaches, they have been adopted even in educational contexts. Dashboards are effectively used not only by teachers – who appreciate the possibility to monitor key indicators of students engagement in visual

[1] http://www.fourwillows.com/interplex.html.

[2] http://www.traductorado.edu.ar/lookup/.

[3] http://www.sdl.com/it/solution/language/terminology-management/multiterm/.

ways – but also by students – who gain greater awareness of their own learning achievements [9].

In a recent paper, Bodily and Verbert [10] perform a comprehensive literature review of student-facing learning analytics reporting systems, including dashboards. The papers reviewed include not only articles describing the functionalities of this type of systems and their experimentations, but also papers describing their design and development processes. An important remark emerges from this analysis: besides describing practical uses of given dashboards, papers should also describe their design and development phases, as these play a crucial role in Learning Analytics. In particular, when designing and developing a dashboard, it is important to:

- identify the key indicators which will be monitored through the dashboard;
- identify the visual elements that should be included into the dashboard for a better visualization of results;
- identify the types of indicators and alert mechanisms that should be implemented into the charts for the different users (learners, teachers).

In the current project, we started designing the dashboard by identifying the glossary activities to monitor (key indicators). The identification of key indicators is strictly related to the learning activities the students are involved in. For example, general data related to platform access and time spent on specific online activities are useful indicators to detect students' participation, but they are not sufficient to provide information about the effectiveness of the learning experience. To this aim, it is extremely important that developers engage with domain experts to jointly identify which activities, in the online system, to trace and which types of measure to report to teachers and, selectively, to students. From our experience, quantitative measures are not always the most suitable option, especially when it comes to the identification of learning achievements. For instance, in our scenario, when populating a glossary, the student has to provide a description of the term s/he is including. In this case, quantitative measures such as the number of terms described or the length of the descriptions do not reveal anything about the quality of the description. Moreover, evaluating the description using automatic procedures is a very complicated task. In cases like this, a dashboard should give teachers the possibility to monitor the students' activities and directly access those elements that allow them to assess the students' learning results.

While designing our dashboard, we made an effort to identify key indicators and visual elements that would really help teachers to monitor salient aspects of the learning processes involved in glossary creation.

Specifically, we decided to divide the dashboard into three main parts:

1. General activities, a section where the teacher would find general information about the students' interactions with the system.
2. Activities on the glossary, a section monitoring specific activities related to the creation of a personal glossary.
3. Secondary activities on the glossary, a section presenting student interactions with the web while populating a glossary with information.

The first part is meant to monitor students' general involvement with the system by detecting activity and inactivity periods. This section aims to help teachers to identify those students who face issues in using the system.

The second part is designed to monitor the student's ability to create and populate a glossary. Here, the dashboard provides information about whether, to what extent, and how the student completed the compulsory and the optional fields, by offering summary and percentage data of the number and types of fields filled in, but also a list of the textual data the student entered in the *description* field. In this case, the evaluation of the quality of the description with respect to the objectives established by the teachers requires manual intervention.

The third part is used to monitor the student's ability to search the Web for information. This section is extremely useful to identify the preferred sources of reference used by students. The view reported in this part of the dashboard can be used to check correspondence between the sources declared by a student in the Source field and the web sites s/he actually visited.

The next section illustrates the tracking system and the data collected.

2.2 Tracking Data for the Dashboard: The Logs and the Proxy

To capture learners' activities, both direct and indirect observation methodologies can be adopted. The latter, which include questionnaires, are mostly based on self-evaluation, and, though suitable to measure the perception of the students about the topic under investigation, may not reflect the actual work done by the learners. For this reason, direct observations, such as behavioural observations, are increasingly captured on a large scale.

When students interact with online systems, direct observations can be collected on remote servers by logging their interactions with the given applications, systems, and services [11]. Many studies have already used log data to analyse learning activities [12–14]. Dumais et al. provide a comprehensive overview of behavioural log data and analysis in the Human and Computer Interaction filed [15].

In particular, they point out that "an important characteristic of log data is that it captures actual user behaviour and not recalled behaviours or subjective impressions of interactions".

In our project, for each section of the dashboard a specific set of indicators was defined. Each indicator is related to student interactions with specific functionalities of the system.

Table 1 lists the indicators that provide a general overview of the activities undertaken by students interacting with the system.

Three types of interactions were selected, in order to detect: (i) interactions with the system (such as login/logout activities), (ii) interactions with the glossary tool and interface (e.g. creating a new term, deleting an existing term, adding new descriptions, and so on), (iii) interactions with the web for search purposes (all the web searches performed by students).

The indicators chosen to monitor the students' activities on the glossary are reported in Table 2. Our Glossary tool requires students to constantly add new entries to the glossary. Each entry contains two term pairs: the Italian term and its translation

Table 1. Indicators used to detect general interactions with the system.

Indicator	Description
System_interactions	Total number of interactions with the system
Glossary_interactions	Number of interactions with the system, considering only the activities connected to the Glossary
Search_interactions	Number of interactions with the system, considering only the activities connected to Web Searches

into English. Moreover, each term is accompanied by a set of compulsory and optional attributes. In particular, students have to specify the topic and subtopic to which the term pair belongs. These inform a classification for the entries added. The students also have to provide a short textual definition of the defined concept. Optionally, they can also fill in the following fields: Pronunciation; Acronym; Phraseology; Uses; and Sources. The Pronunciation field accepts any type of text including IPA (International Phonetic Alphabet) symbols. In the phraseology field students can enter collocations or any other additional information, such as part-of-speech or links to images. The Uses field specifies the linguistic register of the term (e.g. colloquial, technical, etc.). Finally, the Source field is used to specify the main source of information used to fill in the glossary.

Table 2. Indicators used to detect interactions with the glossary tool and interface.

Indicator	Description
Total_terms	Number of terms inserted
Total_concepts	Number of concepts (i.e. descriptions) inserted
Pronunciation_field	Number and percentage of items for which the Pronunciation field was filled in
Acronym_field	Number and percentage of items for which the Acronym field was filled in
Phraseology_field	Number and percentage of items for which the Phraseology field was filled in
Uses_field	Number and percentage of items for which the Uses field was filled in
Source_field	Number and percentage of items for which the Source field was filled in

The third section of the glossary aims to intercept the Web searches done by the students to find information for their glossary. The indicators used in this section are listed in Table 3. Most online learning environments (e.g. Moodle or WebCT) utilize only inbuilt logging facilities. But many language-learning tasks require students to search the Web for information, thus working outside the tool used during the course. These external actions cannot be logged by course management systems such as Moodle. In [16] the Weblog Analysis Tool (WAT) is used to analyse at activity level the log file data of learners' interactions collected within a Web-based learning environment (a courseware website), in order to gain information about the tasks that the learners had engaged in and to determine the achievement of educational objectives.

Table 3. Indicators used to detect interactions with the Web.

Indicator	Description
Used_sources	Percentage of sources used by students
Proxy_list	Proxy source list

The study by Perez-Paredes et al. [17] goes beyond this and uses the log files of a proxy server to analyse which websites students visited to fulfil their task. But this requires a controlled environment, like a classroom, where the course manager can fully control Internet access or has the privilege to install logging software on the students' computers. Other studies have used screen-capturing software like Camtasia or Adobe Connect to record students' learning activities [18]. But these recordings have to be analysed manually; thus the number of subjects is limited by the number of evaluators. Such a method can also be considered more obtrusive than server-side logging.

In the current system, we have developed a novel tracking framework that allows researchers to track all the pages a student views during a learning session without requiring changes on the student's computer. The system tracks also external websites, such as Wikipedia.org or Google.com. Furthermore, it is not limited to classroom use, so students can access it from home and use online resources as they normally would. This makes our system very unobtrusive compared to previous approaches. The information traced through this framework is then used to provide charts showing the percentage of different types of sources used by students, and the actual web pages visited while working on the glossary in LearnWeb.

Furthermore, we trace mouse movements and keyboard input by users, in order to detect their active interactions with web pages. Previous studies did at most consider the time spent by a user on a website. To that end, they often used rough guesses, such as the timespan between two subsequent web requests. This is a very simple measure that does not recognize periods of inactivity (for example when the user temporarily leaves the computer to get a cup of coffee). We named our system Web Analytics Proxy Service (WAPS). This tracking system is available to other researchers under the domain www.waps.io.

2.2.1 Technical Description of the Web Analytics Proxy Service

The main challenge in tracking users' Internet activities is that web server log files are usually only accessible to the server's owner. For example, the operator of a Moodle instance can easily log every request a user makes to the system, but when the user leaves the platform and opens an external webpage, for example to check a term at www.linguee.it, all the actions happening on this external page are outside the scope of the Moodle operator. Hence, the user's activity there cannot be tracked, at least without installing special tracking software on the user's computer.

To overcome this problem, we have implemented a proxy service that keeps users on our server, which allows us to log their activities. When a user follows a link to an external website, such as www.linguee.it, they are directed to a subdomain on our server, e.g. www.linguee.it.waps.io. Our service issues a request to the actual web resource at www.linguee.it and forwards the response to the user. To make sure that the user receives exactly the same response s/he would get without the proxy service, it is crucial to send the same HTTP header information that we received from the user to the actual resource as well. This includes information such as the user's preferred language, browser type and cookies.

The returned page will most likely contain links to other pages on the same or other domains. To make sure that the user does not leave our proxy, which would interrupt the tracking, we modify all the hyperlinks on the page to point to our proxy service. This is done by parsing the HTML code and modifying attributes like *src* or *href* which typically contain URLs. Modern websites make excessive use of JavaScript and some create HTML content dynamically or retrieve it through AJAX calls. This content may contain links which cannot be altered by our proxy server. Therefore we inject a JavaScript code snippet in each proxy response. This snippet modifies all the dynamically created hyperlinks to point to our proxy service.

With regard to tracking, the proxy server can create logs which contain simple information such as the browser model, URL and date when a specific website was visited by a user. To gather more in-depth information, we use JavaScript to record the user input actions, such as mouse movement, scrolling, clicking and typing. We also record when the browser window loses the focus, i.e. when the user switches to another browser tab or puts the whole browser window into background.

For each input action our system records the time and the position on the page. To limit the log size and the transferred data, we record up to 3 mouse positions per second while the mouse is moved. The log data is accumulated into batches and sent asynchronously to our tracking server; this way the browsing experience is not influenced by the tracker. This data is used to calculate how active a user was on a page. For these purposes, we treat all the subsequent actions taking place within a sliding window of five seconds as a single continuous action and we assume that the user was active during the whole timespan between the first and last action. A dedicated interface shows all pages viewed by the user in chronological order.

3 The LearnWeb Platform and Its Glossary Tool

3.1 The LearnWeb Environment

We implemented the Learning Analytics Dashboard outlined in the previous section by integrating it in the LearnWeb environment. LearnWeb is a learning and competence development platform that provides advanced features for searching, organising and sharing distributed resources in an environment that allows users to work both individually and collaboratively [19]. This platform provides users with a search interface for retrieving and sharing resources across various Web 2.0 services, such as YouTube, Flickr, Ipernity, Vimeo, and Bing, as well as LearnWeb itself.

The platform is characterized by an iterative evaluation-driven design-based research approach [20]. The system has been developed at the L3S research center in Hannover through continuous collaboration between researchers and practitioners. Such collaboration is fundamental in order to cyclically assess and improve the functionalities of a system [21], tailoring them to practitioners' needs.

The current release of the system provides several innovative features designed to support teachers and students in individual and collaborative learning tasks. These features include:

1. searching, sharing and aggregation of different learning resources distributed across various Web 2.0 repositories;
2. annotation facilities, such as tagging and commenting;
3. collaborative writing with the integrated Open Office tool;
4. specific functionalities to support language learning activities, such as TED talk transcripts annotation [22];
5. automatic logging of students' actions.

The system has recently been enhanced with a tool for creating glossaries, specifically developed to support the learning activities of students of interpreting. The glossary tool is described in the following section.

3.2 The Glossary Tool

The Glossary tool was inspired by scientific literature on interpreting [1, 2, 7, 23], and it was designed to meet the needs of students training in interpreting. From the user perspective, in LearnWeb a glossary is a type of resource, on a par with images, videos and text files. From a technical perspective, a glossary is a database that may host a potentially infinite number of entries.

Each entry is composed of at least two terms (a term pair), i.e. the source term and its translation into another language. Synonyms in the source or target languages can be added to a given entry (as pointed out by Rogers in [24] synonyms are very frequent in technical and scientific language); thus, depending on the presence of synonyms, each glossary entry may include two or more terms. Each term in a glossary entry is accompanied by attributes corresponding to given fields in the glossary interface; these extra fields are aimed at enriching the description of the term.

In the experimentations described in this paper the glossary was set for the English-Italian language pair, but the interface can be easily adjusted for other language pairs. Figure 1 shows the interface the student sees when inputting a new entry. Figure 2 shows what the glossary looks like when a few term pairs have already been inputted.

Each time a user wants to add a new entry to the glossary, s/he is presented with the fields listed below:

- Topic 1 (compulsory field): the student is required to select the general topic under which s/he wants to classify the given term pair. A list of topics is provided in a dropdown menu.

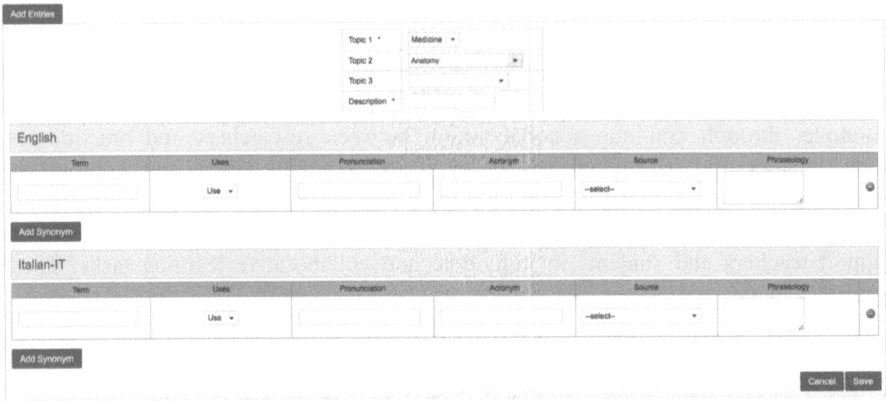

Fig. 1. The interface the student sees when inputting a new entry. (Color figure online)

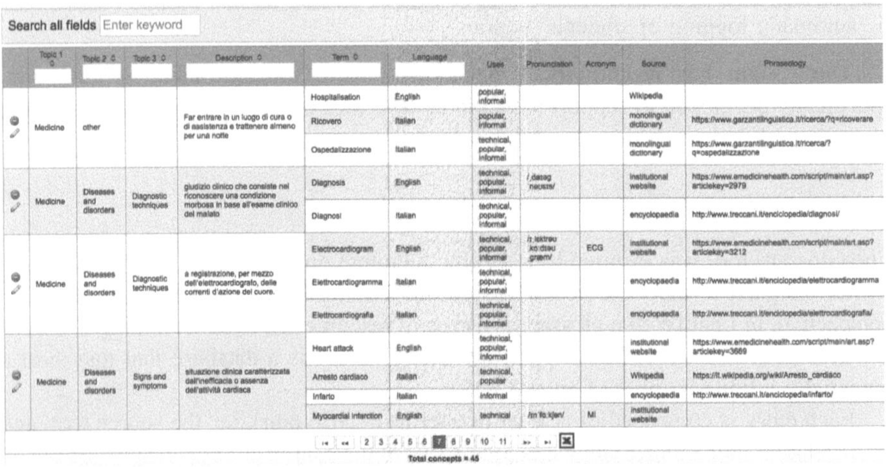

Search all fields Enter keyword

Topic 1	Topic 2	Topic 3	Description	Term	Language	Uses	Pronunciation	Acronym	Source	Phraseology
Medicine	other		Far entrare in un luogo di cura o di assistenza e trattenere almeno per una notte	Hospitalisation	English	popular, informal			Wikipedia	
				Ricovero	Italian	popular, informal			monolingual dictionary	https://www.garzantilinguistica.it/ricerca/?q=ricoverare
				Ospedalizzazione	Italian	technical, popular, informal			monolingual dictionary	https://www.garzantilinguistica.it/ricerca/?q=ospedalizzazione
Medicine	Diseases and disorders	Diagnostic techniques	giudizio clinico che consiste nel riconoscere una condizione morbosa in base all'esame clinico del malato	Diagnosis	English	technical, popular, informal	/ˌdaɪəg ˈnəʊsɪs/		institutional website	https://www.emedicinehealth.com/script/main/art.asp?articlekey=2979
				Diagnosi	Italian	technical, popular, informal			encyclopaedia	http://www.treccani.it/enciclopedia/diagnosi/
Medicine	Diseases and disorders	Diagnostic techniques	a registrazione, per mezzo dell'elettrocardiografo, delle correnti d'azione del cuore.	Electrocardiogram	English	technical, popular, informal	/ɪˌlektrəʊ ˈkɑːdɪəʊ ˌgræm/	ECG	institutional website	https://www.emedicinehealth.com/script/main/art.asp?articlekey=3212
				Elettrocardiogramma	Italian	technical, popular, informal			encyclopaedia	http://www.treccani.it/enciclopedia/elettrocardiogramma
				Elettrocardiografia	Italian	technical, popular, informal			encyclopaedia	http://www.treccani.it/enciclopedia/elettrocardiografia/
Medicine	Diseases and disorders	Signs and symptoms	situazione clinica caratterizzata dall'inefficacia o assenza dell'attività cardiaca	Heart attack	English	technical, popular, informal			institutional website	https://www.emedicinehealth.com/script/main/art.asp?articlekey=3669
				Arresto cardiaco	Italian	technical, popular			Wikipedia	https://it.wikipedia.org/wiki/Arresto_cardiaco
				Infarto	Italian	informal			encyclopaedia	http://www.treccani.it/enciclopedia/infarto/
				Myocardial infarction	English	technical	/ɪnˈfɑːkʃən/	MI	institutional website	

2 3 4 5 6 7 8 9 10 11

Total concepts = 45

Fig. 2. The glossary when term pairs have been inputted. (Color figure online)

- Topic 2 and Topic 3: these fields are meant to help the student to classify the entries according to a logical and functional ontology. In the current experiment, the students were guided in the selection of Topic 2 by means of a dropdown menu containing options provided by the teacher. Topic 3, on the other hand, is open text box.
- Description (compulsory field): the students are invited to enter a short definition of the concept that is linguistically realized by the given term pair. This field is meant to draw the student's attention to the meaning of the terms, rather than the terms themselves. Furthermore, being a searchable text box, the description field also allows users to retrieve specific terms even when one does not remember them. Finally, from a technical perspective, the Description field is the element that keeps

the source and target terms, their synonyms and all the other attributes together to form a single entry.

- Term EN (compulsory field): this is the field where to enter the English term.
- Term IT (compulsory field): this is the field where to enter the Italian term.
- Pronunciation: a text box which accepts any type of characters, including IPA (International Phonetic Alphabet) ones.
- Acronym: a text box to enter acronyms, if any.
- Phraseology: a text box with no restrictions in terms of number of characters. Its size in the database automatically adjusts to its contents. This box can be freely used by students to enter as many collocations and colligations as they want, but also any type of information which have no specific place in the glossary interface, such as part-of-speech information, and links to online images.
- Uses: draws the student's attention to linguistic register by means of three options (Technical, Popular, and Informal). There is also the possibility to select all the three options at once.
- Sources: here the student should specify the primary source of information used to fill in the glossary fields. The dropdown menu includes a list of possible sources, such as: Wikipedia; encyclopaedia; monolingual dictionary; bilingual dictionary; scientific/academic publication; institutional website; Linguee or Reverso.

As reported above, only four of the given fields are compulsory; these are the ones that represent the minimum amount of information necessary to make up a glossary. All the other fields are optional. Moreover, all fields and menus can be customized to the teachers' needs, upon request.

Finally, the student can delete an existing entry or term at any time, by clicking on the red round icon in Figs. 1 and 2. Existing entries can be modified by clicking on the pencil icon in Fig. 2.

Various types of searches can be performed in glossaries. In particular, the 'Search all fields' box allows students to retrieve all the glossary entries that include a given word in any of the glossary fields. Finally an Excel icon allows students to download the entire glossary or filtered results in Excel format for printing.

3.3 Dashboard Interface

The LearnWeb environment integrates the glossary dashboard for both teachers and students.

The teacher dashboard provides an overview of the activities carried out by the students. As explained in Sect. 2, the activities are organized into three main groups. Particular attention is given to the activities the students carry out on the glossary (Fig. 3) and to the sources of information they use (Fig. 4). The charts in the dashboard are based on the indicators listed in Tables 1 and 2.

If the teacher selects a specific time span, the graphs and tables update accordingly. Furthermore, specific students can be filtered out from the general group.

In fact, in this integrated dashboard, teachers can visualize the activities of an individual student by clicking on the correspondent student ID. Like group views, the detailed view for each student consists in a set of charts related to: (i) the student's

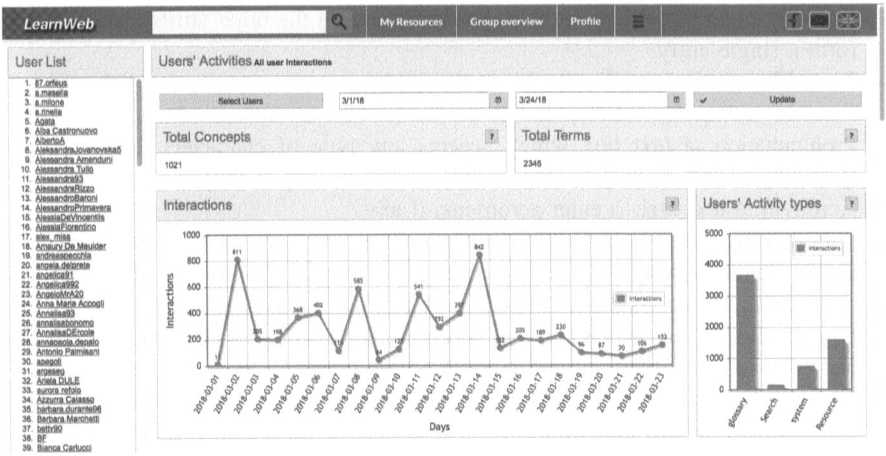

Fig. 3. Teacher dashboard - View of the students' general activities.

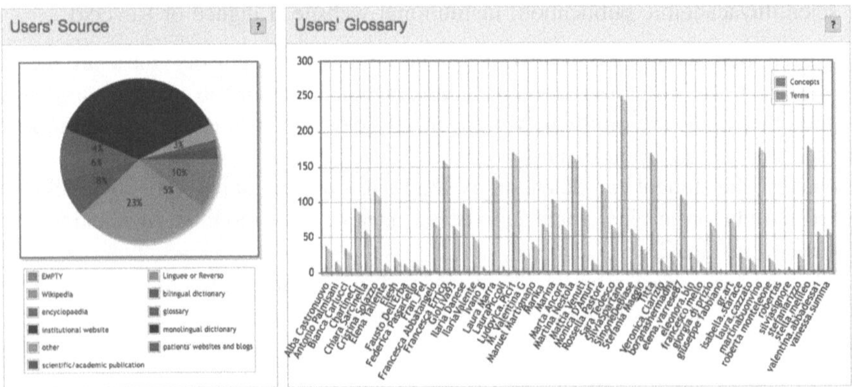

Fig. 4. Teacher dashboard - View of the students' main sources of information. (Color figure online)

general activities, (ii) his way of organizing and populating the glossary, and (iii) his searches on the Web for information (Fig. 5).

The student dashboard has been designed to enable student's self reflection on the learning activities related to the creation of the personal glossary. In particular, an alerting system has been included to allow individual students to view their standing and progress with respect to the group's average. Small symbols in red, green and yellow respectively indicate whether the student's progress is under, over or equal to the average of the group. The students should be explained that these symbols are not forms of assessment of their learning progress, but mere indicators of a student's relative status as regards the task, compared to the rest of the class.

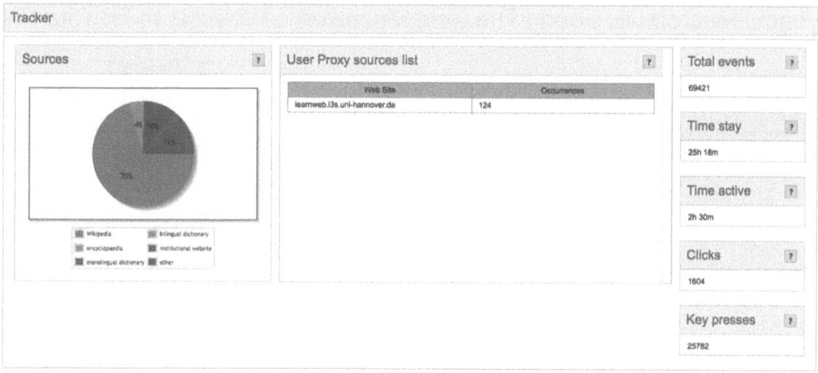

Fig. 5. Teacher dashboard - View of a student's searches on the Web for information. (Color figure online)

Owing to the WAPS, the dashboard also shows statistics of the web searches performed by the students while working on a glossary, including the time spent on a specific site and how long the student was active (moving the mouse, scrolling, clicking or typing). The interface also shows a list of the web sites viewed by the student, in chronological order (Fig. 6). In this particular case, the user first searched for "small intestine" on the LearnWeb platform. Next he opened www.linguee.com and searched for the Spanish and Italian translations of this term. Afterwards he returned to LearnWeb and added his findings to his glossary. Finally, he opened a Wikipedia article.

Url	Title	Total events	Created at
http://it.wikipedia.org.secure.waps.io/wiki/Intestino_tenue	Intestino tenue - Wikipedia	203	2017-03-16 19:09:36.0
http://learnweb.l3s.uni-hannover.de/lw/showGlossary.jsf?resource_id=...	Glossario - Learnweb	3012	2017-03-16 19:08:17.0
http://www.linguee.com.waps.io/english-italian/search?query=small%2...	small intestine - Italian translation – Linguee	186	2017-03-16 19:06:26.0
http://www.linguee.com.waps.io/english-spanish/translation/small%20in...	small intestine - Spanish translation ? Linguee	38	2017-03-16 19:06:18.0
http://learnweb.l3s.uni-hannover.de/lw/search.jsf?query=small+intestin...	Cerca - Learnweb	84	2017-03-16 19:06:13.0

Fig. 6. Dashboard view of a student's web searches [25].

Through the "playback" feature, the teacher can see the student's actions step by step (Fig. 7). To this aim, the system displays the page at exactly the same window size the user viewed it and visualizes the mouse movements recorded. The timeline at the top of this window shows periods and types of activity/inactivity during the specific page session. Yellow indicates mouse movements, and red scrolling or clicking. Grey indicates inactivity.

Fig. 7. The "playback" window [25]. (Color figure online)

4 Testing the Glossary Tool and the Learning Analytics Dashboard

4.1 Methodology

The Glossary tool and the Learning Analytics dashboard were first tested on a group of 34 AM students attending an Italian university, in a module on consecutive interpreting. At the beginning of the module, the teacher presented LearnWeb and the Glossary tool, and explained the rationale of each field. As regards the Phraseology field, the teacher suggested it could be used in a rather open way, i.e. not only to enter collocations, but also any other pieces of information they deemed useful. The students were then invited to individually create a personal LearnWeb glossary on medical topics. The teacher also clarified that she expected them to build up their glossaries on a daily basis, as home activity in preparation for the interpreting exam. Finally, the students were instructed on how to use the platform for searching the web for reference material and were informed that all their actions would be tracked, including the web sites they visited. No one denied permission to track the actions. The students kept on building their glossaries throughout the academic term, until the day of the exam. The testing phase, thus, stretched over a period of about 3 months.

Twenty days after the beginning of the module, the students were asked to fill in a short questionnaire[4] aimed at collecting their opinions on the user-friendliness of the platform and of the Glossary tool. Using 9-point Likert scales, the questionnaire asked the students to assess the following dimensions:

[4] The questionnaire was created using the open source tool Limesurvey.

1. General appreciation of the system (terrible – wonderful).
2. Easiness of use of the system (difficult – easy).
3. Personal reaction to using the system (frustrating – satisfying).
4. System's power (inadequate power – adequate power).
5. Enjoyment in using the system (dull – stimulating).
6. System's flexibility (rigid – flexible).
7. System's interface (confusing – very clear).
8. User-friendliness in creating a glossary (very difficult – very easy).
9. Glossary's easiness of use (very difficult – very easy).
10. User-friendliness in searching the Web from within LearnWeb (very difficult – very easy).

The questionnaire also asked the students to list three negative and three positive aspects of the Glossary and to freely add further comments. The results of the students' answers are summarized in Sect. 4.2.1.

Finally, in keeping with the iterative evaluation-driven design-based research approach that characterizes this platform, the students' answers and suggestions led to a second version of the glossary tool. This updated version and the dashboard were tested with a group of 60 undergraduates attending a module of liaison interpreting revolving around tourism discourse. The students used the Glossary tool throughout an academic term. As in the previous case, they were introduced to the tool and its features in class, but were asked to create and populate a personal glossary at home, in preparation for the exam. The teacher used the dashboard in a fashion similar to the one described in previous paragraphs. Two differences distinguish this experiment from the previous one: this second experiment did not test the WAPS tracking system, because the teacher asked the students to use the material provided in class as reference material for their glossaries, and no extra web searches were needed; the students were asked to bring a printed copy of the glossary at the exam and hand it out to the teacher. At the end of the course, the students were invited to fill in the online questionnaire. The updated version of the system was rated and commented by 19 students. The results of the students' answers to the online questionnaire are summarized in Sect. 4.2.2.

Both teachers used the dashboard to monitor the students' use of the glossary, checking the amount and kind of information they entered in the various fields, and giving students in need personalized feedback. The teachers' comments on the glossary and dashboard were collected through personal interviews. Their comments are summarized in Sect. 4.2.3.

4.2 Results

4.2.1 Testing the First Version of the Glossary Tool – Questionnaire Results

The platform and the Glossary tool seem to have been generally appreciated by the students taking part in the first experimentation of this integrated system. Table 4 reports how the ten dimensions considered scored in the student's questionnaires.

Table 4. Questionnaire results – Average scores.

Dimension	1	2	3	4	5	6	7	8	9	10
Average score	6.9	7.0	6.7	7.1	7.3	6.7	7.3	8.0	7.5	6.7

Measured on a 9-point scale, the platform in general (Dimensions 1–7) scored on average around 7. The Glossary tool (Dimensions 8–9) scored slightly higher, with an average score of 8 as regards the easiness to create a new glossary, and 7.5 as regards the easiness to fill in the glossary. Searching the Web from within LearnWeb (Dimension 10) scored slightly lower, but still positive (6.7).

The students' replies to our request to list three positive features confirmed that all the existing features were appreciated, with different students showing appreciation for different features. Fairly common answers were that that the system had stimulated the students to create and expand their glossaries.

In their replies to our request to list three negative features, the students suggested the following:

1. To add a field for images.
2. To expand the range of items in the Topic 1 drop-down menu, thus making it possible to create glossaries on topics other than medicine.
3. To support the creation of multilingual glossaries (more than two languages).
4. To include the possibility to order glossary terms alphabetically.
5. To add an explicit indication of the number of entries in the glossary.

Comments 2, 4, and 5 were immediately accepted and implemented, thus bringing about the updated version of the tool which was tested by undergraduate students.

4.2.2 Testing the Updated Version of the Integrated System – Questionnaire Results

As regards the general questions about the system and the glossary, the undergraduate students' average rates – reported in Table 5 – are not substantially different from the MA average rates. As mentioned before, Dimension 10 (Searching the Web from within LearnWeb) was not tested with this group of students.

Table 5. Questionnaire results – Average scores.

Dimension	1	2	3	4	5	6	7	8	9
Average score	6.5	7.6	6.6	7.1	7.1	6.4	6.8	7.8	7.9

The students' replies to our request to list three positive and three negative features, and to add further comments showed general appreciation for the existing glossary fields, and in particular of:

- the Phraseology box;
- the Pronunciation field;
- the Synonym feature;

- the auto-saving of glossary entries;
- the indication of the number of entries in the glossary.

However, about 25% of the students mentioned difficulties is exporting the glossary and printing it out. Some students also signalled that deleting a glossary entry was far too easy, in that it only requires a single click and no confirmation box appears; this had led, in some cases, to the accidental deletion of an entire entry, which then had to be recreated from scratch.

4.2.3 Teachers' Comments on the Dashboard

The MA teacher fully appreciated the dashboard and used it to provide remedial feedback during the academic term. For example, about a month after the beginning of her module, the dashboard's graphs/tables showed that a few students were systematically underusing the Phraseology or the Pronunciation fields; the teacher spoke to these students individually and helped them to understand the importance of these elements. Others students appeared to be disregarding the teacher's recommendations and resorted primarily or exclusively to dictionaries as reference resources for the glossary entries; these students were individually helped to understand the importance of using content-based resources, rather than language-based ones. In the following weeks, the students who had received personalized feedback changed their approach to the task, and their new behaviours were visible in dashboard. Detailed descriptions of how this dashboard helped to identify students in need, and of the patterns of student behaviour in the glossary task observed during this first experiment are provided in [25].

The undergraduate teacher appreciated the dashboard and the information it provides, in so far as it offers constant monitoring of each student's engagement with the task and progress in the creation of the glossary. She observed some students' difficulty in distinguishing between technical and non-technical terms, and noticed that many students had problems in deciding what should go in the Term field and what in the Phraseology field. Like her students, the teacher observed that the printed glossaries produced by most students were neither clear nor functional. Finally, she asked for the possibility to have direct access to the students' personal glossaries in order to check the correctness of each glossary's term pairs. This last request was immediately implemented, and at the time of writing, it is already available to the teachers. Based upon the teachers' and students' comments, we are currently discussing alternative ways to download and print out the glossary, and we are thinking of creating a student manual providing suggestions on and examples of how to gain the greatest advantage from the use of this glossary tool.

5 Conclusions

The current paper has described the design and development of an integrated system aimed at supporting students of interpreting in vocabulary building. The Glossary tool guides students in the creation of highly informative bilingual glossaries; the Web Analytics Proxy Service traces student searches on the web for reference material; the

LearnWeb platform – where the Glossary tool, the WAPS and the dashboard are embedded – tracks the students interactions with the glossary; and the dashboard offers graphic representations of selected data for the benefit of both teachers and students. The dashboard was specifically designed to allow teachers to monitor the students' approaches to this particular task and to provide individual remedial feedback, if necessary. The dashboard is also intended to spur students to keep on a par with the rest of the class, by seeing their status compared to the rest of the class.

The paper also reports the results of the experimentation of the described integrated system with two groups of students specializing in interpreting (an MA group and an undergraduate group), and two different teachers. The undergraduate group used the system after a few secondary features suggested by MA students had been implemented. This is in keeping with LearnWeb's iterative evaluation-driven design-based research approach.

The usability and efficacy of the integrated system was assessed by means of questionnaires and interviews. The results of the experiments suggest that this integrated system manages to achieve its goals and provides students and teachers of interpreting with an innovative online tool that fosters and supports vocabulary building. In fact, in both experiments, the system was judged user-friendly and highly useful by both students and teachers. The students generally declared that the Glossary interface had stimulated them to create and expand their personal glossaries. Furthermore, some parts of the glossary, such as the Phraseology box, the Pronunciation field, and the Synonym feature, were specifically appreciated, while no field in the glossary was deemed useless. Both students and teachers appreciated the possibility to download and print out the glossary, but asked for a different implementation of this feature. The teachers considered the dashboard very useful to monitor the students' commitment to the study of vocabulary, their understanding of the importance of content and context information, and their Web search strategies. They also declared that it is very useful to identify students in need of personalized remedial feedback.

From a research perspective, the system collected a large amount of data which could provide insight into student approaches to vocabulary learning and glossary building. These data include: the time spent by students filling in the glossary; the time spent searching the Web for information; the websites visited while looking for suitable content and language resources; the primary sources used for filling in the glossary; the type of data the students entered in the Phraseology field. Cluster analysis of these data could outline different profiles of student behaviour.

References

1. AIIC: Practical guide for professional conference interpreters. aiic.net, 1 December 1999. Accessed 2 Apr 2017. http://aiic.net/p/628
2. Gile, D.: The interpreter's preparation for technical conferences: methodological questions in investigating the topic. Conf. Interpret. Transl. **4**(2), 7–27 (2002)
3. Moser, B.: Simultaneous interpretation: a hypothetical model and its practical application. In: Gerver, D., Sinaiko, H.W. (eds.) Language Interpretation and Communication.

NATOCS, vol. 9, pp. 353–368. Springer, Boston (1978). https://doi.org/10.1007/978-1-4615-9077-4_31
4. Seleskovitch, D.: Interpreting for International Conferences: Problems of Language and Communication. Pen and Booth, London (1978)
5. Pochhacker, F.: Introducing Interpreting Studies. Routledge, Abingdon (2003)
6. Gile, D.: Basic Concepts and Models for Interpreter and Translator Training, vol. 8. Benjamins, Amsterdam/Philadelphia (2009)
7. Fons i Fleming, M.: Do your glossaries excel? aiic.net, 14 September 2009. http://aiic.net/p/3315. Accessed 31 Aug 2017
8. Jiang, H.: A survey of glossary practice of conference interpreters. aiic.net, 21 April 2015. http://aiic.net/p/7151. Accessed 31 Mar 2017
9. Schwendimann, B.A., et al.: Understanding learning at a glance: an overview of learning dashboard studies. In: Proceedings of the Sixth International Conference on Learning Analytics & Knowledge (LAK 2016), pp. 532–533. ACM, New York (2016). https://doi.org/10.1145/2883851.2883930
10. Bodily, R., Verbert, K.: Review of research on student-facing learning analytics dashboards and educational recommender systems. IEEE Trans. Learn. Technol. **10**(4), 405–418 (2017). https://doi.org/10.1109/TLT.2017.2740172
11. Agudo-Peregrina, A.F., Iglesias-Pradas, S., Conde-González, M.A., Hernández-García, A.: Can we predict success from log data in VLEs? Classification of interactions for learning analytics and their relation with performance in VLE-supported F2F and online learning. Comput. Human Behav. **31**, 542–550 (2014). https://doi.org/10.1016/j.chb.2013.05.031
12. Mazza, R., Dimitrova, V.: Visualising student tracking data to support instructors in web-based distance education. In: Proceedings of the 13th International World Wide Web Conference on Alternate Track Papers & Posters, pp. 154–161. ACM (2004)
13. Mazza, R., Bettoni, M., Faré, M., Mazzola, L.: Moclog–monitoring online courses with log data. In: Retalis, S., Dougiamas, M. (eds.) Proceedings of the 1st Moodle Research Conference (2012)
14. Zhang, H., Almeroth, K.: Moodog: tracking student activity in online course management systems. J. Interact. Learn. Res. **21**(3), 407–429 (2010)
15. Dumais, S., Jeffries, R., Russell, D.M., Tang, D., Teevan, J.: Understanding user behavior through log data and analysis. In: Olson, Judith S., Kellogg, Wendy A. (eds.) Ways of Knowing in HCI, pp. 349–372. Springer, New York (2014). https://doi.org/10.1007/978-1-4939-0378-8_14
16. Ceddia, J., Sheard, J., Tibbey, G.: Wat: a tool for classifying learning activities from a log file. In: Proceedings of the Ninth Australasian Conference on Computing Education, ACE 2007, vol. 66, pp. 11–17. Australian Computer Society, Inc., Darlinghurst (2007)
17. Perez-Paredes, P., Sanchez-Tornel, M., Alcaraz Calero, J.M., Jimenez, P.A.: Tracking learners' actual uses of corpora: guided vs non-guided corpus consultation. Comput. Assist. Lang. Learn. **24**(3), 233–253 (2011)
18. Bortoluzzi, M., Marenzi, I.: Web searches for learning. How language teachers search for online resources. Lingue Linguaggi **23**, 21–36 (2017)
19. Marenzi, I., Zerr, S.: Multiliteracies and active learning in clil - the development of LearnWeb 2. 0. IEEE Trans. Learn. Technol. **5**(4), 336–348 (2012)
20. Marenzi, I.: Interactive and collaborative supports for CLIL: towards a formal model based on digital literacy. In: Content and Language Integrated Learning (CLIL) by Interaction, pp. 75–99. Peter Lang, Frankfurt am Main (2014)
21. Wang, F., Hannafin, M.J.: Design-based research and technology-enhanced learning environments. Educ. Technol. Res. Dev. **53**(4), 5–23 (2005)

22. Taibi, D., Chawla, S., Dietze, S., Marenzi, I., Fetahu, B.: Exploring ted talks as linked data for education. Br. J. Educ. Technol. **46**(5), 1092–1096 (2015)
23. Setton, R.: From practice to theory and back in interpreting: the pivotal role of training. Interpreters' Newsl. (15), 1–18 (2010)
24. Rogers, M.: Terminological equivalence: probability and consistency. In: LSP Translation Scenarios, pp. 101–106 (2007)
25. Taibi, D., Bianchi, F., Kemkes, P., Marenzi I.: Learning Analytics for interpreting. In: Proceedings of the 10th International Conference on Computer Supported Education, CSEDU, vol. 1, pp. 145–154, ISBN 978-989-758-291-2 (2018). https://doi.org/10.5220/0006774801450154

How to Apply Problem-Based Learning in a Managed Way? A Case in Computing Education

Simone C. dos Santos[1(✉)], Gustavo H. S. Alexandre[1,2], Ariane Nunes Rodrigues[1], and Priscila B. Souza[1]

[1] Centro de Informática, Universidade Federal de Pernambuco - UFPE, Recife, Brazil
{scs,anr,pbs}@cin.ufpe.br, gugahenrique@gmail.com
[2] CESAR School, Brum Street, Recife, Brazil

Abstract. The continuous advancement of Information Technology and the range of industries and services dependent on technology have required profound changes in the education of software professionals. In fact, the education of these professionals must include diverse skills (technical and non-technical), in order to enable them to solve real problems that impact the lives of companies and people. In this scenario, active learning approaches can make a lot of difference, when applied effectively, with well-defined educational goals and continuous follow-up and feedbacks. One of these approaches that are working well in Computer Education is the Problem-Based Learning (PBL) approach. PBL uses real problems as an instrument to develop skills such as holistic knowledge, business understanding, task management and group work, essential in the software professional. In this context, this paper describes a case of an undergraduate course in Information Systems, conducted in the PBL approach. In order to guarantee the application of PBL in an effective way, a Framework for PBL application in the teaching of Computing, described by Santos and Rodrigues (2016) was used. This framework systematizes the application of PBL in the four stages Plan, Do, Check and Act (based on the management cycle of Deming), which are repeated in learning cycles aligned to educational objectives. As the main results of this experience, the following stand out: a proposal for applying PBL in a managed way, based on a Framework for Computer Education; benefits of using the Framework; possibilities for improvements in this approach.

Keywords: Active learning · Computing education · PBL · Case report

1 Introduction

An Information and Communication Technology (ICT) is everywhere and everywhere. Institutions generally rely on ICTs to not only become efficient but to continue to carry out their activities.

In this scenario, the education of the professionals in Computing area has undergone several transformations to adapt to the demands of the labor market, in the face of

B. M. McLaren et al. (Eds.): CSEDU 2018, CCIS 1022, pp. 287–309, 2019.
https://doi.org/10.1007/978-3-030-21151-6_15

continuous technological changes and increasingly complex and integrated applications. One of the main changes concerns to need of holistic view of different subjects, prioritizing educational objectives based on the development of skills and abilities, rather than knowledge about isolated content disconnected from practices. This change is reflected in the most recent versions of the main curricula in the Computing area ACM/IEEE Computing Science [1] and ACM/IEEE Software Engineering [2], which stand out as principles the real problem-solving ability, project management experience and the ability to critically analyse solutions. All of these principles are multidisciplinary and developed from the work in group and real labour experiences.

In addition, it requires a change of posture of the student, who needs to have a self-initiative in the search for knowledge and in the application of this to actually solve problems, as well as in the posture of the teacher, who leaves the role of the holder of the solution, to a collaborator who guides and evaluates results, giving continuous feedback to students throughout the resolution process. From this motivation, this paper describes a case study of an Enterprise Management Systems (EMS) course, part of an undergraduate course in Information Systems (IS). In order to align the purpose of this course to labour market demands, we chose to adopt the Problem-Based Learning approach (PBL), considering its increasing popularity in this area [3–11].

PBL is defined in [12] as an instructional method of teaching and learning, which is able to develop the ability to apply diverse knowledge to solve problems, through teamwork and individual attitudes as self-initiative, critical vision and reflection of the learning process. The authors of this paper also understand that for an effective PBL approach it is necessary to preserve its principles and manage its processes throughout learning cycles, within an essentially practical environment. Despite the benefits of PBL, evidences identified in [7] indicate that there are difficulties regarding the application of PBL and verification of its results. The lack of knowledge about the methodological fundamentals of PBL, aligned with disjointed ideas about the operationalization of the method, common in innovations, are aspects that contribute to low interest and incoherence in its application.

In order to ensure a manageable implementation of the PBL approach, this case uses a PBL framework for computer teaching published in [13]. This framework proposes the management of PBL in learning cycles based on the Management Cycle of Deming (Plan-Do-Check-Act), supported by processes and artifacts that facilitate the planning, execution, monitoring and realization of continuous improvements along the teaching and learning process. From this study it was possible to understand the importance of a management process that allows: to plan PBL based on essential elements; to execute the learning process supported by continuous evaluations and feedbacks; and to improve the learning process along the course.

This paper is organized in 6 sections. Section 2 describes the PBL approach, highlighting its principles and characteristics, as well as commenting on the planning of the teaching and learning process in this approach and proposed solutions in this context. Section 3 describes the research method used in the design of the Framework used as a solution proposal. Section 4 presents in more detail the elements of the Framework, whose application in an information systems management course is detailed in Sect. 5. Finally, Sect. 6 presents the conclusions and final considerations of this work.

2 Problem-Based Learning

In this section, the theoretical and methodological references that support this article are presented. Section 2.1 describes the PBL method and its principles. Next, Sect. 2.2 presents some important considerations regarding the planning of the teaching and learning process to adopt the PBL method and finally in Sect. 2.3 structured approaches will be presented to facilitate the adoption of the PBL method.

2.1 Definition, Characteristics and Principles

Problem-Based Learning (PBL) is a teaching-learning method that aims to acquire knowledge and develop attitudes and skills through problem-solving. The method began in 1968 at the McMaster Medical School Medical School and was introduced by physician Howard Barrows [14].

Although the method originated in medical courses, it has been applied in courses in the area of Computing and obtaining good results. Since 2006, the research group *iNnovative Educational eXperience in Technology* (N.E.X.T) of the UFPE Informatics Center has been dedicated to the studies and applications of the PBL method in courses in Computer Science, Information Systems and Software Engineering.

The dynamics of PBL are very different from traditional learning, where students usually work on projects far from the reality of the market, under conditions and restrictions imposed by the teacher (teacher-centered approach), which aims to explain a large amount of content and consequent low practical application. In PBL, students are the center of the learning process, and if the problem being solved and the learning environment are authentic, more prepared for the professional reality the students will be. In addition, the skills and abilities developed in PBL are consequences of intense collaborative and investigative work. In traditional teaching, students tend to work individually, often with little interaction and knowledge sharing. This process does not favor the development of interpersonal skills such as communication, leadership, planning, but focusing almost always in technical knowledge. Computer students acquire knowledge in technologies, processes and development methods, while the interpersonal skills, important to solve problems, are little explored.

The PBL method is based on principles [15]. In [9], based on four key studies, ten essential PBL principles were defined that guide an effective PBL approach. The 10 PBL principles are: 1. All learning activities must be anchored on a task or problem; 2. The learner should feel that he/she owns the problem, and is responsible for his/her own learning; 3. The problem should be real; 4. The task and the learning environment should reflect the reality of the professional market; 5. The learner needs to own the process used to work out the solution to the problem; 6. The learning environment should stimulate and at the same time challenge the learner's reasoning; 7. The learner should be encouraged to test his/her ideas against alternative views and contexts; 8. The learner should have the opportunity and support to reflect on the content try, and the learning process; 9. The learning is collaborative and multidirectional; 10. PBL is supported by the planning process and continuous monitoring.

In [10] the authors propose the distribution of the 10 principles in 5 key elements to be exploited in the adoption of the PBL methodology: problem, environment, content, human capital and process.

2.2 Planning of the Teaching-Learning Process and PBL Learning

The implementation of the independent PBL method is a complex activity because it requires a change in both student and teacher attitudes. It also involves changes in the classroom infrastructure so that, in the course of the PBL course, it can achieve the benefits that the approach provides. Another aspect is that the adoption of PBL is not prescriptive, that is, there is no single formula to be followed for the method to be adopted [16].

Faced with the complexity of implementing PBL, it is necessary to carry out a planning so that it is possible to avoid the improper use of the method and thus to avoid that the critical aspects of the process contained in the PBL approach are neglected and to guarantee the realization of course in the PBL approach with due alignment between theory and practice throughout the teaching-learning process.

In [17] corroborates with the above thinking and says that constructivist instruction, including PBL, does indeed require more intensive analysis and planning to create a rich learning situation that guides and engages students in learning activities designed to help them to build the knowledge and skills required. Most importantly, comprehensive analysis and planning allow teachers/tutors to guide student learning in a more flexible and holistic way. Without a complete cognitive map and understanding of the capacity of the PBL problem, the teacher/tutor will likely guide students with their own preference for solving the problem, rather than guiding students to deal with the problem in different ways.

2.3 Approaches to PBL Implementation

In order to provide support to PBL implementation, the few available proposals have been focus on different aspects of the "problem element". For [18] problem-building needs to gain more attention because aligning the quality of problems with learning objectives is a challenge that has an effect on learning. The author presents the 3C3R model as a conceptual framework for the conception of problem ideas. The model name highlights central components related to C's (content, context, connection); and R's (researching, reasoning, reflecting) as processing components. The central components have the function of establishing a basis for the definition of the problems, and the processing components aim to facilitate the students' involvement in the resolution process. Even if this artifact can contribute to the planning stage, there are no considerations regarding the management of the application of the problem and follow-up of the learning. Having effective problems by component descriptions does not make the teaching and learning process effective, even if it is one of the factors that contributes to the results. In [17], the author proposes a process for designing problems in nine steps. This process is indicated to assist in the application of the 3C3R model.

Another solution to be highlighted is the VU-PBL framework used by Victoria University in Australia for computing science and engineering courses. The VU-PBL framework consists of four main components: key elements, PBL principles, PBL cycle and PBL levels. The key elements are four (problem design, facilitation, engagement and evaluation). They make up the central part of the strategically defined cycle for the effective implementation of PBL. In order for each element to be effectively considered in the implementation, ten principles are distributed among them. The cycle is intended for the student, who can lead learning process through seven steps. The cycle and its steps are similar to the PBL process defined by Barrows [19]. In fact, these solutions highlight isolated parts of the implementation process of the PBL, with few operational and managerial supporting to this approach, considering the entire management cycle.

In [20] describe a tool called PBL Planner Toolkit that consisting of a Canvas PBL and a set of 40 cards intended to guide the planning of teaching in the PBL approach. The tool is intended to be used by all educators who wish to carry out teaching planning in PBL Computing courses. Especially novice professor who have low experience in conducting educational planning, professor with low level of knowledge in the PBL approach or both. Each component of this tool is presented in the following sections. A digital version of PBL Toolkit is available at http://www.pblplanner.com. Course planning with the PBL approach using the toolkit is divided into 3 phases: Planning, Revising, and Sharing.

Phase 1 - Planning: To carry out this phase it is important that there is participation of the people who will act as teachers, tutors and coordinator. First, separate the cards according to their respective fields on the canvas. Planning participants should answer questions from card 1 through 40 and set responses in the corresponding fields.

Phase 2 - Revising: The purpose of the review phase is to check issues that have raised questions during planning as well as some aspect that has not been fully answered. It is also important to make sure that the dependencies between the fields are properly aligned. For example the objective fields with those of evaluations in which the first defines the objective and in the second how to measure if it has been reached.

Phase 3 - Sharing: The final phase aims to build an action plan that should list all tasks and artifacts planned during the planning phase. The action plan should contain, in addition to the task list and artifacts, the deadline for creation, the status of the task or artifact, and who is the owner. With the creation of the action plan, a version of the teaching plan is generated (baseline), which can undergo adaptations and improvements throughout its implementation.

3 The Framework By-Cycles

In [13], the authors defined a framework to apply PBL in teaching of Computing. This framework aims to facilitate the management of teaching processes in the PBL approach through techniques and management models. Intended for the pedagogical team, this instrument indicates a set of actions that need to be considered at each step of the Plan-Do-Check-Act cycle of Deming (as shown in Fig. 1), relating roles and responsibilities to the actors for an effective application of the PBL approach.

The components of this framework are: (1) x*PBL* [10], as a methodology specific to the framework that considers techniques and management tools; (2) *PBL-Process*, as a PBL process consists of steps that help conduct the methodology, as well as steps to

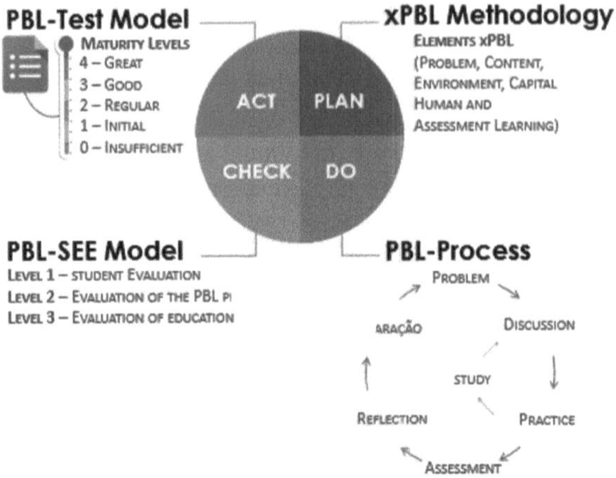

Fig. 1. Steps of PBL framework [32].

encourage the student to the learning process; (3) *PBL-SEE* [21] as an authentic assessment model to verify the student's performance, PBL and teaching process; (4) *PBL-Test*, process maturity model in PBL. The following sections highlight component details and their relationship to the framework steps.

3.1 Plan: XPBL Methodology

Based on the principles of the PBL approach, xPBL considers management techniques to facilitate the implementation of the teaching process [10]. Purposely, the five elements that make up the xPBL defined to ensure adherence to the principles process, envision characteristics necessary for the PBL process. The elements refer to: (1) Problem, an essential aspect in learning in this approach, reflects realism and complexity similar to real contexts; (2) Environment, related to the definition of an authentic learning environment that reflects the actual context of the professional market; (3) Human Capital, with evidence to the roles and responsibilities of the pedagogical team in the planning, execution and follow-up of the process; (4) Content, as an essential part to support the theoretical basis of the problem solving process, consistent with the context of the problem; And (5) Processes, for the adequacy of evaluation processes inherent to the learning format in PBL. The Table 1 summarizes the PBL principles presented in [9] to the elements of xPBL.

Thus exposed, consider the planning process xPBL requires consider and define aspects of the five elements. According to the authors, a plan of action guided by the 5W2H technique sees to it that the five elements are defined in a clear and organized way because they obtain answers to questions such as: "What?", "Who?", "Where?", "When?", "Why?", "How?" and "How much?". As an effective management technique, 5W2H sees to it that activities associated with each xPBL element are broken down, analysed and summarized during the planning stage. The authors objectively considered information about what should be done and when, or who will conduct a certain activity and when, while they were defining each element.

Table 1. Association xPBL and principles PBL [9].

xPBL elements	Principles of PBL
Problem	1. All learning activities are anchored on a task or a problem; 2. The learner should feel he/she owns the problem, and is responsible for his/her own learning; 3. The problem should be real; and 6. The learning environment should stimulate and at the same time challenge the learner's reasoning
Environment	4. The task and the learning environment should reflect the reality of the professional market
Human capital	9. The learning is collaborative and multidirectional
Content	5. The learner needs to own the process used so as to work out the solution to the problem; 7. The learner should be encouraged to test his/her ideas against alternative views and contexts
Process	8. The learner should have the opportunity and support to reflect on the content learned and the learning process; 10. PBL is supported by planning processes and continuous monitoring

3.2 Do: Process PBL

The PBL-process was set to meet the dynamics of learning in PBL. With immersive learning characteristics in problem solving practices, have a process to run consistently the learning cycle becomes essential.

Originally, the term "PBL Process" was adopted by Barrows to represent a set of activities that could lead to PBL learning for medical students. The Barrows process [22] is defined as a tutorial process and has ten activities: (1) Presentation of the problem; (2) Hypothesis questions; (3) Solution Attempt; (4) Survey of Learning Issues; (5) Group work planning; (6) Independent Study; (7) Share information and discussions; (8) Application of knowledge to the problem; (9) Presentation of solutions of the group; and (10) Evaluation. The activities of the Barrows process, with the exception of the first one, are designed solely by students. In the perspective of executing a process of teaching and learning in PBL, in addition to the student conducting the resolution process, the pedagogical team also performs actions to conduct the process in accordance to the teaching approach.

An ideal process for PBL should be cyclical with steps directed to the pedagogical team and the student. The PBL-process is a seven step process for an iterative execution of learning cycles: (1) Preparation, the pedagogical team defines specifications of the methodological context and learning environment; (2) Problem, step for presentation of real problems by real clients; (3) Discussion, when student groups can identify solution possibilities supported by the Delisle resolution process [14] And raise learning needs; (4) Practice, possibility for application of methods, models, theories to the problem context; (5) Study, moment to meet the learning needs identified by the group; (6) Assessment, opportunity for verification of learning and skills development; And (7) Reflection, in-depth analysis of different aspects of the learning process. In the PBL process, the "Preparation - Problem - Assessment" steps guide the pedagogical team to conduct the process. The steps "Discussion - Study - Practice - Reflection" involve the student in the resolution process for collaborative, self-directed, practical and reflexive learning, necessary for the PBL approach. During a learning cycle, it is important to note that steps 3, 4 and 5 do not necessarily take this order. A team can, for example, identify the need for the study before the practice or, if they already have conditions, practice immediately.

3.3 Check: The PBL-SEE Model

As a model aligned with PBL, its use is indicated for software engineering since it is based on valuation models processes used by software industry professionals [9]. In this case, the Check step of the framework is supported by this component in order to verify if the learning objectives were completely achieved, but also the process faithfully adheres to the PBL principles. In summary, the model is composed of three levels: student evaluation (level 1), evaluation of the PBL process (level 2) and evaluation of education (level 3).

To define level 1, the elements of xPBL, the Revised Bloom's Taxonomy (RBT) [23], and the authentic evaluation model [24] were used as main references.

The xPBL (described in Sect. 3.1) was used to guarantee the alignment between the steps Plan and Check.

The Revised Bloom's Taxonomy (RBT), keeping the six levels in verbs: to remember or reproduce ideas (verbs: recognizing, playing); to understand, explaining an idea/concept in one's own words (verbs: interpreting, summarizing); to apply of knowledge to a new and concrete situation (verbs: implementing, carrying out); to analyze, dividing information into parts, being able to understand the interrelationship between them (verbs: organizing, differentiating); to evaluate based on criteria, standards and norms (verbs: checking, criticizing); to create a new vision or solution based on the knowledge and skills previously acquired (verbs: producing, planning). From these structure, it was possible define five educational objectives:

1 To know and understand concepts and fundamentals applicable to problem solving;
2 To apply acquired knowledge to solve problems;
3 To evaluate proposed solutions against the actual client's criteria;
4 To assess one's own interpersonal skills and those of one's team;
5 To analyze and create (or adapt) resolution processes that best apply to the problem situation.

After defined objectives, evaluation strategies were used, with the purpose of verifying their accomplishment. To define these strategies, it was used the authentic assessment model described in [25] and [26–28]. In [25], Tai & Yuen define authentic assessment strategies in the PBL context from three perspectives: Content, related to the knowledge acquired by students; Process, related to the ability to apply that knowledge to solve problems; and Output, related to the products and artifacts generated as a result. Santos and Soares [26–28] enhanced this proposal and added two dimensions to the assessment process: Performance, which refers to a subjective analysis of the student's interpersonal characteristics, developed in the PBL approach; and Client Satisfaction, based on assessment criteria in the client's perspective of the solution.

So, for level 1, five perspectives are considered: (1) Content, for the possibility of verifying the appropriation of knowledge acquired by the students throughout the resolution process; (2) Process, as indicative to verify the ability to apply knowledge in the resolution process defined by the team; (3) Output from the delivery of solutions (products) created to address the context of the problem; (4) Performance, through the subjective analysis of interpersonal characteristics by the students (self assessment) and their team (peer review); and (5) Customer satisfaction, when considering an evaluation from the perspective of the client, with criteria for the defined solution and aspects directed to the performance of the team. Table 2 shows the association between the elements of xPBL, educational objectives and the evaluation strategies.

Table 2. Association xPBL, educational objectives and evaluation.

xPBL elements	Educational objectives	Evaluation strategies
Problem	To apply acquired knowledge to solve problems	Output evaluation
Environment	To evaluate proposed solutions against the actual client's criteria	Client satisfaction assessment
Human capital	To assess one's own interpersonal skills and those of one's team	Performance evaluation
Content	To know and understand concepts and fundamentals applicable to problem solving	Content evaluation
Process	To analyze and create (or adapt) resolution processes that best apply to the problem situation	Process assessment

Level 2 of the model uses the PBL-Test as described in the following subsection. Finally, level 3 focuses on getting information about the planning and teaching program, from the perspective of the students. At this level, the teacher is also evaluated under criteria that refer to skills inherent in teaching practice, as well as ethical aspects.

3.4 Act: PBL-Test Model

In the Framework, the act step maintains focus on the continuous improvement of the PBL process from the application of a test called "PBL-Test" [9], in order to identify possible methodological deviations that may render the fidelity of the approach unfeasible. This model is based on the need to evaluate the maturity of the PBL process regarding the execution of its principles, aligned to level 2 of the PBL-SEE model.

The PBL-Test is consisting of 10 objective and standardized questions are related to one PBL principle: (1) Problem (s) at the core of the educational proposal; (2) Learner as the owner of the problem; (3) Authenticity of the problem or task; (4) Authenticity of the learning environment; (5) Driving the solving the problem process; (6) Complexity of the problem or task; (7) Evaluation and analysis of how the problem was resolved; (8) Reflexion on the content learned and the learning process; (9) Collaborative and multidirectional learning and (10) Continuous Assessment.

In this case, a test with ten questions of multiple choices, referring to the principles, must be filled under the optics, perception and experience of human capital. For each evaluation, a score of 0 to 10 points can be obtained. All the answers are computed from an arithmetic average of the scores to generate the test result and thus identify the level of maturity of the process: (1) level 0 or insufficient (average < 7); (2) level 1 or initial ($7 \leq$ general average < 8); (3) level 2 or regular ($8 \leq$ general average < 9); (4) level 3 or good ($9 \leq$ general average < 10); and (5) level 4 or excellent (general average $= 10$). Once the level is identified, it is up to the PBL tutor, along with the pedagogical team, to identify strategies that can be implemented considering the principles that have had the most impact in the execution of the PBL process.

This assessment becomes effective when at least more than two verifications are performed in the running learning cycle so that improvements can be implemented in a timely manner. By the recommendation of the model, all the human capital defined by the pedagogical team, students and coordinators, needs to be involved in this evaluation.

4 Method

The guidelines for the scientific method which shapes the different stages of this research study, can be found in Design Science Research (DSR), a research method which involves analyzing the use and performance of artifacts that are designed to understand, explain and improve the behavior of specific factors in the domain of Information Systems [29]. The basic principle of DSR is that the knowledge, understanding and problem solving are acquired in the construction and application of an artifact within the context of a specific problem. In this context, the DSR method was adopted in five steps:

(1) *Understanding the Problem* to obtain a clearer understanding of PBL, its principles and characteristics that, in the view of several authors, govern the PBL method. It was possible to identify the challenges and any particular obstacles that might face the PBL method. As a result, a list of problems regarding the management of PBL was highlighting, such as the following: how to apply a PBL approach, the difficulty of setting out a procedure to assist the students with problem-solving, the complexity of assessment, among other factors.
(2) *Suggestions step* was to make conjectures about how processes and management models can be used to facilitate the application of PBL approach. After this, it was possible to design a model for PBL planning [10] and an assessment model aligned to this planning [21]. As a result, a conceptual model of the Framework was originated (see Fig. 1).
(3) *Development step* was to define the PBL Framework, considering all steps of the PDCA cycle. This led to the design of a maturity model of PBL based on its

principles [9] and propose a PBL process to support the solving-process by students.

(4) *Assessment step* was to understand the preparation, application and analysis of the artifacts, together with the end users, with the aim of determining, in the first moment, the applicability of the Framework. This resulted in the setting out of improvement in Framework components along several experiences of use [10, 11, 13, 30].

(5) *Conclusion stage* was to understand what we learn. It should be mentioned that the assessment procedure foresees future cases.

5 Experience Report

The Framework PBL was applied in an Enterprise Management Systems (EMS) course, part of an undergraduate course in Information Systems (IS). This course has a total of 60 h distributed in 4 months. The objective of the course was to enable students to design and implement management information systems, considering their requirements for business success. The course had 29 students with a mean age of 20, 3 were female and 26 were male. The following subsections describe the application of the Framework in each PDCA steps, emphasizing the main interventions related to PBL managing in this course.

5.1 Planning

Regarding the PBL planning, the five elements of xPBL were considered.

With respect to the *learning environment*, 29 students were divided into 7 teams: 3 teams with 5 students; 2 teams with 4 students and 2 teams with 3 students. Of the 29 students with a mean age of 20, 3 were female and 26 were male. The criteria for team formation were: professional experience, professional interest (manage, model solutions or program) and the identification of the profile of the student (artisan, guardian, idealist and rational), being identified by the application of the simplified version of the MBTI - Myers-Briggs Type Indicator [31]. To support the communication process and facilitate the distribution of course educational materials, the following tools have been adopted: Google Drive and WhatsApp group. Each team was able to freely choose the process of planning and managing their project. The only request of the pedagogical team to the students was to make possible the monitoring and follow-up via WEB of the planning and development of the projects. For planning, six teams adopted the Trello tool and one team adopted the Pivotal tracker tool. For development teams used Google Drive as a repository of documents. As for the classroom, it consisted of a blackboard, besides to individual chairs, which could be grouped together to facilitate group work. Although the ideal environment needs to have the same configuration of work environments in the industry, it was not an obstacle to running the course. The students still had five laboratories inside the Computer Center with computers to carry out their activities.

About the *problem* definition, the pedagogical team tried to identify real projects with business partners of the respective university, seeking possible clients to bring their real problems to the teams. As a way to meet the educational goals and competencies associated with the course, the teaching team oriented potential clients that the problems to be presented should be concern to the Enterprise Management Systems context. During the second week of class, three invited clients came to the classroom and presented a set of real problems which the teams could freely choose the one that interested them the most. All clients were managers in the implementation of business management systems, one of them SAP partner.

Considering the *human capital* involved, the teaching staff of the course called the pedagogical team consisted of one teacher and two tutors (one PBL tutor, and one technical tutor). In general, tutors aimed to continuously support the teaching-learning process of students. Specifically, the role of the PBL tutors was to support the execution of the xPBL methodology [10] used in the course. And the technical tutors had the function of supporting the students in the specific subjects of the course. During class, there was always the presence of at least one PBL tutor and a technical tutor attending the project follow-up meetings. Complementing the human capital of the course, there was the role of the project manager who was a student belonging to his respective team and elected by the team itself. The other members of the team worked in the role of developers of management systems. Finally, the real client was an IT professional with real and specific demands on business management systems.

The *content* that was worked on in the discipline served as support for students throughout the problem solving process. The main reference of the content was the book Management Information Systems [32]. Moreover, in order to present the concepts of the PBL approach, a lecture on PBL and its principles was given to the students. Then a lecture and a dynamic on the problem solving process according to the Delisle model [14], another lecture on critical success factors in the implementation of management systems and finally a lecture on stakeholder management.

Finally, the evaluation *process* was applied in all dimensions of the PBL-SEE [21]. Here, only two dimensions are presented: the first one related to students assessment (Content, Process, Results, Performance and Customer Satisfaction); and the second dimension with focus on degree of maturity of the PBL approach, from the perspective of students, and the use of PBL-Test model. The results of these evaluations will be further detailed in Sect. 3.3.

5.2 Doing

In order to help students to better understand the problem chosen and propose a more adequate solution to it, was developed a dynamic that made use of Delisle problem-solving model [14]. The model is composed of four aspects that must be observed: (1) Ideas: possible solutions to the problem; (2) Facts: information about the problem; (3) Hypotheses, identification of learning problems to solve the problem and; (4) Plan of Action: strategies, information resources and other information that lead to the resolution of the problem.

Once the understanding of the chosen problem was clearer, each team had to formalize the problem describing it in some ways such as the context of the problem, its causes and complexity, the target audience, customer needs, and so on. To help in describing the problem, were given to the teams a questionnaire model that reflected these aspects. Teams were also asked to describe their initial proposals for solutions through questions that guided students about the criteria for evaluating possible solutions, problem solving strategies, needed resources, and benefits for the client.

The Enterprise Management Systems (EMS) course was conducted over four learning cycles, with the respective goals:

- 1st. Cycle (*Understanding the problem*): the objective of this cycle was to evaluate if the teams identified a viable problem, considering the time and effort constraints imposed by the course schedule and team formation; If the students understood the causes and impacts of the problem in question; If the teams defined the roles and responsibilities of each member in the problem solving process; If they planned and scheduled the necessary actions to initiate a EMS project. This cycle marked the beginning of the project, so its main focus was "planning".
- 2nd. Cycle (*Proposal of solutions*): this cycle had as main focus to evaluate the maturity of the students in the understanding of the problem from interactions with the real clients and teamwork, describing specifically one solution within a defined project scope. This cycle was responsible for the delimitation of one solution, therefore, focused on the "scope" of the product to be delivered.
- 3rd. Cycle (*Prototyping a solution*): The purpose of this cycle was to evaluate the ability of teams to prototype a solution, in accordance with the requirements of the real client and users. This cycle focused on the design of an IS solution, therefore, focused on the "system design".
- 4th. Cycle (*Delivery a solution*): finally, this last cycle had the objective of evaluating students' understanding of the problem solving process as a whole, as well as the proposed solution and the necessary requirements for its implementation and effective adoption. The aim of this cycle was to understand the "solution" as a whole.

It is important to emphasize that the definition of these cycles had as reference the problem solving process of managerial information systems defined in [32]. From the objective of each cycle, it was possible to define the necessary evaluations, having as main reference the PBL-SEE assessment model [21], an integral part of the PBL framework. For this case, only the results of levels 1 and 2 of the PBL-SEE will be presented in this paper.

5.3 Checking

To develop the essentials skills the student assessment, recommended by PBL-SEE model was applied in accordance with the five perspectives (Content, Process, Output, Performance and Client Satisfaction). Table 3 shows the types of assessment conducted within each module, and highlights the instrument used for the assessment: subjective test, one with focus on process resolution concepts and other with focus on knowledge about the project decisions; the Meeting to start the Project (Kick-off); the Project monitoring meeting or remote monitoring (status report); the final presentation, to delivery the solution.

Table 3. Types of assessment per learning cycle [32].

#Cycle	Individual assessment (summative)		Group assessment (formative)		
	Content	Performance	Process	Output	Client
1	–	–	Kick-off	Kick-off	Kick-off
2	1st subjective test	Questions form	1st status report	1st status report	1st status report
3	2st subjective test	Questions form	2st status report	2st status report	2st status report
4	–	–	Final presentation	Final presentation	Final presentation

The 1st. Cycle and the 4th. Cycle were related to the initial and the end of the project steps, respectively. Thus, only the evaluations from the group perspective (Process, Output and client satisfaction) were applied. The individual evaluations of Performance and Content aspects are not adequate in these situations, when much information is missing or the project is already finalizing. As for the 2nd. and 3rd. cycles, all five perspectives (process, output, client satisfaction, performance and content) were applied. The results are presented and discussed in the following subsections. For the calculation of the students' overall performance in the course, it was used the following formula:

*20% * AA(Content) + 20% * AA(Process) + 20% * AA (Output) + 20% * AA(Performance) + 20% * AA(Client satisfaction),*

where "AA" corresponds to the arithmetic mean of the scores related to each perspective, when there is more than one score.

Regarding the Content perspective of the student assessment model, two subjective tests were applied in the 2nd. and 3rd. learning cycles.

The first test had the objective of the students' understanding of the problem solving process, regarding the implementation of a EMS for the respective real client. As a result, the general average of the class was 3.19, considering an interval of 1 to 5, with 57% of students with a performance equal to or greater than the desired average (equal to or greater than 3.5).

It is worth to emphasize that, on the 2nd. learning cycle, the teams had already structured the problem and delimited with greater clarity the scope of the solution. However, the results of this test showed that there was a difficulty in the teams to plan their projects, to define tasks and schedules compatible with their resources. This was happened because the students didn't define a consistent resolution process, which is a responsibility assumed by teacher in the traditional approach. For this, the content related to project management was reinforced.

The second test, held at the end of the 3rd. Cycle, had the objective of verifying the participation and contribution of each member in his/her team. The questions were also asked according to the resolution process, but the answers should be instantiated within the reality of each project. This test had a very interesting result, as it proved the students' maturity in conducting their projects and the different but consistent point of view that each one had on what his team was solving. From this context, it was also identified that the majority of students was active participant in their projects, all of them were engaged in their projects. The general average of the class reached 4.22, with 90% of the students with marks above the desired average. Table 4 shows the overall average of the teams from the perspective of Content in each test, with better performance for the teams T1, T3 and T6.

Table 4. Evaluations in the perspective of content [32].

Criteria	T1	T2	T3	T4	T5	T6	T7
1° Exam	4	3.375	3.1	3.17	1.92	3.56	2.94
2° Exam	4	4	4.75	3.8	3.25	4.62	4.6
General averages	4	3.68	3.9	3.5	2.58	4	3.77

In the perspective of Performance, two exams were applied on the middle of second and third learning cycles. Eight competences were assessed: self-initiative, commitment, collaboration, innovation, communication, learning, planning and analysis, as shown in Table 4. Due to the subjectivity of this analysis, this perspective used a scale of five values, with the following meanings: (1) "did not meet expectations"; (2) "partially met them"; (3) "met them"; (4) "met them very well"; (5) "exceeded expectations". This review was conducted by the PBL/Technical tutor and applied in the self-assessment format and evaluation in pairs (known as the 180° evaluation), where each member of a team was rated by his/her colleagues, anonymously.

Since this was undertaken by means of an online research tool, sophisticated individual reports could be obtained for each student, which showed the results of the assessment of colleagues in his/her team and his/her own assessment in a consolidated and graphic way, for each assessment criterion, including subjective comments. From their individual report, the students can have a sense of their performance in teamwork in the view of their team members, highlighting their strengths and points of improvement.

On analysing Table 5, it can be seen that teams T3 and T6 stand out with respect to the performance of their members, in the eight perspectives mapped. On comparing with the perspectives of Content, we see that there is a direct relationship between the best results of Performance especially in criteria Learning, Planning and Analysis, considered on the content exams.

The evaluations focused on group performance (Process, Output and Client Satisfaction) were applied in all learning cycles, conducted in the Status Report meetings, with the presence of the teacher (as a specialist in MIS), Technical tutors (as specialist in project management), PBL tutors and real clients.

In the perspective of "Process", the teams were evaluated by a technical tutor, who monitored the projects during four meetings: one Kick-off, two Status Report (SR) meetings and the final presentation. At the SR meetings, each team always

Table 5. Evaluation in the perspective of performance [32].

Criteria	T1	T2	T3	T4	T5	T6	T7
Self-initiative	3.58	3.59	3.59	2.84	3.72	3.75	3.76
Commitment	3.62	3.89	3.89	2.94	3.84	3.88	3.50
Collaboration	3.58	3.81	4.11	3.18	3.84	4.06	3.54
Innovation	3.32	3.27	3.78	2.84	4.06	4.06	3.38
Communication	3.40	3.76	3.83	3.07	3.39	3.72	3.44
Learning	3.68	3.72	3.83	3.00	3.89	4.06	3.48
Planning	3.42	3.56	3.39	2.63	3.83	3.81	3.32
Analysis	3.52	3.60	3.89	2.99	3.78	4.13	3.52
General averages	3.52	3.65	3.83	2.94	3.79	3.93	3.49

answered five questions: "What is the objective of your project?"; "What's the plan?"; "What has been done?"; "What are the strengths?"; and "What are the points of improvement?". As criteria for evaluation in this perspective, the following were defined: (1) Clarity in presentation; (2) mastery of the presentation; (3) Completeness when considering the five questions; (4) understanding of Planning. Each indicator could take on one value from a simple scale of five values: "1 - Insufficient; 2 - Regular; 3 - Good; 4 - Very Good; 5 - Excellent".

As to the perspective of Output, this was focused on analysis of the content of the presentations of the projects in the monitoring meetings. These analyses were conducted under the following criteria: (1) Context of the project; (2) Problem description; (3) Planned solution; (4) Value proposal; (5) Validation of the proposal. Once again, the same simple scale of five values was used. These evaluations were conducted by teacher.

The evaluation of client satisfaction was based on the following criteria: projection of confidence in interviews; understanding of the problems; clarity of presentation; quality of the solutions proposed; level of planning. This assessment used the same value scale as the perspectives of Process and Output, and was conducted by the client of the respective solution present in the Status Report meetings. Figure 2 summarizes the results of the teams in these three perspectives.

Below is a brief description of each project developed by the teams:

Team 1 Project: Tool for corporate training.

Team 2 Project: Organization's maturity diagnostic tool for deploying management systems.

Team 3 Project: Tool for mapping departments and teams to create an interactive organization chart.

Time 4 Project: Knowledge management process and workshops on how to do knowledge management.

Team 5 Project: A game for corporate training.

Team 6 Project: Information system design to combat waste and loss of food products due to management and logistics issues related to products.

Team 7 Project: Software Development for Demand Management (Acquisition of Software/IT Services).

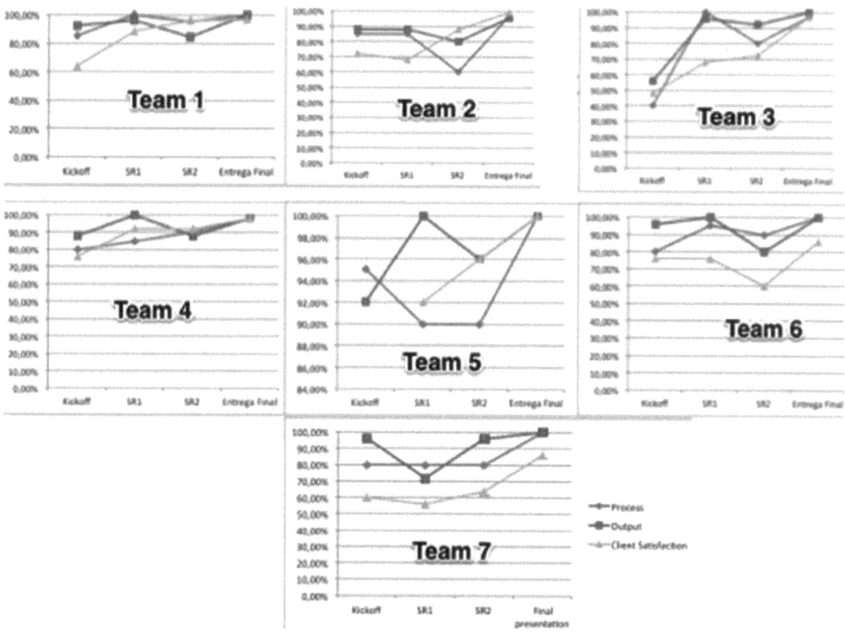

Fig. 2. Evaluations in the perspective of process, output and client satisfaction [32].

On analysing the graph in Fig. 2, we see that the performance of most of the teams improved throughout the stages of the life cycle of the project. Turning to the performance of teams T2, T3 and T5, we moreover see a significant improvement between the 1st monitoring (Kick-off) meeting and the final delivery. We can also see the difficulty of the teams concern to Process aspect, as verified in content exams. Another interesting behaviour observed in this chart was the natural "relaxation" of the teams that obtain excellent performances, when we compare the results of SR 1 and SR 2 for both Process and Output aspect. It is common for teams to concentrate on other priorities when they see that the challenges were met in full at that moment, and thus this has an impact on future activities and hence their performances in the following reviews.

Finally, the results of the teams in Client perspective show us a strong alignment between teams and their respective client. It is worth mentioning, that the involvement of the real customer in the evaluation process is crucial to the PBL approach, given that the stakeholder who will benefit from the solution cannot be left aside. This was one of the points that the teacher most worked on after the kick-off of the project: namely, the need to bring the customer to the center of the project, keeping him/her continuously close to the processes and validating each stage of the project with him. This reinforcement led to greater performances throughout the project in this perspective as shown in Fig. 2.

From the five perspectives of student evaluation (individual and group), radar-type graphics were generated, which summarized, in a visual way, the performance of each team. Figure 3 shows the four-team radars for illustration purposes. These graphics were generated twice, for 2nd and 3trd cycles.

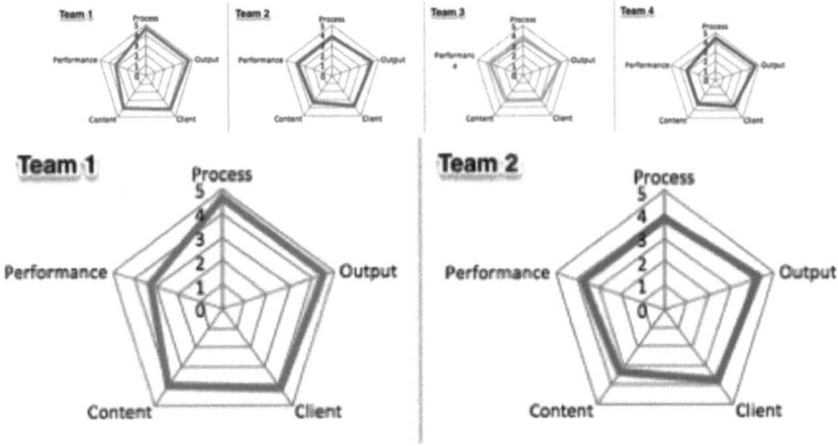

Fig. 3. Student assessment by radar graphics [32].

These graphs represent well the profile of each team, highlighting their strengths and weaknesses. Each respective graph can be used by the team to identify points that need to be better managed within the learning process, such as the process of problem solving and validation of solutions; And by the student groups themselves, which, based on these results, can seek improvements related to teamwork, better distribution of internal tasks and individual needs for further study, among other initiatives.

5.4 Acting

The PBL-Test applications were carried out in two strategically defined milestones during the planning: (1) during the second cycle, after the kick-off of the projects; (2) the third cycle, after the first status report on the solutions. It was defined that, in these milestones, the students would already be able to present their perceptions before what they had already experienced with the process. Tests were applied by two PBL tutors ("guardian of the method"), verifying if the execution of the PBL process was in accordance with the PBL principles. Table 6 summarizes these results.

For both assessments, an average percentage of 84.8% of class responses was maintained. As the purpose of the model, the PBL-Test considers that methodological deviations can be identified.

In summary, the results show that the level of maturity of the process was 2 (regular) for both applications, with a mean of 8.22 and 8.40. This score indicates that the teaching process evaluated is significantly adherent to the PBL principles. Given the results by principle, the PBL tutors, together with the pedagogical team, defined strategies that could improve the adherence of these principles to the process. For this,

Table 6. PBL-Test results [32].

Principles of PBL	1st Evaluation	2nd Evaluation
1. Problem(s) at the core of the educational proposal	0.82	0.88
2. Learner as the owner of the problem	0.82	0.85
3. Authenticity of the problem or task	0.94	1.00
4. Authenticity of the learning environment	0.58	0.56
5. Learner drives the problem-solving process	0.78	0.85
6. Complexity of the problem or task	0.90	0.83
7. Assessment of how the problem was solved	0.80	0.75
8. Reflection on the content learned and the learning process	0.88	0.88
9. Collaborative and multidirectional learning	0.90	0.90
10. Continuous assessment	0.90	0.90
Overall average	8.22	8.40

the results were presented and discussed with the tutors-mediated group in order to identify information that could substantiate the result.

Principles 4 and 5 were those that presented a lower score in the first application, compared to the others.

The main strategies established considered the promotion of reflection among the students so that they could perceive that the defined learning environment reflects real situations. The learning environment could not be characterized as a simulation, a situation assumed by the professor in face of their professional experiences, because the students deal directly with the clients that approved the demands, besides experiencing aspects inherent to the practice of project management (deadlines for delivering artifacts, costs, solution quality, and process risks, among others). It is believed that the lack of adequate infrastructure to promote a collaborative learning environment is the factor that contributed to the result of the second application of the test, being less than the first one. This was due to the structure of the classroom for expository class (chairs lined up, professor's slate and digital projector), almost always requiring improvisation for group work.

For Principle 5, as a strategy to encourage self-directed learning, that is necessary to conduct the resolution process, it was decided that all teams would need to adopt a collaborative tool to manage activities and thus facilitate the conduct of the resolution process by the teams and monitoring by the technical tutor. One can see that the implemented strategies contributed to the adherence of the principles since the result was increased in the second application.

After the application of the second evaluation of the PBL-Test, students' impressions regarding the execution of the discipline were collected through a form. They were able to comment anonymously on what were the strengths and weaknesses. Listed below are some of these comments:

Strengths:

- Exit the comfort zone and stimulate the search for information.
- Feedback from clients and the teacher.
- Well-defined follow-up.
- Interaction with real clients.
- Consistency with the practical world.

Weaknesses:

- Encourage more student participation with bonuses.
- Greater focus on theoretical knowledge, making it clearer how each theory interacts with projects.
- Increased number of clients to choose from students.
- Greater clarity in the definition of evaluation criteria.
- It improves the way the PBL methodology is presented.

6 Conclusions

Although it was born in the 60's in medical education, the Problem-Based Learning (PBL) approach has been used with quite positive results in computer teaching in the last two decades. Its characteristics based on collaborative work, student self-initiative and practical application of knowledge have a very strong alignment with the way ICT professionals work in the market. Therefore, its use has been growing in educational institutions that seek a way to differentiate themselves by innovating their pedagogical approaches. However, many challenges remain on the way to PBL. To apply PBL so that its benefits are achieved requires a very high effort from all the actors involved, either by the pedagogical team, who need to plan and manage their processes carefully or by the students who need to be active actors in the process of learning.

With this motivation, this article proposes the application of PBL in a managed way, from a Framework described in [13]. Based on Deming's PDCA (Plan-Do-Check-Act) cycle, this Framework enables the planning, execution, control, and enhancements to the PBL process across an educational unit. To demonstrate its application, the article describes a case of an undergraduate course in Information Systems, within a period of 1 semester.

In the Plan step, the Framework makes use of a methodology based on guidelines for the application of PBL in the teaching of computing, denominated by xPBL. xPBL is based on five manageable elements (problem, learning environment, human capital, content and assessment process) and recommendations that guide how to plan these elements so that the principles of the approach are preserved. Educational objectives are also defined in this step, allowing the structuring of learning cycles (Do step), accompanied by the application of the authentic evaluation model PBL-SEE [21] (Check step). The PBL approach itself is also evaluated from a maturity model called PBL-Test [9] (Act Step).

In the case discussed in this paper, during the planning stage it was defined the participation of a real client who presented their real problems related to IS deployment (relevant and complex), bringing authenticity to the learning environment. The pedagogical team was formed by the teacher, technical tutor, PBL tutor and the real client, who supported student teams throughout the problem-solving process and partial solution evaluations.

The content proposed by the teacher and tutors was not the only source of information for searching for solutions since it included feedback from the experts (teacher and tutors), the field surveys and interviews with users and clients of information systems.

The evaluations were applied in a formative way, through project monitoring, content evaluations and interpersonal skills assessments (360-degree performance evaluation). These evaluations allowed continuous monitoring of problem-solving, allowing the pedagogical team to intervene in order to redirect teams in search of better solutions.

Finally, the PBL approach was also monitored for compliance with its principles, from the PBL-Test measuring instrument, part of the Act Stage Framework. This monitoring showed a high degree of compliance, above 80%.

About improvements identified, from the perspective of the students, it is important to emphasize the need to instill students' participation more broadly within the team; to stimulate the students in the search of theoretical knowledge, discussing among all the viability or better way of applying them; the participation of a greater number of real customers and; clarity in the definition of evaluation criteria.

From the point of view of the pedagogical team, it is possible to highlight the support of information systems in the management of the learning process, considering the evaluation model proposed by the PBL Framework and the defined educational objectives.

It is also planned as a future improvement, building a website to support dissemination of the PBL Framework, allowing access to its artifacts, systems and application cases.

References

1. Draft, S.: Computer Science Curricula (2013)
2. ACM/IEEE: Software Engineering 2014 - Curriculum Guidelines for Undergraduate Degree Programs in Software Engineering. ACM, New York (2015). https://www.acm.org/education/SE2014-20150223_draft.pdf, https://www.acm.org/education/curricula-recommendations. Accessed 02 June 2018
3. Martin, K., Chinn, D.: Collaborative, problem-based learning in computer science (2005)
4. Tuohi, R.: Assessment in problem based learning connected with it engineering education. Presented at the International Conference on Engineering Education & Research, Melbourne, Australia, pp. 2–7, December 2007
5. Peng, W.: Practice and experience in the application of problem-based learning in computer programming course. In: International Conference on Educational and Information Technology (2010)
6. Zaharias, P., Belk, M., Samaras, G.: Employing virtual worlds for HCI education: a problem-based learning approach. In: Proceeding CHI EA 2012. Extended Abstracts on Human Factors in Computing Systems, pp. 317–326 (2012)

7. Oliveira, A.M.C.A., dos Santos, S.C., Garcia, V.C.: PBL in teaching computing: an overview of the last 15 years. In: Frontiers in Education, Oklahoma. IEEE Education Society (2013)
8. Panwong, P., Kenemavuthanon, K.: Problem-based learning framework for junior software developer: empirical study for computer programming students. Wirel. Pers. Commun. **76**, 603 (2014)
9. Santos S.C., Figuerêdo, C.O., Wanderley, F.: PBL-test: a model to evaluate the maturity of teaching processes in a PBL Approach, FIE, Oklahoma, EUA (2013)
10. Santos S.C., Furtado F., Lins W.: xPBL: a methodology for managing PBL when teaching computing, FIE, Madrid, Spain (2014)
11. Santos, S.C., Alexandre, G.H.S., Rodrigues, A.: Applying PBL in project management education: a case study of an undergraduate course. In: The 45th Annual Frontiers in Education (FIE), El Paso - Texas. Frontiers in Education: Launching a New Vision in Engineering Education (2015)
12. Savery, J.R.: Overview of problem-based learning: definitions and distinctions. Interdiscip. J. Probl.-Based Learn. **1**(1), Article 3 (2006)
13. Santos, S.C., Rodrigues, A.: A framework to apply PBL in computing education. FIE, Erie, Pennsylvania (2016)
14. Delisle, R.: How to Use Problem-Based Learning in the Classroom (1997)
15. Savery, J.R., Duff, T.M.: Problem based learning: an instructional model and its constructivist framework. Educ. Technol. **35**, 31–38 (1995)
16. Maltese, R.: Project Based Learning, 25 Projects for 21st Century Learning. Dog Ear Publishing, Indianapolis (2012)
17. Hung, W.: The 9-step problem design process for problem-based learning: application of the 3C3R model. Educ. Res. Rev. **4**, 118–141 (2009)
18. Hung, W.: The 3C3R model: a conceptual framework for designing problems in PBL. Interdiscip. J. Probl.-Based Learn. **1**, 6 (2006)
19. Barrows, H.S.: Problem-Based Learning (PBL) (2001). http://www.pbli.org/pbl/pbl.htm. Accessed 20 Dec 2015
20. Alexandre, G.H.S., Santos, S.C.: PBL planner toolkit: a canvas-based tool for planning PBL in software engineering education CSEDU, Funchal (2018)
21. Santos, S.C.: PBL-SEE: an authentic assessment model for PBL-based software engineering education. Trans. Educ. **60**, 120–126 (2016)
22. Barrows, H.S.: Problem-Based Learning (2001)
23. Krathwohl, D.R.: A revision of bloom's taxonomy: an overview. Theory Pract. **4**, 212–218 (2002)
24. Herrington, J., Herrington, A.: Authentic assessment and multimedia: how university students respond to a model of authentic assessment. High. Educ. Res. Dev. **17**(3), 305–322 (1998)
25. Tai, G.X.L., Yuen, M.C.: Authentic assessment strategies in problem based learning. In: ICT: Providing Choices for Learners and Learning, Singapore, pp. 983–993 (2007)
26. dos Santos, S.C., Soares, F.S.F.: Authentic assessment in software engineering education based on PBL principles: a case study in the telecom market. In: Proceedings of the 2013 International Conference on Software Engineering. IEEE Press, pp. 1055–1062 (2013)
27. Vaishnavi, V., Kuechler, W.: Design Research in Information Systems (2004)
28. Britain, S., Liber, O. (eds.): A framework for pedagogical evaluation of virtual learning environments (1999)
29. Monte, A.C., Rodrigues, A., Santos, S.C.: A PBL approach to process management applied to software engineering education. In: Frontiers in Education, Oklahoma. IEEE Education Society (2013)

30. Myers, I.B.: Gifts Differing: Understanding Personality Type". Davies-Black Publishing, Mountain View (1980)
31. Laudon, K.C., Laudon, J.P.: Sistemas de informação gerenciais: administrando a empresa digital. Tradução Arlete Simille Marques (2004)
32. Alexandre, G., Santos, S., Rodrigues, A., Souza, P.: Applying and managing PBL - An experience in information systems education. In: Proceedings of the 10th International Conference on Computer Supported Education, CSEDU, vol. 2, pp. 57–67 (2018)

Practical Software Engineering Capstone Course – Framework for Large, Open-Ended Projects to Graduate Student Teams

Timo Vasankari and Anne-Maarit Majanoja(✉)

Department of Future Technologies, University of Turku, Turku, Finland
{timo.vasankari,anne-maarit.majanoja}@utu.fi

Abstract. For students, capstone project represents the culmination of their studies and is typically one of the last milestones before graduation. Participating in a capstone project can be an inspiring learning opportunity or a struggle due various reasons yet a very educative learning experience. During the IT capstone project students practice and develop their professional skills in designing and implementing a solution to a complex, ill-defined real-life problem as a team. This paper reflects on organizing IT capstone projects in computer science and software engineering Master programmes in a Sino-Finnish setup, where the projects are executed in a framework provided by a capstone project course. We describe the course framework and discuss the challenges in finding and providing ill-defined challenges with meaningful real-life connection for project topics. Based on our observations complemented with students' feedback we also propose areas for future development.

Keywords: Capstone · IT student projects · Project-based learning

1 Introduction

During the past years, capstone project has been an important part of the curricula for studies in Information Technology (IT). Based on Merriam-Webster dictionary capstone means: "the high point: crowning achievement". Therefore, the project is the capstone of IT studies where the students use all their acquired skills and knowledge in culminating their academic experience. The main idea behind the capstone course is to provide an opportunity for IT students to demonstrate together, in a team, their true capacity to integrate and apply their knowledge and skills to a real-life (software) engineering problem.

Based on Rasul et al. [28], capstone project is a unique type of learning experience for the students as in capstone project they mainly work in a self-directed approach and are expected to carry out various and numerous tasks related a large problem without

This article is further work extending an earlier conference paper: Majanoja, A-M. and Vasankari, T. Reflections on Teaching Software Engineering Capstone Course. In Proceedings of the 10th International Conference on Computer Supported Education (CSEDU 2018) - Volume 2, pages 68-77.

B. M. McLaren et al. (Eds.): CSEDU 2018, CCIS 1022, pp. 310–327, 2019.
https://doi.org/10.1007/978-3-030-21151-6_16

structured approach provided by teachers. Naturally, the students are not fully out-of-support, but the idea is to transfer the learning process to be student-led instead of teacher-led. While the learning approach is different, also the assessment is based on different aspects. The consistency of the assessment practices of the capstone course needs to be ensured and clearly communicated to the students. As Mills [25], Bramhal et al. [3] and Gardner and Willey [13] identified, the capstone assessment can include various tools from self- and peer-evaluation, process and product assessments, formative and summative assessments (such as the working process and the final outcome of the development), and students self-reflection of their learning in course-diaries/blogs.

The aim of this paper is to reflect on various aspects of organizing capstone projects as courses part of university degree programs. Structured student feedback collected at the end of the course records student experiences and provides data to discuss the relevance of various parts of the course. The students' feedback and teachers' observations are used to provide recommendations for iterative course development at the University of Turku, Finland. The University of Turku and Fudan University, China, have a strategic partnership of collaboration and provide a dual master's degree in Information Technology. Therefore, the two main student groups during the capstone courses were Finnish and Chinese students. In this research we analyse the master level capstone course feedback materials from years 2014 to 2018 and combine the findings with teachers' observations on the courses.

The rest of the paper has been divided into four parts. Section 2 deals with existing research and the theoretical dimensions of Problem-based Project-oriented Learning (POPBL). Section 3 describes the research design. Section 4 presents the findings. Section 5 includes the conclusions and introduces a few tasks for further research.

2 Literature Review

Over the years, one of the most used approaches has been the teacher-centric approach, where the teacher has the full control and authority while lecturing at the front of the class-room. Senge [32] wrote that most people expect to get answers from people above them, because they have grown up in an authoritarian environment and culture. Nowadays, this type of approach does not support the target to prepare students for their future workplace and face constantly changing working environment and requirements. Therefore, the responsibility of learning and own actions need to be pushed onto the students' side. Problem-based learning (PBL) is an example of a student-centered educational model [2, 14, 30] although based on literature PBL's effects are controversial [6, 18, 31]. In PBL approach, students' own learning process is placed at the centre of the educational process by supporting the students to construct their own knowledge, and to develop problem-solving and group work skills [9].

PBL and POPBL based capstone project is one implementation of a student-centric approach to provide opportunities for students to apply their content specific knowledge and workplace skills gained during their several years of studies [8, 10, 22]. The focus is not only on technical skills but also on having the ability to identify non-technical aspects, interaction of those and propose possible solutions [22]. Since the

1980s, the capstone type of learning approach has been part of universities' curriculum [34]. The capstone approach is commonly used, for example, in software development project courses where students design and develop software solutions in teams for external customers [34].

Havelka and Merhout [15] reported IT professional competences that IT professionals should have. In addition to technical aspects, many of the needed skills were non-technical and behaviour related. Havelka and Merhout [15] categorized those skills under four categories: (1) Personal traits (passion, experience, conscientiousness, attitude, character, and flexibility). (2) Professional skills (organization skills, leadership ability, analytic skills, team-oriented, interpersonal skills, and problem-solving). (3) Business knowledge (business concepts, business process knowledge, and organization knowledge). (4) Technical knowledge (enterprise systems, development methods, application software, project management, production data management, architecture, infrastructure, programming, security & control, business intelligence, and communication networks). Practicing these competences is typically at the core of IT domain capstone projects' learning targets.

Reifenberg and Long [29] wrote that students value the capstone experience. Based on Dondlinger and McLeod [8] and Dondlinger and Wilson [7] the capstone experience include challenges, but still the main approach has been favourable. The students reported to gain vital skills and competences, such as, learning new skills when applying prior knowledge; cultural understanding and new appreciation for people within their own culture; interaction and negotiation skills; and self-awareness [7]. At the same time, Reifenberg and Long [29] wrote of the capstone challenges, such as mismatch of expectations, information gaps, misunderstandings and challenges in cooperation among the capstone project team members.

In literature, it has been identified that one of the main challenges in capstone type of course assessment has been the tendency to focus primarily on written or product outcome [16, 21, 32]. This same challenge remains although it has been recognized that the main assessment criteria should be focused on skills developed during the project, such as teamwork, communication, life-long learning, and technical skills. Therefore, the final software program as outcome should not determine the passing grade for the course. Even if the written software does not work, the team can still pass the course if they have achieved the planned learning targets. The capstone course teachers can use a variety of tools and practices to get insight into capstone teams activities, such as self and peer-evaluation, process and product assessments, formative and summative assessments, and students' course-diaries/blogs [3, 13, 21, 25].

Capstone projects can also provide students a valuable opportunity to be exposed to cultural diversity already during their studies when the students operate in a multinational and multi-cultural situation. During the capstone project implementation the team members have to take into account member's national culture impact upon the whole team [11]. Morkos et al. [26] conducted a comparative study between domestic and international students. They found that quite often the domestic students took the leading position, and the teams had to overcome the frustrating situations caused by cultural and language barriers by improving their communication and interaction skills. Morkos et al. [26] pointed that the students may not immediately recognize the lessons they learned from the multicultural situation. The recognition of diversity related lessons happens afterwards.

While the quality and success of final product does not serve well as the main basis for assessment, when the intended learning outcomes emphasize improving problem solving and teamwork skills, the scope of a capstone project may reach to taking the results of the project into operation, providing not only evidence for direct assessment, but also a further viewpoint for students' self-assessment. In engineering education, CDIO has been adopted as a framework for curricular planning and outcome-based assessment [4]. CDIO (Conceiving – Designing – Implementing – Operating) framework, which is developed within engineering, stress engineering fundamentals set in the real-world systems and products, and cover the from understanding the problem to operating the built solution. In the late 1990s it was recognized that fewer faculty members had professional hands-on engineering experience and CDIO started as a reaction to associate engineering students back to the practice of engineering [5–12].

Based on Edström and Kolmos [12], PBL and CDIO target on broader learning outcomes emphasizing the process of becoming a professional, including both skills and personal development. A clear difference between PBL and CDIO can be identified: "*CDIO aims to align the intended learning outcomes with professional practice – and the focus on more appropriate processes for teaching and learning comes as a consequence of that. For PBL, it was the learning process that was aligned with professional practice*" [12]. In other words, PBL focuses on rethinking the process whereas CDIO focuses on rethinking the outcomes. The spirit of the times when the approaches were developed has a direct impact: PBL was developed in the 1960s and 1970s (highly student-centered interpretation) whereas the CDIO was established much later and thereby includes more recent trends (such as, external stakeholder interest).

PBL and CDIO have mutual interest in, for example, problem-, project-, and design-based learning experiences and the lessons learned around organizational change strategies. Therefore, institutions can combine both approaches where the CDIO approach supports a structured process for learning outcomes, and the combination of CDIO and PBL pedagogy supports the development of learning experiences. Using CDIO approach in a capstone course has already been tested in higher education institutes. Two examples of the utilization of CDIO approach:

(1) The principles and standards of CDIO were implemented in the MEng programme in Mechanical and Manufacturing Engineering at Queen's University Belfast [1]. Armstrong et al. [1] found that other courses need to be integrated with the capstone to provide support and add meaning to the topics covered (i.e. constituted learning experience). The syllabus contains technical knowledge, personal and professional skills, interpersonal skills that are developed further during the capstone project (i.e. experimentation and knowledge discovery). Armstrong et al. [1] identified that during the capstone project students mature and become more confident, and they develop their interpersonal skills.

(2) In 2012, a new Capstone Innovation Project course based on the CDIO framework was piloted at Turku University of Applied Sciences [20]. Kulmala et al. [20] identified agile approach and Scrum to ensure successful project management and commitment. They highlighted the criticality of good project management skills: (1) to help students to move from the idea generation phase to implementation phase. (2) to

commit the product owners and users to the development process, (3) to meet and interact with potential clients. Kulmala et al. [20] found the assessment criteria defined in CDIO standards as a challenge to apply in some projects. Also finding the project customers relied on teachers' active role and it was considered should also students participate in the preliminary work to find and meet potential customers before starting the capstone course.

3 Capstone Course Implementation

3.1 The Framework

The software engineering capstone course is a mandatory course in the master level IT studies at the University of Turku. To provide it as a compulsory unit, timely linked to the degree program, and including all the degree program students, it has been organised formally as a traditional course in the teaching program. The course needs to have a clear structure, but at the same time it is important that the teachers only facilitate the students' learning, and the implemented activities are managed by the students themselves to achieve the expected learning outcomes.

One course takes three academic periods, about nine months, and the course is structured with regular predefined classroom activities (e.g., status reports, pitching, demonstrations). The focus of the capstone course is on designing and implementing a proof-of-concept level solution to a fairly complex real-world problem via practical test and try approach. The idea is to provide a situation that simulates various aspects from engineering working life phenomena in a safe environment that also allows failures. Sometimes learning from failures can be a better learning experience than learning from success. Based on our observation, teams that face failures during their project often analyse, identify root causes for their situation and actions, and even are able to take the needed corrective actions. Analysing the causes behind failures during a common class activity provides a viewpoint for students in other teams of these critical project factors.

Capstone project utilizes both PBL and POPBL methods and some elements from Problem-Solving Learning (PSL). As Sotto [33] highlights, it is better that the students are quickly able to practice their knowledge and skills instead of spending significant amount of time to understand the problem. By our experience the nature of problem, often also the field of its origin, determines how soon the team can start experimenting potential solutions. In this course, understanding the problem is given significant time, while however the project teams know from the beginning that they are expected to provide a working solution. They are encouraged to decrease the amount of uncertainty by quickly prototyping potential technologies and partial solutions as part of the design phase, thus the phases of CDIO are applied not separate, strictly one following the other, but overlapping and even sometimes repeating shorter cycles of the adjacent phases. To allow this to materialize, the project is given enough calendar time. The intended learning outcomes (ILOs) defined for this course focus on team working, communication and problem-solving skills. The students practice those skills with preselected project topics stretching out of their comfort zone, while also improving and widening their discipline-specific, in most cases technical, skills.

3.1.1 Project Topics

The teachers spend a significant amount of time to discuss with potential topic owners and prepare the project topics beforehand. After running the course for 4 years, the concept is getting widely known and topics are increasingly suggested to the course (Step 1). Since the main idea of the capstone course is to provide open-ended problems to students, topic owners need to understand and commit to the course goals (Step 2) and accept that they cannot define the expected solution in details or give exact requirements to be implemented, rather describe the problem, user needs and aspects that have impact on the value of a viable solution. In the process of identifying and preparing topics for the project course the initial topic ideas are discussed (Step 3) and, with the influence of teachers, often converted or reformulated from the initial idea the potential topic owner did present (Step 4), or even a new idea, more aligned with the course goals, comes up and is taken further in the process. Our experience is that only few suggested topic candidates are found totally unfit for the project course and once the course concept in working on ill-defined problems is explained, the topic owners mostly accept and even appreciate the more open-ended approach. To do a positive decision on taking a topic further (Step 5) the topic owner needs to commit to the project and allocate time to work with the team. The approved topics are presented to the project course (Step 6) to invite students to project team. A template of topic description is used to give new topic owners guidance on what aspects should be covered in the rather short description that is supposed both to raise interest among the students and appear possible with the knowledge the students have and can be expected to gain during the project. Forming the teams is explained later in 3.1.4.

The process of finding, validating and formulating project topics is summarized in Fig. 1.

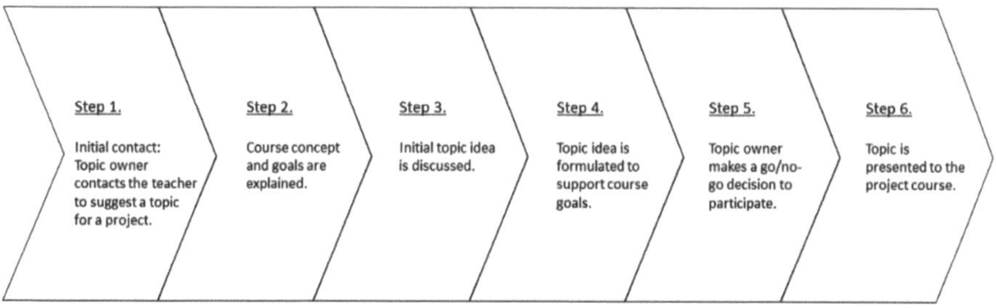

Fig. 1. Process of developing project topic.

Within Fall 2014 – Spring 2018, 46 project teams have been formed to work on their topic. Of these, 12 teams worked on a topic provided by a company, 14 worked on a problem provided by university units representing other disciplines than IT, 4 teams created a product idea responding to a public hackathon or similar challenge, 1 team came up with their own product idea and 15 topics were provided and generated by the department of IT. Since the department offers also another master level course, titled Lean Software Startup method [17], which focuses on the business potential and user value perspectives in developing innovations using the lean startup, the project topic ideas that are based on a students' own business ideas are channeled to that course. This division does not prohibit the capstone teams from considering commercialization of their project results, but business dimension is not systematically discussed as part of the course. The capstone project topics provided by the department of IT, in 2017 renamed as the department of Future Technologies, both serve as a buffer to accommodate the varying course sizes from one course instance to other and allow providing a range of topics that benefit from the full spectrum of modern technologies taught at the department. While in a way home-grown, these topics are chosen and defined so that there can be seen a real-life problem and application area for the solution to be built. Accepted topics typically do not directly relate to the research done the department, but utilize technologies known by a member of the faculty and relate to an application area of his or her personal interest, such as sports. The aim is, that while the topic owner in such case – being one of the teachers - speaks the domain language of the students, defining a viable solution requires understanding a phenomenon or need outside the domain of IT.

3.1.2 Attendance

The practice is that students enrol to the course beforehand. That way the teachers are able to evaluate the students' current level of studies. If the student does not fulfil the requirements (i.e. being master level students), the teachers can inform them to attend the needed courses prior taking the capstone project on coming semesters. Advance enrolment also provides indication on how many teams will likely be formed and thus the number of project topics needed for the next instance of the course.

The full attendance is mandatory, but the demand for 100% presence is adjusted, because students can have situations when they cannot attend (e.g. doctor's appointment or exam on other courses). During every lecture, the attendance is recorded with signature on the student list. That way the teachers can follow-up the attendance (which is one aspect of course evaluation) and also show that teachers care for students' presence. In case of a student missing multiple compulsory sessions, the student needs to agree on activities to compensate for their absence. This kind of social contracts are linked with professionalism [35] and applying those between teachers and students is good practice for working life. That way the students can practice the impact (positive or negative) of unspoken norms and rules.

One of the challenges in organising this course is timing. Typically, the Fudan students spend one academic semester, about six months in Finland. Still, the course takes longer, about nine months. This means that the teams built of students from both universities need to find ways to continue and finalize work even when located in two continents. At the early stage of capstone course implementation, it was found that the Fudan students considered their course related activities ended when they returned back to China and then the Finnish students alone had to finalize the project work. However, during the past few iterations this scheme of thinking has gradually been changed by planning and placing common course activities to the final stage of the project. Also holiday seasons of two cultures impact on the course. For example, the course that starts around January will be finalized around October. This means a summer break in the middle of the course in Finland, and Chinese National Day break in early Fall.

3.1.3 Lectures

The main teaching approach during the capstone project course is on active learning activities. However, due to the high amount of students (35–50 students) some traditional type of lecturing is also included to activate the students in the classroom to further process the topic inside their project teams. Every lecture focuses on a different topic related to the common stage of the projects by providing a short introduction to the students. The idea is to give "mental hooks" for directing their focus on digesting new topics and activities. The capstone course lectures include two parts. One part focuses on project management and communication specific skills. The second part focuses on team work and interaction skills. These lectures and hands-on practices provide the basic knowledge for the students to apply in their project team.

The course utilizes Moodle online tool to share and communicate course related materials. The materials are created by teachers, and there are no specific textbooks to be used during the course. This also encourages students to be active and write their own notes. Earlier research has shown that when students make their own notes, they internalize the topic better [27]. Earlier research indicate that slides can make students passive listeners or they focus on other activities (such as, Facebook, WhatsApp messaging, etc.) as they do not bother to make their own notes.

During the series of lectures the students will give several presentations, such as status reports, project plans and project pitch. The students get assignments during lectures to work independently and then during the next lecture they present the outcomes. Every lecture has a slightly different topic or focus to keep students motivated to work around the project with clear focus areas and deadlines. Although, based on observations, it has been noticed that many of the students are not motivated to listen other teams' presentations.

3.1.4 Project Teams and Forming the Student Teams

Based on experience collected from several capstone course iterations, team dynamics appears to be a core element of success or a serious hindering effect. Since student self-motivation is expected to be one fundamental element to successfully meet numerous project challenges, students' own interests are taken into account and raise of their motivation supported in the process of forming the teams. The process is illustrated in Fig. 2.

At the beginning of the capstone course, teachers and topic owners present the prepared project topics to the class of students. After each presentation, students can ask questions about the topic (Step 1). On another all-class session the class is divided to random groups, number of groups corresponding the number of topics, and a group work is exercised (Step 2). In the workshop all students discuss in groups every topic, one at the time, and the discussion is guided with some questions provided by the teacher. At the end of the workshop, the class gets together and teacher goes through each topic, asking the class what kind of ideas or concerns had come up. Teacher also asks students, who are considering choosing each specific topic, to raise their hand. This workshop is used to both provide students an opportunity to discuss their concerns and interests in respect to the topics available, and create a situation where students discuss aspects of also those topics that may not have been raised their interest when initially presented. For the teachers, the poll at the end gives indication about the popularity of the topics and how the interest in the current class is divided between project topics offered. If a topic is found to be totally uninteresting to the class, it may be dropped out of choices. On the courses run, there has been one such topic on almost every other course.

After the workshop the students are asked to choose the three most interesting topics which they would like to participate in (Step 3). Based on the motivation letters the teachers will form the groups (Step 4).

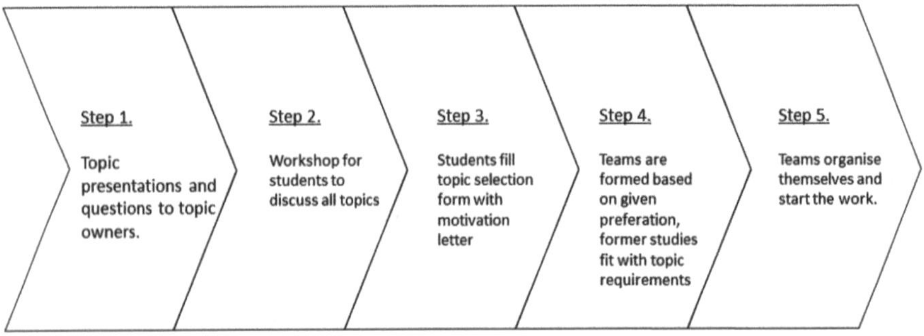

Fig. 2. Process of forming project teams.

The students may not be assigned with the topic they primarily preferred. The teachers spend quite a lot of time to form the groups by reviewing students' prior courses and interests written into the motivation letter to ensure diversity and the topic specific skills needed to succeed. The team size can be slightly adjusted, 1-2 members more or less, to have the students to work on topics they have shown at least some interest, but the aim is that no student is assigned to work on a topic not listed in his motivation letter. The team size is taken into account when discussing the project target with the team and later when assessing the team performance.

Once the teams are formed, the team compositions are announced and the teams are expected to get together and organize themselves (Step 5). At this phase, some students ask for the reasoning behind their placement.

As the course participants consist of students both from the University of Turku and the Fudan University (China), the teachers ensure that every team is multinational. That way it can also be ensured that the teams practice their English language skills during their project work. At the same time, the students also learn to interact with people from different cultures and with way-of-working habits.

Since team working skills are in the core of intended learning outcomes of the course, the team size is normally aimed for minimum of four or five, ideal being five to six, but can reach up to eight students when the topic offers several areas to focus on, and thus provides a larger team ideas how to divide their work. However, larger team size can more easily accommodate "free-riding" type of behavior. In a smaller team members tend to take bigger responsibility for ensuring the overall success and they also support each other around the tasks and competences. In larger teams the division of work and responsibilities requires more attention from teachers.

Quite a lot of the students have working life background or they are even already working in industry. Having prior working life experience can help to excel in capstone projects and reach even more demanding goals, via deeper understanding of what they need to do and what is required from them. In other words, the students are able to fill the knowledge gaps of teachers' presentations with their own practical experience knowledge.

3.2 Project Activities and Course Assessment

3.2.1 Topic Owner Interaction and Project Budget

All of the project teams have an external project topic owner, who is not a teacher on the course. The students interact with the topic owner, often seen as their customer, collect requirements and later present their solution proposal. Ideally the topic owner is an external/industry representative, but as noted earlier, research groups and researchers from the University of Turku have also been in this role. By default, the teams have very small budget that can limit their activities and technology choices. In the case that building the solution for a topic requires access to specific technology, topic owner is expected to provide this.

3.2.2 Project Implementation

The project team assigns different roles to its members during the project activities. One of the key roles is that team leader, who usually is also responsible for customer communication. The idea is to learn to manage communication between the team and its project stakeholders.

Project planning is an important phase, because it shows how well and to what depth students have understood the problem and the requirements. The idea is to review and revise the project plan several times during the capstone course. The first plan is the first best guess, but the main lesson is that the project plan needs to be updated and re-estimated regularly. The idea is also to practice how to divide a complex tasks into smaller implementable entities. That way the students also practice how to schedule activities and what is the impact if they do not take the responsibility or ownership of implementing the tasks. Based on our observations we have identified ownership of the activities to be the most relevant success factor. If the students feel the ownership of the project, they are also willing to invest time and effort to the outcome and interaction.

The project teams also meet regularly with the teachers to discuss the details of their project. These sessions provide a tool for the teachers to assess the dynamics of interaction in the team and their potential need for support or advice to improve the situation.

3.3 Technologies and Tools Supporting Learning Outcomes

As the teams are allowed and expected to organise themselves, they also have freedom in choosing the tools they use, while the nature of the topic sets some requirements for technologies, e.g. specific type of sensors, to be used. Each team is required to keep a project repository to store their digital outcomes, and teachers are given access to it.

Each team presents their choice of tools in their presentations in order to share experience and provide best practices within the course.

Used tools include common file sharing tools, such as Dropbox, Google Drive, etc., task boards like Trello, distributed version control systems like Git. These tools are used regardless of the technologies related to building the actual project result.

Technologies experimented in building the project outcomes have included various sensor technologies, app and web development frameworks, AI and machine vision algorithms and flexible computing platforms specially designed for learning purposes, such as Raspberry Pi. In some cases, a program-controlled device like a drone or model racing car has been used as the platform for the solution built.

4 Results and Analysis

4.1 Students' Feedback Analysis

To evaluate how the course succeeds in guiding students to the intended learning outcomes we analysed the student feedback collected at the end of the capstone courses. The focus in this study was to analyse if the students report development in skills related to the intended learning outcomes on the course. The student feedback is collected by using online survey tool after the course. At the beginning of the capstone course, the assessment process including self and peer-evaluations was introduced to the students. After the course the students self-evaluated their own participation and contribution to their project. They also provide an evaluation for each of their team members. These self-reflected evaluations provide to teachers an insight into the team's operation and how the work load was balanced among the team members.

The students identified technical skills as essential to succeed in their capstone project. Three examples from the student feedback: "Technical support is really necessary", "The biggest problem was to do software project without actual programmers" and "We are all expected to understand and implement software programs. This was a huge issue in my group". Based on the feedback material it was possible to identify that technical aspects could be seen as potential discipline knowledge gaps and were one of root causes to teams' challenges.

The students identified various technical topics (Table 1) as development areas to better succeed in capstone project activities. Also the students' self-evaluation of their prior technical skills indicated that many students did not have the needed technical skills to excel in their capstone project (Fig. 3).

The new situation in which the students independently managed their capstone project and its activities caused question marks for some students. In typical approach teachers give more exact tasks and activities to be performed. However, the capstone project learning target is to practice team skills, take active responsibility on both defining and implementing project tasks, and the accountability remains on the student side.

Based on the feedback results some of the students expected more strict supervision and guidance from the teachers: "*I had a feeling throughout the course that there should have been more supervision that the team members were doing their job*", "*I*

Table 1. Students' self-identified areas for developing their technical skills (in [23]).

Algorithms and analytical skills: - Algorithm and algorithm analysis - Mathematical modeling - Learning analytics - Data-analytics
Programming: - C/C ++ - Java courses - Object-oriented programming courses - Web programming - Python programming
Networks and Databases: - Network knowledge - Database technologies - Network and Operation systems
Other technical skills: - Cloud computing - Software and HTML design - Graphical design - Robotics - Geographical information systems and developing geo-informatics software - IoT devices - App development (Android or iOS) - Version control

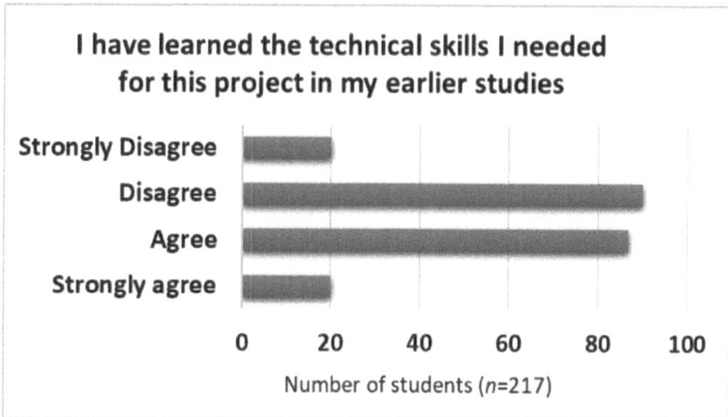

Fig. 3. Sufficient technical skills to succeed in a capstone project.

wish we can get more supervision in the course, because our team was confused sometimes", and "*Provide more detailed directions and motivating or pushing teams to start the project activities*". Yet, some of the students recognized that the supervision should come from inside the team, such as to be conducted by the project manager/leader: "*There should have been more supervision that the team members were doing their job. However I think this should be something that is the responsibility of the project manager not the person managing the course. Maybe this should be emphasized more when talking about the role of the project manager*". Some students also proposed to have a teaching assistant who would focus on supporting a specific team: "*I hope each project team can have one assistant teacher who is familiar with the project so that we can get the necessary help*".

Also motivation and interaction aspects caused some concerns. One of the key success factors to succeed in capstone project is student's own motivation. If a student does not have the needed motivation, it can affect the rest of the team. Few examples from the student feedback: "*Kick out unskilled and unmotivated students*", "*Capstone required a lot of motivation and hard work. Students of IT department are not usually very eager to make suggestions nor working without someone pushing them forward.*" Some even proposed direct approaches to deal with unmotivated or non-participative team members who negatively impacted on their team working: "*I can only come up with two ways to improve motivation towards team working: either punishing students for not doing anything relevant or encouraging them to improve their teamwork skills*".

The interaction and experience sharing with the fellow capstone teams could provide opportunities to learn and cooperate. Sharing situations and challenges could provide a new kind of reflection window to team working: "*I would have some interaction session with other groups on how they are managing the project, what difficulties they are facing and what went so well, are we facing the similar kind of situations? This way we could figure out the common problems and complete the project better*". The communication between the different capstone project teams was very little and limited to the common all-class sessions. The interest to work together with other teams was identified: "*I hope we could have an open working atmosphere to exchange ideas and solutions with other teams*".

Based on the student feedback, the majority of the students reported skill improvements or they learned new technical or project management skills during their capstone project (Fig. 4). As an example, the students reported: "*I got valuable*

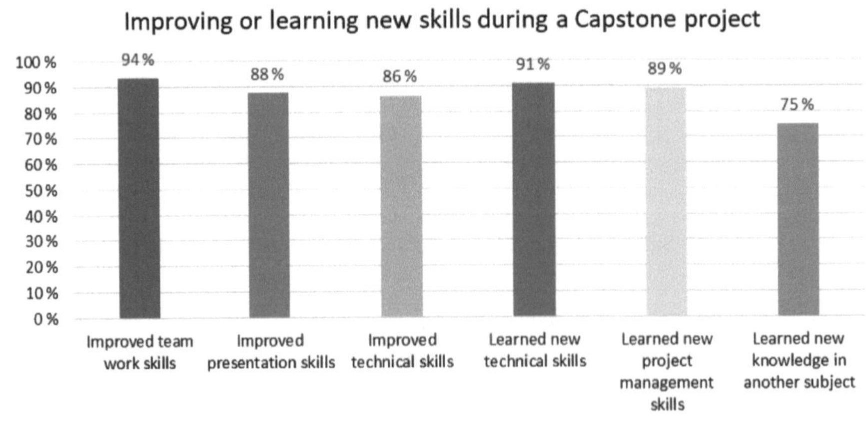

Fig. 4. Students' self-evaluation of their skill development after the Capstone course.

information on project management and leadership and got to practice my presentation skills". "*It is the first formal project course I have ever taken and most of the skills needed are new for me. So I have learned new things which makes me feel happy*".

Some students also identified that the capstone project was an opportunity to practice the skills and knowledge gained during the several years of studies: "*I believe the whole idea of a Capstone project is to employ the skills and competences learned in school and working life*". The students identified team working skills as an outcome of the capstone project: "*I liked the practical teamwork approach for common problems that required learning new skills and problem solving with different types of people. An eye-opening experience*".

The capstone project also provided an opportunity to learn new knowledge in another subject and thereby expanding the students' skills and working life capabilities.

4.2 Analysis and Recommendations for Further Course Development

Based on the student feedback, teachers' observations and hands-on experience, the following focus areas and recommendations for further development were identified.

Clarify the goals of capstone project experience. At the beginning of the capstone course, it is important to highlight to the students the opportunity to apply and deepen the knowledge and skills acquired in their studies and extend their academic experience by thinking critically and creatively during their capstone project. The capstone project provides a safe environment and an opportunity to demonstrate their proficiency in various areas and thus can be used as an asset on job markets.

Highlighting the importance of student commitment to the project and the team. Students' commitment has a key role in the success of a capstone project. This course is quite unique in making the students mainly responsible for their activities, schedules, team work practices, atmosphere, and deliverables. The teacher provides support, but the students have to take the initiative to raise the need for support and guidance. Still, some students try to push the responsibility back on teachers and stay passive waiting for more instructions. During the recent iterations of the capstone course the expectation for the students active role has been discussed more both at all-class sessions and when teacher meets individual teams. More communication and educating the learning method at the beginning of the course needs to be highlighted.

More focus on technical studies. The students need to gain the basic technical knowledge in their pre-capstone studies. Capstone project provides a tool for students to conduct self-evaluation of their current professional skills. For the university the success level of capstone projects gives input for planning how to teach these technical skills at right, early-enough points in curriculum.

Interaction between the capstone teams. A more low-profile interaction between teams could enable sharing and reflecting team challenges without the pressure of presenting the case to the entire class. Topics and situations encountered in capstone projects could be discussed in small groups being a mixture of several capstone teams. The groups would share a summary of their discussion and reflected viewpoints.

Having assistant teachers and technical support. Quite many of the students experienced challenges with technical aspects during their project. Due to budget limitations, various practical exercises on earlier courses have been reduced [24]. In the project students may also operate with technologies they are not familiar with and they need more technical support. Therefore, it is recommendable to have more resources for technical support and course assistants to support the capstone teams.

Expanding the course together with other faculties. While the majority of the students on past capstone project teams have been students of IT, providing a viable solution to most project topics could have benefitted from an interdisciplinary team. Engaging other subjects and faculties on IT focused projects could provide opportunities. To succeed, the project topics should systematically be developed together with other faculties. Linking IT and business students is a realized approach (e.g. [19]). In a multidisciplinary university such as University of Turku, several disciplines could ideally be involved.

5 Conclusions

The capstone project implemented in a team can facilitate learning on many aspects; team working and problem-solving skills, and extending graduate students discipline-specific knowledge and skills aligned by requirements and limitations set in real-life scenarios. From the vast variety of problems and challenges, choosing topics accommodating a sufficiently open, ill-defined challenge yet with a goal that can be defined and achieved using the skills in a team of postgraduate students, typically most of them still with little practical experience, while related to the technical domain of their studies, is a challenge itself. With the strong impact of student motivation present, the topic should appear interesting yet not overwhelmingly complicated to motivate the students in challenging them to take the project seriously and even give their best effort to it. The experience shows that some moderation is often needed to the topics suggested, initially but also while the project is in execution and the actual performance and capabilities of the team becomes evident.

The aim of a capstone project is to provide students a safe environment to practice their current knowledge and abilities, and experiment the diversity cultures, perspectives and even academic disciplines. Further target is to strengthen students' ability to think critically, communicate efficiently and use various technologies, both as project tools and as components of a viable solution. In addition, the capstone project provides a lesson about commitment towards social responsibilities, leadership, providing service to others, and how the lack of commitment affects the whole project team.

This study set out with the aim of describing and discussing the arrangements of capstone project courses in University of Turku, Department of Future Technologies, and to provide recommendations for developing the course and its supporting curriculum. To form our recommendation the students' feedback was analysed and conclusion reflected against teachers' observations. The aim of the course has been in setting a framework that accommodates all IT master students to do a capstone project as part of their degree program in a timely way.

Based on the analysis it was identified that technical aspects cause significant challenges to students. Quite many of the challenges culminate around the students' limited practical programming skills and the capstone course currently as such does not have the resources to provide detailed technical guidance in all team specific issues. Therefore, more focus is needed on strengthening students' technical skills on their earlier studies before joining the master level capstone course.

The results of this study also indicate students' challenges to perceive their student-led role being in charge of all of the activities instead of following the traditional teacher-led approach. The change from rather passive receiver to active doer can be challenging. Students' prior working life experience has a positive effect on the whole team. Those teams are found to achieve deeper understanding of what they are required to do and more effectively fill the knowledge gaps with their practical experience. Thus, the teams with such earlier experience, are seen to reach higher excellence in the quality of their project results.

We acknowledge the limitations of this study as the results come from operations of only one university, yet serving a student population with two significant subgroups: students with their undergraduate IT degree from Finnish university system and students with comparable degree from Chinese universities. At the same time, however, the results are well aligned with the existing capstone research and discourse.

Future research should search for a systematic model for student assessment combining self-assessment, peer-assessment and teacher and topic owner viewpoints. Further, experimenting how to effectively support filling the fundamental knowledge gaps during the project is seen viable for the course execution. Also the relevance of the capstone project as a self-assessment tool for students' working life capabilities is a topic of further interest.

References

1. Armstrong, P.J., Kee, R.J., Kenny, R.G., Cunningham, G.: A CDIO approach to the final year capstone project. In: 1st International CDIO Conference and Collaborators' Meeting, Queen's University, Kingston, Ontario, Canada (2005). http://www.cdio.org/knowledge-library/documents/cdio-approach-final-year-capstone-project
2. Barrows, H.S.: Problem-based learning in medicine and beyond: a brief overview. New Dir. Teach. Learn. **68**, 3–12 (1996)
3. Bramhall, M., Short, C., Lad, R.: Professional reflection and portfolios to aid success and employability. The annual Australasian Association for Engineering Education, Melbourne, Australia (2012). http://www.aaee.com.au/conferences/2012/documents/abstracts/aaee2012-submission-20.pdf
4. CDIO: The CDIO initiative is an innovative educational framework producing the next generation of engineers (2018). http://www.cdio.org/about
5. Crawley, E.F.: The CDIO Syllabus: a statement of goals for undergraduate engineering education: MIT CDIO Report #1. Accessed 21 Apr. www.cdio.org/framework-benefits/cdio-syllabus-report
6. Dochy, F., Segers, M., Van den Bossche, P., Gijbels, D.: Effects of problem-based learning: a meta-analysis. Learn. Instr. **13**(5), 533–568 (2003)
7. Dondlinger, M.J., Wilson, D.A.: Creating and alternate reality: critical, creative, and empathic thinking generated in the "global village playground" capsone experience. Think. Ski. Creat. **7**(3), 153–164 (2012)

8. Dondlinger, M.J., McLeod, J.K.: Solving real world problems with alternate reality gaming: student experiences in the global village playground capstone course design. Interdiscip. J. Probl.-Based Learn. **9**(2), Article 3 (2015)
9. Dolmans, D.H., De Grave, W., Wolfhagen, I.H., Van der Vleuten, C.P.: Problem-based learning: future challenges for educational practice and research. Med. Educ. **39**(7), 732–741 (2005)
10. Dunlap, J.: Problem-based learning and self-efficacy: how a capstone course prepares students for a profession. Educ. Technol. Res. Dev. **53**(1), 65–83 (2005)
11. Duran, V., Popescu, A.-D.: The challenge of multicultural communication in virtual teams. Procedia – Soc. Behav. Sci. **109**, 365–369 (2014)
12. Edström, K., Kolmos, A.: PBL and CDIO: complementary models for engineering education development. Eur. J. Eng. Educ. **39**(5), 539–555 (2014)
13. Gardner, A., Willey, K.: Student participation in and perceptions of regular formative assessment activities. The annual Australasian Association for Engineering Education, Melbourne, Australia (2012). http://www.aaee.com.au/conferences/2012/documents/abstracts/aaee2012-submission-55.pdf
14. Gwee, M.C.: Globalization of problem-based learning (PBL): cross-cultural implications. Kaohsiung J. Med. Sci. **24**(3), 14–22 (2008)
15. Havelka, D., Merhout, J.W.: Toward a theory of information technology professional competence. J. Comput. Inf. Syst. **50**(2), 106–116 (2009)
16. Jawitz, J., Shay, S., Moore, R.: Management and assessment of final year projects in engineering. Int. J. Eng. Educ. **18**(4), 472–478 (2002)
17. Järvi, A., Taajamaa, V., Hyrynsalmi, S.: Lean software startup – an experience report from an entrepreneurial software business course. In: Fernandes, J.M., Machado, R.J., Wnuk, K. (eds.) ICSOB 2015. LNBIP, vol. 210, pp. 230–244. Springer, Cham (2015). https://doi.org/10.1007/978-3-319-19593-3_21
18. Kirschner, P.A., Sweller, J., Clark, R.E.: Why minimal guidance during instruction does not work: an analysis of the failure of constructivist, discovery, problem-based, experiential, and inquiry-based teaching. Educ. Psychol. **41**(2), 75–86 (2006)
19. Kruchten, P., Lawrence, P., Dahl, D., Cubbon, P.: New venture design – interdisciplinary capstone projects at UBC. In: Proceedings of the 2nd Annual CEEA Conference: Memorial University St. John's, Newfoundland 6–8 June 2011 (2011). https://ojs.library.queensu.ca/index.php/PCEEA/article/view/3637
20. Kulmala, R., Luimula, M., Roslöf, J.: Capstone innovation project – pedagogical model and methods. In: Proceedings of the 10th International CDIO Conference, Universitat Politècnica de Catalunya, Barcelona, Spain, 16–19 June 2014 (2014). http://www.cdio.org/node/6098
21. Lawson, J., Rasul, M., Howard, P., Martin, F.: Getting it right: assessment tasks and marking for capstone project courses. In: Capstone Design Conference: 2014 Conference Proceedings (2004). http://www.capstoneconf.org/resources/2014%20Proceedings/Papers/0017.pdf
22. Lehmann, M., Christensen, P., Du, X., Thrane, M.: Problem-oriented and project-based learning (POPBL) as an innovative learning strategy for sustainable development in engineering education. Eur. J. Eng. Educ. **33**(3), 283–295 (2008)
23. Majanoja, A.-M., Vasankari, T.: Reflections on teaching software engineering capstone course. In: Proceedings of the 10th International Conference on Computer Supported Education (CSEDU 2018), vol. 2, pp. 68–77 (2018)
24. Majanoja, A.-M., Taajamaa, V., Leppänen, V., Sutinen, E.: The transformation challenge of IT education and training in higher education and industry. In: Proceedings of the 9th International Conference on Computer Supported Education (CSEDU 2017), vol. 2, pp. 240–247 (2017)

25. Mills, J.: Multiple assessment strategies for capstone civil engineering class design project. The annual Australasian Association for Engineering Education, Melbourne, Australia (2007)
26. Morkos, B., Summers, J.D., Thoe, S.: A comparative survey of domestic and international experiences in capstone design. Int. J. Eng. Educ. **30**(1), 79–90 (2014)
27. Mueller, P.A., Oppenheimer, D.M.: The pen is mightier than the keyboard - advantages of longhand over laptop note taking. Psychol. Sci. **25**(6), 1159–1168 (2014)
28. Rasul, M.G, Nouwens, F., Swift, R., Martin, F., Greensill, V.C.: Assessment of final year engineering projects: a pilot investigation on issues and best practice. In: Rasul, M.G. (ed.) Developments in Engineering Education Standards: Advanced Curriculum Innovations, Chapter 5, pp. 80–104 (2012)
29. Reifenberg, S., Long, S.: Negotiating the client-based capstone experience. Int. J. Teach. Learn. High. Educ. **29**(3), 580–588 (2017)
30. Savin-Baden, M.: Problem-based Learning in Higher Education: Untold Stories. Open University Press, Buckingham (2000)
31. Schmidt, H.G., Van der Molen, H.T., Te Winkel, W.W.R., Wijnen, W.H.F.W.: Constructivist, problem-based learning does work: a meta-analysis of curricular comparisons involving a single medical school. Educ. Psychol. **44**(4), 227–249 (2009)
32. Senge, P.: Systems thinking. Exec. Excel. **13**(1), 15–16 (1996)
33. Sotto, E.: When Teaching Becomes Learning: A Theory and Practice of Teaching. Bloomsbury Publishing, London (2007)
34. Vanhanen, J., Lehtinen, T.O.A., Lassenius, C.: Teaching real-world software engineering through a capstone project course with industrial customers. In: First International Workshop on Software Engineering Education Based on Real-World Experiences EduRex, pp. 29–32 (2012)
35. Vu, M.T.: The social contract: On university English teacher professionalism, structure and agency. In: Leite, L. (ed.) Transitions in Teacher Education and Professional Identities, ATEE Annual Conference Proceedings 2014, pp. 483–492 (2015)

A Systematic Mapping Study on Game Elements and Serious Games for Learning Programming

Adriano Lages dos Santos[1(✉)], Maurício R. A. Souza[2], Marcela Dayrell[2], and Eduardo Figueiredo[1]

[1] Federal University of Minas Gerais, Belo Horizonte, MG, Brazil
{adrianolages, mrasouza, figueiredo}@dcc.ufmg.br
[2] State University of Montes Claros, Montes Claros, Brazil
mdayrell@unimontes.br

Abstract. This work aims to verify how serious games and their composing elements are used and evaluated to support learning programming. Serious games have been used as a tool to support learning in several areas and subjects. To achieve its educational goals, a serious game must consist of a set of game elements that are related to the learning outcomes. In Computer Science, educators are also using serious games and their elements to enhance learning of programming-related disciplines, which are often considered challenging by first-year students. To achieve our goal we defined three research questions: (1) What are the serious games for learning programming? (2) What are the game elements in the serious games for learning programming? and (3) What is the empirical strategies and methods used to evaluate existing game elements? A systematic mapping study on the use and evaluation of game elements for learning programming was conducted. Our systematic literature search found 27 elements of games distributed in 43 serious games. The elements of games are present in 39 primary studies that date from 2007 to 2016. The elements of games more reported in the literature were: Fantasy, Goal, Level, Point System, and Quest. Our results also indicate that game elements are only evaluated indirectly by means of their serious games. Furthermore, we identify some shortcomings in primary studies found, such as the lack of systematic evaluation, for instance, by means of controlled experiments and the low number of quantitative studies.

Keywords: Serious games · Game elements · Programming · Education · Learning

1 Introduction

Serious games are important tools for many educational areas and educators are using games to improve traditional classes. Serious games for learning programming provide students with a way to reinforce knowledge acquired in classroom. Students can also learn programming concepts without being in direct contact with an educator, allowing students to learn anywhere and anytime [1]. Serious games combine different elements,

B. M. McLaren et al. (Eds.): CSEDU 2018, CCIS 1022, pp. 328–356, 2019.
https://doi.org/10.1007/978-3-030-21151-6_17

such as levels, leaderboards, point system, and bosses, to achieve its learning goals [2]. These game elements, if used properly, can promote learning and boost student interest [3]. However, the right combination of elements may contribute to the success or failure of a serious game. Additionally, developing a good game is not an easy task. It demands time and resources and requires programming and graphic design abilities [4]. These factors may hinder the development and use of games in the academia.

Computer Science also benefit from the use of games and their composing elements to provide students a more enjoyable way to learn the fundaments of programming [5]. In the context of programming education, serious games are often evaluated using subjective feedback collected via questionnaires from the students after play sessions [6]. However, students evaluate the games as a whole and, so, they do not evaluate specific game elements that compose these games. As a result, data on the effectiveness of each game element for learning is not gathered. Thus, educators do not have information about which game elements have contributed positively and negatively for learning programming. Such feedback could provide valuable lessons on how each game element contributes for the student learning, engagement, and motivation when playing serious games. Therefore, educators would benefit from guidelines about the use of specific game elements.

Other works in the literature investigate how game elements are related to learning outcomes. Wilson et al. [7], conducted a systematic revision of studies that relates the game elements with learning objectives in the context of the education in general, not specifically for programming. Souza et al. [8] evaluated two game elements used in an experiment in a discipline of software engineering in a university. The study evaluates the effectiveness of the use of these elements taking into account the students' opinion. Battistela et al. [9] conducted a systematic revision to identify games for teaching of several knowledge areas of the computer science. The work makes a division of the games for levels of learning (cognitive, skill and affectionate) objectives, but does not take game elements in consideration. Our work differs from the other related works because we perform a systematic mapping study to identify and verify how game elements are evaluated in the context of learning programming. To the best of our knowledge, we could not find any work in the literature that aims to identify how game elements are evaluated in the context of learning programming.

In this context, this paper extends our previous work [10] by expanding and deepen a systematic mapping study on use and evaluation of game elements for learning programming. Our goal is to investigate the programming educational literature in order to: (i) identify the game elements used in serious games for learning programming and (ii) understand how these game elements are evaluated. Additionally, we expect to identify possible research gaps and trends for future investigations. With respect to our previous work [10], this paper expands the analysis and discussion about the use and evaluation of game elements. We also include a new research question to investigate which are the serious games for learning programming in literature, their characteristics and game elements, and what knowledge areas of learning programming these games aim to cover.

The selection of primary studies was accomplished with a systematic search in five bases of data: ACM Digital Library, IEEE Xplore, Science Direct, Springer Link, and Wiley Online Library. In order to select relevant primary studies, the search was based on combinations of keywords derived from the study goal. We executed automatic searches in the scientific databases using selected keywords. We filtered the studies retrieved from automatic searches to exclude papers not aligned with the study goals. We defined inclusion and exclusion criteria (detailed in Sect. 3) to define which primary studies would be selected and which would not be.

We identified 39 primary studies, which mention or use 27 different game elements in 43 serious games for learning programming. We then identified and mapped the game elements used in each game and the evaluation strategies used. Surprisingly, we did not find any study that objectively and directly evaluates game elements. Due to this negative result, we focus on the indirect evaluation of game elements by means of their comprising serious games. With respect to this indirect evaluation of game elements, only a small number of studies provide quantitative data to support their results.

In summary, the main contributions of this work are:

- We present a list of game elements recurrently used in the development of serious games for learning programming.
- We look at how primary studies evaluate the game elements and if the primary studies show which game elements contribute positively and negatively to learning programming.
- We found that primary studies evaluate the serious games as a whole and not game elements individually. Based on this negative result, we discuss the importance of evaluating each game element individually.
- We present a list of serious games to learn programming in higher education found by a systematic mapping study conducted in five scientific databases.
- We present the characteristics of each serious game and the knowledge area of learning programming that the serious game is covering.

The remainder of this paper is organized as follows. Section 2 provides the current state of art about game-elements and serious games for learning programming. In Sect. 3, we describe the design of this systematic mapping study. Section 4 presents the results of the study. Section 5 discusses the results on how serious games for learning programming can be used and improved. Section 6 discusses the threats to validity of the study while we discuss the related work in Sect. 7. Section 8 concludes this research paper.

2 Background

The goal of this study is to identify elements existing in games to learning programming. When we refer to learning programming, we are referring to learn algorithms and data structures, not only basic concepts but also advanced ones. In this section, we document some of these game elements (Sect. 2.1) and background about learning programming and complexity knowledge areas according to ACM Computer Science Curricula 2013 – CS2013 (Sect. 2.2).

2.1 Game Elements

Game elements are a set of components that compose a game [3]. In some studies, game elements are also called game attributes [3]. In fact, terminology and description for game elements are not uniform in the literature. Souza [11] discuss the lack of a standard definition and nomenclature for game elements. For instance, emblem [12] and badge [13] are two names for the same game element, which are visual rewards given to the user and identify user achievements in the game.

Previous works have tried to define a unified taxonomy for game elements, but there is no consensus in the community about it [14]. Several authors propose different strategies to categorize game elements [14, 15]. However, several authors [2, 3] end up using their own definitions, according to the needs of the research. This lack of standardization in element names makes it difficult to unify results of studies that use or evaluate game elements.

Research on which game elements constitute the core of a game is conducted since the 80 s. Previous work defined that game elements such as, challenge, curiosity, control, and fantasy, constituted a core of a game [16, 17]. Other works expanded this view to incorporate other elements, such as roles of a player, conflicts, even rules, goals, and constraints [18, 19].

Bedwell [3] present a taxonomy to define game elements for educational purposes. They surveyed the literature on game elements related to education and identified the most recurring game elements. The work is generalist and it does not consider specific areas of learning, such as programming.

Werbach [2] propose a pyramid that organizes game elements in three categories: dynamics, mechanics, and components. Components compose the base of the pyramid, with the mechanics group in the middle and dynamics on top. Dynamics contain the main aspects of a serious game. They are conceptual elements in a serious game. Examples of elements in this group are: Constraints, Emotions, Narrative, Progression, and Relationships. Mechanics contain the basic process that directs users to engage with content and continue to drive the action forward. Examples of mechanics are: Challenges, Feedback, Competition, and Cooperation. Components are less abstract than the first two categories and are tools that can be employed to motivate user in the environment of interest. Examples are Achievement, Avatar, Badge, Combat, Leaderboard, and Level.

Table 1 document definitions of some game elements and we cite some works that they appear. There are more than 40 game elements documented in literature.

2.2 Learning Programming

Algorithms are a fundamental knowledge for students of Computer Science. A good software system depends of the algorithms chosen and the various layers of implementation. Design of algorithms is important to performance of all software systems. Furthermore, as stated by the 2013 ACM & IEEE Computer Science curricula (CS2013) [22], the study of algorithms provides insights into the intrinsic nature of the problem and possible solutions independent of programming language, hardware, or other implementation aspects.

Table 1. Game elements and their descriptions.

Game element	Description
Challenge	Ideal amount of difficulty and improbability of obtaining goals. A challenging game possesses multiple clearly specified goals, progressive difficulty, and informational ambiguity. Challenge also adds fun and competition by creating barriers between current state and goal state [2]
Fantasy	Make-believe environment, scenarios, or characters. It involves the player in mental imagery and imagination for unusual locations, social situations, and analogies for real-world processes. The player is also required to take on various roles in which they are expected to identify [3]
Rule	Rules establish criteria for how to win. Specific, well-defined rules and guidelines are a necessary component for an effective educational game. Three types of rules exist: (a) system rules (i.e., functional parameters inherent in the game), (b) procedural rules (i.e., actions in game to regulate behavior), and (c) imported rules (i.e., rules originating from real world [7]
Level	An indication of a reached a milestone, a level in a game. Levels are often defined as point thresholds, so that players can automatically level up based on their participation or use levels to indicate status and control access to content on the game [20]

According to CS2013, students have to develop the ability to select the appropriate algorithms for a set of problems. The knowledge area of CS2013 responsible for defining how algorithms should be addressed in Computer Science courses is "Algorithms and Complexity". This knowledge area defines the main skills for students to design, implement, and debug algorithms to solve problems.

The Algorithms and Complexity knowledge area is divided in seven sub-areas. Table 2 lists the three areas considered in this study: (i) algorithmic strategies, (ii) fundamental data structures and algorithms, and (iii) advanced data structures, algorithms, and analysis. We select these three areas because we are mainly concerned in finding elements from serious games to learn algorithms and data structures.

Table 2. Selected knowledge areas according to ACM Computer Science Curricula 2013 [10].

Name	Description
Algorithmic Strategies - AS	Brute-force, greedy, divide-and-conquer, and recursive algorithms. Dynamic programming, reduction
Fundamental Data Structures and Algorithms - FDS	Binary search. Insertion sort, selection sort, shellsort, quicksort, mergesort, heapsort. Binary heaps. Binary search trees, hashing. Representations of graphs. Graph search, unionfind, minimum spanning trees, shortest paths. Substring search, pattern matching
Advanced Data Structures, Algorithms and Analysis - ADS	Balanced trees, B-trees. Topological sort, strong components, network flow. Convex hull. Geometric search and intersection. String sorts, tries, Data compression

The other four areas are related to automata and complexity analysis. They are: (iv) basic analysis, (v) basic automata, computability and complexity, (vi) advanced computation complexity, and (vii) advanced automata theory and complexity.

3 Study Settings

This section presents the goal of this study and its experimental steps. Section 3.1 presents the study goal and research questions. Section 3.2 explains the research method and steps we followed. Section 3.3 discusses the search strategy applied to mine relevant scientific databases. Section 3.4 shows the selection process filtering only relevant papers for this study. Lastly, Sect. 3.5 shows the strategy for data extraction and summarizing the results.

3.1 Goals and Research Questions

The goal of this study is to identify game elements existing in serious games for learning programming. By learning programming, we mean all aspects to learn algorithms and data structures, from basic algorithms and data structures to advanced ones. More formally, we define the goal of this study based on the GQM [23] as follows: to identify and analyze game elements from the purpose of understanding their use and evaluation, in the context of serious games for learning programming, from the perspective of researchers, educators, and students. To achieve this goal, we defined three research questions:

RQ1. What are the serious games for learning programming? The expected outcome is a list of games categorized by algorithms and complexity knowledge areas from CS 2013.
RQ2. What are the game elements in the serious games for learning programming? The answer is a list of game elements that are in existing serious games. We also aim to categorize these elements.
RQ3. What are the empirical strategies and methods used to evaluate existing game elements? The expected answer is a mapping between game elements and the type of empirical studies used to evaluate them [24].

3.2 Experimental Steps

To achieve the study goal (Sect. 3.1), we conducted a systematic mapping study – SMS. SMS is a secondary study method that systematically (i.e., based on a structured and repeatable process or protocol) explores and categorizes studies in a research field. It also provides a structure of the types of research reports and results that have been published [25]. Additionally, we expect to identify possible research gaps and trends for future investigations.

We have conducted the SMS in the period of May/2017 to September/2017; following four steps adopted described as follows [25].

- **Step 1 – Definition of Research Questions:** we defined three research questions, based on the study goal, to establish the scope of the systematic study (Sect. 3.1);
- **Step 2 – Conduct Search:** based on the research questions, we defined and performed a replicable method for searching and retrieving papers in five selected scientific databases (Sect. 3.3);
- **Step 3 – Study Selection:** we defined and applied a systematic method for selecting only the relevant papers for this study (Sect. 3.4);
- **Step 4 – Data Extraction and Analysis:** we finally summarized the relevant data from the primary studies (Sect. 3.4) and present the study results (Sect. 3.5).

Four researchers participated in the planning and execution of the study: an undergraduate student in Information Systems, two Ph.D. students in Computer Science, and a Ph.D. associate professor. Two Ph.D. students conducted the searches in scientific databases and conducted the process of inclusion and exclusion of primary studies. The undergraduate student participated in the phase of extraction of information from the selected studies. All phases were supervised by the Ph.D. associate professor, which validated all stages of the study and participated in discussions on the SMS strategy.

3.3 Search Strategy

To identify possible relevant primary studies for data extraction, the search was based on (i) trial searches using combinations of keywords derived from the study goal and (ii) the execution of automatic searches in the scientific databases using search strings. Initially, we selected relevant keywords related to three major concepts: (a) education; (b) algorithms and data structures; and (c) games. The resulting keywords per major concept were:

- Education: teach; learn, education, train;
- Algorithms and data structures: algorithm, data structures, program;
- Games: game, edutainment, playful;

We defined search strings by grouping keywords in the same domain with the logic operator "OR" and grouping the three major concepts with the logic operator "AND". We then executed automatic searches in five scientific databases, using and adapting (when necessary) the search string. The databases were ACM Digital Library[1], IEEE Xplore[2], Science Direct[3], Springer Link[4], and Wiley Online Library[5]. We selected these databases because they have a large amount of relevant conferences and journals indexed for Computer Science. We limited the results of automatic searches to return only papers written in English and published from 2007 to 2016, due to the high number of results retrieved. We do not include 2017 because this year has not yet finished.

[1] https://dl.acm.org/.

[2] http://ieeexplore.ieee.org/Xplore/home.jsp.

[3] http://www.sciencedirect.com/.

[4] https://link.springer.com/.

[5] http://onlinelibrary.wiley.com/.

3.4 Study Selection

We filtered the studies retrieved from automatic searches to exclude papers not aligned with the study goals. In this step, the four researchers defined and applied the following inclusion and exclusion criteria.

Inclusion Criteria: Studies whose focus was on proposal, usage, discussion or evaluation of serious games for learning programming in undergraduate courses.

Exclusion Criteria: Papers not written in English; studies whose the main focus was elementary and high school education; studies formatted as short papers (less than 3 pages); studies not published as either journals or conference papers; and duplicated studies.

The study selection process was executed in two phases: (i) in the first selection phase, we read titles and abstracts and removed studies that did not comply with inclusion criteria; (ii) in the second selection phase, we downloaded all papers, read their introduction and conclusion, and removed studies that matched any exclusion criteria.

Table 3 presents the number of papers selected in each phase. It is important to observe that the automatic searches returned a high number of primary studies (#papers column in Table 3). This high number of results is expected by the use of general terms in the search string, such as algorithm and programming. In particular, these terms commonly appear in other contexts not related with programming. Due to the high number of results, we only evaluated the first 500 records of each database.

Table 3. Study selection process [10].

Source	# Papers*	1st selection	2nd selection
ACM Digital Library	143.577	51	10
IEEE Xplore	658.195	136	21
Science Direct	36.956	9	1
Springer Link	78.921	14	4
Wiley Online Library	112.347	8	3
Total	1.029.996	218	39

*Given this high number of results, we evaluate only the first 500 records of each database.

Figure 1 shows the overlapping results between databases. In case of different papers reporting the same study (e.g., journal and conference papers with the same title), only the most recent and/or most complete was kept in the final list of primary studies.

Four researchers executed the selection process, and the other two researchers resolved any conflict regarding the inclusion or exclusion of studies. In case of different papers reporting the same study (e.g., journal and conference papers with the same title), only the most recent and/or most complete was kept in the final list of primary studies.

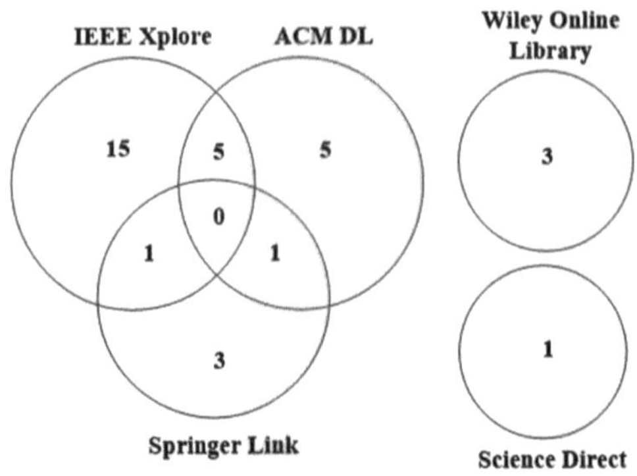

Fig. 1. Distribution of primary studies per database.

3.5 Data Extraction and Summary

Regarding the knowledge areas of Computer Science that are been covered by the games, our SMS relies on the ACM 2013 Computer Science Curricula that defines knowledge areas that compose the curricula for learning programming. To answer RQ1 we use the strategy to classify games to learning programming by CS2013 Knowledge areas. To evaluate the primary studies found in literature, we also used a set of quality criteria [26] detailed in the Table 5 in Sect. 4. These criteria are used to evaluate the primary studies, regarding their methodology, results, evaluation, quality of references, and others. To answer RQ2, we used the strategy to classify and map the groups of game elements found [27]. This strategy defines three groups of game elements: components, dynamics, and mechanics. Finally, regarding the evaluation of games and composing elements (RQ3), we adopted the classifications proposed by [24]. That is, we investigated (i) if the evaluation strategies rely on quantitative or qualitative analysis of the data and (ii) what empirical strategy is used – i.e., case study, experiment, or survey. We consider a quantitative study when it relies on statistical analysis of the data. Studies are considered qualitative when only qualitative discussions are made.

4 Results

In this section, we present the results of the systematic mapping study. Section 4.1 provides an overview of the primary studies selected for this study. Section 4.2 shows the results of a quality assessment of the selected primary studies. Sections 4.3 to 4.5 describe the results for the research questions RQ1 to RQ3, respectively.

4.1 Overview

We selected 39 primary studies published between 2007 to 2016. Figure 2 presents a histogram with the frequency of selected primary studies per year. This result suggests that serious games for learning programming in computer science courses are balanced between years. That is, 5 primary studies were selected per year, except for the years of 2008, 2011, 2013, and 2016.

Our results found 43 serious games distributed over 39 primary studies. In fact, we expected that the number of primary studies describing serious games to learning programming would be higher and we consider 43 a small number. We also found several serious games for this purpose available online, yet not published, such as CodinGame[6], Code Wars[7], Codemancer[8], Code Warriors[9] and Code Combat[10]. In this study, we did not consider these games since our focus is to evaluate primary studies indexed in scientific bases.

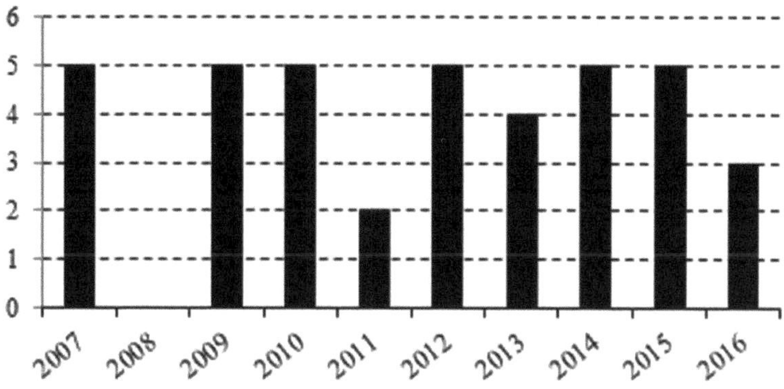

Fig. 2. Timeline of primary studies [10].

Figure 3 shows the distribution of studies was 20.5% in journals (8 studies) and 79.5% (31 studies) in conferences. Table 4 summarizes the most recurring publication venues and their respective counting of selected primary studies. The conferences and journals with greater occurrences of primary studies were FIE (3 studies), SIGSE, ITHET and IEEE Transactions on Education (2 studies each). We listed only publication venues that have two or more primary studies selected in this study. Frontiers in Education, for example, is a conference recognized by researchers in the area of education, where there are opportunities to discuss new strategies for higher education, including teaching in computer science. There are also journals of recognized quality that are in our results, such as Computers and Education, where we found 1 paper. The largest number of conference publications can come from the fact that researchers want to publish fast their preliminary results of experiments with games for learning programming in conferences. Some of them later publish journal extended papers with a greater amount of additional information with respect to the conference paper.

6 https://www.codingame.com/.

7 https://www.codewars.com/.

8 http://codemancergame.com/.

9 http://www.codewarriorsgame.com/.

10 https://codecombat.com/.

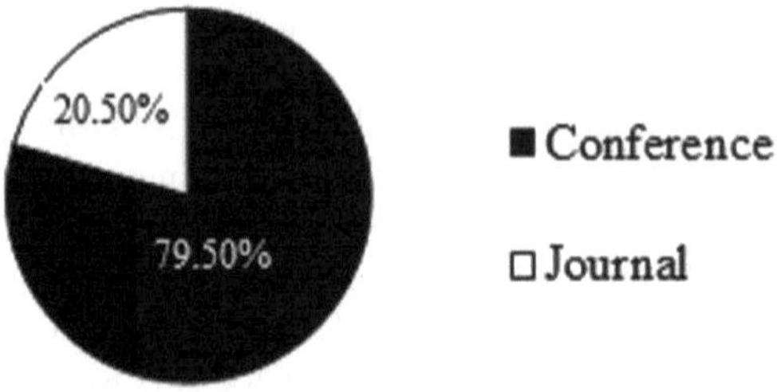

Fig. 3. Distribution of primary studies per venues [10].

In the remaining of this paper, we used unique identifications (AuthorName<year>) when referring to primary studies. For instance, Bishop2015 refers to the paper "Code Hunt: Experience with Coding Contests at Scale" published in proceedings of the International Conference on Software Engineering (ICSE) in 2015. In the appendix of this study we provided the complete list of primary studies and the publication venues.

Table 4. Publication venues for games to learning programming [10].

# Studies	Publication venues
3	IEEE Frontiers in Education (FIE)
2	ACM Technical Symposium on Computer Science Education (SIGSE)
2	IEEE Information Technology based Higher Education and Training (ITHET)
2	IEEE Transactions on Education

4.2 Quality of Selected Studies

We used quality criteria to evaluate primary studies with respect to their methodology, objectives, results, references, and other points [26]. We adopted seven quality criteria, to evaluate the primary studies: (i) Does the primary study clearly describe educational goals? (ii) Has the research methodology been appropriate to address the research objectives? (iii) Is the primary study proper referenced? (iv) Has the proposed game been tested with students? (v) Was there an appropriate assessment of the data collected? (vi) Does the work present results consistent with its educational objectives? (vii) Does the study compare their proposals with related work?

Figure 4 presents the results of the quality evaluation. A study scores one point for each criterion if it fully satisfies that criterion, 0.5 point if it partially satisfies it, or zero if the criterion is not satisfied. The total score of each primary study is the sum of the scores for all quality criteria. Therefore, the total value a primary study can range from zero to seven. According to Fig. 4, 16 primary studies score a total of one point in quality criteria, three studies score 1.5 point, 13 primary studies score 2.5 points, and 7 studies scores 6 points. No study scored points in quality criteria which checks if a primary study compares their proposal with others. The quality criterion with higher attendance was related to the clear description of educational goals. The other five quality criteria had low accordance with the primary studies. We observed an overall low quality considering our criteria. That is, only six studies obtained more than 70% of the points in the quality criteria established for this study. The main shortcomings we observed are that they do not expose the outcomes of the proposed approach. They neither explain the methodology they followed to develop their games nor their evaluation strategy.

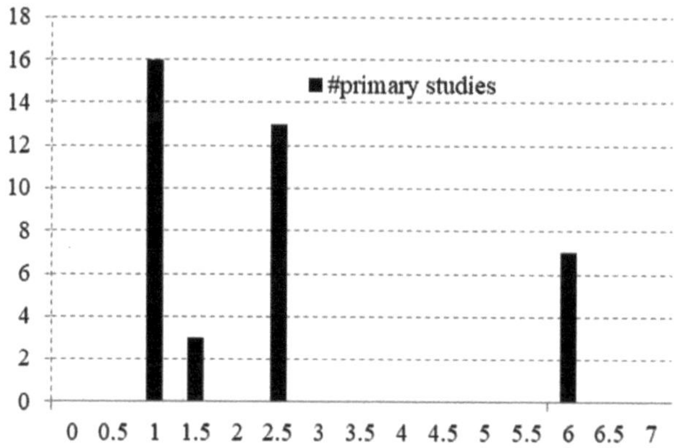

Fig. 4. Quality evaluation of the primary studies [10].

Table 5 presents the seven quality criteria chosen to evaluate the primary studies found in our systematic mapping study. For all quality criteria, we also present in Table 5 how these criteria are scored. For example, according with our quality criteria 1 QC1, which aims to verify if a primary study clearly describes its educational goals, we score 1 point if the study clearly describes educational goals. If the study partly describes its educational goals, we score 0.5 point. Lastly, if the study does not describe its educational goals, we do not score any point to this study in this quality criteria.

Table 5. Quality criteria to evaluate primary studies [10].

ID	Quality criteria of primary studies	Score		
		Yes (1)	Partly (0, 5)	No (0)
QC1	Does the primary study clearly describe educational goals?	If the study clearly describe educational goals	If the study partly describe educational goals, omitting some goals	If the study does not describe the educational goals
QC2	Has the research methodology been appropriate to address the research objectives?	If the methodology is appropriate to achieve research objectives	If the methodology is not totally clear	If the methodology has problems or is not described

(continued)

Table 5. *(continued)*

ID	Quality criteria of primary studies	Score		
		Yes (1)	Partly (0, 5)	No (0)
QC3	The primary study is proper referenced?	If the references are in agreement with the area of the study and are relevant	If the references are partly in agreement with study	If the study has insufficient references and irrelevant ones
QC4	Has the proposed game been tested with students?	If the study tested the proposed game with students	For this QC we consider only yes or no	If the study does not tested the proposed game with students
QC5	Was there an appropriate assessment of the data collected with the use of the game by the students?	If the study conduct a quantitative analysis with the collected data	If the study conduct a qualitative analysis with the collected data	If the study does not assess the data collected with students
QC6	Does the work present results consistent with its educational objectives?	If the study show results with consistent data supporting educational objectives	If the study partly described results to support educational objectives	If the study does not show results consistent with educational objectives
QC7	Do the authors compare their proposals with the work of other authors?	If the study compare the proposed game with other games in the same area of study	For this QC we consider only yes or no	If the study does not compare the proposed game with other games in the same area of study

4.3 Serious Games to Support Programming Learning

In this section, we discuss the results for the first research question:

"**RQ1.** *What are the serious games for learning programming?*"

As mentioned in Section A, 43 games were found distributed over 39 primary studies. Some studies report more than one game. Table 6 (in Appendix) presents the games to learn programming found in literature and presents the characteristics of each game. Table 6 presents the game name, the identifier of the work that this game has appeared and the knowledge area that the game was classified. Also, for each game we show their characteristics regarding if the game has graphical user interface (GUI), if the game is digital (DIG), if provides user guide (USG). Moreover, we verify if the games are available online (ONL), if the games provide examples (EXS) and if the game are in development phase (DEV). The table also inform that a game is open source (OPS) and if this game is available for download (DOW).

Table 6. Games to learning programming and its characteristics.

Game Name	Identifier	CS 2013 knowledge area	GUI	DIG	USG	ONL	EXS	DEV	OPS	DOW
Program your Robot	Kazimoglu2012	FDS	●	●	○	○	○	●	○	○
Bomberman	Wong2007	FDS	●	●	○	○	○	●	○	○
Sorting Casino	Hakulinen2011	FDS	○	○	●	○	●	○	○	○
LadyBuggin	Bowles2007	FDS	●	●	○	○	○	●	○	N/A
CodeHunt	Bishop2015	FDS	●	●	●	●	●	●	○	○
Puzzle-Game	Melero2012	FDS	●	●	○	○	○	○	○	○
Binary Search Game	Shabanah2010	FDS	●	●	○	○	○	○	○	○
Snakes And Ladders	Rossiou2007	FDS	●	●	○	○	○	○	○	○
EleMental	Chaffin2009	FDS	●	●	○	○	○	○	○	○
Age of Computers	Sindre2009	FDS	●	●	○	○	●	○	○	●
Wu's Castle	Eagle2009	FDS	●	●	○	○	○	○	○	○
Saving Princess Sera	Barnes2007	FDS	●	●	○	○	○	○	○	○
ViRPlay3D2	Jimenez-Diaz2007	FDS	●	●	○	○	○	○	○	○
Bots	Hicks2010	FDS	●	●	○	○	○	○	○	○
Web-based MMORPG	Chang2010	FDS	●	●	○	○	○	○	○	○
Hit Typing	Mitamura2012	FDS	●	●	○	○	○	○	○	○
Serious Cube	Mitamura2012	FDS	●	●	○	○	○	○	○	○
3D action game	Mitamura2012	FDS	●	●	○	○	○	○	○	○
Programming learning game	Mitamura2012	FDS	●	●	○	○	○	○	○	○
jLegends	Tsalikidis2016	FDS	●	●	○	N/A	○	○	○	○
SecondLife (modified)	chen2009	FDS	●	●	○	○	○	●	○	○
JeliotConAn	Moreno2013	FDS	●	●	○	N/A	○	●	○	○
Lost in Space	Laguna2014	FDS	●	●	○	○	○	●	○	○
Path finding	Karapinar2012a	ADS	●	●	○	○	○	●	○	○
Learning version of pacman game	Khenissi2013	FDS	●	●	○	○	○	○	○	○
Binary Apple Tree	Karapinar2012b	ADS	●	●	○	○	○	○	○	○
CodeCraft	Ventura2015	FDS	●	●	○	○	○	○	○	○
ResourceCraft	Jiau2009	FDS	●	●	○	N/A	○	○	○	○
Gaps1.0	Rais2011	FDS	●	●	○	○	○	○	○	○
Alice2.0 (modified)	Rais2011	FDS	●	●	○	○	○	○	○	○
Orea	Ansari2014	FDS	●	●	○	○	○	○	○	○
Classcraft	Sanchez2016	FDS	●	●	●	●	●	●	○	○
DOROTHY	South2013	FDS	●	●	○	○	○	○	○	○
PlayAndLearnDS	Kaur2015	FDS	●	●	○	○	○	○	○	N/A
DSLEP	Costa2014	FDS	●	●	○	○	○	○	○	○
SpaceGame	Coelho2013	FDS	●	●	○	○	○	○	○	○
Second Life (modified)	Esteves2010	FDS	●	●	○	N/A	○	●	○	○
The Stack Game	Dicheva2016	FDS	●	●	○	○	○	○	○	○
Space Traveler	Zhang2015	FDS	●	●	○	○	○	○	○	○
Who wants to be an OOP expert?	Alhazbi2010	FDS	●	●	○	N/A	○	○	○	○
Recursive Runner	Zhang2014	ADS	●	●	○	○	○	○	○	○
Super Mario Bros for Learning	Wassila2012	FDS	●	●	○	○	○	○	○	○
No bugs Snack bar	Vahldick2015	FDS	●	●	○	○	○	○	○	○

Table 6 presents the name of the games found and their characteristics. Regarding to CS 2013 knowledge areas, 41 games (95%) support learning of Fundamental Data Structures and Algorithms (FDS). On the other hand, only two games (5%) support learning of Advanced Data Structures, Algorithms and Analysis (ADS) and none targets Algorithmic Strategies (AS). In order to rate the games shown in Table 6, we use only game descriptions provided in the articles where these games were presented. From the descriptions of the games and their operation, we classify the games according to the knowledge areas of algorithms and data structures.

Regarding the games found, only Sorting Casino (Hakulinen2011) is neither digital (DIG) nor has graphical interface (GUI). This game is a card game with the objective to promote learning of sorting algorithms. As can be seen in Table 6, the vast majority of the games found does not have a user guide (USG) and are not available online (ONL). Similarly, many games do not provide examples of how to use game. This lack of information may have occurred because most of the games were designed for use in the classroom rather than online, and the authors of the games choose to pass the instructions directly to the students. About games in development (DEV), only 10 games are still under development according to the authors and new functionalities will be added in future. No game found is open source (OPS). About games that need to be installed on the computer, only one game, namely Age of Computers, is available for download (DOW).

4.4 Game Elements to Support Programming Learning

In this subsection, we discuss the results for the research question:

"**RQ2.** *What are the game elements in the serious games for learning programming?*"

We found 27 game elements distributed over 43 serious games. Table 7 lists these game elements and classify them in three categories: dynamics, components, and mechanics [2]. The number inside parenthesis after each game element corresponds to the number of games that the element has been found. In the group of dynamics, four elements were found, being Fantasy the most used element (17 games in total). In the group of components, we found nine elements. The most used elements in this group are Level (36 games), Quest (16 games) and Avatar (14 games). On the other hand, we found 14 elements in the group of mechanics. Goal (21 games) and Point System (16 games) are the most used elements of the mechanics group.

Table 7. Game elements found in serious games [10].

Game elements group	Game elements
Components	Level (36), Quest (16), Avatar (14), Virtual Good (5), Boss Fight (4), Hint (4), Leaderboard (3), Combat (1), Card (1)
Dynamics	Fantasy (17), Meaning (5), Constraint (4), Progression (3)
Mechanics	Goal (21), Point System (16), Reminder (6), Time Pressure (5), Change Difficult (4), Progressive Disclosure (3), Competition (3), Achievement (3), Win State (3), Cooperation (2), Resource Acquisition (2), Badge (2), Loss Aversion (1), Turns (1)

We note in Table 7, that only six elements (i.e., Avatar, Fantasy, Goal, Level, Point System, and Quest) were used more than ten times. On the other hand, each game uses only a few elements. That is, the average of 8 game elements per game. In Sect. 5, we further discuss about the usage of game elements.

4.5 Evaluation of Game Elements to Support Programming Learning

In this subsection, we discuss the results for the research question:

> "**RQ3.** *What are the empirical strategies and methods used to evaluate existing game elements?*"

In short, we found no study that directly evaluate game elements. The primary studies described evaluation strategies that focused on the game as a whole. However, we believe that evaluating each game element individually is important because they are directly related to how players interact with the game. In addition, evaluating the game elements may give us insights on what game elements are more impactful for a specific audience (in our case, students learning programming, for instance). This in-depth analysis may also provide objective results on why such elements are important in creating a better playing/learning experience.

Given this negative response for RQ2, we opted to investigate how the serious games, in which the game elements are found (RQ1), were evaluated. We mapped two facets: the type of empirical study and the empirical strategy. The type of empirical study means whether the game elements were found in qualitative or quantitative studies. The empirical strategies indicate if the primary study reports a case study, an experiment, or a survey.

Figures 5, 6, and 7 map game elements (components, dynamics, and mechanics, respectively) to the type of empirical study and empirical strategy adopted in the primary studies in which they are found. The numbers inside bubbles in the facet of empirical study represent the number of elements per study type. For example, the element Level appears in 36 studies: 32 qualitative studies and 4 quantitative studies. In the empirical strategy facet, the number inside bubbles means the number of times that a game element appears in studies that adopt one of the empirical strategies listed. If a study does not report any evaluation method, we report that evaluation of the game element is not available.

Usually, studies describe case studies where educators apply the games in classrooms and describe their observations. Surveys are used to collect feedback from students playing games. Only few studies (Chaffin2009, Sindre2009, Eagle2009, Hicks2010, Laguna2014 and Bishop2015) provide quantitative data to support their results. However, none of these evaluation strategies mention any link between game elements and the observed outcomes.

In total, 19 studies used both experiment and survey empirical strategies and 21 studies used both Case Study and Survey to evaluate game elements. There was no case of studies that used experiment and case study together, as well as, there were no case of studies that used the three strategies at same time to evaluate their game elements.

With respect to the types of empirical studies, we found a total of 6 quantitative studies and 33 qualitative studies. These numbers may indicate that researchers are

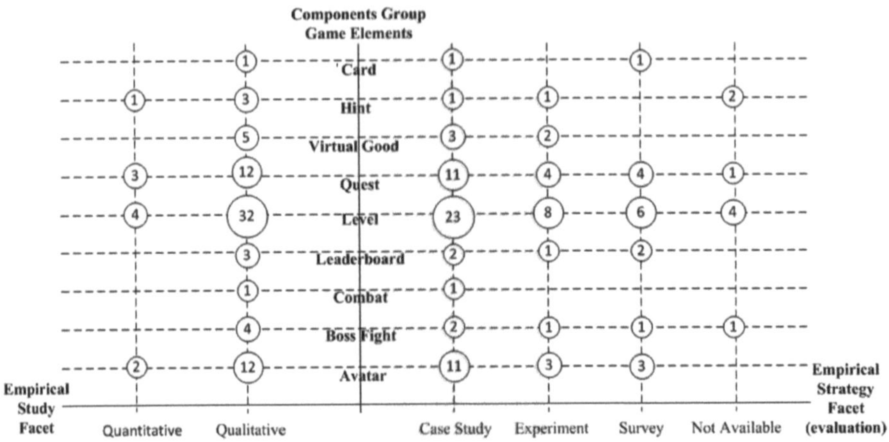

Fig. 5. Game elements of the components group and evaluation strategies [10].

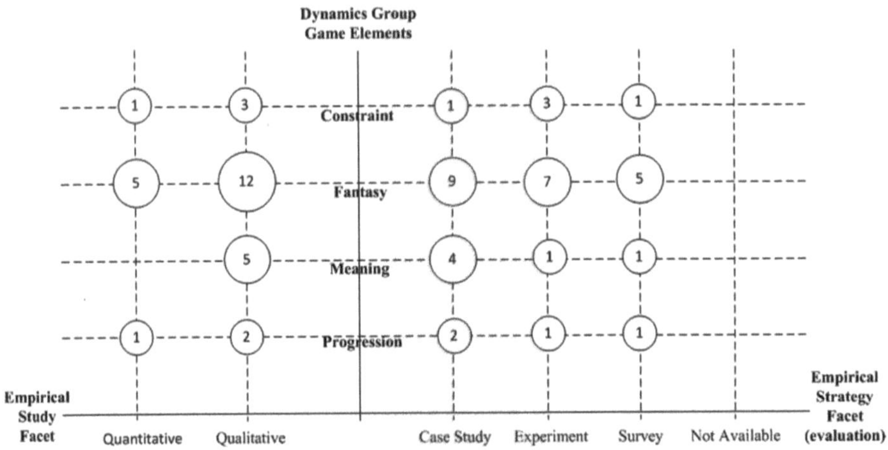

Fig. 6. Game elements of the dynamics group and evaluation strategies [10].

focusing more on collecting and describing perceptions on the game experiences than on providing statistical evidences of the effectiveness of their approaches.

We also verified the number of primary studies that conducted tests of the proposed serious games with users. We found 22 primary studies that tested game with users (56% of total studies), versus 17 studies that have not tested serious games with users (44% of total). About studies that tested serious games with users, 15 studies tested the proposed serious games with a number of users between 1 to 50, while 4 studies tested with a number of users between of 51 to 100 and 3 studies performed tests with more than 101 users. The low number of studies with a reasonable population size is a possible reason for the preference for qualitative studies.

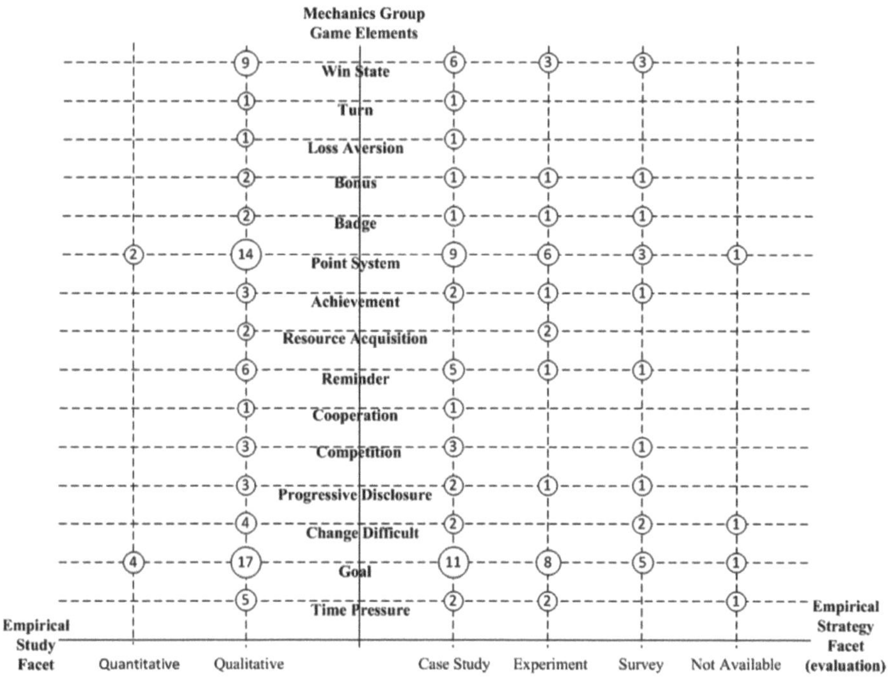

Fig. 7. Game elements of the mechanics group and evaluation strategies [10].

The number of game elements of the components group and how they are evaluated are show in Fig. 5. The numbers inside bubbles on the facet of empirical study means the number of elements per study type. For example, the element level appears in 36 studies, being these, element level appears in 32 exploratory studies and 4 explanatory studies. On the other side, on empirical strategy facet, the number inside bubbles means the number of times that a game element has been evaluated by one of the empirical strategies listed. For example, the game element cards in Fig. 5 were evaluated two times, one time with survey and one time with case study. The cards element appears in only one primary study which the empirical study type is exploratory and this element was evaluated under two empirical strategies in the same study. There are primary studies that have used more than one empirical strategy to evaluate game elements. If a study does not report any evaluation method, we report that evaluation of the game element is not available.

Figure 6 presents the evaluation strategies of the game elements contained in dynamics group. In this group, all elements were evaluated by the three types of strategies (survey, case study and experiment). Moreover, there were no occurrences of studies in which assessment methods were not available. The element level, was the element of game that most appeared among the elements of the components group. Appearing in a total of 36 studies and most of their evaluations were done through case studies. For the group of components, most assessments of game elements were made using case studies.

Figure 7 presents the evaluation strategies for elements of the mechanics group. In this group, we found some elements in studies that not present their evaluation strategies. Furthermore, in mechanics group, we have the major number of elements, and in the same time the smaller number of elements being in quantitative studies. Only the elements goals and point system were found in explanatory studies. Another point to be highlighted is that the game elements of the mechanics group, few elements were not evaluated with any type of strategy. In addition, in the group of mechanics, four elements were evaluated with only one type of empirical strategy.

5 Discussion

In this section we discuss our results presented in Sect. 4.

5.1 Quality of the Studies and Serious Games Found in Literature

We consider that the number of serious games to learn programming found in literature is small. We found 43 serious games in 39 primary studies. This small number of serious games contradicts the common sense, since there are several serious games to learn programming available on the internet (some of them are mentioned in Sect. 4.1). Our hypothesis about this number of serious games to learning programming present in scientific studies is due to three reasons. First, the research of serious games for learning programming is recent (we found relevant results from 2007), and researchers and educators are still developing new ideas and over time. Second, developing a game involves high financial, time and personnel costs that may be deterrent for educators [4].

Third, serious games to learn programming are properties of private companies seeking profit and may not be interested in publishing scientific studies. In our study, we found only one game related to a private company: Code Hunt (Bishop2015), from Microsoft. Code Hunt is free.

In Sect. 4.2, we show the results of the quality evaluation of the primary studies found. Only seven studies scored more than 70% on the proposed quality criteria. The majority of the primary studies found have some shortcomings, regarding their methodology, evaluation with subjects, assessment of data collected during test with students and description of game and how it works. Despite the fact that this quality assessment is related to the purpose of this present study, and to the attendance of the primary studies to our research questions, these criteria should be considered by researchers and educators when writing similar studies.

The simplicity of the serious games caught our attention. Several serious games are only one screen games, such as, Binary Search Game, JeliotConAn, and Gaps 1.0. As mentioned before, the quality of serious games might be related to the costs to develop a game. Hence, some researchers and educators do not have enough resources to develop a high-quality game. However, as far as we are concerned, no primary study reported difficulties and challenges in developing serious games for learning programming.

On the other hand, we found studies and serious games with high quality. Code Hunt, a game to learn programming, is a game that presents puzzles to users, and the user has tips, examples and user guide to help the user to understand the game and its mechanics. Furthermore, Code Hunt scored 6 points in our quality evaluation. The game Lost in Space (Laguna2014) is an example of good game developed by researchers and educators. The game is well structured and it has been tested with students. In addition, the data collected was assessed with statistical tests. Laguna2014 scored 6 points in our quality evaluation.

Regarding ACM CS2013 areas, only two areas are covered by the serious games found in the primary studies. The area with more coverage was the area of FDS – Fundamental Data Structures with 41 proposed serious games to learning programming in this area. The area of ADS – Advanced Data Structures had two proposed serious games. This result can be related to the fact that educators are concerned with development of serious games to help students learn the fundamentals of programming. Since, the programming fundamentals are the core knowledge for many other areas of computer science.

5.2 Few Game Elements Are Used in Programming Learning Games

We note that only a group of six elements (avatar, fantasy, goal, level, point system and quest) were used in more than ten serious games. We found other 21 game elements that are scarcely used in the primary studies. The average number of game elements per game is eight. We consider this number low; since we have an elevated number of game elements available in literature, although the number of game elements used does not necessarily define the quality of games. We can speculate that the development of these games is often driven by researchers and educators, who are not game designers, or have little experience with this discipline.

The lack of evaluation of game elements prevents us from discussing which game elements are more important, or from measuring how much the addition of new elements would improve the evaluation of a game by its users. We are not aware of the correct number of elements a game must have to achieve greater success among users.

Other studies already warned the use of elements of the same type, as in the case of a recent literature review [11] that cited that for games in software engineering, elements such as point system and levels are recurrently used. This low variability in the use of game elements can be caused by unfamiliarity of the authors of the game who were not aware of other elements of games during the development phase of the game.

Once again, it is important to note that these six elements mentioned above are important to a game. We do not find in the literature any paper that evaluates the elements of games directly. Hence, we cannot measure how much the addition of new elements will make a game for programming learning to be better evaluated by users. In addition, we also do not know what the correct number of elements a game must have to achieve greater success among users. Meanwhile, only these six elements do not seem sufficient to make a good game to learn programming, since there are other interesting game elements such as, challenges between users, boss fight, change difficult, and other presented in 21 game elements found in this literature review.

5.3 Shortcomings in Game Elements Evaluation

Some primary studies such as Rais2011a and Hakulinen2012 and other 22 studies (56% of total) tested the proposed serious games with users. However, the majority of studies do not adequately evaluate serious games for learning programming with users. For example, Rais2001, Karapinar2012, and Jiau2009 do not evaluate the opinions of the users about the proposed serious games for learning programming. In total, only eight studies (20% of total studies) report the opinion of users, as said by users, about the proposed game. Other studies that surveyed users only report in the results that users like the game and that educational objectives are achieved or that the result of game was successful, without further evidences. The studies that presented these shortcomings are in the group of 33 qualitative studies found in our systematic mapping study.

In some primary studies Alhazabi201, Barnes2007, Chaffin2009, Eagle2009, Rossiou2007, Zhang2014, Zhang2015 and Melero2012, students reported that the use of serious games is effective. Some studies report that the traditional classes to learn programming with slides and blackboard overwhelm students (Barnes2007, Chaffin2009). Students need to practice coding, not only at home, but also in the classroom. Students have doubts and these concerns can be shared with educator and other colleagues in classroom. With serious games, students report that the learning became pleasant, with more chances for the student to overcome the fear of learning programming and demystifying its difficulty.

Only six primary studies present a quantitative research. These studies are: Chaffin2009, Sindre2009, Eagle2009, Hicks2010, Laguna2014 and Bishop2015. These primary studies present a well structure research paper, allied with controlled experiment, consistent, statistical analysis of the data obtained from experiment with users. We believe that researchers focus on describing preliminary results to share their experiences and somehow show that their game was used in an academic environment, even if it lacks a more comprehensive analysis of the quality of the game.

We believe that there is an opportunity to capture additional insights on how students interact with serious games and what is the link between game elements and the reception of the games.

In none of the primary studies found, there was an explicit evaluation of the game elements of the proposed games. Studies that evaluated games, evaluated only the games as a whole. When the studies do this type of evaluation, they are not taking into consideration which element of game contributed more effectively to the learning of the users in programming. From the studies found, it is not possible to know which elements contributed in the best and worst way to the learning of the users. Every game has strong and weak points and these points are related to game elements. This lack of analysis of game elements creates a research opportunity to assess which game elements are most effective for programming learning.

In Sect. 4.4 we did an indirect analysis of how game elements were evaluated, since these elements were not directly evaluated by the authors of the primary studies. We note that just as there were few quantitative studies, few elements were evaluated with the empirical strategy of experiment. Some reasons why primary study authors do not evaluate game elements individually may be due to the fact that they have not thought of building a game as a set of elements that contribute to the success of the game, or for reasons of time to complete the research or publication deadlines.

6 Threats to Validity

This section discusses the different threats to validity related to this study with respect to the four groups of threats to validity [24]: internal validity, external validity, construct validity and conclusion validity. We also discuss how the threats are addressed to minimize the probability of their impact on our results.

Internal Validity. Internal validity concerns the question whether the effect is caused by the independent variables or by other internal factors that can affect the validity of the experiment [24]. In this sense, a limitation of this mapping study concerns the reliability of its results. The reliability has been addressed as much as possible by involving three researchers, and by having a strict protocol which was piloted and hence evaluated. If the study is replicated by another set of researchers, it is possible that some studies that were removed in this review could be included. Similarly, some studies we selected could be excluded by others. However, in general we believe that the internal validity of this study is high given the use of a systematic procedure, repetition of the search protocol by two researchers, and discussion between three researchers.

External Validity. External validity is related to the ability to generalize the results to other environments, such as to classrooms [24]. A major external validity to this mapping study was the identification of primary studies. The search for the primary studies was conducted in five large scientific databases, namely ACM Digital Library, IEEE Xplore, Science Direct, Wiley Online Library, and Springer Link in order to capture as much as possible relevant studies and to avoid all sorts of bias. However, the quality of search engines could have influenced the completeness of the identified primary studies. For instance, our search may have missed those studies whose authors have used other terms to specify their proposed games for learning programming. In addition, we search for relevant terms only in the title and abstract of their papers.

Construct Validity. Construct validity is related to what extent the operational measures that are studied really represent what the researcher have planned and what is investigated according to the research questions [24]. We are not aware of any bias we may have been introduced during the construction of the study protocol. However, from the selection perspective, a construct validity threat could be biased judgment. In this study, the decision of which studies to include or to exclude and how to categorize the studies could have been biased and thus pose a threat. For instance, a possible threat in the selection process is to exclude some relevant studies. To minimize this threat both the processes of inclusion and exclusion were piloted by at least two researchers. Furthermore, potentially relevant studies that were excluded were documented for further verification.

Conclusion Validity. Threats to conclusion validity are related with issues that affect the ability to draw the correct conclusions from the study [24]. From the reviewers' perspective, a potential threat to conclusion validity is the reliability of the data extraction from the primary studies, since not all information was obvious to answer the research questions and some data had to be inferred. Therefore, in order to ensure the validity, sometime cross-discussions among the paper authors took place to reach a common agreement. Furthermore, in the event of a disagreement between the two researchers, a third reviewer acted as an arbitrator to ensure a position to be reached.

7 Related Work

In this section, we discuss the related research on the use and evaluation of serious games and their elements to learn programming in superior education.

Regarding the identification of how game elements are evaluated in relation of empirical strategies, to the best of our effort, we did not identify any study that proposes this type of work to the date of our investigations. No primary study considered evaluating the game elements that composed a game. Instead, authors only evaluated the serious games as a whole entity.

Malone and Lepper [17] conducted experiments using a serious game with children to see which game elements make learning more fun. The authors identified that the elements that contribute most to the learning in these experiments were: curiosity, sensory, fantasy, cooperation, and competition objectives.

Wilson *et al.* [7] conducted a systematic review in the literature to understand the "state of play" regards to learning outcomes and game attributes. The authors also seek out what specific game attributes have an impact on learning outcomes. Furthermore, authors identify gaps in this research area. Wilson *et al.* found 18 game elements in literature review, but they focused the discussions of the work on a subset of seven game elements. Their work focuses the discussions on how game elements are related to learning objectives, regardless of area of knowledge.

Souza *et al.* [8] performed an experiment introducing two game elements, namely badges and leaderboards, in an introductory Software Engineering course. The goal of the study is to evaluate the students' perception on the impact of these elements in their motivation towards the course. The study of Souza *et al.* is not related to learning programming and it uses concepts of gamification; that is, the use of game elements in non-games contexts [27]. However, it reinforces the importance of evaluating game elements individually. Since each element can positively and negatively impact the motivation of students in a course. Their results suggest that the badge element was better evaluated by the students than the leaderboards element. Students report that the badge element reinforces even to the teacher that the student is engaging in discipline and that badges could be exchanged for bonus grades.

Tihomir *et al.* [28] conducted a study that aimed to examine the quality of serious games designed for learning programming from students' perspective and an empirical study was carried out. Study participants were students enrolled in different courses at two Croatian higher education institutions. Authors used two games to evaluate the students' opinions: LightBot and Code Combat. The work focuses on evaluating games in aspects like: learnability, reliability, accessibility, helpfulness, effectiveness, playfulness, and satisfaction. The authors did not focus in evaluate the game elements present in the chosen serious games.

Battistella *et al.* [9] conducted a systematic revision to identify games for teaching of several knowledge areas of the computer science (software engineering, networks, computer fundamentals, programming, etc.). The work makes a division of the games for levels of learning (cognitive, skill, and affectiveness) objectives, but it does not take game elements in consideration. Our work differs in the sense that we perform a systematic mapping study to identify and verify how game elements are evaluated in the context of learning programming. The work of Battistella *et al.* does not verify how games are evaluated by students or by the authors of primary studies selected. The work is like a census of all existing games in computer science areas.

Petri *et al.* [6] performed a comprehensive study on how serious games for computing education are evaluated. The goal of their study is to present the state of the art on how games for computing education are evaluated. Therefore, the authors performed a systematic literature review on 112 relevant papers, describing 117 studies on the evaluation of games for computing education. The authors show that there is a need for more rigorous evaluations as well as methodological support in order to assist game creators and instructors to improve such games as well as to systematically support decisions on when or how to include them within instructional units. The conclusion of Petri *et al.* is in agreement with our conclusions about the quality of the primary studies found in our study.

Research in literature about serious games to learning programming provides opportunities to research what game elements are more effective to learning programming, since we do not find any study that addresses this type of research. Another opportunity for research is a creation of guidelines to evaluate game elements in learning programming and the development of a framework that provides information about what game elements should be used in different types of contexts to learning programming.

8 Conclusion

This study presented a systematic mapping study to identify serious games present in literature to learn programming and how game elements are used to support learning programming. We mined five scientific databases (IEEE Xplore, ACM Digital Library, Springer Link, Wiley Online Library and Science Direct) and retrieved 39 primary studies, from 2007 to 2016. These primary studies describe 43 serious games with 27 game elements distributed over them.

The results of this work have practical implications for how to report serious games for learning programming in scientific articles. In this study we created seven quality criteria to evaluate the primary studies found in the literature and the results show quality problems related to the objectives of the articles, data analysis in the experiments carried out, article methodology and other criteria. It is important that authors wishing to write articles to report serious games should keep in mind that it is important to evaluate games consistently and report data clearly and objectively. We note from our results that quantitative analyzes are rarely used to report results from experiments with games for learning programming.

Developing games with quality demands high financial costs, as well as personnel and time costs. Another issue evaluated in our work is related to games developed and our results show that most games are simple. The simplicity of the serious games caught our attention. Several serious games are only one screen games. However, as far as we are concerned, no primary study reported difficulties and challenges in developing serious games for learning programming.

Some recurring issues in learning programming motivate the use of game-related approaches that require students to experience real-world issues of software development. It is difficult to provide convincing examples of some aspects of programming in traditional lectures and practical projects, given the limitations of these formats. Game-related approaches have been used to overcome some of these limitations. The use of serious games brings to students the possibility to practice with pleasure and make programming fun even in academic contexts.

The main challenge of this study was to evaluate the primary studies found. Since many studies do not adequately report their methodologies, as well as all the characteristics of the proposed serious games. A considerable number of studies do not clearly structure their learning goals. Many studies also do not adequately evaluate the proposed serious games with students. No study found directly evaluated the link between game elements and learning outcomes for learning programming. More studies are required to assess the effectiveness of specific game elements.

The number of studies with serious games to learn programming in superior education was low in scientific publications. The majority of online serious games are not published in scientific articles. The scientific community of serious games to learn programming need more serious games shared in scientific venues. We expect to provide educators and researchers an overview of the state of the art in the literature of serious games to learn programming, and highlight that there is room for new research, and there is a need for researchers to publish their results.

For future work, we plan to evaluate how game elements are related to learning outcomes, conducting experiments using serious games in academic context, and evaluate how the elements of these games contribute to learning.

Appendix

List of the Selected Primary Studies and Publication Venues

[Alhazbi2010] Saleh Alhazbi, Loay Sabry Ismail. "Supportive Online Learning Environment to Improve students' Satisfaction in Object-Oriented Programming Courses", International Congress on Engineering Education.

[Ansari2014] Nazneen Ansari, Noopur Parikh, Anagha Narvekar, Manjiri Phatapekar, Anita Yadav. "GamEd - Learning Data Structure Algorithm using Computer Game", International Conference on Advances in Engineering & Technology.

[Barnes2007] Tiffany Barnes, Heather Richter, Amanda Chaffin, Alex Godwin, Eve Powell, Tiffany Ralph, Paige Matthews, Hyun Jordan. "Game2Learn: A study of games as tools for learning introductory programming concepts", SIGCSE Technical Symposium on Computer Science Education.

[Bishop2015] Judith Bishop, R. Nigel Horspool, Tao Xie, Nikolai Tillmann, Jonathan de Halleux. "Code Hunt: Experience with Coding Contests at Scale", Proceedings of the 37th International Conference on Software Engineering (ICSE – JSEET Track).

[Bowles2007] John B. Bowles. "Cell Phone Games for a CS2 Data Structures Course", Proceedings of the 45th annual southeast regional conference ACMSE.

[Chaffin2009] Amanda Chaffin, Katelyn Doran, Drew Hicks, and Tiffany Barnes. "Experimental Evaluation of Teaching Recursion in a Video Game", ACM SIGGRAPH Symposium on Video Games.

[Chang2010] Maiga Chang and Kinshuk. "Web-based Multiplayer Online Role Playing Game (MORPG) for Assessing Students Java Programming Knowledge and Skills", IEEE International Conference on Digital Game and Intelligent Toy Enhanced Learning.

[Chen2009] Yan Chen, Ching-Song Wei, Jiann-Gwo Doong. "A 3D Virtual World Teaching and Learning Platform for Computer Science Courses in Second Life", IEEE International Conference on Computational Intelligence and Software Engineering.

[Coelho2013] Antonio Coelho, Enrique Kato, João Xavier, Ricardo Goncalves. "Serious Game for Introductory Programming", International Conference on Serious Games Development and Applications.

[Costa2014] Estevan B. Costa, Armando M. Toda, Marcell A. A. Mesquita, Jacques D. Brancher. "DSLEP (Data Structure Learning Platform to Aid in Higher Education IT Courses)", International Journal of Social, Behavioral, Educational, Economic, Business and Industrial Engineering.

[Dicheva2016] Darina Dicheva, Austin Hodge, Christo Dichev, Keith Irwin. "On the Design of an Educational Game for a Data Structures Course", International Conference on Teaching, Assessment, and learning for Engineering.

[Eagle2009] Michael Eagle, Tiffany Barnes. "Experimental Evaluation of an Educational Game for Improved Learning in Introductory Computing", ACM Technical Symposium on Computer Science Education.

[Esteves2010] Micaela Esteves, Benjamim Fonseca, Leonel Morgado and Paulo Martins. "Improving teaching and learning of computer programming through the use of the Second Life virtual world", British Journal of Educational Technology.

[Hakulinen2011] Lasse Hakulinen. "Card Games for Teaching Data Structures and Algorithms", Koli Calling International Conference on Computing Education Research.

[Hicks2010] Andrew Hicks. "Towards Social Gaming Methods for Improving Gamebased Computer Science Education", International Conference on the Foundations of Digital Games.

[Jimenez-Diaz2007] Guillermo Jiménez-Díaz, Mercedes Gómez-Albarrán, Pedro A. González-Calero. "Pass the Ball: Game-based Learning of Software Design", Entertainment computing - ICEC.

[Karapinar2012a] Zehra KARAPINAR, Arafat SENTURK, Sultan ZAVRAK, Resul KARA, Pakize ERDOGMUS. "A game to test pointers: path finding", Information technology Based Higher Education and Training.

[Karapinar2012b] Zehra KARAPINAR, Arafat SENTURK, Sultan ZAVRAK, Resul KARA, Pakize ERDOGMUS. "Binary Apple Tree: A game approach to tree transversal algorithms", Information technology Based Higher Education and Training.

[Kaur2015] Navneet Kaur, G Geetha. "Play and learn DS: Interactive and gameful learning of data structure", International Journal of Technology Enhanced Learning.

[Kazimoglu2012] Cagin Kazimoglu, Mary Kiernan, Liz Bacon, Lachlan Mackinnon. "A serious game for developing computational thinking and learning introductory computer programming", Cyprus International Conference on Educational Research.

[Khenissi2013] Mohamed Ali Khenissi, Fathi Essalmi, Mohamed Jemni. "A learning version of pacman game", Information and Communication technology and Accessibility.

[Laguna2014] Ángel Serrano-Laguna, Javier Torrente, Borja Manero, Baltasar Fernandez-Manjon. "A game engine to learn computer science languages", IEEE Frontiers in Education.

[Melero2012] Javier Melero, Davinia Hernández-Leo, Josep Blat. "Considerations for the design of mini-games integrating hints for puzzle solving ICT-related concepts", International Conference on Advanced Learning Technologies.

[Mitamura2012] Tamotsu Mitamura, Yasuhiro Suzuki, Takahumi Oohori. "Serious Games for Learning Programming Languages", IEEE International Conference on Systems, Man, and Cybernetics.

[Moreno2013] Andres Moreno, Erkki Sutinen, Carolina Islas Sedano. "A game concept using conflictive animations for learning programming", IEEE Games Innovation Conference.

[Rais2011] Aimi Elliyana Rais, Shahida Sulaiman, Sharifah Mashita Syed-Mohamad. "Game-based Approach and its Feasibility to Support the Learning of Object-Oriented Concepts and Programming", Malaysian Conference in Software Engineering.

[Rossiou2007] Eleni Rossiou and Spyros Papadakis. "Educational Games in Higher Education: a case study in teaching recursive algorithms", Education in a Change Environment Conference.

[Sanchez2016] Eric Sanchez, Shawn Young, Caroline Jouneau-Sion. "Classcraft: from gamification to ludicization of classroom management", Education and Information Technologies.

[Shabanah2010] Sahar S. Shabanah, Jim X. Chen, Harry Wechsler, Daniel Carr, Edward Wegman. "Designing Computer Games to Teach Algorithms", International Conference on Information Technology.

[Sindre2009] Guttorm Sindre, Lasse Natvig, and Magnus Jahre. "Experimental Validation of the Learning Effect for a Pedagogical Game on Computer fundamentals", IEEE TRANSACTIONS ON EDUCATION.

[South2013] David South, Austin Ray, Kevin Thomas, Stephanie Graham, Shiloh Huff, Sarah Rainge, Mary Shuman, Mohan Sridharan, Susan D. Urban, Joseph E. Urban. "DOROTHY: Integrating Graphical Programming with Robotics to Stimulate

Interest in Computing Careers", Proceedings of Alice Symposium on Alice Symposium.

[Tsalikidis2016] Konstantinos Tsalikidis, George Pavlidis. "jLegends: Online game to train programming skills", IEEE International Conference on Information, Intelligence, Systems & Applications (IISA).

[Vahldick2015] Adilson Vahldick, Antonio Jose Mendes, Maria José Marcelino. "Analysing the Enjoyment of a Serious Game for Programming Learning with two Unrelated Higher Education Audiences", European Conference on Games Based Learning.

[Ventura2015] Matthew Ventura, John Ventura, Chad Baker, Grant Viklund, Randall Roth, Jonas Broughman. "Development of a Video Game that Teaches the Fundamentals of Computer Programming", IEEE SoutheastCon.

[Wassila2012] Debabi Wassila, Bensebaa Tahar. "Using Serious game to simplify algorithm learning", International Conference on Education and e-Learning Innovations.

[Wong2007] Wai-Tak Wong and Yu-Min Chou. "An Interactive Bomberman Game-Based Teaching/Learning Tool for Introductory C Programming", Transactions on Edutainment.

[Zhang2014] Jinghua Zhang, Mustafa Atay, Emanuel Smith, Elvira R. Caldwell, Elva J. Jones. "Using a Game-Like Module to Reinforce Student Understanding of Recursion", IEEE Frontiers in Education Conference.

[Zhang2015] Jinghua Zhang, Mustafa Atay, Elvira R. Caldwell, Elva J. Jones. "Reinforcing Student Understanding of Linked List Operations in a Game", IEEE Frontiers in Education Conference.

References

1. Zhang, F., Kaufman, D., Fraser, S.: Using video games in computer science education. Eur. Sci. J. **10**(22), 37–52 (2014)
2. Werbach, K., Hunter, D.: For the Win: How Game Thinking Can Revolutionize Your Business. Wharton Digital Press, Philadelphia (2012)
3. Bedwell, W.L., Pavlas, D., Heyne, K., Lazzara, H.E., Salas, E.: Toward a taxonomy linking game attributes to learning: an empirical study. Simul. Gaming Interdisc. J. **43**(6), 729–760 (2012)
4. Folmer, E.: Component based game development – a solution to escalating costs and expanding deadlines? In: Schmidt, H.W., Crnkovic, I., Heineman, G.T., Stafford, J.A. (eds.) CBSE 2007. LNCS, vol. 4608, pp. 66–73. Springer, Heidelberg (2007). https://doi.org/10.1007/978-3-540-73551-9_5
5. Kazimoglu, C., Kiernan, M., Bacon, L., MacKinnon, L.: Learning programming at the computational thinking level via digital game-play. Proc. Comput. Sci. **9**, 522–531 (2012)
6. Petri, G., Wangenheim, G.C.: How games for computing education are evaluated? A systematic literature review. Comput. Educ. **107**(2017), 68–90 (2017)
7. Wilson, K.A., et al.: Relationships between game attributes and learning outcomes: review and research proposals. Simul. Gaming: Interdisc. J. **40**(2), 217–266 (2009)

8. Souza, M.R., Veado, L.F., Constantino, K., Figueiredo, E.: Gamification in software engineering education: an empirical study. In: Proceedings of the 30th International Conference on Software Engineering Education and Training (CSEE&T), pp. 107–115
9. Batistella, P.E.: Games for teaching computing in higher education – a systematic review. IEEE Technol. Eng. Educ. (ITEE) **1**(3) (2016)
10. dos Santos A.L., de A. Souza M.R., Figueiredo, E., Dayrell, M.: Game elements for learning programming: a mapping study. In: Proceedings of the 10th International Conference on Computer Supported Education, CSEDU, vol. 2, pp. 89–101 (2018)
11. Souza, M.R., Veado, L.F., Moreira, R.T., Figueiredo, E.: A systematic mapping study on game-related methods for software engineering education. Inf. Softw. Technol. (2017)
12. García, F., Mario, P.P., Cerdeira-Pena, A., Penabad, M.: A framework for gamification in software engineering. J. Syst. Softw. (JSS) **132**, 21–40 (2017)
13. Hamari, J.: Do badges increase user activity? A field experiment on the effects of gamification. Comput. Hum. Behav. **71**, 469–478 (2017)
14. Dicheva, D., Dichev, C., Agre, G., Angelova, G.: Gamification in education: a systematic mapping study. Educ. Technol. Soc. **18**(3), 75–88 (2015)
15. Zichermann, G., Cunningham, C.: Gamification by Design: Implementing Game Mechanics in Web and Mobile Apps. O'Reilly Media, Sebastopol (2011)
16. Malone, T.W.: Towards a theory of intrinsically motivation instruction. Cogn. Sci. **4**, 333–369 (1981)
17. Malone, T.W., Lepper, M.R.: Making learning fun: a taxonomy of intrinsic motivations for learning. In: Aptitude, Learning and Instruction. Cognitive and Affective Process and Analyses, vol. 3, pp. 223–253 (1987)
18. Gredler, M.E.: Educational games and simulation: a technology in search of a research paradigm. In: Handbook of Research for Educational Communications and Technology, pp. 521–540 (1996)
19. Thiagarajan, S.: Team activities for learning and performance. In: Handbook of Human Performance Technology, pp. 518–544 (1999)
20. Garris, R., Ahlers, R., Driskell, J.E.: Games, motivation and learning: a research and practice model. Simul. Gaming: Interdisc. J. **33**, 441–467 (2002)
21. ACM & IEEE: Computer Science Curricula 2013: Curriculum Guidelines for Undergraduate Degree Programs in Computer Science (2013)
22. Basili, V.: Software modeling and measurement: the Goal/Question/Metric paradigm, p. 24. Technical report (1992)
23. Wohlin, C., Runeson, P., Höst, M., Ohlsson, M.C., Regnell, B., Wesslen, A.: Experimentation in Software Engineering: An Introduction. Kluwer Academic Publishers, Norwell (2000)
24. Petersen, K., Feldt, R., Mujtaba, S., Mattsson, M.: Systematic mapping studies in software engineering. In 12th International Conference on Evaluation and Assessment in Software Engineering (EASE) (2007)
25. Kitchenham, B., Charters, S.: Guidelines for performing systematic literature reviews in software engineering. Technical report EBSE-2007-01. School of Computer Science and Mathematics, Keele University (2007)
26. Deterding, S., Dixon, D.: Gamification: using game design elements in non-gaming contexts. In: Extended Abstracts on Human Factors in Computing Systems (CHI) (2011)
27. Orehovački, T., Babić, S.: Inspecting quality of games designed for learning programming. In: Zaphiris, P., Ioannou, A. (eds.) LCT 2015. LNCS, vol. 9192, pp. 620–631. Springer, Cham (2015). https://doi.org/10.1007/978-3-319-20609-7_58

Algorithms and Logic as Programming Primers

Pia Niemelä[1(✉)], Antti Valmari[2], and Simo Ali-Löytty[3]

[1] Pervasive Computing, Tampere University of Technology, Tampere, Finland
pia.niemela@tut.fi
[2] University of Jyväskylä, Jyväskylä, Finland
[3] Mathematics, Tampere University of Technology, Tampere, Finland

Abstract. To adapt all-immersive digitalization, the Finnish National Curriculum 2014 (FNC-2014) 'digi-jumps' by integrating programming into elementary education. However, applying the change to mathematics teachers' everyday praxis is hindered by a too high-level specification. To elaborate FNC-2014 into more concrete learning targets, we review the computer science syllabi of countries that are well ahead, as well as the education recommendations set by computer science organizations, such as ACM and IEEE. The whole mathematics syllabus should be critically viewed in the light of these recommendations and feedback collected from software professionals and educators. The feedback reveals an imbalance between supply and demand, i.e., what is over-taught versus under-taught, from the point of the requirements of current working life. The surveyed software engineers criticize the unnecessary surplus of calculus and differential equations, i.e., continuous mathematics. In contrast, the emphasis should shift more towards algorithms and data structures, flexibility in handling multiple data representations, and logic: in short – discrete mathematics. The ground for discrete mathematics should be prepared early enough, started already from primary level and continued consistently throughout the secondary till tertiary education. This paper aims to contribute to the further refinement of the mathematics syllabus by proposing such a discrete mathematics subset that especially supports the needs of computer science education, the focus being on algorithms and data structures, and logic in particular.

Keywords: K–12 computer science education · Programming in mathematics syllabus · Digital skills gap · Professional development of software professionals · Effectiveness of education · Continuous vs. discrete math · Computational vs. specificational thinking

1 Introduction

Digitalization triggers pressure to change the current education system. Both domestic and multinational governing bodies have recognized the skills gap

B. M. McLaren et al. (Eds.): CSEDU 2018, CCIS 1022, pp. 357–383, 2019.
https://doi.org/10.1007/978-3-030-21151-6_18

between computer science and the growing need for a digitally fluent workforce. Consequently, the EU has outlined a strategy for improving e-skills for the 21st century to foster competitiveness, growth, and jobs. Just-published technical reports provide guidance for educators and politicians at the European level [1,2], highlighting the pervasive and ubiquitous nature of digitalization. The digital literacy, responsible use of technology, and civic participation are thus relevant to everybody. In consolidation, digitally skillful workers are more likely to keep their positions and, if displaced, are re-employed more quickly than employees without digital skills [3].

The skills gap concerns not only the lack of SW professionals but also the quality of their skills. The STEM shortage paradox highlights the peculiarity of having hard-to-fill open positions and at the same time an excess of graduates who cannot find a job [4,5]. One explanation is the skills mismatch. In compliance, employers point out the candidates' shortcomings, such as the incapability of breaking down problems into manageable chunks and solving them, and the gaps in technical, data modeling, and analytical skills. In the US, for example, the skills related to data analysis, database skills, data management, and statistics outnumber other requested digital competencies of job advertisements [6].

The promotion of computer science (CS) education is global. In consequence, a number of countries all over the world have already introduced CS into their K–12 curricula. In line with others, FNC-2014 comprises algorithmic thinking and adapting good coding conventions as CS contents that are included in the mathematics syllabus [7], see Table 1:

Table 1. Computing-related additions in FNC-2014. Typically, a student is 6–7 years old in Year 1.

	Years 1–2	Years 3–6	Years 7–9
Digital competence	Using digital media, technological fluency	Impact of technology, tech-integration	
Math	Step-by-step instructions	Visual programming	Algorithmic thinking, good computing conventions
Crafts		Robots, automation	Embedded systems, own artifacts

In pursuit of consistent CS support, the entire mathematics syllabus should be reviewed along with these newly introduced additions. Thus, this study asks:

- RQ1: What elementary mathematics syllabus areas should be strengthened for the anticipated CS emphasis?
- RQ2: Are there mathematics syllabus areas that are currently overemphasized from this viewpoint?
- RQ3: According to the feedback from software engineers, is the current CS-supportive syllabus missing any crucial points?

First, Specifying the Discipline of CS and Relating it to Mathematics chapter reviews the discourse of CS as a scientific discipline, its neighboring disciplines, and the learning targets of mathematics in anticipation of supporting CS. Related Work introduces already-existing directives and recommendations of institutions that aim at building flexible future software engineers, such as ACM/IEEE. There, we focus on suggested mathematics courses in particular. For an age-appropriate reality check, we reflect on the elementary-level mathematics and computing syllabi of current strong performers in CS, i.e., the UK and US. Results and Discussion cross-expose the recommendations with feedback from in-service software engineers by focusing on the mathematics topics that are the top-scorers in profitability. To sum up, Conclusions sketch a hypothetical learning trajectory for a CS support attached to the corresponding topics in the mathematics syllabus.

2 Specifying the Discipline of CS and Relating It to Mathematics

Most natural sciences and engineering disciplines rely on calculus, differential equations, and linear algebra as a mathematical foundation appropriate for continuous phenomena [8]. Systems relying on such phenomena can be adequately tested. For instance, a bridge does not need tests for all possible loads between zero and a maximum value. Testing the maximum load under typical and extreme weather conditions suffices. In contrast, Parnas highlights the different nature of software [9]. Unlike bridge load tests, testing a piece of software with typical and extreme values does not guarantee the expected behavior with untested values. Furthermore, software is rarely concise enough to be tested inside out, and unlike mathematical theorems, it is not comprehensively checked by other experts in the field. Thus, frequent errors and failures are common [10].

As we will discuss later, computer scientists have suggested topics such as logic, formal grammar, and set theory as an appropriate mathematical basis for mastering software and improving its quality. In addition, the importance of algorithmic thinking has been revealed. In traditional engineering degree programs, classic mathematics and physics are included early on. The rationale is to develop a suitable mindset, that is, a way of thinking that facilitates profound learning of engineering topics. The basis is constructed already in elementary school physics and mathematics. Similarly, professional computer science and software development need a suitable mindset that should be developed before studying the bulk of the software topics. However, because software cannot be appropriately mastered with mechanisms suited for continuous phenomena, this mindset is not the same as that of, say, an electrical engineer.

The discussion about the educational needs in Finland suffers from a poor distinction between Computer Science (CS), Software Engineering (SWE), and Information and Communication Technology (ICT). For more than a decade, the Finnish mobile phone company Nokia was very successful and its educational needs had a significant impact on the Finnish educational discourse. In addition to SW engineers, Nokia needed expertise in the fields of hardware, radio technology, and signal processing. Therefore, SWE and ICT were emphasized instead of CS, with SWE largely perceived analogous to traditional engineering, less through its relation to CS. As a consequence, Finnish scholars and educators have only partially conceived the special character of CS and SWE as disciplines distinct from ICT, thus requiring a different educational foundation, which implies changes to the mathematics syllabus as well.

To clarify the conceptual difference, we define the relation of CS to SWE more closely. Parnas equates it to the relationship between physics and electrical engineering [11, p. 21]: physics belongs to the natural sciences, which target an understanding of a wide variety of phenomena, whereas electrical engineering is an engineering discipline striving to create useful artifacts. Although electrical engineering is based on physics, it is neither a subfield nor an extension of it. Analogously, CS is a science, and SWE is an engineering discipline based on CS. Therefore, CS degrees must focus on the underlying computational phenomena and the acquisition of new knowledge of these, while SWE degrees concentrate on implementing trustworthy, human-friendly software cost-effectively.

In regard to mathematics, the latest specifications of Association for Computing Machinery (ACM) and Institute of Electrical and Electronics Engineers (IEEE) explicate the similarity of required skills both in CS and SWE [12,13]. Even if CS is more scientific as a discipline and more deeply grounded in mathematics, SW engineers benefit from more theoretically-oriented CS education and discrete mathematics to be able to implement quality software. Hence, the conceptual difference does not diverge the required mathematics and CS fundamentals. Consequently, Meziane and Vadera concluded, '*There is very little difference between the SWE and CS programs currently offered in English Universities*' [14].

3 Related Work

3.1 ACM Recommendations

The standards developed by the ACM promote CS as a discipline, and in compliance, provide normative recommendations for teaching CS at the tertiary level. The recommendations are used as a premise in curriculum planning in a number of Finnish universities. The CS concepts introduced in the first courses are important either for their own sake or for further topics. Obviously, the first fundamental concepts are also the most evident candidates in the considerations of advancing basics at the elementary school level.

CS Knowledge Areas of ACM. ACM introduces Curriculum Guidelines for Undergraduate Degree Programs in Computer Science (ACM-CS2013) [12]. The material is divided into Knowledge Areas (KA) and further to Knowledge Units (KU) that match with no particular course, instead, courses may incorporate topics from one or multiple KAs. Topics are divided into Core and Elective, and the Core is further subdivided into Tier-1 (to be fully completed) and Tier-2 (at minimum 80% coverage). The KAs with the most Tier1 hours are, where time allocation is thought to correlate with the importance of a topic:

1. Software Development Fundamentals (43 h)
2. Discrete Systems (37 h)
3. Algorithms and Complexity (19 h)
4. Systems Fundamentals (18 h).

The natural flow of concepts is to introduce Software Development Fundamentals (SDF) by simultaneously strengthening the mathematical foundation with Discrete Systems (DS). In descending order of allocated hours, Algorithms and Complexity (AL) come next, where mastering common algorithms is considered general CS knowledge. Complexity considerations consist of evaluating the efficiency of algorithms based on their execution time and consumed resources. Systems Fundamentals (SF) give an insight into system infrastructure and low-level computing by acquainting students with computer architecture, main hardware resources and memory, and, e.g., sequential and parallel execution.

From the list above, items 2 and 3 link closely with mathematics. According to ACM, DS comprises the following areas in descending order of emphasis (Tier-1 + Tier-2 hours): Proof Techniques (11), Basic Logic (9), Discrete Probability (8), Basics of Counting (5), Sets, Relations, and Functions (4), and Graphs and Trees (4). AL, in turn, consists of basic and advanced KUs of Analysis, Strategies, Fundamental Data Structures, Automata, Computability, and Complexity. Algorithms and data structures are at the center of gravity of SDF, besides the introduction of the programming basics.

The Most Relevant Mathematics to Support CS. ACM-CS2013 highlights the tight and mutual interdependence between mathematics and CS. However, ACM-CS2013 focuses on the common denominator part, instead of being prepared for a full range of different career options specifically. Thus, only directly relevant requirements are specified for the KA of DS, such as the elements of set theory, logic, and discrete probability. On the other hand, ACM-CS2013 states that '*while we do not specify such requirements, we note that undergraduate CS students need enough mathematical maturity to have the basis on which to then build CS-specific mathematics*'. It also mentions that '*some programs use calculus ... as a method for helping develop such mathematical maturity*' [12].

Thus, the recommendations make a distinction between such mathematics that is an important requirement for all students in the faculty, in distinction to mathematics that is relevant only to specific areas within CS, exemplified by linear algebra that '*plays a critical role in some areas of computing such as graphics and the analysis of graph algorithms. However, linear algebra would not necessarily be a requirement for all areas of computing*' [12].

If discrete mathematics – including logic – were emphasized in the elementary school mathematics curriculum, an age-appropriate and tested subset of ACM

Basic Logic could be found in the National Curriculum and GCSE Mathematics of the UK. The UK has taught discrete mathematics already for a longer period, see Sect. 3.3. In programming, logic is frequently employed, not only when implementing conditions in selections and iterations. Subsequently, university-level logic targets more sophisticated and far-reaching knowledge than these. Basic Logic of DS introduces such topics as normal forms, validity, inference rules, and quantification.

Although the domain of probability associates significantly weaker to the programming fundamentals than logic, for instance, it gives readiness for various prominent topics. These topics include the analysis of average-case running times, randomized algorithms, cryptography, information theory, as well as games.

3.2 SWEBOK Recommendations

The Guide to the Software Engineering Body of Knowledge (SWEBOK) of the IEEE breaks down the mathematical foundations into smaller knowledge areas [15]. Because of their direct mathematics linkage, we focus on both Chaps. 13 and 14 of the guide in particular, i.e., Computing and Mathematical Foundations.

Computing Foundation comprises algorithms and data structures. The chapter classifies data structures based on following dichotomies: linear – nonlinear, homogeneous – heterogeneous, and stateful – stateless. For instance, linear structures organize items on one dimension (lists, stacks), in contrast to nonlinear structures exemplified by trees and heaps. Well-designed data structures accelerate data storage and retrieval; the efficiency of algorithms depends significantly on the selection of a suitable data structure. Appropriate data structures foster algorithm development. When the effects of selected algorithms and data structures are combined, performance and memory consumption may range from poor to extremely efficient.

Chapter 14 highlights CS as applied mathematics. The foundational KAs concentrate on logic and reasoning as the essences that a SW engineer must internalize in particular. The chapter describes mathematics as a tool of studying formal systems, widely interpreted as abstractions on diverse application domains. These abstractions do not limit to numbers only, but in addition comprise symbols, images, and videos.

The following subtopics constitute the foundational KAs of mathematics. The topics are divided by us into continuous (c) and discrete (d) mathematics. The assumption is that the order implies their importance:

1. Sets, Relations, and Functions (c/d)
2. Basic Logic (d)
3. Proof Techniques (d)
4. Basics of Counting (d)
5. Graphs and Trees (d)
6. Discrete Probability (d/c)
7. Finite State Machines (d)

8. Grammars (d)
9. Numerical Precision, Accuracy, and Errors (c)
10. Number Theory (d)
11. Algebraic Structures (d).

Immediately, a notably smaller portion of continuous mathematics compared with traditional engineering education leaps out. In particular, calculus, differential equations, and linear algebra are conspicuous by their absence. Instead, several topics target a better position of underlying logic (2, 3); and primers for data types, data structures and algorithms (1, 4, 5, 9, 11). In addition, the subtopics of Basics of Counting (4), and Discrete Probability (6) and Number Theory (10) scaffold a deeper understanding of probability and cryptography. Numerical Precision, Accuracy, and Errors (9) section reveals underlying HW and memory specifics that have an effect on, for instance, the resolution of measurements and impossibility of expressing most real numbers precisely.

3.3 CS-Supportive Mathematics Syllabi of the UK and the US in K–12

For comparison, we went through the National Curriculum (UKNC) and General Certificate of Secondary Education (UKGCSE) of the UK [16–18], and the Core Curriculum of the US (USCC) [19], see Table 2. In UKNC and USCC, all the suggested mathematics syllabus areas remain at the basic level, which is necessary taking into account elementary students' rudimentary abstraction skills. In addition to reducing its complexity, the new content should be carefully bridged with the prior knowledge by starting early enough, proceeding in spiral revisits, and by exploiting lots of different type of exercises including hands-on exercises and visual clues. To ensure mathematics-compatibility, a hypothetical learning trajectory is sketched and further extended to the proposed CS topics. Next, we will review potential discrete mathematics contents in UKNC and USCC starting from algorithms and data structures, logic, sets, statistics and probability, and ending up with linear algebra.

Algorithms and Data Structures. In UKNC, the definition of algorithms in KS1 is followed by studying the behavior of selected algorithms in KS2, after which the key algorithms are digested. The CS syllabus of the GCSE sets a few learning targets for algorithms: at a minimum, binary search and merge sort are to be introduced [17]. In USCC, since CS is not compulsory, algorithms are not that pertinently present, however, computing strategies used in problem solving, are perceived as algorithms. Paper-and-pencil calculations provide affordances of applying such algorithms, for example, long division may be systematized as the strategy of 'divide, multiply, subtract, drop the next free number, repeat'. Because of all-immersive digitalization, many such educational sweet-spots are missed, e.g. phone books for demonstrating search algorithms.

Table 2. Mathematics syllabi (KS = key stage, G = grade, HS = high school. In the UK, each key stage covers several grades ranging from two to four; KS4 is followed by the GCSE exams.)

	UKNC	USCC
Algorithms	KS1: understand what algorithms are KS2: use logical reasoning to explain the functionality of simple algorithms KS3: key algorithms of searching and sorting, such as binary search and merge sort GCSE: data handling and algorithms visualized with flowcharts	G3: algorithms in problem solving heuristics, e.g., based on place value in addition/-subtraction G5: the same with multiplication G6: and division
Logic (in CS)	KS2: logical reasoning, e.g., in explaining the functionality of simple algorithms KS3: Boolean logic (AND/OR/NOT)	General: Construct viable arguments and critique the reasoning of others. Logical progression of statements
Sets	KS3: enumerate sets, unions/intersections, tables, grids and Venn diagrams KS4: data sets from empirical distributions, identifying clusters, peaks, gaps and symmetry, expected frequencies with tables, trees and Venn diagrams	G6: data sets, identifying clusters, peaks, gaps, symmetry G7: random sampling to generate data sets HS: interpreting differences in shape, center and spread of a distribution
Stat Prob	Chart interpretations (K2), distributions/ rel. frequencies, bivariate data, P scale: 0–1, P of mutually exclusive events (K3); bigger samples, population, histograms, scatter and box plots, combined dependent events (K4)	Variability (G6), generalizations and random sampling (G7), bivariate data (G8)
Linear algebra	KS4: (in Geometry) translations as 2D vectors, addition and subtraction of vectors, multiplication with a scalar, diagrammatic and column representations GCSE: transformations & vectors	HS: addition, subtraction, multiplication of matrices, multiplication with a scalar, identity matrix, transformations as 2 × 2 matrices

Logic. The basics of logic are present in UKNC. A comprehensive subset is provided, yet in the UK Boolean logic is currently included in the computing and not in the mathematics syllabus. However, Boolean logic would also fit well in the mathematics syllabus as a consistent continuum of studying inequalities and their truth values. A readily field-tested elementary syllabus is found in GCSE CS [17] as well. It contains the following topics:

- binary and hexadecimal notations
- binary addition and shift
- Boolean values (*true*, *false*)
- Boolean operators (AND, OR, NOT)
- truth tables.

In USCC, logic is substituted by logical thinking as part of critical thinking skills and consistency in arguments. In addition collaborative learning techniques are utilized, in particular sociomathematical norms [20]. Yackel and Cobb emphasize the need for a rationale and justification for a solution. It is a mathematics teacher's duty to challenge students to invent multiple alternatives ending up with the same result. Among the presented alternatives, the class should evaluate the most sophisticated and elegant method.

Sets, Statistics, and Probability. Sets may be employed to illustrate nested number sets of natural numbers ($\mathbb{N}$), integers ($\mathbb{Z}$), and reals ($\mathbb{R}$) that match with variable types (*unsigned*, *int*, *float*) in programming. However, due to differences in how, e.g., reals appear in both, we note that this juxtaposition is prone to misconceptions. For instance, in:

```
int x=1; float y=x/2;
```

division may produce a value of zero depending on the programming language selected. All the same, not every *int* is necessarily a *float*, in contradiction to the mathematics subset relation of $\mathbb{Z} \subset \mathbb{R}$. In mathematics, sets are a basic abstraction of containment, likewise in programming, they could be exploited as a cognitive scaffold that assists in understanding e.g. collections and their operations. The same operations are exploitable even if the collection type would change from a set to an array, a list, a vector or a matrix. Therefore, set theory would be useful in any mathematics syllabus designed to support CS. Currently, sets are a part of UKNC, but absent from USCC and FNC-2014. Sets prompt types in programming and they can be utilized in abstracting both primitives and collections. UKNC specifies the syllabus of sets containing the following topics:

- sets visualized by Venn diagrams
- set operations: subset, proper subset, intersection, and union, combinations of these
- sets represented as lists, and
- set and its complement.

Statistics and probability have only a small role in the conceptual core of CS, however they are useful tools for further studies, e.g., statistical analyses in STEM reports or probability exploited in game applications.

Linear Algebra. Linear algebra basics are included in the USCC as matrices and basic operations, and as vectors and transformations in UKNC, whereas they are missing from the FNC-2014. However, linear algebra basics could be a beneficial addition, even if supported by ACM-CS2013 only as an elective mathematics topic. The need for matrices is increasing, because of topicality of their application areas. Hence many libraries, e.g., in Python exploit them extensively. As a topic, matrices and vectors (that can be handled as matrices) belong together. Matrix manipulations, such as transformations (scaling, translation, reflection and rotation) are especially applicable in many popular fields of graphics, animations and game engines. In addition, matrices are extensively exploited in machine learning, data analysis, and pattern recognition.

4 Method

This study complies with the scope of curriculum theory [21], and its key question of what knowledge is the most valuable and how the knowledge should be constructed in order to ensure consistent proceeding. Here, we are concerned with the educational and sociological aspects due to the aim of improved employability and filling the digital skills gap. This study is restricted to elementary mathematics and compares FNC-2014 with UKNC and USCC [16,19,22] and with the recommendations given by the ACM and IEEE [12,15]. The comparison exploits content analysis in searching for the mathematics syllabus anticipated to be the most useful for CS students.

In addition to the comparison, the effectiveness of the university-level SWE studies reflects back to the curriculum design. We do not collect any new data but reuse the data of existing studies [23–26]. The results of the previous studies are cross-correlated to confirm their validity in order to draw conclusions about the most profitable mathematics topics.

5 Results and Discussion

In this section, we first review the feedback from the field: SW professionals evaluate the curriculum topics according to their profitability in working life. Being informed of both the recommendations and criticisms of the current realization, we summarize the necessary mathematics syllabus content and bridge the learning trajectories from elementary to higher education mathematics.

5.1 Feedback from SW Engineers

To evaluate the effectiveness of their education, SW engineers have scored the profitability of plenty of curriculum topics [23]. An imbalance between supply and demand was discovered and as a remedy, the author recommends putting less emphasis on the topics of minor importance – or teaching them in a way that makes them more relevant to SWE students. The study was run in the year 1997 and repeated in 1998. The differences between outcomes remained modest. In 1998, the sample size was $N = 181$, and the survey consisted of 75 topics of CS, SWE, etc. A few years later, in 2004, Kitchenham et al. conducted a research focusing on the curricula and graduates of four British universities [26]. The methodology was somewhat different and so was the obtained list of the most under-taught topics. The findings regarding mathematics were, however, the same.

Then in 2009, a decade after Lethbridge's original research setup, Puhakka et al. published an analogous study conducted in Tampere University of Technology [24] ($N = 212$). Out of the original 75 subtopics, three were removed because of their not being common in Finnish curricula. Both sub-figures of Fig. 1 illustrate the differences between math-related perceptions among SW professionals in the examined cohorts of US and Finland. First, we observe that the results correlate surprisingly well, taking into account a timespan and continent switch. The scientifically significant values of R^2 are 0.88 in the upper, and 0.91 in the lower figure.

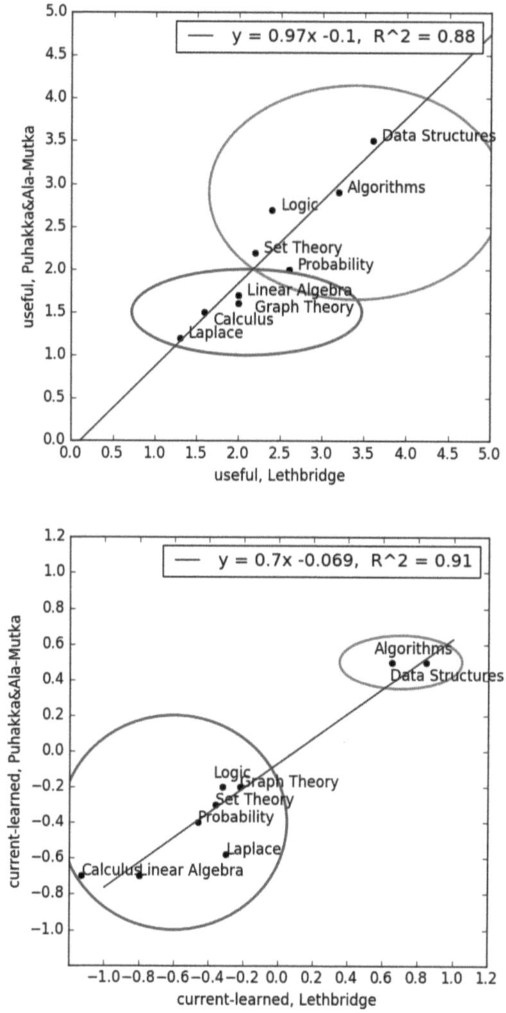

Fig. 1. The comparison of usefulness and adequacy of mathematics education evaluated by SW professionals [23,24] ($N = 181$; $N = 212$), originally in [8]. (Color figure online)

The green circles in sub-figures designate the areas considered either useful (the upper) or in need of more emphasis (the lower) to build work-life competence of SW professionals. The lower sub-figure, however, demonstrates the rarity of topics in need of more emphasis. Negative values indicate a post-graduate knowledge loss, whereas positive values a knowledge gain, in other words, inadequate learning of such topics in higher education. The latter sub-figure is visually telling. Only algorithms and data structures are in need of more emphasis. In addition to these, the Lethbridge top-ten consists of no other mathematical, but instead, such items as negotiation, human-computer interaction, and leadership.

In comparison with both previous surveys, Surakka separates the sample into the cohorts of SW engineers, academics (professors, lecturers) and students, see Fig. 2. The winner is again clear: algorithms and data structures, also the prominence of discrete mathematics compared with continuous mathematics is unchallenged, yet the bias has an academic flavor: discrete mathematics scores the highest among professors and lecturers (3.1).

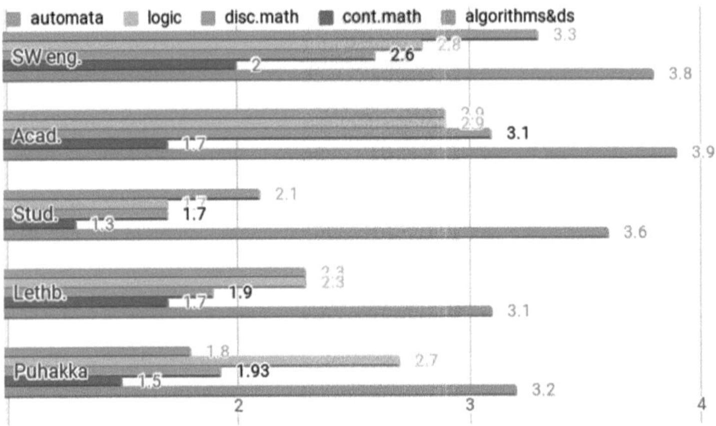

Fig. 2. The mathematics areas perceptions [1(not important), 4(very important)] of Surakka's engineers, academics, and students contrasted with Lethbridge and Puhakka et al.; $N = 11, 19, 24; 181; 212$ – respectively. Originally in [8].

5.2 TEK, Aarresaari

The society follows the effectiveness measures of higher education. In a yearly basis, the association of Academic Engineers and Architects in Finland, TEK, collects the feedback of university graduates. The latest survey, 2017 TEK graduate survey, is referred to update the current emphasis areas of the graduates [27, p. 21].

Unfortunately, in regard to mathematics, the granularity of the survey is more coarse-grained than in the previous studies examined. The more general information addresses the importance of certain skills, such as problem solving and information retrieval skills. Only two aspects are studied more than anticipated by their importance, i.e., the difference of importance – learned in studies is negative. The two areas are 'knowledge of the research of the own field' and 'mathematics and natural sciences', that is, they are learned more than actually needed in working life. In comparison, 'practical application of theories' is one of the top-scorers. 'Problem solving' is regarded the most important skill among graduates, and after project management and oral communication skills, analytical thinking also scores highly. In Aarresaari data, learning skills in overall and self-regulatory skills in particular are valued the highest, exemplified by such skills as 'ability to learn' and 'self-steerability/initiative' [28]. These key areas intimately reflect the current requirement of a flexible workforce capable of recreating itself based on the current need. Also analytical thinking skills and problem solving score high. In contrast, 'theoretical skills' are valued much lower to their applicative counterparts, and 'theoretical knowledge of one's own domain' and 'mathematics and natural sciences' actually count among few topics over-taught, i.e., during their studies, the graduates learn them maybe too theoretically without exploiting the learned content in practice.

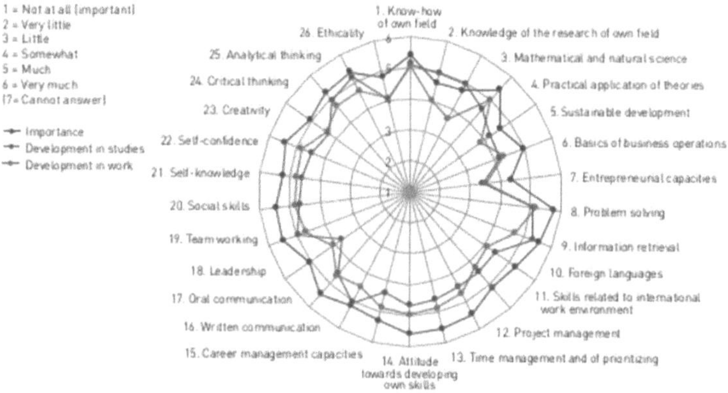

Fig. 3. TEK graduate survey in 2017; $N = 1985$.

The TEK survey for university graduates confirms the findings of over-taught topics: 'knowledge of the research field' and 'mathematical and natural science', see Fig. 3. Even if the theoretical aspects of one's research field are over-emphasized, the practical application of theories is yet insufficient. Moreover, the resolution is partly lost in bundling mathematics and natural sciences together. Lethbridge/Puhakka/Surakka studies suggest chemistry being constantly among the low-scorers, whereas parts of mathematics, especially those fostering algorithmic and logical thinking, are appreciated.

In the TEK and Aarresaari survey, high-valued self-regulatory skills are seconded by such practical aspects that can be situated under the broader umbrella concept of 'specificational thinking'. These skills comprise, e.g., communication and negotiation skills with a client as part of user-centered design. However, the specificational thinking in its entirety is more about modeling and abstracting data, which as topics were absent from these surveys. Specificational thinking will be treated more thoroughly in Sect. 5.5.

5.3 CS-Supportive Mathematics for Primary and Secondary Education

In constructing a strong basis for CS, both ACM and SWEBOK emphasize discrete mathematics, confirmed by the feedback from the field. After programming basics, ACM values discrete systems as the second most prominent, and algorithms, data structures, and complexity as the third most prominent KAs, whereas the in-service SW engineers appreciate the latter more. In SWEBOK, nine out of eleven mathematics KAs comprise discrete mathematics. Spearheading in CS, the UK invests in discrete mathematics already at the elementary level and, in addition, provides CS as a subject of its own right that allows more in-depth topics.

Algorithmic Thinking. In pondering the difference between the mindsets of mathematicians and computer scientists, Knuth points out that computer scientists need to be concerned about algorithms and their computing specifics, such as the notion of complexity or economy of operations [29]. Denning equates algorithmic and computational thinking [30], which he, in turn, associates with general problem solving [31]. When solving a problem, it is beneficial to start by decomposing it to smaller solvable subproblems that may be implemented as subroutines in a code. At its simplest, an algorithm may thus be understood as a subroutine, a sequence of commands that can be called repeatedly as many times as desired [32, for instance]. Figure 4 suggests dividing the algorithms into the following sub-topics:

1. The introduction of the key algorithms of searches and sorts. These can be trained without computers as well.
2. Complexity considerations.
3. Data structures and corresponding operations.

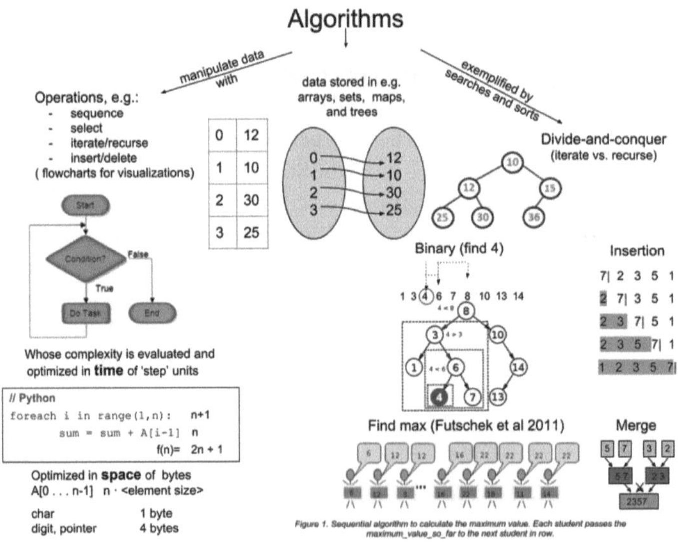

Fig. 4. Algorithms at elementary level.

Algorithmic thinking has been brought within reach of school or even preschool children with multiple initiatives such as [33], and without utilizing computers, as demonstrated by the CS-unplugged movement [34], and algorithmic plays [35]. Puzzles and games can be very educative and thought-provoking, thus this approach is also exploited by a number of universities in familiarizing students with algorithms [36]. Unplugging removes the extra cognitive load of knowing the programming details. To be acquainted with well-known algorithms, binary-search and merge-sort are considered an age-appropriate start, backed up with the CS syllabus of UKNC.

In general, a student should learn to save resources, i.e., time and memory, as a part of good coding conventions. In algorithm development, it is crucial to select an appropriate algorithm and data structure for a task. In consequence, a student must be aware of the consequences of poor choices, where estimating the complexity of the algorithm is educative. The combined effect of algorithm and data structure can be huge. In extending the data amounts, the differences highlight further. The same control structures are applicable as usual, i.e., sequencing, selection, iteration and recursion. In visualizing the control flow, a flow chart is educational. Iterations and recursions, especially if nested, can easily increase the number of iterations.

Data Structures: Sets and Other Representations. In programming-oriented mathematics, data structures can be seen as an application of set theory that conceptualizes collections. Sets are missing from FNC-2014, whereas UKNC defines a functional subset visualized in Fig. 5. Sets (naïve set theory) in UKNC are a gentle kick-start for the set theory, familiarizing students with different notations, e.g., the interchangeable use of either a list or a Venn diagram (excluding some special cases). A number of basic concepts are introduced, such as a set and its complement, a universe, and a subset. Set operations cover union and intersection.

In programming, collections are of various types: a set is an unordered collection of values where no value may occur twice, a list an ordered collection where the same value may occur multiple times, and a map a collection of values identified by keys; the map may also be interpreted as a representation of a mathematical function. Data structures should introduce the very basic structures, such as arrays, lists, maps and optionally also more sophisticated tree structures, and demonstrate the efficiency of each basic operation of adding, deleting, and selecting (searching). Sorting can be interpreted as an application of search in compliance with divide-and-conquer heuristics: after an item is found and in the right position, search is applied iteratively till all items are sorted.

Multiple external representations (MERs) elucidate the data and problem from different perspectives. For example, a function may be represented as an expression, a curve, a map from 'argument set' to 'image set', a table with two columns, or a function machine. Flexibility in moving from one representation to another indicates a deeper understanding of the concept [37], which facilitates problem solving. Wilkie and Clark denote representational flexibility as fluency

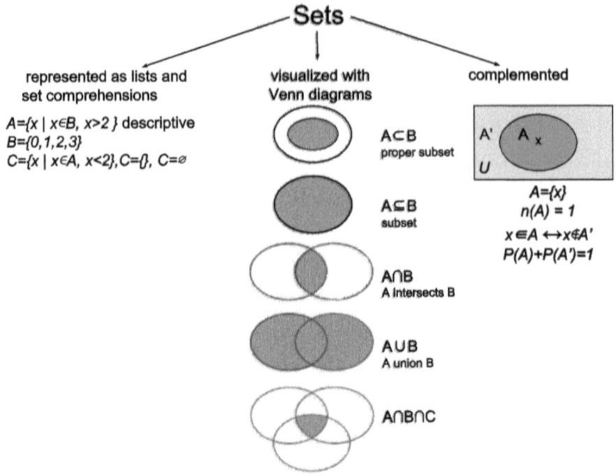

Fig. 5. Sets in UKNC.

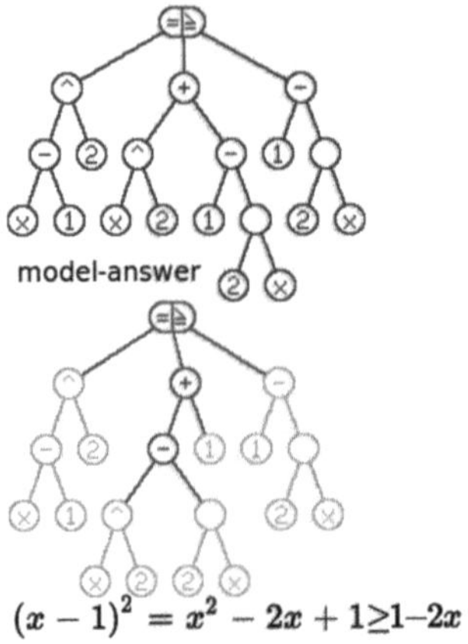

Fig. 6. A tree representation of an arithmetic relation chain, and a failed attempt to yield a similar tree [8].

with the order of operations; commutative, associative, and distributive laws; and equivalence of expressions [38]. In programming, representational fluency is practiced, e.g., with the syntactic diversity of operations, such as addition: $x+y$, $+(x, y)$, or $(+\ x\ y)$. Figure 6 illustrates the use of the MathCheck learning tool [39] in studying the relationship between textual and tree representations. Such exercises aim at training the precedence and left- and right-associativity rules in particular. The exercises help students to grasp the distinction between semantics and syntax by differentiating between associativity as a semantic notion and left- and right-associativity as syntactic notions. Furthermore, the example in Fig. 6 reveals that the relation operators ($=$ and $\geq$, and so on) are neither left- nor right-associative unlike arithmetic operators ($+$, $-$, and so on). Consequently,

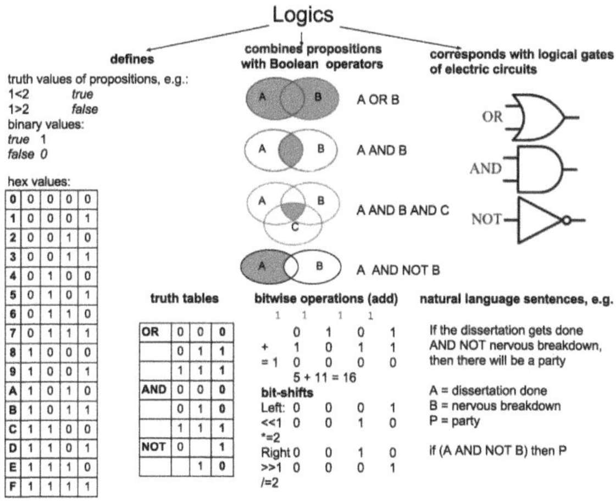

Fig. 7. Logic in UKNC [8].

in $x = y \geq z$, the first comparison result is not passed as an argument to the second, but instead, a Boolean AND is performed on both. Thus, drawing $=$ as a child of $\geq$, or vice versa, would be misleading. Being even, the relation operators must share the root of a tree as Fig. 6 illustrates. This also makes it explicit that although y occurs only once, both comparisons use it as an argument.

In problem solving, the ability to model and abstract the data is crucial. USCC specifies Modeling as a syllabus area of HS mathematics [19,40]. It links to a broader pedagogical idea of using the open-ended problems of everyday life by combining skills from mathematics, statistics and technology, and '... *and the ability to recognize significant variables and relationships among them. Diagrams of various kinds, spreadsheets and other technology, and algebra are powerful tools for understanding and solving these problems.*' Although modeling, say, a banking system for implementation as software is fundamentally different from modeling a physical or statistical problem, the need to recognize and formalize the essential aspects of the problem is common. Specificational thinking is necessary for both SW engineers and their customers to reach a common vision.

Logic. In formalizing CS, a formula, $CS = mathematics + logic$, proposed by Dijkstra, aims at describing its distinctiveness [41]. In accordance, he calls students to learn formal mathematics and logic to construct a well-grounded basis for CS. UKNC points out that already at the elementary level a novice programmer needs simple Boolean logic, at least the operators of AND, OR and NOT, and their combinations, see Fig. 7. In the same context, UKNC introduces logic gates in circuits, thereby creating a link between CS and physics (electronics).

To skim other logic uses, we reviewed ACM course descriptions. The logic applications were proofs, correctness, the combinational and sequential logic of state machines, and in addition to these, reasoning that targets translating

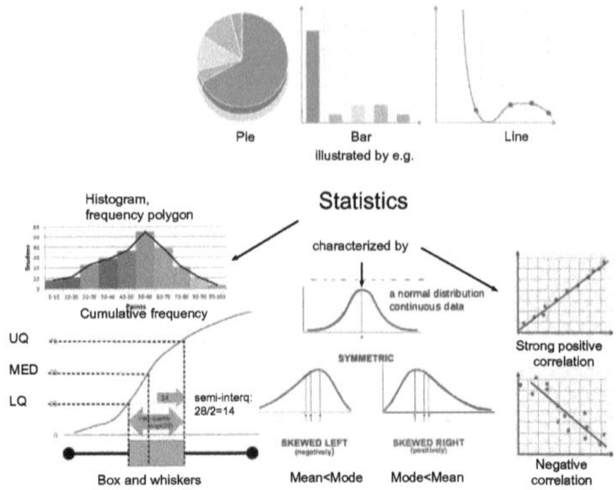

Fig. 8. Statistics in UKNC [8].

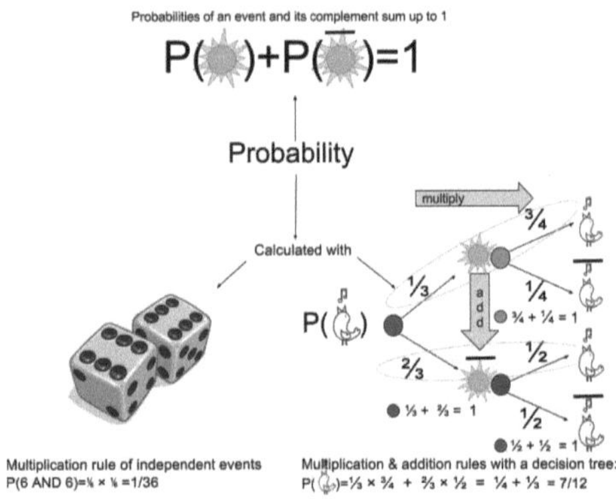

Fig. 9. Probability in UKNC [8].

natural language (e.g., English) sentences into predicate logic statements. Such a skill would stand out in specificational thinking in Sect. 5.5.

Statistics, Probability. The syllabus areas of statistics and probability are inter-related at the elementary level, justifying combining the topics under the same label. Building the knowledge base and gaining experience of these topics may be initiated, for instance, by collecting the data of concrete phenomena, such as measuring the heights of students of a class and constructing a histogram of the heights of the class. Students should be capable of reading and interpreting these charts. For instance, the shape of the height histogram should resemble the typical bell-shape of a normal distribution making it timely to introduce the concepts of mean, median, and mode in this context. In addition to histograms, the alternative way of representing this information is to construct a cumulative frequency chart, in the UKNC subset visualized in Fig. 8, the left bottom corner. Ultimately, information could be reduced to a box-and-whiskers chart.

Venn diagrams and relative frequency charts prompt probability. The relative frequency of an event, e.g., which percentage of students are in the range of 140–150 cm, provides an obvious scaffold to investigate the probability of a randomly-selected student being 140–150 cm tall, and prepares for generalizations concerning bigger populations. In Venn, the bin of 140–150 cm students can represent the set A, where the complement set of $\overline{A}$ represents all the students not within this height category. In the universe of this class (or any other), a selector will get either a student from the set A or its complement $\overline{A}$ with 100% probability, i.e., $P(A) + P(\overline{A}) = 1$. In Finnish elementary mathematics, probability links closely with statistics in the described manner. UKNC progresses further by including the multiplication and addition rules, see Fig. 9. In the figure, a decision tree clearly demonstrates that the sun either is shining or not, no other options exist. As a consequence of the shining sun, a bird will sing more probably. Furthermore, the tree assists in constructing the combined probabilities correctly: the multiplication rule applies horizontally to each branch at a time, and the products are added vertically. In a tree, all the probability branches of one joint must sum up to one. For statistics, and probability, UKNC specifies a valid and deliberately planned mathematics syllabus for an elementary level that could be emulated as such in FNC-2014.

5.4 CS-Supportive Mathematics at High School

In the Finnish high school system, CS is not provided as a subject of its own. Instead, the cross-curriculum thread of digital competence started at elementary level continues as the utilization of CS and practicing technological fluency throughout the high school. After completing the first course of mathematics (MAY1), a student either chooses honors mathematics (the MAA* courses), or regular mathematics (the MAB* courses) [42]. The respective courses are listed in Table 3. This study concentrates on honors mathematics in particular, which comprises ten compulsory courses (MAY1-MAA10), and three optional courses (MAA11–MAA13), because of its partial support for discrete mathematics. The courses of discrete mathematics consist of 'Number theory and proofs' (MAA11) and 'Algorithms in mathematics' (MAA12) that are currently optional.

In HS, algorithms are introduced only in the elective courses of 'Number theory and proofs' (MAA11), and 'Algorithms in mathematics' (MAA12). Closest to logic is the elective MAA11 with conjunctives and truth values. Instead, we propose a compulsory status for these courses to ensure a proper support for CS. Due to the proposal, some compulsory courses ought to be converted as optional as a fair exchange. Maybe the advanced courses of derivation and integration could be potential candidates, since the SW engineers' feedback manifest the excess of continuous mathematics, such as calculus. Moreover, the electric version of matriculation examination will be taken into use in the year 2019 implying hands-on exercises with computers. The developing of these questions is currently proceeding. In anticipation of this change, mathematics teachers should prepare their students to master the required applications and programmable environments.

Table 3. High school mathematics divided in MAA* and MAB* courses and grouped by learning trajectories (stat. and prob., logic, algorithms, cont.mathematics, and geometry), see Fig. 11.

stat. and prob.		arithmetic(logic/algor. in yellow)		cont.mathematics		geometry	
course	description	*course*	description	*course*	description	*course*	description
MAB5	stat. and prob.	MAY1	numbers,sequences	MAB2	expression,equations	MAB3	geometry
(MAB8)	stat. and prob. II	MAB4	modeling,patterns	(MAB7)	mathematics.analysis		
		MAB6	commercial math				
MAA10	prob. and stat.	MAY1	numbers,sequences	MAA2	polynomials	MAA3	geometry
	combinatorics	MAA8	root,log functions	MAA6	derivative	MAA4	vectors
		(MAA11)	number theory,proofs	MAA9	integral calculus	MAA5	analytic g.
		(MAA12)	algorithms in math	(MAA13)	adv.calculus	MAA7	trigonometry

5.5 Specificational Thinking

In the SW engineers' feedback, specificational thinking and related skills become ever more pronounced. Specificational thinking shares certain analogies with computational thinking, and it could be described as its practical cousin. Taken that computational thinking comprises the theoretical basis and the acquaintance of a software process, at least in the abstract, specificational thinking extends to the real working life and project-based conditions, where the threads of modeling and user-centric design mix in, see Fig. 11. Modeling implies both data modeling and conceptual visualizations in order to describe the system. User-centered design attempts to ensure such products that respond to users' expectations and needs, which starts by specifying user requirements, often referred to as user stories in agile project management.

As a complementary part of the negotiation skills that were highly appreciated in the SW graduate surveys, capturing all the essentials in a specification benefits from an adequate amount of domain knowledge and observations as a typical practice of user-centered design. Translating all the information and observations as clearly-worded specifications – while minimizing the chances for misunderstandings – requires a sense of the nuances of a spoken language, preciseness, and the capacity for recognizing the sentences as implicit logical propositions. First, use cases and requirements are defined together with a customer. It is difficult to design SW so that it meets the needs of its end users. Indeed, [10] lists twelve common causes for SW project failures. Three of them are unrealistic or unarticulated project goals; badly defined system requirements; and poor communication among customers, developers, and users. We believe that *specificational thinking* alleviates these problems: to provide usable and user-friendly products requires a fair reflection on the actual needs and expectations of end users, and clothing them as precise specification text.

In writing a good specification, it is hard to anticipate all its consequences, especially if one is not a professional, which is illustrated by the next example. A man sitting in a wheelchair tried to buy winter boots at one supermarket, in Helsinki [43]. For the purpose, he had received a voucher worth at most 70 euro granted by social security authorities. However, the shoes did cost 74.50 euro. The remaining part, 4.50, the man would have paid himself. However, a cashperson refused and appealed to the instructions. After a while, a superior of the cashperson arrived, the next arrival being a safeguard. Finally, an outsider paid the winter boots from her own money to resolve the awkward stalemate. Afterwards, the supermarket analyzed what went wrong. Cashpersons had been given a written specification of how to process the social security vouchers: first, check the maximum value of a voucher, then, a purchase not exceeding that value. The cashperson obeyed the instructions literally. However, this was not the intention, but instead, to prevent from using the vouchers as worth of more than their maximum, i.e., they are no reduction coupons. The supermarket fixed the instructions and returned the money to the customer who had paid the boots.

At first glance, this incident may seem to have nothing in common with SW development, however, it illustrates such defects in specificational thinking that are a major source of problems throughout an SW process: it is very hard to see the unintended consequences in advance. Beforehand, the authors may think that they have written a decent specification; afterwards, it is self-evident to everybody that it allows some drastic and unintended interpretations. Commonly, a failure scenario is considered too improbable, too crazy, to worry about, until it does occur. Concerning software project failures more generally, the subtitle of [10] is '*We waste billions of dollars each year on entirely preventable mistakes*'. The publication lists many examples and argues, '*Even organizations that get burned by bad software experiences seem unable or unwilling to learn from their mistakes.*'

Another aspect of specificational thinking is the ability to choose an appropriate representation for the data and required operations. In bigger organizations, it is a duty of an SW architect to translate the specification into an architectural design, often illustrated as UML diagrams. To be capable of making efficient and unambiguous designs requires technical skills, awareness of the variety in possible data structures, and their implications for efficiency and required resources. For instance, Fig. 10 shows two fragments of Tampere region bus timetables:

Line 2 Rauhaniemi–Pyynikintori

05	10 36 48
06	00 12 24 36 48
07	00 14 26 38 50
08–14	02 14 26 38 50
15	02 07 14 26 38 50
16–18	02 14 26 38 50

Line 55 Vesilahti–Tampere

A	B	C	D	E	F
06:20	06:35	-	06:50	06:59	07:25
07:30	07:45	08:02	08:05	08:15	08:41
08:40	08:55	-	09:07	09:17	09:39
-	09:45	-	09:57	10:07	10:29
-	-	-	10:40	10:50	11:12

Fig. 10. Two fragments of bus timetables (Monday–Friday).

On the left, full hours are shown in the first column, and the rest of each line lists departure times in minutes after the full hour. On the right, each line represents a route via bus stops from A to F: departure times are shown stop-by-stop; '-' denotes no visit. Students could be asked to discuss the advantages and disadvantages of these two representations, and possible justifications for each.

In avoidance of the unintended consequences and bad design, it is crucial to admit the very existence of these specificational problems, them necessitating specificational thinking to be taken seriously. To exercise it at elementary level, an educative and sufficient learning objective would be to deal with real and open-ended specification problems. For instance, a teacher could ask a student to write instructions for another student to follow. The instructions may describe, say, a location of an object hidden in the schoolyard. Afterwards, the students should discuss how the instructions were to be improved to find the object even quicker. By the same token as those 'follow-my-instructions' games, programming can provide epistemologically productive learning experiences. Papert claims that, '*... in teaching the computer how to think, children embark on an exploration about how they themselves think. The experience can be heady: Thinking about thinking turns the child into an epistemologist*' [44]. Sooner or later, a novice will notice that a computer functions differently from what he intended because it obeyed his instructions precisely. The situation is akin to the example of buying boots, where reaching a common understanding between humans was tricky, yet a computer is even more stubborn in its obedience.

The modest goal of these exercises is that in a future our students will be more discerning and resourceful in specifying and implementing SW projects than decision makers of today.

5.6 The Learning Trajectories Bridged from Elementary to Higher Education Mathematics

To track the consistent proceeding in learning, we draft a hypothetical syllabus of CS-supportive mathematics by enhancing it with discrete mathematics. For learning proceedings, 'learning trajectory' is the selected theoretical framework rooted in Piaget's cognitive constructivism [45] and active learning theories [46]. It targets a definition of a consistent path for a learner to follow. The path should consist of well-justified building blocks. Figure 11 illustrates the learning trajectories as vertical dashed lines, dedicated to each topic proposed in the previous sections: algorithms and data structures that comprise sets, logic, statistics, and probability. The trajectories are crossing through four horizontal layers of Elementary mathematics, computational thinking, HS mathematics, and Tertiary mathematics. In Finland, only elementary education is compulsory, whereas continuing to high school or tertiary education is elective.

The learning trajectories of algorithms and data structures, and logic are marked with light green and blue to highlight their prominence. Currently, the elementary mathematics syllabus in FNC-2014 does not define any specific learning targets for the topics except that of 'algorithmic thinking' anticipated to start with problem solving and decomposition. In programming, the decomposition implies a program's division into subroutines. In algorithms, the introduction of the simplest sort and search algorithms would be a natural learning goal. Data structures are prompted by number sets of natural numbers ($\mathbb{N}$), integers ($\mathbb{Z}$),

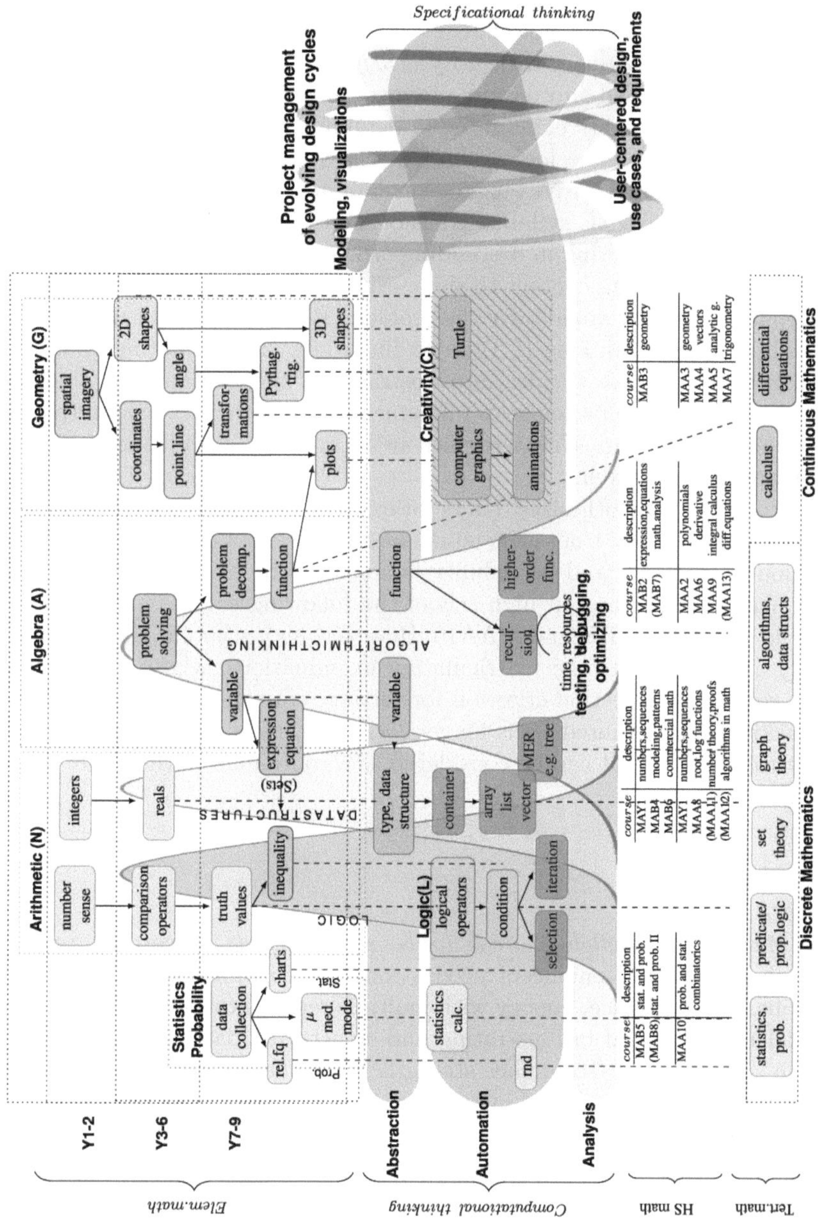

course	description
MAB5 (MAB8)	stat. and prob. stat. and prob. II
MAA10	prob. and stat. combinatorics

course	description
MAY1 MAB4 MAB6	numbers,sequences modeling,patterns commercial math
MAY1 MAA8 (MAA11) (MAA12)	numbers,sequences root,log functions number theory,proofs algorithms in math

course	description
MAB2 (MAB7)	expression,equations math.analysis
MAA2 MAA6 MAA9 (MAA13)	polynomials derivative integral calculus diff.equations

course	description
MAB3	geometry
MAA3 MAA4 MAA5 MAA7	geometry vectors analytic g. trigonometry

Fig. 11. Hypothetical learning trajectories bridged from the FNC-2014 elementary to higher-education mathematics. (Color figure online)

and reals (ℝ) that match with variable types (*unsigned*, *int*, *float*) in programming. In addition to simple primitives, types in CS can be more complex, such as primitive containers of arrays, lists, and vectors. Structuring data in various ways, modeling and visualizing it, assists in raising the abstraction level, thus ultimately in problem solving as well.

The second most prominent trajectory is logic. Like algorithmic thinking, in FNC-2014, logic is included only as a requirement of logical thinking. However, in programming, logic is highly exploitable in defining the conditions in selection and iteration structures. The logic subset in Fig. 7 proposes enhancements to mathematics, physics, and native language syllabi in Y7–9. To add further value to this age range, the UKNC syllabus areas of statistics and probability (Figs. 8 and 9) were worth considering in descending order of importance. However, due to time constraints, adding content to the mathematics syllabus is problematic. CS, as a separate subject, would solve the problem. Below elementary mathematics, the computational thinking (CT) layer illustrates the computing enhancement and how the process divides into abstraction, automation, and analysis phases. In this layer, the mathematics fundamentals have their CS counterparts. The schedule in mathematics Y7–9 implies an appropriate introduction order of the CS fundamentals as well.

In regard to the hypothesized trajectories, sets are unfortunately missing from the FNC-2014, both from elementary and high school education, whereas the situation of statistics and probability is much brighter. They start already at the elementary level, and in high school the following courses are allocated for the topic: MAB5, MAB8, and MAA10. However, high school is elective, and, regrettably, rigidly targets the matriculation examinations, whose importance has lately grown as a selection criterion for tertiary education. Tertiary mathematics elucidates the required skills for modern SWE by representing the most prominent topics only that can be considered as a continuum of the trajectories sketched in the figure.

6 Conclusions

- *RQ1: Mathematics syllabus areas to be strengthened?* According to the reviewed studies, SW engineers need stronger algorithms and data structure skills. In accordance, fluency with multiple representations and modeling is considered beneficial in illustrating and structuring data, thus improving problem solving skills. To further strengthen the theoretical basis primarily necessitates the inclusion/teaching of logic, and secondarily set theory, statistics, and probability. In increasing discrete mathematics, the UKNC mathematics and CS provide an exemplar to emulate in elementary education in Finland.

  However, discrete mathematics does not benefit only future SW engineers, but all students in becoming generally educated and acquainted with CS. Even though continuous and discrete mathematics are posed as opposite, in practice, they are deeply interconnected and complement each other. Natural sciences continue to exploit continuous mathematics as before, so continuous mathematics must keep a significant role in the curriculum. However, to meet the challenges of digitalization, we believe that it is beneficial to move emphasis from continuous to discrete mathematics.

- *RQ2: The overemphasized mathematics syllabus areas?* Curriculum planning is a zero-sum game. If the volume of discrete mathematics were increased, some areas ought to be decreased correspondingly. The proposal is to move some emphasis from continuous to discrete mathematics already at the elementary level. To get all the suggested content to fit in the mathematics syllabus is challenging, thus adding CS as a separate subject is a distinct option.
- *RQ3: Missing but crucial topics to support CS?* The feedback from the SW engineers emphasized soft and practical skills more than hard and theoretical ones. For example, problem solving, and communication and negotiation skills, as well as other project managerial skills are valued high. In real projects, a freshman SW engineer faces the challenge of capturing the real needs and expectations of a customer and being capable of verbalizing them as unambiguous textual specifications and a design for an implementation team. For instance, USCC defines HS Modeling for structuring data, and the area could be subset age-appropriately for the elementary level. These skills constitute a substantial part of what we refer to as 'specificational thinking'.

  However, mathematics is by far the only subject to practice specificational thinking. In essence, with such cross-curricula skills as good oral communication skills, appropriate observation and interview techniques, critical and analytical thinking that imply logical thinking, and conceptual modeling skills, students are more likely to excel in specificational thinking. Thus, achieving the goal should be a combined effort of the subjects of native language, mathematics, and why not social studies and philosophy, if available.

Further Studies. The emphasis shift from continuous to discrete mathematics must be executed in an evidence-based manner, i.e., the learning outcomes must be carefully evaluated in co-operation with pedagogical experts both in elementary and higher education. To advance this approach further, the results should speak for themselves. To achieve the full potential of discrete mathematics in higher education, traditional '*Advanced Engineering Calculus*' would need its discrete mathematics counterparts, say, '*Programmers' Introduction to Automata and Formal Languages*' or '*Set Theory for Software Engineers*', which indisputably explicate the benefits of the renewed mathematics syllabus for the good of CS.

Acknowledgments. Thanks to the Academy of Finland (grant number 303694; *Skills, education and the future of work*) for their financial support.

References

1. Redecker, C., Punie, Y.: European framework for the digital competence of educators: DigCompEdu. EUR - Scientific and Technical Research Reports. The European Commission's Science and Knowledge Service (2017)
2. Bocconi, S., et al.: Developing computational thinking: approaches and orientations in K-12 education. In: EdMedia: World Conference on Educational Media and Technology, pp. 13–18. Association for the Advancement of Computing in Education (AACE) (2016)
3. Peng, G.: Do computer skills affect worker employment? An empirical study from CPS surveys. Comput. Hum. Behav. **74**, 26–34 (2017)
4. Harris, M.: The STEM shortage paradox. Phys. World **27**, 56 (2014)
5. Smith, E., White, P.: A 'great way to get on'? The early career destinations of science, technology, engineering and mathematics graduates. Res. Pap. Educ. **32**, 231–253 (2017)
6. Beblavý, M., Fabo, B., Lenearts, K.: Demand for digital skills in the US labour market: the IT skills pyramid. CEPS Special Report No. 154/December 2016 (2016)
7. Finnish National Board of Education: Finnish National Curriculum 2014 (2014)
8. Niemelä, P., Valmari, A.: Elementary math to close the digital skills gap. In: CSEDU 2018 Conference, vol. 10 (2018)
9. Parnas, D.L.: Software aspects of strategic defense systems. Commun. ACM **28**, 1326–1335 (1985)
10. Charette, R.N.: Why software fails. IEEE Spectr. **42**(9), 42–49 (2005)
11. Parnas, D.L.: Software engineering programs are not computer science programs. IEEE Softw. **16**, 19–30 (1999)
12. ACM&IEEE: Computer Science Curricula 2013: Curriculum Guidelines for Undergraduate Degree Programs in Computer Science. Technical report, 20 December 2013 (2013)
13. Ardis, M., Budgen, D., Hislop, G., Offutt, J., Sebern, M., Visser, W.: Software engineering 2014: curriculum guidelines for undergraduate degree programs in software engineering. Joint Effort of the ACM and the IEEE-Computer Society (2014)
14. Meziane, F., Vadera, S.: A comparison of computer science and software engineering programmes in English universities. In: 17th Conference on Software Engineering Education and Training (CSEE&T 2004), Norfolk, VA, USA, 1–3 March 2004, pp. 65–70. IEEE Computer Society (2004)
15. Bourque, P., Fairley, R.E., et al.: Guide to the Software Engineering Body of Knowledge (SWEBOK (R)): Version 3.0. IEEE Computer Society Press, Washington, D.C. (2014)
16. Department of Education: National Curriculum in England. Key stages 3 and 4 framework document (2014)
17. GCSE: GCSE subject content for computer science (2015). https://www.gov.uk/government/uploads/system/uploads/attachment_data/file/397550/GCSE_subject_content_for_computer_science.pdf
18. Brown, N.C., Sentance, S., Crick, T., Humphreys, S.: Restart: the resurgence of computer science in UK schools. ACM Trans. Comput. Educ. (TOCE) **14**, 9 (2014)
19. Core Standards Organization: Mathematics Standards—Common Core State Standards Initiative (2015)
20. Yackel, E., Cobb, P.: Sociomathematical norms, argumentation, and autonomy in mathematics. J. Res. Math. Educ. 458–477 (1996)
21. Pinar, W.F.: What is Curriculum Theory?. Routledge, Abingdon (2012)

22. English Department for Education: National Curriculum in England: Computing programmes of study (2013)
23. Lethbridge, T.C.: What knowledge is important to a software professional? IEEE Comput. **33**, 44–50 (2000)
24. Puhakka, A., Ala-Mutka, K.: Survey on the knowledge and education needs of Finnish software professionals. Tampere University of Technology, Department of Software Systems (2009)
25. Surakka, S.: What subjects and skills are important for software developers? Commun. ACM **50**, 73–78 (2007)
26. Kitchenham, B., Budgen, D., Brereton, P., Woodall, P.: An investigation of software engineering curricula. J. Syst. Softw. **74**, 325–335 (2005)
27. TEK: TEK graduate survey 2017 (2017)
28. Aarresaari net: The ingredients of building a successful career in year of 2016 (2017)
29. Knuth, D.E.: Algorithmic thinking and mathematical thinking. Am. Math. Mon. **92**, 170–181 (1985)
30. Denning, P.J.: The profession of IT Beyond computational thinking. Commun. ACM **52**, 28–30 (2009)
31. Denning, P.J.: Remaining trouble spots with computational thinking. Commun. ACM **60**, 33–39 (2017)
32. CSTA: Computer science standards (2016)
33. Liukas, L.: Hello Ruby (2015). A childrens' book available in 22 languages
34. Taub, R., Armoni, M., Ben-Ari, M.: CS unplugged and middle-school students' views, attitudes, and intentions regarding CS. ACM Trans. Comput. Educ. (TOCE) **12**, 8 (2012)
35. Futschek, G., Moschitz, J.: Developing algorithmic thinking by inventing and playing algorithms. In: Proceedings of the 2010 Constructionist Approaches to Creative Learning, Thinking and Education: Lessons for the 21st Century (Constructionism 2010), pp. 1–10 (2010)
36. Lamagna, E.A.: Algorithmic thinking unplugged. J. Comput. Sci. Coll. **30**, 45–52 (2015)
37. McGowen, M., DeMarois, P., Tall, D.: Using the function machine as a cognitive root (2000)
38. Wilkie, K.J., Clarke, D.M.: Developing students' functional thinking in algebra through different visualisations of a growing pattern's structure. Math. Educ. Res. J. **28**, 223–243 (2016)
39. Valmari, A., Kaarakka, T.: MathCheck: a tool for checking math solutions in detail. In: SEFI 2016 Annual Conference Proceedings, pp. VK.1–VK.9. European Society for Engineering Education (2016)
40. Core Standards Organization: High School: Modeling (2017). http://www.corestandards.org/Math/Content/HSM/
41. Dijkstra, E.W., et al.: On the cruelty of really teaching computing science. Commun. ACM **32**, 1398–1404 (1989)
42. Finnish National Board of Education: Finnish National Core Curriculum for General Upper Secondary Education (2015)
43. Aamulehti: Pyörätuolissa istuvaa miestä nöyryytettiin Prisman kassalla – 'Olemme sydämestämme pahoillamme' (2017)
44. Papert, S.: Mindstorms: Children, Computers, and Powerful Ideas. Basic Books, Inc., New York (1980)
45. Piaget, J.: Piaget's theory of cognitive development. In: Childhood Cognitive Development: The Essential Readings, pp. 33–47 (2000)
46. Clements, D.H.: Linking research and curriculum development. In: International Research in Mathematics Education, p. 599 (2002)

An Evaluation of the Reliability, Validity and Sensitivity of Three Human Mental Workload Measures Under Different Instructional Conditions in Third-Level Education

Luca Longo[1,2(✉)] and Giuliano Orru[1]

[1] School of Computing, College of Sciences and Health, Dublin Institute of Technology, Dublin, Republic of Ireland
luca.longo@dit.ie

[2] ADAPT: The Global Centre of Excellence for Digital Content and Media Innovation, Dublin, Republic of Ireland

Abstract. Although Cognitive Load Theory (CLT) has been researched for many years, it has been criticised for its theoretical clarity and its methodological approach. A crucial issue is the measurement of three types of cognitive load conceived in the theory, and the assessment of overall human cognitive load during learning tasks. This research study is motivated by these issues and it aims to investigate the reliability, validity and sensitivity of three existing self-reporting mental workload instruments, mainly used in Ergonomics, when applied to Education and in particular to the field of Teaching and Learning. A primary research study has been designed and performed in a typical third-level classroom in Computer Science, and the self-reporting mental workload instruments employed are the NASA Task Load Index, the Workload Profile and the Rating Scale Mental Effort. Three instructional design conditions have been designed and employed for the above purposes. The first design condition followed the traditional explicit instruction paradigm whereby a lecturer delivers instructional material mainly using a one-way approach with almost no interactions with students. The second design condition was inspired by the Cognitive Theory of Multimedia Learning whereby the same content, delivered under the first condition, was converted in a multimedia video by following a set of its design principles. The third design condition was an extension of the second condition whereby an inquiry activity was executed after the delivery of the second condition. The empirical evidence gathered in this study suggests that the three selected mental workload measures are highly reliable. Their moderate face validity is in line with the results obtained so far within Ergonomics emphasising and confirming the difficulty in creating optimally valid measures of mental workload. However, the sensitivity of these measures, as achieved in this study, is low, indicating how the three instructional design conditions, as conceived and implemented, do not impose significantly different mental workload levels on learners.

B. M. McLaren et al. (Eds.): CSEDU 2018, CCIS 1022, pp. 384–413, 2019.
https://doi.org/10.1007/978-3-030-21151-6_19

Keywords: Cognitive Load Theory · Cognitive load types · Human Mental Workload · Instructional design · Direct instructions · Cognitive Theory of Multimedia Learning · Inquiry methods · Community of Inquiry · Reliability · Validity · Sensitivity

1 Introduction

Cognitive Load Theory (CLT) has been designed to guide instructional designers and practitioners keen to develop instructional resources aimed at promoting the activities of learners, increase their performance and optimise their learning [8,56]. Although CLT has been investigated for many years, developing a set of guidelines aimed at creating effective instructional designs, it has been subjects of multiple critiques due to its theoretical clarity [54] and its methodological approach [15]. In detail, a central problem is the measurement of the overall cognitive load of learners while performing learning activities [43]. Three types of cognitive load have been conceptualised and identified within CLT: intrinsic, extraneous and germane. These are the fundamental assumptions that compose the theory itself. The intrinsic load can be influenced by the familiarity of the learners on a given subject or the intrinsic difficulty and complexity of the learning material to be exploited. The extraneous load can altered by the procedure used to design, organise and deliver instructional material. The germane load is influenced by the effort exerted by learners for handling information, development and automation of schemas in their brains. However, taking into consideration the Popperian's view on critical rationalism [47], CLT cannot be treated a scientific theory due to the lack of clear procedures to measure its fundamental building blocks - the cognitive load types - and thus their empirically validation. As a consequence the theory is believed not to be falsifiable [15]. in other terms, the scientific value of the Cognitive Load Theory and all the other theories built upon the notion of cognitive load [15,16] still lack empirical validation. The main research challenge in this area concerns the development of reliable and valid measures of the cognitive load types and the development of overall measures of cognitive load that can be applied in the general field of Education and in the specific field of Teaching and Learning. Unfortunately, although significant advances in Educational Psychology, limited research has been done towards the development of cognitive load assessment techniques [1,2,6,10,45]. The situation is similar in the more specific field of Teaching and Learning [19,45,57].

A domain in which cognitive load has been extensively researched and applied is Ergonomics [64] (Human Factors). In this discipline, the construct of mental workload (MWL), almost overlapping with the construct of cognitive load, has a long history with a plethora of applications for example in the field of aviation [18,24,25] and automotive industry [5]. In these applications, several assessment procedures, both uni-dimensional and multi-dimensional, have been proposed [7,64]. As a consequence, several MWL measures exist in the literature. Similarly, various criteria for validating these measures have been recommended highlighting the continuous interest on MWL research [52]. Taking a broad view, the main logic behind measuring mental workload, in Ergonomics, is to quantify the amount of mental activity devoted to performing a task for predicting human performance and in turn system performance [7]. In Education, the goal is analogous: the logic behind measuring mental workload is to quantify the mental cost of performing a learning task with the objective of predicting the performance of a learner and in turn estimate learning.

This research study is an attempt to bridge the gap present in educational psychology concerned with the measurement of cognitive load by adopting existing measures of mental workload borrowed from Ergonomics. The aim of this study, initiated in [29,42] and extended here, is to evaluate the reliability, validity and sensitivity of three mental workload measures from ergonomics, namely the multidimensional Nasa Task Load Index [18] and Workload Profile [59] as well as the unidimensional Rating Scale Mental Effort [66]. A primary research study has been designed including the comparison of three different instructional design conditions in a third-level master module. The first condition includes the delivery of instructional material using a traditional one-way direct instruction approach (lecturer to students). The second design condition includes the conversion of the instructional material of the first condition into multimedia videos developed by following a set of design principles developed within the Cognitive Theory of Multimedia Learning [36]. The third design condition extends the second design condition by adding a collaborative group activity inspired by the concept of Community of Inquiry [4,13] aimed at extending understanding. Figure 1 summarises this research by presenting its key components, the limitations as emerged in literature, the design of a primary research experiment as well as its evaluation.

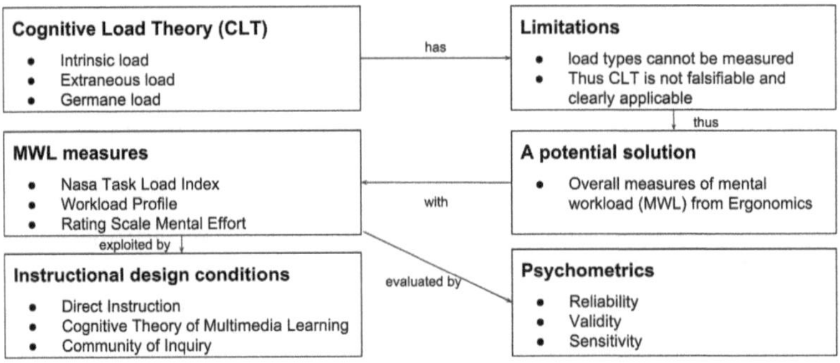

Fig. 1. Summary of the primary research, its motivation and its main components.

The rest of the paper is shaped as below. Section 2 introduces Cognitive Load Theory and its cognitive load types. It follows a description of the general issues surrounding other cognitive load-based theories and a brief presentation of state-of-the-art mental workload assessment techniques in Ergonomics, with their advantages and limitations. Afterwards, the paper puts the focus on three self-reporting mental workload procedures because of their adoption in this research. Cognitive Theory of Multimedia Learning, its design principles as well as the Community of Inquiry paradigm, a social constructivist approach for teaching, are described to provide the reader with those relevant notions for understanding the planned experiment. Section 3 focuses on the construction of a primary research experiment with human learners, detailing the methodology and formalising the research hypotheses. Sections 4 and 5 respectively present experimental results and critically discuss them emphasising the contribution to the body of knowledge. Section 6 concludes the paper and introduces future work.

2 Theoretical Background

2.1 Cognitive Load Theory

Cognitive Load Theory (CLT) [56] has been conceived as a form of guidance for instructional designers eager to create resources that are presented in a way that encourages the activities of the learners and optimise their performance, thus their learning [8]. CLT is an approach that considers the limitations of the information processing system of the human mind [61]. The intuitive assumption behind this theory is that if a learner is either underloaded or overloaded, learning is likely to be adversely affected. In detail, the assumption of Cognitive Load Theory is that the capabilities of the human cognitive architecture devoted to the processing and retention of information are limited [39] and these limitations have a straight influence on learning. Unfortunately, the experience of mental workload is highly likely to be different on an individual basis, changing according to the learner's cognitive style, the own education and training [44]. As a consequence, modelling and assessing cognitive load is far from being a trivial activity. In his seminal contribution, [56] have proposed three types of cognitive load:

- intrinsic load - this is influenced by the unfamiliarity of the learners or the intrinsic complexity of the learning material under use [2,55];
- extraneous load - this is impacted by the way the instructional material is designed, organised and presented [9];
- germane load - this is influenced by the effort devoted for processing information, for the construction and automation of schemas in the brain of the learners [44].

Intrinsic cognitive load is considered being static, extraneous load should be minimised [40] and germane load promoted [11]. Cognitive Load Theory, although highly relevant for instructional design and with a plethora of theoretical material that has been published in the last few decades, has a fundamental, open and challenging problem: the measurement of its three cognitive load types [10,43,54]. Unfortunately, there is little evidence that these three types are highly separable [9,12,58]. Similarly, to date, there is little evidence about the ways the three different types of load can be coherently and robustly measured [14,43]. According to the traditional critical rationalism proposed by Karl [47], CLT cannot be considered a scientific theory because some of its fundamental assumptions cannot be tested empirically and are thus not falsifiable [15]. To be scientific, the measurement methods about a hypothesis must be sensitive to the different types of load. CLT must provide empirical demonstrations about the cognitive load types (its fundamental assumptions). As a consequence, the main research challenge is the development of a valid measure of cognitive load and the demonstration of the scientific value of Cognitive Load Theory and all the other theories built upon it [15,16]. CLT has mainly been developed by educational psychologists and evolved over almost three decades of research endeavour in the field of education. Despite the theoretical evolution of this theory, and the many ah-hoc, domain and context-specific applications based upon it, the practical measurement of cognitive load has not been sufficiently investigated in education. In contrast to this, the situation is different in the field of Ergonomics, where more effort has been devoted towards the development of cognitive load assessment techniques. In this discipline, cognitive load is mainly referred to as human Mental Workload (MWL), a well known psychological construct [7,61,64].

2.2 Human Mental Workload

The concept of human Mental Workload (MWL) has a long history in the fields of ergonomics and psychology, with several applications in the aviation and automotive industries. Although it has been studied for the last four decades, no clear definition of MWL has emerged that has a general validity and that is universally accepted [7,27,49]. The main reason for assessing MWL is to measure the mental cost of performing a certain task with the goal of predicting operator and system performance [7]. MWL is an important design criterion: at an early system design phase not only can a system or interface be optimised to take workload into consideration, but MWL can also guide designers in making appropriate structural changes [33,63]. Modern technologies such as web applications have become increasingly complex [23,28,32], with increments in the degree of MWL imposed on operators [17,22]. The assumption in design approaches is that as the difficulty of a task increases, perhaps due to interface complexity, MWL also increases and performance usually decreases [7]. In turn, errors are more frequent, there are longer response times, and fewer tasks are completed per time unit. When task difficulty is negligible, systems can impose a low MWL on operators: this should be avoided as it leads to difficulties in maintaining attention and increasing reaction time [7]. In the following sections it is shown how MWL can be measured and the formalisms to aggregate heterogeneous factors towards an overall index of mental workload. This review of current solutions is aimed at identifying both reasons why a more generally applicable measure of MWL has not yet been developed, and the key characteristics of MWL representation and assessment.

Measures of Mental Workload. The measurement of mental workload is a vast and heterogeneous topic as the related theoretical counterpart. Several assessment techniques have been proposed in the last 40 years, and researchers in applied settings have tended to prefer the use of ad hoc measures or pools of measures rather than any one measure. This tendency is reasonable, given the multi-dimensional property that characterises mental workload [26,31,41]. Many approaches to operationalise mental workload as a computational concept have been proposed as in [25,30,41,49,50]. Similarly, Various reviews attempted to organise the vast amount of knowledge behind MWL measures and assessment techniques [7,27,62,65]. In general, the measurement techniques of MWL can be classified into three broad categories:

- *self-assessment measures* including self-report measures and subjective rating scales;
- *task performance measures* which consider primary and secondary task measures;
- *physiological measures* which are derived from the physiology of the operator.

The class of *self-report measures* is often referred to as subjective measures. This category relies on the subjective perceived experience of the interaction operator-system. Subjective measures have always appealed many workload practitioners and researchers because it is strongly believed that only the person concerned with the task can provide an accurate and precise judgement with respect to the mental workload experienced. Various dimensions and attributes of mental workload are considered in self-report measures. These include demands, performance, effort as well as individual differences such as the emotional state, attitude and motivation of the operator [5,30]. The class of subjective measures include multi-dimensional approaches such as the NASA Task Load Index [18], the Subjective Workload Assessment Technique [48], the Workload Profile [59] as well as uni-dimensional approaches such as the Rating Scale Mental Effort [66], the Subjective Workload Dominance Technique [60] and the Bedford scale [51]. These measures and scales are mostly close-ended and, in case multidimensional, they have an aggregation strategy that combines the dimensions they are built upon to an overall index of mental workload. The class of *task performance measures* assumes that mental workload practitioners and, more generally system designers, are typically concerned with the performance of their systems and technologies. The assumption is that the mental workload of an operator, when interacting with a system, acquires importance only if it influences system performance. As a consequence, it is believed that this class of techniques is the most valuable options for designers. According to different reviews [7,62], performance measures can be classified into two sub-categories: primary task and secondary task measures. In primary-task methods the performance of the operator is monitored and analysed according to changes in primary-task demands. Examples of common measurement parameters are response and reaction time, accuracy and error rate, speed and signal detection performance, estimation time and tapping regularity. In secondary-task assessment procedures, there are two tasks involved and the performance of the secondary task may not have practical importance, but rather may serves to load or to measure the mental workload of the operator performing the primary task. The class of *physiological measures* includes bodily responses derived from the operator's physiology, and it relies on the assumption that they correlate with mental workload. They are aimed at interpreting psychological processes by analysing their effect on the state of the body, rather than measuring task performance or perceptual subjective ratings. Example includes heart rate, pupil dilation and blinking, blood pressure, brain activation signals as measured by electroencephalograms (EEG) and muscle signals as measured by electromyograms (EMG). The principal reason for adopting physiological measures is because they do not require an overt response by the operator and they can be collected continuously, within an interval of time, representing an objective way of measuring the operator state.

Subjective measures are in general easy to administer and analyse. They provide an index of overall workload and multi-dimensional measures can determine the source of mental workload. However, the main drawback is that they can only be administered post-task, thus influencing the reliability for long tasks. In addition, meta-cognitive limitations can diminish the accuracy of reporting and it is difficult to perform comparisons among raters on an absolute scale. However, they appear to be the most appropriate types of measurement for assessing mental workload because they have demonstrated high levels of sensitivity and diagnosticity [52]. *Task performance measures* can be primary or secondary. Primary-task measures represent a direct index of performance and they are accurate in measuring long periods of mental workload. They are capable of discriminating individual differences in resource competition. However, the main limitation is that they cannot distinguish performance of multiple tasks that are executed simultaneously by an operator. If taken in isolation, they do not represent reliable measures, though if used in conjunction with other measures, such as subjective ratings, they can be useful. Secondary task measures have the capacity of discriminating between tasks when no differences are detected in primary performance. They are useful for quantifying the individual's spare attentional capacity as well as short periods of workload. However, they are only sensitive to large changes in mental workload and they might be highly intrusive, influencing the behaviours of users while interacting with the primary task. *Physiological measures* are extremely good at monitoring data on a continuous interval, thus having high measurement sensitivity. They do not interfere with the performance on the primary task. However, the main drawback is that they can be easily confounded by external interference. Moreover, they require equipment and tools that are often physically obtrusive and the analysis of data is complex, requiring well trained experts. In the experimental study carried out in this research, subjective mental workload measures have been adopted because they are easy to be administered in a typical third-level classroom. Primary and secondary task measures would have been intrusive and would have influenced the natural behaviour of learners in the classroom. Physiological measures would have been physically obtrusive, requiring expensive equipment to be attached to the body of each learner. The next sections describe the three MWL assessment techniques adopted in the current study, describing their formalism to produce a quantifiable score of mental workload.

2.3 Subjective Workload Measures

The NASA Task Load Index (NASATLX) instrument is a subjective self-assessment measure of mental workload [18]. It has been extensively applied within Ergonomics in many socio-technical domains, and validated mainly in the transportation industry [18,52]. The measure is built upon six dimensions that are thought to affect mental workload, as described in a number of papers [24,29,34]. Each dimension is assessed with a self-reported judgement by a human, and a weight for each dimension is computed through a paired comparison across dimensions. A subject, after executing a task, is required to express, for each possible pair of the 6 dimensions, (binomial coefficient, $\binom{6}{2} = 15$), a preference indicating which of the two had a greater contribution to mental workload while executing the underlying task. A weight w for a given dimension is the number of times it was picked as preference in the pairwise procedure. Given the 6 dimensions of the Nasa Task Load Index, each weight is therefore in the range 0 (not relevant) to 5 (more important than any other dimension). The final mental workload score is inferred as a weighed average, taking into account each subjective rating for a dimension d_i and the correspondent weights w_i (Eq. 1). For comparison purposes in this research, the overall measure is scaled within $[1..100] \in \Re$. The questionnaire can be found in Table 13 (Appendix).

$$NASATLX : [0..100] \in \Re = \left(\sum_{i=1}^{6} d_i \times w_i \right) \frac{1}{15} \quad (1)$$

The Workload Profile (WP) is a mental workload assessment procedure [59] developed upon the Multiple Resource Theory [61]. According to this theory, humans are seen as having different capacities or 'attentional resources' related to:

- *stage of information processing* – perceptual/central processing and response selection/execution;
- *code of information processing* – spatial/verbal;
- *input* – visual and auditory processing;
- *output* – manual and speech output.

As described in other articles [24,29,34], each dimension is assessed through subjective rates and an individual, after task completion, is required to rate the proportion of attentional resources elicited while performing the task itself. This self-reporting is done expressing a quantity within the range $0..1 \in \Re$. A rating of 0 indicates that the task performed placed no demand while 1 that it required maximum attention. The overall measure of mental workload is a sum of the 8 rates d (Eq. 2). For comparison purposes in this research, the overall measure is scaled within $[1..100] \in \Re$. The questionnaire associated to the Workload Profile measure can be found in Table 14 (Appendix).

$$WP : [0..100] \in \Re \qquad WP = \frac{1}{8}\sum_{i=1}^{8} d_i \times 100 \tag{2}$$

The Rating Scale Mental Effort (RSME) is a unidimensional mental workload assessment procedure that is built upon the notion of effort exerted by a human over a task. As described in other contributions in the literature [24,29,34], a subjective rating is required by an individual through an indication on a continuous line, within the interval 0 to 150 with ticks each 10 units [66]. Example of labels such as 'absolutely no effort', 'considerable effort' and 'extreme effort' are used along the line (Appendix, Table 12). The overall mental workload of an individual coincides to the experienced exerted effort indicated on the line (Eq. 3). On one hand, although simplicity, the RSME has demonstrated a good degree of sensitivity across different empirical studies. However, on the other hand, it has shown a poor diagnostic power [66].

$$RSME : [0..150] \in \Re \tag{3}$$

2.4 Cognitive Theory of Multimedia Learning

Another cognitivist theory of learning is the Cognitive Theory of Multimedia Learning (CTML) [35,36]. It is strongly connected to other learning theories, including Sweller's Cognitive Load Theory. CTML is based upon three assumptions (Fig. 2):

- dual-channel assumption - this assumption has been inspired by the dual-coding approach of [46] whereby two separate channels are available for processing information in the human brain, namely the auditory and the visual channel;
- limited processing capacity assumption - in line with the Baddeley's model of working memory [3] and following the assumption of Cognitive Load Theory [56], each channel has a finite, limited capacity;
- active processing assumption - learning is an active process for the selection, filtering, organisation of new information and its integration with prior knowledge.

Humans are capable of processing a finite amount of information in each channel at a given time. In details, according to CTML, the human brain does not interpret multimedia instructions composed by words, auditory and pictorial information in a mutually exclusive way. Instead, these types of information are firstly selected and then dynamically organised to produce schemas, which are mental logical representations. Schemas are cognitive constructs in which information is organised for storage in long-term memory. Similarly, they can organise simpler elements in a way that these can subsequently act as elements

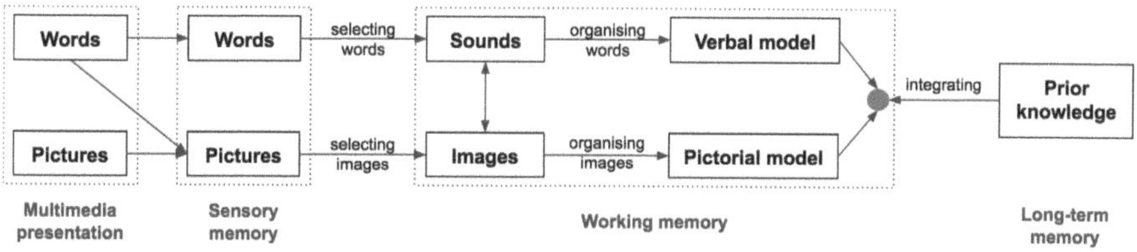

Fig. 2. The model behind Cognitive Theory of Multimedia Learning.

in higher-order schemas. Learning coincides with the development of complex schema as well as the transferring of those learned procedures from controlled processing to automated processing. This shift empties working memory that can then be used for other cognitive processes. [37] suggested five ways for representing words and pictures while information is processed in memory. These are particular stages of processing information. The first stage is represented by words and pictures in the multimedia presentation layer. The second stage includes the acoustic (sounds) and iconic representation (images) in sensory memory. The third stage coincides the sounds and images within working memory. The fourth stage, always within working memory, concerns with the verbal and pictorial models. The fifth stage relates prior knowledge, (the schemas), stored in long-term memory.

Mayer proposed a set of design principles for creating instructions aligned to the above assumptions and stages. Readers can obtain more information on the principles in [38]. Generally speaking, these design principles suggest to provide learners with coherent instructional material in the form of verbal and pictorial information. Coherent information aims to guide learners in the selection of the relevant words and pictures and reduce the cognitive load in each elicited channel. CTML is strictly connected to the Cognitive Load Theory because its twelve principles can be grouped according to the three types of loads - reducing extraneous load: coherence, signaling, redundancy, spatial contiguity, temporal contiguity; managing intrinsic load - segmenting, pre-training, modality; fostering; germane load - multimedia, personalisation, voice, image. These principles have emerged from more than 100 studies conducted in the field [38]. In addition to these, advanced principles have been proposed by Mayer in a number of papers, and recently updated [35]. This demonstrates how CTML is a dynamic theory, suggesting how its principles should not be taken rigidly, but as a starting point for discussion and experimentation. Cognitive Theory of Multimedia Learning has been described for providing the readers with those key elements necessary for the comprehension of the primary research experiment presented in this paper.

2.5 The Community of Inquiry

A Community of Inquiry (COI) can be defined as a group formed by people interacting within a social context with the goal of investigating the limits of a problematic concept by means of a dialog [13]. 'Dialog' is not a discussion nor a conversation. On one hand, a discussion is a persuasive debate where participants explain their own ideas in at attempt to persuade the other participants. It is a competitive dialectical exchange of ideas that usually ends up with the definition of the correct one, emphasising a winner. On the other hand, a conversation is a spontaneous exchange of ideas and sharing of information. There is no a well-defined way of conversing, leaving learners to develop and build the conversation entirely on their own. The expected outcome is that learners can transfer learned concepts to a new context, and thus expanding their vocabulary and abilities. Instead, a dialog focuses on the thinking of the group as a whole, with the objective of processing certain information aimed both at expanding individual and group knowledge as well as to increase understanding [4].

A pedagogical framework built upon the above definition of dialog is the 'Philosophy for Children' proposed by Lipman [20] and exploited in the project NORIA [53]. This framework proposes a set of questions aimed at exercising the cognitive abilities of a learner and at developing a higher level of thinking. Lipman, in his work [21], presents a model of reasoning considered to be a genuine and fundamental aspect of any instructional process: the complex thinking. This model is an educational process composed by three ways of thinking: critical, creative and caring thinking. The critical thinking is based upon the formulation of judgements and it is commanded by the criteria of logic, it is self-corrective and sensitive to a context. The dialogue elicits the capacity to think about the thinking (metacognition). In order be understood by others participants within a dialogue, a learner has to clearly explain owns ideas. This communicative requirement leads to a self-correction activity sensitive to the underlying context. The creative thinking is similar to critical thinking in the way of formulating judgements. However, these judgements are strictly related to the underlying context. This type of thinking is self-transcendent and sensitive to the criteria of logic but not governed by them. The caring thinking aims to develop practices regarding the substantial and procedural reflection connected to the resolution of some problem. It is sensitive to the context and it requires metacognitive processes of thinking in order to formulate practical judgments. Within the Community of Inquiry, the development of complex thinking occurs in a process of discovery learning. This process embraces the three type of thinking and it focused on generating and answering philosophical and cognitive questions on logic (critical thinking), aesthetic (creative thinking) and ethic (caring thinking). The Community of Inquiry paradigm has been described for providing the readers with those key notions necessary for the comprehension of the primary research experiment presented in this paper.

3 Design and Methodology

A primary research has been designed to investigate the reliability, validity and sensitivity of the three selected subjective mental workload measures (NASA, WP, RSME). An experiment has been conducted in the School of Computing at the Dublin Institute of Technology, Ireland, in the context of an MSc module: 'Research design and proposal writing'. This module is taught both to full-time and part-time students. The main difference between full-timers and part-timers is the way classes are planned. Full-timers attend 12 classes within an academic semester, of 2 h each, on a day of the week. Part-timers attend 4 classes of 6 h, within an academic semester and each class is scheduled on a Saturday and are usually separated by a period of 3 to 4 weeks of inactivity. Full-timers have usually no break during their classes, while part-timers, given the long day in the classroom, have two to three breaks (coffees and lunch). In this research study, conducted over a period of three years (from 2015 to 2017), four topics were delivered to different groups of students, both full-timers and part-timers, in the first part of each academic semester: 'Science', 'The Scientific Method' 'Planning Research' and 'Literature Review'. The remaining topics, taught in the second part of semester, were focused more on practical activities whereby students had to put in practice the theoretical notions provided in the first part of the semester. Three instructional conditions were designed. The first condition included the delivery of instructional material using a traditional one-way direct instructional approach (lecturer to students). The second design condition included the conversion of the instructional material of the first condition into multimedia videos developed by following a set of design principles proposed within the Cognitive Theory of Multimedia Learning [36] (as described in Sect. 2.4). The third design condition extends the second design condition by adding to it a collaborative group activity inspired by the notion of Community of Inquiry [4,13] aimed at extending the understanding of learners (as described in Sect. 2.5). Here the cohort of students is divided into groups composed by 3 or 4 persons performing a collaborative activity. In detail, the differences between the first and the second condition are described in Table 15, grouped by the underpinning principles of the CTML. The details of the activity carried out in the third condition are explicated in Table 16. Figures 3 and 4 respectively summarise the instructional conditions and the entire research design.

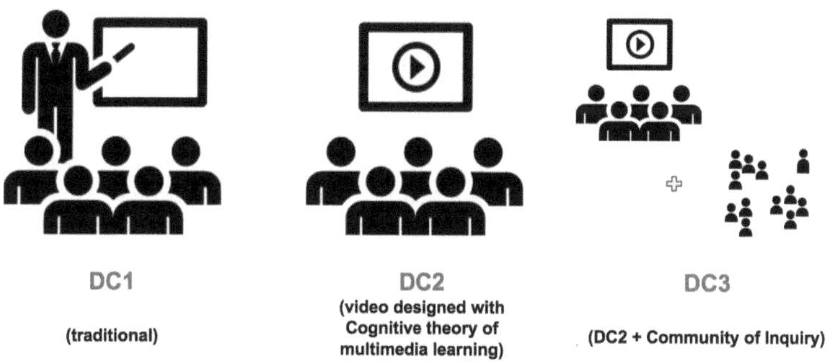

Fig. 3. Differences between the three instructional design conditions.

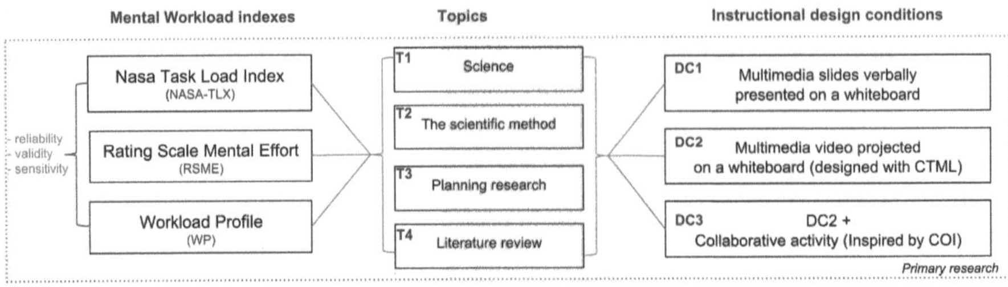

Fig. 4. Layout of the design of the experiment: three mental workload measures evaluated over three design conditions and three taught topics.

Informally, the research hypotheses are that the NASA Task Load Index, the Workload Profile and the Rating scale mental effort are reliable and valid measures of mental workload when applied in an educational context. If this will be the case, then the extent to which these measures can discriminate the selected topics, the three instructional conditions as well as the classes delivered will be investigated by computing a measure of their sensitivity. Table 1 lists the criteria for evaluating the selected mental workload measures, their definition, the associated statistical test and the expected outcome. Note that both forms of validity are expected to be moderate. A high degree of face validity would imply that participants could subjectively and precisely assess the construct of mental workload as good as the selected MWL measures. Therefore these measures would not have reason to exist as participants can precisely assess mental workload autonomously. Similarly, a high degree of convergent validity would imply that two different measures assess the construct of mental workload exactly in the same way, but given the known difficulties in measuring mental workload itself, the chances that this occurs are low. Thus, a positive moderate correlation is expected for both types of validity, underlying reasonable relationships between selected MWL measures.

Table 1. Criteria for the evaluation of different mental workload assessment techniques, their definition, associated statistical tests and the expectations for this primary research.

Criteria	Definition	Statistical test	Expectation
Reliability	The consistency/stability of a MWL measure	Cronbach's Alpha	High
Validity (face)	The extent to which a MWL measure is subjectively viewed as covering MWL itself	Pearson/Spearman correlation	Positive & moderate
Validity (convergent)	The degree to which two measures of MWL, theoretically related, are in fact related	Pearson/Spearman correlation	Positive & moderate
Sensitivity	The extent to which a MWL measure is able to detect changes in instructional design conditions, topics and classes	ANOVA + t-test/ U-test	Moderate

3.1 Participants and Procedure

Different cohorts of part-time and full-time students participated in the experimental research and attended the MSc module ‘Research design and proposal writing’ across different academic semesters between 2015 and 2017. These cohorts of students attended the four topics (T1–T4) listed in Fig. 4. Some cohort received the first instructional condition (DC1), some other the second (DC2) and some other received the third instructional condition (DC3). At the end of each topic (class), students were asked to fill questionnaires in, aimed at quantifying the mental workload experienced during the class. In details, the three selected self-reporting mental workload assessment techniques, as described in Sect. 2.3, were used in the experimental study: the NASA Task Load Index, the Workload Profile and the Rating Scale Mental Effort. The NASA-TLX and the WP are multi-dimensional and thus require participants to answer a number of questions (Tables 13 and 14 in Appendix). To facilitate the completion of each questionnaire and not to overwhelm students with many questions, two groups were formed within the same class, one receiving the NASA-TLX and one the WP. Eventually, both the groups received the RSME questionnaire (Table 12 in Appendix). The rationale was that, being RSME uni-dimensional, adding one further question to the previous questionnaires was deemed reasonable. In summary, the groups of each class are as below:

- (IRa) MWL instruments received by group A: the NASA-TLX + the RSME
- (IRb) MWL instruments received by group B: the WP + the RSME.

Table 2 summarises the number of students across the design condition received, the number of classes for each design condition, across the topics and overall totals.

Table 2. Number of classes, number of students grouped by mental workload instruments received (IRa: NASA-TLX + RSME; IRb: WP + RSME) across design conditions (DC1-3) and topics (T1-4) as well as their totals.

Design condition	T1			T2			T3			T4			Totals
	Classes	Students		Classes	Students		Classes	#students		Classes	Students		
		IRa	IRb		IRa	IRb		IRa	IRb		IRa	IRb	
DC1	2	13	17	2	20	23	1	11	9	2	20	20	133
DC2	2	23	24	2	16	18	2	22	22	1	13	11	149
DC3	1	9	7	1	10	8	2	15	12	1	9	7	77
Totals													
Classes	5			5			5			4			19
NASA		45			46			48			42		181
WP			48			49			43			38	178
RSME		45	48		46	49		48	43		42	38	359

The formation of the two groups for each class was random. Groups were planned to be as balanced as possible. However, some of the student who took part in the experimental study did not fully complete the administered questionnaires or they left the class before its administration, therefore associated data was discarded. Students were instructed about the study and were required to sign a consent form. This documentation was approved by the ethics committee of the Dublin Institute of Technology. Students had the right to withdrawn at any time during the experiment and collection of data.

4 Results

Table 3 presents the descriptive statistics showing the average (avg), the standard deviation (std) and the Shapiro-Wilk test (W) of normality of the distributions, of the mental workload scores obtained across the different topics and the mental workload assessment techniques (NASA, WP, RSME), grouped by design condition (DC1–DC3) and topic (T1–T4) along their p-value (p-val). As it is possible to assess from Table 3, the p-values (p-val) of the Shapiro-Wilk test (W) obtained for the NASA-TLX and the WP measures are greater than the chosen alpha level ($\alpha = 0.05$), thus, the null hypothesis that the data came from a normally distributed population cannot be rejected (is accepted). However, for the RSME measure, in most of the cases (highlighted), the p-values are lower than the alpha value, thus scores do not follow a normal distribution.

Table 3. Average, standard deviation and Shapiro-Wilk test (W) with p-value (p) at 95% confidence level of the mental workload scores by measure, topic and design condition.

Topic	Design	Mental Workload measures								
		NASA			WP			RSME		
		avg	std	W(p)	avg	std	W(p)	avg	std	W(p)
T1	DC1	43.6	08.6	0.96(0.69)	58.6	18.8	0.98(0.99)	42.2	20.5	0.89(0.00)
T2	DC1	51.9	11.9	0.95(0.40)	51.9	15.1	0.95(0.27)	57.0	23.0	0.97(0.25)
T3	DC1	50.2	12.8	0.91(0.25)	50.2	15.9	0.91(0.29)	54.9	20.8	0.90(0.04)
T4	DC1	48.3	11.5	0.95(0.32)	56.6	10.9	0.96(0.61)	53.3	20.8	0.97(0.25)
T1	DC2	41.8	17.2	0.98(0.90)	49.2	15.2	0.95(0.34)	45.4	18.6	0.95(0.03)
T2	DC2	50.2	10.8	0.97(0.86)	57.2	09.7	0.95(0.36)	62.0	17.3	0.94(0.06)
T3	DC2	43.5	12.2	0.96(0.43)	51.9	14.1	0.94(0.20)	46.5	18.2	0.94(0.02)
T4	DC2	52.2	16.4	0.96(0.74)	45.5	19.2	0.90(0.17)	59.0	19.0	0.91(0.04)
T1	DC3	38.5	11.3	0.94(0.54)	60.0	14.8	0.85(0.12)	38.0	22.6	0.94(0.31)
T2	DC3	48.2	12.5	0.97(0.88)	50.8	10.3	0.89(0.25)	65.1	24.2	0.85(0.01)
T3	DC3	45.4	14.6	0.98(0.93)	58.6	13.1	0.96(0.77)	51.8	20.2	0.92(0.04)
T4	DC3	48.3	07.6	0.98(0.96)	60.3	11.7	0.96(0.78)	60.3	24.5	0.85(0.01)

4.1 Reliability

To assess the reliability of the selected mental workload measures, the Cronbach's Alpha has been employed. It measures the internal consistency of the items of a multi-dimensional instrument, that means, how closely related these items are as a group. For this reason, the Rating Scale Mental Effort is not subject to reliability analysis as it is uni-dimensional. Table 4 shows the Cronbach's Alpha coefficients of the other two selected multidimensional mental workload measures (NASA-TLX and the WP), across all the topics (T1–T4) and the instructional design conditions (DC1-DC3). In most sciences, a reliability coefficient of .70 or higher is considered acceptable to infer that a scale is a consistent measure of a construct. Therefore, both the NASA-TLX and the WP can be considered reliable respectively with a coefficient of 0.73 and 0.847. To confirm this high reliability, Cronbach's Alpha has been computed also across each topic and instructional condition (Table 5). The alpha scores are mostly above 0.6 for the NASA-TLX and 0.8 for the WP strongly suggesting how these measures have an inherent good reliability.

Table 4. Overall reliability of the multidimensional mental workload measures with sample size, related number of items in the scales and associated Cronbach's Alpha.

Instrument	Sample size	# of items	Cronbach's α
NASA	181	6	0.730
WP	178	8	0.847

Table 5. Reliability of the multidimensional MWL measures computed with the Cronbach's α, grouped by topic (T1-4) and design condition (DC1-3).

Topic	Design condition	Mental workload measures			
		NASA-TLX		WP	
		Size	α	Size	α
T1	DC1	13	0.63	17	0.91
T2	DC1	20	0.69	23	0.87
T3	DC1	11	0.59	9	0.93
T4	DC1	20	0.65	20	0.81
T1	DC2	23	0.84	24	0.83
T2	DC2	16	0.56	18	0.67
T3	DC2	22	0.66	22	0.81
T4	DC2	13	0.81	11	0.92
T1	DC3	9	0.72	7	0.88
T2	DC3	10	0.79	8	0.64
T3	DC3	15	0.80	12	0.83
T4	DC3	9	0.24	7	0.80

4.2 Validity

To assess the validity of the three MWL measures, two sub-forms have been selected, namely face and convergent validity. The former validates the extent to which a MWL measures is subjectively viewed as covering the construct of MWL itself while the latter validates the degree to which two measures of MWL, expected to be theoretically related, are in fact related. To assess face validity, a question on overall MWL has been designed and asked to students straight after the completion of each class and before starting to fill the MWL questionnaires in (Table 17). The answers to this new question have been correlated to the scores of the selected MWL measures (NASA-TLX, WP, RSME), as listed in Table 6.

Table 6. Face validity of the mental workload assessment instruments, namely the Nasa Task Load Index, The Workload Profile and the Rating Scale Mental Effort, the sample size, the Pearson and Spearman correlation coefficients.

Instrument	Sample size	Pearson r	Spearman ρ
NASA	181	0.49	0.47
WP	178	0.39	0.40
RSME	359	0.42	0.41

To assess convergent validity, the MWL scores produced by the multidimensional NASA-TLX and the WP measures have been correlated against the MWL scores of the unidimensional RSME measure. This test was possible because a participant filled in either the questionnaire associated to the NASA-TLX or WP, and at the same time the RSME. Correlation between the NASA-TLX and WP cannot be computed because no participant received the questionnaires associated to these measures at the same time. Both the Pearson (parametric) and the Spearman's Rank (non-parametric) correlation coefficients have been employed for computing validity. Both parametric and non-parametric tests have been employed because not all the distributions of Table 3 were normal. Tables 6 and 7 respectively shows the correlations for face validity and convergent validity.

Table 7. Convergent validity of the mental workload assessment instruments, sample size, Pearson and Spearman correlation coefficients.

Instrument	Size	Pearson r	Spearman ρ
NASA-TLX vs RSME	181	0.49	0.47
WP vs RSME	178	0.29	0.31

4.3 Sensitivity

The sensitivity of the selected MWL measures has been computed by checking whether the distributions of their scores are statistically significant different across the topics (T1–T4), the instructional design conditions (DC1–DC3) and the classes (C1-19). Figure 5 depicts the boxplots of these distributions for visual inspection.

Formally, a Kruskal-Walllis analysis with a 95% confidence interval has been conducted. This is equivalent to a one-way analysis of variance on ranks and it is a non-parametric method for testing whether samples originate from the same distribution. This has been chosen because not all the distributions of Table 3 are normal. As it is possible to see from Table 8, some statistical significant difference was spotted across topic and classes, but not for instructional design conditions.

Table 8. Comparison of distributions of the workload scores using the Kruskal-Wallis test with 95% confidence interval (Chi-squared, degrees of freedom and p-values).

Group by	NASA			WP			RSME		
	X^2	DF	p-val	X^2	DF	p-val	X^2	DF	p-val
topic (T1-T4)	10.91	3	0.012	0.22	3	0.973	35.66	3	<0.0001
design condition (DC1-3)	2.44	2	0.293	3.43	2	0.179	0.146	2	0.9290
class (C1-19)	20.25	18	0.318	33.30	18	0.015	45.42	18	0.0003

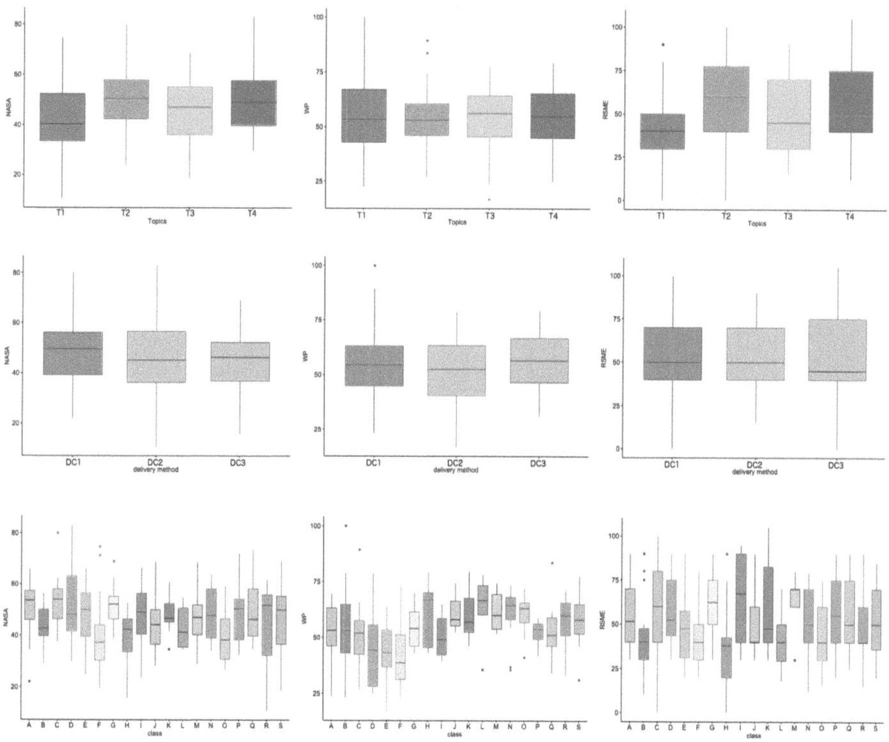

Fig. 5. Boxplots of the distributions of the mental workload scores by measure (NASA, WP, RSME) grouped by topic (T1–T4), design condition (DC1-3) and class (A–S).

The Kruskal-Walllis test does not precisely tells which distributions are statistically significantly different. Thus, the Wilcoxon-Matt-Whitney test (or Mann-Whitney U-test) was employed only where a difference was spotted by the Kruskal-Wallis test. It is a non-parametric test for comparing the means of two groups that are not normally distributed. Table 9 lists the comparisons across topics of the NASA-TLX and RSME scores. Tables 10 and 11 respectively list the comparisons of the WP and RSME scores by classes. From Table 9, the NASA-TLX was able to produce scores significantly different twice across six comparisons while the RSME five times out of six, demonstrating higher sensitivity across topics. The WP, out of all the possible comparisons across classes, was able to produce scores significantly different 22 times out of 171 (Table 10), while the RSME 46 out of 171 (Table 11), showing a higher sensitivity across classes.

Table 9. P-values of the pairwise U-test with 95% confidence interval by topic.

Topic	NASA			RSME		
	T1	T2	T3	T1	T2	T3
T2	0.002	-	-	<0.00001	-	-
T3	0.196	0.095	-	0.020	0.0006	-
T4	0.014	0.596	0.241	<0.0001	0.237	0.0241

Table 10. P-values of the pairwise U-test with 95% confidence interval by class for the Workload Profile scores

Class	WP																	
	A	B	C	D	E	F	G	H	I	J	K	L	M	N	O	P	Q	R
B	0.93	-	-	-	-	-	-	-	-	-	-	-	-	-	-	-	-	-
C	1.00	0.684	-	-	-	-	-	-	-	-	-	-	-	-	-	-	-	-
D	0.47	0.27	0.36	-	-	-	-	-	-	-	-	-	-	-	-	-	-	-
E	0.29	0.13	0.38	1.00	-	-	-	-	-	-	-	-	-	-	-	-	-	-
F	0.28	0.06	0.19	0.93	0.70	-	-	-	-	-	-	-	-	-	-	-	-	-
G	0.72	0.75	0.38	0.13	0.03	0.02	-	-	-	-	-	-	-	-	-	-	-	-
H	0.36	0.43	0.20	0.12	0.02	0.03	0.58	-	-	-	-	-	-	-	-	-	-	-
I	0.88	0.56	1.00	0.38	0.23	0.09	0.35	0.16	-	-	-	-	-	-	-	-	-	-
J	0.37	0.53	0.23	0.24	0.08	0.06	0.31	0.81	0.18	-	-	-	-	-	-	-	-	-
K	0.26	0.29	0.18	0.06	0.02	0.02	0.37	0.94	0.11	0.83	-	-	-	-	-	-	-	-
L	0.11	0.39	0.06	0.09	0.03	0.02	0.12	0.72	0.13	0.71	0.53	-	-	-	-	-	-	-
M	0.15	0.31	0.12	0.09	0.01	0.01	0.18	0.72	0.09	1.00	0.83	0.58	-	-	-	-	-	-
N	0.10	0.34	0.06	0.07	0.01	0.01	0.18	0.78	0.12	1.00	0.86	0.72	0.96	-	-	-	-	-
O	0.15	0.27	0.06	0.01	0.01	0.01	0.20	0.75	0.07	1.00	0.89	0.39	1.00	0.64	-	-	-	-
P	1.00	1.00	0.86	0.20	0.14	0.06	0.61	0.34	0.63	0.28	0.16	0.03	0.14	0.03	0.02	-	-	
Q	0.96	0.83	0.80	0.17	0.19	0.09	0.66	0.52	1.00	0.37	0.26	0.15	0.14	0.09	0.06	0.93	-	
R	0.38	0.51	0.17	0.10	0.02	0.01	0.55	0.65	0.21	0.69	0.82	0.22	0.48	0.36	0.57	0.18	0.27	-
S	0.35	0.64	0.25	0.12	0.03	0.02	0.49	0.91	0.22	0.64	0.79	0.34	0.67	0.54	0.84	0.33	0.41	0.93

Table 11. P-values of the pairwise U-test with 95% confidence interval by class for the Rating Scale Mental Effort scores.

Class	RSME																	
	A	B	C	D	E	F	G	H	I	J	K	L	M	N	O	P	Q	R
B	0.09	-	-	-	-	-	-	-	-	-	-	-	-	-	-	-	-	-
C	0.43	0.03	-	-	-	-	-	-	-	-	-	-	-	-	-	-	-	-
D	0.46	0.01	0.81	-	-	-	-	-	-	-	-	-	-	-	-	-	-	-
E	0.27	0.33	0.07	0.04	-	-	-	-	-	-	-	-	-	-	-	-	-	-
F	0.05	0.95	0.01	0.01	0.34	-	-	-	-	-	-	-	-	-	-	-	-	-
G	0.25	0.01	0.86	0.58	0.01	0.01	-	-	-	-	-	-	-	-	-	-	-	-
H	0.02	0.49	0.01	0.01	0.10	0.33	0.01	-	-	-	-	-	-	-	-	-	-	-
I	0.19	0.01	0.59	0.42	0.02	0.01	0.60	0.01	-	-	-	-	-	-	-	-	-	-
J	0.50	0.45	0.24	0.14	1.00	0.45	0.09	0.18	0.11	-	-	-	-	-	-	-	-	-
K	0.57	0.03	0.91	0.84	0.15	0.02	0.62	0.01	0.58	0.20	-	-	-	-	-	-	-	-
L	0.03	0.88	0.01	0.01	0.17	0.57	0.01	0.67	0.01	0.36	0.03	-	-	-	-	-	-	-
M	0.23	0.06	0.75	0.57	0.03	0.01	0.95	0.01	0.52	0.20	0.96	0.01	-	-	-	-	-	-
N	0.62	0.24	0.18	0.16	0.60	0.22	0.06	0.07	0.05	0.69	0.31	0.10	0.14	-	-	-	-	-
O	0.14	0.76	0.04	0.01	0.60	0.77	0.01	0.26	0.01	0.60	0.04	0.41	0.02	0.29	-	-	-	-
P	0.67	0.07	0.71	0.83	0.13	0.02	0.58	0.01	0.27	0.35	0.80	0.01	0.59	0.28	0.06	-	-	-
Q	0.91	0.10	0.35	0.35	0.32	0.06	0.17	0.02	0.13	0.45	0.56	0.03	0.30	0.57	0.12	0.57	-	-
R	0.38	0.28	0.08	0.05	0.93	0.37	0.01	0.09	0.03	0.88	0.15	0.25	0.02	0.55	0.57	0.16	0.32	-
S	0.80	0.21	0.33	0.28	0.46	0.14	0.14	0.06	0.09	0.67	0.35	0.07	0.30	0.78	0.22	0.50	0.82	0.46

5 Discussion

Two multidimensional and a unidimensional subjective mental workload (MWL) measures, borrowed from the discipline of Ergonomics, have been employed in a novel primary research experiment within Education. The former are the Nasa Task Load Index [18] and the Workload Profile [59] while the latter is the Rating Scale Mental Effort [66]. These measures have been applied in a typical third-level classroom in the context of a module taught in the School of Computing, at the Dublin Institute of Technology. The experiment included the quantification and analysis of the experienced mental workload of different cohorts of students who were exposed to three different instructional design conditions and four topics. An analysis of the reliability of the two multidimensional MWL measures has been performed through a quantification of their internal consistency. In details, Cronbach's Alpha has been employed to assess the relation of the items associated to each MWL assessment technique. An obtained alpha value of 0.73 for the NASA task Load Index suggested that all its items share high covariance and probably measure the underlying construct (mental workload). The situation is similar for the Workload Profile with an even higher alpha of 0.847. Although the standards for what can be considered a 'good' alpha coefficient are entirely arbitrary and depend on the theoretical knowledge of the scales in question, results are in line with what literature recommends: a minimum coefficient between 0.65 and 0.8 is required for reliability.

Having reliable multidimensional measures of mental workload, an analysis of their validity has been subsequently performed, extended also to the selected unidimensional MWL measure, namely the Rating Scale Mental Effort. In detail, two forms of validity were assessed: face and convergent validity. The former validity indicates the extent to which the three employed MWL measures - the

Nasa Task Load Index (NASA-TLX), the Workload Profile (WP) and the Rating Scale Mental Effort (RSME) - are subjectively viewed as covering the construct of MWL itself by students. The latter validity indicates the degree to which the two multidimensional measures of MWL are theoretically related with the unidimensional measure. The obtained positive Pearson and Spearman correlation coefficients suggest how the three MWL measures are moderately correlated to the overall mental workload self-reported by students (correlations between $0 - 39 - 0.49$), thus demonstrating, as expected, moderate face validity. Similarly, the achieved positive Pearson and Spearman correlation coefficients show the expected moderate relationships that exist between the two multidimensional MWL measures (NASA-TLX and WP) and the unidimensional MWL measure (RSME), thus demonstrating moderate convergent validity. Eventually, with highly reliable and moderately valid MWL measures, their sensitivity was subsequently computed. Sensitivity referred to the extent to which the three selected MWL measures were able to detect changes of MWL scores across the four topics, the three instructional design conditions and the nineteen classes delivered over a period of 3 years. In detail, sensitivity was assessed through a non-parametric analysis of the variance of the MWL scores by adopting the Kruskal-Walllis test. This test was able to detect some statistical significant difference of the MWL scores across topic and classes, but not for instructional design conditions. Subsequently, an extended analysis of these detected differences was performed by a pairwise comparison of the MWL distributions employing the Wilcoxon-Matt-Whitney test (or Mann-Whitney U-test). The test showed how the NASA Task Load index was able to detect some of the differences in MWL scores only across topics while the Workload Profile only across classes. However, the unidimensional Rating Scale Mental Effort scale succeeded in detecting differences in MWL scores across topics and classes. None of the three measures was able to detect differences in MWL scores across the design conditions suggesting how they did not really impacted the variation of mental workload experienced by students. Figure 6 summarises the findings visually comparing the reliability, validity and sensitivity of the three selected mental workload measures.

Intuitively, given the strong reliability and moderate validity achieved by these measures, it is reasonable to infer that the design principles from the Cognitive Theory of Multimedia Learning - applied to design the second instructional condition - and the application of the Community of Inquiry approach - employed to design the third instructional condition - were, in this primary research, as not effective as expected, despite the different expectation. This research contributes to the body of knowledge by offering an alternative application of existing measures of mental workload, mainly adopted within Ergonomics, in Education, and in particular within the field of Teaching and Learning. Additionally, the experiment proposed in this study is in line to the Popperian's view of falsifiability because it is transparent and can be replicated and eventually falsified. Every attempt aimed at falsifying the findings achieved in this research is not seen as a negative pursuit but rather a positive endeavour because it is aimed at increas-

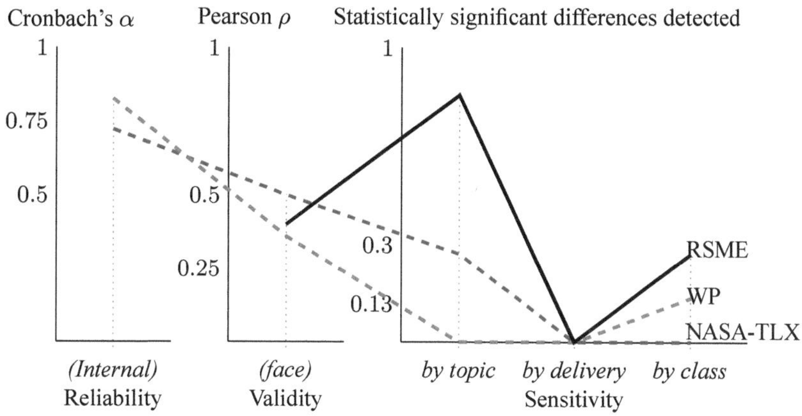

Fig. 6. Comparison of the reliability, validity and sensitivity of the Nasa Task Load Index (NASA-TLX), the Workload Profile (WP) and Rating Scale Mental Effort (RSME).

ing our understanding of mental workload as a construct applied within Education, Teaching and Learning for evaluating the efficiency of various instructional approaches.

6 Conclusions

The research conducted in this paper was an attempt to investigate the reliability, validity and sensitivity of three well known self-reporting mental workload (MWL) measures, mainly used within Ergonomics, within third-level education. A primary research study has been designed and executed to gather self-reported data by different cohort of students of a post-graduate module in Computer Science. In details, four different topics of a module on 'research design and proposal writing' were repeatedly delivered using three different instructional approaches over a period of 3 years. The first design approach included the delivery of theoretical material by employing a traditional direct instruction method employing slides projected to a white-board that included textual and pictorial information. The second approach included the delivery of the same theoretical material through multimedia videos built by employing a set of principles from Cognitive Theory of Multimedia Learning [38]. The third design approach included the extension of the second approach with a collaborative group activity for students inspired by the Community of Inquiry paradigm [21]. Evidence strongly suggests how the three MWL measures are reliable when applied in a typical third-level classroom. Results demonstrated their moderate validity, in line with the validity achieved in other empirical experiments within Ergonomics. On the contrary, their sensitivity was very low in discriminating the mental workload scores of the three different instructional design conditions. However, given the high reliability and modest validity of the three MWL measures, the achieved sensitivity might be reasonably attributed to the minimal impact of the way the three instructional design conditions were designed.

Future work will include the replication of this primary research across other instructional design conditions, topics and third-level modules as well as the development of a hybrid scale that takes into account the strengths and limitations of the three mental workload assessment instruments adopted in this research.

Appendix

(See Tables 12, 13, 14, 15, 16, 17 and Figs. 7, 8, 9).

Table 12. The Rating Scale Mental Effort.

Please indicate, by marking the horizontal axis below, how much effort it took for you to execute the task you have just completed.

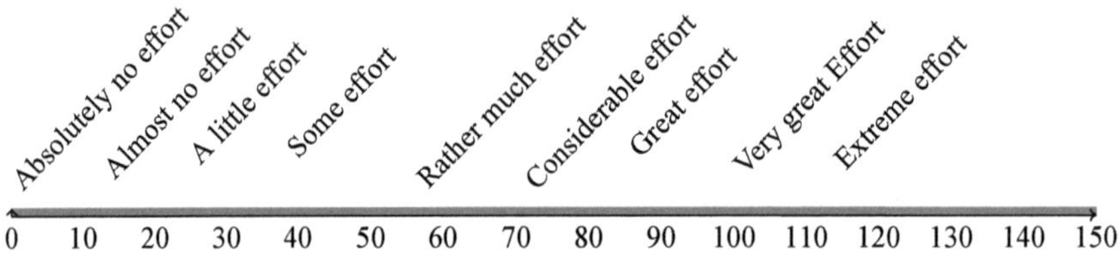

Table 13. The NASA Task Load Index (NASA-TLX).

Label	Question
NT_1	How much mental and perceptual activity was required (e.g. thinking, deciding, calculating, remembering, looking, searching, etc.)? Was the task easy or demanding, simple or complex, exacting or forgiving?
NT_2	How much physical activity was required (e.g. pushing, pulling, turning, controlling, activating, etc.)? Was the task easy or demanding, slow or brisk, slack or strenuous, restful or laborious?
NT_3	How much time pressure did you feel due to the rate or pace at which the tasks or task elements occurred? Was the pace slow and leisurely or rapid and frantic?
NT_4	How hard did you have to work (mentally & physically) to accomplish your level of performance?
NT_5	How successful do you think you were in accomplishing the goals, of the task set by the experimenter (or yourself)? How satisfied were you with your performance in accomplishing these goals?
NT_6	How insecure, discouraged, irritated, stressed and annoyed versus secure, gratified, content, relaxed and complacent did you feel during the task?

Table 14. The Workload Profile (WP).

Label	Question
WP_1	How much attention was required for activities like remembering, problem-solving, decision-making, perceiving (detecting, recognising, identifying objects)?
WP_2	How much attention was required for selecting the proper response channel (manual - keyboard/mouse, or speech - voice) and its execution?
WP_3	How much attention was required for spatial processing (spatially pay attention around)?
WP_4	How much attention was required for verbal material (e.g. reading, processing linguistic material, listening to verbal conversations)?
WP_5	How much attention was required for executing the task based on the information visually received (eyes)?
WP_6	How much attention was required for executing the task based on the information auditorily received?
WP_7	How much attention was required for manually respond to the task (eg. keyboard/mouse)?
WP_8	How much attention was required for producing the speech response (eg. engaging in a conversation, talking, answering questions)?

Table 15. Design of the instructional condition 2 using the principles of Cognitive Theory of Multimedia Learning and its differences with condition 1 grouped by load type.

Principle	Load type	Design condition 1	Design condition 2
Coherence	Extraneous	Any extraneous material was kept to minimum	
Signaling	Extraneous	Cues, in the form of relevant keywords, with a larger font size	Cues (relevant keywords), popped-in in the video to emphasise the organisation of essential material
Redundancy	Extraneous	Graphical aids and use of narratives	Most of text was removed, offloading one channel (eyes); graphical aids and the use of narratives
Spatial contiguity	Extraneous	Corresponding words and pictures were placed beside each other and not in different slides or screens	
Temporal contiguity	Extraneous	Corresponding words and pictures were presented at the same time	Corresponding words (verbally transmitted) and pictures were presented at the same time

(*continued*)

Table 15. (*continued*)

Principle	Load type	Design condition 1	Design condition 2
Segmenting	Intrinsic	The instructional material was presented in a single unit	The instructional material is presented in segments, separated by video transitions
Pre-training	Intrinsic	No pre-training was offered to students	
Modality	Intrinsic	Printed text is kept in the slides and verbally explained	Printed text is removed, offloading one channel (eyes) and verbally explained (ears.)
Multimedia	Germane	Words and pictures	
Personalisation	Germane	Words are presented using a conversational style and not a formal style	
Voice	Germane	The words are spoken by the lecturer and not by an artificial machine voice	
Image	Germane	No video was used, thus no speaker's image was available	The lecturer's image was most of the time kept in the video, sometimes using the full space available or using half-space, with the second half used for important pieces of text/pictures. Other times, the image was removed and important sentences were textually presented full screen

Table 16. Dialogical activity set for the third design condition inspired by the Community Inquiry paradigm.

Which are the most important concepts explained during the lesson?
Through a dialogue with the members of your team, talk about these concepts, try to define them and try to eliminate misunderstandings

Table 17. Question and scale designed for investigating the face validity of the mental workload assessment measures.

How much mental workload the teaching session imposed on you?

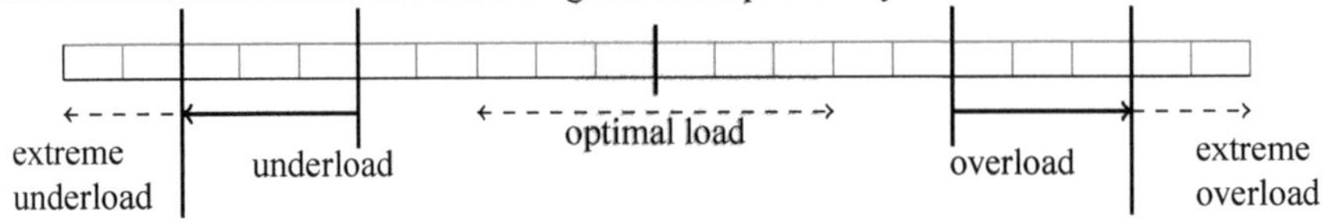

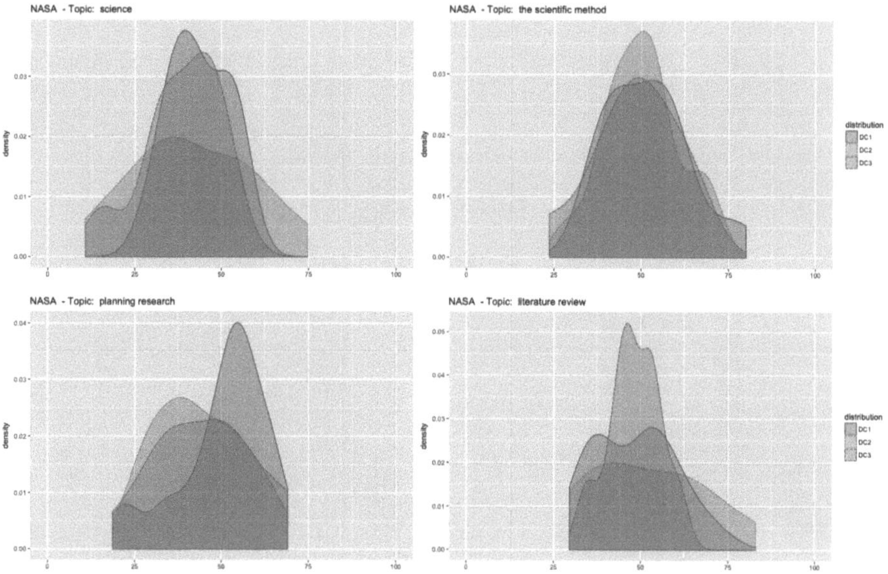

Fig. 7. Density plots of the distributions of the mental workload scores by topic (T1–T4) and design condition (DC1-3) for the NASA Task Load Index

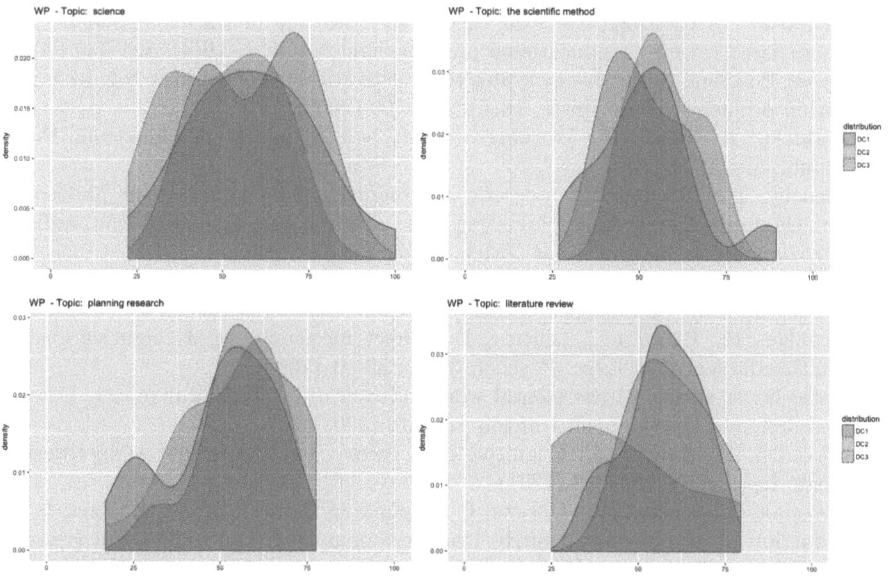

Fig. 8. Density plots of the distributions of the mental workload scores by topic (T1–T4) and design condition (DC1-3) for the WorkloadProfile

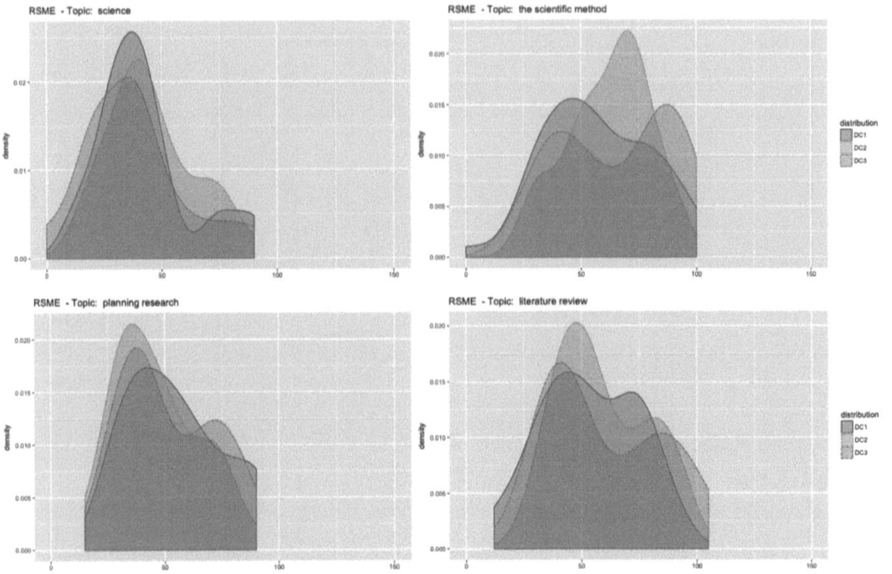

Fig. 9. Density plots of the distributions of the mental workload scores by topic (T1–T4) and design condition (DC1-3) for the Rating Scale Mental Effort.

References

1. Artino Jr., A.R.: Cognitive load theory and the role of learner experience: an abbreviated review for educational practitioners. AACE J. **16**(4), 425–439 (2008)
2. Ayres, P.: Using subjective measures to detect variations of intrinsic cognitive load within problems. Learn. Instr. **16**(5), 389–400 (2006)
3. Baddeley, A., Hitch, G.: Working Memory, vol. 8, pp. 47–90. Academic Press, Cambridge (1974)
4. Bleazby, J.: Autonomy, democratic community, and citizenship in philosophy for children: dewey and philosophy for children's rejection of the individual/community dualism. Anal. Teach. **26**(1), 30–52 (2006)
5. Brookhuis, K.A., de Waard, D.: Monitoring drivers' mental workload in driving simulators using physiological measures. Accid. Anal. Prev. **42**(3), 898–903 (2010)
6. Brunken, R., Plass, J.L., Leutner, D.: Direct measurement of cognitive load in multimedia learning. Educ. Psychol. **38**(1), 53–61 (2003)
7. Cain, B.: A review of the mental workload literature. Technical report. Defence Research and Development Canada Toronto (2007)
8. Chandler, P., Sweller, J.: Cognitive load theory and the format of instruction. Cogn. Instr. **8**(4), 293–332 (1991)
9. Cierniak, G., Scheiter, K., Gerjets, P.: Explaining the split-attention effect: is the reduction of extraneous cognitive load accompanied by an increase in germane cognitive load? Comput. Hum. Behav. **25**(2), 315–324 (2009)
10. De Jong, T.: Cognitive load theory, educational research, and instructional design: some food for thought. Instr. Sci. **38**(2), 105–134 (2010)
11. Debue, N., van de Leemput, C.: What does germane load mean? An empirical contribution to the cognitive load theory. Front. Psychol. **5**, 1099 (2014)

12. DeLeeuw, K.E., Mayer, R.E.: A comparison of three measures of cognitive load: evidence for separable measures of intrinsic, extraneous, and germane load. J. Educ. Psychol. **100**(1), 223 (2008)
13. Dewey, J.: The Child and the Curriculum. University of Chicago Press, Chicago (1902). No. 5
14. Dixon, P.: From research to theory to practice: commentary on Chandler and Sweller. Cogn. Instr. **8**(4), 343–350 (1991)
15. Gerjets, P., Scheiter, K., Cierniak, G.: The scientific value of cognitive load theory: a research agenda based on the structuralist view of theories. Educ. Psychol. Rev. **21**(1), 43–54 (2009)
16. Goldman, S.R.: On the derivation of instructional applications from cognitive theories: commentary on Chandler and Sweller. Cogn. Instr. **8**(4), 333–342 (1991)
17. Gwizdka, J.: Distribution of cognitive load in web search. J. Am. Soc. Inf. Sci. Technol. **61**(11), 2167–2187 (2010)
18. Hart, S.G.: NASA-task load index (NASA-TLX); 20 years later. In: Human Factors and Ergonomics Society Annual Meeting, vol. 50, pp. 904–908. Sage Journals, San Francisco (2006)
19. Kirschner, P.A.: Cognitive load theory: implications of cognitive load theory on the design of learning. Learn. Instr. **12**(1), 1–10 (2002)
20. Lipman, M., Sharp, A.M., Oscanyan, F.S.: Philosophy in the Classroom. Temple University Press, Philadelphia (1980)
21. Lipman, M.: Thinking in Education. Cambridge University Press, Cambridge (2003)
22. Longo, L.: Human-computer interaction and human mental workload: assessing cognitive engagement in the world wide web. In: Campos, P., Graham, N., Jorge, J., Nunes, N., Palanque, P., Winckler, M. (eds.) INTERACT 2011. LNCS, vol. 6949, pp. 402–405. Springer, Heidelberg (2011). https://doi.org/10.1007/978-3-642-23768-3_43
23. Longo, L.: Formalising human mental workload as non-monotonic concept for adaptive and personalised web-design. In: Masthoff, J., Mobasher, B., Desmarais, M.C., Nkambou, R. (eds.) UMAP 2012. LNCS, vol. 7379, pp. 369–373. Springer, Heidelberg (2012). https://doi.org/10.1007/978-3-642-31454-4_38
24. Longo, L.: Formalising human mental workload as a defeasible computational concept. Ph.D. thesis. Trinity College Dublin (2014)
25. Longo, L.: A defeasible reasoning framework for human mental workload representation and assessment. Behav. Inf. Technol. **34**(8), 758–786 (2015)
26. Longo, L.: Designing medical interactive systems via assessment of human mental workload. In: International Symposium on Computer-Based Medical Systems, pp. 364–365 (2015)
27. Longo, L.: Mental workload in medicine: foundations, applications, open problems, challenges and future perspectives. In: 2016 IEEE 29th International Symposium on Computer-Based Medical Systems (CBMS), pp. 106–111, June 2016
28. Longo, L.: Subjective usability, mental workload assessments and their impact on objective human performance. In: Bernhaupt, R., Dalvi, G., Joshi, A., Balkrishan, D.K., O'Neill, J., Winckler, M. (eds.) INTERACT 2017. LNCS, vol. 10514, pp. 202–223. Springer, Cham (2017). https://doi.org/10.1007/978-3-319-67684-5_13
29. Longo, L.: On the reliability, validity and sensitivity of three mental workload assessment techniques for the evaluation of instructional designs: a case study in a third-level course. In: Proceedings of the 10th International Conference on Computer Supported Education, CSEDU 2018, Funchal, Madeira, Portugal, 15–17 March 2018, vol. 2, pp. 166–178 (2018)

30. Longo, L., Barrett, S.: Cognitive effort for multi-agent systems. In: Yao, Y., Sun, R., Poggio, T., Liu, J., Zhong, N., Huang, J. (eds.) BI 2010. LNCS, vol. 6334, pp. 55–66. Springer, Heidelberg (2010). https://doi.org/10.1007/978-3-642-15314-3_6
31. Longo, L., Barrett, S.: A computational analysis of cognitive effort. In: Nguyen, N.T., Le, M.T., Świątek, J. (eds.) ACIIDS 2010. LNCS, vol. 5991, pp. 65–74. Springer, Heidelberg (2010). https://doi.org/10.1007/978-3-642-12101-2_8
32. Longo, L., Dondio, P.: On the relationship between perception of usability and subjective mental workload of web interfaces. In: IEEE/WIC/ACM International Conference on Web Intelligence and Intelligent Agent Technology, WI-IAT 2015, Singapore, 6–9 December, vol. I, pp. 345–352 (2015)
33. Longo, L., Kane, B., Hederman, L.: Argumentation theory in health care. In: 25th International Symposium on Computer-Based Medical Systems, Rome, Italy, pp. 1–6. IEEE (2012)
34. Longo, L., Rusconi, F., Noce, L., Barrett, S.: The importance of human mental workload in web-design. In: 8th International Conference on Web Information Systems and Technologies, Porto, Portugal, pp. 403–409. SciTePress, April 2012
35. Mayer, R.: Using multimedia for e-learning. J. Comput. Assist. Learn. **33**(5), 403–423 (2017). jCAL-16-266.R1
36. Mayer, R.E.: Multimedia learning. Psychol. Learn. Motiv. **41**, 85–139 (2002)
37. Mayer, R.E.: The Cambridge Handbook of Multimedia Learning. Cambridge University Press, Cambridge (2005)
38. Mayer, R.E.: Multimedia Learning. Cambridge University Press, Cambridge (2009)
39. Miller, G.A.: The magical number seven, plus or minus two: some limits on our capacity for processing information. Psychol. Rev. **63**(2), 81–97 (1956)
40. Mousavi, S., Low, R., Sweller, J.: Reducing cognitive load by mixing auditory and visual presentation modes. J. Educ. Psychol. **87**(2), 319–334 (1995)
41. Moustafa, K., Luz, S., Longo, L.: Assessment of mental workload: a comparison of machine learning methods and subjective assessment techniques. In: Longo, L., Leva, M.C. (eds.) H-WORKLOAD 2017. CCIS, vol. 726, pp. 30–50. Springer, Cham (2017). https://doi.org/10.1007/978-3-319-61061-0_3
42. Orru, G., Gobbo, F., O'Sullivan, D., Longo, L.: An investigation of the impact of a social constructivist teaching approach, based on trigger questions, through measures of mental workload and efficiency. In: Proceedings of the 10th International Conference on Computer Supported Education, CSEDU 2018, Funchal, Madeira, Portugal, 15–17 March 2018, vol. 2, pp. 292–302 (2018)
43. Paas, F., Tuovinen, J.E., Tabbers, H., Van Gerven, P.W.: Cognitive load measurement as a means to advance cognitive load theory. Educ. Psychol. **38**(1), 63–71 (2003)
44. Paas, F., Van Merrienboer, J.J.G.: The efficiency of instructional conditions: an approach to combine mental effort and performance measures. Hum. Factors: J. Hum. Factors Ergon. Soc. **35**(4), 737–743 (1993)
45. Paas, F.G., Van Merriënboer, J.J., Adam, J.J.: Measurement of cognitive load in instructional research. Percept. Mot. Skills **79**(1), 419–430 (1994)
46. Paivio, A.: Mental Representations: A Dual Coding Approach. Oxford Psychology Series. Oxford University Press, Oxford (1990)
47. Popper, K.: Conjectures and Refutations: The Growth of Scientific Knowledge. Routledge, Abingdon (2014)
48. Reid, G.B., Nygren, T.E.: The subjective workload assessment technique: a scaling procedure for measuring mental workload, Chap. 8. In: Hancock, P.A., Meshkati, N. (eds.) Human Mental Workload, Advances in Psychology, vol. 52, pp. 185–218. North-Holland (1988)

49. Rizzo, L., Dondio, P., Delany, S.J., Longo, L.: Modeling mental workload via rule-based expert system: a comparison with NASA-TLX and workload profile. In: Iliadis, L., Maglogiannis, I. (eds.) AIAI 2016. IAICT, vol. 475, pp. 215–229. Springer, Cham (2016). https://doi.org/10.1007/978-3-319-44944-9_19
50. Rizzo, L., Longo, L.: Representing and inferring mental workload via defeasible reasoning: a comparison with the NASA task load index and the workload profile. In: Proceedings of the 1st Workshop on Advances in Argumentation in Artificial Intelligence Co-Located with XVI International Conference of the Italian Association for Artificial Intelligence (AI*IA 2017), Bari, Italy, 16–17 November 2017, pp. 126–140 (2017)
51. Roscoe, A.H., Ellis, G.A.: A subjective rating scale for assessing pilot workload in flight: a decade of practical use. Technical report TR 90019. Royal Aerospace Establishment, March 1990
52. Rubio, S., Diaz, E., Martin, J., Puente, J.M.: Evaluation of subjective mental workload: a comparison of SWAT, NASA-TLX, and workload profile methods. Appl. Psychol. **53**(1), 61–86 (2004)
53. Satiro, A.: Jugar a pensar con mitos: este libro forma parte del Proyecto Noria y acompaña al libro para niños de 8–9 anos: Juanita y los mitos. Octaedro (2006)
54. Schnotz, W., Kürschner, C.: A reconsideration of cognitive load theory. Educ. Psychol. Rev. **19**(4), 469–508 (2007)
55. Seufert, T., Jänen, I., Brünken, R.: The impact of intrinsic cognitive load on the effectiveness of graphical help for coherence formation. Comput. Hum. Behav. **23**(3), 1055–1071 (2007)
56. Sweller, J., Van Merrienboer, J., Paas, F.: Cognitive architecture and instructional design. Educ. Psychol. Rev. **10**(3), 251–296 (1998)
57. Sweller, J.: Cognitive load theory, learning difficulty, and instructional design. Learn. Instruct. **4**(4), 295–312 (1994)
58. Sweller, J.: Element interactivity and intrinsic, extraneous, and germane cognitive load. Educ. Psychol. Rev. **22**(2), 123–138 (2010)
59. Tsang, P.S., Velazquez, V.L.: Diagnosticity and multidimensional subjective workload ratings. Ergonomics **39**(3), 358–381 (1996)
60. Vidulich, M.A., Ward, G.F., Schueren, J.: Using the subjective workload dominance (SWORD) technique for projective workload assessment. Hum. Factors Soc. **33**(6), 677–691 (1991)
61. Wickens, C.D.: Multiple resources and mental workload. Hum. Factors **50**(2), 449–454 (2008)
62. Wilson, G.F., Eggemeier, T.F.: Mental workload measurement, Chap. 167. In: Karwowski, W. (ed.) International Encyclopedia of Ergonomics and Human Factors, 2nd edn, vol. 1. Taylor and Francis (2006)
63. Xie, B., Salvendy, G.: Review and reappraisal of modelling and predicting mental workload in single and multi-task environments. Work Stress **14**(1), 74–99 (2000)
64. Young, M.S., Brookhuis, K.A., Wickens, C.D., Hancock, P.A.: State of science: mental workload in ergonomics. Ergonomics **58**(1), 1–17 (2015)
65. Young, M.S., Stanton, N.A.: Mental workload: theory, measurement, and application. In: Karwowski, W. (ed.) Encyclopedia of Ergonomics and Human Factors, 2nd edn, vol. 1, pp. 818–821. Taylor & Francis (2006)
66. Zijlstra, F.R.H.: Efficiency in work behaviour. Doctoral thesis. Delft University, The Netherlands (1993)

An Exercise in Reverse Engineering for Safety-Critical Systems: An Experience for the Classroom

Emanuel S. Grant(✉) and Pann Ajjimaporn

University of North Dakota, Grand Forks, ND 58202, USA
emanuel.grant@engr.und.edu

Abstract. There have been multiple software system failures and successes that have led to milestone events since the inception of software development. One can harken back to the Y2K problem of the late 1990s that led to a great demand in reverse engineering activities in academia and the industry. Fast-forward to the 21st century and one observes that reverse engineering lacks emphasis in USA academia. This issue is exemplified by the high demand for software systems in new and expanding software application areas, which has resulted in systems being implemented before the requirements and design phases have been completed. Towards the maintenance of such systems, it is necessary to conducted reverse engineering for the derivation of software documentation for requirements and high-level and low-level design. When this scenario exists in the domain of safety-critical system, particularly in the aviation industry, reverse engineering takes on greater value because such software systems must undergo development regulations and certification restrictions. This work reports on the experienced gained from conducting reverse engineering on an industry-based software system as a university project. The software system addressed a problem in the domain of aviation and was treated as a safety-critical system. The reverse engineering methodology applied was based on the RTCA DO-178C Software Considerations in Airborne Systems and Equipment Certification specification for onboard avionic software systems.

Keywords: Software engineering · Reverse engineering · Modelling notation · UML · Activity diagram · Safety-critical systems · Pedagogy · Curriculum

1 Introduction

1.1 Historical Perspective

Since the introduction of high-level programming, research efforts in software development methodologies and modelling notations have produced several notable ones, namely model-driven [1], component-based [2], and Agile methodologies [3], along with Coad/Yourdon [4], Shlaer/Mellor [5], and Unified Modelling Language (UML) [6] modelling notations. One goal of the research and the production of these software development methodologies and notations has been to address the "software crisis" that was first identified in the late 1950s [7]. The software crisis may be defined as the

B. M. McLaren et al. (Eds.): CSEDU 2018, CCIS 1022, pp. 414–432, 2019.
https://doi.org/10.1007/978-3-030-21151-6_20

inability of developers to deliver reliable software systems in a timely and cost-effective manner. The software crisis is greater today than it has ever been, because of the increasing complexity and domains of application in which software systems are being deployed in todays' business and personal spheres.

The early proliferation of software development methodologies and notations did not resolve the many issues associated with the software crisis but added another layer of complexity to the realm of software development. Inter-project ventures were stymied by a project developers' unfamiliarity with the methodology and notation of another of the inter-projects methodologies. The problems arising from this overgrowth of methodologies and notations were arrested with the merger of multiple modelling notations into a single representation; the UML and the methodologies coalescing around model-based software development methodologies [1].

The evolution and amalgamation of methodologies and notations, over the early 15 years are captured in Fig. 1, which was produced by Guido Zockoll, Axel Scheithauer & Marcel Douwe Dekker. It should be noted that as of this date (second quarter 2018) the UML is at version 2.5, sysML is at version 1.5, BPMN is at version 2.0.2, and xUML is at version 1.1. These modelling notations have been developed by the Object Management Group (OMG) and the latest versions are not necessarily the ISO adapted version of the modelling notations. Figure 2 is an extrapolation of the Fig. 1 to illustrate the evolution of the main notations and methodologies from 2008 to current time.

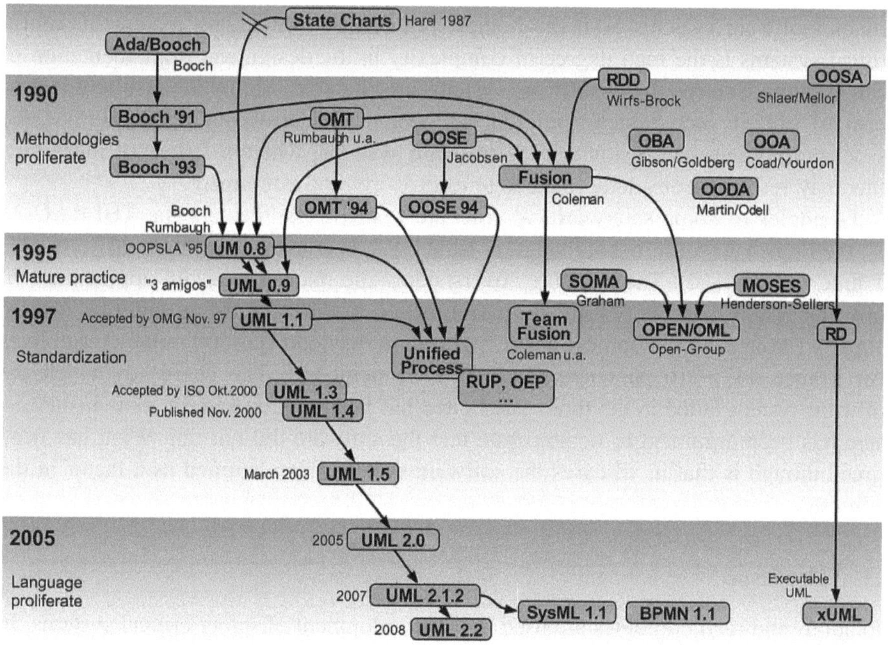

Fig. 1. Evolution of object-oriented methods and notations 1980s – mid 2000s.

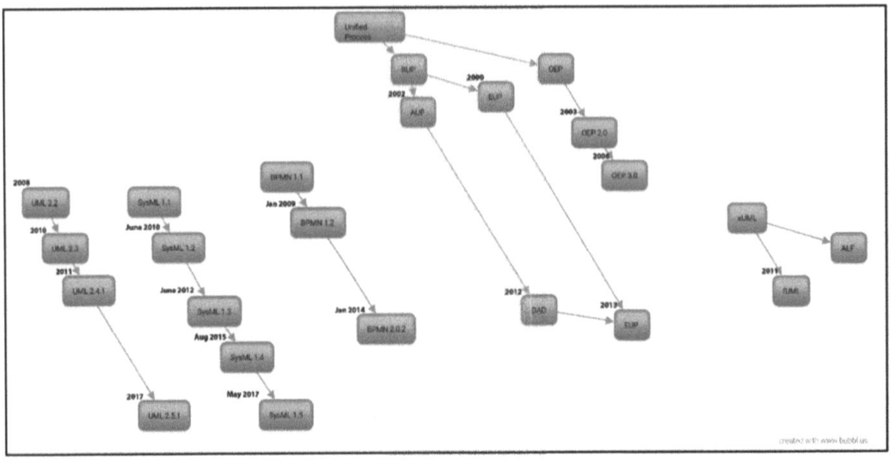

Fig. 2. Evolution of object-oriented methods and notations mid 2000 – present.

1.2 Current State

Notwithstanding the availability of the UML as the de facto industry-standard software modeling notation and accompanying methodologies such as the Rational Process, the software crisis is still an ever-present phenomenon of the software development industry. In the domain of safety-critical systems, the need to deliver correct and reliable software systems is at the highest priority. A challenging feature of safety-critical systems is the high degree of complexity in the design and implementation of such systems. Safety-critical software systems are characterized by the resulting loss or harm to life, if such systems fail during operation. Correspondingly, there is the associated domain of mission-critical software systems, wherein failure of those systems may result in considerable damage to property and equipment.

Examples of some safety-critical software systems' failures are the THERAC-25 [8], the French Arian-5 rocket inaugural launch [9], and Air France flight 447 (AF447) of June 1, 2009 [10]. These failures overshadow the many successful applications of software systems in safety-critical environments, because of the prohibitive cost in property (Ariane-5 development cost US$7 billion, payload US$500 million), and lives (Air France 447, 216 passengers and 12 crewmembers). The degree to which the software system failed in the three cases cited has been argued and, in some instances, there has been argument to demonstrate that the software did not fail. What has been agreed though is that in all cases the software system was identified as a factor in the failures.

1.3 The Issue

Notations and methodologies are used in the development of safety-critical systems. In the USA, many of the software development methodologies, notations, and standards use in the software development industry were defined within the professional world; independence of the curricula of tertiary software development/engineering programs.

This situation results in a disconnect between the pedagogy of the classroom and the practices of the workplace, because of the pace of introducing these industrial-driven notations and methodologies within academia. Examples of some of these are, FUSION [11], SCADE [12]. In the circumstance where there is collaboration on a software development project between academia and industrial partners there arise opportunities for academia to incorporate some of the concrete practices of the industry into related curricula to be more responsive to the desired skill-set of such program graduates. This report documents one such experience in the development of a software system to manage the assignment of commercial aircrafts to airport terminal gates with multiple and conflicting gate-assignment restrictions. The following sections of the manuscript documents the background, in terms of the scope, deliverables, methodology, and pedagogy. The next section documents the experience of the project, followed by a discussion of the educational benefits derived from the project. The final section presents a summary in the form of a conclusion and a look at future work in this area.

2 Background

2.1 Reverse Engineering Support

A search of two publication websites for books/articles on a set of common software development subjects produced the list as presented in Table 1. The Amazon website search produced a hit list of only 799 publications with the subject Reverse Engineering, which represents 0.24% of the total eight subjects searched. The ACM Digital Library produced a list of 169,298 instances of articles that references the subject Reverse Engineering, which represented 11.80% of the total eight subjects searched. The inference drawn from this data is that while there is a high number of publications, implying a corresponding high-level of research, on the subject of reverse engineering in academia; there is a significantly lower level of publication on this subject in the professional publication realm. This inference leads to a possible conclusion that there is a significantly lower level of support for teaching the subject in academia, as the availability and use of an established text book on the subject is crucial at the undergraduate level. This situation may then lead to a lower than desired teaching of reverse engineering as a first-class subject in many computer science undergraduate program curriculum.

A further search of the computer science program courses descriptions of eight US universities for the subject Reverse Engineering produce the results of Table 2. The data search of Table 2 does not imply that reverse engineering is not included in the curricula of these institution; what is evident is that the term "reverse engineering" does not appear in the available descriptions of the universities courses/programs. In the Editorial paper titled "Should Reverse Engineering Remain a Computer Science Cinderella?" [13], Christian Mancas, examined reverse engineering form the legal. Ethical, and security perspectives and concluded that it is a necessary tool for discovery and learning. The author concluded that reverse engineering is a "Cinderella both in colleges, universities, and research labs…" [13], and students and researchers should be encouraged to work in this area.

Table 1. Software development subject search result.

Subject	Amazon	Amazon %	ACM DL	ACM DL %
Requirements Engineering	4,000	1.22	208,352	14.52
User Interface Design	2,000	0.61	247,196	17.23
Requirements Analysis	4,000	1.22	167,266	11.66
Object-Oriented Design	7,000	2.14	205,428	14.32
Object Oriented Programming	9,000	2.75	146,678	10.22
Software Programming	100,000	30.60	183,038	12.76
Programming	200,000	61.20	107,672	7.50
Reverse Engineering	**799**	**0.24**	**169,298**	**11.80**
Totals	326,799	100	1,434,928	100.00
Average	40,849.88	12.50	179,366.00	12.50

Table 2. Search of 8 universities for courses on Reverse Engineering.

University	Yes	No
University of North Dakota		X
Stanford University		X
Georgia Tech		X
Massachusetts Institute of Technology		X
Carnegie Mellon University		X
California Institute of Technology		X
Florida Atlantic University		X
Rochester Institute of Technology		X

2.2 Safety-Critical System Development

Within the domain of safety-critical systems the use of standardized software development methodologies is crucial to the successful completion of such systems. For avionic software systems development, the RTCA organization has developed a standard, the DO-178C - Software Considerations in Airborne Systems and Equipment Certification [14] for USA software development. A corresponding European EUROCAE ED-12C Software Considerations in Airborne Systems and Equipment Certification exist for avionic software development in the European territories. These documents set out a series of objectivities, activities, and data items that are required for the certification of onboard avionic systems. DO-178C is a revised standard of its previous version DO-178B, issued in late 2011 to incorporate new guidance regarding the use of object-oriented software development and formal specification techniques in software development. The purpose of DO-178C is "…for the production of software for airborne systems and equipment that performs its intended function with a level of confidence in safety that complies with airworthiness requirements" [14]. In order for a software system to be use onboard aircrafts in the USA, it has to be certified by the USA Federal Aviation Administration (FAA), as set out in the DO-178C Specification.

2.3 Problem Definition

A commercial airline company conducted a review and determined that there was a significant problem with its information system structure. The problem identified was considered to be a "single-point of failure" in the dynamic assignment of aircrafts to airport terminal gates. That single point of failure in the process was the non-documentation and unscientific strategy used for dynamic assignment of aircrafts to terminal gates. The process involves the listing of all aircrafts for assignment and the available gates. Aircrafts are classified based on certain attributes, such as size, capacity, manufacturer, arrival time, departure time, etc. Gates are classified based on certain attributes, such as, location to runway, fuel-port, accessibility, availability time, etc. Other constraints pertain to global considerations, such as available runway, taxiway path to runway, established departure timeframes, etc.

An operator would compile the aircraft and gate lists and generate a standard assignment, based on the previous assignment cycle. The existing software system would then identify any assignment conflicts, which may arise from gate closures, incompatible aircraft-gate assignment, aircraft late or none arrival, etc. The operator would then attempt to resolve the assignment conflicts by reassigning aircrafts based on his/her prior experience of executing this process.

The company recognized the failure that may arise if this system and process were not improved to be more efficient and effective. Consequently, a team of researchers from the University of North Dakota (UND) departments of Aviation and Computer Science were asked to look at the problem and develop a plan to mitigate the potentially problematic system and process. The UND team included researchers in genetic algorithm design and software engineering from the Department of Computer Science; it is the software engineering researchers' work, which is specifically documented in this report. Because of the nature of confidentiality and propriety information of the project, the airline will not be identified and information presented in the report has been sanitized.

2.4 The Software Methodology

The software development methodology applied on this project is now taught in the software engineering course at the University of North Dakota and was derived from a research project on safety-critical system development for avionic software systems. The methodology was applied on the development of an unmanned aerial system (UAS) for monitoring the flight operations of unmanned aerial vehicles (UAVs) in unrestricted airspace. To conduct software development for operation in US national airspace (NAS) domain, the RTCA DO-178C specification was use as the guideline on this project.

The research work conducted with the DO-178C specification was two-fold. In the first phase of the work the DO-178C document was transformed from its textual representation to a graphical representation, in the UML notation. Figure 3 [15], and Fig. 4 [15] present two of the UML package diagram models developed to represent components of the specification. Figure 3 represents the DO-178C specification, software development methodology components requirements as an UML package-level model.

Each package of Fig. 3 was decomposed into a set of UML use case diagrams, class diagrams, and activity diagrams. Figure 4 represents the DO-178C Software Planning Process (Sect. 4 of the DO-178C specification) as an UML Use Case Diagram, wherein the user is the project development team. Figure 4 is one of the models contained in the Software Planning Process 4.0 package of Fig. 3.

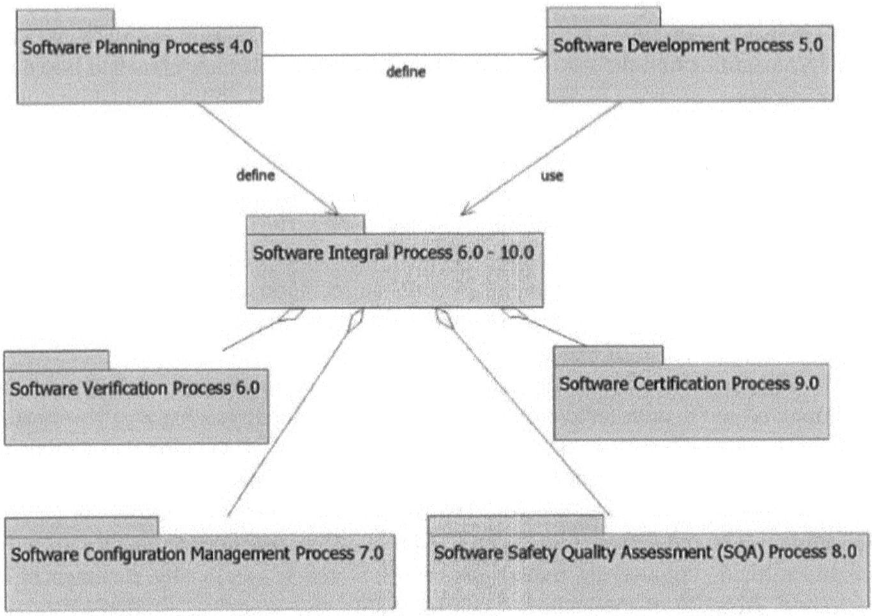

Fig. 3. DO-178C software development UML package-level model [15].

The second phase of the research work with the DO-178C specification is the definition of a model-driven software development methodology that incorporates and is compliant with the DO-178C specification. This methodology is illustrated in Fig. 5 [15] as an UML activity diagram. Figure 5 is an UML activity diagram representation of the requirement-level activities contained in the Software Development Process 5.0 package of Fig. 3. The activities of Fig. 5 are mapped to the respective sections of the DO-178C document, by way of the DO-178C section number being listed in the activities of the model. Figure 5 captures the activities as specified in the DO-178C for the software requirements analysis and design phases; the software implementation (coding), testing, and deployment phases are represented in separate UML activity diagrams. The work reported on in this manuscript is limited to the scope of Fig. 5. The UML models specified in Fig. 5 are specific to this instantiation of the methodology; in other instantiations, other models may be used to satisfy the requirements of either the problem domain or the expertise of the development team.

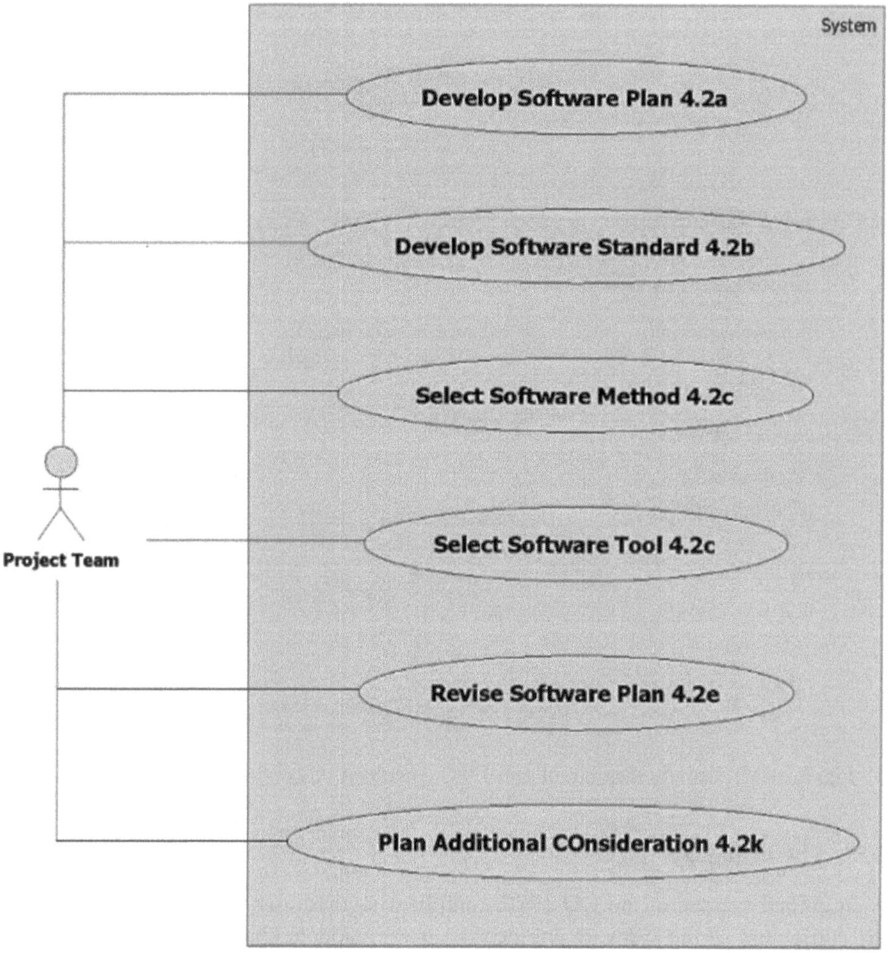

Fig. 4. DO-178C Software Planning Process 4.0 UML use case diagram [15].

A first task requirement of DO-178C Software Planning Process (4.0) is the identification of the software level of development. DO-178C specifies five (5) levels of criticality, designated Level-A through Level-E, with Level-A being the highest and Level E the lowest. Once the software level has been determined then DO-178C Software Development Process (5.0) and Software Integral process (6.0–10.0) specify the required set of activities and data element necessary for certification of the system that is to be developed. The outputs of these activities are the Software Plan (4.2a), Software Standard (4.2b), Software Method (4.2c), and Software Tool (4.2c), as listed in Fig. 5. There may be Additional Considerations, for the particular application domain. On the UAS project no additional considerations was necessary; the use of DO-178C on this project is not required, but was applied as a means to verify the newly defined methodology, as a proof of concept experiment.

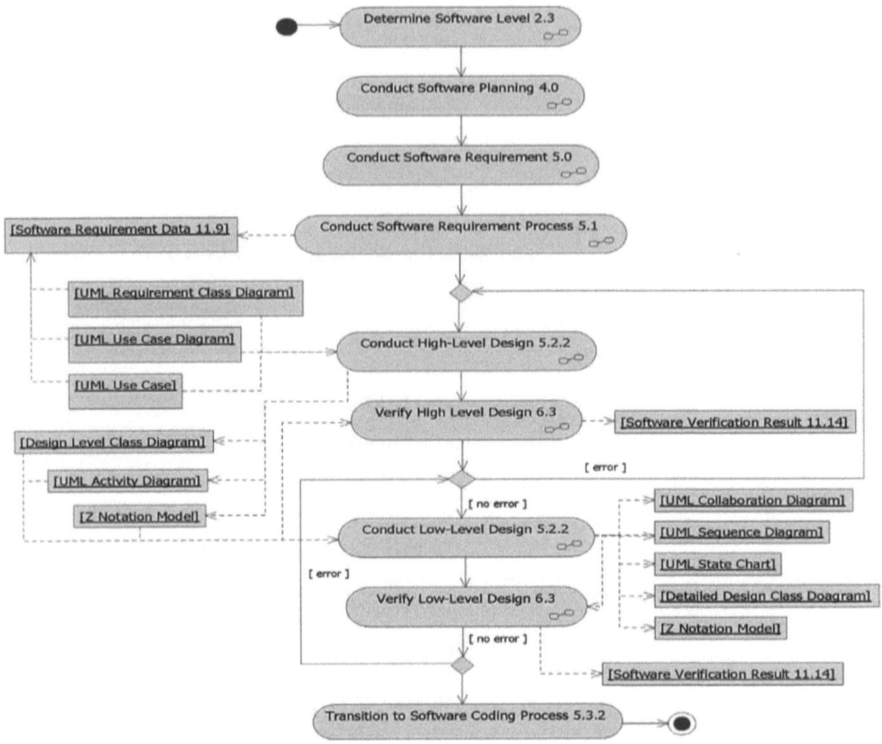

Fig. 5. UML activity diagram of DO-178C compliant model-driven methodology [15].

2.5 The Pedagogy

A simplified version of the DO-178C compliant methodology of Fig. 5 is included in the curriculum of the software engineering undergraduate course and a graduate-level formal specification course in the Department of Computer Science at UND. In the undergraduate-level course, students are taught a number of software development methodologies, and are required to develop a small software system by using the simplified version of the methodology of Fig. 5. In a similar manner at the graduate-level, the students are required to develop a more complex system than that of the undergraduate-level. An additional requirement, at the graduate-level, is that the system is assumed to be at the DO-178C criticality Level-A, thus necessitating the use of rigorous system validation and verification (V&V) techniques as an activity of the development methodology. These V&V activities are executed at the Verify Low Level Design 6.3 and Verify Low Level Design 6.3, of Fig. 5. This formal specification technique involves the derivation of Z notation [16]) representation of the UML models that were developed of the system at the activities of Conduct High Level Design 5.2.2 and Conduct Low Level Design 5.2.2 of Fig. 5.

The two software engineering courses are taught once per year and follow a strict forward engineering life-cycle methodology. The topic of reverse engineering is covered the end of the teaching cycle, subject to the availability of lecture time; teaching time on higher priority topics may be extended thus reducing time for the lower priority topics.

As previously stated from Table 2, a review of the software engineering programs at eight major universities in the USA, did not encounter the term "reverse engineering" as ether a topic or course in any of the listings. Search of the catalogue of two major USA academic publishing firm for textbooks on reverse engineering produced a hit list of 799 and 169,298 items; similar searches for the terms "requirement engineering", "software design" and "code generation" produces kit lists exceeding thousands and hundreds of thousands items, respectively, as presented in Table 2. The implications of these findings have been presented in Sect. 2.1. The additional observation at this point is that there are no publically available examples of how best to incorporate the teaching of reverse engineering, though it is assumed that it is taught at many institutions, but not formally described; as is the case at the University of North Dakota.

3 Project Description

At the start of the project, the Department of Computer Science researchers formed three teams. One team focused on developing the genetic algorithms to implement the aircraft-to-gate assignment solution. The second team focused on the design and implementation of the user interface of the system. The third team focused on the documentation of the system, by way of modelling and verification/validation exercises. The teams are hereinafter referred to as Team I, Team II, and Team III respectively. The content of this report is a documentation of the efforts of Team III on the project. Notwithstanding the fact that the teams worked independent of each other, to a great degree, there was a high level of integration between the teams, as Team II worked on the interface to the genetic algorithms and Team III developed models of both systems for verification and validation, and system documentation. A secondary goal of Team III was the identification and capture of any pedagogical principles for incorporation into the curricula of software engineering courses, taught by the Department of Computer Science.

The teams held joint and separate interviews with the airline's stakeholders; namely managers, system administrators, and operators over the life of the project, and typically had greater number of meetings at the start and end of the project. Meetings at the start of the project were geared towards capturing the full requirements of the system, while meetings towards the end of the project were targeted at system verification and acceptance. At the initial phase of the project, the teams sought to establish a common set of system requirements, coming out of their respective independent and joint meetings with the stakeholders. Once these requirements were finalized, the teams progressed at different rates of work during the early stages of the project. In joint meetings between the teams, Team III determined that their initial models of the system were not synchronized with the work products of the other two teams, as there were supplemental meetings with some of the stakeholders and some requirements were modified, eliminated, or new ones introduced. This realization led to Team III reorganizing their standard approach to the model development activities.

This situation led to a iterative sequencing of work at the "Conduct Software Requirement Process 5.1" of Fig. 5. The models produced at this phase of Fig. 5 was the UML use case diagrams, as the software administrators of the airline company were interested in capturing the dynamic aspect of the system, these models were later fined into as UML activity diagrams at the "Conduct High-Level Design 5.2.2" phase of the Fig. 5 methodology.

3.1 Modified Methodology

Research showed that many software development projects fail because of the inability to deliver the product in a timely and cost effective manner, i.e. the software crisis. Paul Dorsey list ten reasons why systems projects fail [17]. Among the Dorsey's list is the lack of use of an appropriate software development methodology and focusing the development efforts on coding. Teams I and II had initiated what may be best described as an Agile approach to developing the system's user interface and generic algorithm solutions, as they rapidly produce coded components of the system. The teams refined the code, after consultation with the stakeholders, towards having a working system at the earliest.

Team III determined that their initial approach to modelling the system would not be successful; consequently, the team modified the development methodology in use to accommodate the work of the other two teams. This modification was an iterative reverse engineering process that is illustrated in Fig. 6 [15].

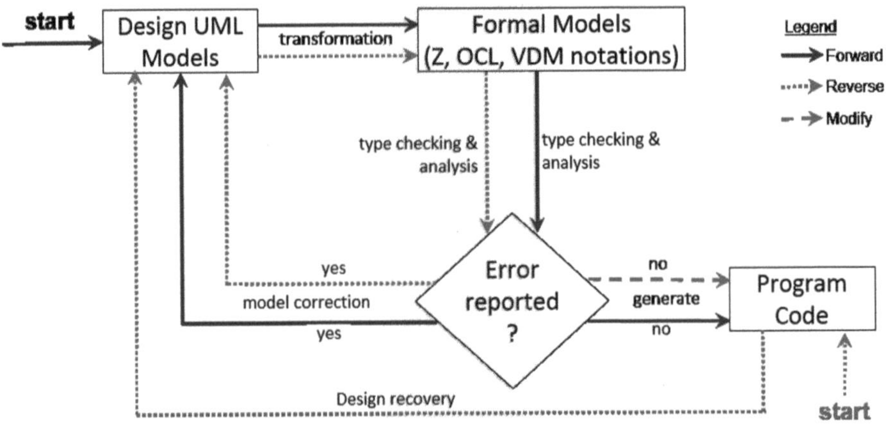

Fig. 6. Reverse-engineering modified model-driven methodology [15].

The process model of Fig. 6 was developed to incorporate a reverse-engineering strategy to complement the forward-engineering activities. This process model also illustrates the use of formal specification techniques for validating the reverse and forward engineering activities. The "Design UML Models" activity of Fig. 6 is congruent with the "Conduct High Level Design 5.2.2" and "Conduct Low-Level Design 5.2.2" of Fig. 5, and the "Formal Models" activity of Fig. 6 is synonymous to the

"Verify High Level Design 6.3" and "Verify Low-Level Design 6.3" activities of Fig. 5. The solid arrowed lines represent the forward engineering path through the process model, while the broken arrowed lines represent the reverse engineering path through the model. The forward engineering process commenced with the "Design UML Models" activities, while the reverse engineering process commenced at the "Program Code" activity of Fig. 5.

This modification to the development methodology then transitioned along the reverse engineering line "Design recovery" line, from the "Program Code" to representative "Design (high and low) UML Models". The UML models were then transformed to a formal representation in the Z notation for analysis during the verification phases of the Fig. 5 methodology. If the models pass the verification, then work transition along the "generate" arrowed lines to the production of "Program Code" of Fig. 6. Otherwise, work transition along the "model correction" arrowed line to the UML models of Fig. 6 and the next iteration of the process commence with the identified errors being corrected in the models.

3.2 Project Implementation

Team I developed the coded program solution for the airline-gate assignment problem by pursuing an Agile-based methodology. The teams held monthly meetings with the airline's stakeholders to present the accomplished goals and establish a new set of goals for the next scheduled meeting. Each iteration resulted in the refinement of achieved goals, accomplishment of established goals, or the definition of new goals. While these sprints were unusually long for a Scrum framework, they proved adequate for this particular domain, because of the complexity of the requirements and the development strategy. Shorter sprints would have produced incomplete goals at the level of granularity that would be understandable to the stakeholders. Team I was successful in developing an application system that was acceptable to the stakeholders. The software system emulated the actions of resolving aircraft-gate assignments in an optimal manner that was equal to or better than that which the experience operator could devise. This ensured that even in the absence of an operator the aircraft-gate assignment conflict resolution would be completed in a timely manner for the airlines operations.

Team II's effort to develop a user interface for the gate-assignment conflict resolution system, was simplified after it was determined that the existing user interface only needed to undergo minor modifications to accommodate the new application system. The modifications involved adding a menu item for executing the aircraft-gate assignment conflict-resolution system. Consequently, the modelling of the user interface system was not conducted by Team III, as the existing documentation for the user interface was assessed to be sufficient for the airlines system administrators.

3.3 Team III Efforts

Team III effort was initially to be the development of requirements-level models that would have been transformed and refined into high-level design models, which would then be verified and validated, as depicted in Fig. 5. These high-level models would then be further transformed/refined into low-level design models then verified and validated before being transformation into code. Team III's initial goal of adhering to the software development methodology of Fig. 5 had to be revised to be now centered on that of reverse engineering the code that was developed by Team I into a set of UML models for the purpose of verification, validation, and system documentation. Team III opted to classify this system as a Level-A DO-178C system, in order to exercise as many of the model-driven methodology's activities, as represented in Fig. 5. The intent was to garner as much pedagogical benefits as possible for incorporation into the software engineering curricula of the department and provide comprehensive system documentation artefact to the stakeholders.

The main UML model developed by Team III was a set of activity diagrams that was implemented at the low-level design phase, as illustrated in Fig. 5. The limitation to producing just one type of UML model was borne out of the airline system administrators' preference for just the necessary models to facilitate any immediate small-scale bug fixes or system modification, versus models to be used for main or long term system evolution.

An aspect of the work conducted by Team III but not a part of the project contracted deliverables was a set of formal specification models of the system that would have been used to conduct formal system verification if there was a need to have the system certified for DO-178C compliance. This formal specification effort was initiated as being done strictly for research purposes and was started at the end of the contracted project period. A sample set of formal specification representations, in the Z notation [], of components of the system is illustrated in Fig. 7. The derivation of the formal specification representations of the system is carried out at the "Verify Low-Level Design 6.3" stage of Fig. 5 and currently at the "Formal Models" stage of Fig. 6.

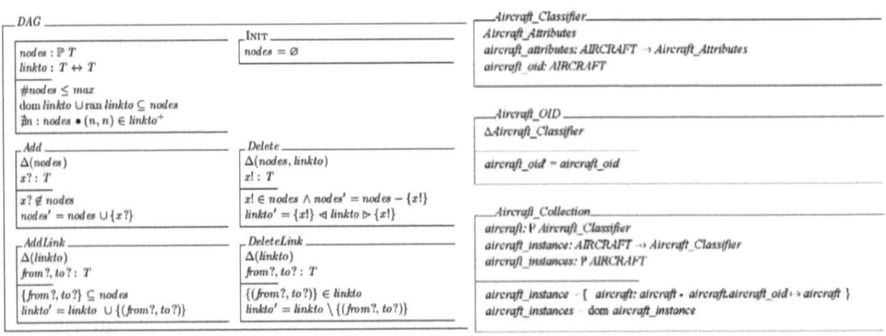

Fig. 7. Example Z notation formal specification.

Sanitized example of a segment of the UML activity diagrams that was developed is presented in Fig. 8 [15]. Figure 8 does not illustrate any significantly unusual activity diagram modelling technique, but with the exception of the listing of some activities with generic titles, such as "Activity 1", "Activity 2", etc. This was done in order to capture very low-level details of the program code, from which the model was reversed engineered. The models were developed in the open-source tool StarUML and the contents of "Activity-Xs" were stored in the documentation fields of the models. As implemented in this activity diagram, "Activity 2" is the snippet of code presented in Fig. 9 [15].

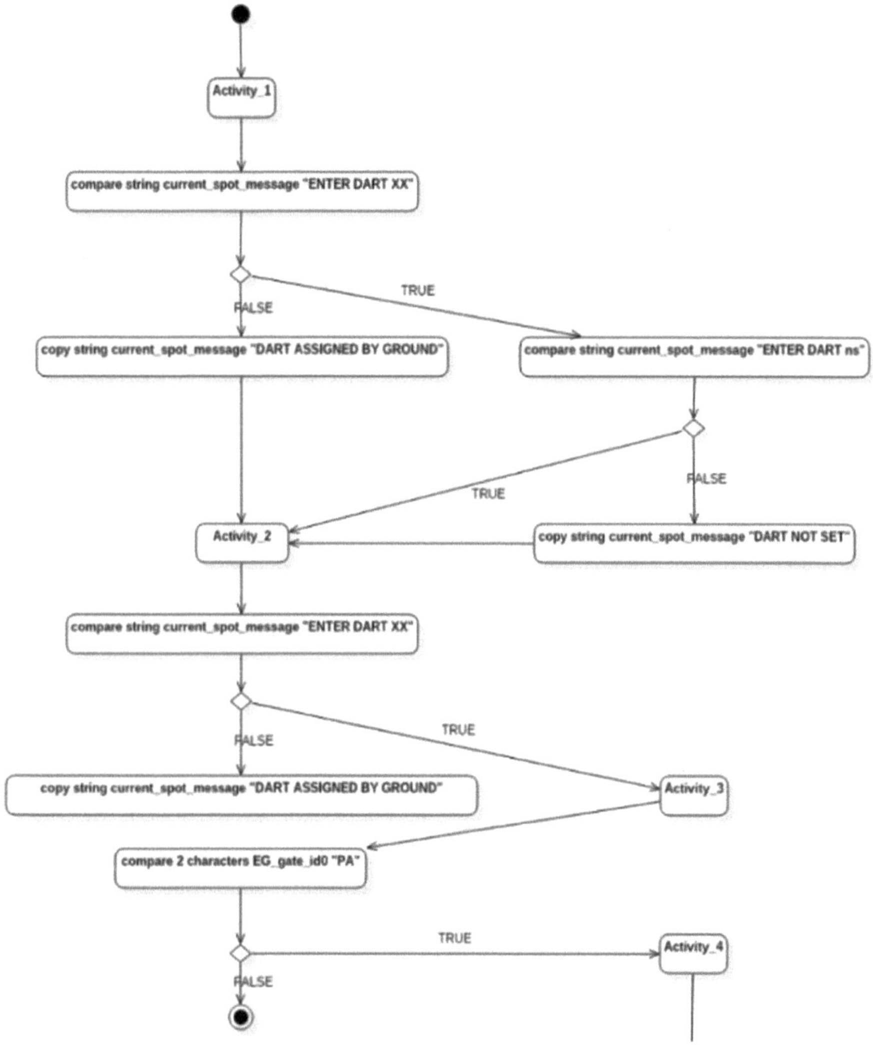

Fig. 8. UML activity diagram of aircraft-gate assignment system [15].

Team I did not implement a fully object-oriented programming paradigm, but partitioned the code-production exercise into modules based on four phases of the operation; (1) list aircrafts and terminal gates, (2) assign aircrafts to gates, (3) generate conflicts, and (4) resolve conflicts.

```
cout << "current_dart_message=" << current_dart_message <<
".xx" << endl;

//  GET GATE NUMBER FOR TITLE
  hold_gaterecno =  gate_recno;
  strcpy (EG_gate_id, gate[gate_recno].id);
  sprintf (title, "GATE  %-4.4s", EG_gate_id);
```

Fig. 9. Code snippet from UML activity diagram [15].

Team III completed the reverse engineering of the models with the assistance of graduate students in the department, under the supervision of faculty researchers. The work was completed over one and one half years. Team III's work was partitioned into two phases; the first phase covers the reverse engineering of the UML activity diagram models, and the second, future, phase will involve the formal verification of the models.

4 Result

Software system performance must always be reliable in the domain of safety-critical systems. These software systems encompass numerous highly complex processing components and have high demands for security and accuracy, in order to safeguard against failure.

With the UML being the de facto notation for software system modeling, there is a need for a more rigorous representation in the domain of safety-critical systems. Transforming UML models into Z equivalent schemas provides a means for formal analysis to accomplish verification and validation of software systems. With the growing demand for software systems in existing, new, and emerging application areas, formal requirements and design phase activities of some software development methodologies are sometimes not enforced. Consequently, industrial practices incorporate reverse engineering as a necessary phase of software system development for those systems that were developed with loose development processes and procedures. The goal of this exercise is to develop the needed software system modelling artefacts for system verification and validation, documentation, and evolution.

In many USA universities, reverse engineering is normally taught as an "add-on" to forward software development methodologies, such as the waterfall, component, and model-driven methodologies. This results in a situation wherein graduates leave these software engineering programs with minimal knowledge on reverse engineering then find themselves in a work environment where reverse engineering is of paramount importance. The experience gained by the faculty researchers on the project documented in this report, and from a prior project on the development of an UAS airworthiness system for monitoring UAVs operation in a restricted airspace, points to the need for a change in the pedagogical approach to reverse engineering.

The student researchers on this project and a prior project, in which reverse engineering was also applied, expressed specific and strong opinions on the need to be taught formal approaches to reverse engineering. Some of these student researchers had participated in internship programs at a variety of industrial organizations and had exposure to reverse engineering tasks. There was a unanimous conclusion that reverse engineering is important to the software development activities in real-world project and consequently, they think the process should be offered in courses on the same level as forward engineering topics.

There was also a consensus among the student researchers that working with code at the start of the project was challenging and this challenge may be alleviated if they had grounding in techniques to re-construct the code, i.e. reverse engineer the code. The students, in question, agreed that their experience did not require them to reverse engineer from code all the way back to requirements, but did see the need to be able to reverse engineer from code to the most detailed low-level design models. They identify the UML activity model as the preferred model as the output from a reverse engineering exercise. The students also noted that from their experience it was easier to reverse engineer procedural code versus object-oriented code.

The faculty researchers have begun the process of revising the curricula of two undergraduate-level and one graduate-level courses in software engineering, at the UND Department of Computer Science, to address this identified disconnect between industrial practice and the pedagogy of the courses. The curricula revision is multi-faceted, with changes in lecture content, assignments, and project requirements at both the undergraduate and graduate levels of teaching. It should be noted that these changes are not intended to be in support of industrial requirements, but are intended provided the graduates with additional knowledge of a software engineering subject that has not been taught at the same level of importance as that of other subjects. This is in recognition that reverse engineering is as important as forward engineering of software systems, and not the scenario of reverse engineering being a new or emerging field of software development; reverse engineering has been happening from the first time one developer had to modify the code of another developer.

Selection of chapters and articles from textbooks and journals on reverse engineering will be listed for reference reading to both groups of students, with some being selected as required reading for each of the two groups. It should be noted that while there is an abundance of textbooks on forward engineering (requirements engineering, software design, and software implementation) there are less known and available textbooks on reverse engineering, which are suitable for academia. Assignments and projects will now include specific work on reverse engineering in a form that is based on the experience from the aforementioned two projects. Critical to the new reverse engineering pedagogy will be an emphasis on Agile software development methodologies as a class of methodologies that fosters the incorporation of reverse engineering techniques.

4.1 The Revised Curriculum

The revised software engineering curriculum will continue to be project-based, but will now include activities in reverse engineering. The software engineering methodology of instruction for the course will continue to be based on a simplified version of the methodology illustrated in Fig. 5. The specific pedagogical topics covered are influenced from the experience on the aforementioned projects. Specifically, students will be introduced to the relationship between forward and reverse engineering, as illustrated in Fig. 6 but without introduction of the formal specification techniques at the undergraduate level. At the graduate level, students will receive instruction in the importance of formal specification to the verification and validation of safety-critical system development. Reverse engineering topics to be covered in the revised curriculum will include, but are not limited to the following:

Use of CASE tools in reverse engineering. Specifically, open source tools will be used, example StarUML, so that students can work on their own time and computers, and facilitate a common software development for the sharing and assessment of course assessment instruments:

- Reverse engineering techniques for object-oriented programming and procedural programming. The software engineering principle of encapsulation, as implemented in object-oriented development and programming adds a layer of complexity to the reverse engineering procedure, consequently requiring slightly different approaches from that procedural design and programming.
- Techniques to manually reverse engineer program codes that include: identifying methods' names, methods' inputs and outputs, and call sequences between methods, when working in an object-oriented software development domain.
- Techniques to identify programming constructs, such as: assignments, iterations, decisions, selections, etc., when working in both procedural and objected-oriented software development environments.
- Techniques for transforming programming code into pseudo-code, as an alternative to graphical modeling notations.
- Techniques for transforming pseudo-code into graphical models, namely UML models, as a more abstract representation of the system that is being reversed engineered.

The teaching strategy applied in the revised curriculum will have the students working in teams to develop a moderately complex system as a forward engineering exercise. Concurrently, the teams will work on reverse engineering the code of a well-known textbook system, such as the library management system [18]. Both project will be preceded by lectures on the fundamental principles of software engineering, and concurrent lectures on detailed and supplemental software engineering topics. Pre- and post-surveys to determine the students' comprehension of the relationship between academia and professional software engineering learning and practices will be conducted. The data from these surveys will aid in improving the curriculum.

5 Conclusion

For computer science and more specifically software engineering education at the undergraduate and graduate levels, the curricula have to undergo constant changes to keep pace with not just the emerging and new technologies, but also with the changes in interest areas. Currently there is focus in the areas of cyber-security that is being driven by the many threats from security breaches and hacks of commercial and government systems. There is also the burgeoning interest, work, and development in the areas of data science, data analytics, big data, and block-chain technologies. With all these new and emerging subject fields it has become a daunting task to keep computer science and its related sub-disciplines (database systems, networking, software engineering, operating systems, etc.) current.

Another issue of curricula development in software engineering is the identification of the need to prioritize a set of topics in a semester of work that is appropriate for the regulation of the institution and provides the graduates with the necessary skill set to make that a productive member of their profession. One challenge in this area is that of recognizing when there is a gap between the content of curricula and the practices of the industry of software development and how to address reducing or eliminating that gap in pedagogy knowledge-delivery and industrial knowledge-requirement. This report documents the experience gained from a collaborative project between academia and industry and how this experience reshaped the curricula of a set of courses.

The project called for the development of a mission-critical software system, albeit, the system was assessed as a safety-critical application for educational purposes. The project was conducted by teams of academic researchers and graduate students. One team conducted a reverse engineering exercise in order to develop a set of graphical UML models, from the program code of the system. These models formed the main artefacts of documentation and verification of the software system. This team had an adjacent project goal of identifying aspects of the project that would be incorporated in the curricula of software engineering courses.

The project successfully achieved the established goal by providing a software system to the stakeholders that was introduced into production within the specified timeframe. The adjacent project goals of identifying pedagogical benefits from the project were realized, as the hypothesis of a knowledge gap existence between the curricula of some USA undergraduate and graduate tertiary software engineering education and industrial practices was exemplified and data collected to address this issue. The outcome is that the curricula of the software engineering courses have been revised to include the teaching of reverse engineering as a first-class topic of the courses under review. The next stage in this curricular revision effort will be to update the official description of the courses to include the term "reverse engineering" to ensure that future searches will provide a yes response for updating Table 2. Future work will seek to evaluate the benefits of this revised pedagogy to the productivity of the graduates from the courses.

References

1. Larman, C.: Applying UML and Patterns, 3rd edn. Prentice Hall, Upper Saddle River (2005)
2. Sharp, J.H., Ryan, S.D.: A theoretical framework of component-based software development phases. ACM SIGMIS Database: DATABASE Adv. Inf. Syst. **41**(1), 56–75 (2010)
3. Salvador, C., Nakasone, A., Pow-Sang, J.A.: A systematic review of usability techniques in Agile methodologies. In: Proceedings of the 7th Euro American Conference on Telematics and Information Systems. ACM (2014)

4. Coad, P., Yourdon, E.: Object-Oriented Design. Prentice Hall, Inc., Upper Saddle River (1991)
5. Shlaer, S., Mellor, S.J.: Object-Oriented Systems Analysis: Modeling the World in Data, 1st edn. Prentice Hall, Upper Saddle River (1988)
6. Booch, G., Rumbaugh, J., Jacobson, I.: The Unified Modeling Language. Rational Software Corporation, Addison-Wesley, Indiana (1997)
7. Glass, R.L.: The software-research crisis. IEEE Softw. **1**(6), 42–47 (1997)
8. Leveson, N.G., Turner, C.S.: An investigation of the Therac-25 accidents. IEEE Comput. **26**(7), 18–41 (1993)
9. Lions, J.: ARIANE 5, Flight 501 Failure, Report by the Inquiry Board, European Space Agency, Paris, France (1996)
10. Bureau d'Enquêtes et d'Analyses: Final Report on the Accident on 1st June 2009 to the Airbus A330-203 Registered F-GZCP operated by Air France flight AF 447 Rio de Janeiro – Paris, Bureau d'Enquetes et d'Analyses France (BEA), Paris, France (2012)
11. Coleman, D.: Object-Oriented Development: The Fusion Method. Prentice Hall, Upper Saddle River (1993)
12. Boulanger, J.-L., Fornari, F., Camus, J.-L., Dion, B.: SCADE: Language and applications. Wiley, Hoboken (2014)
13. Mancas, C.: Should reverse engineering remain a computer science Cinderella? J. Inf. Technol. Softw. Eng. (2013). https://doi.org/10.4172/2165-7866.S5-e001
14. RTCA: Software considerations in airborne systems and equipment certification. DO-178C. Radio Technical Commission for Aeronautics (RTCA), Washington DC, USA (2011)
15. Grant, E., Ajjimaporn, P.: Pedagogical benefits from an exercise in reverse engineering for an aviation software system. In: Proceedings of 10th International Conference on Computer Supported Education (CSEDU), Madeira Portugal (2018)
16. Potter, B., Sinclair, J., Till, D.: An Introduction to Formal Specification and Z. Prentice Hall, Upper Saddle River (1996)
17. Dorsey, P.: 10 Reasons why systems projects fail. Technical report, Dulcian, Inc. (1998)
18. Singh, D.: C++ Library management system project - Source code of program, CPP for school. C++ Tutorial for School Students, Ghaziabad, India (2010)

Digital Media and Informal Learning: Alteration Mechanism and Captured Episodes

Otto Petrovic(✉)

Institute for Information Science and Information Systems,
Karl-Franzens-University of Graz, Graz, Austria
otto.petrovic@uni-graz.at

Abstract. The main part of human learning happens en passant and outside of the formal education system - called informal learning. Even pupils and students spend more time in front of digital media screens than in formal settings inside schools. Consequently, their learning is strongly impacted by the use of digital media in everyday life. Nevertheless, current research, educational practice, and design of learning systems have their focus mostly on courseware and distance education for formal settings. The current study captures 373 informal learning episodes in everyday life of 77 learners in the domains of cognitive, affective, and psychomotor learning. Autovideography is used based on the day reconstruction method (DRM) and selected self-monitoring (SSM). Additional episodes are captured applying participatory action research (PAR) in extensive field studies in different cultures. The episodes are analyzed using qualitative content analysis and grounded theory based on selected learning theories to develop a category system of alteration mechanism for Learners' perception sphere. The study shows that digital media do not alter informal learning in a simple cause-effect relationship but in a complex system of effects. Learners perception sphere obtain altered conditions for information assimilation on a learning topic. That can lead to informal learning in the cognitive, affective, and psychomotor domain. Related research with a focus on information assimilation and learning as media pedagogy, cognitive science, or learning psychology can use those identified mechanism for a differentiated view on digital media and consequently for more specific and sustainable results. One mechanism identified is the extension of linear learning content to a multi-dimensional perception sphere that is characterized by high interactivity, personalization, associativity, contingency, and often playfulness. Learners should become aware of the differences between the secondary experiences formed by that mechanism and primary experiences in the physical world to adjust their perception and media usage. Educators can respond by conveying key skills qualification as well as linking problems, processes, and contents between formal and informal settings. An important next research step is capturing and analyzing learning episodes in additional cultural areas to allow a fresh, quite different view on the widely discussed phenomena of digital divide.

Keywords: Teaching in the digital age · Learning in the digital age · Alterations by digital media · Informal learning · Day reconstruction method · Participatory action research · Autovideography

B. M. McLaren et al. (Eds.): CSEDU 2018, CCIS 1022, pp. 433–469, 2019.
https://doi.org/10.1007/978-3-030-21151-6_21

1 Introduction

Since the coming up of computers we deal with the question: how can we use them to enhance learning? In 1945, Vannevar Bush wrote in his article “As We May Think” about a future technology named *Memex*: “A device in which an individual stores all his books, records, and communications, and which is mechanized so that it may be consulted with exceeding speed and flexibility. It is an enlarged intimate supplement to his memory” [6, p. 108]. He anticipated the Personal Computer and Hypertext, which shape our learning today. In 1962, Doug Engelbart proposed using computers to augment learning [14]. Some years later, he developed the system Augment, already supporting collaborative knowledge working. Ted Nelson introduced in 1965 a computer system which enabled nonsequential writing and reading as well as cross-referencing and annotating. He called it Hypertext, anticipating the World Wide Web [40]. With the advent of the Arpanet in 1968, followed by the Internet and World Wide Web in the early 1990s, teaching become more and more impacted by computers and network technologies. For a detailed discussion of the interrelationship of learning and innovations in technology, going back to speech, writing, and printing see [19].

In those early days of computer networks, universities were pioneers in developing and using them for organizing collaborative research work and supporting teaching. They surpassed enterprises and usage by students in daily life significantly and were forerunners in using email, computer conferencing, video conferencing, and computer-based training. But now the times they are a-changing. Development is mainly driven by private enterprises and usage time shifted from inside universities out to learners' daily life. Computers, networks, and digital media have become ubiquitous.

[16] shows for the age group between 16 and 64 years in an average of 36 countries (n = 153.501) around the world a daily use time of 4,3 h. That time includes use of online TV, press and radio as well as games and social networking. Not included are online activities like browsing the web and e-commerce. Also, not included is the booming field of Internet of Things (IoT). The tight integration of the physical world with computer-based system supports people when performing daily activities, often without any conscious perception by the user. Examples are smart homes, intelligent transportation systems, or self-monitoring devices like fitness trackers.

Another impressive indicator for ubiquity of computers, networks, and digital media is the worldwide coverage of mobile communication networks. [23] reports that 95% of the global population live in an area which is covered by a mobile-cellular network whereby 87% live within the coverage of a broad-band network (3G or higher) facilitating mobile internet.

Despite that impressive ubiquity of computers, networks, and digital media in daily life, the focus of using them for teaching is still on dedicated software systems to support the transfer of knowledge from the teacher to the learners. Examples are massive open online courses (MOOCs), adaptive learning systems, or intelligent tutoring systems, mostly developed and implemented by universities themselves.

One of the best-known examples is the widespread learning management software *Moodle*, introduced in 2002 to help educators in creating online courses. Nowadays, educators are challenged by learners which are using totally different systems in their everyday life on a much bigger scale – and they learn a lot in doing so. Moodle is currently used by 130 million of users [39], whereas its counterparts in everyday life are used by more than two billion (Facebook), one and a half billion (WhatsApp) or one billion (WeChat). Therefore, the software systems used by teachers to support learning are mostly strange and unfamiliar to learners.

But not only to move from proprietary, university-based learning software systems to widespread everyday life systems is an opportunity for teachers to support learning. Also, the jump from the classroom with its formal learning settings into *everyday life* is an opportunity. In OECD countries 15-year-old spend on average 2,6 h a day in the classroom. A teacher is doing so for 1,9 h [41]. Thus, pupils spend around nine tenth of their time outside of traditional learning settings. And they use digital media heavily during that time, often also during night time using digital sleeping trackers. That ubiquitous usage impacts learning much more than the use of dedicated systems in formal settings.

The main part of human learning happens en passant as a by-product of something else, mostly outside of an educational institution, and is naturally embedded in human life. It is non-intentional with no a priori objectives. We call this kind of learning informal learning. Young people spend, even during their life span with the highest share of formal education, more time in front of digital media screens than in formal settings inside schools. Better understanding of digital media's alteration mechanism should help to improve practice of informal learning by learners, methods of teaching, and envisioning and design of new learning environments.

The aim of the present study is to have a better understanding of digital media's alteration mechanism to enable learners and teachers to choose, combine and utilize different mechanism in the best possible way. Therefore, the focus of the present study is to understand the alteration mechanism of digital media which are used by learners in their everyday life and not on dedicated courseware like MOOCs or systems for distance education. Just talking about the possibility to learn everywhere and at any time is not enough, because that has already been a consequence of the invention of writing and book printing. To broaden the perspective, which is currently focused on transferring knowledge from teacher to learner, deeper insights into characteristics of related learning theories and epistemologies are necessary.

To gain a better understanding for digital media's alteration mechanism on learner's perception sphere, we firstly capture real-life learning episodes via pictures, videos, and text annotations in the domains of cognitive, affective, and psychomotor learning. Next, we analyze the learning episodes through the 'glasses' of the two main learning theories of the 20th and 21st century, objectivism and constructivism, to identify basic alteration mechanisms. Finally, we develop a category system for those mechanisms. On that basis we can give first proposals for how teachers can guide learners in the process of informal learning in the digital age and how they can bridge informal with formal learning.

2 Informal Learning

2.1 Formal, Non-formal, and Informal Learning

Learning in general can be defined as acquiring new or modifying existing knowledge, skills, competencies, and perceptions which lead to alterations in thinking, feeling, and behavior. Depending on the chosen definition of learning and its measurement, only around 25% of it happens in formal or non-formal settings. *Formal* learning is systematic organized learning within a formal learning system like universities or schools with specified objectives and degrees awarded by the system. *Non-formal* learning is similar but conducted outside of the formal learning system, e.g. in organizations for further education, vocational training settings, or youth organizations. Also, self-study with certain learning objectives, e.g. watching a recorded lecture or using a learning app is part of non-formal learning.

The predominant part of learning happens in informal settings. In those, learning is not the main aim, it happens en passant as a by-product of something else, e.g. playing a game on the computer, competing in a bike race, or cheating during an exam. Very often the contexts for informal learning are day-to-day situations but it can also be a formal learning setting where informal learning is not intended. Normally, informal learning doesn't lead to a formal degree, whereby the formal acknowledgment of outcomes is a widely-discussed topic. Informal learning can happen in different contexts: Family, school, work, leisure time, or social communities [1, 10, 20].

In summary, informal learning is characterized by:

- Non-intentionality
- Absence of structure
- Absence of a priori set objectives
- Occurrence in day-to-day situations outside of educational institutions
- No formal degree
- Ongoing, pervasive, and natural connection with life
- Domains of learning

As shown in the section on methodology in Sect. 4, real-life learning episodes are captured by learners in the form of videos, pictures, and annotations. The first step of analysis is assigning them to certain learning domains. For the purposes of this study, considered learning domains are based on the well-established and widely discussed taxonomy of learning objectives by Benjamin Bloom and his colleagues [5, 29]. However, as informal learning has per definition no a priori defined learning objectives, we focus more on outcomes than on objectives and use the notation of *domains*.

The focus of learning in the *cognitive domain* is the ability to recall facts, methods and processes. Bloom and his colleagues identified six categories of cognitive learning outcomes with different levels of difficulty, in that the first must be mastered before the next. The first level, knowledge, comprises remembering facts, definitions, basic concepts, or answers without necessarily understanding what they mean. Understanding means to be able to explain information to oneself and others. Apply covers the capability to use those facts, definitions, or concepts to solve well-structured problems with a 'correct' answer. Analyze covers comparing and elaborating differences and similarities between information bits to solve semi- and unstructured problems. Synthesis means to merge and combine facts with creative ideas to create novel and unique answers to problems. Finally, the sixth level called evaluation, covers the capability to make critical judgements based on solid knowledge.

Learning in the *affective domain* [28] focusses on perceptions, attitudes, emotions, feelings, values, and norms. The basic level is receiving, the precondition for the other levels. It covers the willingness to listen, to give attention to a certain topic, and to follow up with something. The next level, responding, comprises learner's active participation expressed by a certain reaction like asking questions, sharing information, or giving some likes. Valuing occurs if the learner associates a certain value to the content learned from their personal point of view and develops a willingness to be involved. Organizing is putting together different information, ideas, and attributed values and embed them into one's own mental model. Finally, characterizing is building abstract implicit and explicit knowledge on a certain domain and to become willing to change behavior, lifestyle, and way of life.

Learning in the *psychomotor domain* [3] concerns physical coordination and movement in relationship with cognitive and affective processes. Examples are handwriting, doing sports, operating a complex machine like a car, or playing a computer game. Imitate means the ability to replicate the actions of others based on observations. To reproduce standardized actions from memory or instructions is called manipulate in that taxonomy. Perfect covers to perform actions without external interventions and to demonstrate and explain them to others. Articulate comprises the capability to perform actions in a non-standard way, in different context, or using alternative tools and instruments. Finally, embody means performing actions in an automatic, intuitive way appropriate to the given context.

2.2 Theories of Learning as Point of View

To find different alteration mechanism of digital media we study their impact in real world learning episodes. As those episodes are very complex, like every real-world phenomenon, we must reduce complexity by using a certain point of view, a dedicated 'lens', in form of a theory of learning. Many of those theories were generated during the last decades and centuries. They should explain how people learn and act by applying them on observations in the field. For the purposes of this study we will look at learning episodes through the lens of objectivism and constructivism and their related subcategories. For an in-depth analysis of these theories as well as their relationships to epistemology see [19].

The *objectivist* point of view posits knowledge as existing objectively beyond our minds, as finite truth. It is based on the dualism of one's own mind and the world around it. The focus of behaviorist learning theories is how particular behavior is changed by certain learnings. Cognitivism tries to overcome those limitations of behaviorism by understanding the 'black box' of the human mind. Its' focus is to understand mental processes to promote learning effectively.

Constructivism refers both to a learning theory (how humans learn) and to an epistemology (the nature of knowledge). It postulates that humans construct their own knowledge of the world by experiencing and interacting. Thus, knowledge is dynamic and changing, constructed and negotiated in social context, rather than something absolute and finite. The teacher's task is no longer only to transfer his knowledge to the brains of students effectively but to help them build their own knowledge by creating supporting environments. Glasersfeld [15] emphasizes, that memorization and rote learning are not useless. But to solve problems that are not exactly presented during instruction the student requires conceptual understanding, the ability to rearrange memorized facts just as abstract building blocks and to relate them to already learned processes fitting challenges of a novel problem situation.

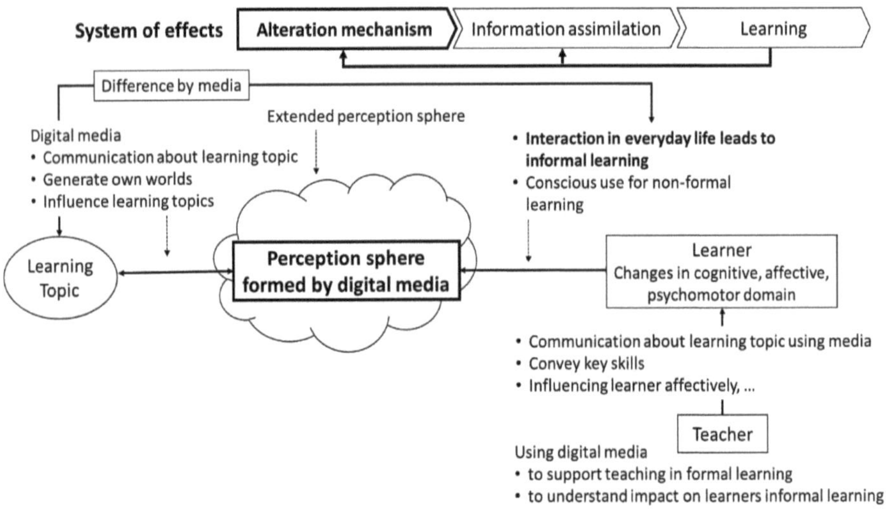

Fig. 1. System of effects in which digital media can alter informal learning.

Collaborativist learning theory is based on constructivism and emerged with the advent of networked computers. The basic assumption is that computer networking creates new opportunities to share multiple perspectives, to foster reflective thinking skills, and to build a multidimensional and multidisciplinary understanding instead of putting emphasis on one 'correct' answer. Learning happens by interacting with others using online environments. An example is the significant increase in using self-monitoring devices which create content in form of vital and performance data and to share it with millions of peers on fitness platforms like Strava (www.strava.com) and Garmin Connect (connect.garmin.com). Increased awareness of exercise and nutrition as well as self-responsibility for one's own fitness and health are resulting learnings [43]. Figure 5 shows the analyzing process of such a learning episode within the current study.

3 Digital Media and Its System of Effects

3.1 Media as Communication

For the scope of the present study, media should be defined as 'means or channels of communication between humans, machines and humans, or among machines, forming a perception sphere for the participants of the communication process'. We do not see media just as means to represent and transport a certain part of reality, but rather to communicate a certain *view* on reality. That view is built by the creator of the communication content and is shaped by his individual social and cultural background, political intentions, personal capabilities, or business interests. On the other hand, media is perceived individually by each recipient depending on his personal background – see also the discussion of the constructivist view in Sect. 2.3. For a more in-depth discussion see [47] and quoted literature.

Because of this, media are not a substitution for reality, but a means to communicate individually perceived reality. The content of this communication process forms a perception sphere for the participants to perceive secondary experiences as discussed in Sect. 3.2.3.

3.2 The System of Effects in Which Digital Media Can Alter Informal Learning

Digital media do not alter learning in general or informal learning directly, deterministically and simultaneously in the sense of a cause-effect-chain. They can change informal learning by bringing alterations into a complex system of effects as shown in Fig. 1 and discussed in system theory [51].

Digital media's alteration mechanism, which build the focus of the present study, create changed conditions for the learner to perceive aspects of the learning topic. For learning, those functions have in the first instance to be utilized by the learner in form of perceiving and assimilating altered information on the learning topic. Afterwards, that information can lead to learning processes by the learner, expressed by changes in the cognitive, affective, or psychomotor domain. That learning influences in form of feedback loops further information assimilation just as selection and use of certain digital media.

Aspects of Learning

Figure 1 shows the learner with changes of knowledge, skills, competencies, and perceptions which lead to alterations in thinking, feeling, and behavior. In this way, we defined learning in the cognitive, affective, and psychomotor domain. A main research question in this area is: *How does learning change in the context of digital media, considering the process as well as the outcomes?* Disciplines involved in such questions are mainly *learning theory, learning psychology, cognitive science, and pedagogy*. This question is not in the domain of the present study, but elements from those research areas are very valuable fundamentals.

Aspects of Information Assimilation Using Media

A prerequisite for learning is *information assimilation* [4] whereby this information is received by communication processes. The teacher communicates with learners referring to a certain learning topic using different media like speech, writing on the blackboard, textbooks, or digital media. The aim is to support learning on the selected topic. Choosing and shaping these topics is based on values and norms of the society, political and ethical decisions, curriculums of the formal learning system as well as on personal interests of teachers and learners. Also, conveying key skills qualification as discussed in Sect. 6.1 or influencing learners affectively, e.g. by increasing their interest in the learning topic, are important activities of the teacher. The connection to digital media is twofold. Firstly, the teacher can use digital media to support his own teaching within *formal learning settings* using e.g. massive open online courses (MOOCs) or adaptive learning systems (ALS). Secondly, he can use certain digital media by himself to better understand them and gain an impression of impacts on informal, everyday learning of his learners. That aspect is widely underestimated but has major significance regarding the importance of learner's informal learning in the context of digital media. *Which media teachers should use to support teaching and how they should do it* is the main research area of pedagogy, especially media pedagogy. This will not be a point of focus in the present study but is discussed based on identified media's alteration mechanism in Sect. 6.

A main question from *communication science* is: *how does the interaction processes between an individual and media form his perception sphere?* This interaction process together with the related information assimilation is a prerequisite for learning. A main question within this domain is: which media are used by which groups of humans and for what reasons?

Aspects of Perception Sphere Formed by Digital Media

Digital media together with other media and complex psychological and social structures form learner's extended perception sphere. That is mainly the focus of *psychology, sociology, ethnography, and media studies*. The latter have a special interest in the difference by media. Media is not the representation of a learning object, this would enable primary experiences for learners, but it enables the communication about it, allowing learners to form secondary experiences. This secondary experience is always based on individual interests and intentions of the creator of the media, in the context of digital media as well as of lectures, printed newspapers, books, or documentary movies in TV. At the same time, that secondary experience is also contingent on learner's individual perception. The spread between those two experiences of learners is the difference by media [47].

The perception sphere in general and particularly that one formed by digital media has besides communicating about a learning object two other functions. It generates its one world, quite far of or totally decoupled from the physical world and related primary experiences. To know about that function of digital media can be an important key skills qualification for learners, e.g. in the context of video gaming and eSport: To be able to distinguish between the world generated by the perception sphere formed by digital media on the one hand and the physical world on the other. That difference generated by media is the core question of *media studies*. The perception sphere covers a third important function: It influences attributes of the physical object. For example, political communication is often aligned to the functions of certain media used. Because of this recursive relationship between media and object, the naive belief of media representing the physical world becomes logically impossible.

When new, extended, or changed mechanism of media appear, as witnessed in the case of digital media during the last years, the perception sphere alters. Learners can use alterations in forms of new or advanced learning systems like online courses or learning apps consciously with clear learning aims in form of non-formal learning as defined above. Examples are vocabulary training apps or research in electronic journals for writing a course paper.

The focus of the present study are not those alterations of the perception sphere in relation with formal or non-formal learning, but rather with *informal learning*. When learner's perception sphere is changed by digital media's alteration mechanism, also learner's interaction with it in daily routines will change. This natural behavior in everyday life is the starting point and context for informal learning. An example is performing a multiplayer videogame and learning informally about social behavior in virtual spaces.

Digital media's alteration mechanism are mostly not totally new – depending on the level of abstraction. At a very high abstraction level, nothing is new. We can trace back the phenomena of fake news to the manipulated information created about the battle between Ramses II (1303-1213 BC) and the Hittites using lapidary hieroglyphs. Everywhere-everytime learning is possible since the invention of writing and book printing, and the echo chamber effect is widely spread in traditional newspapers doing market research in the reader market to better shape their content. It is the core aim of the present study to identify digital media's alteration mechanism on a more sophisticated level, because they differ significantly in their subtle mechanism, speed, geographical and demographical reach, dissemination, involved actors, or underlying interests. Therefore, informal learning gains fresh opportunities as well as risks within the system of effects.

To identify digital media's alteration mechanism and to present exemplary learning episodes using them is the core of the present study. The value of those results is the following. Firstly, research dealing with digital media in learning theory, learning psychology, cognitive science, or pedagogy should obtain a more differentiated view on digital media than is currently the case. Today, digital media is most often described using general terms such as Internet, email, social media, or computer mediated communication. Those highly aggregated terms often result in generalizing formulated research output. On the other hand, when more specific results are presented, those are based on a certain form of the general type of digital media with high variation between different forms, not allowing for conclusions about the general term used. For example, the term social media covers user generated content in digital newspapers, activities in messenger services, multiplayer videogames and eSports, or by means of vital and performance sensors directly linked to athletes. Therefore, research findings can be valid only for a certain form of a general term with very quickly changing properties due to technology innovations. Thus, the results of the present study should give a much more sophisticated view on digital media's alteration mechanism allowing for more differentiation in the disciplines by focusing on 'information assimilation' and 'learning' in the system of effects shown in Fig. 1.

Secondly, the results of the present study should allow *learners* to become aware of the difference through media, but not only on the 'What' but also on the 'How' based on identified alteration mechanism. This allows learners to better understand what they are doing, possible gains and risks associated with it, and adjusts their perception as well as their media usage. That seems to be one of the most important key skills in the age of digital.

Thirdly, *teachers* should be able to better understand learners informal learning in every day settings on a much more differentiated level than 'using the smartphone every time' or 'playing computer games intensively'. This allows for more sophisticated linking between formal and informal settings just like the conveying of key skills as discussed in Sect. 6. As a side effect, teachers learn to use digital media in formal settings better aligned with their own teaching.

Finally, researchers in related fields, learners, and teachers can benefit from the results in form of *properties of digital media*, the alteration mechanism, instead of certain product categories or brands like email, social media, or Facebook. Product categories and brands change their characteristics very quickly and often have a very short lifecycle on the market due to rapid technological changes and changes in user adoption. Using properties instead allows the reconfiguration of identified alteration mechanism to best fit new or enhanced digital media in learner's perception sphere independently from a present product category or brand.

3.3 Primary Media Functions

The focus of the present study are digital media's alteration mechanisms in learner's perception sphere. Thus, the center of analysis are *not* empirical findings on changes in different learning settings caused by digital media or recommendation for using digital media in the context of learning but *enabling factors* for such changes facilitated by digital media. This allows us firstly, to better understand the reasons for observed changes in learning and their relationship to digital media and secondly, to envision and design new learning environments. The starting point for the category system of alteration mechanisms are *primary media functions* defined as properties of media to support handling of the communication content [26, 50].

Create and delete allows to produce and delete communication content e.g. symbols like letters, pictures, videos, drawings, or models. An example of using this primary function is to make pictures and videos with omnipresent smartphones. Normally, the creator of a content assumes its permanency until someone deletes it. Thus, deletion is a related function of media. Examples of digital medias alteration in deletion are Snapchat with its value proposition of deletion after some seconds or issues in the violent discussion on the 'right to be forgotten' within the universe of digital media.

Arrange and link facilitates the organization of communication content. By arranging, the content is grouped together in spatial proximity within a certain perception sphere. Examples are digital documents stored in the same folder or organic results of Google search. Thus, arranging is not a characteristic of the content itself as the spatial proximity is generated by human intervention or software algorithm without changing the content entity. Linking implies a reference within the communication content to some other showing relationships. Therefore, it is a property of the communication content. Examples of using that primary function are hypertext links or recommendations on e-commerce sites. Arrange and link are the core functions for creating a perception sphere, contrary to a single linear information entity. Thus, arrange and link is one of digital media's most powerful alteration mechanism for learner's perception sphere.

Transmit and access comprises the exchange of information content between humans, humans and machines, or directly between machines without human intervention as discussed in the context of internet of things [44]. A core characteristic of transmit is the existence of a certain addressee of the communication content. Therefore, transmit leads to push communication in one-to-one, one-to-many, many-to-one, or many-to-many settings. Examples for using that alteration mechanism are sending emails or making video calls. Contrary to transmit, access doesn't require any intervention of communication content's creator after creation. Others access the content in the perception sphere in a pull mode based on their access rights. Examples are accessing a web site or the use of social media groups.

3.4 Types of Digital Media

After the widespread use of the personal computers and the launch of the Internet in 1989 followed by the rise of social media around 2004, settings like computer based training and intelligent tutoring systems, followed by MOOCs (massive open online learning), PLEs (personalized learning environments) and ALS (adaptive learning systems), and online communities of practice became parts of learning processes [19], (Kindle-Position 4178). As those systems are designed and used to support formal learning, they are not the focus of the present study. In the present study, the focus lies on digital media used by learners in their everyday life, e.g. popular social media sites, online games, or browsing the World Wide Web. Figure 2 shows the use of widespread forms of digital media and compares it with traditional media. For an extensive review of different ways to build a typology of digital media see [49].

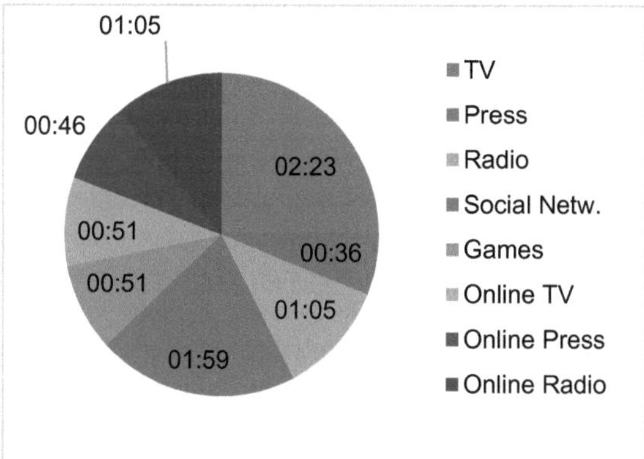

Fig. 2. Daily media consumption in hours, n = 153.501, age 16–64, 36 countries around the world (source: [16, 45]). Other online activities like browsing and e-commerce not included.

The focus of Fig. 2 is on media, whereby its content is *generated by humans*, like online press. Currently, software agents often called *bots* strongly gain in importance for all primary media functions mentioned above. They can be embedded in other software, act invisibly to human users, and create, arrange, and transfer communication content automatically without human intervention. Further types of communication content generated by machines are performance and vital data in the field of self-monitoring captured by sensors [43] or results of search engines and recommender systems.

4 Methodology

The main aim of the present study is to better understand the alteration mechanism of digital media for learner's perception sphere. This broadened understanding can help improve practice of informal learning by learners, methods of teaching, and to envision and design new learning environments. Therefore, the research question is: *What are digital media's alteration mechanism for learner's perception sphere?* It's not the aim to find representative results for a certain population or to evaluate a certain technical system. Thus, the methodology applied is selected by its added value to gain insights into digital media's alteration mechanism and not its representativeness for a certain population by testing hypothesis, as is often the goal of quantitative methods.

4.1 Main Elements of Methodology Used

Why observations and not questionnaires?

As the main aim of the present study is to identify digital media's alteration mechanism, we must deal with widely unknown questions in two domains. Firstly, as we do not know the alteration mechanism, we cannot ask participants for them in a questionnaire format as neither the researcher nor the participants are fully aware of them. If we would ask participants, we would get memories of only partly consciously perceived impacts of digital media. This challenge is similar to researching life satisfaction in contrast to happiness. The first can be measured with questionnaires and retrospective questions like: Are you satisfied with your income, your social relations, your personal success? On the contrary, happiness is built by sequentially linked moments of perceptions and feelings. It can be best captured at the time of occurrence. For a detailed discussion see [24].

For the aims of the present study we mainly apply observations by learners themselves as well as by researchers to capture data. We are aware of difficulties to control extraneous variables, which can be managed more easily using questionnaires or controlled lab experiments. Also, the research effort expressed in time and money needed is significantly higher than for questionnaires or lab experiments. Nevertheless, observations of everyday life learning episodes are applied. This is due to the primary aim being the discovery of different alteration mechanism of digital media and not the obtaining of results of a behavior within a certain population with a high external and internal validity and aiming to generalize results. To better understand the unobservable processes within participant's perception sphere, we supplement observations by focus groups with participants just as well as questionnaires filled out simultaneously or within some hours of media usage.

Why field study and not experimental lab setting?

As informal learning happens en passant while doing other things, it is a major aim to *not* control as many extraneous variables as possible. This would strongly contrast with the main characteristic of informal learning: happening en passant, by accident, and triggered by other activities. We are aware that the uniqueness of each observational situation in the field makes it difficult to generalize results and apply them to other occasions. This lower external validity seems to be acceptable as we do not want to find causal chains between certain digital media and alterations in learner's behavior. Rather the identification of frequently occurring alterations mechanism of digital media is the main research aim.

Why intercultural?

Many studies on digital media and informal learning are limited to bachelor students taking a related course. According to [22] 68% of research subjects in a sample of hundreds of studies in world's top psychology journals came from the United States, and 96% from Western industrialized nations. Of the American subjects, 67% were undergraduates studying psychology. Those studies have a strong focus on internal validity and statistical significance. To conclude from this very narrow view on digital media usage to general alteration mechanism on informal learning would imply a certain kind of cultural imperialism in the sense: all people in the world are using, or should use, the same digital media with the same consequences for the same aims of learning. That view would on the one hand neglect technical innovations especially from Asia, which are widely unknown or at least not widespread in the western hemisphere, such as WeChat or Alibaba. On the other hand, significantly different cultural backgrounds like the use of WeChat as a social control mechanism in China shaped by Confucianism are neglected. Thus, we have a strong motivation on doing our research in different countries, also in remote areas and unusual learning situations, not for comparing different cultures but for finding additional alteration mechanism.

Why use of screen capturing and videos and not behavioral tracking?

Use of digital media gives the opportunity to track user behavior automatically. Examples are pages visited, search queries, click streams, content displayed or purchases in eShops. For the aims of the present study we do not use automated tracking, but we ask learners to capture screencasts from its own usage behavior via the mobile phone or personal computer and annotate them by voice comments directly during media usage. Alternatively, the learners produce a video clip from the learning episode, e.g. of flying a drone. Immediately after finishing the captured learning episode they filled out a questionnaire to give more insights into their usage motivation and the perceived alterations in learning due to its media usage. In this way we gain deeper insights into digital media's alteration mechanism, because the learner is no longer a black box.

Why qualitative content analysis based on videographics and not semi-quantitative data analysis?

For data capturing also vital sensors are used to measure delivered power, hearth rate variability, running speed, or oxygen saturation in muscles. Those devices deliver quantitative raw data which could be used for quantitative empirical research. We capture that data, but we do not use them directly in the present study. Many studies on digital media usage are *semi quantitative*. That means, that the raw data are qualitative, captured by interviews and questionnaires based on participant's memories or opinions. Afterwards, these qualitative data are used for quantitative data analysis that results in quantitative results with a strong focus on internal validity and significance.

For the purposes of this study qualitative content analysis [30] based on videographics [21] is used as the main research methodology with a strong emphasis put on quality criteria as described below. This allows us to capture informal learning episodes in everyday life while they are happening, gain insights into alterations and an in-depth understanding. On that basis, digital media's alteration mechanism can be identified iteratively and step by step during the research process embedded in theoretical frameworks following the principles of grounded theory [8].

It is not the aim of the present study to describe causal relationships between digital media usage and informal learning in form of models, interrelationships, and numeric evidence to predict future impact. This would be the field for quantitative research. For the long history of the discussion regarding those apparent conflicting research methodologies as a detailed description of qualitative content analysis see [9, 30, 37].

4.2 Data Capturing

The methodology used for capturing learning episodes in the field *by learners themselves* in form of videos pictures, and annotations is based on autovideography and photovoice [17, 54, 59]. Video gained in importance tremendously during the last decade. At YouTube, 300 h of video are uploaded every minute and five billion videos are watched every single day by 30 million daily visitors [38]. Thus, streamed video has become not only a major source for informal learning but also a familiar means of communication. Whereas the most common source for scientific content analysis is still text as well as for presenting scientific work [21].

In the present study the learners capture informal learning episodes perceived as being significantly changed by digital media. Mostly a screencast software is used on their own smartphones and personal computers to record the clickstream during a certain learning episode and to annotate it by voice comments simultaneously. For learning episodes outside the smartphone/personal computer context, e.g. flying a drone, a video sequence is recorded by smartphone. In total, 77 learners captured, annotated, and edited 373 learning episodes between October 2017 and May 2018.

Episodes are also captured by researchers, using participatory action research (PAR) [27]. That methodology applies also screencasts and videography approaches but is extended with video capturing devices like action cams, vital sensors like power meters, SmO2 measurement, and speed meters. The resulting video recordings are edited and further annotated immediately after the learning episode or together with others at the evening.

To analyze that data, qualitative content analysis and grounded theory [8] is applied, subsequently to ten years of preceding studies with several hundreds of participants as shown in [42].

Capture Stream 1: Day Reconstruction Method (DRM)

The aim of the first capture stream, the day reconstruction method (DRM) is to obtain learning episodes within a seven-day period in learner's everyday life. It's not the aim to capture the whole seven-day period to gain results which are representative for a participant's life but rather to have the opportunity to capture the most interesting episodes, impacted by digital media significantly. The method is based on the widely recognized work of the Nobel prize winner Kahneman [24], for detailed instrument documentation see [25].

Diploma students were instructed at the beginning of their work in fundamentals of informal learning, digital media, the aims of the ongoing research work, and the processes of the day reconstruction method. They also studied basic literature on those topics. To extend the reach of participants outside students of economics and information systems they recruited further participants by themselves. Finally, 27 learners captured, annotated, and edited 299 learning episodes.

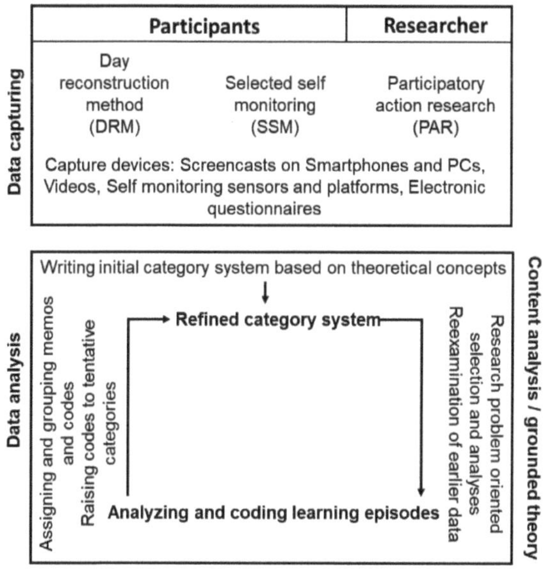

Fig. 3. Methodology used to gain insights into digital media's alteration mechanism (source: [45]).

At the beginning of the study learners completed a questionnaire regarding their usage behavior of digital media including devices, software, and services. Additionally, they are asked for demographic data. Within the following period, learners capture three or four learning episodes every day by using a screencast software on their smartphones or personal computers and annotate them during recording with voice overlays. Alternatively, they film a certain usage behavior with their smartphone. The main selection criteria for capturing a learning episode are: it happens in everyday life or during breaks in formal education or vocational trainings, it happens en passant while doing something else, there are no clear learning goals, there is a clear connection to digital media, and informal learning is changed significantly.

After recording, they edit the video clip and fill out one row in the 'short note' questionnaire on the same device used to capture the episode. The main elements of this description of the episode are a title, beginning and end time, the reason for the episode, a description of activities fulfilled, and the learnings perceived. For each captured learning episode, the learners complete a questionnaire every evening describing perceived alteration mechanism. The questions are based on the theoretical background of learning domains as shown above including cognitive, affective, and psychomotor learning and the preliminary category system of alteration mechanism.

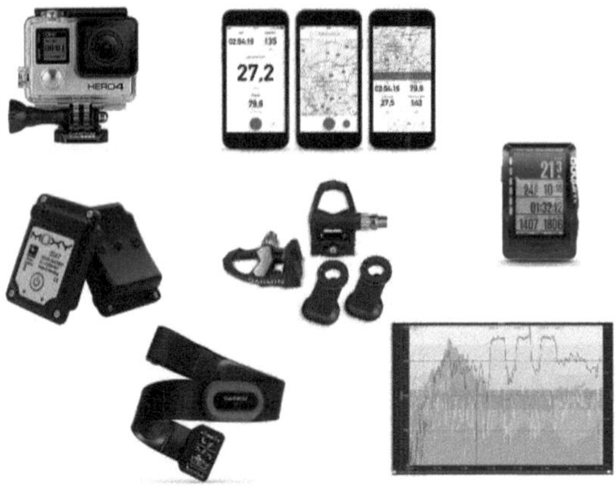

Fig. 4. Vital and performance sensors connected with social sharing platforms used in the PAR-stream.

Capture Stream 2: Selected Self-monitoring (SSM)
In the SSM-stream 50 participants of bachelor and master courses capture learning episodes perceived as significantly altered by digital media. The capture procedure and the questionnaires are the same as in the DRM-stream. The main difference between the two streams is the added team phase in the SSM-stream. After finishing recording and editing their individual learning episodes, the participants discuss the results in teams of five and select the best episodes according to the criteria shown in the section on the DRM-stream. Afterwards, they present their results to the researcher team to discuss them. According to the results of this discussion process the group refine their episodes or produce additional ones. Finally, they write a course paper on the presented learning episodes, describing their trigger for creating a episode, the actions fulfilled, the learnings in the cognitive, affective, and psychomotor domain and finally assigning them to different alteration mechanism of digital media. In total, 74 episodes were selected by the groups, analyzed in detail and presented to other learners and the research team.

Capture Stream 3: Participatory Action Research (PAR)
Capturing of learning episodes within the PAR-stream is done by researchers and not learners. Its aim is to supplement the DRM- and SSM-stream in the following areas: Firstly, not only students and their peers in highly developed countries are involved. Rather, the focus is on everyday situations in remote areas of different countries, thereby also involving learners which are far off any university relationship and atmosphere. An example is the significantly different use of smartphones in Uganda, powered by little solar panels, for mobile banking. It is done, without any involvement of a bank, to pay certain obligations like the apartment rent by transferring calling credits to the creditor. They use the same notion of mobile banking, but with a totally different impact on their everyday life and their learning. This capture stream should avoid the strong bias often found in empirical studies focused on undergraduate students from Western industrialized nations [22] and associated conclusions, e.g. on the topic of digital divide.

Fig. 5. Analysis of road biking in South Korea considering different learning domains (source: [45]).

Secondly, quantitative data are collected using different sensors and dedicated software to measure alterations especially in the psychomotor domain and their impact on the cognitive and affective domain. Figure 4 shows some of the devices used by the researcher. Action cams support capturing of psychomotor activities and synchronous annotation of perceived learning effects especially in the affective domain which can be hardly captured retrospectively with traditional methods. Additionally, route planning software and GPS tracking is used, mainly impacting the cognitive domain. SmO2 sensors are applied to measure oxygen accumulation as indicator for psychomotor activities. Also, power meters are used to measure performance data in relation with vital functions and to share them on platforms with millions of participants (for details see [43]). Finally, chest straps are applied to measure hearth frequency and HF-variability together with social sharing activities. Especially those sharing activities of vital and performance data show a strong alteration of informal learning in all three learning domains.

Besides self-observation using performance and vital sensors, social sharing platforms, and dedicated software, researchers capture unusual every day learning episodes of others in significantly different contexts than the DRM- and SSM-stream can deliver. An example is shown in Fig. 5. An important aim of the PAR-stream is to identify and capture learning episodes in learning domains which are not covered by the DRM- and SSM-stream, as well as alteration mechanism not captured in-depth within DRM and SSM. Those are mainly episodes in rural areas where digital media are used in different ways and for different aims.

To capture unusual learning episodes in everyday life contexts, the researchers travel to remote areas by public transportation and bicycle. This allows for significantly different insights in digital media's alteration mechanism due to the closeness to learners' everyday life situations. This very tedious, time consuming, and expensive kind of data capturing pays off because of the considerably different, significantly deeper, and surprising insights into digital medias alterations. It's an essential requirement to fulfill the corner point of 'understanding' as given above describing the basic elements of the methodology.

4.3 Data Analysis

The process of data analysis and its interrelationship with data capturing is shown in Fig. 3. Basically, it follows the principle of grounded theory [7, 8] and qualitative content analysis. The aim is to capture qualitative data about informal learning episodes to generate and extend theory about alteration mechanism of digital media inductively. Starting point is the main research question: *What are digital media's alteration mechanism on learner's perception sphere?* In a first step, well-established concepts on epistemology issues of learning just as on different learning domains are selected with a focus on informal learning. Simultaneously, literature on basic mechanism of digital media is reviewed and systematically grouped by certain research questions and methodology issues. Based on that, an initial category system of alteration mechanism is written based on primary media functions as has been described above. Afterwards, empirical results from captured learning episodes are coded and the used category system is reviewed, refined, and extended iteratively during the whole process of data capturing. Same or similar alteration mechanism are grouped together, and groups of mechanism are assigned to main groups. During this process, the research team looks out for coherent mechanisms, plausible relations between them, and aims to reach an exhaustive category system of digital media's alteration mechanism. The main guideline during the analysis is the additional value of categories concerning the research questions.

The analyzing process of the learning episodes is performed by three researchers with the software MAXQDA. The first step of the research analysis is to assign the learning episodes, or certain parts of them, to one or more learning domains. For this, the learning episodes were analyzed according to the main characteristics of cognitive, affective, and psychomotor learning. If single parts of the learning episode were related to different learning domains, those parts were marked and assigned within MAXQDA separately.

A very valuable source for assigning learning episodes, or certain parts of them, to learning domains and tentative alteration mechanism are learner's annotations as part of the captured learning episodes. They express learners' view on altered learning domains and involved alteration mechanism. Those annotations are supplemented by the questionnaires completed by the learners daily.

Additionally, the researchers facilitated group meetings with 26 learners arranged into groups of five. In meetings that lasted at least 75 min, the learners discuss with the researchers selected learning episodes in detail, especially activities performed and the motivation behind them, perceived learning alterations, and involved alteration mechanism. The facilitators, which also code the learning episodes, make extensive notes to better understand the learning episodes and further increase intercoder reliability.

4.4 Ensure Compliance with Quality Criteria

Special attention is paid to quality criteria of qualitative research as discussed by [30, p. 201]. *Internal validity* should ensure reliability, trustworthiness, compliance with rules, and intersubjective traceability. All captured data are documented in form of annotated videos captured by learners themselves. Simultaneously to or only some hours after data capturing, questionnaires are filled out by participants to better understand the context of the learning episode. To ensure a high intercoder reliability memos are used extensively. Many episodes are coded by more than one researcher, followed by in-depth review meetings to discuss reasons for different coding results. Also, the joined facilitated focus group meetings increased intercoder reliability. The learners also annotated the videos with the categories and used them in the questionnaire. The categories are shown in this publication and have also been used for coding the captured video sequences.

External validity should enable generalizability and transferability of results to ensure their relevance not only for the analyzed learning episodes. In quantitative research this should be obtained by random or quota sampling, many participants, and sophisticated statistical methods. Due to the relatively small number of participants in qualitative research, other methods must be used. A central aspect is that 'truth' in the sense of the correct representation of states or events of an external world is replaced by *'viability'*. Findings are viable if they prove adequate in the context in which they were created. Thus, they must be seen in a context of problems to be solved, goals, and purposes. For a detailed discussion of viability see [15, 35]. To obtain a high degree of viability, the following measures were carried out. In peer briefings, experts comment methodological issues as well as findings. The performed focus groups with participants allow feedback on findings, especially on digital media's alteration mechanism. Very important for ensuring a high degree of viability are the extended field phases in all three streams of data capturing. Within the DRM and SSM stream, participants capture learning episodes in their natural environment and not in an artificial situation as is the case with laboratory experiments or traditional survey research. In the PAR stream, the researchers spent many weeks in remote areas and different cultures to study digital media usage. The triangulation of those three approaches allows for different views on digital media's alteration mechanism and ensures a high level of viability.

5 Findings

Table 1 shows digital media's core alteration mechanism for learners' perception sphere as identified after several iterative cycles between analyzing and categorizing captured learning episodes on the one hand and theoretical views from learning theory and epistemology on different learning domains on the other. This categorization is neither exhaustive nor mutually exclusive. In traditional broadcast media like printed newspaper the three domains of *create and delete, arrange and link, and transmit and access* mostly form a linear step-by-step sequence of activities, ranging from writing an article by an editor to reading the newspaper by the reader. In a perception sphere formed by digital media this is not the case. An activity in one domain immediately triggers mechanism in another one, whereas this alteration initiates further mechanism. One communication activity is mostly impacted by different related alteration mechanisms at the same time. The resulting interdependent communication contents form the perception sphere. Communication content is not only created by humans or machines explicitly as autonomous entities. Also, its dynamic structure due to *arranging and linking* those entities forms content. Additionally, a certain browsing behavior creates a new perspective on communication content and also leads to altered content within the perception sphere. Relations between content in form of spatial proximity like search results or semantical proximity due to linking, create new content and become important parts of the perception sphere. Also, the behavior in *accessing* creates new content, e.g. due to tracking user behavior and deduced recommendations such as 'most read' or 'other users also looked at …'. Those examples show the *multiple forms of generating communication content in learner's perception sphere* formed by digital media in contrast to linear broadcast content like a lecture, book or educational film.

The alteration mechanisms in Table 1 should be interpreted as *enabling factors* for higher degree of freedom in forming content and relationships within a perception sphere. They shouldn't be viewed as totally new capabilities or as inevitable improvements or deteriorations for informal learning. They are part of the system of effects discussed in Sect. 3.2.

Table 1. Digital media's alteration mechanisms for learners' perception sphere.

Domain of alteration mechanism	Alteration mechanism
Create and delete	1. Medialization 2. Omnipresent means of production 3. Real time reach 4. Copy-ability without loss and marginal costs 5. Traceability 6. No doubtlessness of deletion
Arrange and link	1. Divisibility 2. Multi-perspectivity 3. Associativity
Transmit and access	1. Efficient transmission 2. Immediacy 3. Searchability 4. Interactivity and Contingency 5. Ubiquity

5.1 Digital Media's Alteration Mechanism

The following section shows the main effects of digital media on learner's perception sphere. Consequently, they lead to changed conditions for information assimilation as a basis for informal learning. This altered perception sphere is characterized by:

- *High interactivity*: Learners are engaged into multipoint communication processes with peers using also symbols, pictures, and video heavily.
- *Personalization*: Perception spheres of learners differ significantly considering place and time of interaction, geographical scope, substance, and media used.
- *Associativity:* The perception sphere is characterized by a boundless network-like structure instead of a limited linear one.
- *Contingency*: The substance as well as the processes within the perception sphere are in principal open and depend significantly on learner's perception and media usage. An example is different clicking behavior in browsing a hypermedia structure, generating a totally different perception sphere after some clicks.
- *Playfulness*: The perception sphere offers more opportunities for playful interaction due to symbols, pictures, and video as content instead of speech and text only. It is also often 'gamificated' considering substance and processes and structured similarly to games. Also, the absence or decreased involvement of traditional authorities like parents or teachers in the perception sphere may increase its playfulness.

The author wants to *emphasize strongly* that those are characteristics of learners' perception sphere formed by digital media but not necessarily neither of learners extended perception sphere nor of informal learning as a whole, also including information assimilation and learning processes as shown in Fig. 1. The increase of a certain characteristic due to digital media can be compensated or even overcompensated by

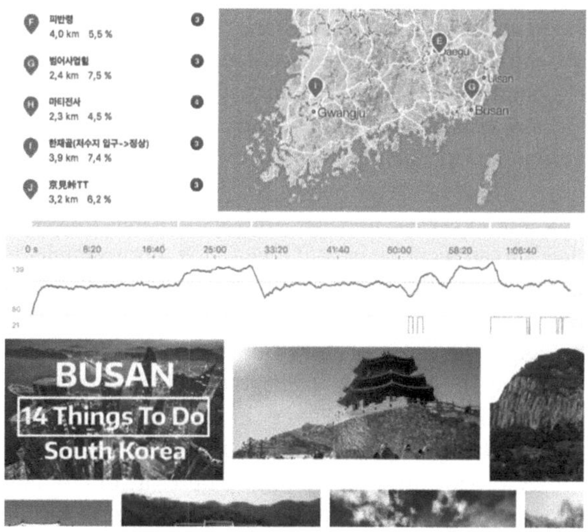

Fig. 6. Tracing a bike ride opens informal learning opportunities on local history, culture and geographic (source: [45]).

alterations in those other parts of the system of effects. For example: By using highly interactive, associative video games instead of a book with its simple letters forming a linear text, the capability of the human mind to build associations, to imaging certain characters, or to feel the atmosphere of the story can decrease, not only in the human part of the system of effects but also regarding the whole experience. The simple statements that digital media 'lead' to more interactive learning should be scrutinized critically.

Create and Delete

Medialization means the representation of a certain communication content by digital media instead of physical environments. A learning episode found in the present study in the psychomotor domain shows playing tennis with Nintendo's Wii in front of a screen instead of on a physical tennis court. This medialization leads to a medial difference [47] between the physical environment and the learning environment formed by digital media. Therefore, the learning environment doesn't represent the physical environment but becomes a new perception sphere with its own information content, linkage, forms of access (swinging the virtual tennis racket), and social rules. For the learner, it is 'reality' like playing on the court, but a different one. From a constructivist point of view, both realities are created by the learner himself. Nintendo's game designers have that in mind and don't try to imitate the physical game perfectly but exploit digital media's alteration mechanism. A further lucid learning episode found was to remotely control a drone. The medial difference to a human which cannot fly is so big that together with the alteration mechanism of multi-perspectivity sustained affective learning is stimulated, particularly considering values and norms. Informal learning happens more and more in environments which are created by humans and machines instead of by evolution's respectively God's design.

Traditional media requires rare and expensive means of production like presses, broadcasting stations, and complex logistic systems. Means of production of digital media are *omnipresent* in form of smartphones, personal computers, computerized things of daily life, and the Internet. The ubiquitous use of digital media alters learners' perception sphere continuously, largely independently from intentions, structures, and activities of the formal education system and its teachers. That means, that learning happens more and more independently from traditional authorities like parents, teachers, or publishers.

Digital media's omnipresence together with its efficient transmission of communication content leads to an increase in *real time reach*. For example, immediately after writing a blog post it can be read by thousands and millions of other people as well as by machine-based agents. This works similarly for real time sharing of performance and vital data on fitness platforms as shown in Fig. 5. No layouts, printing, physical distribution, or scanning to make the content readable by machines is necessary. Therefore, learners' perception sphere covers more content with promptness as core value. This content can also be used immediately for critical analysis and embedding in one's own point of view, both are often seen as the opposite of promptness. Promptness and in-depth analysis happen in the learning episode shown in Fig. 5.

While creating communication content, it can be copied without loss in quality, with no or extremely low marginal cost, and without much time needed. This *Copy-ability* leads to a significant increase in content in form of text, pictures, video, and linkages between them, and consequently leads to a strongly extended perception sphere for informal learning. Increased demands concerning affective capabilities are a consequence, particularly at the level of receiving, including awareness and willingness to hear, and giving attention to a certain issue. This alteration mechanism could be a fruitful connecting point between informal learning and formal settings with teachers – not only by 'teaching' media literacy but mainly by building a scaffold to learn informally at the levels of awareness and willingness during daily life behavior.

Traceability is mostly seen as an alteration mechanism for the domain of transmission and access. But it also strongly alters the creation of content. Every activity with digital media is traced, whether someone wants that or not – otherwise digital media wouldn't work technically. Google's organic search results as important communication content are strongly based on the search behavior of humans and machines. Tracing user behavior enables recommendations on e-commerce sites as personalized news feeds. Whereas the tracing is always done by machines, its object can be the behavior of humans, for example clicking patterns, or of machines, such as web crawlers which generate around a third of the Internet traffic. The results of tracing can be analyzed and used by humans or automatically by machines like the personalized arrangement of content by Facebook, which permanently creates new content. The consequence of this alteration mechanism is more communications content on the one hand and an increased richness of it on the other. As shown in Fig. 6, tracing vital and performance data from one's own bike ride or from live tracking shared by peers on platforms like Strava, Garmin Connect, or Komoot opens up possibilities for informal learning on geographic characteristics of the environment, recommended sightseeing opportunities, or historical and cultural insights into cities along the route. This alteration mechanism can bridge psychomotor activities with informal learning within the cognitive and affective domain.

The alteration mechanisms of copy-ability, efficient transmission, and real time reach lead to *no doubtlessness of deletion*. Immediately after creation, the communication content can be disseminated widely within the whole Internet and other networks with or without human intervention. Due to the impossibility of knowing the number of indistinguishable copies of certain content and their current storage location, it's hard to imagine that somebody can guarantee the full removal of certain communication content. That is the root of the discussion on 'the right to be forgotten', started by [36] and taken up by the European Commission afterwards. This alteration mechanism expands possibilities for informal learning as it extends the perception sphere with content, which otherwise would be deleted or disappeared. On the other hand, it can also inhibit learner's willingness to share opinions and personal data, and thus, also opportunities for one's own and other's informal learning shrink.

Arrange and Link

Divisibility allows to split communication content into any number of packages for re-arranging and separate sharing. A widespread example are playlists for audio and video files. This alteration mechanism can be directly led back to technical implications of digitalization, specifically discretization of signals. It facilitates micro learning, using small packages of learning content 'on-demand', e.g. while using a software product.

These packages are context sensitive and personalized, considering learner's actual need in real time, often resulting from a quick Google search. Consequently, en passant micro learning in the sense of informal learning increasingly replaces formal learning in traditional seminars on using certain software.

Multi-perspectivity allows the arrangement of communication content, or certain parts of it, in spatial proximity to other content. Because of this changed context, the content gain added value which can be used within altered information assimilation. An example is displaying blog posts arranged by author, date, certain predefined topics, or tags. In a broader sense, also individual browsing after querying a search engine creates a unique perspective on existing content. It's unlikely that another user searching for the same item in the same content will apply the same browsing sequence. Thus, every user generates its own perspective depending on its clicking and browsing behavior. That multi-perspectivity results in alterations in the cognitive learning domain, for example by finding different applications of a certain mathematical formula. The learner can gain a deeper understanding and can bring his knowledge from the low level of recalling the formula to applying it for different problems.

Associativity is best known by hyperlinks embedded in communication content and by recommender systems. Because of this embedding, the content itself changes and gains a new quality. This alteration mechanism is closely related to multi-perspectivity and both are core building blocks of digital media's alteration mechanism for learner's perception sphere. It does not only lead to alterations in the cognitive learning domain as shown in the example above, but also in the affective one. Associativity helps the learner to explore communication content triggered by a sudden perception, desire, emotion, or just by chance. Thus, he can gain awareness for a new issue, explore it immediately, and induce different valuing of a certain domain. For example, someone hears streamed music from a certain musician on a tablet computer or PC, learns that the artist changed his name several years ago, searches in Google to find out why, and ends up reading about a different religion largely unknown to him so far. At the same time, this is an example for wandering off the point caused by associativity and how hard it can be to stay attentive and concentrated on what you are doing at the moment. Thus, we speak in this study of 'alterations' and not 'improvements' for learners' perception sphere.

The alteration mechanism of arrange and link facilitates the shift from a mostly linear, self-contained content like a book or a movie to a multidimensional and borderless perception sphere. *Therefore, associativity is probably the most important alteration mechanism for learner's perception sphere.*

From the perspective of social systems theory, that perception sphere is an autopoietic system, characterized by a high level of contingency [34]. Its participants are not only humans but also machines controlled by algorithm, equipped with self-learning capabilities based on artificial intelligence. Those algorithms include functionalities similar to learning in the affective domain like giving *attention* to a certain issue, for example by an adapted search strategy. Examples for alterations in *responding* are automatic generated Likes or blog posts, and highly personalized intelligent agents changing *habitual behavior*. Currently, those algorithms try to catch up to human intelligence which is 'strong' particularly because of three capabilities: defining its own problem to be solved, specifying and adapting the problem-solving algorithm by itself, and modifying hardware during the process of problem solving, like changes in synapses of the human brain. When machines and their embedded algorithms achieve that goal and the algorithm are no longer programmed by humans but by machines themselves, the point of singularity is reached [33].

Transmit and Access

Efficient transmission as an alteration mechanism is widely discussed and facilitates the transmission of more communication content without loss of quality, and with no or very low time delay and marginal costs. It's in the focus of infrastructure projects and is discussed comprehensively from a theoretical point of view, like in economic theories including transaction cost and principal agent theory. It has its origin directly in the technical capabilities of digitalization, is the basis for other alteration mechanism and will be discussed together with them.

Immediacy is the counterpart to the alteration mechanism of real time reach as discussed above in the section on 'create and delete'. The time lag between the creation of a certain communication content and learner's awareness of it shrinks significantly or disappears entirely. More and more content with high promptness become available. Because of disintermediation of intermediaries like journalists, publishers, or teachers also authenticity of communication content can increase. For a fruitful use of that authenticity in relation with a strongly increased quantity of communication content, key skills out of the affective domain like awareness, giving attention, responding, valuing, and organizing should be further developed. This need can become a valuable trigger for informal learning processes.

Searchability is mainly based on medialization, traceability, and efficient transmission. It facilitates search for a certain content, relations to other content, for meta information like author, date and place of creation, or certain tags made by users. The search can be triggered by humans or by machines; also, the results can be used by both. Because of the alteration mechanism of efficient transmission, the search can be done with no or very little time needed and marginal costs within huge quantities of communication content. From a constructivist point of view, search results are not a characteristic of the underlying communication content, but they *are* the content. Only the results of transmit and access can be perceived by humans and by machines. Therefore, search and access tools are not neutral means for better use of the perception sphere, but they are very significant content creators within it.

Interactivity is characterized by the relation of certain communication content to several previous ones [48]. Interactivity is facilitated and used by human and machine-based participants of the perception sphere and creates new communication content within it together with the alteration mechanism of associativity. *Contingency* means, that the outcome of a certain interaction is open in principal [34]. Consequently, it is the content for learning also. Interactivity and contingency together with arrange and link create the most significant alterations for informal learning and lead to a strong decrease of learning control by traditional authorities like educators, parents, or publishers. Simultaneously, it creates for the learner altered conditions to construct own knowledge as core characteristic of learning from a constructivist point of view.

Ubiquity means that communication content is available anytime and everywhere. The perception sphere for informal learning is no longer limited to human teachers, textbooks, natural environment or smartphones and gaming consoles. It includes more and more everyday objects like a pair of glasses, watches, refrigerators, LED lamps or sensors for vital and performance data as discussed above in the context of Internet of Things. As informal learning often happens en passant in everyday life, ubiquity highlights the importance of looking beyond digital media dedicated developed for learning like courseware or distance education.

5.2 Selected Informal Learning Episodes

Learning Episode in the Cognitive Domain

Figure 6 shows a path crossing South Korea, planned in a web-based route planner. By clicking certain points of interests and cities, the system calculated the best suited path for a certain mean of transportation. The proposal is based on the street conditions as well as routes already used by hundred thousand other travelers. Those peers comment certain points along the route and upload associated pictures and videos. Routes are not only planned manually but also uploaded from already accomplished trips. Those routes are tracked by a GPS based computer, like a bike computer or GPS watch, during riding and uploaded via the Internet to the routing platform. If not marked private by the user, every route is searchable and reusable by others. Those features are enabled by the alteration mechanism *traceability* of the domain *create and delete* just as *efficient transmission* of the domain *transmit and access*.

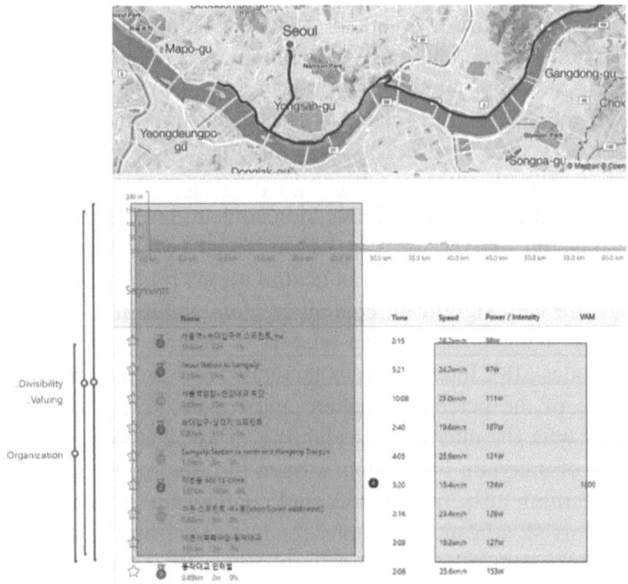

Fig. 7. Informal learning in the affective domain enabled by the alteration mechanism 'divisibility' and 'multi-perspectivity' from the domain 'arrange and link'.

The major alteration mechanism is based on *interactivity and contingency* from the domain of *transmit and access* as well as *associativity* from *arrange and link.* By clicking on points of interest on the interactive route the user can jump to different locations along the path to explore them. That information is linked to related content in the web, e.g. from Wikipedia. The example in Fig. 6 shows the use of a stored Four River Path across South Korea, modified by the user according to his concerns like visiting the headquarters and development centers of Samsung in Seoul and LG in the city of Gumi. By clicking on the hyperlinked information, the user jumped to more information about those two companies and further on coincidentally to information on OLED display technology. That use flow is enabled by the alteration mechanism of *associativity* from the domain of *arrange and link*, enabling informal learning significantly in the cognitive domain. Due to additional information regarding points of interest along the route the *knowledge* about history, culture, and geographic is enlarged. Due to associative linking of related information it can be put into context, fostering its *understanding*. *Synthesis* as higher level of learning in the cognitive domain is altered by merging and combining that information with own ideas and recommendations of peers to a route which is unique according to one's own considerations and interests in people, culture, and history – resulting in a unique route, enriched with associated information. All that is achieved en passant while doing route planning.

Learning Episode in the Affective Domain

Figure 7 shows a screenshot from the running and cycling platform *Strava*, analyzed with MAXQDA. *Strava* is one of the leading social platforms for capturing, sharing, and comparing performance and vital data of bicycle riders and runners. In 2017, 8,4 billion kilometers of cycling were tracked by GPS systems on rider's bikes and transmitted for storing and sharing on the Strava platform. 136 million of runs were uploaded and 2,3 billion kudos, acknowledgements for extraordinary performances, were attributed by peers [11, 52].

One major alteration mechanism in this learning episode is *traceability* from the domain *create and delete*. The GPS based bike computer traces the route together with the speed. The power meter shown in Fig. 4 measures the performance data in watt and the chest belt meters the current hearth frequency. Thus, geocoded moving data are stored together with performance data associated with vital data while generating them. As a standalone system, that would already strongly support learning in the *psychomotor domain*. But the core value proposition of Strava comes from the affective domain. Due to the alteration mechanism of *efficient transmission* from the *domain of transmit and access,* data are shared on the platform after finishing the ride or run. The alteration mechanism of *divisibility and multi-perspectivity* from *arrange and link* supports comparing data with one's own performances in the past as well as with those of peers. To achieve that, data have to be divided and regrouped according to different perspectives.

A core functionality of Strava are segments, certain parts of the traced route. They allow us to compare the one's own performance and vital data like speed, hearth frequency, and power with those of others within that certain part of the route. The platform not only shows rankings, also for different age and weight groups or by gender, but also awards recognitions like king of mountain. Because of this alteration mechanism Strava evolved from capturing data to sharing them with millions of other peers – an impossible thing outside of the world of digital.

By doing that, informal learning strongly happens en passant in the affective domain. *Receiving* is altered, as the impact of regular training on fitness and health is shown vividly and engagingly. But also, the motivation gained through the comparison and awarding features impacts receiving in form of increased awareness of self-responsibility for one's own personal fitness and health. Therefore, that digital media can change *valuing* one's own mental and bodily wellbeing. Finally, emotions as part of affective learning are strongly involved, much more so than in any other domain and is nowhere as strongly observable as in sport competitions. How far this emotional involvement can go shows the prosecution of Strava because of the tragic death of a descending bicycle rider, chasing a new time record in a segment [53].

Learning Episode in the Psychomotor Domain

Figure 5 shows a racing bicycle rider stopping to analyze his route, vital, and performance data while smoking a cigarette – a quite unusual learning episode. The starting point for digital media alteration mechanism is *traceability* from the domain of *create and delete*. It allows capturing the route, speed, performed power, and vital data with sensors as shown in Fig. 4. By the alteration mechanism of *efficient transmission* from the domain *transmit and access,* those data are transferred in real time from the sensors to applications on the smartphone and if configured further on to internet-based platforms for sharing. This is facilitated by the alteration mechanism of *ubiquity*. Almost all racing bike riders use bike computers to capture those data and store them in databases using the ubiquitous smartphone to control the sensors, store data temporarily, and bridge the bike computer with the platforms in the Internet. Those computers can be connected with other platforms, with coaches and medical doctors for advice, and with ecommerce platforms.

In this learning episode, the *psychomotor domain* is mainly affected. To navigate according to the route on the GPS system within a power level advised by the coach and being permanently measured by the power meter is an informal psychomotor learning on the level of manipulate. Dynamic re-routing supported by the GPS system alters the ability to perform those actions in a non-standard way after a detour or a wrong turn and thus psychomotor learning on the articulate level. Finally, after thousands of kilometers of riding with a power meter, the rider becomes capable of automatically riding in the right performance zone, adjusting performance output according to route, wind, weather, and current physical fitness. Psychomotor learning on the level of embody took place.

6 Starting Points for Teachers

The following section will present some starting points for teachers to use digital media's alteration mechanism to support learning objectives. They include two main approaches. Firstly, *key skills qualification* within formal settings should enable learners to use digital media's alteration mechanism in appropriate ways. On the other hand, *formal and informal learning should be bridged* by combining problems to be solved, learning processes, and learning content from both areas. For example, a problem can be raised in a formal teaching session and can be solved using learning processes and learning content from a digital video portal used en passant in the context of informal learning.

This section should *not* be viewed as a collection of advices nor as scientifically proved causal chains between applying certain alteration mechanism and learning outcomes. In domains where such rules can be used, human teachers will be probably substituted by computer systems very soon, because the implementation of certain rules in form of an algorithm is a strength of computers that is hard to beat by humans. The following starting points should rather support teachers in finding *fresh approaches* that are appropriate for his/her aims and teaching style to also support learners in the informal part of learning.

What most teachers should become more aware of is the increased importance of informal learning in the digital age and the associated alteration mechanism of digital media. The increased importance is due to more opportunities being available for learning outside the classroom. This process started with the invention of writing, followed by printing. Both *decoupled learning from the presence of a teacher* and increased the perception sphere as a biotope for informal learning significantly. Due to search engines, video archives, or digital encyclopedias, learners are living in a considerably enlarged perception sphere. They also have much more communication channels due to social media and eSports. At the same time, *former environments* for informal learning are shrinking. One example is the erosion of traditional family structures due to all-day schooling, a changed view on parents as role models, or increased number of single parents and divorces. Therefore, teachers should also be aware that learners pick up content, which was previously mainly taught in formal education, differently. Now they are picked up according to their own processes, while selecting their own perspective and picking certain parts of a learning domain highly individually with no direct control of teachers or other traditional authorities. Examples are learning in the field of history, politics, or recent events somewhere in the world.

6.1 Key Skills Qualification

Key skills can be defined as "a range of essential skills that underpin success in education, employment, lifelong learning and personal development" [56]. In the context of the present study, key skills qualification should help learners to reach learning aims striven by the formal education system. Thus, teachers can train such skills in formal settings, used by learners outside the classroom in informal learning context. Examples for key skills are communication, application of numbers, working with others, problem solving, or improving one's own learning in the digital age.

Due to the significantly enlarged perception sphere available for learners, *selecting and evaluating information* is an important affective as well as cognitive key skill. Teachers can explain basic concepts of evaluating information and ask learners to apply them in their social media channels as discussed below. Afterwards, the teachers evaluate those concepts together with their experiences in informal settings. A useful concept to identify fake news is: What is the core message, from whom does it come, why does that person know that, what are the personal aims of that person in communicating it? Learners can use that concept to identify fake news in the old Egyptian history, in traditional media, as well as in social media.

Another example for a key skill bridging formal with informal learning settings that is not so widely recognized and discussed but with tremendous future importance, is *living with embedded systems*. These are computer systems with a certain function within a larger mechanical or electrical system. Examples are assisted living facilities with medical monitoring and emergency communication devices, virtual assistants like Amazon's Alexa or Apples' HomePod. or the embedded systems used in the present study and shown in Fig. 4.

Adoption of embedded systems can lead to significant informal learning in the affective and psychomotor domain but requires also certain key skills in those fields. In the affective domain teachers can increase learner's perception on already implemented ubiquity of embedded systems in daily life and possibilities on how to handle associated privacy issues. An example is round-the-clock tracking by cellular phone operators. Also, to valuing embedded systems for certain use and to apply them as a natural extension of one's own 'self', as the Smartphone is perceived currently, are relevant topics. To support learners' willingness to change behavior, embedded systems can be used mandatorily in some settings, as some universities are already doing with fitness trackers to implement a fitness scheme [55]. A main part of digital media's alteration mechanism discussed above are based on those embedded system, often discussed in the context of Internet of Things (IoT). Probably, they will alter informal learning in the future at least as much as the smartphone did in the past.

6.2 Link Informal Learning with Formal Learning Context

eSports are a form of competition using videogames, mostly performed as organized multiplayer video game competitions between professionals [18]. Tournaments are held in arenas with thousands of on-site spectators. It is discussed to include eSports in the Olympic program and to initiate mandatory drug controls. The worldwide turnover is higher than that of the film industry and in Germany higher than that of the first and second soccer league combined. It becomes more and more a *substitute for traditional social media* as a social relations and communication sphere, especially in the age group between 12 and 30 years [46].

An interesting starting point for teachers is to link informal learning happening in the context of *eSports* with formal learning processes just as learning content. Those games are very emotional and based on different feelings, associated with the type of game. Game's content and processes as well as the social interaction with other players is a *remarkable field for informal learning* in the affective domain. Teachers' understanding of learner's motivation to follow up with a certain game setting, to actively participate, to value the game, to organize the complex social and technical elements, and the impact on learner's lifestyle can give fresh ideas for organizing formal learning processes. Also linking learning content from the eSports domain with formal settings can be applied. For example, strategy video games can be the starting point for explaining and discussing theories of business strategies in formal settings.

As discussed above, an important key skills qualification is to *evaluate information*. Teachers can elaborate learning topics e.g. in the field of world politics, history, or sociology with learners in the context of their recent informal learnings from social media and user generated content. They can discuss the process to evaluate information from those sources, also in comparison to traditional media. Thus, not only content-related informal cognitive learning can be extended to formal settings, but also applying evaluation methods of information can be trained. Finally, the highest level of cognitive learning, evaluation, can be linked between informal and formal settings.

6.3 Link Formal Learning with Informal Learning Context

The other side of the coin is to link formal learning with informal learning context. Both approaches are similar, but the starting point differs. The author of the present study used this approach in the perennial project D-Move [42]. The first step was to teach methods, in formal settings, for optimizing user experience of information systems. Thus, the problem-solving strategy came from the formal setting. Afterwards, learners were asked to capture real world experiences with a great deal of improvement opportunities with their Smartphones. The problem to be solved came from the informal context. Learners annotate, post, and shared them with their colleagues using a joined blog to discuss them electronically. Finally, the findings were further elaborated and evaluated according to user experience methods in formal settings. This approach is *quite different to traditional case study teaching* as the learner do not to have to envision certain situations, but they experience it in daily life.

Learning is supported in the *cognitive domain* by acquire, understand and use knowledge on user experience methods, and evaluate them based on everyday experiences. In the *affective domain*, learners willing to give attention to user experience issues is impacted, they respond by capture their own experiences, organize different information and ideas and form their own mental model on user experience.

An example for linking formal learning in the domain of *psychomotor* with informal learning context is *soldering as part of electrical engineering* education. Basic skills taught in formal settings inside the lab can be extended with advices in digital video portals where learners spent some hours every day. They can enlarge their psychomotor capabilities by trying different approaches in soldering own devices in their spare time. Thus, several levels of psychomotor learning are impacted. Firstly, the learner replicates the teacher's soldering technique. At the level of articulate, he/she applies those skills in the different context of own devices and finally becomes able to solder in an automatic, intuitive way.

6.4 Support Informal Learning During Formal Settings

Mostly, informal learning happens outside classrooms, but it can also take place as a side effect of formal education inside the classroom. An interesting example started ten years ago in a Viennese high school. Pupils were taught common learning subjects one hour every day while pedaling on an ergometer, equipped with a writing desk. During the last years the experiment was extended to other school in Austria, Germany, and Sweden, each of them accompanied scientifically. Compared to reference classes, learners of the ergometer class became better at concentrating, became more attentive in class, showed better blood values and results in psychomotor test, had a better development of their body mass index (BMI), and showed less aggressions towards their schoolmates [13] (Table 2).

Table 2. Examples for teacher's starting points using digital media's alteration mechanism to support informal learning.

	Cognitive domain	Affective domain	Psychomotor domain
Key skills qualification	Evaluating information	Living with embedded systems	
Link informal learning with formal learning context		Processes and contents of eSports	
Link formal learning with informal learning context	Improvements in customer experience		Soldering in electrical engineering
Support informal learning during formal settings	Ergometer class in high school		

This example has a close relation to the world of digital, as this age group shows a significant decrease of sports and physical activities due to spending more time in front of displays. The WHO reports, that in Austria around a third of elementary school children suffer from overweight [58]. Thus, the ergometer class can be considered as a response to digital media's alteration mechanism of ubiquity. We would like to underline, that teacher's response to alteration mechanism shown in this study *do not have* to be always an increased usage of digital media. An example is Michael Sandel, a recognized authority in the digital age, with millions of views in his video channels. He bans all electronic devices during his lectures [32].

The ergometer class covers all three learning domains. The *cognitive domain* is addressed indirectly via better concentration and more attentiveness to classes on subjects in the cognitive domain like mathematics or history. In the *affective domain*, learners in the ergometer class perceive the value of physical activities for personal wellbeing expressed by less aggression and changes in lifestyle. They also experience the value of physical activities for concentration and attentiveness.

The *psychomotor domain* is affected directly, beside relations with the cognitive and affective domain, by learning how to pedal on a bike and writing on a console while following the teacher's talk. This is a valuable preparation for behavior in road traffic.

7 Conclusion and Further Research

The main part of learning in the cognitive, affective, and psychomotor domain happens outside the classroom en passant while doing something else and without clear learning objectives. This informal learning mostly happens without any intervention from the formal education system. It significantly gains in importance due to learner's broadened perception sphere formed by digital media.

Digital media do not alter learning in general or informal learning in particular in a simple cause-effect relationship but in a complex system of effects. They form learner's perception sphere by different alteration mechanism as analyzed in the present study. Therefore, learner's everyday life interaction with this perception sphere obtains altered conditions for information assimilation regarding the learning topic. This can lead to changes in the cognitive, affective, and psychomotor domain as we defined learning.

The deeper understanding for digital media's alteration mechanism within learner's perception sphere could be a useful input for more specific and differentiated results in disciplines with focus on information assimilation and learning including learning psychology, cognitive science, media pedagogy, or media studies.

The impact of digital media on learner's perception sphere is much more than the widely discussed and applied everywhere-everytime learning, which is already possible since the invention of writing and printing. The present study shows significant alterations due to digital media in the domain of create and delete, arrange and link, and transmit and access. Those mechanisms lead to everyday life environments with high interactivity, personalization, associativity, contingency, and often playfulness in contrast to linear, predefined content mostly used in formal learning settings.

Based on those identified alteration mechanism, learners can get an increased awareness on differences between secondary experiences in their perception sphere formed by digital media and primary experiences in the physical world. This allows learners to better understand possible gains and risks associated with digital media and their alteration mechanism, and to adjust perception as well as media usage - one of the most important key skills in the age of digital.

The presented findings should enable teachers to better understand informal learning in every day settings. Examples for widely undervalued and little understood alterations are living with embedded systems as well as video gaming and eSports. Both are no longer futuristic visions but part of learners' everyday life. This deepened understanding allows for more sophisticated linking between formal and informal settings just as conveying key skills for the digital age. The response of teachers should be based on learning aims, personal teaching styles, and linking with learners every day perception sphere. In any case, it should not be only an increased usage of digital media.

Teachers' main starting points are conveying key skills qualification to use digital media's alteration mechanism in an appropriate way outside the classroom and to link problems, processes, and content between formal and informal learning. Today, educators have their focus mostly on digital media supporting their teaching, like courseware or distance education, turning a blind eye to the main part of students' learning – the informal part. To fully utilize digital media's alteration mechanism, educators should neither stick to pure transfer of knowledge nor retreat to a facilitator role, the latter of which is empty of content. By linking with learner's perception sphere formed by digital media, she/he can head for being a renowned source of knowledge *and* focus on the interaction process, introduce appropriate concepts of the discipline, and help to reach intellectual convergence. If this convergence is replaced by fully individualized learning styles and contents, social cohesion will shrink, as people can no longer communicate among each other due to the lack of mental connectability.

The presented findings could also be useful for future technologies and systems, as the alteration mechanism are characterized by properties and are not based on certain product categories or brands. This allows for reconfiguration of the properties to best fit new or enhanced digital media in learner's future perception sphere.

The methodology used triangulation of self-observation, participatory action research with extended field phases, and surveys within some hours of media usage. That results in high amount of research effort expressed in time, costs, and laborious work to capture 373 informal learning episodes of 77 learners via videographics and interpret them with qualitative content analysis. Controlling internal and external validity is quite different than in traditional survey research. But the implemented methodology helps to identify not only certain 'known unknows' but also to search for 'unknown unknowns. The extensive use of videographics mainly in form of annotated screencasts and videos of real-life learning episodes is a first step to overcome limitations of the traditional representation of research results in form of static text, figures, tables, and pictures. This allows research questions, strategies, and results which are closer to learner's real life – and to fulfil Wittgenstein's proposition in a deeper sense: 'Whereof one cannot speak, thereof one must be silent.' (German: 'Wovon man nicht sprechen kann, darüber muss man schweigen', [57]).

Future research will cover a deeper analysis of captured learning episodes to further refine and evaluate the category system of alterations, also with a focus on selected learning domains, for example on the affective domain and self-monitoring of vital and performance data. Also, capturing learning episodes in additional cultural areas is planned to better understand differences in digital media's alterations in learners' perception sphere. That should allow a fresh and quite different view on the widely discussed phenomena of *digital divide*, which today is mostly seen from a limited cultural and historical background.

Acknowledgments. The author is thankful to Rene Haras and Olivia List for their support in collecting data. Some of the content in this paper, especially in Chapter 5, was already published in author's conference paper [45].

References

1. Ainsworth, H.L., Eaton, S.: Formal, Non-formal and Informal Learning in the Sciences. Eaton International (2010)
2. ARD/ZDF: Onlinestudie 2017 – Kern-Ergebnisse (2017). http://www.ard-zdf-onlinestudie.de/files/2017/Artikel/Kern-Ergebnisse_ARDZDF-Onlinestudie_2017.pdf. Accessed 24 Nov 2017
3. Atkinson, S.P.: Adaptation of Dave's Psychomotor Domain (2014). https://spatkinson.wordpress.com/tag/daves-taxonomy. Accessed 10 Nov 2017
4. Bateson, G.: Steps to an Ecology of Mind: Collected Essays in Anthropology, Psychiatry, Evolution, and Epistemology. University of Chicago Press (2000)
5. Bloom, B., Englehart, M., Furst, E., Hill, W., Krathwohl, D.: Taxonomy of Educational Objectives: The Classification of Educational Goals. Handbook I: Cognitive Domain. Longmans, Green, New York (1956)
6. Bush, V.: As we may think. Atlantic Monthly **176**(1), 101–108 (1945)
7. Glaser, B.G., Strauss, A.L.: The Discovery of Grounded Theory: Strategies for Qualitative Research. Aldine, Chicago (1967)

8. Charmaz, K.: Constructing Grounded Theory: A Practical Guide Through Qualitative Analysis. SAGE Publications (2014)
9. Cohen, L., Manion, L., Morrison, K.: Research Methods in Education. Routledge, London and New York (2018)
10. Council of Europe: Strategies for Learning Democratic Citizenship. Strasbourg (2000)
11. Dailymail: Globally cyclists clocked up 4.5 BILLION miles and Regent's Park is the UK's most popular bike route (2017). http://www.dailymail.co.uk/travel/travel_news/article-5215117/Strava-GPS-training-app-reveals-amazing-2017-statistics.html. Accessed 31 May 2018
12. Dave, R.H.: Psychomotor levels in developing and writing behavioral objectives. In: Armstrong, R.J. (ed.) Developing and Writing Behavioral Objectives. Educational Innovators Press, Tucson (1970)
13. Der Standard: Ergometerklasse: Bessere Schulleistungen durch Radeln (2018). https://derstandard.at/2000075195520/Ergometerklasse-Bessere-Schulleistungen-durch-Radeln. Accessed 1 June 2018
14. Engelbart, D.: Augmenting Human Intellect: A Conceptual Framework (SRI Summary Report AFOSR-3223). Stanford Research Institute, Menlo Park (1962)
15. Von Glasersfeld, E.: A constructivist approach to teaching. In: Steffe, L.P., Gale, J. (ed.) Constructivism in Education, pp. 3–15. Erlbaum, Hillsdale (1995)
16. Globalwebindex: The most important 2017 trends to look out for (2017). https://www.globalwebindex.com/reports/trends-17. Accessed 4 June 2018
17. Goo Kuratani, D.L., Lai, E.: TEAM Lab - Photovoice Literature Review (2011). http://teamlab.usc.edu/Photovoice%20Literature%20Review%20(FINAL).pdf. Accessed 10 Nov 2017
18. Hamari, J., Sjöblom, M.: What is eSports and why do people watch it? Internet Res. **27**(2), 211–232 (2017)
19. Harasim, L.: Learning Theory and Online Technologies. Taylor and Francis. Kindle-Version (2017)
20. Harring, M., Witte, M., Burger, T. (eds.): Handbuch informelles Lernen – Interdisziplinäre und internationale Perspektiven. Weinheim und Basel: Beltz (2016)
21. Heath, Ch., Hindsmarsh, J., Luff, P.: Video in Qualitative Research. SAGE Publications, London (2010)
22. Henrich, J., Heine, S.J., Norenzayan, A.: The weirdest people in the world? Behav. Brain Sci. **33**(2–3), 61–83 (2010)
23. International Telecommunication Union: ICT Facts and Figures 2016 (2016). https://www.itu.int/en/ITU-D/Statistics/Documents/facts/ICTFactsFigures2016.pdf. Accessed 2 Nov 2017
24. Kahneman, D., Krueger, A.B., Schkade, D.A., Schwarz, N., Stone, A.A.: A survey method for characterizing daily life experience: the day reconstruction method. Science **306**(5702), 1776–1780 (2004)
25. Kahneman, D., Krueger, A.B., Schkade, D., Schwarz, N., Stone, A.: The Day Reconstruction Method (DRM): Instrument Documentation (2004). https://dornsife.usc.edu/assets/sites/780/docs/drm_documentation_july_2004.pdf. Accessed 26 May 2018
26. Keil-Slawik, R., Selke, H.: Forschungsstand und Forschungsperspektiven zum virtuellen Lernen von Erwachsenen. In: Arbeitsgemeinschaft Qualifikations-Entwicklungs-Management Berlin (eds.). Kompetenzentwicklung 1998 – Forschungsstand und Forschungsperspektiven. Münster: Waxmann-Verlag, pp. 165–208 (1998)
27. Kindon, S., Pain, R., Kesby, M.: Participatory action research: origins, approaches and methods. In: Kindon, S., Pain, R., Kesby, M. (eds.) Participatory Action Research Approaches and Methods. Routledge, London and New York (2007)

28. Krathwohl, D.R., Bloom, B.S., Masia, B.B.: Taxonomy of Educational Objectives, the Classification of Educational Goals. Handbook II: Affective Domain. David McKay Co., Inc., New York (1973)
29. Krathwohl, D.R.: A Revision of Bloom's Taxonomy: An Overview. Theory into Practice, Autumn 2002, pp. 212–218 (2002)
30. Kuckartz, U.: Qualitative Inhaltsanalyse (2012)
31. Methoden, Praxis. Computerunterstützung, Beltz Juventa: Weinheim und Basel
32. Neue Zürcher Zeitung: Der Aufstieg des Populismus ist eine Reaktion auf die Verarmung des öffentlichen Diskurses (2018). https://www.nzz.ch/feuilleton/aufstieg-des-populismus-ist-eine-gegenreaktion-auf-die-verarmung-des-oeffentlichen-diskurses-ld.1379811. Accessed 28 May 2018
33. Kurzweil, R.: The Singularity Is Near: When Humans Transcend Biology. Viking (2005)
34. Luhmann, N.: Social Systems. Translated by Bednarz, J. Jr. with Baecker, D. Stanford University Press (1996)
35. Maturana, H.R., Varela, F.: The Tree of Knowledge: The Biological Roots of Human Understanding. Shambhala (1992)
36. Mayer-Schönberger, V.: Delete: The Virtue of Forgetting in the Digital Age. Princeton University Press, Princeton (2011)
37. Mayring, Ph.: Qualitative content analysis: theoretical foundation, basic procedures and software solution (2014). http://nbn-resolving.de/urn:nbn:de:0168-ssoar-395173. Accessed 23 May 2018
38. MerchDope: 37 Mind Blowing YouTube Facts, Figures and Statistics (2018). https://merchdope.com/youtube-statistics/. Accessed 26 May 2018
39. Moodle: Moodle statistics (2018). https://moodle.net/stats/. Accessed 5 May 2018
40. Nelson, T.H.: Computer Lib: You Can and Must Understand Computers Now; Dream Machines: New Freedoms Through Computer Screens—A Minority Report, Self-published (1974)
41. OECD: Education at a Glance 2017 (2017). http://www.oecd.org/education/education-at-a-glance-19991487.htm. Accessed 6 May 2018
42. Petrovic, O.: D-Move: ten years of experience with a learning environment for digital natives. In: Proceedings of the 9th International Conference of Computer Supported Education, Porto 21–23 April 2017, pp. 315–322 (2017)
43. Petrovic, O.: Self-monitoring: a digital natives' delphi embedded in their everyday life. In: Proceedings of the 4th European Conference on Social Media, Lithuania 3–4 July 2017 (2017)
44. Petrovic, O.: The internet of things as disruptive innovation for the advertising ecosystem. In: Siegert, G., von Rimscha, M.B., Grubenmann S. (eds.) Commercial Communication in the Digital Age. Information or Disinformation?. de Gruyter, Berlin/New York (2017)
45. Petrovic, O.: Digital media's alteration mechanism for informal learning. In: Proceedings of the 10th International Conference on Computer Supported Education, Madeira, Portugal, 15–17 March 2018 (2018)
46. Petrovic, O.: Lesen ist unmittelbares Glück, Neue Zürcher Zeitung, 27 February 2018 (2018)
47. Pietraß, M.: Informelles Lernen in der Medienpädagogik. In: Rohs, M. (ed.) Handbuch Informelles Lernen, pp. 123–142. Springer VS, Wiesbaden (2016)
48. Rafaeli, S.: Interactivity: from new media to communication. In: Hawkins, R.P., Wiemann, J.M., Pingree S. (eds.) Sage Annual Review of Communication Research: Advancing Communication Science: Merging Mass and Interpersonal Processes, 16, Beverly Hills, pp. 110–134 (1988)
49. Salaverría, R.: Typology of digital news media: theoretical bases for their classification. Mediterranean J. Commun. **8**(1), 19–32 (2017)

50. Selke, H.: Sekundäre Medienfunktionen für die Konzeption von Lernplattformen für die Präsenzlehre, Dissertation, Paderborn (2008)
51. Stichweh, R.: Systems theory. In: Badie, B., et al. (eds.) International Encyclopedia of Political Science. Sage, New York (2011)
52. Strava: 2017 in Stats (2018). https://blog.strava.com/2017-in-stats/. Accessed 31 May 2018
53. Velonews: Family sues Strava over descending death (2012). http://wwwvelonews.com/2012/06/news/family-sues-strava-over-descending-death_224889. Accessed 31 May 2018
54. Wang, C., Burris, M.A.: Photovoice: concept, methodology, and use for participatory needs assessment. Health Educ. Behav. **24**(3), 369–387 (1997)
55. Wearable: Fitbits are now mandatory for students at a university in Oklahoma (2016). https://www.wareable.com/fitbit/fitbits-mandatory-students-university-oklahoma-2250. Accessed 3 June 2018
56. Welsh Assembly Government: Education, Lifelong Learning and Skills (2006). https://web.archive.org/web/20060514103238/http://new.wales.gov.uk/about/departments/dells/?lang=en. Accessed 3 June 2018
57. Wittgenstein, L.: Logisch-Philosophische Abhandlung. In: Ostwald, W. (ed.) Annalen der Naturphilosophie, 14 (1921)
58. World Health Organization: WHO European Childhood Obesity Surveillance Initiative (COSI) (2018). http://www.euro.who.int/en/health-topics/disease-prevention/nutrition/activities/who-european-childhood-obesity-surveillance-initiative-cosi. Accessed 5 June 2018
59. Woodgate, R.L., Zurba, M., Tennent, P.: Worth a thousand words? Advantages, challenges and opportunities in working with photovoice as a qualitative research method with youth and their families. Forum: Qual. Soc. Res. **18**(1) (2017)

As One Size Doesn't Fit All, Personalized Massive Open Online Courses Are Required

Nour El Mawas[1(✉)], Jean-Marie Gilliot[1], Serge Garlatti[1], Reinhardt Euler[2], and Sylvain Pascual[3]

[1] CIREL(EA 4354), University of Lille, Lille, France
nour.el-mawas@univ-lille.fr,
{jm.gilliot,serge.garlatti}@telecom-bretagne.eu
[2] LabSTICC, University of Brest, Brest, France
reinhardt.euler@univ-brest.fr
[3] Education Sector, Immanens, Palaiseau, France
s.pascual@immanens.com

Abstract. Most of the time, lifelong learners have different backgrounds, abilities, experiences and prior knowledge. This is especially true in case of MOOCs that can reach a large number of learners but the same content is proposed for learners. According to the low average completion rate for MOOCs, the "one size fits all" policy is not relevant. This paper aims to define the functional and technical architecture to personalize content in Massive Open Online Courses in a Lifelong Learning (LLL) perspective to overcome these drawbacks. The main goal of the European project ITEA 3, called MOOCTAB to create a Tablet-based platform dedicated to LLL using an on-demand cloud based MOOC platform with a personalized content. Our approach is applied on a Java course where we present the domain model modelled in the LMAP editor and the learner model for three different learners.

Keywords: Personalization · MOOCs · Learner model · Course model · Lifelong Learning

1 Introduction

Lifelong Learning (LLL) refers to systematic and purposeful learning throughout a person's life involving formal (schools) and informal (work, recreation, leisure, social relations, family life) domains [5]. The original concept of Massive Open Online Courses (MOOCs) is to offer free and open access courses for a massive number of learners from anywhere all over the world [19]. Access to and effective use of relevant information and continuously learning in MOOCs is essential for lifelong learners. LLL as a concept has gone through many changes over the years especially with the arrival of MOOCs and the increase of their learning resources. Acknowledging this, professional learning has become a central asset for MOOC providers [21]. The number of courses (started/scheduled) has grown from about 100 MOOCs in 2012 to more than 2000 new free online course every month in 2018, with a duplication of the number of courses between 2015 and 2016. However, according to [9] by the International

B. M. McLaren et al. (Eds.): CSEDU 2018, CCIS 1022, pp. 470–488, 2019.
https://doi.org/10.1007/978-3-030-21151-6_22

Review of Research in Open and Distributed Learning, the average completion rate for MOOCs has only been about 6%. There is a growing trend of researches in the possibility of MOOC personalisation and adaptation in order to improve users' engagements, and hence reduce MOOCs' drop-out rate problem [15].

In order to understand the reason behind this low rate, we have relied on the MOOCs annual report published by the *École Polytechnique Fédérale de Lausanne* (EPFL) [20] as EPFL is one of the first universities to experiment with MOOCs, and among the few in Europe to integrate the use of MOOCs on its own campus.

The motivation that drives users to register to an EPFL MOOC varies according to the need of each learner. Six reasons are behind the registration to the MOOC: Finding a new job, getting a promotion, meeting family expectations, earning a higher salary, solving a specific problem, and helping to pass class. The "solving a specific problem" motivation is the main motivation for 60% of the courses. The academic degrees held by users of the EPFL MOOCs are very diverse. The highest degree obtained are high school, associate degree, bachelor degree, master degree, and doctoral degree. The percentage of MOOC users who are currently enrolled in an educational program is low. Only 34% of registered learners are students (including part-time students). The remaining enrolees are not in an educational program. Therefore, it is important to understand that users do not have the same background.

The diversity of users' background who followed a MOOC is a key issue [10]. For example, in the matter of the Analyse Numérique course, 34% of learners have Mathematics, Computers, Engineering backgrounds, 21% of learners have Architecture, Civil Engineering backgrounds, 12% of learners have Education and Training, 2% of learners have Business, Finance, Sales, Management backgrounds, 4% of learners have Arts, Design, Entertainment backgrounds, 13% of learners have Construction, Food, Utilities, Healthcare, Life Sciences backgrounds, and 2% of learners have Legal, Administration, Social Services backgrounds. It means that learners do not have the same prior knowledge for this course.

In this context, the motivation behind our research work is that (1) differences exist among learners in terms of background, ability, experience, prior knowledge, and (2) MOOC platforms unify the educational content to all learners without taking into account these differences. According to [14], learners' personalization and social learning are essential concepts in Lifelong and Life wide Learning contexts. The next challenge is about how to insure adaptive learning that gives each student a personal experience in a MOOC. [1] also believes that MOOCs should offer student-centred learning for effective and quality education in order to meet each individual learner's learning expectations in MOOCs. Furthermore, [12] and [11] point out that MOOCs environment is convenient for offering personalized contents and feedbacks to learners based on their learning goals. This is because MOOCs provides learning flexibility and sense of independence between learners and teachers, which are important when implementing personalization in technology enhanced learning.

This work takes place within the context of the European MOOCTAB (Massive Online Open Course Tablet) project. Its main goal is to create a Tablet-based platform dedicated to LLL (primary, secondary, higher and continuous) using an on-demand MOOC platform with a personalized content. The MOOCTAB project in-tends to offer a cloud based European MOOC on Demand platform with a Plug & Play approach deployable in Europe and developing countries. This platform is based on existing technology bricks and existing open source platforms like edX. Note that this work is an extension of our previous research paper [6].

The paper is organized as follows. Section 2 proposes the theoretical background of the study. Section 3 presents several existing solutions for personalized MOOCs. Section 4 details our scientific positioning and defines our functional and technical solution. Section 5 is dedicated to the application of our approach on a Java course. Finally, Sect. 6 summarizes this paper and presents its perspectives.

2 Theoretical Background

In this section, we discuss theoretical background directly related to the personalized of MOOC content [6].

Personalization is the process of providing relevant content based on individual user preferences or behaviour [18]. It is the explicit user model that represents user knowledge, goals, interests, and other features that enable the system to distinguish among different users [3].

In the e-learning field [17], personalization is education, where participants have different learning objectives, depending on their learning needs. The training is customized, so this is possible, and personalized instruction may also provide opportunities for differentiation and individualization. In this context, differentiation is education, where participants have the same learning goals, but the teaching method varies so they adapt to the individual student's needs. Individualization is teaching, where the participants also have the same learning goals, but participants can move forward at different speeds and relate to a particular content area or a given activity in different ways, and teaching is tailored to individual needs.

According to [7], personalization is classified in categories: Link Personalization, Content Personalization, Context Personalization, Authorized Personalization and Humanized Personalization. In this paper, we focus on content personalization. [8] defines four forms of content personalization: information filtering systems, recommender systems, continuous queries, and personalized searches. Information filtering systems screen out irrelevant data from incoming data streams and distribute relevant data items according to a user profile. Recommender systems have automated the everyday procedure of relying on recommendations from other people whenever personal experience is not sufficient for making choices. Continuous queries are issued only once and executed continuously over the database. Personalized searches are based on the observation that "to enhance user searches one needs to take into account the fact that different people find different things relevant". In our research work, we are interested in the form of information filtering systems.

To allow the personalized content, we need to model the learner. The model must depend on the learner himself and the domain which is the course in our case. The next section details existing projects on MOOC personalization. Note that we consider the personalization as a specific concept of the adaptation where adaptation is based on the personal preferences and background of the learner.

3 Related Work

In this section, we consider existing projects related to personalized MOOCs and we deduce important elements to ensure this personalization [6].

3.1 The MOOC Personalization for Various Learning Goals Project

The MOOC Personalization for Various Learning Goals project is a project funded by the Bill and Melinda Gates foundation. It aims to identify how students' goals are expressed through their activities on the edX learning platform, and how they evolve over time.

The objectives of this project were: (1) classify student learners by learning goals; (2) cluster learners by engagement with the platform, comparing various groups by learning outcomes (i.e., certificate attainment), and aiming to predict user transition from one cluster to another; (3) study how the clustering could be used for platform customization and personalization of learning experience.

This research was expected to proceed in the context of HarvardX, (Harvard's division for online learning) and to be based on the data on 17 HarvardX courses running on the edX platform, focusing on 5 courses that must be completed by December 2013. Since December 2013, there are no research papers that concern the project.

3.2 The POEM Project

The POEM (Personalised Open Education for the Masses) project aims at designing a platform that reconciles Massive Education—as with the strong development of MOOCs (Massive Open Online Courses)—with Personalized Education. According to [4], one of the important concepts that allows personalized education is the deconstruction of courses and curricula into hundreds and thousands of short independent units that will interact together as a complex system. The objective is then to get these thousands of small independent courses to self-organize into optimal pedagogical paths that allow individual students to validate curricula as fast as possible depending on their personal skills, aims and previous knowledge. POEM is developed under Creative Commons and will be as interoperable with edX. Students involve in many individual and collective educational activities for their mutual benefit: assessment, inter-tutorship and construction of dynamical Knowledge Maps of domains to provide different learning paths to learners.

3.3 The Knowledge Map on Khan Academy

Khan Academy proposes math courses with a knowledge map that makes learning objectives and individual progress available to learners. The motivation behind the map is that learners miss an overview of how all the math exercises tie in together. The concept of the Knowledge Map is behind the Math Missions in the sense that exercises build on another and basic concepts are introduced before advanced ones. This knowledge map is in forms of skill-meter (display and badges) [16]. It contains a starry night, containing all of the stars. The stars represent lessons. Yellow stars with a blue border are lessons, users are proficient at, green borders mean recommended lessons, and others are lessons that are not recommended. An orange border means a lesson a user should review. It also tells the user how skills are connected to each other. The Knowledge Map also has a navigation bar, with which students could search for a particular skill.

3.4 The ECO Project

[2] proposes the European ECO (Elearning, Communication and Open-data: Massive Mobile, Ubiquitous and Open Learning). The motivation behind this project is that MOOCs are proving to be inconsistent with the European standards for formal higher education due to their low-level of learner support and lack of an enriched pedagogical approach. This project introduces the notion of sMOOCs ("social" MOOCs) which provides a learning experience marked by social interactions and participation.

The sMOOCs are accessible from different platforms and through mobile devices and integrated with participants' real life experiences through contextualization of content via mobile apps and gamifications. It also supports adaptive learning strategies and ubiquitous, pervasive and contextualized learning. ECO sMOOCs have the potential to adapt to the changing intentions of participants during the course.

3.5 The aMOOC Project

[19] proposes an adaptive MOOC (aMOOC) platform, providing a strong pedagogical framework and a personalized learning experience in a MOOC learning environment. The aMOOC allows for different ways to organize content, offering different context and perspective for learners. It also aims to identify the way a learner would like to learn by conducting diagnostic assessments on the learning preference. It uses assessment results to provide continuous intelligent feedback that motivates and provides guidance to overcome concept deficiencies and maximize learning performance.

In this project, learning strategies are related to five learning pedagogies: apprentice (learning through mentor–student interaction), incidental (learning through case study), inductive (learning through example), deductive (learning through application), and discovery (learning through experimentation). The content of the aMOOC is presented to students based on the learning style of preference. For example, in the incidental learning study, learning happens primarily within a context of case studies. Content provided by the expert is sequenced in ways that explain the events involved in the case study.

3.6 Discussion

This state-of-the-art allows us to define important elements for our content personalization approach (Table 1): learning goals, learning experience, learning recognition, learning path, and content granularity.

Note that for clarity reasons, in Table 1, E1 refers to learning goals, E2 to learning experience, E3 to learning recognition, E4 to learning path, E5 to content granularity,

P1 refers to the MOOC Personalization for Various Learning Goals project, P2 to the POEM project, P3 to the knowledge map on Khan Academy, P4 to the ECO project, and P5 to the aMOOC project.

The learning goals are a key element in content personalization. It is a very personal decision that has its roots in a social environment providing examples, discussions and opportunities. A learner has a set of realistic and achievable goals and based on these goals the content must be delivered to him. The learning experience refers to Learning by doing which takes place through on-the-job and leadership experiences. The learning recognition is important in our approach. It acknowledges achievements and constitutes certified evidence. It includes formal learning such as diplomas, certificates, and recommendations. The learning path makes learning objectives and individual progress available to learners. It allows an overview of how all learning concepts tie in together and where is the learner's current position in the learning path. The content granularity is related to the pieces of learning content that are combined to form the whole MOOC content. For example, if a content package is comprised of only a few pieces of large grained learning content then re-sequencing them to form a new learning path for another learner may not be possible. This issue is paramount in the delivery of any personalized content.

Table 1. Important elements/levels for content personalisation based on existing projects [6].

	Learning			Visualisation	Content
	E1	E2	E3	E4	E5
P1	✓	–	✓	–	–
P2	–	✓	–	✓	✓
P3	–		–	✓	–
P4	–	✓	–	–	–
P5	–		–	✓	–

These elements can be categorized in three levels (Table 1): (1) the learning level includes learning goals, learning experience, and learning recognition; (2) the visualization level includes the learning path; (3) the content level includes the content granularity.

To highlight all these ideas, we are going to detail in the next section our approach that takes into account these elements and provides innovative solutions in this domain.

4 Our Proposed Approach

In this section, we present an overview of our approach. Then we detail our functional architecture and our Domain/Learner Models before discussing the presence of our elements categorized in three levels as defined in Sect. 3.6 [6].

4.1 An Overview of Our Approach

The difference between a course completion in a classic MOOC and in our approach is the personalization of the course content.

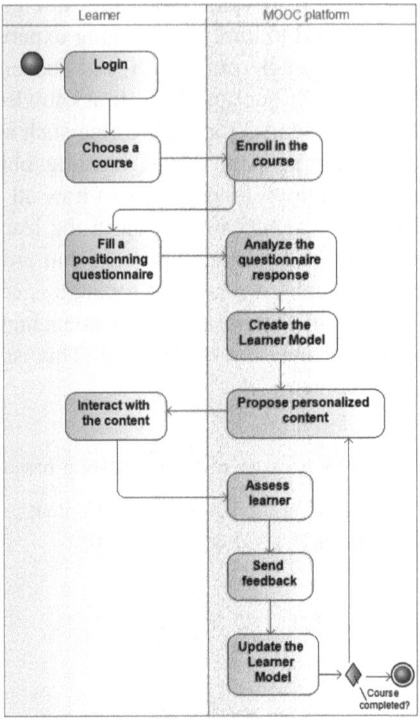

Fig. 1. The course completion [6].

Figure 1 shows how the personalization occurs during the course completion. The learner logins in the MOOC platform. He can, therefore, choose a course to take. Before starting the course, the platform asks him to fulfil a positioning questionnaire. This questionnaire is about the current professional situation, his diplomas, his certifications, and the platform permission to access to his LinkedIn profile. Once the questionnaire is submitted by the learner, the platform analyses the questionnaire response and creates the Learner Model for the learner.

Note that the Learner Model is addressed in Sect. 4.2. Based on the Learner Model and while the course is not completed, the platform proposes a personalized content to each learner who can interact with it. Then the learner will be evaluated on this specific content before updating his Learner Model.

In the next section, we will detail our functional architecture that allows this personalization.

4.2 Our Functional Architecture

Our learning architecture (Fig. 2) is designed in order to be compliant with different MOOC platform architectures. In general, MOOC platforms distinguish two main components dedicated to different steps in the course lifecycle: the Content Management System (CMS) and the Learning Management System (LMS). The CMS is used to manage students' enrolment, track students' performance, and create/distribute course content. The LMS focuses on course management including user registration, tracking courses, recording data from learners, and analysis purposes.

In our vision, we consider three main roles: the pedagogical engineer, the teacher, and the learner. In a standard course creation, the pedagogical engineer has to provide the course structure and populate it with the course content. In our approach, the course structure is becoming a part of the Domain Model (DM). We propose an LMAP editor that enables to define the structure of the Domain Model with related content and provision of potential exercises. The LMAP editor replaces the classical linear description of a course in traditional platforms while the content description does not change. When the DM is created, the course structure and content are up-loaded by the pedagogical engineer in the LMS.

When the learner will access the course, he will get personalized content through our "Course Navigation" plug-in. Content will be proposed according to his own current Learner Model (LM). He can also visualize his current progress through the LM Dashboard and point specific topics in the DM. Other MOOC activities such as forums and quizzes are maintained in our approach.

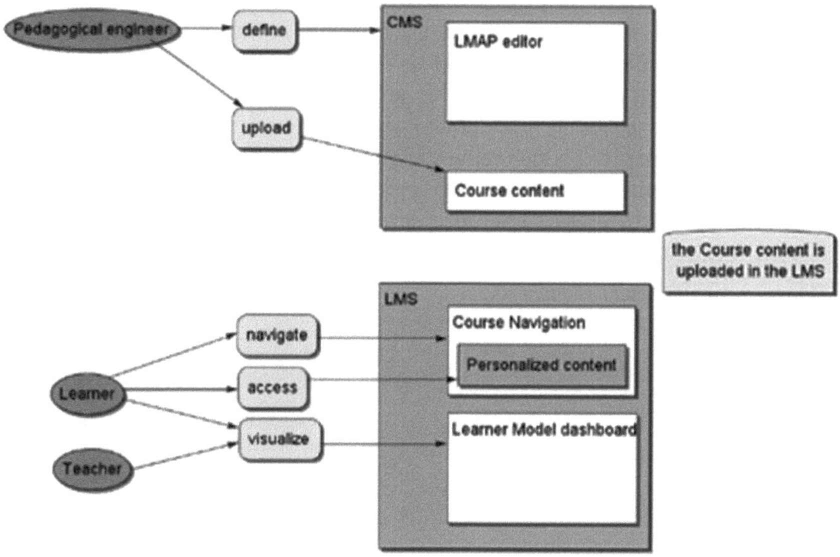

Fig. 2. Our functional architecture [6].

Teachers have standard access to learner progress and productions on the platform. They have also aggregated access to LM of the learners registered in their course.

Now we will detail the domain and the Learner Models which are main elements in our approach.

4.3 Domain and Learner Models

Our Domain Model is shown in Figs. 1 and 3. It has three layers: subject, topic, and concept. The Domain Model is composed of a set of subjects, each subject is composed of many topics, and each topic refers to many concepts.

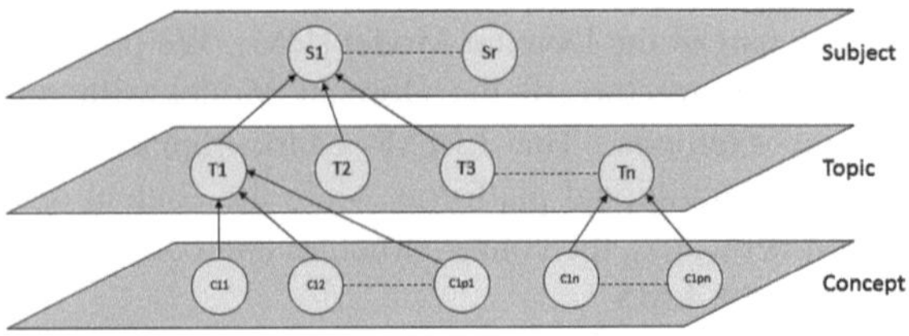

Fig. 3. The structure of our Domain Model [6].

Our Learner Model (Fig. 3) is based on the Generic Bayesian Student Model (GBSM) [13]. It is composed of two different kinds of variables: knowledge and evidential variables. Knowledge variables (K) represent students' knowledge (either declarative or procedural knowledge, but also skills, abilities, etc.). These are the variables of interest in adaptive e-learning systems, in order to be able to adapt instruction to each individual student. Their values are not directly observable (i.e., they are hidden variables). In the GBSM, all knowledge variables are modelled as binary, and take two values: 0 (not-known) and 1 (known).

Evidential variables (Q), which represent students' actions, are directly observable. For example, the results of a test, question, problem solving procedure, etc. The values of such variables will be used to infer the values of the hidden knowledge variables. In the GBSM, evidential variables are also considered to be binary, with values 0 (incorrect) or 1 (correct).

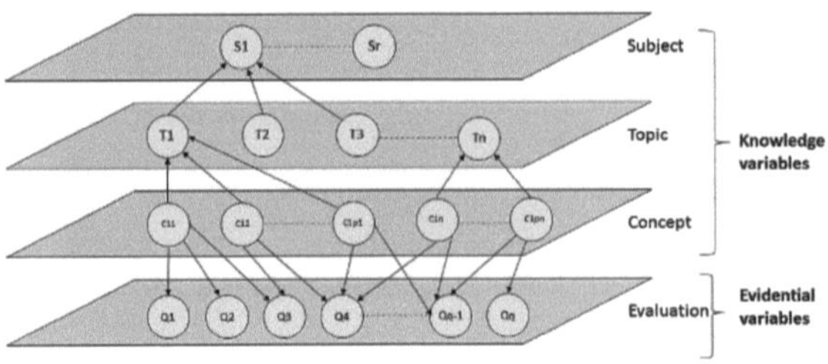

Fig. 4. The structure of our Learner Model [6].

In Fig. 4, there are two types of relationships: aggregation relationships and causal relationships. Aggregation relationships are between knowledge nodes (basic concepts, topics and subject). Causal relationships are between knowledge and evidential nodes (concepts and evaluations).

4.4 Our Conceptual Architecture

Technically, our conceptual architecture (Fig. 5) relies on three main components: the learner environment, the Learning Record Store (LRS), and the Learning Map (LMAP) core.

The learner environment is composed of different learning tools. The LMS platform is the main component of this environment. It contains the Course Navigation module that gives the learner a personalized access to content. In the learner environment, MOOCs are central but there are also other assessment platforms and social networks offering learning services.

Since we have different learning services and platforms, we need to collect learning experience and performance data from many different sources and present them in a meaningful way. That is why we choose the use of the LRS that supports the open standard, xAPI (Experience Application Performing Interface). In this way, all learning traces collected from the learner environment are transferred to the LMAP core via the LRS. Note that a statement (to be approved by the teacher) can be made by the user himself based on a certification or on a previous/current job.

The Learner Models are dynamic and must be updated. As such, we used the LMAP core to (1) store the Domain and the Learner Model, and (2) update the Learner Models.

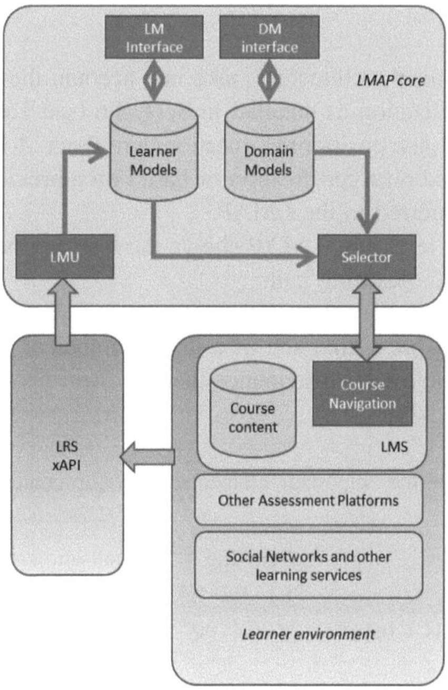

Fig. 5. Our conceptual architecture [6].

In the LMAP core, we have two main components and two interfaces. The main components are the Learner Model Updater (LMU) and the Selector. The LMU updates the Learner Model based on new assessments and learner achievements collected by the LRS. The Selector chooses the personalized content from the Domain Model according to the current Learner Model. The access to the models is provided separately by the Domain Model (DM) Interface and the Learner Model (LM) Interface. The DM interface enables Domain Models creation, modification, and deletion. It is defined for the DM editor in the CMS. The LM interface enables achievement updates, and access. It enables interactions with the learner and the teacher through LM Dashboard in the LMS.

Our first implementation is based on the edX platform, as it is the main open source platform with an active developers' community. We have developed xAPI connectors in order to collect learner traces of statements. Course Navigation is integrated by using LTI standard that permits seamless integration of external components.

As we explain in Sect. 4.3, the pedagogical engineer defines the Domain Model. The Domain Model is created via the LMAP editor which we have developed for this purpose. The frontend of our LMAP editor is based on Javascript, html, css, and svg. The backend is created using open source software LAMP (Linux-Apache-Mysql-PHP) server technology and PHP-framework Symfony 2. When the pedagogical engineer adds a new element (subject, topic, concept, or evaluation) in the LMAP editor, he needs to define properties below: the name of the element (label), its priority, the order it has in relation to other elements, its acquisition link (link to an online content), its acquisition mode, its validation link (if it exists), its validation approval, and the number of hours and weeks for acquisition.

4.5 Discussion

Our functional and technical architectures take into account the important elements for MOOC content personalization as detailed in Sect. 3.6 (see Table 2).

At the learning level, the positioning questionnaire (Sect. 4.1), the statements made by the user himself based on a certification or based on a previous/current job, and all learning traces are transferred to the LMAP.

At the visualization level, the LMAP shows the learning path of the learning and his current position in the learning path.

At the content level, we have three layers of granularity: subject, topic, and concept (Sect. 4.3). These layers are comprised of a large number of pieces of small grained learning content which allow to re-sequence them to form personalized learning paths for each learner.

Table 2. The presence of the important elements/levels for content personalization in our approach [6].

	Learning			Visualisation	Content
	E1	E2	E3	E4	E5
Statements + traces	✓	✓	✓	–	–
LMAP	–	–	–	✓	–
3 layers of granularity	–		–	–	✓

To summarize, in this research work, we propose a functional and a technical architecture to allow personalized content for each learner who attends a MOOC course.

5 A Java Course Case Study

In this section, we apply our approach on a Java course. We present the domain model modelled in the LMAP editor and the learner model for three different learners. The LMAP editor and some learner models are also shown on the following website: http://www.spoc.pro. Indeed, Immanens launched the commercial exploitation of "SPOC PRO", a cloud professional training. It is an outcome of the MOOCTAB Project.

5.1 The Domain Model of Programming Languages

The Java is a programming language. As we explain previously, the domain model is dedicated for a specific domain and its structure is detailed in Fig. 3. In our case, the domain is the programming languages. The domain is a set of subjects. In our case, subjects are different programming languages like Python, Ruby, Java, C, PHP, and JavaScript. Each subject is composed of many concepts. Figure 6 shows an extract of the domain model of programming languages. This model is produced by The LMAP editor detailed in Sect. 4. For clarity reasons, we present only some topics and concepts of the Java subject. In Fig. 5. Our technical architecture. Figure 5, the subject Java has three topics: introduction to Java, basic constructs, and OOP concept. The topic basic constructs include six concepts: primitive data types, variables and the assignment statement, how to run the example programs, input and output, floating point input, control statement (if, loops, while, for).

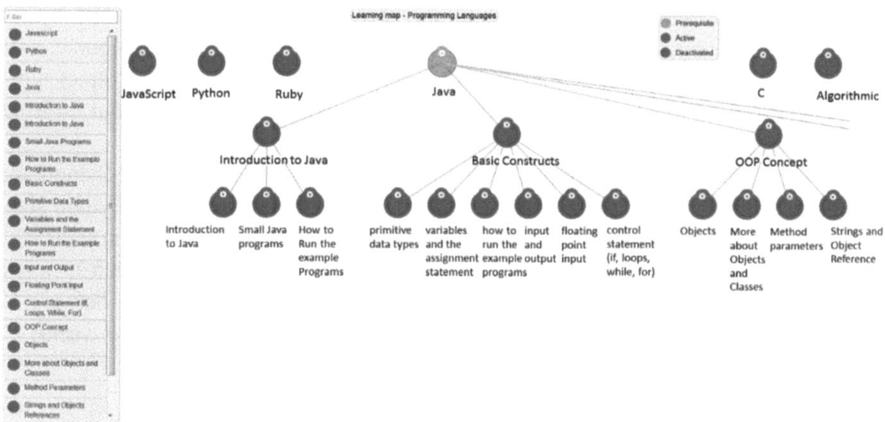

Fig. 6. An extract of a domain model in the LMAP editor. (Color figure online)

5.2 An Example of Three Different Learners

In this section, we present the application of our approach on different learners who want to attend a java course on a MOOC. Note that structure of a learner model contains also evaluation nodes (see Fig. 4). For reasons of clarity, these nodes are not presented in Figures Figs. 7, 8, and 9.

Consider the following example; Bill a Beginner in programming, Charles is a C programmer, and Elise is an Engineer who has developed skills through attending Java programming and algorithms courses.

Bill, Charles, and Elise are motivated to try our personalized content MOOC approach and they decide to subscribe to a Java course. The question raised involves discerning how initially, our approach is unable to provide any meaningful content suggestion to the three learners? This is the well-known cold-start problem.

In fact, the learner model is initiated from three different inputs:

- The positioning questionnaire (Sect. 4.1),
- A statement (to be approved by the teacher) made by the user himself based on a certification,
- A statement (to be approved by the teacher) made by the user himself based on a previous/current job.

Note that the time is a very important factor in our approach because knowledge can be forgotten with time. That is why every time the learner gives a new input, he must define when it goes back.

In concrete terms, Bill declares in the position questionnaire that he has never written a single line of code. Our platform proposes to him the full course of Java. The estimated effort for his personalized content is about 48 h, he needs to spend approximately 4 h of coursework per week for 12 weeks.

Charles owned a C programming certification from Coursera one week ago. He developed professional skills at work from various positions. Consequently, since Charles has already a good knowledge in programming, just equivalence syntax between Java & C and few exercises about the new syntax are proposed to him by our platform. Those exercises will also introduce algorithmic approach of the course, with some basic examples. Object programming will be introduced through abstract types and generalization. The estimated effort for his personalized content is about 24 h, he needs to spend approximately 4 h of coursework per week for 6 weeks.

Elise has a diploma in Computer Science. She declares that she took a Python and algorithmic courses five years ago. As a result, Elise is potentially expert in Python algorithmic but needs a refresher course in these two fields. Her personalized content starts with a short introduction to Java constructs and a focus on key differences between Java and Python with some exercises. The estimated effort for his personalized content is between 12 and 24 h, she needs to spend between 3 and 6 h of coursework per week for 4 weeks.

5.3 The Learner Models of Three Different Learners

In our case study, we have three learners: Bill, Charles, and Elise. Bill is a beginner in programming languages. Charles is an expert in C programming (certification from

Coursera one week ago) and he held various positions. Elise has a diploma in Computer Science and she took a Python and algorithmic courses five years ago. Our main contribution is that our platform takes into account these differences between Bill, Charles, and Elise in terms of background, prior knowledge, diplomas, and professional experience. That is why the three learners has three different learners Model. Learners can visualize their learner models through the Learner Model dashboard. Each element (subject, topic, concept, or evaluation) in the Learner model can have 5 statuses: Validated, pending, Unavailable, Failure, and ToDo.

As explained in Sect. 5.2, Bill needs to attend the full course of java. His learner model is based on the domain model and it is composed of all Concepts and evaluations of the Java Topic. Figure 7 shows an extract of Bill learner model. All the subjects (Javascript, Python, Ruby, Algorithmic…) except the Java are unavailable to

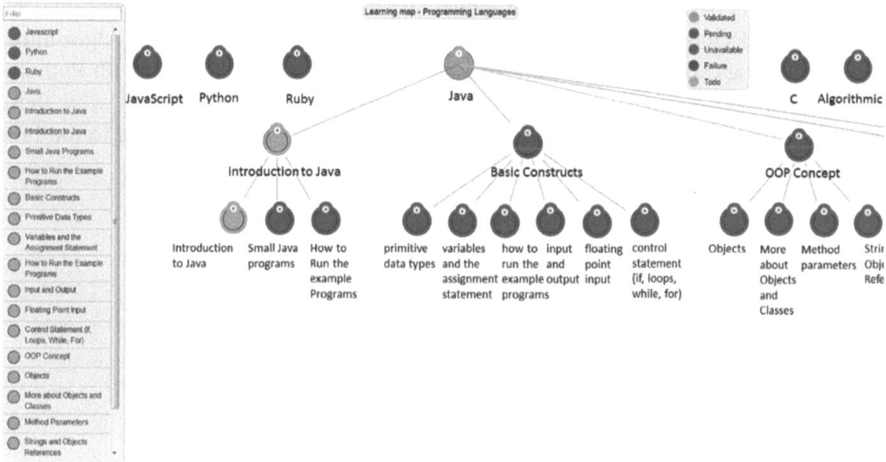

Fig. 7. An extract of Bill Learner Model in the Learner Model dashboard. (Color figure online)

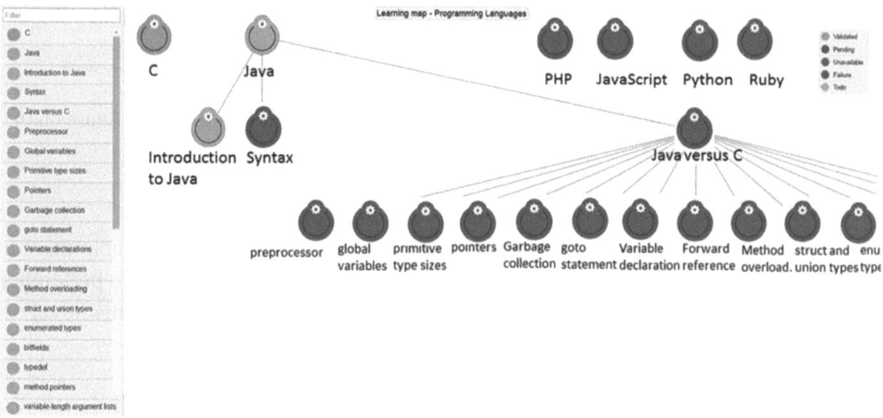

Fig. 8. An extract of Charles Learner Model in the Learner Model dashboard. (Color figure online)

him. He needs to focus only on the Java subject, he needs to learn Java concepts in order (first “introduction to Java”, second “basic constructs”, third “OOP concept” …). That is why “Introduction java” is blue (ToDo status). Once this concept is validated, it will be green and the concept “Small Java programs” will be blue.

Let us go to Charles case (Fig. 8). As discussed in Sect. 5.2, Charles needs to learn the syntax in Java and the difference between Java and C. His learner model is based on the domain model and it is composed of some concepts and evaluations of Java (The syntax and the difference with C) and he needs to start first by the introduction to Java topic before moving to the Syntax topic and finally to the Java versus C topic. This why the introduction to Java is in blue (ToDo status). The topic C is validated in his model (coloured in green).

In the case of Elise (Fig. 9), she needs to attend a refresher course about Python and Algorithmic and then she will learn the difference between Java and Python. Her learner model is based on the domain model and it is composed of some concepts and evaluations of Python (refresher course), some concepts and evaluations of Algorithmic (refresher course) and some concepts and evaluations of Java (difference with Python). She can start by Python or Algorithmic refresher course. This explains why these subjects are in blue (ToDo status). Once they are validated, Elise can move to the Java subject.

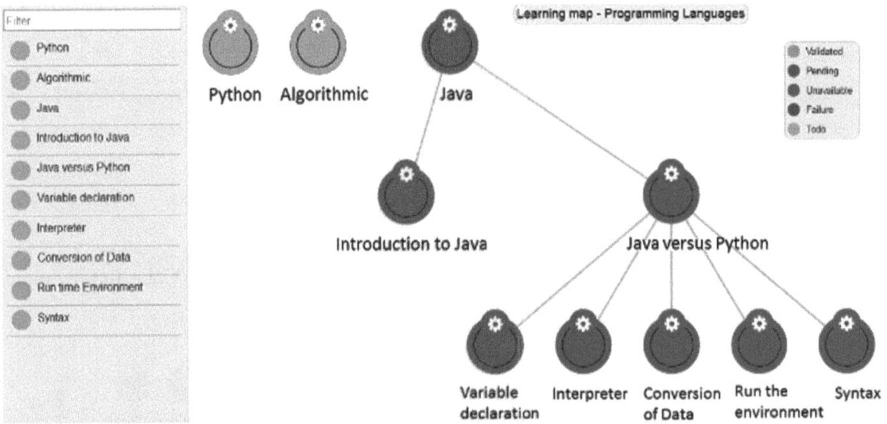

Fig. 9. An extract of Elise Learner Model in the Learner Model dashboard. (Color figure online)

5.4 Discussion

Bill, Charles, and Elise have a concept map/a graphic path indicator, these help them to visualize the structure of the domain knowledge of the course. The sequence preference in the concept map differs from a learner to another depending on his level of knowledge, his background, and his learning goals.

Table 3. Different learning paths.

	Java	C	Python	Algorithmic
Bill	Full course	–	–	–
Charles	Syntax in Java + equivalence between Java and C	✓	–	–
Elise	Java versus Python	–	Refresher course	Refresher course

For example, Elise must begin with a refresher course in Python and Algorithmic before attending the Java course (according to her personalized content).

While Charles and Bill start directly start by the Java course but with two different paths (see Table 3). Our approach therefore meets all the criteria set out in Sect. 3.6.

To summarize, in this research work, we propose a set of criteria, a functional and a technical architecture to allow personalized content for each learner who attends a MOOC course.

6 Conclusion and Perspectives

This research addresses the problem of "One Size Fit All" policy in Massive Open Online Courses for Lifelong learners. The study focuses on how to address the different learners (in terms of background, ability, experience, prior knowledge). In other words, the main issue is how to personalize content in MOOCs to the different learners and to increase the completion rate. According to the literature, no existing approach can meet our requirements to personalized MOOCs, to support of learner's level of knowledge, learner's background, learning goals, navigation preference, and the presence of a concept map for the course and a graphic path indicator. Thus, a functional and technical solution to our problem is proposed to personalized content in MOOCs and to provide more choices for learners. In others words, the goal is to increase the learning outcome and the average completion rate.

Now, we have to refine our learner and domain models and to implement them before deploying our solution in classrooms in France and Turkey for the MOOCTAB Project. To evaluate our approach, we will focus on results about the domain knowledge acquired by learners. To estimate the learning for a controlled period of time, learners will be divided into two groups: the first one will attend a course on a standard MOOC platform and the second one will attend the same course on our personalized MOOC platform. The learner selection will be based on a preliminary questionnaire to test learner prerequisites and to drive down inequalities in knowledge. The questionnaire will have to minimize knowledge heterogeneity of the two groups according to the knowledge addressed in the course. To evaluate the platform, learners' traces such as learning outcomes (i.e., course completion, course grades) and parameters related to the platform use (time spent on watching videos, on answering questions, on passing an exam) will be gathered and analyzed. These interaction data will be used to compare the various learners in the two groups. Next, we will consider how learners' interactions with the platform evolve over time to track changes in their learning goals.

To support our conceptual architecture, the MOOCTAB infrastructure (Fig. 10) relies on: (i) a web server in a cloud architecture with the role of hosting MOOCs contents and the global information system; (ii) some embedded servers hosting classroom-level information (called classroom servers or MOOCTAB Boxes) and used by teachers; (iii) tablets used by learners to interact with classroom level information and software. Synchronization processes are required between the Web server and the classroom servers, and between the classroom servers and the tablets.

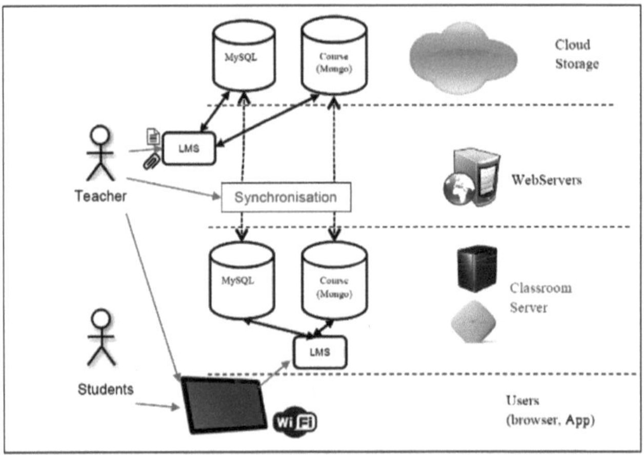

Fig. 10. The MOOCtab infrastructure.

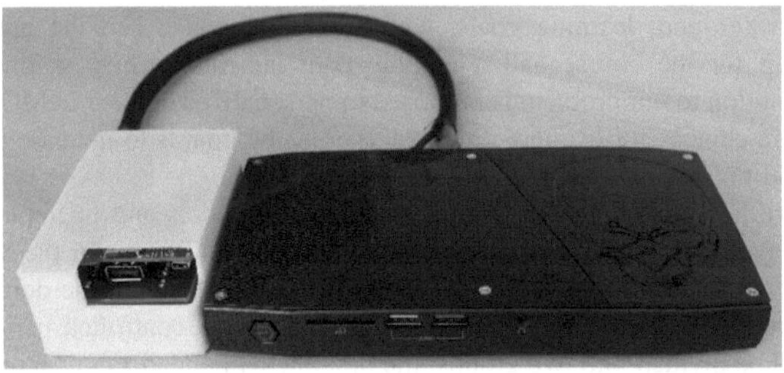

Fig. 11. A MOOCtab Box and a card reader for authentication.

The Classroom Server of MOOCtab Box has two main purposes: (i) It is a standalone server in a classroom; (ii) a teacher can store and update courses by connecting to the cloud server. In the MOOCtab project, every student will use a tablet as learning support. To make the lessons' contents available for the students, a MOOCtab Box is used as middle support, where students and teachers can connect using their own wireless tablet.

This MOOCtab Box – an Intel NUC - (Fig. 11) contains the whole data needed for the learning sessions, and the means to authenticate authorized students. It can work out of any connection as a standalone server. The students and the teacher of a specific lesson access different resources depending on their role in the lesson. The MOOCtab Box can also be used as official support for exams. A strong user authentication is achieved by identifying and authenticating the user using her student Id card (Fig. 11). The device authentication is achieved by using a device manufacturer certificate and associated keys that are stored in the tablet secure element. These credentials enable to authenticate the device to be sure that it respects the needed configurations.

Acknowledgements. This research was supported by The ITEA 2 (Information Technology for European Advancement) Massive Online Open Course Tablet, MOOCTAB (2014-2017) project.

References

1. Amo, D.: MOOCs: experimental approaches for quality in pedagogical and design fundamentals. In: Proceedings of the First International Conference on Technological Eco-System for Enhancing Multiculturality, pp. 219–223. ACM (2013)
2. Brouns, F., et al.: A networked learning framework for effective MOOC design: the ECO project approach (2014)
3. Brusilovsky, P., Maybury, M.T.: From adaptive hypermedia to the adaptive web. Commun. ACM **45**, 30–33 (2002)
4. Collet: POEM (Personalised Open Education for the Masses). In: Educpros: actua-lités et services pour les professionnels de l'éducation (2013). http://www.letudiant.fr/educpros/. Accessed 18 Nov 2017
5. Cropley, A.J.: Some guidelines for the reform of school curricula in the perspective of lifelong education. Int. Rev. Educ. **24**, 21–33 (1978)
6. El Mawas, N., Gilliot, J.-M., Garlatti, S., Euler, R., Pascual, S.: Towards personalized content in massive open online courses. In: 10th International Conference on Computer Supported Education. SCITEPRESS-Science and Technology Publications (2018)
7. Germanakos, P., Mourlas, C.: Adaptation and personalization of web-based multimedia content. In: Digital Multimedia Perception and Design, pp. 284–304 (2006)
8. Ioannidis, Y., Koutrika, G.: Personalized systems: models and methods from an IR and DB perspective. In: Proceedings of the 31st International Conference on Very Large Data Bases, p. 1365. VLDB Endowment (2005)
9. Jordan, K.: Initial trends in enrolment and completion of massive open online courses. Int. Rev. Res. Open Distrib. Learn. **15** (2014)
10. Kizilcec, R.F., Piech, C., Schneider, E.: Deconstructing disengagement: analyzing learner subpopulations in massive open online courses. In: Proceedings of the Third International Conference on Learning Analytics and Knowledge, pp. 170–179. ACM (2013)
11. Knox, J., Ross, J., Sinclair, C., Macleod, H., Bayne, S.: MOOC feedback: pleasing all the people. Invasion of the MOOCs 98 (2014)
12. McLoughlin, C.E.: The pedagogy of personalised learning: exemplars, MOOCS and related learning theories. In: EdMedia: World Conference on Educational Media and Technology, pp. 266–270. Association for the Advancement of Computing in Education (AACE) (2013)
13. Millán, E., Descalço, L., Castillo, G., Oliveira, P., Diogo, S.: Using Bayesian networks to improve knowledge assessment. Comput. Educ. **60**, 436–447 (2013)
14. Sloep, P., et al.: A European research agenda for lifelong learning. Int. J. Technol. Enhanced Learn. **3**, 204–228 (2011)

15. Sunar, A.S., Abdullah, N.A., White, S., Davis, H.C.: Personalisation of MOOCs: the state of the art (2015)
16. Thompson, C.: How Khan Academy is changing the rules of education. Wired Mag. **126**, 1–5 (2011)
17. U.S. Department of Education Office of Educational Technology: Transforming American Education - Learning Powered by Technology. National Education Technology Plan (2010)
18. Vignette Corp.: Personalization Strategies-Fit Technology to Business White Paper (2002)
19. Yousef, A.M.F., Chatti, M.A., Schroeder, U., Wosnitza, M., Jakobs, H.: A review of the state-of-the-art. In: Proceedings of CSEDU, pp. 9–20 (2014)
20. MOOCs Annual Report 2015. Center for Digital Education, Ecole Polytechnique Fédérale de Lausanne (2016)
21. MOOCs Find Their Audience: Professional Learners and Universities | EdSurge News. https://www.edsurge.com/news/2017-07-06-moocs-find-their-audience-professional-learners-and-universities. Accessed 3 Jul 2018

Intermediaries in eHealth Education

Janne Lahtiranta[1] and Anne-Maarit Majanoja[2(✉)]

[1] Department of Management and Entrepreneurship, University of Turku, Turku, Finland
janne.lahtiranta@it.utu.fi

[2] Department of Information Technology, University of Turku, Turku, Finland
anne-maarit.majanoja@utu.fi

Abstract. As in other industry-related fields, information technology and business are becoming intertwined in health care. This has changed the field profoundly, including the way people work, communicate and conduct their everyday affairs. This change is ongoing, and the future of health care and technology is unknown. However, one thing is certain: this change calls for new kinds of professionals who are able to work in a field that has become multi-faceted and convoluted, and able to meet the changing requirements of the eHealth industry. In the following, the focus is on industry-oriented eHealth education, how it can be enabled in the context of higher education in Finland and what kind of intermediary roles are needed. The results are based on a practically oriented pilot in which new forms of industry-oriented education were examined and put into practice.

Keywords: Industry-oriented education · eHealth · Health care information systems · Health care technologies

1 Introduction

Advanced digitalization, an ongoing industrial paradigm shift [20], is changing the world in new and often unanticipated ways. It alters our behaviour, the ways we interact with each other – how we learn and how we teach – and it even has an impact on the fundamental notion of what it means to be a human.

Digitalization has already created benefits for many, and it will continue to do so in the coming years. However, even if it may seem to be, digitalization is not axiomatic, nor can it be taken for granted; talented people are needed to see the ongoing shift through.

Universities, especially Humboldtian science universities, are often blamed for stagnation. They are seen as slow to react to economic developments in the surrounding world [7, 21], and establishing new courses and degree programs often takes years [9]. To counter these arguments, and to develop a sustainable and networked approach to

This article is further work extending an earlier conference paper: Lahtiranta, J. and Majanoja, A-M. Industry-oriented Education in eHealth. In Proceedings of the 10th International Conference on Computer Supported Education (CSEDU 2018) – Volume 2, pages 411–419.

B. M. McLaren et al. (Eds.): CSEDU 2018, CCIS 1022, pp. 489–506, 2019.
https://doi.org/10.1007/978-3-030-21151-6_23

industry-oriented education, a project called 'Working Life Oriented Open University Education' was established in 2015. In the project, Finnish polytechnics, universities and industrial partners collaborated in the three distinct fields of (1) health and social services, (2) bio-based economy and (3) information and communication technologies (ICT).

The project, funded by the European Social Fund (2015–2018), consisted of three pilots, one in each of the three fields. These were stand-alone pilots; in other words, they were implemented autonomously in order to take the distinct characteristics of each field into account and to create different practices to be investigated by an external evaluator later in the project. Each pilot was charged with the specific tasks of (a) developing a method for industry-oriented education and (b) testing the method in practice.

In the pilots, the development took the form of 'inspect-and-adapt' cycles in concurrent implementations with a specific focus (Fig. 1), in the spirit of the Agile approach [5]. Due to the differences in the fields, and the autonomy of the pilots, the length and number of cycles was not predefined or limited. In some pilots, the most practical solution was to emphasize dialogue with the organizations, focus on business priorities and implement a single cycle in which the defined method was tested.

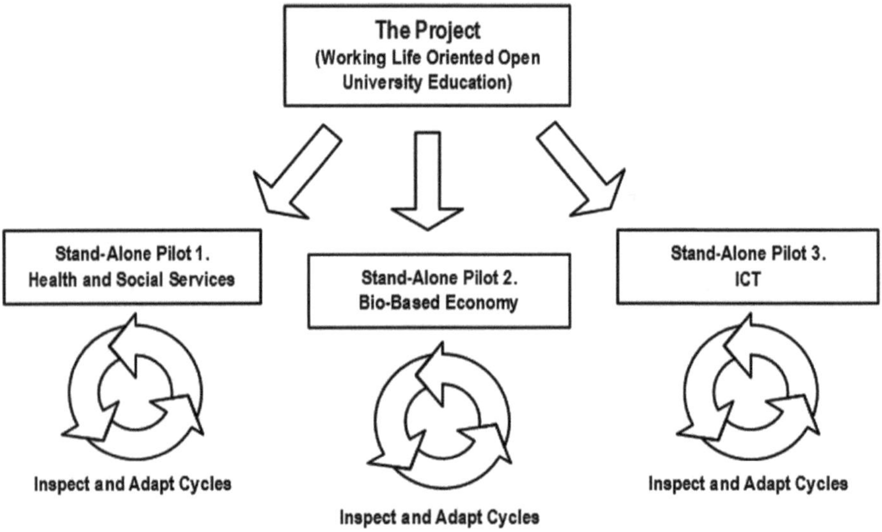

Fig. 1. Overall project and pilots (in [19]).

In the following, the focus is on the ICT pilot (Fig. 1, stand-alone pilot 3), and more specifically on one of its implementations that was carried out during the first half of 2016 in the field of health and wellbeing technologies (eHealth). This implementation is referred to as the eHealth pilot.

2 eHealth Pilot

Health care is one of the fields most influenced by digitalization. It not only changes the way of working in the field, but it also has a tremendous impact on how responsibilities and duties, and even power, is delegated [15–18]. eHealth is also one of the most promising fields in terms of business growth in Finland [14]. While other fields have been in decline in recent years, eHealth has been expanding. For example, in 2017, health technology exports in Finland grew to €2.2 billion, 5.3% up on the previous year. In the longer run, exports have grown steadily during the past 20 years, yielding a fivefold increase. At the same time, the export surplus increased to €1.1 billion in 2017, giving a total of €10.75 billion for 1996–2017 (Fig. 2). The performance is well in line with global trends, where the growth estimate of the domain is 5.1% ([10], p. 3). In other national estimates (ibid., p. 3), the growth in exports is more drastic (€10–20 billion) for the coming years. The underlying reason for these estimates is the currently ongoing health, social services and regional government reform in Finland, which will provide a reference market for ‘next generation’ products and services (ibid., p. 3).

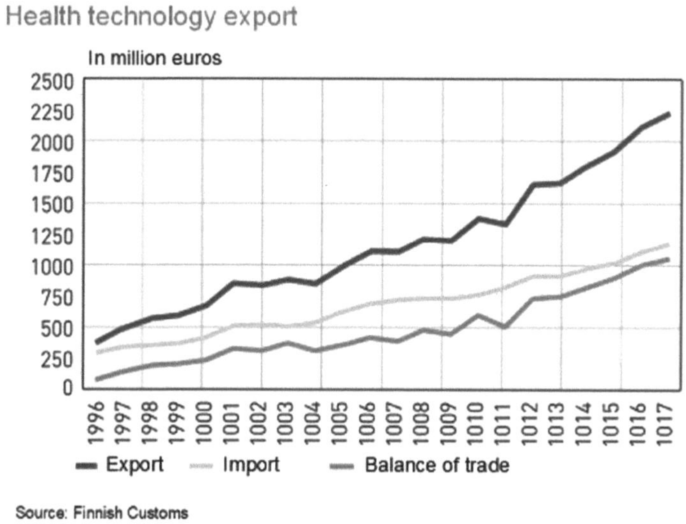

Fig. 2. Health technology exports (source: Finnish Customs).

eHealth is not a new field or a sudden ‘booming star’ in Finland. It has been on the rise since 1996, and there is no indication that the situation will change in the near future. One indicator of this is a survey conducted in late 2015 amongst health technology companies by the Finnish Health Technology Association (FiHTA) and Saranen Consulting. According to the survey, the majority of the companies working in the field were planning to hire new personnel in 2016 [25].

Another indicator of relevance is the changing health care infrastructure in Finland. There are currently four major health care digitalization projects in Finland, with two of them focusing on implementing a new Electronic Health Record (EHR). One of the EHR projects, Apotti, focuses on the public health service providers operating in the metropolitan area (i.e. the greater Capital Region). Apotti is currently in the early stages of implementation, and the project recruited approximately 150 health technology professionals in early May 2016. The second EHR project, Una, focuses on providers operating outside the metropolitan area. It is currently (as of September 2017) in the early stages of implementation, and it is estimated that the acquisition of the core components will begin in late 2017.

The remaining two health care digitalization projects, Virtual Hospital and Digital Self-care Services (ODA), focus on implementing new electronic services, such as virtual clinics (cf. [16]), in basic health care (ODA) and in specialized health care (Virtual Hospital 2.0). While the actual costs associated with the projects are still unclear, it is estimated that the cost of the EHR projects alone will be in the region of €1 billion [12], of which Apotti will account for €575 million (over the ten-year timeframe) [1].

The ongoing development in the field has created an acute demand for technology professionals who possess (a) a domain-specific skill-set from the field of ICT and (b) at least a basic understanding of how the health care field operates. In order to understand what these skills are, and what kind of ‘hybrid professionals’ the field needs, the first implementation of the ICT pilot focused on eHealth.

Digitalization creates new opportunities for health care, but it also provides opportunities for the education field, as different digital devices, modalities and ways of reaching students have become available. However, new tools and ‘gadgets’ alone do not inspire learning; it is important to focus on the content and incorporate real-life elements into education. One well-employed approach is to combine online courses [6] and to mix the course content with the challenges emerging in the domain of application. In this, a constant dialogue with domain experts from industry is essential.

2.1 The Framework

On the level of the overall project, the work was organized in stand-alone pilots focusing on a specific field. Within the pilot focusing on the field of ICT, the work was organized further as ‘inspect-and-adapt’ cycles and concurrent implementations with a more refined focus (Fig. 1). In the ICT pilot, one of the implementations focusing on eHealth (i.e. the eHealth pilot) organized the work even further by employing a more specific methodological framework.

The employed framework was based on the work of Stewart and Hyysalo [26], and on previous work by Stewart [27], on the roles of cybercafés in the 1990s. Their work on intermediary roles in the development and appropriation of new technologies defines intermediaries as individuals who (a) facilitate user innovation and (b) link user innovation to supply-side activities, such as marketing, branding or product development [26].

Using a more down-to-earth or bland definition, intermediaries can be seen as ‘go-betweens’; these are individuals who bring different people together and help them in the appropriation and generation of new technologies (or, taking a broader scope, innovations). As such, an intermediary is not a fixed concept or a profession; it is more akin to a role. There are different kinds of intermediary roles in different fields of business, and their alignment in the hierarchy and composition of different actors (producers, consumers, patients, physicians, etc.) commonly varies [17].

What is common to different intermediary roles is that they have an impact on shaping the end-user experience, or even entire markets. For example, when an intermediary operates between an electronic service and an end-user, the intermediary is in a position to shape the expectations, and in some cases the outcome, of the mediated service. In the case of electronic health care (or banking) services in particular, this is a position of power (ibid.).

The three-tiered framework created by Stewart and Hyysalo [26] categorizes the primary roles of an innovation intermediary as (1) facilitating, (2) configuring and (3) brokering. While the framework is more generic when compared to work in the field (cf. [3–13]), it can be applied to a wide range of domains, from technology to health (cf. [17]), and to industry-oriented education.

In Stewart and Hyysalo's framework [26], facilitating refers to activities in the core of industry-oriented education. It is about 'providing opportunities to others', either by managing resources, influencing regulations, setting local rules or by educating. Facilitating also highlights the managerial aspects of industry-oriented education, as the activities involve 'creating spaces' (ibid.) of various types (such as social, cultural or physical), or their combinations (for example, a network of educators and appropriately equipped facilities). From an industrial point of view, facilitation is about interaction, generating new opportunities and creating an encouraging atmosphere for a continuous dialogue between the demand and the supply sides of labour.

The creation of spaces used in facilitating is intertwined with configuring, which, as defined by the original authors (ibid.), is both technical and symbolic. While technical aspects are present, for example when certain properties (such as connectivity) of a product are configured to meet the needs of the end-users, the symbolic side of configuring has deeper meanings and connotations. Symbolic configuring conveys the meaning of use – how relevant the technology is from the perspective of different stakeholders (users, sponsors, suppliers, etc.). As such, symbolic configuration is about value and applicability – how well the provider side has succeeded in incorporating the views of the user side in their technology. The relation between the two 'sides' can be regarded as a symmetric one, as symbolic configuring incorporates the viewpoint of the provider side as well, and how the technology is intended to be used. In this symmetricity, the expectations of both sides share common ground.

The third activity in their framework (ibid.) is brokering. As the name suggests, the activity is present, for example, when the intermediaries raise 'support for the appropriation process from sponsors and suppliers' (ibid.). When an intermediary negotiates on behalf of a particular stakeholder in order to get new partners involved in a project, or when a particular space is defended by an intermediary, the actions of an intermediary fall into this category. While brokering is in the framework the most direct activity for an intermediary in the axis of user side and provider, it is also among the most vulnerable ones. If an intermediary fails in brokering, the result may represent itself in the form of a lack of commitment and interest. In other words, as the 'bridge' cannot be built, there is no common ground.

2.2 The Framework and the eHealth Pilot

In the eHealth pilot, a three-tiered framework was used in (a) outlining the needed skill-set, (b) organizing the lectures and (c) setting up the platform used in education. As such, the role of the intermediary [26] became intertwined with the concept of a product owner – a key stakeholder in the project implemented according to the Agile approach [5].

Defining the skill-set, and gaining an understanding of what kind of professionals are needed in the field, was done personally, brokered by a domain specialist. Instead of formal questionnaires, public seminars or workshops, representatives working in the organizations were met face-to-face (when possible). These meetings were flexible and informal; there was no written agenda or minutes and they were organized on the terms of the representatives (time and place).

The free-spirited meetings allowed room for exploring additional topics in addition to the skill-set and the expert profile. These included ongoing projects, potential avenues for future collaboration and the organizations themselves. It followed from this that the meetings were also about facilitating and brokering, linking organizations together, and not just about the project.

In relation to the goals of the eHealth pilot, the primary result of these 18 meetings was the collection of topics the organizations considered relevant in the field (Fig. 2). The topics covered the field of eHealth on a wide scale. While some of the topics were extremely specific, related to a single technology or standard, others were vaguer by nature and reflected the concerns of the potential employers.

Example: 'We have this problem that is not really related to technology. When a person starts working in the company, he or she is rather young, typically in [their] late twenties. Most of them have never been seriously ill, [and] neither have their parents. A consequence of this is that they [new employees] do not know how the field [of health care] works, or how it is organized. They can't separate a health centre from a university hospital' [Lahtiranta, personal communication, translated].

The topics were also prioritized using a simple and straightforward method; if the organizations specifically pointed out that a certain topic was vital for their business, or if a topic was repeatedly mentioned in other meetings, it was considered essential (indicated by a circle in Fig. 3).

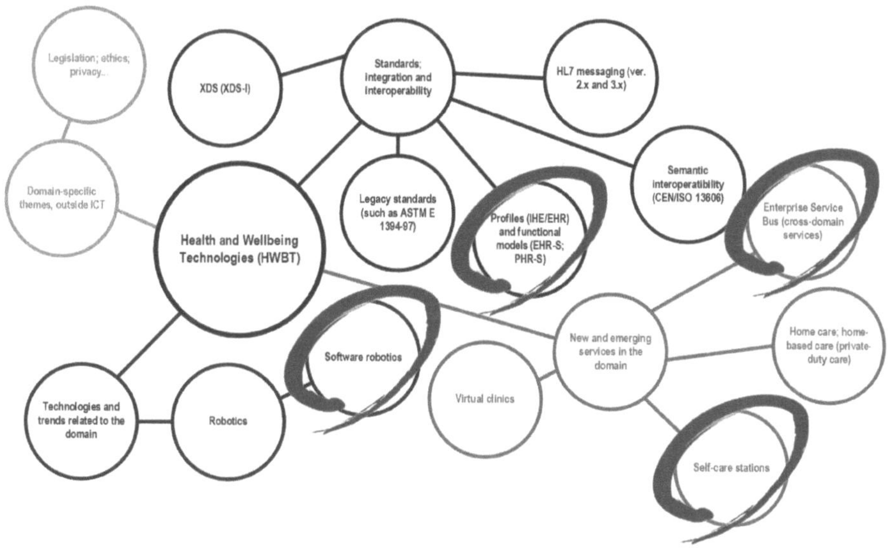

Fig. 3. Topics (a sample) (in [19]).

In total, 55 topics of different degrees of specificity were identified. In order to analyse these in more detail, they were grouped using the following categories: (a) standards; integration and interoperability, (b) new and emerging services in the domain, (c) technologies and trends related to the domain and (d) domain-specific themes outside ICT. Individual topics were distributed according to the following table (Table 1).

Table 1. Categories and topics (in [19]).

Category	Distribution
Standards; integration and interoperability	18
New and emerging services in the domain	10
Technologies and trends related to the domain	18
Domain-specific themes outside ICT	9
Total	**55**

In the next phase, the topics were re-grouped into more concrete groups based on their thematic and contextual similarities (if there were any). For example, certain European Union directives (93/42/EEC, 90/385/EEC and 98/79/EC) formed a group related to validation and verification. In the case of messaging, certain standards (ASTM E 1394-97 and HL7 ver. 2.x) formed a group of their own due to the similarities in structure and function. These groups were called thematic groups.

On a more abstract level, the thematic groups took the shape of two distinct collections: introductory and advanced. The topics regarded as introductory related to the nature and organization of health care and social services (e.g. legislation, funding, etc.). The remaining topics, the advanced ones, related to a specific function or standard, such as the Cross Enterprise Document Sharing (XDS) standards (Table 2).

Table 2. Thematic groups (a sample) (in [19]).

Thematic group	Content description	Learning outcomes
Coding, classification and ontologies	Coding, classification and ontologies have a long history in the field of health care. They are an essential part of service provisioning today, and they are embedded into most communication standards in the field	During the lecture(s), an introduction to ontologies is provided, and some of the most common coding and classification systems (such as SNOMED CT and ICD-10) are briefly introduced
	In the health care domain, information is commonly exchanged in (asynchronous) messages. Some of these messages based on 'legacy standards' were developed in the 1990s but are still in use	Starting with ASTM E 1394-97, continuing to HL7 2.x messaging, and later on to the up-to-date HL7 v3 messaging, the lecture(s) outline the used standards and provides practical examples of their use
Messaging	Profiles and functional models provide a summary of the envisioned functions for specific information systems, such as EHR. Furthermore, profiles (such as IHE integration profiles) define conformance criteria for such systems	The lecture(s) depicts the most relevant functional models today (such as PHR-S and EHR-S) and (localized) integration profiles used in the field. In addition, the lecture (s) provides a cursory glance at IHE Scheduled Workflow (SWF) and an introduction to IHE organization (focusing on the national special interest group)
Profiles and functional models	Coding, classification and ontologies have a long history in the field of health care. They are an essential part of service provisioning today, and they are embedded into most communication standards in the field	During the lecture(s), an introduction to ontologies is provided, and some of the most common coding and classification systems (such as SNOMED CT and ICD-10) are briefly introduced

As Table 2 shows, thematic groups formed the backbone of the actual lectures. Content and learning outcomes were defined for each of the formed groups based on the literature, domain knowledge and earlier discussions with the companies. In addition, thematic 'arcs' were discussed; how the themes are linked to each other, the actual scope and the extent to which the themes overlap (for example, in the case of legislation and EU directives).

There were no funds reserved for outsourced services, such as marketing or lectures, in the eHealth pilot. One consequence of this was that the lecturers had to be recruited from industry, domain organizations, standards development organizations, universities and government. In all, 49 different organizations were contacted.

As the language of the lectures was English, it was possible to recruit lecturers internationally. The recruitment process was also used for collecting feedback on the original topics, thematic groups and on the planned 'arcs'. As such, the process itself formed a reflective inspect-and-adapt cycle of its own, executed in the spirit of Agile development [5].

The recruitment process further defined the thematic groups as actual lecture content. While the original topics (Fig. 3) were considered an accurate representation of the industry and the needs of the organizations, the availability and expertise of the lecturers defined the final content and the amount of lectures (per thematic group). For example, in addition to giving a generic lecture on trends related to the field, the lecturers insisted on delving deeper into specific trends, such as corporate wellness, which was considered particularly important.

As the lectures were delivered in English and the recruitment of lecturers was global, the most practical way of offering lectures was online. Some of the lectures were webinars with a live audience and lecturer, while others were recordings produced specifically for the project. The lectures were recorded using the Adobe Connect web conferencing software service, and they were offered via the open-source learning platform and course management system known as Moodle.

Employing the taxonomies of the used methodological framework [26], these two (Adobe Connect and Moodle) were the technical elements of the 'space' configured for the purposes of the eHealth pilot and used for facilitating expertise and knowledge on eHealth.

There were five steps involved in the process from definition to implementation, or from collecting topics to giving actual lectures (Fig. 4). First, the topics were collected in free-form meetings with one or two representatives of organizations operating in the eHealth field. These included companies, standards development organizations, universities and research organizations and government. The meetings were face-to-face when possible. The collected topics were prioritized and grouped thematically, including assemblages of topics with similarities or that were close to each other context-wise.

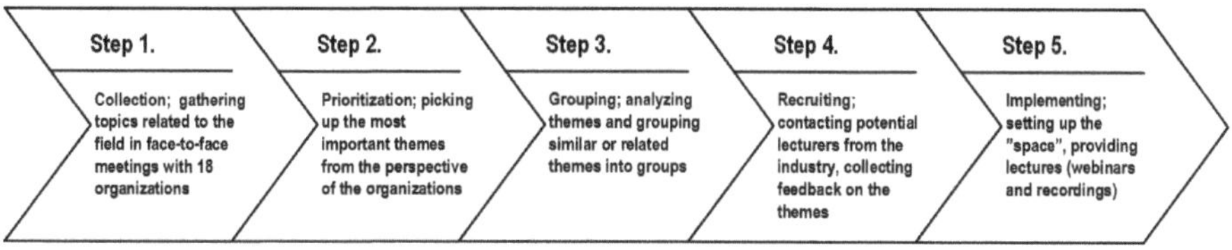

Fig. 4. Steps 1–5, from definition to implementation (in [19]).

The thematic groups formed the backbone of the actual lectures and were used in recruitment. At that time, the groups were also subject to feedback from potential lecturers. The actual lectures were formed based on the thematic groups and lecturers' feedback, including their expertise and interests. Finally, the lectures were provided via an electronic teaching platform, or the 'space'.

Even though the process is depicted as a linear one in Fig. 4, certain steps were repeated. For example, the composition of thematic groups changed during the recruitment process, resulting in regrouping. Figure 4 also depicts how different intermediary roles were aligned during the overall process. While the content was brokered by a domain specialist (steps 1–3), the practical arrangements (steps 4–5) were primarily – if not always solely – brokered and configured by the academic officers. In the following, the challenges related to the work of the academic officers are discussed in more detail.

2.3 Practical Arrangement of Lectures

Organizing a novel course, especially on a new domain with tight coupling to industry, can be quite demanding for academic officers working in the Open University. The practicalities require a lot of planning, scheduling, brokering and marketing, significantly more than in the case of a more typical or 'academic' course.

The lectures and the related materials (handouts, assignments, etc.) were agreed directly with the lecturers. During the course of arranging these practicalities, it was discovered that sometimes the language used in the course was a challenge for some of the lecturers, as they were not used to giving lectures in English. This was considered too demanding by some of the lecturers, who lost interest in the project.

Another motivational aspect was financial, as some of the lecturers refused to participate due to the low level of compensation offered. As discussed earlier, the eHealth pilot did not have any funding to cover lecturing costs. Thus, one of the findings of the pilot is that investment is needed if the plan involves incorporating experienced industry specialists into the education.

Organizing the actual lectures with the potential lecturers caused some challenges for the Open University's academic officers as the lecturers asked for detailed instructions on, for example, the domain-specific technical aspects of their topic. Understandably, the officers were not able to answer these kinds of questions given that they did not possess sufficient technical expertise on the domain.

Another challenge for the Open University's academic officers was contacting industry specialists, as they did not have the required network and did not share the same 'language'. The academic officers felt calling the potential lecturers and discussing the practicalities in-depth was quite demanding.

Thus, during the eHealth pilot, four types of challenges were identified from the perspective of the academic officers. (1) Scheduling the lectures (brokering). Sometimes, it was a challenge to reach lecturers from the industry side in order to arrange the schedule of the lectures. Commonly, the lecturers answered after the schedule was set, which required changing the course setup and structure; eventually, the effects of this were also evident to the students.

As an example, it was initially planned for some of the lectures to be available online prior to issuing assignments, and it was intended that the assignments would be based on the contribution. However, the lectures and the assignments were 'out of sync', which caused fundamental problems for the organizers and the students.

(2) Scheduling of the academic officers (facilitating). Some of the scheduling problems originated from the officers, which were a direct consequence of the somewhat 'stop-go' nature of the course. Planning and practical arrangements (Fig. 4, steps 4–5) required significantly more time than was originally estimated; even a partial restructuring of the timetable took up academic officers' entire working days. The officers were not assigned solely to the course, and they had other duties to which to attend.

(3) Setting up the online course (configuring). The original idea was to organize the course as a series of online lectures, or webinars, which could be attended by everyone interested. The focus group was not limited, as the course was intended as a low-threshold introduction to the field and to the relevant actors (organizations, companies, researchers, etc.). However, due to the practical challenges and problems in scheduling, a decision was made to implement (to 'reconfigure') the course as an online course with limited access in the Moodle learning environment. Even though the course was organized as a closed one (in contrast to a MOOC, c.f. [2]), it was successful in facilitating, namely in bringing together students from health care and from the technology side.

(4) Student recruitment (brokering). This eHealth-focused course was a new addition to the curricula of the Open University. As such, it needed a new marketing approach, as it was not enough to simply add the course to the list of those available. At first, the course was marketed using traditional methods, such as via the university's webpages and email distribution lists. However, it quickly became clear that in order to reach the intended audience – potential students interested in operating in a field that combines technology and health care – social media channels had to be utilized as well. In doing this, LinkedIn, Facebook and Twitter were the primary channels. In addition, an interview that focused on the overall project was published in one of Finland's leading newspapers. This was a real boost in terms of marketing.

Despite the practical challenges described above, the course was conducted successfully, with an extremely strong connection to industry.

3 The Pilot and the Project

The 'Working Life Oriented Open University Education' project was executed from 2015–2018. Based on the preliminary analysis (2018) of the individual pilots (Fig. 1), the approach adopted in the eHealth pilot differed somewhat from the other ones at the level of practice. In the following, these differences are discussed.

In the Bio-based Economy pilot, the approach was to identify relevant courses offered by the open universities operating in Finland. The results of the pilot included a catalogue of the identified courses; students could choose one or more courses from the catalogue based on their preferences.

In addition to the catalogue, an introductory course called ‘New Viewpoints to Bio-based Economy’ was developed as an online course in the pilot. The purpose was to help students understand how they can create an appealing skill-set and a student portfolio of their own related to the business domain.

In the Health and Social Services pilot, the focus was on course collections instead of individual courses. These collections were built around specific topics, such as child welfare and developing child and youth services. All courses were provided by the open universities, or open universities of applied sciences, and they already existed in the curricula. Unlike in the eHealth pilot, the focus of the Health and Social Services pilot was on cooperation between different education providers, including what kind of processes are needed and how practicalities (student enrolment, course credits, invoicing, etc.) can be managed.

In the Health and Social Services pilot, a series of web-based seminars (i.e. webinars) on four different topics were also provided as part of specific collections. Some of the webinars were developed in cooperation with other pilots when the topic of the webinar was related to the specific domain (such as ICT). Based on the feedback collected during the pilot, the webinars were regarded as a good way to integrate specific topics into course collections. With these kinds of cross-disciplinary collections, it was possible to highlight aspects that otherwise would have attracted less attention (such as usability, integration, etc.).

When compared to the ICT pilot, and more specifically to the eHealth pilot (one of the ‘inspect-and-adapt’ cycles in the ICT pilot, see Fig. 1), the premise was different, and so were the measures taken. There were no appropriate eHealth-related courses to pick from, and therefore the content had to be produced from ‘square one’. In doing this, the innovation of the pilot emerged. Instead of implementing the content of the pilot based on the current curricula, it was possible to use the expectations of the industry as a starting point.

To summarize, the Bio-based Economy and Health and Social Services pilots focused primarily on developing practicalities and making connections between different educators. In comparison, the ICT pilot, and the eHealth pilot specifically, focused on bridging activities – how to bring the industry and the educators together.

The steering group of the overall project was satisfied with the findings of the ICT pilot, with some challenges and opportunities identified. While proving that it is possible to implement academic education from the industry point-of-view, the pilot also underlined some challenges in the way open universities currently operate in Finland.

As the other pilots and experiences drawn from the eHealth pilot suggest, the managerial side of affairs requires the bulk of the work, and is commonly (if not solely) at the centre of development activities in Finnish open universities. It follows from this that focusing on the operative side (in other words, industry collaboration) is rarely a viable avenue.

3.1 From Pilot to Practice

Over the course of the project (2015–2018), global economics changed. In 2015, the economy was largely in decline, while by 2018 it was booming. In Southwest Finland in particular, the ICT sector faced a ‘positive structural change’ in 2018, and ICT professionals were in high demand. This economic alteration provided the project personnel with unique insights into the way the ICT labour market changed in the region. Even though global economics were improving during the final quarter of the project, unemployed ICT professionals often struggled to get new work. While the reasons for this are without doubt multiform and complex, one of the possible explanations is the industry-education mismatch. The ICT professionals were 'products of their time' (education and work experience), meaning they did not necessarily possess the skills that were relevant during the economic boom.

Following this assumption, it can be argued that Finnish universities and open universities should have a more active role in lifelong learning – in the kind of education that aims to meet the current needs of industry. This line of thought is in line with current developments in the Finnish education sector, as the Ministry of Education and Culture [24] has granted a separate €10 million fund for higher education for retraining and upgrading qualifications in the field of ICT.

Taking this speculative discussion further, the open universities could provide more specific courses or master-level courses in the field of ICT, instead of focusing on more generic (bachelor-level) courses. This kind of approach could potentially provide more opportunities for 'working people' to update their knowledge and skills.

In the ICT field, students in Finland can be regarded as being working people, as it is common for students to be employed during the early stages of their studies. It follows from this that attending traditional face-to-face learning is rarely an option for those working full-time. This calls for new kinds of teaching methods and pedagogical approaches – something more than online access to recorded webinars. In addressing this, the eHealth pilot was a first step in the right direction as it combined elements from online courses, webinars, group work and face-to-face sessions, thus emphasizing the schedules of working people.

Continuing with the pedagogical viewpoint, there were two lessons of particular importance. The first was script writing; how to create an entire series of lectures (including content and exercises) in close collaboration with lecturers from industry. The second was networking; how to contact and manage industry connections. In order to excel in providing industry-oriented education, good connections with the domain companies is essential, and a prerequisite for successful brokering.

While the five-step process (Fig. 4) was developed based on the eHealth pilot, there are no restrictions in applying it to other business domains. In Finnish ICT education in particular, where a large number of assignments (master's thesis, capstone projects, etc.) come from industry (c.f. [23]), the five-step process may serve to bridge business and ICT, thus creating new kinds of 'hybrid' professionals similar to those working in the field of eHealth.

3.2 What Did the eHealth Pilot Lack?

The eHealth pilot was principally about the domain. The topics covered were mainly technological aspects or aspects related to the workings of the sector (funding, organization, service processes, etc.). As a learning outcome, the students gained an elementary understanding of how the domain operates, and received directions for future studies.

In a context broader than that of the thematic groupings (Table 2), the content of the pilot had three branches: (1) Basics; how the domain works and the 'gears shift'; (2) Systems; what technologies are used in the domain, and how they relate to the clinical work; and (3) Specifics; the kind of standards, ontologies and so on that the information systems use in their operation. In other words, the thematic groups formed a hierarchical de-composition that cut through the health care sector, primarily from the technological point of view. While this was essentially what the industry called for, some (well-known) themes could be used for expanding the education provided in the pilot.

(1) Technology. eHealth is about 'e' and 'health'. While the eHealth pilot focused more on the 'health', there is also a need for the 'e'. The ICT companies operating in the health care domain need domain-independent technology skills as well, and a common job advertisement is for a Full-Stack Developer – a programmer who is able to work on front-end and back-end portions of an application. These kinds of professionals need skills such as HTML/CSS, JavaScript, SQL, REST and so on.

(2) Project management. Another domain-independent skill of importance is project management. Simply put, this is crucial in developing high-quality products and services in a timely and cost-effective manner. Common approaches applied in the field of ICT include Agile/Scrum, Prince 2, and Kanban (to name just a few).

(3) Communication and negotiation. In the field of eHealth, running development projects is somewhat like politics; different individuals from different professional backgrounds need to work together. The need for these kinds of 'soft skills' is essential today, as the commonly employed project management frameworks (such as Agile/Scrum) place more responsibility on the individual developers. Consequently, the developers often work directly with the actual end-users and other primary stakeholders (cf. [22]).

To summarize, while domain knowhow is vital, it can only be used to a certain degree without other (basic) skills required of a ICT professional today (and vice versa). In order to educate professionals that can operate in the changing tides of today's technology development, a comprehensive education framework that integrates industry-oriented continuing education is needed.

4 Recommendations

Looking back to the eHealth pilot, and more precisely to the five steps depicted in Fig. 4, the following recommendations can be made. These are not intended to be domain or project specific, meaning they can be applied to the field of industry-oriented education as a whole.

Use a domain expert as an intermediary (Step 1). Regardless of the domain, planning industry-oriented education requires an understanding of the industry. Without a solid understanding of the domain in question, eliciting information from different sources (stakeholders, literature, media, etc.) is a challenge.

The domain itself – its processes, terminology, hierarchy, and so on – may pose a challenge for the uninitiated, and more so if the domain is a hybrid one, as it is in the case of eHealth. In eHealth, domain understanding is not just about technology; depending on the emphasis, it is also about health care, social services and wellbeing.

Domain expertise is related to another important requirement: networks. Without them, there is a risk that a certain stakeholder group will go unnoticed, and that its views will not be incorporated appropriately in the planning. For example, in the field of eHealth, different standards development organizations, such as the HL7, are of particular importance.

Prefer face-to-face meetings (Step 1). The personal touch matters. In the eHealth pilot, the representatives of different organizations appreciated doing things 'on their terms' (time, place, etc.). A direct result of this way of working was a more laid-back atmosphere, and the possibility to act as an intermediary. In other words, to bring issues to the table that would otherwise have been ignored or left off the official agenda.

Meeting face-to-face was also a matter of efficiency. Instead of communication via email or phone, it was easier to control the flow of the meetings to ensure that everyone was engaged and participated and contributed to the eHealth pilot.

Prioritize! (Step 2). Collecting singular themes was not enough in the eHealth pilot; it required further work to thin them out. Prioritization of the individual themes based on the corporate needs was the first step in the right direction. A simple method based on the number of times a theme was brought up, combined with the emphasis placed on it in the meetings, was sufficient.

However, this analysis could have been strengthened by analysing future trends provided by organizations such as Gartner or Forbes (cf. [8]). This kind of analysis would have given more back to the organizations, and even challenged them to reconsider their current position and future avenues in the field. The analysis could even have helped in brokering [26], if common ground had been identified in the fields of expertise and interest.

Sharpen up and clarify (Step 3). As the process of planning industry-oriented education moves towards more practical issues, such as organizing lectures, structuring content into manageable content is essential, particularly if the lectures are provided by more than one person or involve external professionals. In this, defining content and learning outcomes, and creating thematic arcs that linked themes together, was a valuable tool in the eHealth pilot.

Inspect and adapt (I&A) (Step 4). Reflecting on the current state of the project and comparing the results based on the goals is a basic practice employed in most project management paradigms. Instead of performing analysis retrospectively, iterative and incremental inspect-and-adapt cycles were performed during the eHealth pilot in the spirit of the Agile approach [5].

Each meeting with a company provided an opportunity for reflection on the themes gathered up to that point. The most natural reflection point, where the 'whole' (i.e. thematic groups) could be evaluated for the first time instead of the 'parts' (individual themes), was during the recruitment. At that point, the actual lectures, and the emphasis of the education as a whole, started to take shape.

Resource adequately (Step 4). Another recommendation that originates from the generic project management paradigms relates to adequate resourcing. There was a single step in the eHealth pilot during which resourcing was found to be insufficient: recruiting. Professional lecturers rarely come cheap, or free of charge, especially if the topic of the lecture is a current one. In the eHealth pilot, the whole field was a current one, especially in Finland, and certain themes even more so (such as the Fast Healthcare Interoperability Resource, or FHIR). The lack of resources made recruiting potential lecturers a challenge.

Another aspect related to resources and recruiting that had an impact on the content of the lectures was the HL7 membership. Even though the national organization collaborated and contributed, the international HL7 organization was understandably reluctant to contribute, as the organization responsible for the education was not a member at that time.

Advocate (Step 5). A traditional best practice originating from project management is advocating. A well-managed project needs a 'champion' [4], an unfeigned and authoritative character who carries the weight of the project. In the eHealth pilot, this practice should have been put into proper use as the project stumbled at a critical point, specifically during the handover from planning the course to producing the webinars and recordings.

Revalidate (overall process). Industry-oriented education needs periodic revalidation (unless it is intended as non-recurring education), and more so if the domain is a rapidly evolving one, as in the case of eHealth. During the eHealth pilot, two basic types of revalidation were discussed: (1) calendar-based revalidation and (2) trigger-based revalidation.

Calendar-based revalidation could occur yearly or bi-yearly depending on the field. During the process, the education as a whole could be scrutinized. Depending on the implementation of the education, this could be done at the same time as the practicalities are organized (time, place, lectures, etc.) or within a specific timeframe.

Trigger-based revalidation was seen as a narrower process; instead of looking at the education as a whole, single topics or thematic groups could be scrutinized. The trigger, a real-world event, could be the release of a new standard, law or directive, or the announcement of a project in need of specific expertise (such as the Apotti [1] project discussed earlier).

While these mechanisms were never put into actual use due to the nature of the ICT pilot (Fig. 1), they were considered as mechanisms that could be used in maintaining the original connection with the industry.

5 Conclusions

Industry-oriented education often contravenes the higher education provided in Humboldtian science universities. In higher education, the underlying paradigms are often static (such as in natural sciences), and may remain so for decades. In industry-oriented education, the paradigms shift and change in conjunction with economic fluctuations, development trends and even the whims of consumers. In other words, it changes when the underlying business does.

While fundamental, this difference in paradigms does not mean that industry-oriented education cannot be provided in the curricula of science universities. However, doing so requires flexibility; a different mind-set, different practices and new kinds of intermediary roles that bridge industry and science. It can be argued that this kind of flexibility is a necessity in the current research funding climate, where competition is fierce. In order to become a credible partner in securing funding and other assistance, higher education needs to pay more attention to the needs of industry. This is vital today, and will be tomorrow.

In order to understand how the education aligns in the supply-use axis from the perspective of industry, and what kinds of skills are expected from the eHealth professional of today, constant dialogue is needed. In achieving this, intermediary activities are essential, and educators themselves become intermediaries. This expands the skill-set of a modern educator and calls for active networking. The findings of the eHealth pilot represent the first steps in the right direction as part of a grander scheme to balance higher education and industry demands.

Acknowledgements. The project called "*Working Life Oriented Open University Education*" (2015–2018) on which the paper bases on was funded by the European Social Fund. The project partners were University of Turku, Diaconia University of Applied Sciences, University of Helsinki, University of Eastern Finland, Karelia University of Applied Sciences, JAMK University of Applied Sciences, University of Jyväskylä, Åbo Akademi University, and Yrityssalo Ltd.

References

1. Apotti: Apotti: usein kysytyt kysymykset (2017). http://www.apotti.fi/usein-kysytyt-kysymykset/. Accessed 4 Oct 2017
2. Baggaley, J.: MOOC rampant. Distance Educ. **34**(3), 368–378 (2013)
3. Bessant, J., Rush, H.: Building bridges for innovation: the role of consultants in technology transfer. Res. Policy **24**(1), 97–114 (1995)
4. Cash, C., Fox, R.: Elements of successful project management. J. Syst. Manag. **43**(9), 10–12 (1992)
5. Cohn, M.: Agile Estimating and Planning. Prentice Hall, Upper Saddle River (2005)
6. El-Bishouty, M.M., Chang, T.-W., Graf, S., Chen, N.-S.: Smart e-course recommender based on learning styles. J. Comput. Educ. **1**, 99–111 (2014)
7. Fathi, M., Wilson, L.: Strategic planning in colleges and universities. Bus. Renaissance Q.: Enhancing Qual. Life Work **4**, 91–103 (2009)
8. Forbes: Top Five Digital Transformation Trends in Health Care (2017). https://www.forbes.com/sites/danielnewman/2017/03/07/top-five-digital-transformation-trends-in-healthcare/. Accessed 4 Oct 2017
9. Gerson, E.M.: The interaction of research systems in the Evo-devo juncture. In: Love, A.C. (ed.) Conceptual Change in Biology. BSPHS, vol. 307, pp. 441–457. Springer, Dordrecht (2015). https://doi.org/10.1007/978-94-017-9412-1_20
10. Healthtech Finland: Terveyttä ja kasvua teknologialla (2018)
11. Terveysteknologian vuosi (2018). http://healthtech.teknologiateollisuus.fi/sites/healthtech/files/terveysteknologian_vuosi_2018.pdf. Accessed 20 Apr 2018
12. Helsingin Sanomat: Una avaa yli miljardin euron pelin. Helsingin Sanomat, 4 September 2015. http://www.hs.fi/kotimaa/a1441254356635. Accessed 20 Apr 2016
13. Howells, J.: Intermediation and the role of intermediaries in innovation. Res. Policy **35**(5), 715–728 (2006)

14. Kauppalehti: Terveysteknologian vienti rikkoi ennä-tyksiä. Kauppalehti, 9 April 2015. http://www.kauppalehti.fi/uutiset/terveysteknologian-vienti-rikkoi-ennatyksia/AjFvuGRg. Accessed 4 Oct 2017
15. Koskinen, J.S.S., Knaapi-Junnila, S.: Information technology – the unredeemed opportunity to reduce cultural and social capital gaps between citizens and professionals in healthcare. In: Kimppa, K., Whitehouse, D., Kuusela, T., Phahlamohlaka, J. (eds.) HCC 2014. IAICT, vol. 431, pp. 333–346. Springer, Heidelberg (2014). https://doi.org/10.1007/978-3-662-44208-1_27
16. Krausz, M., Ward, J., Ramsey, D.: From telehealth to an interactive virtual clinic. In: Mucic, D., Hilty, Donald M. (eds.) e-Mental Health, pp. 289–310. Springer, Cham (2016). https://doi.org/10.1007/978-3-319-20852-7_15
17. Lahtiranta, J.: New and emerging challenges of the ICT-mediated health and well-being services. Doctoral thesis. Turku Centre for Computer Science (2014). http://www.doria.fi/handle/10024/96886. Accessed 4 Oct 2017
18. Lahtiranta, J., Koskinen, J.S.S., Nurminen, M.: Sensemaking in personal health space. Inf. Technol. People **28**(4), 790–805 (2015). https://doi.org/10.1108/itp-09-2014-0214
19. Lahtiranta, J., Majanoja, A.-M.: Industry-oriented education in eHealth. In: Proceedings of the 10th International Conference on Computer Supported Education (CSEDU 2018), vol. 2, pp. 411–419 (2018)
20. Lasi, H., Fettke, P., Kemper, H., Feld, T., Hoffman, M.: Industry 4.0. Bus. Inf. Syst. **4**(1), 239–242 (2014). https://doi.org/10.1007/s12599-014-0334-4
21. Lozano, R., Lukman, R., Lozano, F.J., Huisingh, D., Lambrechts, W.: Declarations for sustainability in higher education: becoming better leaders, through addressing the university system. J. Clean. Prod. **48**(1), 10–19 (2013). https://doi.org/10.1016/j.jclepro.2011.10.006
22. Majanoja, A.-M., Avikainen, P., Leppänen, V.: The impact of agile software development approach on software developers' responsibilities. In: Rocha, Á., Correia, A.M., Adeli, H., Reis, L.P., Costanzo, S. (eds.) WorldCIST 2017. AISC, vol. 569, pp. 581–591. Springer, Cham (2017). https://doi.org/10.1007/978-3-319-56535-4_58
23. Majanoja, A.-M., Vasankari, T.: Reflections on teaching software engineering capstone course. In: Proceedings of the 10th International Conference on Computer Supported Education (CSEDU 2018), vol. 2, pp. 68–77 (2018)
24. Ministry of Education and Culture: Osaavan työvoiman saatavuutta turvataan uusila 10 miljoonan euron muuntokoulutuksila (2017). http://minedu.fi/artikkeli/-/asset_publisher/osaavan-tyovoiman-saatavuutta-turvataan-uusilla-10-miljoonan-euron-muuntokoulutuksilla. Accessed 1 June 2018
25. Saranen Consulting: Terveysteknologia-alalle tulossa yli tuhat uutta työpaikkaa ensi vuonna (2015). http://wwwsaranen.fi/uutiset/terveysteknologia_alalle_tuhat_tyopaikkaa/. Accessed 4 Oct 2015
26. Stewart, J., Hyysalo, S.: Intermediaries, users and social learning in technological innovation. Int. J. Innov. Manag. **12**(3), 295–325 (2008). https://doi.org/10.1142/S1363919608002035
27. Stewart, J.: Cafematics: the cybercafé and the community. In: Gurstein, M. (ed.) Community Informatics, pp. 320–338. Idea Group Publishing (2000). http://dx.doi.org/10.4018/978-1-878289-69-8.ch015

Detecting and Addressing Design Smells in Novice PROCESSING Programs

Ansgar Fehnker(✉) and Remco de Man

Formal Methods and Tools Group, Faculty of Electrical Engineering, Mathematics and Computer Science, University Twente, Enschede, The Netherlands
ansgar.fehnker@utwente.nl

Abstract. Many novice programmers are able to write code that solves a given problem, but they struggled to write code that adheres to basic principles of good application design. Their programs will contain several design smells which indicate a lack of understanding of how to structure code. This applies in particular to degrees in which programming, and by extension software design, is only a small part of the curriculum.

This paper defines design smells for PROCESSING, a language for new media and visual arts that is based on *Java*. This includes language specific smells that arise from the common structure that all PROCESSING programs share. The paper also describes how to detect those smells automatically with static analysis. This tool is meant to support teaching staff with providing feedback to novices on program design.

We applied the tool to a large set of student programs, as well as programs from the PROCESSING community, and code examples used by textbooks and instructors. The latter gave a good sense of the quality of resources that students use for reference. We found that a surprising number of resources contains at least some design smell. The paper then describes how to refactor the code to avoid these smells. These guidelines are meant to be practical and fitting the concepts and constructs that are known to first-year students.

1 Introduction

Programming has become an increasingly important subject for many different disciplines. First, programming was only important for technical disciplines. Nowadays, also novices in less technical disciplines learn some programming. Within these degrees, programming, and by extension software development, is just one subject among others. The curriculum will offer only limited room to teach principles and practices of software application design.

This paper is based on the experience in the first year of *Creative Technology* (CreaTE) at the University of Twente. CreaTe equips students with skills and knowledge required to develop creative and innovative human-centered applications. Programming is an integral part of the curriculum. First-year students are introduced to the PROCESSING language, a recent derivative of Java for electronic

B. M. McLaren et al. (Eds.): CSEDU 2018, CCIS 1022, pp. 507–531, 2019.
https://doi.org/10.1007/978-3-030-21151-6_24

art, new media, and visual design. It is a good fit for first-year CreaTe students, as its philosophy – as exemplified by a thriving community – is very close to the design philosophy of CreaTe. It prepares the ground for teaching more generic languages, such as Java and C++, as well as for teaching languages used in physical computing, such as the Arduino sketch language.

For novices, programming is often difficult. At the end of the first-year, students will be able to write code that effectively solves a given problem, but have trouble with applying principles of good application design. As soon as they have to build bigger applications, they find it difficult to understand, maintain or extend their own or other students code. Lack of exposure to principles of software design frustrates good students, who cannot progress beyond a certain point, and hinders struggling students, who are facing unnecessary complexities of their own making. An experiment with the block-based *Scratch* language has shown that badly written code can lead to decreased system understanding by programmers themselves but also for more experienced programmers that review the code [1].

The field of software development has developed in the last decades a set of principles and practices that guide good application design. Their aim is to make code understandable, maintainable, and extendable. A *design smell* is an indicator of poor design [2] that may negatively affect these aims. In programs by novice programmers, these smells are often symptoms of not understanding design principles or how to put them into practice. Giving quality feedback on application design to these programmers is especially important, and justifies the need for automated tools that assist programming educators.

This paper studies design smells in PROCESSING, a language developed by Casey Reas and Ben Fry in the 2000s for visual arts and new media [3]. PROCESSING lowers the bar to producing interactive applications and offers built-in methods for 2D and 3D graphics and for handling user input events, and a host of libraries for graphics, audio and video processing, and hardware I/O. It is a subset of *Java*, and omits, for example, certain object-oriented concepts of the *Java* language. These simplifications allow students to create a simple application in just a few lines of code.

While PROCESSING is a subset of *Java*, design smells that have been developed for Java do not always translate to PROCESSING. One reason is that PROCESSING consciously omits certain features, such as a system of access control. In PROCESSING all fields are `public` by design, which by itself would be considered a design smell in *Java*. Another reason is the established practice of the PROCESSING community. It is not uncommon in PROCESSING programs for objects to access and change fields of other objects directly. This would be considered poor practice in *Java*.

However, just because the language does not explicitly enforce certain coding practices, does not mean that students should not be exposed to the ideas behind them. Processing is only an introductory language, and CreaTe students will proceed to common general-purpose languages like Java, C# and C++. At that point, prior exposure to essential design concepts will be beneficial to understand advanced language features in those languages.

The software development community has learned that certain practices lead to poor code, regardless of language particularities. We have to strike a balance between keeping the benefits of a simplified language while introducing well-known object-oriented design principles. While it is technically possible to use any *Java* keyword or syntax in PROCESSING, and teach "*Java* by stealth", we choose instead to teach PROCESSING as it is defined by its inventors, and introduce design in the form of design smells that are to be avoided.

The definition of these smells in this paper is informed by a manual analysis of PROCESSING code from two different sources: student code, and community code. This paper will introduce customisations of existing design smells to PROCESSING, and in addition, define design smells that are particular to PROCESSING. All PROCESSING programs have a shared basic structure, with the same predefined methods for event handling and status variables. This common structure makes them suspectable to common violations of good design principles, violations you usually will not find in *Java* programs.

The paper then describes how automated static analysis tools can be used to detect these smells. The tool is applied to code from three sources: student code, community code, and code examples used by textbooks and instructors. This analysis gives a good sense of common design problems in PROCESSING, their prevalence in novice code, and the quality of resources that students use for reference.

This paper is an extended version of the work presented in [4]. We refined the definition of some of the PROCESSING specific smells such that they fit better with the accepted practice and extended the prior work with a discussion of recommended refactorings.

The contributions of this paper are as follows:

1. Defining design smells for PROCESSING code and assess to what extent these occur the most in novices as well as publicly available code.
2. A static analysis tool that detects those smells automatically.
3. A discussion of proposed refactorings that will address these smells and improve the overall design of the programs.

The next section discusses the background and work related to the subject. Section 3 describes the design smells, Sect. 4 the results of the manual code analysis. Section 5 discusses the implementation of automated detection tools for the earlier defined design smells. Section 6 validates the effectiveness these tools on code from different sources. In Sect. 7 we discuss possible refactoring that address the smells. The final section contains the conclusion and the discussion.

2 Background and Related Work

2.1 PROCESSING

The PROCESSING language was created to make programming of interactive graphics easier since the creators noticed how difficult it was to create simple interactive programs in common programming languages such as *Java* and *C++* [3]. It is based on *Java*, but hides certain language features such as access control of field and methods, while providing a standard library for drawing interactively on screen. Each program created in PROCESSING has a `draw()` method which is run in a loop to animate the drawings on the screen. Because the PROCESSING programs are primarily meant for creating interactive sketches, they are also called *sketches*.

2.2 Code Smells

A code smell is defined as a *surface indication* which usually corresponds to a deeper problem in the system. This means that a code smell only identifies a code segment that most likely has some correspondence with a deeper problem in the application design. The code smell itself is merely an indication for possibly badly written code, hence the name *code* smell. An experienced programmer would by seeing the code immediately suspect that something odd is happening, without always directly knowing the exact cause of the problem.

Code smells are widely used in programming education to give feedback to novice programmer code. Existing research has determined the most important code smells defined by standard literature on professional programming [5]. The code smells found in this study were used for the assessment of novice's code. This resulted in a framework that could be used for the assessment of novice's code in general. This framework covered nine criteria for code quality, of which two are related to design: decomposition and modularization.

Most recently, studies were conducted on the occurrence of code smells in block-based languages such as *Microsoft Kodu* and *LEGO MINDSTORMS EV3*. In [6] it was reported that *lazy class*, *duplicate code* and *dead code* smells occur the most. Another study on *Scratch* code from the community and on code of children new to programming showed comparable results [7]. The *duplicate code* smell is closely related to multiple design smells.

2.3 Design Smells

Design smells are structures in the design that indicate a violation of fundamental design principles and negatively impact design quality [2]. Although design smells seem to originate as part of code smells, design smells are usually more abstract. Design smells imply a deeper problem with the application design itself. Design smells are more difficult to detect using static code analysis, since design smells are related to the application as a whole, as opposed to parts of the code.

There is only little research on design issues in programming education. In 2005, a large survey was conducted in order to gain a better understanding of problems that students face when learning to program [8]. This study found that abstract concepts in programming are not the only difficulty that novice programmers are facing. Many problems arise when novices have to perform program construction and have to design the program.

2.4 Static Code Analysis

Static code analysis analyzes code without executing or compiling the code. Static analysis is used in industry to find problems with the structure, semantics, or style in software. This includes simple errors, like violations of programming style, or uninitialized variables, to serious and often difficult to detect errors, such as memory leaks, race conditions, or security vulnerabilities.

A popular automated feedback tool that is based on static code analysis is *PMD*. PMD finds code style issues as well as code smell issues. PMD works for multiple programming languages and custom rules can be implemented in *Java*. PMD was used in [9] to investigate to what extent PMD covers 25 common errors in novice's code. It furthermore linked the common errors to misunderstood concepts, in order to give students appropriate feedback on the root cause of the error.

Keunig et al. reviewed 69 tools for providing feedback on programming exercises [10]. They found that the majority of tools use testing based techniques, and most often they point to programming mistakes, which could be called code smells. They found only one tool that uses static analysis to explain misunderstood concepts. The tool, CourseMarker [11], offers a range of tools, among them also a tool to analyse object-oriented diagrams for design issues.

This paper is an extended version of the work presented at the *10th International Conference on Computer Supported Education (CSEDU)* [4]. This extended paper uses a refined definition of the PROCESSING specific smells and presents updated results. It elaborates, furthermore, in detail on how to refactor code to achieve a better overall structure.

3 Design Smells for PROCESSING

This section presents eight design smells as well as rules for good design that apply to PROCESSING. Four of these are specific to PROCESSING. They are a consequence of the predefined basic structure of PROCESSING programs, which leads to smells that will not appear in common *Java* programs.

The other four design smells are based on existing design smells in *Java*. While PROCESSING is a subset of Java, design smells that have been developed for Java do not always translate directly. One reason is that PROCESSING consciously omits certain features, such as a system of access control. In PROCESSING all fields are public by design, which by itself would be considered a design smell in *Java*. Another reason is the predefined basic structure of all PROCESSING program, with its predefined methods and status variables for event handling. In *Java* event handlers that handle multiple tasks by branching are considered a design smell [12], but in PROCESSING, this is the only way to handle multiple events.

3.1 Code Bases

The occurrence of the design smells in actual code is determined by manual and semi-manual analysis of programs from two sources. The first source consists of two batches of code written by novice programmers of the degree *Creative Technology* at the *University of Twente*. The first batch of 79 programs was written for the final tutorial in the programming course, whilst the second batch of 61 programs was written as the final project for the same course. Both batches are written by the same group of students and all code is provided anonymously.

The second source is community written code. This batch of 178 programs originates from www.openprocessing.org and was retrieved on the 20th of May 2017. We selected the most popular code, i.e. programs that received most likes by community members since the community has been active. Sketches from this source might contain professional code, but also poorly written code. This source is of particular interest to us, as students will use the examples that they find on this site for inspiration for their own project.

3.2 Processing Specific Design Smells

These design smells are specific to Processing and relate to best practices when creating a sketch in Processing.

3.3 Pixel Hardcode Ignorance

The pixel hardcode ignorance smell refers to having no abstraction for positioning elements that are drawn in the sketch. Instead of modelling objects with a position or size that can be represented on screen they treat Processing as an advanced drawing tool for rectangles and ellipses.

In the following example, a rectangle and car are drawn, both hardcoded in pixels.

```
void draw() {
  //Pixels are hardcoded
  rect(30, 40, 10, 20);
  car.draw();
}

class Car {
  //Partial class
  PImage image;

  void draw() {
    //Position is hardcoded in pixels
    car(image, 60, 60);
  }
}
```

In this case, moving, scaling or animating the sketch is difficult and in more involved sketches code duplication will occur. It will be difficult to impossible to reuse the code in a different context or turn it into a proper object.

This smell is related to "magic numbers", the use of literals instead of variables and constants. This is considered a code smell in other languages, but both community code as well as standard textbooks on Processing use magic numbers liberally. This is in part simply because PROCESSING does not use the concept of user defined constants. Failure to abstract from the position of a graphical element, however, will often prevent them from producing working, extendable or maintainable animations. This elevates this smell to a design smell. Use of magic number for other purposes, such as margins or sizes is accepted practice.

3.4 Jack-in-the-box Event Handling

The Jack-in-the-box event handling smell, a form of decentralised event handling, occurs when a novice programmer uses the global event variables in processing to perform event handling outside of dedicated event handling methods. PROCESSING defines global variables such as `mouseX`, `mouseY`, `mouseButton`, `key` or `keyPressed`. These global variables can be requested from anywhere in the code, but are meant to be used inside the event handling methods, such as `keyTyped()`, `mouseMoved()`, or `mousePressed()`.

A novice programmer may actually choose to not use these methods, and use the variables directly from other parts of the code, such as:

```
void draw() {
  if (keyPressed && key == 'B') {
    fill(0);
  } else {
    fill(255);
  }
}
```

In this example, the `fill(int)` method changes the color of the drawings as soon as the key 'B' is pressed. Although this code will work perfectly, it is smelly, since events can better be handled through the `keyPressed()` method, as follows:

```
int color = 255;

void keyPressed() {
  if (key == 'B') color = 0;
}

void keyReleased() {
  if (key == 'B') color = 255;
}

void draw() {
  fill(color);
}
```

This code has the same functionality but handles the keyboard event inside the `keyPressed()` method, which is considered more readable and maintainable. Programmers of PROCESSING sketches should always use the methods for event handling instead of putting event variables everywhere in the application.

This smell often causes students to struggle with debugging, as it becomes very difficult to trace changes on the screen to events, and vice versa. The name of the smells refers to the surprise many students or teachers feel when they find in some remote part of the program code that unexpectedly handles events. And often is the cause of intricate bugs.

3.5 Drawing State Change

In PROCESSING, the `draw()` method runs in a loop to redraw elements on the screen, unless `noLoop()` is used in the `setup()` method. Although the `draw()` method is meant for drawing objects on the screen as part of the sketch, it can be used as any other method, which makes it possible to change the state of the sketch during execution. While this should only be used to animate objects, it is often used for calculations and updates. These which should happen in a different place, preferably in methods that belong to an object and update its state.

3.6 Decentralized Drawing

The decentralized drawing smell occurs in PROCESSING sketches if drawing methods are called in methods that are not part of the call stack of the `draw()` method. All things drawn on the screen should always be drawn in either the `draw()` method itself, or in methods that are (indirectly) called by the `draw()` method. They should not occur in methods like the `setup()` method or the event handling methods. You might find that the event handler will directly draw something on the screen, instead of changing the state of an object, which then changes the representation of the object.

3.7 Object-Oriented Design Smells in PROCESSING

The smell mentioned in this section are known smells of languages such a *Java*, and are also common in PROCESSING code. However, they may have to be adapted to fit with the particularities and practices of PROCESSING.

3.8 Stateless Class

A stateless class is a class that defines no fields. It only defines methods that get data via parameters. In *Java* classes of this kind are sometimes called utility classes and are perfectly allowed. They help moving out computations and manipulators from stateful classes. This has some benefits, such as the stateless classes being completely immutable and therefore thread safe [13].

In PROCESSING, stateless classes are considered a design smell. Since PROCESSING allows having global methods in a sketch (which are defined in the hidden parent class of the sketch), utility methods should be defined here. Stateless classes should rarely or never occur in a PROCESSING sketch.

3.9 Long Method

The long method design smell is a smell that is directly related to the method length code smell. When a method exceeds a certain size, the method performs too many actions and should be split or shortened. Methods that have this design smell usually perform multiple algorithms or computations in one method, when they actually should be split into multiple methods.

Table 1. Result of manual analysis for the three different sets of programs.

Set	Number of programs	LoC per program	Smells per program	Smells per 1000 LoC	Programs with some smell
Novices (tutorial)	79	154.4	2.0	13.1	88.6%
Novices (finals)	61	310.3	3.1	10.0	98.4%
Community code	178	162.7	1.9	11.4	86.0%

3.10 Long Parameter List

The *Long Parameter List* design smell occurs when a method accepts too many parameters. When a method exceeds a certain amount of parameters, the method either performs too many tasks, or a (sub)set of the parameters actually should be abstracted as part of an object.

3.11 God Class

The *God Class* smell denotes complex classes that have too much responsibility in an application. It is detected by combining three software metrics: the *Weighted Methods Count* (WMC), the *Access To Foreign Data* (ATFD) metric and the *Tight Class Cohesion* (TCC) metric. The *God Class* smell is defined more in-depth in the book *Object-Oriented Metrics in Practice* [14].

In PROCESSING, the parent class of the sketch has a great chance of being a God class because programmers have access to all fields and functions defined on the top-level at all times. This can cause child classes to interleave with the parent class which causes the metrics to go bad quickly. A God class is considered bad design since it reduces maintainability and readability.

4 Design Smells in PROCESSING Code

In the previous section, eight design smells that apply to PROCESSING are discussed. Analysis of code from publicly available sources as well as student code has been done to determine how often these design smells actually occur. Table 1 shows the results of the manual analysis. They show the how many smells are present in a program. The results take to account whether a smell is present, not how often. Programs often make the same mistake consistently; one novice program, for example, had 106 instances of the *pixel hardcode ignorance* smell, i.e. 106 graphics commands with hardcoded pixels. Here we count this as one program exhibiting the *pixel hardcode ignorance* smell.

The results show that programs for the final project are about twice as large as programs written for the tutorial, with 154.4 lines of code against 310.3 in the finals. In the tutorial code, we find on average 2.0 of the eight considered smells, in the final project 3.1. This is in part due to the fact that the final projects are larger. The number of smells per line code decreases slightly in the code written for the final project. Overall smells occur very frequently in novice code, with close to 88.6% of all tutorial code, and even 98.4% of final projects containing at least one smell.

Table 2. Percentages of programs in different sets that exhibit a given design smell.

Smell	*Novice (tutorial)*	*Novice (finals)*	*Community code*
Pixel hardcode ignorance	29.1%	49.2%	33.7%
Jack-int-the-box event handling	62.0%	85.2%	32.0%
Drawing state change	20.3%	42.6%	55.6%
Decentralized drawing	5.1%	6.6%	5.6%
Stateless class	2.5%	9.8%	1.7%
God class	3.8%	16.4%	10.7%
Long method	72.2%	80.3%	36.5%
Long parameter list	7.6%	19.7%	10.1%

The results for novices may not be surprising since novices are still learning how to program. Surprising is, however, the number of community programs that do contain one or more smells. 160 out of 178 programs that were analyzed contained one or more code smells. There could be multiple reasons causing this. It could be that the community code is mostly written by inexperienced programmers, but it is also likely that to PROCESSING programmers the rules for good design are unclear or less important. This is of course caused by PROCESSING being a language without the history and broad usage of other languages, which led in those languages to widely accepted programming guidelines. Within PROCESSING the focus often lies on quickly producing visually appealing prototypes, instead of on building software systems that will have to be extended and maintained.

It is interesting to know is which design smells occur the most in the different sets of programs. Table 2 has an overview of the occurrences of each analyzed smell in each set. As we can see from this overview, the three most occurring smells are the long method, pixel hardcode ignorance and Jack-in-the-box event handling smells. Also, the drawing state change smell occurs in many community programs, while this smell occurs less inside novices programs. This might be caused by the novices assessment. They are asked as part of the assessment to implement classes, something that community programmers do not necessarily have to do.

5 Automated Detection

This section discusses the implementation of rules used for automated detection of the earlier discussed design smells. The PMD framework is used to implement the rules, which means that each rule can be used in combination with PMD to detect design smells in PROCESSING code.

5.1 PROCESSING Code Analysis in PMD

In order to make analysis of PROCESSING code with PMD possible, the PROCESSING sketches are converted to *Java* code, using the `processing-java` binary. Since PMD already has a grammar and supporting functions for *Java*, only the rules still need to be implemented. The rules implemented as part of this study detect the design smells inside the resulting *Java* files.

Converting the PROCESSING code to *Java* has some important side effects. For example, the sketch is converted to one *Java* class with all additional classes inserted as inner classes of this class. This is because the additional classes need access to the PROCESSING standard library, which is defined by the class `PApplet` in *Java*. The generated class extends `PApplet` to have access to all PROCESSING functions. These functions can then be used by the methods, but also by the inner classes.

If a PMD rule is violated, a violation is added to the PMD report. The rules implemented as part of this study detect when a design smell is found and reports them as a violation to PMD.

5.2 Design Smell Detection

Each design smell in this study is implemented as one PMD rule. All rules are implemented as an `AbstractJavaRule`, which means that PMD can execute them on *Java* files. Each smell has a different implementation discussed in the following sections.

5.3 Pixel Hardcode Ignorance

The pixel hardcode ignorance smell is implemented by checking each method invocation expression. When an expression calls a method, this expression is compared against the list of drawing functions in PROCESSING. A function matches the expression if and only if the name of the method is equal to the method name called by the expression, the number of parameters specified in the expression does match the number of parameters expected by the method, and the scope of the expression does not define another method with the same name and arguments (e.g., the method is not overridden). When the expression matches the method call of a drawing method, then all parameters that define the position in pixels are checked for being a literal value. When the method is called with a literal value for one parameter that is defined in pixels, a violation is created. In that case, the program contains the pixel hardcode ignorance design smell.

This rule has been slightly modified since [4], to align with the common practice in PROCESSING to define the size of graphical elements as literal values. The definition used in this paper considers only whether the position of an element is hardcoded, while it will not warn if, for example, the width or height is. Fehnker et al. discussed in [15] three dimensions for assessing static analysis warnings: severity, incidence, and correctness. While the definition in [4] was technically correct, and pointed to a definite violation (in contrast to a potential violation), it found many warnings that PROCESSING programmers will not consider severe enough to change the code. In this paper, we use a definition of the smell that will not warn about these less severe instances of *Pixel Hardcode Ignorance.*

5.4 Jack-in-the-box Event Handling

The *Jack-in-the-box Event Handling* smell uses possible call stacks to determine which methods are allowed to use global event variables. This smell required to extend PMD with a detection algorithm. The detection algorithm of the smell consists of two steps.

First, the rule checks which of the predefined PROCESSING event methods are implemented and used by the program. Of these methods, all possible method call stacks are evaluated and saved, as long as the methods can only be called from event handling methods. This detection is done by the exclusive call stack as described in [16].

The second step of the detection algorithm goes over all expressions in the code. If the expression is not defined inside one of the methods saved earlier, it is checked for the usage of global event variables. If an expression uses the global event variables, then a violation is created.

5.5 Drawing State Change

The drawing state change smell detection algorithm also consists of two steps. In the first step of the algorithm, the algorithm determines all methods that are called as part of the *draw sequence.* This is done by the non-exclusive call stack algorithm as described in [16]. All methods that are part of this sequence are saved for use in step 2.

In step 2 of the algorithm, each expression inside the *draw sequence* is checked for the usage of variables that are defined in the top-level scope (e.g., the main class of the program). If such a variable is used, and the expression is a self-assignment or the variable is used as the left-hand side of an expression, then the variable is mutated, indicating a drawing state change. In that case, a violation is created because the state of the application has changed.

5.6 Decentralized Drawing

The decentralized drawing smell detection rule is implemented using a similar algorithm as the *Jack-in-the-box Event Handling* smell. In the first step of the algorithm, all methods that are exclusively called as part of the *draw sequence* are determined. This is done by the exclusive call stack algorithm as described in [16]. These methods are saved for use in step 2.

In step 2 of the algorithm, for each expression in the program, it is checked if it is called by a method that is part of the exclusive call stack as determined in step 1. If the expression is not part of the *draw sequence*, it is checked if the expression is a method call. When an expression calls a method, this expression is compared against the list of predefined drawing functions of PROCESSING. Like the implementation of the pixel hardcode ignorance detection algorithm, a function matches the expression if and only if the name of the method is equal to the method name called by the expression, the number of parameters specified in the expression does match the number of parameters expected by the method, and the scope of the expression does not define another method with the same name and arguments. When the expression matches the method call of a drawing method, then a violation is created.

5.7 Stateless Class

The stateless class smell detection rule is implemented by going over all class and interface definitions. When the definition is an inner class, not an interface, and not defined abstract, then the fields declared in the class are checked. If the class does not declare any fields, then a violation is created and the class is considered stateless.

Please note that the algorithm only runs on inner classes, which are in PROCESSING, i.e. just the classes that are defined by the programmer. The top-level class which declares the main program is not checked, since in the PROCESSING language, this is not seen as a class.

5.8 Long Method

The long method smell detection rule is implemented using the same algorithm PMD uses to check the method count of *Java* classes. The rule uses the NCSS (Non-Commenting Source Statements) algorithm to determine just the lines of code in the method. When this exceeds 25, a violation is reported.

5.9 Long Parameter List

The *Long Parameter List* smell detection rule is implemented using the same algorithm as PMD's existing rule `ExcessiveParameterList`. For each method definition, the amount of accepting parameters is counted. If this count exceeds 5, then a violation is reported.

5.10 God Class

The *God Class* smell detection rule is re-implemented based on the rule that was provided by PMD to detect the God class in *Java* files. A shortcoming of this algorithm is that it calculates the needed metrics, the Weighted Methods Count (WMC), the Access To Foreign Data (ATFD) metric and the Tight Class Cohesion (TCC) metric, one time for the whole compilation unit. That means the rule does not take into account inner classes as different classes. This makes sense for *Java* programs, in which inner classes should not be used for defining new standalone objects. In PROCESSING, however, all classes are in the end inner classes of the main program class. Therefore, these classes should be seen as different objects and have their own calculated software metrics.

The new implementation calculates the WMC, ATFD and TCC metrics for each inner class separately. If one of the inner classes violates these metrics, then this class is considered a God class, as opposed to the whole file being a God class. Then for this class, a violation is added.

5.11 Design Limitations

The usage of PMD as static code analysis framework introduces some design limitations to the detection of design smells. This section discusses these limitations.

An important limitation of PMD is the call stack detection. To determine which methods are called from a certain method, PMD makes use of the name of the method and the number of arguments that the method is called with. Because PMD has very little knowledge about the type of each variable, it cannot distinguish between different overloaded methods. Also, if a method is called on an object, PMD might not always be able to detect the type of the object the method is called on, which causes the method detection to fail. This limitation affects the rules that actually try to detect method calls. The pixel hardcode ignorance smell might not always report the right overloaded method in the violation, for example. This is however not of great consequence. The feedback is not entirely correct, but the smell detection is. In the Jack-in-the-box event handling and decentralized drawing rule, this limitation might lead to false positives, since it was impossible to detect the entire event handling stack or *draw sequence* respectively. For the drawing state change smell, it might lead to false negatives because it was impossible to detect the entire *draw sequence*.

Another limitation of the proposed rules is the handling of object constructors. Since constructors are handled differently than method definitions in PMD, not all rules will work correctly on them. Constructors will, for example, never be detected as part of the event handling stack or *draw sequence*. This means the Jack-in-the-box event handling and decentralized drawing rule will always report violations when using global event variables or drawing methods inside constructors. For the same reason, the change of program variables from a constructor will not cause the drawing state change rule to detect a violation.

Despite these limitations, it is expected that the detection will work fine on most of the programs. This will be validated in the next section.

Table 3. Results for the automated analysis, as checked by the proposed PMD rules.

Set	Number of programs	Lines of code per program	Smells per program	Smells per 1000 lines	Programs with some smell
Novices (resit)	17	297.7	2.8	9.3	100.0%
Textbook examples	149	40.1	0.8	19.8	51.7%
Course material	31	82.1	0.5	5.9	29.0%

6 Validation

To assure that the proposed PMD rules can indeed detect design smells in Processing applications, we consider two criteria. The first is if they are capable to detect smells on a new set of programs. The second is the false positive rate of the warnings.

6.1 Applicability

To assure the rules can be applied to a broader set of programs than the ones used in the manual analysis performed earlier, the PMD rules were executed on three new sets of programs that have different behaviour. The first set is a new set of novices programs written for the same final project, as were the programs from the set that we considered before. The difference is that these are submissions for a resit. Students had to take the resit most commonly because their initial submission was found to be lacking. The second set contains code examples from our first year programming course that uses Processing; examples provided by lecturers and assistants. The third set of code examples are taken from the website `learningprocessing.com`. They are the example accompanying the first 10 chapter of the textbook *Learning Processing* [17]. These are the chapters that are covered in the course.

Table 3 shows the results for the different sets as detected by the PMD rules. It is apparent that novice's code differs significantly from the course and textbook example, not just because it contains many more lines of code. The code examples for the course and code from the textbook do not contain as many smells as the novice sets. However, it still seems striking that sketches from these sources contain this many code smells.

The high number of smells is explained in part because both sets also contain examples of "messy" code, which is effectively code that is meant to be improved by the student. It also includes examples from the first weeks that illustrate basic concepts, before more advanced concepts are taught. For example, canonical Processing examples on the difference between global and local variables will exhibit the *Drawing state change* smell, since drawing the state change is a very visual illustration of the difference. However, the course material and textbook examples contain also smells that should be improved. We will discuss some possible refactorings in Sect. 7.

Table 4. Percentages of programs in different sets that exhibit a given design smell. Compare with Table 2.

Smell	*Novice (resit)*	*Textbook examples*	*Course material*
Pixel hardcode ignorance	35.3%	23.5%	6.5%
Jack-int-the-box event handling	76.5%	18.1%	19.4%
Drawing state change	41.2%	21.5%	6.5%
Decentralized drawing	0.0%	13.4%	6.5%
Stateless class	29.4%	0.0%	0.0%
God class	0.0%	0.0%	0.0%
Long method	82.4%	2.7%	9.7%
Long parameter list	11.8%	0.0%	0.0%

Table 4 splits the results by smell. This table shows each of the PMD rules on an untested set of programs. Only the *God Class* smell was not present in the new sets. This is of course also in part because the code in the course and textbook set are significantly smaller than the programs in the novice sets.

Interesting is that the *Stateless Class* smell occurs much more frequent in programs submitted for the resit, than in any other set. Some students were told that they have to use classes to structure the code; they introduced stateless classes, to make a – somewhat misguided – effort towards this request.

6.2 False Positives

The false positive rate tells how many of the warnings were incorrect. This rate is important because it determines the value that users will attach to a warning. For this analysis, we consider a technical definition of correctness, as defined in [15]. For example, the course material contains a program with a *Long Method* smell. The method in questions has 27 instead of the specified maximum of 25 lines of code. While the warning is technically correct – the method is too long – splitting the method into two part would feel artificial, as it draws one single, slightly more complicated graphical element. The warning is not a false positive and will be counted as a correct warning, even though an individual developer may have good reasons not to act upon it.

The results in Table 5 show that there was one false positive for *Pixel Hardcode Ignorance*. This student program used `pushMatrix` and `popMatrix` in combination with `translate` and `rotate` to move and rotate a graphical element. In PROCESSING there is a practice to use `pushMatrix` and `popMatrix` as a pair to define local blocks of code where the coordinate system is manipulated. Within these local blocks the position can be considered to be relative.

However, semantically, `pushMatrix` refers to the global coordinate system stack. It is just good practice to always use `pushMatrix` and `popMatrix` pairs to make the effect local. The false positive arose because the student used `pushMatrix` and `popMatrix` separated from the actual drawing. Closer inspection of the control flow showed that it was overall correct, despite the warning.

To analyse this correctly would mean to have a full semantic model of coordinate transformations, something that would exceed the capabilities of PMD.

The false positives found for the *Decentralised Drawing* smell are caused by an idiom that caused the call stack to be incorrect. This idiom occurred in particular in community code, which accounts for 18 of the 21 false positives. The false positive rate for this checks seems high, unfortunately, addressing this would require to modify the presentation of the call stack, as provided by PMD, which is outside of the scope of this paper.

Table 5. Frequency of false positives per design smell.

	Warnings	*False positives*	
Pixel hardcode ignorance	157	1	0.6%
Jack-int-the-box event handling	202	0	0.0%
Drawing state change	183	0	0.0%
Decentralized drawing	61	21	34.4%
Stateless class	16	0	0.0%
God class	6	0	0.0%
Long method	192	0	0.0%
Long parameter list	38	0	0.0%
Total	855	22	2.6%

Not counted as false positives were 3 instances of the *Decentralised Event Handling* smell, that pointed to dead code. Technically the warning is correct, as the code contains drawing instructions that are not part of call stack of the main `draw` routine, simply because this code is not part of any call stack. Different programmers may disagree whether this dead code is a problem that needs to be addressed.

From this table, it is easy to see that the long parameter list, long method, and stateless class smells are easy to detect. After all, they are just counting rules. It is fairly easy to count lines of code or count the number of defined parameters for a method. In the same way, counting the number of variables defined for a class is fairly simple.

All things considered, the results are satisfying. Especially when compared to the state of the art in static code analysis tools, as reported in [18], a rate of 2.6% of false positives can be considered to be low. Our analysis is helped because we can make certain assumptions about PROCESSING code. For example, converting PROCESSING code to *Java* will make sure that all classes of a sketch are part of one file, which means that all code definitions can be detected inside that file. These assumptions can be exploited in the PMD rules to improve the analysis.

7 Refactorings

The previous section defined the design smells and discussed how to detect them. This section will discuss the causes as well make suggestions how to refactor the code. The refactorings are meant to be practical and suitable for novice programmers. This, for example, excludes patterns in the spirit of the Gang-of-Four [19], since novice programmers are not yet familiar with the required concepts to competently implement those patterns.

7.1 Pixel Hardcode Ignorance

In novice's code, this smell occurs because there is no abstraction from drawing elements having a location as opposed to an object having a location on the screen. Students often view PROCESSING as a type of scripting language for a drawing application, instead of a fully fledged programming language. Graphical objects still have a static position on the screen directly written as pixels inside the program.

A typical example would be the following part of a program that is meant to display parts of a *hamburger*.

```
stroke (0);
fill(#E80000);
rect(263, 254, 60, 8);
rect(200, 254, 60, 8);
rect(137, 254, 60, 8);
```

These line of code fail to capture that they are conceptually related to a graphical object, a hamburger, and more importantly, that the position is determined by the position of the hamburger.

A basic refactoring would be to introduce position variables. For simple programs that consist only of the main class these would most likely be global variables, such that they can be updated by other methods. The exercise to introduce position variables will also clarify which drawing instruction belongs to which graphical object in the animation. In the following example, all three rectangles are part of the hamburger.

```
stroke (0);
fill(#E80000);
rect(hamburgerX+63, hamburgerY, 60, 8);
rect(hamburgerX,    hamburgerY, 60, 8);
rect(hamburgerX-63, hamburgerY, 60, 8);
```

This prepares the ground for the next step, namely to determine which parts deserve their own class. Once classes are introduced, global variables that relate to the hamburger will become part of the `Hamburger` class. In the course we use the following rule of thumb: if you can legitimately ask "Where is the hamburger?", then the hamburger deserves variables modelling the position.

A more sophisticated refactoring uses `pushMatrix` and `popMatrix`. The command `pushMatrix` pushes the matrix representing current coordinate system onto a stack. The program can then use transformations and rotations to achieve the desired result. Calling popMatrix will then restore the previous coordinate system afterwards. The following would be the corresponding refactoring of the hamburger code snippet:

```
stroke (0);
fill(#E80000);
pushMatrix();
translate(hamburgerX,hamburgerY);
rect(63, 0, 60, 8);
rect(0,  0, 60, 8);
rect(-63,0, 60, 8);
popMatrix();
```

Note, that in this code, the first two arguments of the call to rect are not absolute positions, even though they are literals. They are relative to the new origin after translation to the position of the hamburger. The width and height however are literals. In other languages novices would usually be encouraged to avoid such magic numbers, and be asked to introduce constants instead. However, textbooks on PROCESSING do not introduce constants; it is not a official feature of the language. It is possible to use the final keyword from Java, however this is then strictly speaking no longer PROCESSING. In PROCESSING it is accepted and normal to use literals for dimensions of graphical elements.

It is important to note that pushMatrix and popMatrix work on a global stack. This means that there is no syntactic requirement to use them in pairs. However, it is established practice to have each pushMatrix matched by a popMatrix in the same block. The single false positive for the *Pixel Hardcode Ignorance* smell was caused by a program that separated pushMatrix, popMatrix, and the drawing into different methods.

7.2 Drawing State Change

The drawing state change smell occurs for different reasons. One of the reasons is the programmer wanting to animate an object by incrementing, decrementing a global counter on each redraw. This is particularly the case for programs in the very first weeks, that only contain the main class. In this case, it is usually possible to replace the global variable by the predefined frameCount variable. In most other cases this can be fixed because the calculated value should actually be part of an object. This means the global variable should become a field, and a method to update the object should take care of manipulating its value.

7.3 Jack-in-the-box Event Handling and Decentralized Drawing

We will deal with these together because they are other two aspects of the same problem: not distinguishing between event handling, drawing, and updates of the state.

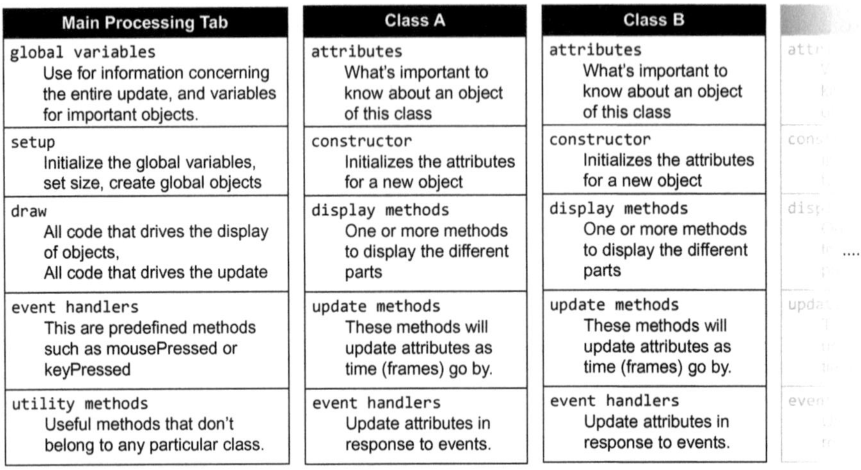

Fig. 1. Suggested structure for simple interactive PROCESSING applications.

The *Jack-in-the-box Event Handling* smell occurs for two main reasons. The first reason is the opportunity to decentralize event handling. Because PROCESSING has a multitude of global variables for event handling, it is tempting to work around the event methods. This usually leads to code that is littered with small bits of event handling.

Another reason for this to happen is drawing on the position of the mouse pointer, which is done in many programs. The best solution is to use instead the `mouseMoved()` method in combination with a position variable used for drawing. Unfortunately, the easiest method, and the first students see in community code and teaching material is to use the global variables `mouseX` and `mouseY` directly and everywhere where it is convenient.

The *Decentralized Drawing* smell is happening for less obvious reasons. Some novices treat PROCESSING as a sophisticated drawing application, and do not yet understand that PROCESSING is a fully fledged programming language. Also, some novice students have the misconception that drawing is a way to record a state change.

To address these two smells we recommend distinguishing in the code between the three main task of a PROCESSING program: (1) Displaying a graphical object, (2) updating the state of these object from frame to frame, (3) and handling events. Figure 1 gives a recommended structure that will be applicable to most interactive applications that are developed by novices.

Each interesting graphical object in the application should be modelled as a class that encapsulates the relevant state and provides the methods to display, update, and handle events that relate to object. The rule of thumb we give to students is that "If you see a monster on the screen, we want to see a monster class in the project."

The structure in Fig. 1 entails that drawing should ideally happen in draw methods of the corresponding object. These should be only called from the main draw method, or draw methods of other objects. Separate from these should be update-methods that are executed with every frame of the animation. These methods update the state in response to the passing of time. These have to be called from the main draw method, or from other update methods.

Separate from draw- and update-methods should be event handling methods, which should be called from the event handling methods in the main class, such as `mouseMoved()`, or from other event handling methods. This ensures that it is possible to track the calls from the main class to the relevant event handler, which help during debugging. The event handling methods are ideally also the only methods that use global event variables such as `keyCode` or `keyPressed`.

The structure given in Fig. 1 distinguishes between the model, the display, and event handling, not unlike the Model-View-Controller pattern. However, here we separate these horizontally within a class, instead of vertically into separate classes. Our structure is closer to the structure that is also present in *openFrameworks* [20], a toolkit for interactive application based in C++. Note also that this structure uses composition of objects as the main mechanism to compose systems, instead of inheritance. In the first year of CreaTe inheritance is only covered cursory; a more thorough treatment of inheritance takes place when languages such as Java, or C++ are introduced.

7.4 Stateless Class

The stateless class smell is mostly caused by the programmer not understanding the principle of object-oriented programming. The programmer moves out long methods by putting them in separate classes which are used as utility classes, which is considered bad design in PROCESSING. It is also caused by the programmer failing to grasp a central object-oriented concept, namely that data should be bundled with associated methods operating on that data. Refactoring means to determine whether these methods belong to an object or are general purpose methods. In the latter case, it is usually best to keep them in the main class of the PROCESSING application.

7.5 Long Method

In more than half of the programs, long methods are caused by drawing complex structures that have to be split into different parts or even different objects. In such cases it may be better to divide the code into smaller methods, however, as mentioned in Sect. 6.2, this depends on the case. In most other cases, the long method smell is caused by putting all application logic inside one method. This is of course fundamentally bad design and should be changed.

7.6 Long Parameter List

Novice programs that contain the *Long Parameter List* smell mostly have this smell because they define methods as a way to combine a set of methods into one. They want to repeatedly draw some structure with slightly different parameters, so they put the small sequence of functions inside a method with a lot of parameters. In most cases, the best way to fix this is by creating an object out of the structure that the programmer wants to draw.

7.7 God Class

The *God Class* smell only occurs in a small set of programs and is caused by the programmer not understanding the responsibility of its defined classes. Each class defined by the programmer has multiple responsibilities or one responsibility is divided over multiple classes. This causes these classes to communicate heavily with the global parent scope, pushing the metrics of the program to bad values. It can be fixed by reconsidering the responsibilities of each class.

7.8 Application to Course Material

We applied these recommended refactorings to the course material that we developed ourselves. The main problem was *Jack-in-the-box Event Handling.* It was in most cases easy to move the problematic code out to the predefined event handling methods. This has two added advantages; one is that it gives more attention this often neglected feature of PROCESSING; the other is that it also makes the code more readable. For example, instead of an object chasing the mouse, it is now converging to an explicit `target`, and the `target` is changed by moving the mouse. It makes the relation between the target and the mouse explicit. Changing the code to having other events change the aim is now easily accomplished. Other programs that were refactored contained the *Long Method* and *Pixel Hardcode Ignorance* smell.

The 31 refactored programs now contain two "messy" programs that contain combined 6 smells. These are intentionally poor programs that students have to improve. It contains one program that explains the difference between value and reference passing, which intentionally uses drawing to illustrate the difference, and an example that illustrate an array algorithm, by manipulating and drawing the content of a global array. Finally, it still contains one other example with a long method as discussed before. It was decided not split this method, also to convey that smells are just indicators of potential problems instead of mandatory guidelines. The number of programs with smells reduced from 9 to 5. This includes the two messy programs. Instead of 0.5 smells per program (Table 3), the examples now contain only 0.3 smells on average; or 0.15 if we take disregard the two intentionally "messy" programs.

8 Conclusions and Future Work

This paper applied the concept of design smells to PROCESSING. The new design smells that we introduced relate to common practice by novice programmers, as well as the PROCESSING community. In addition, we identified and adapted relevant object-oriented smells, that also apply to PROCESSING. We showed the relevance of these new and existing smells to PROCESSING code, by manual analysis of novice code and code by the PROCESSING community. We found that a majority of programs by novices and by the community contain at least some PROCESSING related design smell. This is particularly true for the newly proposed PROCESSING specific smells.

For the eight identified design smells, we implemented customised checks in PMD. These proposed rules were checked against the manually analyzed sets of PROCESSING sketches to estimate the false positive rate. They were then applied to a new set of code to demonstrate their wide applicability. The results show that the proposed way of detecting design smells performs well on the code examples used in this study. This analysis also revealed that even course material and textbook examples exhibit, to a somewhat surprising extent, design smells.

This led us to discuss suggested refactoring that will improve the overall design of the application, and reduce the number of smells. We applied these refactoring to the course material that we developed for the course.

This work produced along the way also the first static analysis tool for PROCESSING. It created an automated pipeline, defined new rules, and customized existing rules, all to accommodate PROCESSING specific requirements.

This study has introduced a selected set of design smells that apply to PROCESSING. In the future, more research on design smells will be needed to further develop design guidelines for PROCESSING. This paper made a start with discussing some potential refactorings, and by applying them to our own course material. As such this made a first effort towards the future work discussed in [4], which this paper extends. This paper refined the definition of some of the PROCESSING specific smells such that they match more closely the accepted practice, and extended the prior work with a discussion of recommended refactorings. It will take more effort to review other publicly available material and to initiate and contribute to the discussion on the importance of application design within the PROCESSING community.

This paper presents a tool for automated detection and discusses its accuracy and applicability. Future research has to investigate the most effective use of these tools; whether students should use them directly, or only teaching assistants, to help them with providing feedback, how frequently to use them, and if and how to intergrade them into peer review, assessment, or grading.

In order to make novice programmers aware of design smells and good application design, guidelines for application design should be provided. These guidelines can be used to give quality feedback on the code of novice programmers as well as helping them understand the rules of application design.

In the recent years, a lot of research has been performed on automated feedback frameworks for students using static code analysis, which primarily look at styling issues and possible bugs. Although successful in providing feedback on these aspects of the code, few give feedback on the application design. Feedback generated by industrial software development tool is mostly based on software metrics, such as cyclomatic complexity. These concepts are, not surprisingly, poorly understood by novice programmers. They will not understand the feedback, nor will it help them to gain a deeper understanding of object-oriented application design. The concept of design smell may prove to be easier for novices to grasp.

The sources and analysed programs that were used in this paper will be available at http://wwwhome.ewi.utwente.nl/~fehnkera/smell/.

References

1. Hermans, F., Aivaloglou, E.: Do code smells hamper novice programming? A controlled experiment on scratch programs. In: ICPC 2016, pp. 1–10 (2016)
2. Suryanarayana, G., Samarthyam, G., Sharma, T.: Refactoring for Software Design Smells: Managing Technical Debt, 1st edn. Morgan Kaufmann Publishers Inc., San Francisco (2014)
3. Reas, C., Fry, B.: Processing: A Programming Handbook for Visual Designers and Artists. The MIT Press, Cambridge (2007)
4. Man, R., Fehnker, A.: The smell of processing. In: Proceedings of the 10th International Conference on Computer Supported Education, vol. 2 (2018)
5. Stegeman, M., Barendsen, E., Smetsers, S.: Towards an empirically validated model for assessment of code quality. In: Koli Calling 2014, pp. 99–108. ACM, New York (2014)
6. Hermans, F., Stolee, K.T., Hoepelman, D.: Smells in block-based programming languages. In: 2016 IEEE Symposium on Visual Languages and Human-Centric Computing (VL/HCC) (2016)
7. Aivaloglou, E., Hermans, F.: How kids code and how we know: an exploratory study on the scratch repository. In: ICER 2016. ACM, New York (2016)
8. Lahtinen, E., Ala-Mutka, K., Järvinen, H.M.: A study of the difficulties of novice programmers. SIGCSE Bull. **37**, 14–18 (2005)
9. Blok, T., Fehnker, A.: Automated program analysis for novice programmers. In: HEAd 2017, Universitat Politecnica de Valencia (2016)
10. Keuning, H., Jeuring, J., Heeren, B.: Towards a systematic review of automated feedback generation for programming exercises. In: ITiCSE 2016. ACM, New York (2016)
11. Higgins, C.A., Gray, G., Symeonidis, P., Tsintsifas, A.: Automated assessment and experiences of teaching programming. J. Educ. Resour. Comput. **5**, 5 (2005)
12. Lelli, V., Blouin, A., Baudry, B., Coulon, F., Beaudoux, O.: Automatic detection of GUI design smells: the case of Blob listener. In: Proceedings of the 8th ACM SIGCHI Symposium on Engineering Interactive Computing Systems, EICS 2016. ACM (2016)
13. Goetz, B.: Java Concurrency in Practice. Addison-Wesley, Upper Saddle River (2006)
14. Lanza, M.: Object-Oriented Metrics in Practice: Using Software Metrics to Characterize, Evaluate, and Improve the Design of Object-Oriented Systems. Springer, Heidelberg (2006). https://doi.org/10.1007/3-540-39538-5
15. Fehnker, A., Huuck, R., Seefried, S., Tapp, M.: Fade to grey: tuning static program analysis. Electron. Notes Theor. Comput. Sci. **266**, 17–32 (2010)
16. de Man, R.: The smell of poor design. In: 26th Twente Student Conference on IT, University of Twente (2017)

17. Shiffman, D.: Learning Processing: A Beginner's Guide to Programming Images, Animation, and Interaction, 2nd edn. Morgan Kaufmann Publishers Inc., San Francisco (2016)
18. Okun, V., Delaitre, A., Black, P.E.: Report on the static analysis tool exposition (SATE) IV. NIST Spec. Publ. **500**, 297 (2013)
19. Gamma, E., Helm, R., Johnson, R., Vlissides, J.: Design Patterns: Elements of Reusable Object-oriented Software. Addison-Wesley Longman Publishing Co., Inc., Boston (1995)
20. Perevalov, D., Tatarnikov, I.S.: openFrameworks Essentials. Packt Publishing, Birmingham (2015)

Investigating Embodied Music Expression Through the Leap Motion: Experimentations in Educational and Clinical Contexts

Adriano Baratè, Luca A. Ludovico(✉), and Eleonora Oriolo

Laboratorio di Informatica Musicale (LIM),
Dipartimento di Informatica "Giovanni Degli Antoni",
Università degli Studi di Milano, Via Celoria 18, 20133 Milano, Italy
{adriano.barate,luca.ludovico}@unimi.it,
eleonora.oriolo@studenti.unimi.it
http://www.lim.di.unimi.it

Abstract. This paper describes a computer-based approach to foster embodied musical expression. The proposed system captures user's hand gestures through a Leap Motion controller, and the signals thus generated are sent to a software tool that converts movements into music notes. When applied to an educational or a rehabilitation context, this solution may foster the development of communication and motor skills by using free-hand interaction. The conceptual framework was experimented in two contexts: technologically-augmented music lessons in a primary school, and music therapy sessions for the rehabilitation of physically and intellectually impaired people.

Keywords: Leap Motion · Music education · Embodied music expression · Music therapy · Computer-supported education

1 Introduction

The practice of a musical instrument may be challenging, above all for young or impaired learners: it requires manual and listening skills, as well as the ability to face the threats typical of a learning environment, such as focusing on a performance goal, gathering feedbacks to improve performance, reinforcing self-confidence, and developing a psychological and behavioral toolkit against pressure and problems [22]. In this sense, ad hoc music learning environments can foster self-regulation abilities [20] by covering a 3-phase cyclical process: forethought, performance or volitional control, and self-reflection [23]. Another aspect related to music practice should not be ignored: the creation of a relationship between movement and the generation of sound [6].

All the mentioned aspects are particularly critical for young learners, who do not master fundamental movement skills [2] and have not fully developed

B. M. McLaren et al. (Eds.): CSEDU 2018, CCIS 1022, pp. 532–548, 2019.
https://doi.org/10.1007/978-3-030-21151-6_25

Fig. 1. The Leap Motion controller (image taken from the official Web site).

higher-order thinking skills [13], and for people with disabilities, due to their physical and intellectual impairment.

The mentioned aspects, which involve self-awareness and encourage self-improvement, are crucial factors in the design and implementation of interfaces to let people actively join music experiences; but, despite the increasing number of enabling technologies and support tools, music expression for untrained people still presents a number of obstacles.

In this work we will analyze the impact of the Leap Motion controller on individual music expression, specifically addressing two categories of users: primary school children and impaired people.

First released in 2012, the Leap Motion is a computer hardware sensor device able to track hand and finger motions as input, requiring no hand contact or touching. This USB peripheral device was originally designed to be placed on a physical desktop, facing upward (see Fig. 1). Using two monochromatic IR cameras and three infrared LEDs, the device observes a roughly hemispherical area to a distance of about 1 meter, catching about 200 frames per second. Data are sent to the host computer, where 3D position of hands and fingers are synthesized by comparing the 2D frames generated by the cameras (see Fig. 2). As demonstrated by independent tests, the overall average accuracy of the controller is about 0.7 mm [32].

In the following, we will discuss the effectiveness of the Leap Motion in order to achieve an intuitive and embodied interaction with music. This approach aims to foster, through music expression, the development of motor and intellectual

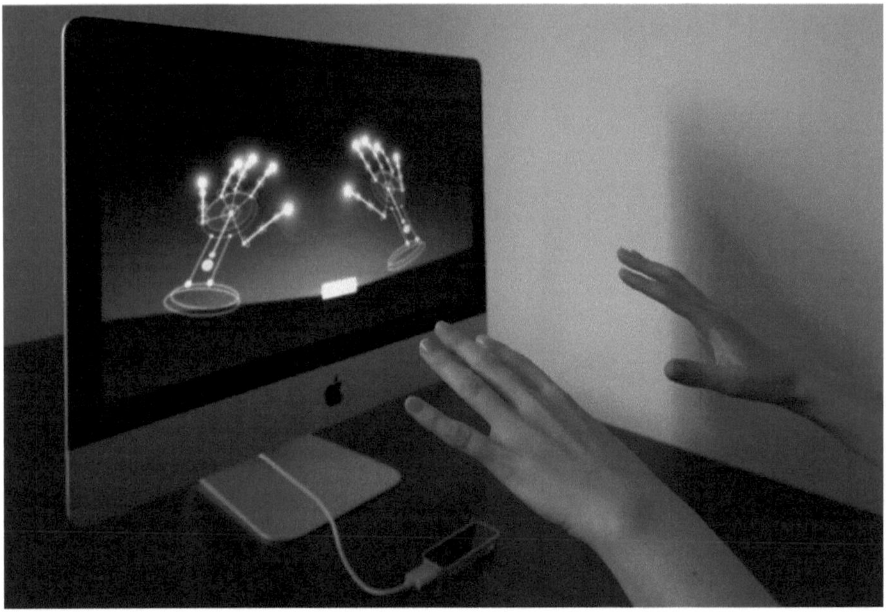

Fig. 2. A software application that shows hand and finger tracking by the Leap Motion (image taken from the official Web site).

skills and social aptitudes in musically untrained children and physically and/or intellectually impaired people.

This work is an extension of the research results presented at the *10th International Conference on Computer Supported Education* (CSEDU 2018) held in Funchal, Madeira, Portugal on 15–17 March, 2018 [1]. In particular, the idea of exporting the conceptual framework from a rehabilitation context to a classroom environment emerged from the question-and-answer session following the presentation.

The paper is structured as follows: Sect. 2 will describe some initiatives dealing with the Leap Motion, Sect. 3 will outline the proposed approach, Sect. 4 will introduce the analysis framework adopted to assess observations, Sects. 5 and 6 will discuss two specific experiences conducted in a classroom and a rehabilitation environment respectively, and, finally, Sect. 7 will draw conclusions.

2 State of the Art

The Leap Motion controller has been already adopted in a number of medical and therapeutic applications. In general, this tool is used to allow free-hand interaction in the treatment of physical injuries, including applications for hand rehabilitation [18,31], gesture recognition to recover the functionalities of upper extremity [5], and stroke rehabilitation [16]. Other works – e.g., [14] and [33] – explicitly address the possibility to treat cognitive and intellectual disabilities.

In music research the potential of the Leap Motion to intuitively generate and/or control a performance is currently under investigation. This technology is seen as a new interface for music expression, as stated in [25], and implementations embrace fields such as sound synthesis and interactive live performance [10].

Much has been written about the sociocultural dimensions of the interface between the human body and technologies. It is worth citing [7,8,11,24], to name but a few. The introduction of new computer technologies such as augmented and virtual reality has risen interest in how the ontology of bodily experience and selfhood are altered via the human/machine interface [26]. Conversely, the ways in which technologies can contribute to the meanings and experiences of the lived body/self with disabilities has been explored to a lesser extent [21].

3 The Proposed Approach

The goal of this experimentation is to let users generate music – in terms of pitch and rhythm – by playing a virtual instrument in a free-hand and no-contact context. The sequence of notes provides a sort of leading voice that the facilitator (either the teacher in a classroom environment or the music therapist for rehabilitation) may accompany thanks to a traditional polyphonic musical instrument, such as the piano or the guitar.

The computer-based system can be easily implemented with commonly available or low-cost hardware and software equipment. Concerning hardware, a computer with a Leap Motion attached is the only requirement. Please note that the Leap Motion controller is a low-cost device: at the moment of writing, it is sold for less than 70€. The only software component required is a specially designed browser application that integrates the LeapJS framework in order to communicate with the hardware device. One of the design goals was to keep both technological requirements and expenses to a minimum, so as to make the implementation simple, cost-effective, and easily reproducible in a number of contexts (e.g., schools, hospitals, etc.).

The browser application allows users to play a virtual musical instrument with a hand movement from the bottom up and vice versa, providing a graphical feedback of the relative position of the hand. The space above the controller is vertically segmented into a number of rectangular areas, each one referring to a different note pitch and represented on screen through a colored section (see Fig. 3). When the distance between hand and controller exceeds a threshold value, this gesture triggers the production of a new sound. If the hand remains in a given area for a predefined amount of time, a new note with the same pitch is performed.

User interaction is based on the use of colors and simple shapes. The interface is deliberately simple and playful, so as to engage young learners (even preschoolers) and to respond to the constraints posed by intellectual disabilities. This is also the reason why tracking potentialities of the device have not been fully exploited: for example, the horizontal position of the hand, the movements produced by the second hand, and even single finger bones could be tracked as well, but the interaction would be less intuitive.

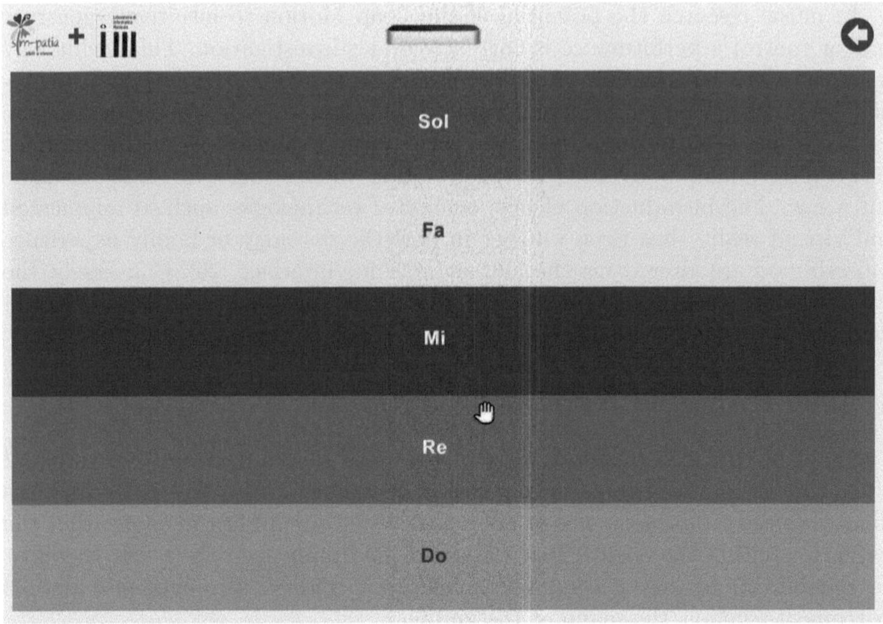

Fig. 3. The main window of the browser interface. Horizontal sections can be customized in color, number and pitch association during the set-up phase. The cursor provides a feedback on the current hand position (image taken from [1]). (Color figure online)

Some parameters of the interface can be customized during the set-up phase, in order to better meet specific needs. First, the capture range can be fine-tuned by determining the minimum and maximum distance from sensors that each user can cover with his/her gestures. The declared range of the device is 25 to 600 mm, but often the movements of users, due to their young age or motor disabilities, are more limited. Moreover, configuring the actual capture area allows to place the device in a non-standard position and orientation.

Another parameter that can be fixed is the number of horizontal sections the total area is divided into, or alternatively their height. This value sets the number of different pitches supported by the interface. For example, preschoolers with no music training can benefit, at an early stage, from a simplified environment. Similarly, paraplegic patients and seriously injured people may experience great difficulty in moving the limbs and pointing precisely. In these cases, it is possible to adopt a setting with few but well-defined areas. Besides, giving the option to perform only a limited number of notes can encourage beginners without causing them a sense of frustration.

Please note that the mentioned parametrization, basically intended to provide the user with a comfortable interface, can be also turned into an instrument of motivation and engagement. For instance, the experimentations described

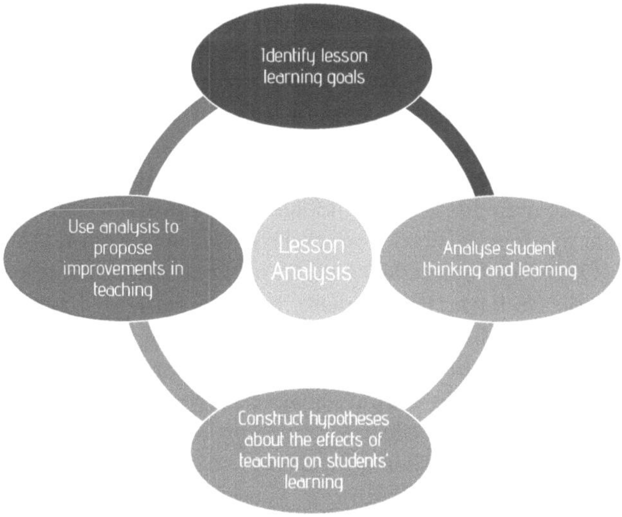

Fig. 4. The questions posed by the Lesson Analysis Framework.

later showed that, after an initial learning and adaptation phase, some users were eager to play with richer and more complex configurations, implying a higher number of notes.

Other customizable parameters were introduced to make such a music experience more engaging. For example, specific pitches can be associated to the horizontal colored areas, thus supporting typical progressions and cadences (e.g., the I-V or I-IV-V progression), scale models (e.g., the pentatonic or the whole tone scale), and altered notes to play in specific keys. Another customization concerns the timbre of the virtual instrument in use, even if in our experimentations we always adopted piano sounds.

The graphical interface was designed keeping simplicity in mind. Implemented as a browser application in HTML5 and JavaScript, the main page presents a number of colored horizontal sections corresponding to pitches and a hand-shaped cursor that provides visual feedback on the rough position of the hand. It would be easy to track and graphically represent further or more precise information: as mentioned above, the Leap Motion technology can track both hands and single finger bones, and the extension framework called LeapJS embeds a detailed 3D visualizer for the hand. Nevertheless, both teachers and music therapists discouraged a finer level of granularity, at least in an early stage, considering this kind of implementation less intuitive and potentially frustrating.

4 The Lesson Analysis Framework

All the experimental activities based on the Leap Motion were filmed and evaluated *a posteriori* in order to test the effectiveness of the proposal.

The observation phase was conducted on the base of a methodology called *Lesson Analysis Framework* [27]. Its conceptual framework centers the analysis of teaching on classroom lessons, which represent natural units in the educational process [12]. The methodology consists of a series of questions that guide teachers through a process of lesson analysis, as shown in Fig. 4.

The first question (Q1) invites the observer to analyze the lesson learning goals: What are the main ideas that students are supposed to understand through this educational approach? Then, the analysis concentrates on student thinking and learning (Q2): Did the students make progress toward the learning goals? What evidence do we have that students made progress (or not)? Considering these aspects leads to the next question, focusing on the impact of teachers' decisions on student learning (Q3): Which instructional strategies supported students' progress toward the learning goals and which did not? Finally, starting from the analysis of the cause-effect relationship between teaching and learning, teachers are asked to improve their educational strategies (Q4): What alternative strategies could the teacher use? How do you expect these strategies to impact on students' progress toward the lesson learning goals? If any evidence of student learning was missing, how could the teacher collect such evidence?

The application of the Lesson Analysis Framework to the evaluation of innovative classroom practices seems natural; conversely, its adoption in a rehabilitation context may sound strange or inappropriate. Nevertheless, we believe that also a music therapy session, even if different from a traditional lesson, can be seen as an educational situation and can be assessed using tools from the teaching domain. In this case, the concept of "computer-based education" assumes a multiplicity of meanings: on the one hand, it implies the use of enabling technologies to teach/learn how to play a virtual musical instrument, on the other it points out a technologically-assisted re-education process in the development or recovery of physical and intellectual abilities.

The results emerging from the evaluation of the Leap Motion technology applied to classroom teaching and music therapy will be detailed in the next sections.

5 Experimentation in a Classroom Setting

The experimentation of the system described in Sect. 3 within a classroom setting aimed to apply the idea of embodied music expression to young students without a specific music training. The Leap Motion controller has been experimented during music lessons in a third-grade class of a primary school.[1] The class, composed by 18 students, was split into two groups of 9 components each. This allowed to design and implement three different didactic situations:

1. *Free embodied music expression*—Young learners belonging to the first group experimented a free use of the virtual instrument, supported by the adaptive

[1] The experimentation took place at the Scuola Elementare Del Centro, Via Cesare Battisti 14, 22036 Erba (CO), Italy.

accompaniment performed on the piano by the music teacher. This gesture-to-sound process encouraged the exploration of musical instrument's possibilities and, after a short training, the development of creative processes;
2. *Reconstruction of a simple music tune*—Students belonging to the second group were asked to follow a predefined melodic contour with their hand gesture, in order to perform a known melody (see Fig. 5). The music fragment to reproduce, short and easy, was expressed using both written note names and the corresponding interface colors. This experiment aimed to revert the gesture-to-sound relationship, encouraging the development of analytical, visual- and motor-memory skills to translate a music tune into movement. In this case, the role of the facilitator was to help students by driving their gesture and singing the tune;
3. *Technologically augmented ensemble music*—The Leap Motion was added to the set of rhythmical instruments usually practiced to make music together. Both groups were involved together in this didactic situation. The use of the virtual instrument allowed the integration of a leading voice within a purely rhythmic context, thus augmenting the expressive possibilities of the ensemble. The music teacher accompanied the experience playing various instruments, e.g., the piano or a percussion.

Concerning the first two experiences, groups were further subdivided into 2 smaller subgroups, made of 4 and 5 children respectively. The idea was to conduct an uninformed experiment on the former subgroup (i.e. students were asked to approach the system with no prior knowledge on its functions), and an informed test on the latter (learners had the possibility to observe their schoolmates from the other subgroup).

Recalling the Lesson Analysis Framework (see Sect. 4), the main learning goal mentioned by question Q1 was apparently easy to identify: fostering the exploration and use of a hand-controlled virtual musical instrument, whose computer-based interface was new for all students. Nevertheless, the experiment presented subtler goals other than developing music skills, such as acquiring awareness about the relationship between sound production and gesture, developing motor memory reinforced by music feedback, and encouraging peer-to-peer interaction among schoolmates.

The second phase of the observation protocol, i.e. the analytical reflection on students' thinking and learning (question Q2), was based on their performances. The tool, suitably configured,[2] demonstrated to be intuitive enough to support music creation processes, even for the "uninformed" subgroup who was administered the free music expression task. The second subgroup, benefiting from the observation of their schoolmates, performed more conscious, controlled, and fluid gestures. In this first didactic situation, the role of the teacher was fundamental to sustain and encourage music expression by an ad hoc music accompaniment. For instance, most students tried to trigger new notes by instinctively following the underlying rhythm.

[2] At first, only 3 pitches with clear tonal functions could be selected by users.

Fig. 5. Performing a music tune through the Leap Motion. The melody to reproduce is shown below the picture.

On the other side, learners approaching the music-tune reconstruction with no prior knowledge experienced greater difficulties, even if guided by the facilitator's singing voice and gesture during an initial phase of exploration. A relevant aspect that emerged during this didactic situation was the spontaneous involvement of observing schoolmates, who tried to help their companion by singing the tune. As we expected, the other subgroup proved to be more skilled, above all regarding motor memory (i.e. the sequence of gestures to follow the melodic contour) and the precise identification of hand positions to produce any given pitch.

After completing the first two didactic situations, groups were switched and could test their abilities by facing more challenging tasks (e.g., a higher number of notes, a longer tune to reconstruct, etc.). Finally, the Leap Motion controller was employed in the context of an ensemble music performance, and the new virtual instrument was perfectly integrated with the percussions normally used by young learners during music lessons.

Question Q3 encourages the formulation of hypotheses about the effects of the educational experimentation. The mentioned tasks were profitably completed even by students who, according to the teacher, were usually less prone to react to educational stimuli. Another aspect clearly emerging from video observations was a noticeable level of attention paid not only by the current user, but also by surrounding schoolmates. Finally, it is worth underlining the establishment of a positive and somehow unexpected peer-cooperation climate, even in those didactic situations that should not promote it. These considerations prove the effectiveness of music as a means to foster interaction, inclusion, and self-reflection.

The final step of the Lesson Analysis Framework, namely question Q4, concerns possible improvements in teaching strategies. In this context, such a reflection involved two aspects: on one side, how to improve the technological solution, in order to better meet the requirements of a classroom setting; on the other side, how to rethink traditional music lessons in primary school so as to take full advantage of this and other computer-based educational tools.

6 Experimentation in a Rehabilitation Context

Scientific research has clearly identified the importance of music in the physical and intellectual rehabilitation of disabled people. In this sense, it is worth mentioning some works that investigate the relationship between music and disability in history, society, and culture, such as [17,19,30].

In literature, the term *enabling technology* designates a technology that alleviates the impact of disease or disability. According to [9], 4 categories can be recognized, according to how their impact is distributed between the individual and the surrounding society:

1. *Therapeutic*—Restoring the original biological function that has been lost or preventing further losses;
2. *Compensatory*—Replacing, fully or partially, a lost biological function by a new function of a general nature;
3. *Assistive*—Allowing to perform a task or activity despite an uncompensated disability or lack of function;
4. *Universal*—Intended for general use.

The approach described below drew full benefit from the features of the Leap Motion, combining its potential in the therapeutic and rehabilitative fields with the possibility for disabled users to intuitively control the parameters of musical expression.

The experimentation took place at an Italian rehabilitation center called *Sim-patia*.[3] Among other ongoing activities, including cognitive and logopedic therapies, manual and creative tasks, etc., music therapy plays a key role at *Sim-patia*. The disabled is invited to develop music-based communication skills through the

[3] Cooperativa Sociale Sim-patia, Via G. Parini 180, 22070 Valmorea (CO), Italy, http://www.sim-patia.it/.

Fig. 6. Music therapy at *Sim-patia* in a "traditional" setting.

interaction with the environment and non-competitive peer cooperation, in the context of group activities guided by a music therapist. Scientific literature – such as [15,28,29] – highlighted the effects of music on the development of memory, language, rhythm, attention, sense-perceptual skills, communication, and relaxation. A traditional music-therapy session at *Sim-patia* is shown in Fig. 6.

In this framework, the solution based on the Leap Motion was experimented in order to improve the interaction of disabled people with music during therapeutic sessions. This activity involved 3 groups of patients, with 8 to 10 participants per group, homogeneous for pathologies: the first group included users with cognitive disabilities and some cases of moderate motor disability, the second group was formed by people up to 25 years old with motor and cognitive disabilities and autism, and the third group was constituted by users in a wheelchair due to traffic accidents. The time schedule was approximatively one hour per group, repeated once a week, organized as follows: 45 min of practical activities plus 15 min of final discussion, open to educators' and patients' comments.

The music therapist working at *Sim-patia* played a key role both in the design and test phases of the experimentation (see Fig. 7). Being a domain expert, his remarks were fundamental to assess the educational valence in the context of physical and intellectual stimulation of people with disabilities.

Progresses in the rehabilitation of patients were assessed by the therapist through the *phenomenological-relational methodology* by Cattaneo [3,4]. The music therapist used an observation form to track improvements along the rehabilitation path. This document, compiled at the beginning and at the end of each session, allowed to evaluate the evolution occurred in the psycho-physical, affective-emotional and cognitive spheres by taking into consideration the three main elements of musical language, i.e. *rhythm*, *melody* and *harmony*, and combining them with the three main dimensions of the human system, namely *movement*, *emotion* and *thought*. For further details, please refer to [1].

Since users had no previous music training and presented different levels of disability, either motor/physical or cognitive/intellectual, the goal of creating melodic awareness in them was not trivial. Rather than providing users with a traditional diatonic scale (e.g., the eight-grade C major scale), the proposed virtual instrument was configured to produce smaller sets of pitches. Even a minimal subset of natural notes – formed, e.g., by C and D – showed to be effective in producing articulated melodic events. In fact, these two pitches can be intuitively associated to the ideas of tension/suspension and rest/conclusion, even better when supported by the adaptive accompaniment of the music therapist.

Complexity, a concept that implies a higher level of difficulty but also an improved expressive potential, was raised by adding notes adaptively, depending on the aptitudes and responses shown by users during the therapy. Patients were motivated to interact with the musical accompaniment, being rewarded by the achievement of richer melodic tunes. Interaction with external musical stimuli was fostered also through a suitable choice of the pitch set. For instance, the pentatonic scale, presenting no halftone interval, is well known for being easily adaptable to any accompaniment, consequently it was extensively used during music-therapy sessions.

In addition to the subjective evaluation by the music therapist, this kind of experience has been evaluated through the principles of the Lesson Analysis Framework enunciated in Sect. 4.

As it regards learning goals (Q1), users were asked to interact with the interface and produce music together with the therapist. The declared goal for patients was to achieve music expression through gesture, but the underlying purpose was to implement rehabilitation tasks by using music performance to stimulate and motivate them.

Regarding the analysis of student thinking and learning (Q2), video observations demonstrated that all involved patients were able to complete their assignments, even in early sessions. The progresses tracked by the therapist showed noticeable improvements in almost all patients, concerning both physical and intellectual rehabilitation. The computer-based system demonstrated to be not only intuitive, but also engaging for impaired users, who, in some cases, asked for more difficult assignments. The average number of notes proposed to users at the end of the rehabilitation path was 5, a relevant result for people with motor disabilities, who usually experience difficulties in precisely pointing an area, and for users with intellectual disabilities, less prone to interact with music.

Fig. 7. A disabled person interacting with the system.

Concerning the gesture range, it is worth underlining that some patients were able to cover the full interval, spanning from 25–50 to 600 mm. In this sense, patients with autism were particularly skilled, but – more surprisingly – also some users with motor disability were able to achieve this remarkable result. From video observations, other punctual results emerged: a user, despite his motor disability, was able to cover the full range of distances and to play a whole 8-grade scale; a second user, affected by quadriplegia, obtained very encouraging results in terms of motion ability; and another user, presenting autism spectrum disorder, was successfully administered a non-trivial 5-grade scale. In general terms, making autistic patients interact with the interface and produce music together with the therapist was a remarkable success. Anyway, this category of users showed innate musical abilities, being able to easily memorize tunes and reproduce them.[4]

Then, the therapist is invited to construct hypotheses about the effects achieved by the educational approach under evaluation (Q3). In this case, the comparison is between music therapy in a traditional setting and a technologically-augmented music experience. Probably, the most noticeable effect was the possibility for users to intuitively perform a leading voice, namely to produce a melodic (and rhythmic) note sequence instead of a purely rhythmic

[4] For further details, please refer to [1].

pattern. A supposed effect was to make patients protagonists of the music experience, and this hypothesis was corroborated by the results achieved in terms of motor performance and level of engagement. Consequently, the adoption of the Leap Motion controller seems very promising in a rehabilitation context.

Finally, some requests for changes and improvements emerged during music therapy sessions (Q4). From this point of view, let us mention: the possibility of managing multiple devices, in order to create a Leap Motion orchestra, thus fostering a better integration among patients within a collaborative and non-competitive environment; an option of track numeric outputs (e.g., the maximum distance reached by patients' hands from the device, the number of notes covered in each session, etc.) in order to automatically integrate evaluation forms; the possibility of introducing special timbres, such as the human voice, to allow impaired users to express themselves by "singing".

7 Conclusion

In this work, we have described a computer-based approach to encourage the interaction of young learners and disabled people with music content. Starting from educational roots and requirements, with the help of experts from different domains (behavioral and rehabilitative medicine, music and musicology, computer science), we have designed and released a framework that was tested in both a school and a clinical context, showing encouraging results.

Based on the Leap Motion, the application implements a simplified and intuitive virtual instrument that gives musically-untrained users the chance to create a music tune, picking available pitches from a user-tailored set. The musical experience is highly customizable, depending not only on the educational or rehabilitation goal to achieve, but also on the skills and motivation developed by users during the experience.

The creation of musical patterns becomes a recognizable element that triggers formal processes. Thanks to sound, the whole psychomotor sphere is stimulated: through live interaction, a gesture produces a clearly recognizable sound feedback, and the effect is the feeling to play and achieve the desired musical result, even in absence of a physical contact.

This computer-based project presented multiple educational meanings. First, thanks to the Leap Motion, young learners and disabled people had the possibility to learn and experience music concepts (e.g., melody, rhythm, harmony, synchronization, etc.) in an intuitive way. Besides, they were encouraged to play in front of their mates or even together in a non-competitive environment, where forms of peer-to-peer cooperation and interaction naturally emerged. Another educational achievement, fostered by engagement and motivation and appreciated by both categories of users, was the desire to overcome one's limits in order to reach new goals, such as a more precise pointing or a higher number of available notes.

The results illustrated in this work should be further validated through a more extensive experimentation, but early achievements are promising and are pushing us to improve the computer-based solution and to implement new functionalities.

Acknowledgements. The authors wish to acknowledge the music therapist Antonio Elia, staff members and patients of the *Cooperativa Sociale Sim-patia*, Valmorea, Italy for experimenting the Leap Motion in a music therapy context. Besides, the authors would like to thank Monica Mengacci, Daniela Pina, third-grade students attending section B and the entire staff of the *Scuola Elementare Del Centro*, Erba, Italy for their support in classroom experimentation. Finally, we are grateful to Veronica Curioni, who coordinated and operatively performed the observation phase on primary school students.

References

1. Baratè, A., Elia, A., Ludovico, L.A., Oriolo, E.: The Leap Motion controller in clinical music therapy. A computer-based approach to intellectual and motor disabilities. In: McLaren, B.M., Reilly, R., Uhomoibhi, J., Zvacek, S. (eds.) Proceedings of the 10th International Conference on Computer Supported Education, CSEDU 2018, 15–17 March 2018, Funchal, Madeira, Portugal, pp. 461–469. SCITEPRESS - Science and Technology Publications, Lda., Setúbal (2018)
2. van Beurden, E., Zask, A., Barnett, L.M., Dietrich, U.: Fundamental movement skills: how do primary school children perform? The Move it Groove it program in rural Australia. J. Sci. Med. Sport **5**(3), 244–252 (2002)
3. Cattaneo, P.: La canzone come esperienza relazionale, educativa, terapeutica. Universal Music MGB Publications, Sesto Ulteriano, San Giuliano Milanese (2009)
4. Elia, A.: Con un fil di voce: dinamiche espressive tra parlato e canto. In: Cattaneo, P., Lopez, L. (eds.) Musicoterapia e Relazione. Franco Angeli, Milano (2017)
5. Gieser, S.N., Boisselle, A., Makedon, F.: Real-time static gesture recognition for upper extremity rehabilitation using the Leap Motion. In: Duffy, V.G. (ed.) DHM 2015. LNCS, vol. 9185, pp. 144–154. Springer, Cham (2015). https://doi.org/10.1007/978-3-319-21070-4_15
6. Godøy, R.I., Leman, M.: Musical Gestures: Sound, Movement, and Meaning. Routledge, Abingdon (2010)
7. Gray, C.H., Figueroa-Sarriera, H.J., Mentor, S.: The Cyborg Handbook. Routledge, Abingdon (1995)
8. Halberstam, J.M., Livingston, I.: Posthuman Bodies. Indiana University Press, Bloomington (1995)
9. Hansson, S.O.: The ethics of enabling technology. Camb. Q. Healthc. Ethics **16**(3), 257–267 (2007)
10. Hantrakul, L., Kaczmarek, K.: Implementations of the Leap Motion device in sound synthesis and interactive live performance. In: Proceedings of the 2014 International Workshop on Movement and Computing, p. 142. ACM (2014)
11. Haraway, D.: Simians, Cyborgs, and Women: The Reinvention of Nature. Routledge, Abingdon (1991)
12. Hiebert, J., Morris, A.K., Berk, D., Jansen, A.: Preparing teachers to learn from teaching. J. Teach. Educ. **58**(1), 47–61 (2007)

13. Hmelo, C.E., Ferrari, M.: The problem-based learning tutorial: cultivating higher order thinking skills. J. Educ. Gifted **20**(4), 401–422 (1997)
14. Iosa, M., et al.: Leap Motion controlled videogame-based therapy for rehabilitation of elderly patients with subacute stroke: a feasibility pilot study. Top. Stroke Rehabil. **22**(4), 306–316 (2015)
15. Karageorghis, C.I., Terry, P.C.: The psychophysical effects of music in sport and exercise: a review. J. Sport Behav. **20**(1), 54 (1997)
16. Khademi, M., Mousavi Hondori, H., McKenzie, A., Dodakian, L., Lopes, C.V., Cramer, S.C.: Free-hand interaction with Leap Motion controller for stroke rehabilitation. In: Proceedings of the Extended Abstracts of the 32nd Annual ACM Conference on Human Factors in Computing Systems, pp. 1663–1668. ACM (2014)
17. Lerner, N., Straus, J.: Sounding Off: Theorizing Disability in Music. Routledge, Abingdon (2006)
18. Liu, Z., Zhang, Y., Patrick Rau, P.-L., Choe, P., Gulrez, T.: Leap-Motion based online interactive system for hand rehabilitation. In: Rau, P.L.P. (ed.) CCD 2015. LNCS, vol. 9181, pp. 338–347. Springer, Cham (2015). https://doi.org/10.1007/978-3-319-20934-0_32
19. Lubet, A.: Music, Disability, and Society. Temple University Press, Philadelphia (2011)
20. Ludovico, L.A., Mangione, G.R.: Self-regulation competence in music education. In: McPherson, M., Nunes, M.B. (eds.) Proceedings of the International Conference e-Learning 2014, EL 2014, pp. 46–54. IADIS Press, Lisbon (2014)
21. Lupton, D., Seymour, W.: Technology, selfhood and physical disability. Soc. Sci. Med. **50**(12), 1851–1862 (2000)
22. Martin, A.J.: Motivation and engagement in music and sport: testing a multidimensional framework in diverse performance settings. J. Pers. **76**(1), 135–170 (2008)
23. McPherson, G.E., Renwick, J.M.: A longitudinal study of self-regulation in children's musical practice. Music Educ. Res. **3**(2), 169–186 (2001)
24. Penley, C., Ross, A.: Technoculture, vol. 3. University of Minnesota Press, Minneapolis (1991)
25. Ritter, M., Aska, A.: Leap Motion as expressive gestural interface. In: Proceedings ICMC—SMC—2014, pp. 659–662 (2014)
26. Riva, G., Baños, R.M., Botella, C., Mantovani, F., Gaggioli, A.: Transforming experience: the potential of augmented reality and virtual reality for enhancing personal and clinical change. Front. Psychiatry **7**, 164 (2016)
27. Santagata, R., Zannoni, C., Stigler, J.W.: The role of lesson analysis in pre-service teacher education: an empirical investigation of teacher learning from a virtual video-based field experience. J. Math. Teach. Educ. **10**(2), 123–140 (2007)
28. Scheufele, P.M.: Effects of progressive relaxation and classical music on measurements of attention, relaxation, and stress responses. J. Behav. Med. **23**(2), 207–228 (2000)
29. Schlaug, G., Norton, A., Overy, K., Winner, E.: Effects of music training on the child's brain and cognitive development. Ann. N.Y. Acad. Sci. **1060**(1), 219–230 (2005)
30. Straus, J.N.: Extraordinary Measures: Disability in Music. Oxford University Press, Oxford (2011)
31. Taylor, J., Curran, K.: Using Leap Motion and gamification to facilitate and encourage rehabilitation for hand injuries: Leap Motion for rehabilitation. In: Handbook of Research on Holistic Perspectives in Gamification for Clinical Practice, pp. 183–192 (2015)

32. Weichert, F., Bachmann, D., Rudak, B., Fisseler, D.: Analysis of the accuracy and robustness of the Leap Motion controller. Sensors **13**(5), 6380–6393 (2013)
33. Zhu, G., Cai, S., Ma, Y., Liu, E.: A series of Leap Motion-based matching games for enhancing the fine motor skills of children with autism. In: 2015 IEEE 15th International Conference on Advanced Learning Technologies (ICALT), pp. 430–431. IEEE (2015)

Intuitive Reasoning in Formalized Mathematics with ELFE

Maximilian Doré[1(✉)] and Krysia Broda[2]

[1] Department of Computing, RWTH Aachen University, Aachen, Germany
maximilian.dore@rwth-aachen.de
[2] Department of Computing, Imperial College London, London, UK
k.broda@imperial.ac.uk

Abstract. In teaching mathematics, theorem provers have been used only seldomly due to their technical nature. Theorem provers like ELFE can bridge the gap between informal and formal reasoning by using automated theorem provers to verify intermediate steps in a proof that are passed over when reasoning intuitively. In this paper we present the inner workings of ELFE and how it can be used to prove lemmas in synthetic geometry. We compare the system to other approaches to formalized mathematics and give an outlook where the development may lead.

Keywords: Formal mathematics · Proof checking · Didactics of mathematics · Interactive theorem proving · Synthetic geometry

1 Introduction

Everyday mathematical practice has been mostly untouched by the advancements in formalized mathematics made in recent years. In particular, teaching mathematics in university is generally still blackboard based. In order to understand mathematical reasoning, students practice writing proofs on paper and wait for the feedback of instructors to improve their understanding. Immediate feedback would greatly increase the learning curve – it is often difficult to see when a proof is complete or what steps are missing.

Such feedback could be provided by machines. And indeed, many attempts have been made to formalize mathematics. Most prominently, the interactive theorem provers ISABELLE and COQ are advanced systems; for instance COQ was used in proving the Four-color-theorem [1]. However, mathematical beginners are overwhelmed by the capabilities of such systems since using them requires a deep understanding of logical calculi.

The goal of this work is to provide users with a system that gives feedback on proofs entered in a fairly natural Mathematical language. Thereby the users are detached from the technicalities of automated theorem provers (ATP). The ELFE system provides a proof of concept that this is feasible and sensible. In the past years, several attempts have been made to create a proof verifier which

B. M. McLaren et al. (Eds.): CSEDU 2018, CCIS 1022, pp. 549–571, 2019.
https://doi.org/10.1007/978-3-030-21151-6_26

accepts mathematical texts written in fair English, one of which System for Automated Deduction (SAD) [2] was most influential and inspirational for our work. The SAD provides an intuitive input language, called ForTheL. However, the user still has to dig into the automated verification process to understand why a proof does not work. The Elfe system in contrast processes the output of background provers and tries to give countermodels to wrong proofs.

```
Include functions.

Let A,B,C be set.

Let f: A → B.
Let g: B → C.

Lemma: g∘f is injective implies f is injective.
Proof:
   Assume g∘f is injective.
   Assume x ∈ A and x' ∈ A and (f{x}) = (f{x'}).
   Then ((g∘f){x}) = ((g∘f){x'}).
   Hence x = x'.
   Hence f is injective.
qed.
```

Fig. 1. Exemplary Elfe text [3, p. 1].

Consider the exemplary proof in Fig. 1 which is in fact a valid Elfe text. After including a background library and introducing specific sets A, B and C and functions f and g, a lemma is proposed that if the composition of f and g is injective, so the firstly applied f must be injective. This lemma is proven by the reasoning that if f maps two elements x and x' to the same element, the composition of f and g must map them to the same elements. Since this composition is injective, it follows that x and x' are the same elements and f is thus injective. Note that $(g \circ f)\{x\}$ denotes the function application of $g \circ f$ which is put in brackets to specify the precedence of the symbols. We will learn in the following how the text is verified.

The remainder of the paper is structured as follows. We first give a brief overview of the implementation in Sect. 2 before introducing the Elfe language and proof structures and justify the correctness of the formalization in Sect. 3. We demonstrate the flexibility of the system by formalizing geometry in Sect. 4. We will evaluate our work in Sect. 5 and compare it with popular current theorem provers in Sect. 6 before concluding with a short discussion in Sect. 7.

The system was first presented at CSEDU [3] and interested readers can find an instance of it online[1].

[1] https://elfe-prover.org.

2 Implementation

The ELFE system can be accessed through a web interface or a command-line interface (CLI) as shown in Fig. 2. The web interface provides an intuitive way of accessing the system's output, while the CLI offers more debugging functionality. After the text is entered via one of its interfaces, it will be parsed into an intermediary representation in first-order logic. This proof representation is presented in Sect. 3.2. The Verifier takes the intermediary proof representation and checks it for correctness by calling several ATPs in parallel. If a proof obligation is wrong, the Verifier tries to extract a countermodel from the background provers. The result of this verification process is then returned to the user via the chosen interface.

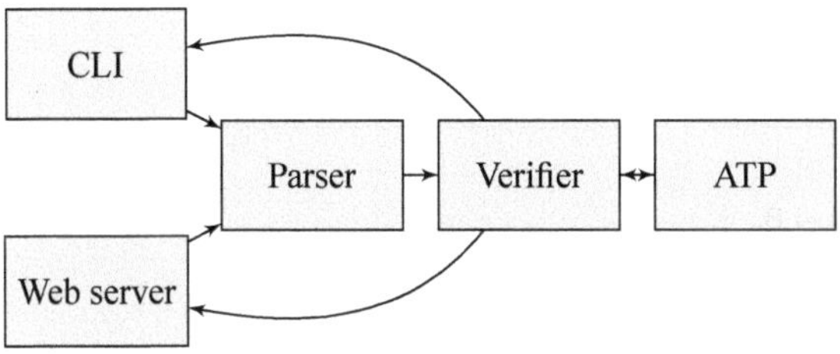

Fig. 2. Architecture of the ELFE system [3, p. 2].

The system is implemented in HASKELL (its source code can be found online[2]). In order to send proof obligations to the background provers, the syntax standard TPTP [4] is used. Since the used ATP can be easily configured, nearly all current systems can be interfaced.

So far, we have used the provers SPASS [5], E PROVER [6] and VAMPIRE [7] due to their performance at the CADE System Competitions [8] alongside the provers BEAGLE [9] and Z3 [10], which do theorem proving modulo background theories. Different provers have varying strengths, for example, E PROVER turned out to be fast in proving lemmas with equality while BEAGLE gave useful countermodels for wrong proof obligations. For this reason, it turned out efficient to call several provers in parallel.

3 ELFE Language

The input language for ELFE is mathematical texts written in a subset of natural mathematical language. We will not introduce the whole feature set in this paper and only examine the exemplary proof of Fig. 1 in the following. Other language constructs like case distinctions or subproofs, which make a text less monolithic, are presented in [11].

In order to verify an ELFE text, we transform it into a special data-structure which implies certain proof obligations. Since this internal proof representation

[2] https://github.com/maxdore/elfe.

uses first-order logic, we will first introduce how to transform the ELFE language into first-order logic. This preprocessing will be presented in Sect. 3.1. Keywords like Then and Hence have special meanings in an ELFE proof and are used to structure a mathematical proof. This structure is captured in an intermediate proof representation which is introduced in Sect. 3.2. The intermediate proof representation implies certain obligations which need to be checked by the background provers. What these are will be explained in Sect. 3.3.

3.1 From ELFE to First-order Logic

First-order logic is used to encode mathematical statements. Most transformations are straightforward from ELFE to first-order logic, e.g., P implies f is injective is transformed to $P \rightarrow injective(f)$. In order to make an ELFE text more legible, three commands introduce meta-language features.

```
Include sets, relations.
Let A,B,C be set.
Notation function: f: A → B.
Definition function: for all f.f: A → B iff
  for all x ∈ A. exists y ∈ B. f[x,y] and (for all y' ∈ B. y = y' or not f[x,y']).
Let f: A → B.
Definition injective: f is injective iff
  for all x ∈ A, x' ∈ A, y ∈ B. f[x,y] and f[x',y] implies x = x'.
Let g: B → C.
Notation composition: g∘f.
Definition composition: (g∘f): A → C and
  (for all x ∈ A. for all y ∈ B. for all z ∈ C. ((f[x,y] and g[y,z]) implies (g∘f)[x,z])).
```

Fig. 3. Excerpt of the functions library [3, p. 4].

The command Include can be used to include the axioms of a background theory. E.g., in our example in Fig. 1 we include the functions library with Include functions. The user can easily create his own background theory since these are written in the ELFE language as well. You can find an excerpt of the functions library in Fig. 3.

The command Notation is used to introduce syntactic sugars. One can write an arbitrary pattern of Unicode characters to define such a pattern, e.g., Notation function: f: A → B. The alphabetical parts of the pattern, i.e., f, A and B are treated as placeholders for arbitrary terms. Thus, all terms of the form

$$*: * \rightarrow *$$

with * being arbitrary terms are subsequently considered instances of the predicate function. For example, g: B → C will be transformed internally to the first-order formula $function(g, B, C)$. Similarly, the notation for composition is defined as g ∘ f. Consider the version of our proof in raw first-order logic in Fig. 4, where the first line of our exemplary ELFE proof Assume g ∘ f is injective is

Lemma: $\forall set(A), set(B), set(C), function(f, A, B),$
$function(g, B, C).\ injective(composition(g, f)) \rightarrow injective(f).$
Proof:
Assume $injective(composition(g, f))$.
Assume $funApp(f, x) = funApp(f, x')$
$\wedge\, in(x, A) \wedge in(x', A)$.
Then $funApp(composition(g, f), x)$
$= funApp(composition(g, f), x')$.
Hence $x = x'$.
Hence $injective(f)$.
qed.

Fig. 4. The injectivity proof without syntactic sugar [3, p. 4].

transformed into Assume $injective(composition(g, f))$. Note that notations can be used both for term and predicate symbols.

The command Let binds a predicate symbol to a variable, effectively assigning a type to a symbol. By writing Let A,B, C be set, we ensure that in all following statements A, B and C have the predicate symbol set. Consider Fig. 4 which shows the injectivity proof after removing meta-level language features. A, B and C are introduced universally quantified as sets in the lemma.

3.2 Statement Sequences

So far, we have only seen how single mathematical statements are transformed into first-order formulas. In order to capture the structure of a proof, we propose a special kind of data-structure, so-called statement sequences. Intuitively, a statement holds a first-order formula with an identifier and a proof. A proof can consist of other statements in order to represent complex proof objects.

Definition 1 (Statement Sequences)
A statement S is a tuple ID × GOAL × PROOF *where*

- ID *is an alphanumeric string which is unique for each statement*
- GOAL *is a formula in first-order logic*
- PROOF *is either*
  ASSUMED *or*
  BYCONTEXT *or*
  BYSUBCONTEXT $Id_1, ..., Id_n$ *or*
  BYSEQUENCE $S_1, ..., S_n$ *or*
  BYSPLIT $S_1, ..., S_n$

A statement sequence is a finite list of statements $S_1, ..., S_n$.

If a statement S is proved BYSEQUENCE $S_1, ..., S_n$ *or* BYSPLIT $S_1, ..., S_n$, *we call $S_1, ..., S_n$ the children of S. If we want to access S from a child S_i, we write S_i.*PARENT. *On the top level, a statement has no parent, thus S.*PARENT = EMPTY.

Consider the example in Fig. 5. We will depict a statement visually in the following as a box with its ID in the upper-left corner. The GOAL of a statement is written in the header of a statement, the PROOF below. A PROOF can take different forms to capture complex proof structures. The axioms of a text however are simply annotated by ASSUMED. For instance, the statements S_{fun} and S_{inj} depict the statements resulting from the definitions in Fig. 3. In the functions library, numerous additional definitions are made which are omitted here. Statements annotated with ASSUMED will be depicted green in the following. Below the axioms, the statement S of the lemma of our text in Fig. 1 follows. In order to prove this statement, we need more advanced proof structures which will be introduced in Sect. 3.3. The statement is depicted red and with a dashed border to indicate that its proof is not complete.

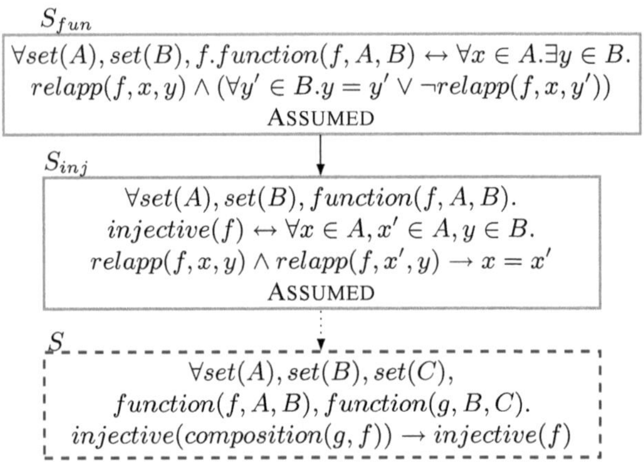

Fig. 5. Exemplary statement sequence [3, p. 5]. (Color figure online)

To give an overview of the other types of PROOF: A proof BYSEQUENCE and BYSPLIT makes it possible to nest more complex derivation sequences. A statement annotated with BYCONTEXT will be checked by the background provers. BYSUBCONTEXT is a special case of this proof type which allows for restricting the context of the statement.

3.3 Proved Statements

Since we want to verify that a text is sound, we need to introduce a soundness criterion for statements. The axioms of a text are entered freely and thus not checked. Conjectures of a set of axioms, like the lemma in our our exemplary proof in Fig. 1, need a more subtle criterion.

First we will define which axioms are considered relevant to a statement. Intuitively, the context of a statement in a statement sequence are all statements "above" it.

Definition 2 (Context of a Statement). *Let $S_1, ...S_n$ be a statement sequence. The context of a statement S_k, $\Gamma(S_k)$, is inductively defined as*

- $\Gamma(\text{EMPTY}) = \emptyset$,
- $\Gamma(S_k) = \{S_1.\text{GOAL}, ..., S_{k-1}.\text{GOAL}\} \cup \Gamma(S_k.\text{PARENT})$.

For example, in Fig. 5, the context of statement S consists of the respective goals of S_{fun} and S_{inj} (as well as other definitions of the library which are omitted here). With that, we can define an appropriate soundness criterion for statements.

Definition 3 (Proved Statement). *Let S be a statement with $S.\text{GOAL} = \phi$. We call S proved iff $\Gamma(S) \models \phi$.*

In other words, a statement is considered proved if it already followed from the theory created by its context. The statements S_{fun} and S_{inj} in Fig. 5 are not proved since they build up the axioms of our theory. The statement S however should follow from these axioms, i.e., should be a proved statement. In order to show that S is proved, we will create a more complex proof object in the following such that correctness of the proof object implies that S followed from its context.

We start by unfolding the outer implication of the lemma. More specifically, we fix specific sets A, B and C and functions f, g. As we see in Fig. 6, this is captured in our data-structure by introducing another statement S_1 such that the proof of S is BYSEQUENCE S_1. We represent proofs BYSEQUENCE by putting the proof inside the statement to prove. The difference between S and S_1 is that we removed the quantifiers and replaced the variables with constants (depicted in blue and with an overline $\bar{A}$ in case the color does not show up).

In order to prove the new goal of S_1, we do a so-called unfolding of the implication. The left hand side is put in the statement S_2 and annotated with ASSUMED such that it is in the context of S_3, which holds the right hand side of the implication.

The whole reduction from S to S_3 is done automatically by the system. It detects if meta-variables are contained in the goal and injects the proof automatically.

With this, we have reduced the problem of showing that S is proved to showing that S_3 is proved. In order to convince us that S_3 is proved indeed implies that S is proved, we will first see that it is sound to fix an universally quantified variable to a constant. This can be done by natural deduction which has been shown to be sound [12]. Concretely, our construction is analogous to the following deduction rule:

$$(\forall I) : \frac{P(a)}{\forall x.P(x)} \quad \text{with } a \text{ not occurring in } P(x)$$

We use this deduction rule in showing the soundness of our construction in Lemma 1.

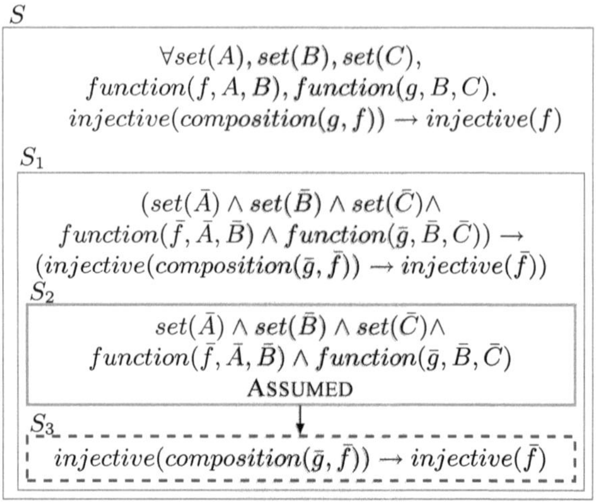

Fig. 6. Unfolding meta-variables [3, p. 6]. (Color figure online)

Lemma 1 (∀ Introduction). *Let S be a statement such that S.*Goal *$=$ $\forall x.P(x)$ and a not occurring in S.*Goal*, S.*Proof *$=$* BySequence $\boldsymbol{S_1}$, $\boldsymbol{S_1}$.Goal *$= P(a)$ and S_1 is proved:*

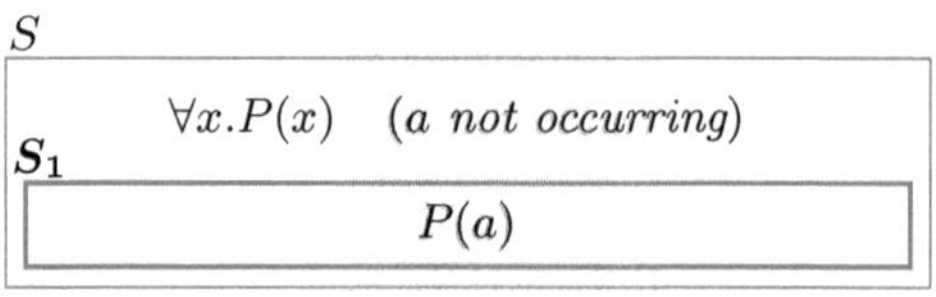

Then S is proved.

Proof. *Since S_1 is proved and $\Gamma(S) = \Gamma(S_1)$, we have $\Gamma(S) \models P(a)$. With $(\forall I)$ it follows that $\Gamma(S) \models \forall x.P(x)$ since a does not occur in $P(x)$.*

Next we have to show that it is sound to assume the left hand side of an implication and deduce the right hand side. Again, this is analogous to a natural deduction rule:

$$(\rightarrow I) : \frac{P \vdash Q}{P \rightarrow Q}$$

This rule is used in the soundness proof in Lemma 2.

Lemma 2 (→ Introduction). *Let S be a statement such that S.*Goal *$= P \rightarrow Q$, S.*Proof *$=$* BySequence $S_1, \boldsymbol{S_2}$, S_1.Goal *$= P$,* $\boldsymbol{S_2}$.Goal *$= Q$ and S_2 is proved:*

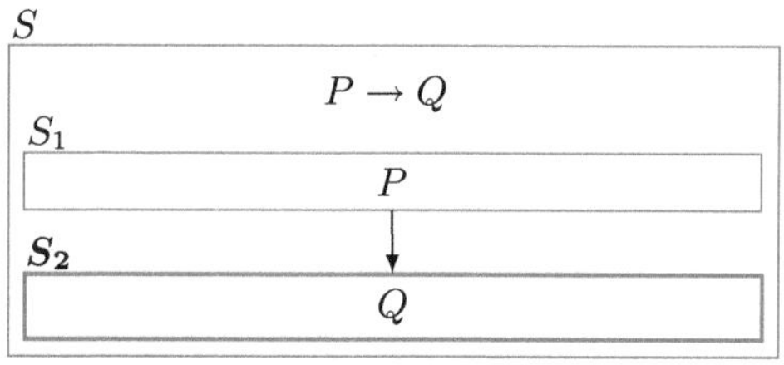

Then S is proved.

Proof. We have $\Gamma(S_2) = \Gamma(S) \cup \{P\}$*. Since* S_2 *is proved,* $\Gamma(S) \cup P \vDash Q$*. With* $(\rightarrow I)$ *it follows* $\Gamma(S) \vDash P \rightarrow Q$.

Now we will construct the proof of S_3 as shown in Fig. 7. In the proof text in Fig. 1, we explicitly wrote Assume $injective(composition(g, f))$. [...] Hence $injective(f)$. Analogous to the unfolding of the implication of S_1 in Fig. 6, we assume the left hand side and now have to prove the right hand side. Again, this is sound as proved in Lemma 2.

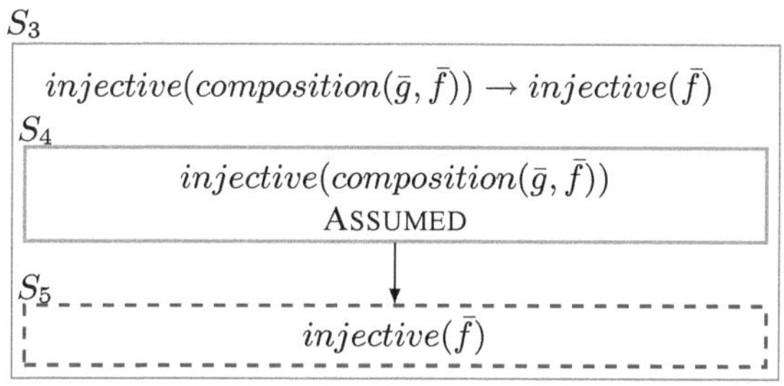

Fig. 7. Unfolding an implication [3, p. 6].

Now, we have to prove that $injective(f)$ holds. In order to do that, the proof in Fig. 1 uses the definition of injectivity: Assume $funApp(f, x) = funApp(f, x') \wedge in(x, A) \wedge in(x', A)$. [...] Hence $x = x'$. In other words, we prove an alternative goal. In order to retain a sound construction, we have to show two things: First, that the alternative goal indeed implies the original goal and second, that the alternative goal holds. This is represented in Fig. 8 by putting two statements S_6 and S_7 below the goal of S_5. This depicts that the PROOF of S_5 is BYSPLIT S_6, S_7. Note that a proof BYSPLIT leads to a division of contexts, i.e., the derived goal of S_6 will not be put into the context of S_7. Thus, the proof BYSPLIT allows for a finer scoping of statements.

The statement S_6 contains the soundness check. Its proof is BYCONTEXT which means that it will be sent to the background provers. If some ATP finds a proof, a statement annotated with BYCONTEXT is considered proved. This is here the case if our definition of injectivity indeed allows us to prove this alternative goal. We will depict statements proved ByContext in orange in the following.

Statement S_7 contains the proof of the alternative goal. Again, the universally quantified variables x and x' are fixed to constants. Afterwards, the implication is unfolded. As shown in Lemmas 1 and 2, this construction is sound.

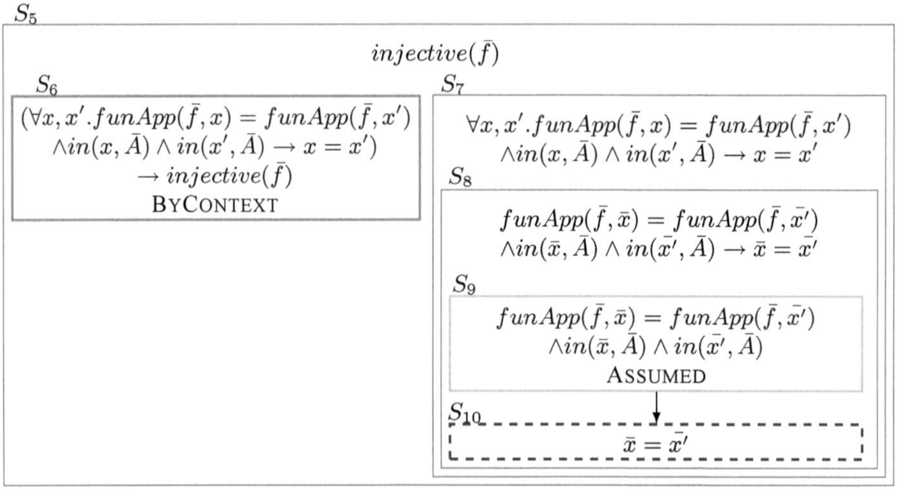

Fig. 8. Proving an alternative goal [3, p. 8]. (Color figure online)

To convince us that a proof constructed BySplit is sound, we have to use two additional natural deduction rules:

$$(\wedge I): \frac{P \quad Q}{P \wedge Q} \qquad (\rightarrow E): \frac{P \rightarrow Q \quad P}{Q}$$

These rules will be used in the proof of Lemma 3 which is an abstract case of our approach in Fig. 8.

Lemma 3 (Splitting a Goal). *Let S be a statement such that S.*Goal *$= P$, S.*Proof *$=$* BySplit *$\boldsymbol{S_0}, \boldsymbol{S_1}, ..., \boldsymbol{S_n}$, $\boldsymbol{S_0}$.*Goal *$= Q_1 \wedge ... \wedge Q_n \rightarrow P$, $\boldsymbol{S_i}$.*Goal *$= Q_i$ and S_i is proved for $i = 1, ..., n$:*

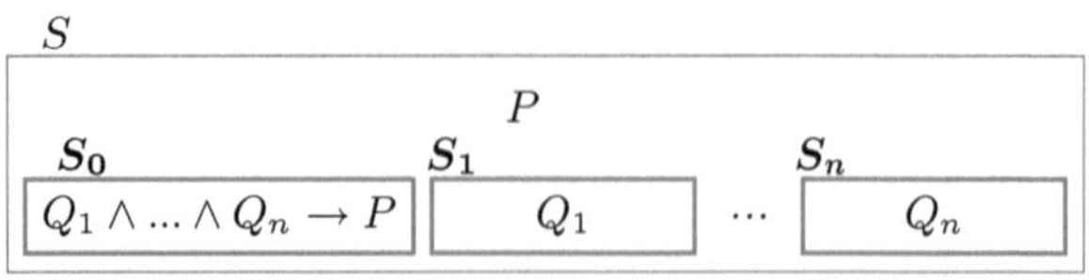

Then S is proved.

Proof. *We have* $\Gamma(S) = \Gamma(S_i)$ *for* $i = 0, \ldots, n$. *With* S_i *proved for* $i = 1, \ldots, n$ *we have* $\Gamma(S) \models Q_i$ *for* $i = 1, \ldots, n$. *With* $(\wedge I)$ *it follows* $\Gamma(S) \models Q_1 \wedge \cdots \wedge Q_n$.

With S_0 *proved we also have* $\Gamma(S) \models Q_1 \wedge \ldots \wedge Q_n \rightarrow P$. *Thus, we can deduce with* $(\rightarrow E)$ *that* $\Gamma(S) \models P$.

The remaining bit to prove is the goal of S_{10}, i.e., that $x = x'$ follows from the context. However, in the text in Fig. 1 the next derivation step is Then $funApp(composition(g, f), x) = funApp(composition(g, f), x')$.. This statement does not change the overall goal we want to prove, but gives a cornerstone to how one can derive the goal. As depicted in Fig. 9, this additional finding will first be verified by annotating statement S_{11} with BYCONTEXT. Afterwards, the actual goal is proved. Since the user gave no additional proving methods, we send the final goal $x = x'$ to the background provers as well.

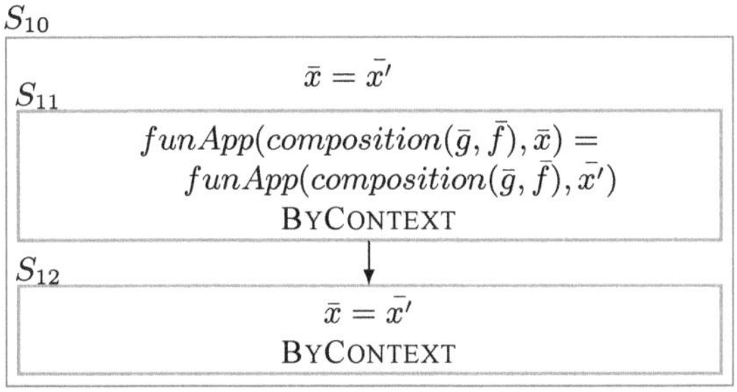

Fig. 9. Giving a cornerstone to a proof [3, p. 7].

If S_{11} can be derived by the background provers already, the theory created by the context of S_{12} is not extended by adding S_{11}. This is formally reflected in Lemma 4.

Lemma 4 (Deriving a Cornerstone). *Let* S *be a statement such that* S.GOAL $= P$, S.PROOF $=$ BYSEQUENCE $\boldsymbol{S_1}, \boldsymbol{S_2}$, $\boldsymbol{S_1}$.GOAL $= Q$, $\boldsymbol{S_2}$.GOAL $= P$ *and* S_1 *is proved:*

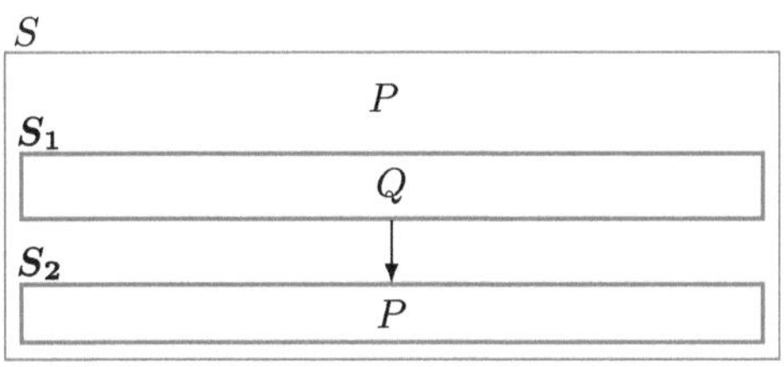

Then S *is proved.*

Proof. *Since* S_1 *is proved, we have* $\Gamma(S_1) \models Q$. *Because of* $\Gamma(S) = \Gamma(S_1)$ *already* $\Gamma(S) \models Q$. *Hence, with* S_2 *proved we have* $\Gamma(S_2) \models P$ *and thus* $\Gamma(S) \models P$.

This completes our construction of the internal proof representation of the lemma in Fig. 1. Three statements S_6, S_{11} and S_{12} are annotated ByContext and will be sent to the background provers. If each of these three statements can be derived from their respective contexts, we can conclude that the original goal of S already followed from its context. The proof of the lemma is then considered sound.

4 Geometry in Elfe

During the development of Elfe, we primarily formalized proofs in discrete mathematics. In this case study we will show that the system can straightforwardly be used to formalize a domain different from sets and relations: Euclidean geometry. We will use an axiomatization of geometry by [13] to create an Elfe library in Sect. 4.1. On this basis, we will formalize a geometry text and compare it to a formalization in Coq in Sect. 4.2 and discuss our findings in Sect. 4.3.

4.1 Tarski's Axiomatization

Tarskis's axiomatization [13] is a formalization of elementary Euclidean geometry. The axiomatization considers points as basic elements and introduces two predicates:

- a-b-c stands for: the points a, b and c are collinear, with b lying between a and c.
- a-b ≡ c-d stands for: the line spanned by the points a and b has the same length as the line spanned by the points c and d.

The axioms can be formalized as depicted in Fig. 10. Introducing new notations in Elfe can be done right away so that writing the axioms is more intuitive than in the original formalization, e.g., a-b-c for collinearity is more concise than $B(abc)$ as used in [13].

The first three axioms for the congruence relation CongrSymm, CongrIdent and CongrITrans ensure that ≡ is an equivalence relation. The Pasch axiom states that in a quadrangle a, b, p and q, the two diagonals a-q and b-p must have an intersection x, compare Fig. 11.

The axiom BetwIdent assures that if a point b is enclosed by the same point a from both sides, the points must in fact be equal.

Tarski's axiomatization models Euclidean geometry of an arbitrary dimension. In order to limit its models to specific dimensions, the axioms LowerDim and UpperDim can be used. We only want to prove lemmas in two dimensions, therefore we need to exclude interpretations with other dimensions. LowerDim ensures that there exists at least one proper triangle and therefore the dimension of our interpretation must have more than one dimension. UpperDim closes the dimension of possible interpretations upwards: Three points equidistant from two points must form a line and cannot leave the two dimensional plane. Thus, it is not possible to construct a three-dimensional model of our axioms.

The other axioms shown in Fig. 10 are not directly used in the following, we refer to [13] for a further explanation.

```
Notation between: a-b-c.
Notation equidistant: a-b ≡ c-d.

Axiom CongrSymm: for all a,b. a-b ≡ b-a.
Axiom CongrIdent: for all a,b,c. a-b ≡ c-c implies a = b.
Axiom CongrITrans: for all a,b,p,q,r,s. a-b ≡ p-q and a-b ≡ r-s implies p-q ≡ r-s.

Axiom Pasch: for all a,b,c,p,q. a-p-c and b-q-c implies exists x. p-x-b and q-x-a.
Axiom BetwIdent: for all a,b. a-b-a implies a = b.

Axiom LowerDim: exists a,b,c. not a-b-c and not b-c-a and not c-a-b.
Axiom UpperDim: for all a,b,c,p,q.
  (a-p ≡ a-q and b-p ≡ b-q and c-p ≡ c-q and not p = q)
  implies (a-b-c or b-c-a or c-a-b).

Axiom SegmentConstr: for all a,b,c,d. exists e. b-e ≡ c-d and a-b-e.
Axiom FiveSegment: for all a,b,c,d,a',b',c',d'.
  (a-b-c and a'-b'-c' and a-b ≡ a'-b' and b-c ≡ b'-c' and a-d ≡ a'-d' and b-d ≡ b'-d'
  and not a = b) implies c-d ≡ c'-d'.
Axiom Euclid: for all a,b,c,d,t. exists x,y.
  (a-d-t and b-d-c and not a = d) implies (a-b-x and a-c-y and x-t-y).
```

Fig. 10. Tarski's axiomatization of geometry in ELFE.

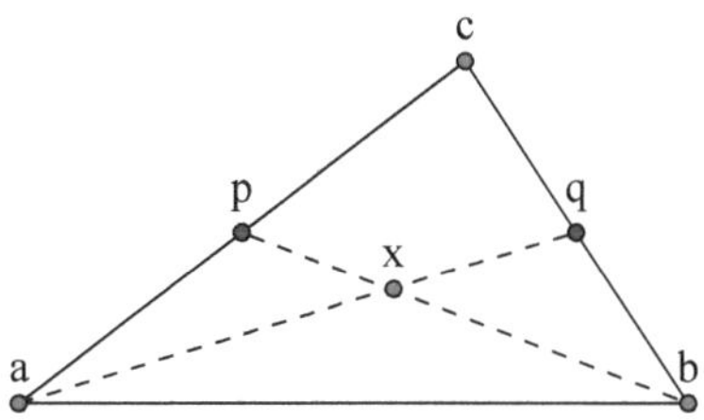

Fig. 11. Axiom of Pasch.

4.2 A Geometrical Proof Text

We will present in the following the proof of a conjecture of Tarski's axiomatization in ELFE and COQ.

The Proof in ELFE. Consider the text in Fig. 12 which states a proof text in geometry by using the previously developed library. The text consists of three lemmas, with the first two being interim observations to derive the third lemma.

The first lemma BetwEquality states that if two collinearities a-b-c and b-a-c hold, then a and b must in fact be equal. Intuitively, we can make this clear with the following diagram, which illustrates the situation in which both collinearities hold:

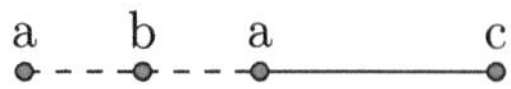

```
Include geometry.

Lemma BetwEquality: for all a,b,c. a-b-c and b-a-c implies a = b.
Proof:
  Assume a-b-c and b-a-c.
  Then a-b-a by BetwIdent, Pasch.
  Hence a = b.
qed.

Lemma ThreeCong: for all a,b,c,a',b',c'.
  a-b-c and a-b ≡ a'-b' and a-c ≡ a'-c' and b-c ≡ b'-c' implies a'-b'-c'.
Proof: qed.

Lemma BetweenCong: for all a,b,c. a-b-c and a-c ≡ a-b implies c = b.
Proof:
  Assume a-b-c and a-c ≡ a-b.
  Then a-b ≡ a-c and b-c ≡ c-b by CongrSymm, CongrlTrans.
  Then a-c-b by ThreeCong.
  Hence c = b.
qed.
```

Fig. 12. An exemplary geometry text.

Therefore, b must lie between a on both sides and a and b collapse to the same point. This exact reasoning is used in the ELFE proof. At first, the antecedent of the main implication of the lemma is assumed. Then it is observed that a-b-a must hold as well. In this case, we have given explicitly which axioms are needed to prove this observation, BetwIdent and Pasch. The restriction of the context can be omitted, in which case the whole background library is given to the ATP. Restricting the context can however clarify why a derivation holds. In our case, the derivation holds as we can retrace with the following reasoning: By instantiating the Pasch axiom with p = b and a = q, we can derive that there exists an x such that b-x-b and a-x-a. With BetwIdent we can derive that b = x and therefore especially a-b-a holds.

The proof of the second lemma ThreeCong is entirely left to the background provers. For our purposes an intuitive account of the lemma is sufficient: If three points a, b and c are collinear, and their respective distances are equal to the distances between three other points a', b' and c', then the latter points cannot span a triangle. Thus, they must be collinear as well.

With these two lemmas we can derive the main lemma of the text: If the point b lies between a and c, and the distances between a and b respectively a and c are equal, then the points b and c are in fact equal. Intuitively, we can elucidate this observation with the following illustration:

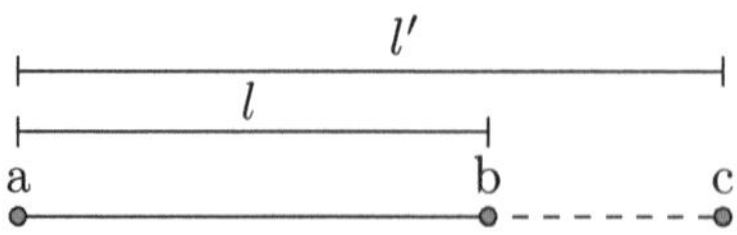

If the two distances l and l' are equally long, then b and c collapse. In the formal proof shown in Fig. 12, we employ the two previously derived lemmas. At first, two other congruences of lines are observed. Note that we restrict the context for the background provers by specifying that our proof should be done only using CongrSymm and CongrlTrans. These lemmas imply that ≡ is an equivalence relation, therefore the congruences hold.

Including the assumption, we now have the three congruences a-b ≡ a-c, a-c ≡ a-b and b-c ≡ c-b such that we can employ the lemma ThreeCong with a' = a, b' = c and c' = b. Hence, we observe that also c lies between a and b.

We now have a-b-c and a-c-b. We cannot directly apply BetwEquality but only after observing that also c-b-a and b-c-a hold. This is due to the symmetry of collinearity, i.e., a-b-c implies that c-b-a. This symmetry property, even though obvious from an intuitive point of view, is not straightforward to prove and involves invoking Pasch, BetwIdent, CongrIdent and SegmentConstr. We can however leave this work the background provers and directly observe that we can apply BetwEquality to finally prove that c and b collapse to the same point.

The Proof in Coq. The last lemma BetweenCong we have just shown is also formalized in Coq in [14, p. 147]. In Fig. 13 you can find an adaption of their proof. The two basic predicates for betweenness and congruence are called Bet and Cong.

We do not give a proof of the intermediate lemmas BetwEquality and ThreeCong and will take them as given. Other properties like symmetry of the betweenness relation BetwSymm, i.e., that Bet A B C → Bet C B A holds, need to be proven prior to the lemma. We refer to the GeoCoq[3] project for a complete formalization of these preliminaries.

The proof idea is similar to the proof we gave in ELFE in Fig. 12. The universally quantified variables and the antecedent of the implication are introduced as assumptions with intros. Then two other congruences Cong B C C B and Cong A B A C are derived. By employing ThreeCong, the collinearity Bet A C B can be deduced. It is necessary to explicitly state from which axioms and intermediate derivations a goal follows by using apply. Finally, we can use the lemma BetwEquality, which is analogous to the one in ELFE in Fig. 12, to prove the final goal C = B. When entering the proof gradually in the command line interface of Coq, all relevant hypotheses and goals are prompted to the user. We use this to illustrate the subproof of H3: Bet A C B. After entering eapply ThreeCong, Coq yields the following proof state:

```
Coq < eapply ThreeCong.

2 subgoals
  A, B, C : Tpoint
  H : Bet A B C
  H0 : Cong A C A B
  H1 : Cong B C C B
  H2 : Cong A B A C
  ============================
  Bet A C B

subgoal 2 is:
 C = B

3 focused subgoals
  A, B, C : Tpoint
```

[3] http://geocoq.github.io/GeoCoq/.

```
ThreeCong: forall A B C A' B' C', Bet A B C → Cong A B A' B' /\Cong B C B' C'
  /\Cong A C A' C' → Bet A' B' C'.
BetwEquality: forall A B C, Bet A B C /\Bet B A C → A = B.
BetwSymm : forall A B C, Bet A B C → Bet C B A.

Lemma BetweenCong : forall A B C, Bet A B C → Cong A C A B → C=B.
Proof.
  intros.
  assert (H1: Cong B C C B).
    apply CongPseudoReflexivity.
  assert (H2: Cong A B A C).
    apply CongSym. apply H0.
  assert (H3: Bet A C B).
    eapply ThreeCong.
    apply H.
    split. apply H2. split. apply H1. apply H0.
  eapply BetwEquality.
  split. all: apply BetwSymm. apply H. apply H3.
Qed.
```

Fig. 13. The exemplary proof in Coq.

```
17      H : Bet A B C
18      H0 : Cong A C A B
19      H1 : Cong B C C B
20      H2 : Cong A B A C
21      ============================
22      Bet ?A ?B ?C
23
24    subgoal 2 is:
25     Cong ?A ?B A C /\ Cong ?B ?C C B
26        /\ Cong ?A ?C A B
27
28    subgoal 3 is:
29     C = B
```

The two goals we want to prove, `Bet A C B` and `C = B`, are depicted in lines 2–13, including the set of hypotheses from lines 4–8. In order to prove the first goal `Bet A C B`, we applied the lemma `ThreeCong`. Therefore instead of showing `Bet A C B`, we have to prove the antecedent of the lemma ThreeCong, i.e., that `Bet ?A ?B ?C` and `Cong ?A ?B A C /\ Cong ?B ?C C B /\ Cong ?A ?C A B` hold for some appropriate `?A, ?B, ?C`. This results in three focused subgoals we need to prove, depicted in lines 15–29.

Next, we apply the hypothesis `H: Bet A B C`:

```
1   Coq < apply H.
2   2 subgoals
3
4     A, B, C : Tpoint
5     H : Bet A B C
6     H0 : Cong A C A B
7     H1 : Cong B C C B
8     H2 : Cong A B A C
9     ============================
10    Cong A B A C /\ Cong B C C B /\ Cong A C A B
```

```

subgoal 2 is:
  C = B
```

By applying the hypothesis, we fix the `?A, ?B, ?C` such that the subgoal `Bet ?A ?B ?C` is proven with `?A = A, ?B = B, ?C = C`. We still have to prove the second subgoal with the three congruences. Since the variables are fixed now, this leads to the new goal `Cong A B A C /\ Cong B C C B /\ Cong A C A B`. The unification procedure makes it apparent in which way exactly the lemmas are applied, the user can thereby retrace which variables are instantiated in which way.

4.3 Discussion

We have seen how geometry can be formalized in ELFE and how it compares to a formalization in COQ. The proof in ELFE captures more intuitive reasoning and allows a user to let the background provers figure out the details. However, this also leads to losing some information why a proof works. In which manner exactly the lemma ThreeCong is applied is not apparent in the ELFE proof. For future work it can be interesting to extract such unifications from the background provers. Currently, the user can restrict the context to allow the background provers to use only some axioms for a derivation. It could be interesting to recover this restricted context by analysing the proofs of the ATP; similar to what the extension SLEDGEHAMMER does for ISABELLE.

Notably, our proof resembles the informal proof given in [14], while the proof formalized in COQ is more cumbersome. The authors note that "some intuitively simple properties are hard to prove in this context" [14, p. 154]. Our approach allows for entrusting ATP with proving laborious lemmas as the lemma ThreeCong. The user therefore can focus on the interesting bits and employ a rather intuitive way of proving. The notations allow for an elegant representation of the axioms and deductions.

5 Evaluation

The ELFE system is currently being tested by students in a discrete mathematics course, we will introduce the didactic practice in Sect. 5.1. We also formalized some more advanced theorems in the system, e.g., Cantor's theorem and the Knaster-Tarski theorem, and will discuss our experiences as well as the system's inherent limitations in Sect. 5.2.

5.1 User Feedback

The system was initially tested with 12 undergraduates of Computing, Mathematics and Electrical Engineering at Imperial College London. Following CSEDU, we are currently evaluating the system with 80 students of the Universidad El Bosque in Colombia. In a course about discrete mathematics they learn

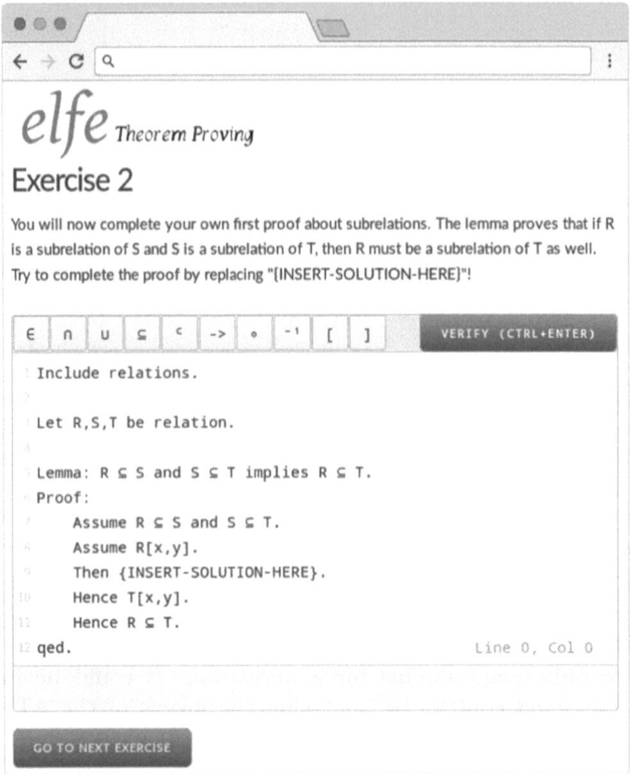

Fig. 14. Task of tutorial.

about relations. The students are introduced to the notions and concepts of the domain in a lecture. Then they are asked to complete a training session at home. For this purpose, the web interface of ELFE was extended so the students can test their proofs at home. A task of the tutorial is depicted in Fig. 14.

The lemma proves transitivity of subrelations. The students are given a scaffolding of the proof, so they only have to insert that also S[x,y] holds. With several examples of this kind, they get to know the proof structures usable in ELFE. In a final task, they are asked to complete a more complex proof on their own, i.e., the statement $\mathsf{R} \subseteq \mathsf{S}$ and S is symmetric implies $(\mathsf{R} \cup (\mathrm{R}^{-1})) \subseteq \mathsf{S}$.

We plan to compare the learning progress with a control group that has not worked with the ELFE system but solved the tasks analogously. The final results of our study are pending as we are still conducting it.

5.2 Limits of the Current System

Since first-order logic is an intuitive way to write down proofs in set theory and relations, proofs in these domains could be written down easily. The Notation command has turned out to be a very powerful construct to ease the readability of proofs. As shown in the geometry case study in Sect. 4, new notations can be introduced easily and make a proof look quite intuitive. Working with the functions library was more complex. Some additional lemmas and function symbols which were introduced to make a proof more readable for humans increase the difficulty for the background provers. If the background provers take too long in proof search, it is hard to assess if a proof itself is wrong or only takes a long time to prove.

Debugging a failing proof is still difficult with the user interface provided by ELFE. In most cases, the raw proof obligations given to the background provers were more helpful in finding bugs by manually deleting and changing the given premises. This is due to constructions like Let which shorten a proof, but also hide what is going on inside the system. BEAGLE was able to provide countermodels to a wrong proof only if the number of premises was limited. Restricting the context of a derivation step increased the success rate significantly. However, for new users it is certainly difficult to relate a countermodel to the entered text since it is given in the raw TPTP format.

Another problem that occurred was that the background provers were too clever. They sometimes found intermediate steps that are not at all obvious for a human reader. This cleverness is particularly problematic with proofs by contradiction. If the background provers find the inconsistency caused by the assumption, all derivations a user may make are trivially also true, even though they do not make sense in the proof.

Writing larger proof texts in straightforward domains as set theory can be easily done in ELFE. However, some properties like well-foundedness are not expressible at all in first-order logic, so it might be expedient for future versions to use higher-order logic at the core of statement sequences.

6 Related Work

The ELFE system is closely related to the SYSTEM FOR AUTOMATED DEDUCTION, which we will introduce in the following. Afterwards, we will take a look at the NAPROCHE system, another project aiming at the verification of natural mathematical language. Most influential for formal mathematics are the interactive theorem provers ISABELLE and COQ, we will conclude with presenting both systems as well as their formalizations of the injectivity proof of Fig. 1.

SYSTEM FOR AUTOMATED DEDUCTION (SAD). The SAD was developed at the University Paris and the Taras Shevchenko National University of Kyiv. It continues the project “Algoritm Ochevidnosti” (algorithm of obviousness) which was initiated by the soviet researcher Victor Glushkov in the 1960s. His goal was to develop a tool that shortens long but “obvious” proofs to users. These omitted parts should be verified by automated theorem provers [15].

SAD uses the input language FORTHEL which allows for expressing mathematical statements intuitively. FORTHEL texts are converted to an ordered set of first-order formulas. The structure of the initial text is preserved such that necessary proof tasks can be defined. These tasks are then given to an ATP. The internal reasoner may simplify tasks and omit trivial statements. Afterwards, the verification status of the text is given to the user. For each proof task, the result of the used ATP is returned. This allows to inspect possible sources of failing tasks, but requires knowledge of how the background provers work [2].

Currently, it is not possible to work with functions in SAD due to the lack of background libraries. Thus, we could not implement the injectivity proof of Fig. 1 in SAD.

Naproche. The Naproche system was a joint project between mathematicians at the University of Bonn and linguists at the University of Duisburg-Essen. Its central goal was to develop a controlled natural language (CNL) which checks semi-formal mathematical texts. The input are texts in a LaTeX style language, consisting of mathematical formulas embedded in a controlled natural language [16].

To extract the semantics of a CNL text, Naproche adapts a concept from computational linguistics: Proof Representation Structures (PRS) enrich the linguistic concept of Discourse Representation Structures in such a way that they can represent mathematical statements and their relations. The semantics of PRS have been researched extensively; however, the project is not continued and has no working version available.

Isabelle. Isabelle is a joint project of Cambridge University and the Technical University Munich. It supports polymorphic higher-order logic, augmented with axiomatic type classes. At present it provides useful proof procedures for Constructive Type Theory, various first-order logics, Zermelo-Fraenkel set theory and higher-order logic [17].

Consider the injectivity proof written in Isabelle in Fig. 15. The predicate inj_on f A expresses that function f is injective on the domain A. The proof structure is close to the one used in Elfe: We introduce arbitrary x and x' which f maps to the same element and conclude that they must have been the same. One has to specify the automated proof tactics and used premises: In our example, the derivations are made by term rewriting using definitions comp_def and inj_on_def from the background library.

In comparison to Elfe, the user is therefore more involved in the automated verification process. Since 2007, Isabelle offers the extension Sledgehammer. By calling several ATP, Sledgehammer tries to determine which premises are important to a goal. It then tries to reconstruct the automated proofs with methods implemented in Isabelle. In fact, the mechanical prove methods needed in Fig. 15 can be found by invoking Sledgehammer.

In a recent study, 34% of nontrivial goals contained in representative Isabelle texts could be proved by Sledgehammer. With this extension, Isabelle allows beginners to prove challenging theorems. The creators note that Sledgehammer was not designed as a tool to teach Isabelle since it focused primarily on experienced users. However, it changed the way Isabelle

```
theory InjectiveComposition
  imports Fun
begin

lemma:
  assumes "inj_on (g ∘ f) A"
  shows "inj_on f A"
proof
  fix x x'
  assume "x ∈ A" and "x' ∈ A"
  moreover assume "f x = f x'"
  then have "(g ∘ f) x = (g ∘ f) x'"
      by (auto simp: comp_def)
  ultimately show "x = x'" using assms
      by (auto simp: inj_on_def)
qed
```

Fig. 15. Proof in ISABELLE [3, p. 10].

```
Require Import Basics.
Definition injective {A B} (f : A → B) :=
  forall x y : A, f x = f y → x = y.
Theorem c_inj (A B C:Type) (f:A→B) (g:B→C):
  (injective (compose g f)) → injective f.
Proof.
  intuition.
  intros x x'.
  pose (f x = f x').
  intuition.
  assert (g (f x) = g (f x')).
  { elim H0. rewrite H0. trivial. }
  auto.
Qed.
```

Fig. 16. Proof in COQ [3, p. 11].

is taught. Beginners do not have to learn about low level proving tactics and how they work but can focus on the proof from a higher level [18].

COQ. COQ is an interactive theorem prover initially developed 1984 at INRIA. It is based on the Curry–Howard correspondence which relates types to classical logic. In order to prove a proposition, one has to construct a term with the type corresponding to the proposition.

Consider the injectivity proof implemented in Fig. 16. Again, the idea of the proof is to show that f x = f x′ implies x = x′. However, we have to explicitly apply rewrite techniques to make the derivation steps. The tactic intuition says that we can assume a left hand side of an implication and then prove the right hand side. Afterwards, we want to make sure that we can just apply g on both sides. We have to rewrite both sides of H0, which stands for f x = f x', in order to get to our assertion. The final goal x = x' is then derived by applying the rewrite technique auto.

As we see, the translation process of mathematical texts to functional programs requires a good understanding of type theory and is not suitable for mathematical beginners.

Consequently, the most prominent current interactive theorem provers are of a deeply technical natural. They are thought of as programming languages that happen to prove theorems, and not digitisations of mathematical language.

7 Discussion

This paper presented ELFE, a system that checks proofs in discrete mathematics. Entered texts are transformed to statement sequences, a special data-structure of first-order formulas. Remaining proof obligations are then checked by background provers. Statement sequences are a powerful intermediate proof representation which can hold manifold proof techniques. The clear soundness criterion allows for extending the proof techniques easily. For example, it might be interesting to allow for proofs via mathematical induction based on the automation of induction [19].

Formalizing domains like geometry is straightforward in ELFE. Proofs can be done in a fairly intuitive manner and are significantly shorter than formal proofs in interactive theorem provers like COQ. This however also leads to a loss of detail. Many ATP return information about the proof of a conjecture which could be used to fill in some of the missing details. The challenge is to present the technical output of the background provers via an intuitive interface. Information that could be given rather easily is which axioms and lemmas were used in a proof. The restriction of a context could thereby be filled in automatically.

ELFE uses ATP as oracles and trusts their results. An extension of ELFE could try to reconstruct proofs found by the background provers. This can be used to gain more trust in the automatic proofs and moreover yielded to the users to give an idea of why a proof works.

One acknowledged structural limitation of ELFE is that it internally uses first-order logic. For example, it is therefore not possible to express well-foundedness of a relation. The recent years have seen interesting advances in automated theorem proving of typed higher-order logic. A new standard for typed higher-order-logic has been added to TPTP which is used by several provers like LEO-III [20] and SATALLAX [21]. A next version of ELFE could use this development in order to provide a more powerful way of expressing mathematics. This requires to introduce a meaningful type system for ELFE.

References

1. Gonthier, G.: Formal proof-the four-color theorem. Not. AMS **55**, 1382–1393 (2008)
2. Verchinine, K., Lyaletski, A., Paskevich, A.: SYSTEM FOR AUTOMATED DEDUCTION (SAD): a tool for proof verification. In: Pfenning, F. (ed.) CADE 2007. LNCS (LNAI), vol. 4603, pp. 398–403. Springer, Heidelberg (2007). https://doi.org/10.1007/978-3-540-73595-3_29
3. Doré, M., Broda, K.: The ELFE system - verifying mathematical proofs of undergraduate students. In: Proceedings of 10th CSEDU, vol. 2, pp. 15–26 (2018)
4. Sutcliffe, G.: The TPTP problem library and associated infrastructure: the FOF and CNF parts, v3.5.0. J. Autom. Reason. **43**, 337–362 (2009)
5. Weidenbach, C., Brahm, U., Hillenbrand, T., Keen, E., Theobald, C., Topić, D.: SPASS version 2.0. In: Voronkov, A. (ed.) CADE 2002. LNCS (LNAI), vol. 2392, pp. 275–279. Springer, Heidelberg (2002). https://doi.org/10.1007/3-540-45620-1_22
6. Schulz, S.: E - a Brainiac theorem prover. AI Commun. **15**, 111–126 (2002)
7. Riazanov, A., Voronkov, A.: The design and implementation of VAMPIRE. AI Commun. **15**, 91–110 (2002)
8. Sutcliffe, G.: The CADE ATP system competition. AI Mag. **37**, 99–101 (2016)
9. Baumgartner, P., Bax, J., Waldmann, U.: BEAGLE – a hierarchic superposition theorem prover. In: Felty, A.P., Middeldorp, A. (eds.) CADE 2015. LNCS (LNAI), vol. 9195, pp. 367–377. Springer, Cham (2015). https://doi.org/10.1007/978-3-319-21401-6_25
10. de Moura, L., Bjørner, N.: Z3: an efficient SMT solver. In: Ramakrishnan, C.R., Rehof, J. (eds.) TACAS 2008. LNCS, vol. 4963, pp. 337–340. Springer, Heidelberg (2008). https://doi.org/10.1007/978-3-540-78800-3_24
11. Doré, M.: ELFE - an interactive theorem prover for undergraduate students. Bachelor thesis (2017)
12. Fitting, M.: First-Order Logic and Automated Theorem Proving, 2nd edn. Springer, New York (1990). https://doi.org/10.1007/978-1-4684-0357-2
13. Tarski, A., Givant, S.: Tarski's system of geometry. Bull. Symb. Logic **5**, 175–214 (1999)
14. Narboux, J.: Mechanical theorem proving in Tarski's geometry. In: Botana, F., Recio, T. (eds.) ADG 2006. LNCS (LNAI), vol. 4869, pp. 139–156. Springer, Heidelberg (2007). https://doi.org/10.1007/978-3-540-77356-6_9
15. Verchinine, K., Paskevich, A.: FORTHEL-the language of formal theories. Int. J. Inf. Theor. Appl. **7**, 120–126 (2000)
16. Cramer, M., Fisseni, B., Koepke, P., Kühlwein, D., Schröder, B., Veldman, J.: The Naproche project controlled natural language proof checking of mathematical texts. In: Fuchs, N.E. (ed.) CNL 2009. LNCS (LNAI), vol. 5972, pp. 170–186. Springer, Heidelberg (2010). https://doi.org/10.1007/978-3-642-14418-9_11
17. Nipkow, T., Wenzel, M., Paulson, L.C.: ISABELLE/HOL: A Proof Assistant for Higher-Order Logic. Springer, Heidelberg (2002). https://doi.org/10.1007/3-540-45949-9
18. Paulson, L.C., Blanchette, J.C.: Three years of experience with Sledgehammer, a practical link between automatic and interactive theorem provers. In: Proceedings of IJCAR 2010, pp. 1–10 (2010)
19. Bundy, A.: The automation of proof by mathematical induction. In: Handbook of Automated Reasoning (2001)
20. Benzmüller, C., Steen, A., Wisniewski, M.: LEO-III version 1.1 (system description). In: IWIL Workshop and LPAR Short Presentations, p. 16 (2017)
21. Brown, C.E.: SATALLAX: an automatic higher-order prover. In: Gramlich, B., Miller, D., Sattler, U. (eds.) IJCAR 2012. LNCS (LNAI), vol. 7364, pp. 111–117. Springer, Heidelberg (2012). https://doi.org/10.1007/978-3-642-31365-3_11

Automatic Evaluation of Students' Discussion Skill Based on their Heart Rate

Shimeng Peng[1], Shigeki Ohira[2], and Katashi Nagao[1(✉)]

[1] Graduate School of Informatics, Nagoya University, Nagoya, Japan
hou@nagao.nuie.nagoya-u.ac.jp, nagao@i.nagoya-u.ac.jp
[2] Information Technology Center, Nagoya University, Nagoya, Japan
ohira@nagoya-u.jp

Abstract. Discussion which consists of several Q&A segments (question and answer pairs) is often considered as one of the most familiar types of intellectual and creative activities at meetings. Evaluating students' answer-quality of Q&A segments in discussion and giving them feedback can effectively help them improve their discussion skills. Considering that the discussion process is a type of cognitive activity, which could result in changes in certain physiological data, such as heart rate (HR) variability (HRV). In this study, we argue that students' HR data can be used to effectively evaluate the answer-quality of their Q&A segments and as a method of automatic evaluation of students' discussion-skill compared with using traditional NLP such as semantic analysis. In order to confirm this, we used a non-invasive device, i.e., Apple Watch, to collect real-time updated HR data of students during their discussions in our lab-seminar environment, their HR data were analyzed based on Q&A segments, and three machine-learning models were generated for evaluation: logistic regression, support vector machine, and random forest. The significant HR and HRV features (metrics) were also discussed using a feature selection method. Comparative experiments were conducted involving semantic data of Q&A statements alone and a combination of HR and semantic data. We also gave an experimental investigation on HR and HRV features robustness on the new data set we collected additionally.

Keywords: Evaluation of discussion skills · Machine learning · Heart rate variability · Learning analytics

1 Introduction

Discussion is one of the most common effective active learning cycle activities in academia by presenter-students organizing and explaining their current research and future plans, participants involving peers and instructors who raising questions and presenter-students answering them, we call question and answer pairs Q&A segments, a way to enhance the interaction with peers and teachers, to generate useful feedback about the presenter-students' learning performance status relating to their specific goals and facilitate knowledge discovery and exchange. There is great significance in analyzing discussion in a scientific way and evaluating its quality to improve students' discussion skills and help them carry out future research activities.

B. M. McLaren et al. (Eds.): CSEDU 2018, CCIS 1022, pp. 572–585, 2019.
https://doi.org/10.1007/978-3-030-21151-6_27

Making full use of discussion data such as audio-and-video, facial expressions, and semantic information can help us evaluate the students' discussion skills. Previously, our lab developed a system called "discussion-mining (DM)" system [1, 2] which provide us with analyzable discussion data, it generates multimedia meeting minutes of lab discussions containing audio-visual and semantic information of Q&A segments given by participants and answered by the discussion presenter-students.

We think that these questions given by participants are useful for helping presenter-students troubleshoot problems that have not been resolved or are ignored at the present stage, at the same time, participants could understand and learn well about the presenter-students' research content through the process of raising questions to them. Given the crucial importance of the questions asked by the participants, ideally we want the presenter-students to give answers that are close to the correct answer, in other words give a high-quality answer. Many high-quality answers given by presenter-students indicates a better discussion ability. Evaluation of answer-quality of Q&A segments is common in the study of high quality answers selection or prediction on the social question-and-answer sites (Q&A site), such as Yahoo! Answers and Answer.com. The aim of this research topic is to automatically categorize answers as good or bad to help users decrease answer searching time. This specific topic has always been analyzed as a Nature Language Processing (NLP) task. Patil and Lee [3] analyzed certain linguistic features to identify expert answers, some previous studies described using contextual features, such as n-gram, to predict the answer quality of Yahoo! Answers [4]. However, the personal characteristics of responders or recorders inevitably decrease the generalization performance of the answer-quality evaluation of Q&A segments.

Considering that the discussion process is a kind of cognitive activity, which could result in changes in certain psychophysiological data, such as heart rate (HR) variability (HRV), several studies have proven that HR is an important index of the autonomic nervous system regulation of the cardiovascular system [5]. Therefore, there has been increasing focus on observing the correlation between HR data and cognitive activities. A study on measuring the HR during three cognitive tasks [6] revealed the affection of cognitive processing on HRV. The stress level also has been assessed during Trier social stress test tasks, a type of cognitive activity, by using HR and HRV metrics [7]. Judging from the large amount of evidence presented, we argue that the HR data of the participants of a meeting can be used to effectively evaluate the answer-quality of Q&A segments, which is helpful in improving participants' discussion skills [8].

In this paper, our starting point is categorizing the answer-quality of Q&A segments of discussions into low quality and high quality according to how correctly a presenter-student answered participants' questions. To validate our argument, we first introduce our proposal systems which generate lab-seminar style meeting data and collect participants' HR during a discussion in real time. We then introduce our evaluation and comparative experiments which adopt three types of binary classification machine-learning methods: logistic regression (LR), support vector machine (SVM), and random forest (RF), as well as the HRV features (metrics), and discuss the evaluation results. Finally, we will describe the system we are going to generate for training and improving students' discussion-skills by taking advantage of the results we made in this study.

2 Discussion Mining System

Seminar-style meetings that are regularly held at university laboratories are places where exchanges of opinions on research occur. Many comments on future work are included in the meeting records. However, as discussions at meetings are generally not recorded in detail, it is difficult to use them for discovering useful knowledge. Our laboratory developed and uses a discussion mining (DM) system that records the content of face-to-face meetings while providing metadata [1, 2]. Looking back on the challenges presented in remarks is essential for setting new goals in activities, but their existence may be buried in many other remarks in the minutes.

In our laboratory at Nagoya University, we have used this DM system to record detailed meetings in the laboratory for over 10 years. The system enables all participants to cooperate together to create and use structured minutes. It is not fully automated, i.e., a secretary manually writes down the contents of speech, and each speaker tags his/her speech. Therefore, we can generate data with high accuracy.

The meeting style supported by the DM system is one in which a presenter explains a topic while displaying slides, and Q&A with the meeting participants is either conducted during or at the end of the presentation.

Specifically, using multiple cameras and microphones installed in a discussion room, as shown in Fig. 1, and a presenter/secretary tool we created, we record discussion content. In the center of the discussion room, there is also a main screen that displays presentation materials and demonstration videos, and on both sides, there are sub screens for displaying information on and images of the participants who are currently speaking.

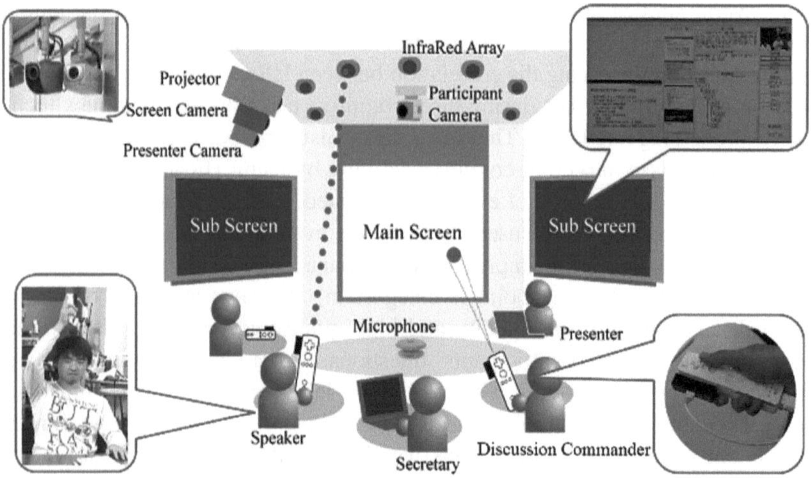

Fig. 1. Overview of discussion mining (DM) system [8].

The DM system records slide presentations and Q&A sessions including participants while segmenting them in time. As a result, content (discussion content), as shown in Fig. 2, is recorded and generated.

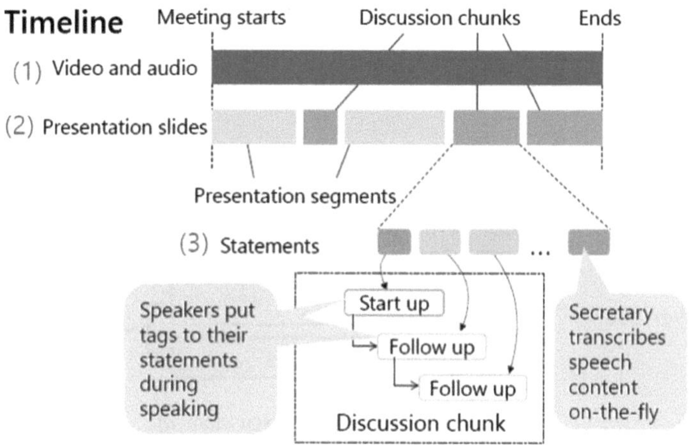

Fig. 2. Structured meeting content [8].

Every participant inputs metadata about his/her speech by using a dedicated device that is called a "discussion commander", as shown in the lower right of Fig. 1, Participants who specifically ask questions or make comments on new topics assign start-up tags to their statements. Also, if they want to speak in more detail on topics related to the immediately preceding statement, they provide a follow-up tag. Furthermore, the system records pointer coordinates, the location of figures and texts in a slide, and information on a button pressed to indicate that one is for or against a statement during a presentation and Q&A session. Information marked on important statements is also recorded.

We also developed a system for searching and viewing recorded data. In this system for browsing discussion content, a user can search the contents of an agenda from a date and participant information, view past discussions similar to the ongoing debate, and effectively visualize the state of a discussion, as shown in Fig. 3.

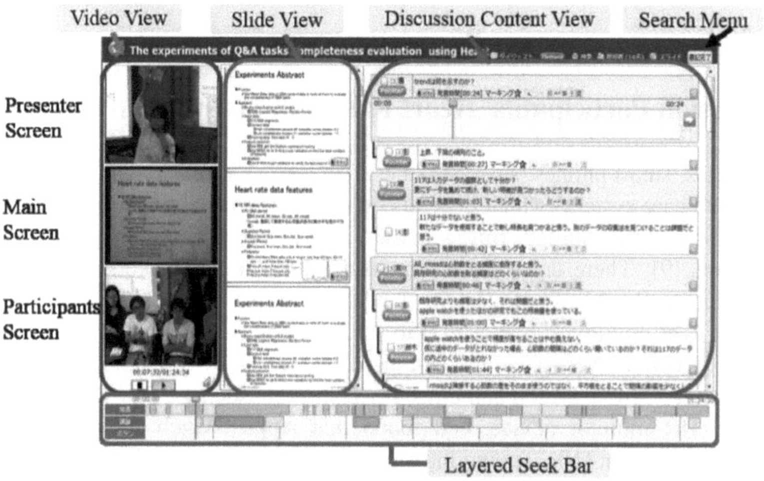

Fig. 3. Discussion browser [8].

The discussion view presents the semantic structures of discussion content and shows all of the recorded questions given by the participants and corresponding answers given by the presenter, which we call Q&A segments, as shown in Fig. 4.

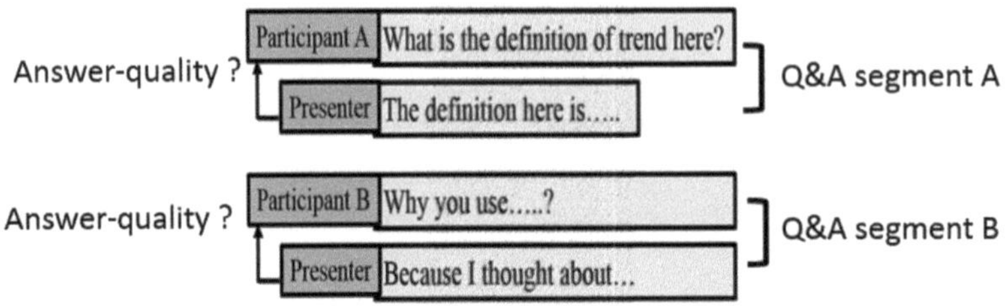

Fig. 4. Q&A segments in discussion [8].

In addition, we also focus on pointing and "referring to" behaviors during meetings. Speakers usually refer to something when making a statement, e.g., "this opinion is based on the previous comment" or "this is about this part of the slide" (while pointing to an image or text in the slide). We assume that a statement with a reference to an object in a slide is strongly related to the topic corresponding to the object. We also assume that two statements during which the speakers point to the same object are about the same topic. Therefore, we concluded that acquiring and recording information on pointing to objects in a slide would facilitate topic segmentation and lead to more precise semantic structuring of discussions. We call an object pointed to in presentation material a "visual referent". We thus developed a system for pointing to and selecting objects in slides that uses the discussion commander mentioned earlier and created a mechanism for acquiring and recording information on pointing to objects in relation to participants' statements.

This system can also extract any part of a figure in a slide and refer to it. In addition, selected or extracted image objects can be moved and magnified by using the discussion commander.

3 Discussion Participants' Heart Rate Data Acquisition System

In recent years, smart phones, smart watches, wireless smart trackers have been widely used in health care systems which depends on recording activities and monitoring vital signs such as calories burned, fitness activity, pulse, weight, HR, oxygen level, and sleep patterns [9]. There are several famous wireless smart trackers, such as Apple Watch, Fitbit series, Microsoft Bands, Jawbone Up, Samsung Galaxy Gear. These devices use light-emitting diode (LED) to measure the frequency at which the blood pumps [10]. Fatema investigated and compared the accuracy difference on monitoring HR data between Apple Watch and other smart trackers such as, Samsung Gear with a professional HR monitor device, and found that Apple Watch showed the highest accuracy and precision [10]. Taking into account the high accuracy of Apple Watch on HR data measurement, and the wide range of uses in the market. In our study, we used

Apple Watch to collect participants' HR data based on our DM system and visualize their HR information during discussions.

3.1 Heart Rate Data Acquisition

In our lab-seminar discussion environment, we asked discussion participants to wear the Apple Watch on their left hand before the discussion as showed in Fig. 5, they should choose their own ID and press the "start" button to start their HR data monitor during the whole discussion, and pressed the "stop" button at the end of the discussion. Through the Health Kit framework on Apple Watch, participants' HR data were acquired almost in real time in 5–7 s intervals. The collected HR and participants' information is displayed on the Apple Watch screen as well as synchronously presented on the HR browser.

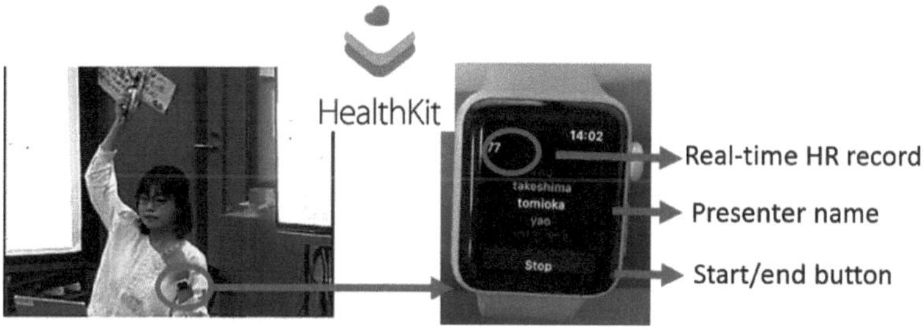

Fig. 5. Discussion participants' heart rate (HR) acquisition [8].

3.2 Heart Rate Browser

The participant's HR information which was accumulated during the heart-rate-data acquisition was presented synchronously in the heart-rate browser with the time line of the corresponding discussion. As shown in Fig. 6, the heart-rate browser consists of three parts: search menu, HR graph, and HR records.

Participants' heart-rate browser has the following three components:

Search menu: The historical HR data and user information can be searched through this search menu at the top of the browser.

HR graph: The graph provides an intuitive way to observe participant's HR data changes throughout the discussion.

HR records: The HR data at each point of the discussion with which the participant's information can be checked.

4 Discussion-Skill Evaluation Based on Participants' Heart Rate

As explained in the previous sections, the DM system we developed records the statements of each participant consist of several Q&A segments during a meeting as the discussion content, including video/audio data and text minutes. As well as, our Heart-rate data acquisition system collects participants' heart rate data during the discussion. Therefore, we can analyze participants' heart rate data based on their Q&A segments generated in discussion and validate our argument that HR of participants can be used to effectively evaluate the answer-quality of Q&A segments during discussions and as an automatic evaluation method in discussion skills evaluation.

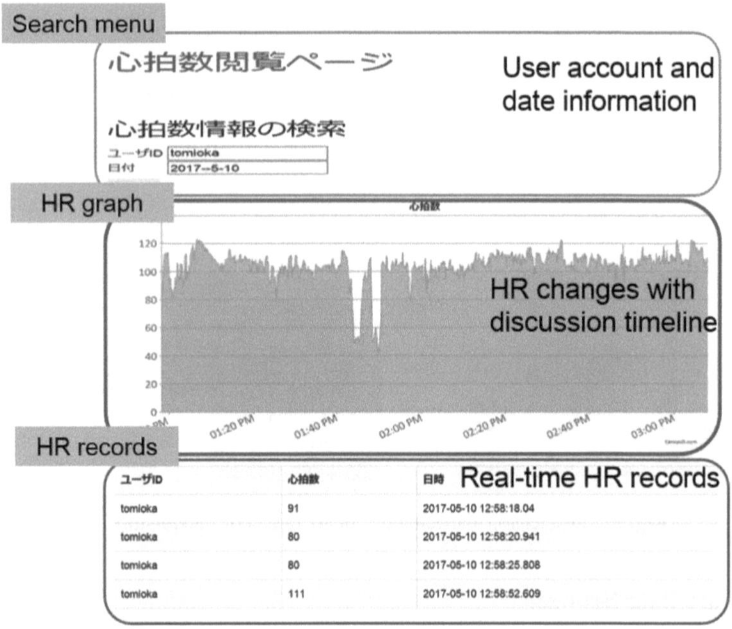

Fig. 6. Discussion participants' heart rate (HR) browser [8].

4.1 Heart-Rate Data Analysis

The complete HR information of a presenter-student during one discussion is displayed in a graph, as shown in Fig. 7, with the Abscissa representing the relative timeline of a discussion, often about 1.5–2 h, the vertical axis showing the corresponding HR value in this discussion. Since we aimed to use participants' HR data to evaluate their discussion skills by analyzing the Q&A segments of discussion. We extracted HR segments corresponding to each Q&A segment from discussion, and described the HR data during three periods as shown in Fig. 8: HR data during question period (blue line), HR data during answer period (orange line), as well as the question and answer periods.

We then computed 18 h and HRV features from all Q&A segments as well as the question and answer periods separately. The HR and HRV features include mean, standard deviation (std.), and root mean square successive difference (RMSSD) from these three periods, which has been proven as an important metric for understanding HRV differences under cognitive activities [11]. The trends in the HR of these three periods were also computed by calculating the difference between two adjacent HR points. If the number of positive differences was more than the negative one, we assumed this HR period shows an upward trend, if not, this HR period shows a downward trend, as shown in the Fig. 8. We used a quadratic curve (red line) to more clearly present the HR trend for readers. We can see that HR during the question period shows a downward trend and an upward trend during answer period.

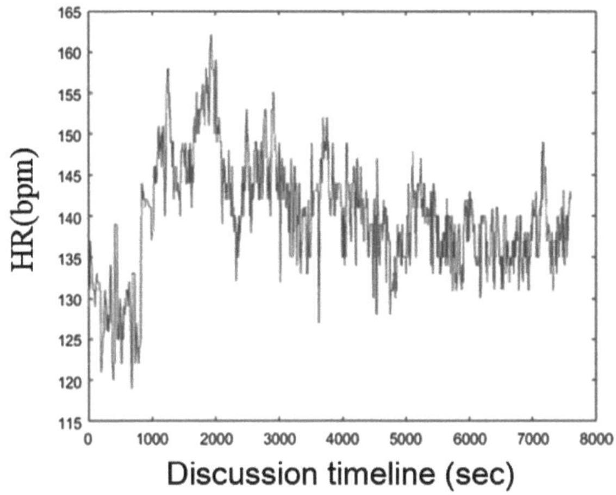

Fig. 7. A participant's complete HR information during a discussion [8].

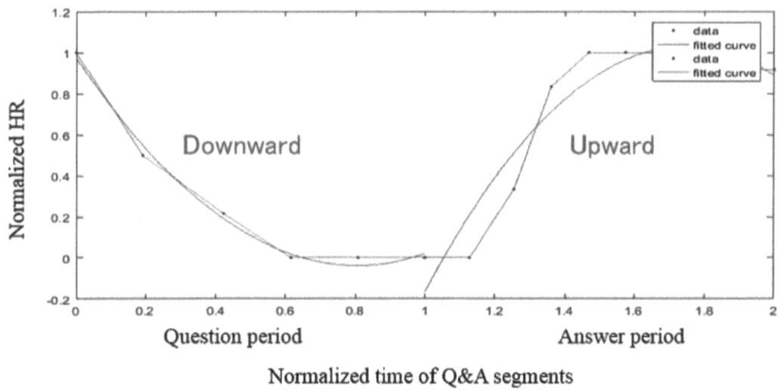

Fig. 8. A participant's HR during one Q&A segment [8]. (Color figure online)

We also divided the HR data of these three periods into the following nine ranges: less than 60 bpm, 60–70 bpm, 71–80 bpm, 81–90 bpm, 91–100 bpm, 101–110 bpm, 111–120 bpm, 121–130 bpm and more than 130 bpm. The mean and std. were calculated to describe the HR appearance-frequency distribution in each range. Table 1 summarizes these 18 features.

Table 1. HR and HRV features (metrics) [8].

HR period	HR and HRV features
Both periods	mean, std., RMSSD, trend
	Freq. all mean, Freq. all std.
Question period	mean, std., RMSSD, trend
	Freq. question mean
	Freq. question std.
Answer period	mean, std., RMSSD, trend
	Freq. answer mean
	Freq. answer std.

4.2 Evaluation Experiments

We performed experimental discussion data collection a total of two times, the first time collecting data for establishing the initial evaluation models based on HR data and the second collecting data for investigating the robustness of HR and HRV features [7]. At first, We collected discussion data from 9 presenter-students from 9 lab-seminar discussions in 4 months, and 12 undergraduate and graduate students and 3 professors made up the participants, the discussions were carried out following the presenter-students' research contents report with the participants asking questions related to the discussion topic then answered by the presenters. There were 117 complete Q&A segments extracted from these 9 discussions, and the answer-quality of these Q&A segments were evaluated by the corresponding participants who asked the questions by gave a score based on a five-point scale; 1 = very poor, 2 = poor, 3 = acceptable, 4 = good, 5 = very good. We obtained 66 high-quality answers with scores from 4–5, and 51 low-quality answers with scores from 1–3.

There were three machine learning models adopted: logistic regression (LR), support vector machine (SVM), and random forest (RF), to carry out binary classification of the Q&A segments' answer quality. About 80% of Q&A segments were randomly selected as a training data set and the remaining 20% as a test data set.

Feature Selection. It would be possible to use all the 18 h and HRV features for these three evaluation models, however this may decrease the performance of the classifiers, particularly because of dimensionality. Therefore, we tried to find the subset of HR and HRV features which could be used to discriminate the two classes with the highest classification accuracy which indicates the highest F-measure. Therefore, on our training data set we used recursive features elimination (RFE) [12], which ranks the features according their importance to the different evaluation models. To determine the best size of the feature subset, we used the RFE with 5-fold cross-validation (RFECV) method. By calculating the F-measure (or F1 score that is the harmonic mean of precision and recall), we extracted the best performing feature subset that could achieve the best evaluation performance for the corresponding models.

For the LR model, we obtained a 0.790 F-measure by using an eight-feature candidate subset and an F-measure of 0.740 by using a seven-feature candidate subset; therefore, we used the eight-feature subset to train our LR model. We obtained an F-measure of 0.805 for the SVM model with 10 h and HRV features we selected in advance. For the RF model, when there were 36 trees (sub-models of RF) and 19 terminal nodes on each tree, we obtained the highest F-measure of 0.870. In this case, we chose an eight-feature subset. Figure 9 lists the evaluation results for each model.

Figure 9 shows three sub-graphs that separately illustrate the best subset of all the HR and HRV features for each model at the top and the feature-importance-ranking results at the bottom. The highest F-measure was obtained when seven or eight key features were included in the subsets for the LR model; therefore, the first seven or eight features surrounded by the red rectangle were considered as two candidate feature subsets for the LR model. Similarly, the first ten features comprised the candidate subset for the SVM model, and there were two candidate feature subsets for the RF model which involved seven or eight features in the ranking list counted from the top.

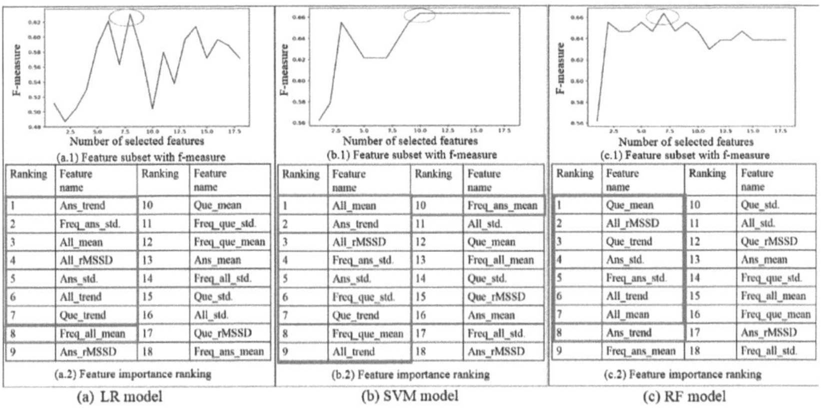

Fig. 9. HR and HRV feature selection for each evaluation model [8]. (Color figure online)

Evaluation Results. For the LR model, we obtained a 0.790 F-measure by using the eight-feature candidate subset and an F-measure of 0.740 when using the seven-feature candidate subset; therefore, we used the eight-feature subset to train our LR model. We obtained an F-measure of 0.805 for the SVM model with the ten HR and HRV features we selected in advance. For the RF model, when there were 36 trees and 19 terminal nodes on each tree we obtained the highest F-measure of 0.870. In this case, we chose an eight-feature subset. Table 2 lists the evaluation results for each model.

Table 2. Evaluation results of each learning model [8].

Evaluation model	F-measure
LR	0.790
SVM	0.805
RF	0.870

Comparing the F-measures of each model, the RF model exhibited superior evaluation performance compared with the LR and SVM models. Considering all three models, the HRV data of participants showed an outstanding performance in evaluating Q&A segments' answer quality. Meanwhile, we focused on seven HRV features: all mean, answer trend, all RMSSD, freq. answer std., answer std., question trend, and all trend, which exhibited the largest effect on all three models.

4.3 Comparative Experiments

In order to further argue that whether the HR and HRV features of discussion participants show better discrimination performance regarding the Q&A segments' answer-quality evaluation than semantic features extracted from participants' statements, we conducted two comparative experiments by generating LR, SVM, RF models based on the semantic features of Q&A statements alone and the combination of them.

We took advantage of 1246 Q&A segments data recorded before in our lab environment and evaluated the answer-quality with the same method as we introduced in Sect. 4.2, 993 high-quality and 253 low-quality Q&A segments were obtained. Morpheme bigram was generated based on these survey Q&A segments and several bigrams were extracted as the certain semantic features if their occurrences were much higher than 0.15%, there were 14 semantic features selected for evaluating the Q&A segments' answer-quality.

The results are shown as Table 3, all of the models received low F-measure when used semantic features alone and RF model obtained a relative higher F-measure even though only 0.583. If compares the evaluation performance of HRV and semantic features. We can clearly see that participants' HR and HRV features brought out excellent discrimination ability regarding Q&A segments' answer quality compared with semantic features in all evaluation models. These results provide favourable evidence regarding our original argument that using participants' HR and HRV features can effectively evaluate the answer-quality of Q&A segments in discussions.

However, we were surprised find that combining the HR data of presenters and semantic data of Q&A statements clearly increased evaluation ability than using each type of data alone. The SVM and RF models obtained a 3 and 4% increase in F-measure, respectively, but there was no obvious increase for the LR model.

Table 3. Evaluation-performance comparison of HRV and semantic features and their combination for each evaluation model [8].

Evaluation model	F-measure		
	HR and HRV features	Semantic features	Combination of HR and semantic features
LR	0.790	0.500	0.790
SVM	0.805	0.540	0.833
RF	0.870	0.583	0.916

Heart Rate Data Robustness Investigation Experiment. To verify the robustness of HR and HRV features, we collected another 8 times' presentation data and extracted a total of 66 Q&A segments. 20% Q&A segments were randomly selected from the new dataset and the previous test dataset together to become new test dataset, remaining Q&A segments with the previous training dataset were used as new training dataset. We generated new evaluation models of LR, SVM, and RF by using the 7 meaningful HRV features, we got a 0.756 F-measure of LR model, a 0.810 F-measure of SVM model and a 0.837 F-measure of RF model. From the evaluation results, HRV data of participants still show a well discrimination performance on new dataset even though has a slight decline of F-measure. We take insight into the Recall score on low answer-quality reorganization in these three HRV models, we achieved a 0.560 Recall of LR model, a 0.780 Recall of SVM model, a 0.650 Recall of RF model, which provides us with favorable evidence that HRV features can be used to effectively recognize the low answer-quality and as a discussion performance evaluation method.

We also verified the robustness of semantic features on this new dataset. We got a similar F-measure with the results on old dataset, however, we got a really low Recall scores, such as 0.060 Recall of LR model, 0.240 Recall of SVM model and 0.480 Recall of RF model, which indicated that the semantic features cannot recognize the low quality Q&A segments.

5 Further Application for Discussion-Skill Training

In this study, we have validated and explained our argument that discussion participants' HR data can be used to effectively evaluate Q&A segments' answer quality in discussion and as discussion-skill automatic evaluation indicators for measuring participants' discussion ability. In order to make our findings applicable, we are going to combine physiological with acoustics and linguistics data of discussion participants to design an effective discussion-skill assessment mechanism to rank their discussion ability and implement a discussion-skill training system to help students improve their discussion ability.

Discussion-Skill Assessment Mechanism. Let the weighted average value of the value of each indicator be the evaluation of one statement, and let the sum of the evaluation values of all statements of a participant be the numerical value expressing that participant's speaking ability in discussions at a meeting. By looking at the changes for each discussion in each meeting, participants will be able to judge whether their discussion skills are rising or stagnating.

Discussion-Skill Training System. We have offer some powerful evaluation indicators regarding participants' answer-quality in discussion which can let us measure participants discussion skills, but, of course, they should be used not only for measurement but also for extending their ability. One way to do this is to visualize the results in an easy-to-understand manner and feed them back to the participants at just the right time.

Participants should make an effort to raise their discussion ability. For that purpose, we are going to generate a training system to evaluate discussion participants' statements during a meeting, points out the problems, and encourages improvement. There are various ways to point this out. Such as display a message on the main screen during or shortly after speaking to let participants calm down and give a more reasonable answer. There is another way to give feedback which regarding low-quality Q&A segments to presenter-students after discussions to encourage them to spend more time on re-understanding the questions, to sort out their research to find more accurate answers, and to strengthen the communication skills to give participants a more understandable description, in the long run, to effectively improve students' discussion performance.

To train the discussion ability, it is necessary to record evaluation results over a considerably long span of time. Changes in short-term evaluation results are effective as a clue to evaluating and improving the performance of the developed system, but this will not be enough to judge whether a person certainly has improved their discussion ability. This is similar to the fact that local optimal solutions do not necessarily become true optimal solutions when optimizing the parameters of machine learning models.

It is often said that human education takes time. We think that discussion skills as well as basic academic ability need to be firmly acquired over the long term. To that end, we believe that we must have a clear guide that becomes a signpost. Without good, clear, and factual guidance, people will lose confidence in themselves. The system for acquiring and evaluating data that we developed is useful for clarifying what can be done to improve what kind of ability.

We believe that discussion ability is a fundamental and important skill that human beings use to perform intellectual activities. Improving this ability is a task that can be said to be essential for many people. However, if visible growth does not appear, people will get bored with such training. We are planning to introduce gamification techniques to solve this problem.

6 Conclusion

In this study, we argued that participants' HR data can be used to effectively evaluate Q&A segments' answer quality in discussion and as a discussion-skill evaluation method compared to using NLP such as semantic analysis.

In order to confirm our argument, we set and implemented two goals. Our first goal was employing a non-invasive device Apple Watch to build a participants' HR data real-time acquisition system and HR data visual browser based on our DM system which generates a multimedia meeting minutes and provides us with analyzable Q&A segment data which make up discussions. Our second goal was to hold an experimental investigation into the use of a participants' HR data collected by our HR acquisition system, to determine whether it can more effectively evaluate answer-quality of Q&A segments than using semantic information from Q&A segments' statements alone.

In order to achieve our second goal, we generated three binary classification models for evaluation: LR, SVM, and RF, and selected the seven most significant features out of all 18 h and HRV features: All mean, Answer trend, All RMSSD, Freq answer std., Answer std., Question trend, and All trend, which had the largest effect on all three models. We obtained an F-measure of 0.790 for the LR model, 0.810 for the SVM model, and 0.870 for the RF model. These results indicate that HR data of participants can be used to evaluate the answer-quality of Q&A segments of discussions. Two kinds of comparative experiments also been done and the results revealed that HR data of participants can exhibit more effective evaluation on the answer-quality of Q&A segments than semantic data, and the combination of two kinds of data could improve the discussion performance evaluation ability to some extent.

Future tasks include long-term participant-based experiments on evaluating discussion skills and on training and on extending the training process to motivate students to continue training on the basis of gamification techniques.

References

1. Nagao, K., Kaji, K., Yamamoto, D., Tomobe, H.: Discussion mining: annotation-based knowledge discovery from real world activities. In: Aizawa, K., Nakamura, Y., Satoh, S. (eds.) PCM 2004. LNCS, vol. 3331, pp. 522–531. Springer, Heidelberg (2004). https://doi.org/10.1007/978-3-540-30541-5_64
2. Nagao, K., Tehrani, M.P., Fajardo, J.T.B.: Tools and evaluation methods for discussion and presentation skills training. Smart Learn. Environ. **2**(5) (2015). https://doi.org/10.1186/s40561-015-0011-1
3. Patil, S., Lee, K.: Detecting experts on quora: by their activity, quality of answers, linguistic characteristics and temporal behaviors. Soc. Netw. Anal. Min. **6**(5), 1–11 (2016)
4. Agichtein, E., Castillo, C., Donato, D., Gionis, A., Mishne, G.: Finding high-quality content in social media. In: Proceedings of the 2008 International Conference on Web Search and Data Mining, pp. 183–194. ACM (2008)
5. Camm, A.J., et al.: Heart rate variability: standards of measurement, physiological interpretation and clinical use. Eur. Heart J. **17**(3), 354–381 (1996)
6. Luque-Casado, A., Zabala, M., Morales, E., Mateo-March, M., Sanabria, D.: Cognitive performance and heart rate variability: the influence of fitness level. PLoS ONE (2013). https://doi.org/10.1371/journal.pone. 0056935
7. Pereira, T., Almeida, P.R., Cunha, J.P., Aguiar, A.: Heart rate variability metrics for fine-grained stress level assessment. Comput. Methods Programs Biomed. **148**, 71–80 (2017)
8. Peng, S., Nagao, K.: Automatic evaluation of presenters' discussion performance based on their heart rate. In: Proceedings of the 10th International Conference on Computer Supported Education, CSEDU 2018 (2018)
9. Jeon, E., Park, H.: Development of a smartphone application for clinical-guideline-based obesity management. Healthc. Inform. Res. **21**(1), 10–20 (2015)
10. El-Amrawy, F., Nounou, M.I.: Are currently available wearable devices for activity tracking and heart rate monitoring accurate, precise, and medically beneficial? Healthc. inform. res. **21**(4), 315–320 (2015)
11. Wang, X., et al.: Genetic influences on heart rate variability at rest and during stress. Psychophysiology **46**(3), 458–465 (2009). https://doi.org/10.1111/j.1469-8986.2009.00793.x
12. Guyon, I., Weston, J., Barnhill, S., Vapnik, V.: Gene selection for cancer classification using support vector machines. Mach. Learn. **46**(1), 389–422 (2002)

Author Index

MIX
Papier aus verantwortungsvollen Quellen
Paper from responsible sources
FSC® C105338

If you have any concerns about our products,
you can contact us on
ProductSafety@springernature.com

In case Publisher is established outside the EU,
the EU authorized representative is:
Springer Nature Customer Service Center GmbH
Europaplatz 3, 69115 Heidelberg, Germany

Printed by Libri Plureos GmbH
in Hamburg, Germany